The Living Elephants

R A M A N   S U K U M A R

THE LIVING ELEPHANTS

Evolutionary Ecology,

Behavior, and Conservation

OXFORD
UNIVERSITY PRESS

2003

UNIVERSITY PRESS

Oxford   New York
Auckland   Bangkok   Buenos Aires   Cape Town   Chennai
Dar es Salaam   Delhi   Hong Kong   Istanbul   Karachi   Kolkata
Kuala Lumpur   Madrid   Melbourne   Mexico City   Mumbai   Nairobi
São Paulo   Shanghai   Taipei   Tokyo   Toronto

Published by Oxford University Press, Inc.
198 Madison Avenue, New York, New York 10016

www.oup.com

Oxford is a registered trademark of Oxford University Press

Library of Congress Cataloging-in-Publication Data
Sukumar, R.
    The living elephants : evolutionary ecology, behavior, and conservation /
by Raman Sukumar.
      p. cm.
    Includes bibliographical references (p.).
    ISBN 0-19-510778-0
    1. Asiatic elephant.   2. African elephant.   3. Wildlife conservation.   I. Title.
QL737.P98 S956 2003
599.67—dc21   20020333995

9 8 7 6 5 4 3 2 1

Printed in the United States of America
on acid-free paper

For Madhav Gadgil
who taught me ecology

Preface

In an article entitled "How many species are there on earth?" in the September 16, 1988, issue of the journal *Science*, the eminent and influential scientist Robert May (now Lord May) observed, almost with a tinge of regret, that the Order Proboscidea topped the list of the number of articles per species of various animal groups that were published annually during 1978–1987. The message of his article was that the study of the vast diversity of smaller-size organisms was being neglected in favor of the larger vertebrates. The recent genetic evidence for two species of African elephants, and the claims of a possible third or even fourth species of African elephant, would alter the articles-to-species ratio, but the Proboscidea would still maintain its top slot. Actually, I think that the defection of the few biologists who study creatures such as elephants and tigers to disciplines such as the classification of beetles would make little difference to our knowledge of beetles but considerably erode our understanding of elephants and tigers, creatures that could act as flagships in conserving beetles and the diversity of our tropical forests.

During the past 20-odd years, my own work as well as that of my research group has actually extended beyond elephants to communities of small and large mammals, rain forest birds, parasites, tropical plants, and even paleoclimate. Yet, in some strange fashion the elephant has been the thread connecting many of these diverse themes—for example, the interaction between elephants and tropical plants, parasite loads in relation to mate choice, and the use of stable carbon isotopes in studying the elephant's feeding habits as well as in reconstructing past climate change. This echoes Wendy O'Flaherty's observations of the elephant-headed god: "One can start from Ganesa and work from there in an unbroken line to almost any aspect of Indian culture."

Some years ago I realized that, in spite of the considerable numbers of articles and books on elephants, there was hardly any volume that provided a broad synthesis of their biology within the framework of modern evolutionary theory. Most of the books either pertained to individual studies of African or Asian elephant populations or were pictorial books (usually with pictures of wild African elephants and captive Asian elephants). This is why I embarked upon this project. I have also tried to provide a better balance between studies of Asian and African elephants than is available in most other volumes. When I began writing this book I had not even planned for a section on the molecular genetics of elephants, as hardly anything was known of this subject; with the rush of articles in recent years this section had to be added. Very soon this part will certainly become hopelessly outdated.

I owe many debts of gratitude to professional colleagues, students, friends, and family for their help and support over the past two decades in making my research and writing possible. I begin by thanking colleagues who reviewed various chapters of this book: Adrian Lister (chapter 1), Mahesh Rangarajan (chapter 2), Bets Rasmussen (chapters 3 and 4), Richard Barnes (chapters 5 and 6), Niranjan Joshi (chapter 7), and Richard Hoare (parts of chapter 8). Needless to say, any errors or omissions are entirely mine.

The late V. Krishnamurthy was always a source of inspiration, wisdom, and support. I was fortunate to spend many, many hours in his company watching elephants or listening to his elephant tales. D. K. Lahiri-Choudhury and I spent long hours discussing and arguing about elephants; this has enriched my knowledge of elephants considerably. J. C. Daniel, the first Chair of the IUCN/SSC Asian Elephant Specialist Group, and his successor, Lyn de Alwis, provided support at important junctures. Charles Santiapillai has been a pillar of support (laced with his special wit) as we presently guide the activities of the specialist group. Jacob Cheeran's calm and reassuring presence has been vital to the success of our radio-telemetry studies, and so has Subrata Pal Choudhury's skills in guiding a dart accurately through the foliage of a rain forest on to an elephant's back. Vivek Menon and Ashok Kumar have been steadfast companions in several elephantine (and some nonelephant) ventures, while Tom Mathew has provided us support at crucial moments (and gently nudged us into action when we were in slumber).

Many other colleagues in India and abroad have chatted about elephants and other organisms, been companions on jungle trips, and have helped in many ways. They include, in no particular order, Anindya Sinha, Ullas Karanth, Vijayakumaran Nair, P. S. Easa, A.J.T. Johnsingh, Adrian Lister, Chris Wemmer, Bets Rasmussen, Heidi Riddle, Lynette and Ben Hart, John Sale, Peter Jackson, Hezy Shoshani, Steve Hubbell, Rick Condit, and Liz Losos.

R. Ramesh has been a long-standing collaborator on elephants and climate change. Lalji Singh, Pruthu Fernando, and Don Melnick have been generous in our collaborative work on elephant genetics.

I have also drawn upon the work of many other colleagues in India and elsewhere for this treatise. In India they include Parbati Barua, Anwaruddin Choudhury, Sushant Chowdhury, Hemant Datye, Ajay Desai, Justus Joshua, Ramesh Kumar, N. Sivaganesan, and Christy Williams. Elsewhere in Asia they include Mohd. Anwarul Islam (Bangladesh), Aster Zhang (China), Jayantha Jayewardene (Sri Lanka), Widodo Ramono and Bambang Suprayogi (Indonesia), Hideo Obara and Masayuki Sakamoto (Japan), Mohd. Khan, Jasmi Abdul, Mohd. Shariff Daim, and Zainal Zainuddin (Malaysia), Khyne U Mar, U Uga, U Aung Than, and U Ye Thut (Myanmar), Mattana Srikrachang, Grishda Lungka and Richard Lair (Thailand), and Nguyen Xuan Dang and Tran Van Thanh (Vietnam). Joe Heffernan, Joe Walston, and Gert Polet have filled in important gaps for the Indochina region.

IUCN—The World Conservation Union—has provided the opportunity for me to discuss elephants in a structured manner with specialists from Asia and other continents. I thank all my colleagues who have volunteered to be part of the Asian Elephant Specialist Group. George Rabb, former Chair of the IUCN's Species Survival Commission, provided tremendous encouragement, while his successor David Brackett has continued to put faith in me. Simon Stuart played an important role in shaping the activities of the Asian Elephant Specialist Group, a role that is now taken over by Sue Mainka. Ulie Seal and Bob Lacy of the Conservation Breeding Specialist Group introduced me to the world of Population and Habitat Viability Analysis.

Several researchers and conservationists who work mainly in Africa have discussed their studies, hosted me, or provided ideas. They include Eve Abe, Richard Barnes, Holly Dublin, Iain Douglas-Hamilton, Richard Hoare, Paula Kahumbu, Malan Lindeque, Cynthia Moss, Steve Njumbi, Loki Osborn, Katy Payne, Joyce Poole, James Powell, Martin Tchamba, John Waithaka, and David Western.

Since the early 1970s I have had the good fortune to interact with and share the field experiences of a large number of forest officers in various states across India. It would be too cumbersome to mention each of them by name but the states they hail from include Tamilnadu, Karnataka, Kerala, Andhra, West Bengal, Uttar Pradesh, Uttaranchal, Jharkhand, Orissa, Assam, Meghalaya, and Arunachal Pradesh. I should, however, mention those responsible for running India's Project Elephant at the Ministry of Environment and Forests, New Delhi: the late S. Deb Roy, Vinod Rishi, Kishore Rao, S. C. Dey, and S. S. Bist. I have gained much in discussing elephant conservation matters with them.

My graduate students, post-docs, and research assistants over the years have made rich contributions to ecological thinking and investigations. Milind Watve thought creatively about elephants, other mammals, and their parasites. C. Arivazhagan and R. Arumugam have followed and registered these elephants and other mammals over many years. Surendra Varma trekked the Asian jungles in search of their elusive elephants. Mukti Roy, Guha Dharmarajan, A. Mathivanan, and N. Baskaran have tenaciously radio-tracked the elephants of West Bengal. Truptha Purohit and Uma Ramakrishnan (Jr.) initiated the work on elephant genetics, while T.N.C. Vidya has comprehensively followed up this line of work. H. S. Suresh, H. S. Dattaraja, K. S. Murali, and Robert John have followed the life history of thousands of trees that sustain elephants. Cheryl Nath has made a successful transition from watching elephants to modeling the growth of trees that provide them shade. T. R. Shankar Raman has begun chasing elephants after completing his dissertation on birds. Kartik Shanker took brief moments off his work on small mammals to watch the largest mammal when it appeared at his study site. Geeta Rajagopalan and Indrani Suryaprakash thankfully kept a safe distance from elephants when they worked on climate change. Venkatesa Kumar, K. Narendran, Kumaran Raju, and R. Saandeep have provided important GIS support. A. Madhusudan has effectively mobilized people in keeping elephants away from their crop fields. Uma Ramakrishnan (Sr.) and J. A. Santosh executed the Periyar poaching model. Gauri Pradhan quickly and competently tackled the problem of tusk inheritance in elephants. K. Manavalan, C. M. Bharanaiah, K. Palani, R. Mohan, and S. Nagaraj have provided logistic support to our team, while trackers Setty, Shivaji, K. Krishna, B. Bomma, and K. Siddhan have kept us all out of reach of the trunks and tusks of elephants.

Arun Venkataraman has enacted several roles—from observing wasps to pursuing dholes; the one most important for elephants (and for me personally) has been to organize and run several programs of the Asian Elephant Research and Conservation Centre. M. O. Sriram has ensured that order prevails over chaos in the functioning of an organization.

As with my earlier books, S. Nirmala organized the entire manuscript from my handwritten script. Her assistance has been invaluable in piecing together the contents of this book. In the final stages of production, Joshua David's careful reading picked up several errors I had missed.

My faculty colleagues at the Centre for Ecological Sciences, Indian Institute of Science, have contributed to a stimulating intellectual atmosphere. Madhav Gadgil not only guided me through my doctoral research, but has since maintained interest in my work. Niranjan Joshi has provided key insights and support on a variety of issues, quantitative and nonquantitative. Vidyanand Nanjundaiah has been a source of knowledge on everything from genes to evolution. N. H. Ravindranath has made it possible for me to move from past climate change to future climate change.

I owe my original interest in natural history to the "Adyar Naturalists Club," although now depleted and dispersed. R. Selvakumar has continued to maintain active interest in my work in spite of migrating to the other side of the globe. A. N. Jagannatha Rao, the only member still rooted to Adyar, and S. T. Baskaran, who has recently completed a round-trip migration, continue likewise. The late Siddharth Buch and the late M. Krishnan helped me not only to refine my photography but also my natural history observations.

Many colleagues and friends readily provided photographs that I could not dig up or match in quality from my collection for this volume: Adrian Lister, Richard Barnes, D. K. Bhaskar, M. Y. Ghorpade, Ben Hart, Richard Hoare, Paula Kahumbu, Adrian Lister, Vivek Menon, Katy Payne, T.N.A. Perumal, Bets Rasmussen, Rei Rasmussen, S. Wijeyamohan, and the Karnataka Police Department. A. G. Ryan and D. K. Bhaskar assisted with preparing the photographs for publication, A. V. Narayan prepared many of the figures, and J. Ramesh sketched the drawings of extinct proboscideans. Michael Long kindly permitted me to reproduce two of his drawings, and Hezy Shoshani likewise allowed me to use a drawing from one of his articles.

I thank several publishers for permissions to reproduce material from their books and journals (individually acknowledged in the respective figures or tables). These constitute an important part of this volume. While every effort has been made to contact copyright holders for permissions to reproduce material, any omissions will be rectified in subsequent editions.

Kirk Jensen, my editor at Oxford University Press, has been patient through the three elephant gestation periods it has taken for me to complete the book.

My work has received funding support from many agencies, institutions, and foundations. The Ministry of Environment and Forests of the Government of India has provided core support for much of the broader research program on conservation biology in southern India over the past 15 years. The Forest Department of West Bengal funded the first phase of our research in their state. Wildlife Trust (U.S.A) has been the major international partner and supporter of the Asian Elephant Research and Conservation Centre. The John D. and Catherine T. MacArthur Foundation, the Liz Claiborne/Art Ortenberg Foundation, Dr. Scholl Foundation, U.S. Fish and Wildlife Service, Rotterdam Zoo, World Wide Fund for Nature, Fauna and Flora International, and Scientific Exploration Society have all provided significant support.

My late parents were broad-minded enough to let their son wander the jungles. I am grateful to my wife Sudha who continues to not only endure my frequent absences from home but also the long bouts of writing when I am at home; I also thank our elder daughter Gitanjali for promising to illustrate my next book, and apologize to our younger daughter Hamsini for the bedtime stories she missed.

I owe special thanks to a wonderful organization for their enduring support over the past 8 years and for ensuring that this book did not exceed three elephant gestations. Wildlife Trust, U.S.A., supported my sabbatical year (2001) and that enabled me to complete a substantial part of this manuscript. While I thank all the staff of Wildlife Trust for their help, my special thanks go to Mary Pearl and Fred Koontz for this enduring support.

Contents

The Living Elephants

Moeritheres, Mastodonts, and Mammoths
Elephant Evolution in Action

1

1.1 Introduction

The evolution of elephants and related forms, collectively known as the proboscideans, is one of the better-recorded tales of mammalian evolution. Since its origin in the late Paleocene Epoch, about 60 million years (My) ago, the order Proboscidea witnessed a spectacular radiation until the end of the Pleistocene Epoch, about 10,000 years ago. The evolutionary course of the proboscideans, marked by an overall increase in body size, also took many seemingly bizarre paths, including extreme dwarfism and morphologies (seen from the fossil record) that only the most daring paleontologist could have otherwise imagined (fig. 1.1). There are many examples of parallel and convergent evolution. During this period, the proboscideans occupied almost every continental habitat type, including swamps, tundra, boreal forests, deserts, savannas, tropical forests, river basins, and high mountains. With the exception of Australia and Antarctica, fossil proboscideans have been found in every continent. Adaptations in anatomy and physiology of the proboscideans were obviously as diverse as the spread of habitats they occupied.

Interest in the story of elephant evolution is probably rivaled only by that of human evolution (and perhaps dinosaur extinctions). One reason is obviously our fascination with creatures larger than we are ourselves. In addition, the bones of large animals are more likely to be preserved and hence discovered and described in greater detail. The largest land mammal ever known is actually not a proboscidean. This was the giant "giraffe rhinoceros" or *Indricoth-*

Figure 1.1
A representation of the diverse array of extinct proboscideans. With the exception of *Moeritherium*, the others are drawn approximately to scale. (Redrawn by J. Ramesh from various sources.)

erium, weighing 15 tons, that lived in Southeast Asia about 25 My ago. Nevertheless, some of the extinct proboscideans did reach a formidable size, even larger than the living elephants.

The Asian elephant (*Elephas maximus*) and the African elephant (*Loxodonta africana*) are the living representatives of more than 160 species of recognized proboscideans. During the Pleistocene, the last ice age, which spanned nearly 2 My until 10,000 years before the present day, myriad proboscidean species

Figure 1.1
Continued.

still flourished across the continents from the Americas to Eurasia and Africa, although a decline was under way. Most of the proboscidean evolution had occurred in the Old World, with successive migrations to the New World. Yet, by the end of the Pleistocene, all but *Elephas maximus* and *Loxodonta africana*, had become extinct, along with a host of other "megafauna." Although the Pleistocene extinctions may not necessarily have been as severe as some of the earlier episodes of "mass extinctions" in the geological record, they were notable for their rapidity and impact on the larger mammals. About half of the mammalian genera greater than 5 kg in body weight became extinct during the late Pleistocene. Only tropical and subtropical Africa and Asia were left with anything like the diversity of larger mammals that flourished until recent times.

The rich fossil remains of the proboscideans housed in museums around the world have yet to be exploited fully by scientists. Henry Fairfield Osborn's monumental work on the Proboscidea, published as two volumes in 1936 and 1942, described 44 genera and about 350 species. Since Osborn's tome, there have been at least two significant volumes on proboscidean evolution. The first, by Vincent Maglio in 1973, is considered the standard volume on the evolution of the true elephants—the family Elephantidae. The second is a multiauthor volume on proboscidean evolution; it was edited by Jeheskel Shoshani and Pascal Tassy (1996a).

As with the taxonomy and phylogeny of other animal or plant taxa, there are usually as many interpretations as biologists, and the Proboscidea have been no exception. In this case, the "lumpers" have latterly prevailed over the "splitters," with the result that only about 39 genera and 163 species were recognized as of 2001 (table 1.1). New fossil discoveries have also pushed back the origin of the proboscideans by several million years. Since its discovery at the turn of the twentieth century, a piglike creature named *Moeritherium*, with fossil remains first recovered from 50-My-old Eocene beds of Egypt by C. W. Andrews, was considered to be the oldest proboscidean. In 1980, a major shift in the geographic origin of the proboscideans occurred with the description by R. M. West of *Anthracobune*, another Eocene genus with proboscidean affinities from the northwestern Indian subcontinent. An African origin for the proboscideans was quickly reasserted with the discovery of *Numidotherium* from the early Eocene of Algeria. More recently, the description in 1996 of *Phosphatherium* from Morocco by Emmanuel Gheerbrant and coworkers not only strengthened the African origin, but also significantly pushed it back to the late Paleocene.

The warm, shallow waters along the fringes of the ancient Tethys Sea, of which the Mediterranean is a remnant, provided the milieu for an extraordinary evolutionary divergence of two orders of mammals—the Proboscidea, which are the largest of the land mammals, and the Sirenia or sea cows, which are strictly aquatic today. Not only are the fossil ancestors of these two mammalian groups found together in the same geological stratum of the Fayum in Egypt, but also they share common features, such as double-apex hearts, with each ventricle separated from the other at the tip. The paleontologist Malcolm McKenna thus created in 1975 the Tethytheria, a superorder encompassing the Proboscidea, the Sirenia, and an extinct order called Demostylia, implying that the closest extant relatives of the elephants were the sea cows. This was a modification of another scheme of classification proposed by the famous evolutionist George Gaylord Simpson, who proposed the Paenungulata, which included the proboscideans, the sea cows, and the hyraxes in addition to four extinct orders. A shared character, such as the carpals or wrist bones arranged serially one above the other, justified this new grouping, termed Tethytheria under the Paenungulata.

Table 1.1
Known geological distribution of proboscidean genera.

Taxon	Geological Record*												Continents†				
	Pa	eE	mE	lE	O	eM	mM	lM	Pl	Ps	eH	lH	As	Af	Eu	NA	SA
Phosphatherium	X	?												+			
Anthracobune		X	X										+				
Moeritherium			?	X	X									+			
Numidotherium		?	X											+			
Barytherium				X	X									+			
Prodeinotherium						X	X	X					+	+	+		
Deinotherium							X	X	X	X			+	+	+		
Palaeomastodon				X	X									+			
Phiomia				X	X									+			
Hemimastodon						X							+				
Eozygodon						X	X							+			
Zygolophodon						X	X	X	?				+	+	+	+	
Mammut							X	X	X	X	X		+	+	+	+	
Choerolophodon						X	X	X	?				+	+	+		
Gomphotherium						X	X	X	?				+	+	+	+	
Amebelodon							X	X	X				+	+		+	
Platybelodon						X	X	X	?				+	+	+	+	
Serbelodon							X	X					+		?	+	
Protanancus							X	X					+	+			
Archaeobelodon						X	X							+	+		
Gnathabelodon							X	X								+	
Sinomastodon								X	X	X			+				
Eubelodon							X									+	
Rhynchotherium							X	X	X							+	
Stegomastodon									?	X						+	?
Haplomastodon									X	X						?	+
Notiomastodon										X							+

Table 1.1
Continued.

Taxon	Geological Record*												Continents†				
	Pa	eE	mE	lE	O	eM	mM	lM	Pl	Ps	eH	lH	As	Af	Eu	NA	SA
Cuvieronius								?	X	X						+	+
Tetralophodon						X		X	X	?			+	+	+	?	
Anancus								X	X	X			+	+	+		
Paratetralophodon								X					+				
Stegolophodon						X	X	X	X	?			+				
Stegodon								X	X	X	X		+	+			
Stegotetrabelodon								X	X				?	+	?		
Stegodibelodon								X	X					+			
Primelephas								X	X					+			
Loxodonta								X	X	X	X	X		+			
Elephas									X	X	X	X	+	+	+		
Mammuthus									X	X	X		+	+	+	+	

Source: Updated from Shoshani and Tassy (1996b).
*Key to geological records: Pa, Paleocene; eE, early Eocene; mE, middle Eocene; lE, late Eocene; O, Oligocene; eM, early Miocene; mM, middle Miocene; lM, late Miocene; Pl, Pliocene; Ps, Pleistocene; eH, early Holocene; lH, late Holocene.
†Key to continents on which remains of these genera were found: As, Asia; Af, Africa; Eu, Europe; NA, North America (including Central America for *Zygolophodon*, *Mammut*, *Rhynchotherium*, *Stegomastodon*, *Cuvieronius*, and *Mammuthus*); SA, South America (including Central America for *Haplomastodon*).

The newest anatomical and biochemical evidence certainly supports the contention that the closest living relatives of the elephants are creatures such as the sea cows (manatees and dugong), the hyraxes, and the aardvarks. A 1999 article by Ann Gaeth and associates on the embryonic development of the African elephant strengthens the aquatic ancestry of the proboscideans and places them closest to the sirenians. The elephant fetus contains a curious structure called the *nephrostome*, a funnel-shaped kidney duct that appears by about the third month in embryonic development, but disappears by about the fifth or sixth month. Nephrostomes are characteristic of freshwater fishes (e.g., sturgeons), frogs, birds, and egg-laying reptiles and mammals (e.g., platypus), but are never found in the embryonic kidneys of present-day viviparous mammals. Their presence in elephants seems to be a throwback to their aquatic ancestry. Other embryonic features in the elephant, such as true intra-abdominal testes, also suggest an aquatic origin.

Although I briefly review proboscidean taxonomy and phylogenetic history (fig. 1.2), my objectives in this chapter are not to provide detailed descriptions of fossil proboscidean morphologies or get into hair-splitting debates of proboscidean relationships. The volumes I mentioned provide very detailed accounts of extinct proboscidean morphologies and phylogeny. Rather, my primary aim in this chapter is to review how climatic and environmental change over the past 60 My may have driven the "adaptive radiations" of the Proboscidea, especially the lines leading up to the living elephants. I also dwell at some length on the possible role of climate change and hunting by humans on the Pleistocene extinctions. Last, I summarize the emerging molecular evidence from genetic (DNA, deoxyribonucleic acid) studies for relationships among the true elephants and for structure, diversity, and phylogeography within and between populations of the African and Asian elephants.

Relating the complex radiation of the proboscideans to climate and habitat change over geological time spans is not an easy task. Our knowledge of the world becomes progressively fuzzier as we go back in time. A series of complex climatic episodes is reduced to an average value over several million years. Reconstructions of ancient habitats may be based on very indirect inferences that are, of necessity, extreme simplifications. The interplay of the earth's orbit around the sun, continental movement, oceanic circulation, climate, and vegetation change in the ancient world is understood only in broad terms. The fragmentary nature of the fossil record also does not help matters. Looking for fossils is often akin to searching for the proverbial needle in a haystack. While natural selection is widely accepted as the major driving force of evolution, all change need not have been an adaptive response. A character may have arisen and persisted in a particular lineage by chance alone, simply because this character was no more disadvantageous than an alternative character.

It is obviously incredibly difficult to reconstruct in detail the niche of particular fossil species and what particular selective forces were acting on it. The extensive literature on proboscidean evolution offers only a few glimpses into this subject, much of it linked to broad trends observed in mammalian evolution. A 1993 account by eminent paleontologist Christine Janis of mammalian evolution, set against the backdrop of geological climate and vegetation change, however, offers an excellent framework. I used her basic sequence of global events and newer information from the literature in tracing the spectacular radiation of the proboscideans across the globe (fig. 1.3).

1.2   *The Paleocene—Ancient origins*

Contrary to popular belief, the mammals were not the last vertebrate class to evolve. They appear in the fossil record during the late Triassic Period over 200 My ago, about 60 My before the birds and only a short time after the first

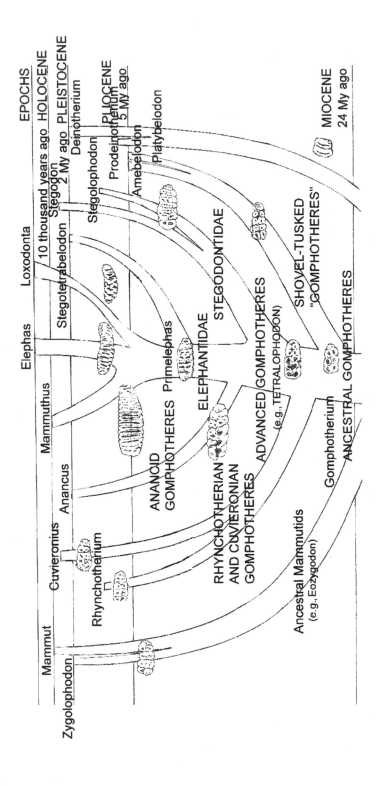

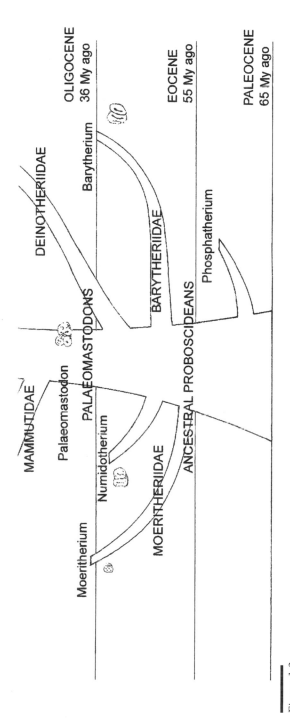

Figure 1.2

A simplified evolutionary tree of the Proboscidea. (Based on Shoshani 1992 with the addition of *Phosphatherium*.)

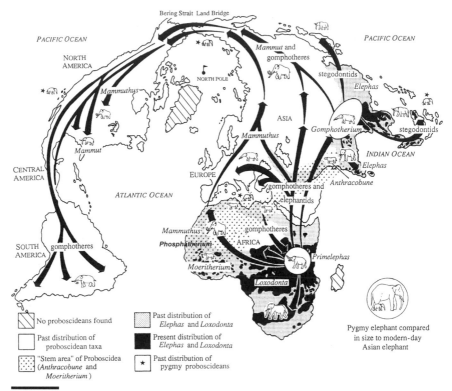

Figure 1.3
A reconstruction of the global distribution of the proboscideans beginning with the
ancestral forms along the shores of the ancient Tethys Sea in present-day northern
Africa. (From Shoshani and Tassy 1996b with the addition of *Phosphatherium*.) The
modern distributional ranges of *Elephas* and *Loxodonta* are more accurately depicted
in appendix 1.

dinosaurs. Mammals, though small, nocturnal, and mostly omnivorous, were
very much in evidence during the Jurassic and Cretaceous Periods, the golden
age of the dinosaurs. By the end of the Cretaceous, 65 My ago (the so-called
K-T boundary), the dinosaurs made their exit in one of the most catastrophic
events of the planet. Whether the dinosaur extinctions were triggered by an
asteroid impact or prolonged volcanic activity in the Indian Deccan, the stage
was now set for the succession of new dynasties—"victors by default" in the
words of Christine Janis.

The Tertiary Period dawned on a world in which the upper range of niches,
in terms of body size, had been vacated. This was an opportunity for mammals
to emerge from their tiny, nocturnal lairs. Yet, they took several million years
to reach even moderately large body sizes.

One possible reason could have been that, during the early Tertiary Period (the Paleocene Epoch, 65–57 My ago), the forests were denser—a consequence of a warmer, wetter world with no dinosaurs to trample the vegetation. Dense forests favor small, tree-dwelling animals over large, ground-dwelling ones. The Paleocene seems to have enjoyed a more equable climate than today, with much less contrast between the equator and the poles. The higher rainfall was more evenly spread over the year. Deciduous forests extended into the polar regions, while tropical type forests covered much of the rest of the globe. There is evidence that forests in North America, for instance, were dense and swampy.

It is in the Paleocene world, not long after the exit of the dinosaurs, that there is now evidence for the existence of a proboscideanlike creature. Dental remains of a small "ungulate," weighing perhaps 10–15 kg, were described in the leading scientific journal *Nature* in 1996 by Emmanuel Gheerbrant, Jean Sudre, and Henri Cappetta. The material was originally obtained by F. Escuillié from a fossil dealer. Although the discoverer and exact origin of the fossil are not known, the fossil was unambiguously traced to the phosphate deposits of Ouled Abdoun Basin in Morocco. The material was named *Phosphatherium escuilliei*. At this time, no inferences have been drawn about the habitat in which the creature lived. The teeth characters indicate a close relationship to another early proboscidean, *Numidotherium koholense*, from northern Africa that lived about 7 My later.

There must be more discoveries and analysis by paleontologists for a better understanding of *Phosphatherium* and its significance not only to proboscidean evolution, but also to the early radiation of the placental mammals.

1.3   The Eocene—Aquatic existence

The global climate turned even warmer by the early Eocene. Tropical type forests expanded further into the Arctic and Antarctic Circles, while seasonal forests thrived at the poles, a most unusual event in the globe's vegetational history. Many of the mammalian orders known today had their origins in the early Eocene. Even higher latitudes saw a proliferation of mammal types. Christine Janis speculates that a globe at its peak warming may have brought about a more phased distribution of rainfall over the year, forcing greater spacing of trees and encouraging undergrowth vegetation. This would have created niches for the evolution of ground-dwelling herbivores. The hoofed mammals, the even-toed artiodactyls (e.g., primitive deer), and the odd-toed perissodactyls (e.g., earliest horse) appeared at this time in addition to the true primates (lemurlike creatures).

It is in the early to middle Eocene that several early proboscideans thrived. The best known of these is *Moeritherium*, a stocky, pig-size, and hippolike creature weighing about 125–250 kg; it lived in small, freshwater bodies or marshy habitat along the fringe of the ancient Tethys Sea. Its remains were first discovered about a century ago in the Fayum Basin of Egypt, but fossils were also later recovered from a wider area in northern Africa.

The dental characters of *Moeritherium* clearly indicate an animal that was a proboscidean archetype. It had six cheek teeth on either side of the upper and lower jaws. The molars were low crowned with simple cusps, a primitive condition known as *bunolophodont*. The second upper and lower incisor teeth protruded into the upper and lower jaws; these were clearly incipient tusks. The skull features suggest that even a short trunk was not present, although one moerithere (*M. lyonsi*) may have had a thick upper lip. The moeritheres were clearly specialized to feed on soft aquatic vegetation.

The 1984 discovery from early Eocene deposits in Algeria of a creature named *Numidotherium koholense* displaced the moeritheres as the oldest Eocene proboscideans. This creature stood 1–1.5 m tall. Its elevated skull with elevated external naris suggests that it had a short proboscis, rather like that of a tapir. Its teeth characters are closer to those of the older *Phosphatherium* (the former having larger teeth) than to the moeritheres. Based on the pattern of wear on the first premolar in the lower jaw, Nick Court has argued that *Numidotherium* specialized in stripping leaves from branches at head height or above. Such a diet is not consistent with the common assumption of a brackish water existence for the early proboscideans.

Before the end of the Eocene, another creature appeared, the enigmatic *Barytherium*, now recognized as a full-fledged proboscidean. Fossil remains of the barytheres go back to the Fayum site in Egypt, although they have also been discovered elsewhere in northern Africa. *Barytherium grave* from the Egyptian site seems to have already reached the size of a modern elephant, while another species from Libya resembled a moerithere in size. The upper jaw shows a large pair of lateral incisors (clearly "tusks"), while the molars were bilophodont (cusps arranged in pairs). Although *Barytherium* is not considered a mainstream proboscidean, it is considered to be related to another puzzling proboscidean—*Deinotherium*—which appeared at a later stage, along an evolutionary branch that was to reach a dead end after a very long run.

An African origin for the proboscideans was seriously challenged by the discovery of the anthracobunids from older Eocene rocks in the northwestern Indian subcontinent. Five genera (*Anthracobune, Ishatherium, Jozaria, Lammidhania,* and *Pilgrimella*) have been described from sites in Pakistan and India. The dentition of the anthracobunids is relatively unspecialized, with a full complement of teeth that included three incisors, one canine, four premolars, and three molars on either side of the upper and lower jaws. *Pilgrimella* was the size of a river hog, with a weight of about 125 kg. These unspecialized mammals lived in brackish water and clearly fed on soft vegetation in aquatic habitats. There has been much debate on whether the anthracobunids are proboscideans. The present view, strengthened by the cladistic analysis of Pascal Tassy, is that these are indeed proboscideans.

The Eocene fossil record thus reveals a diverse assemblage of mammals, several of them with proboscidean affinities, inhabiting a wide area in semi-aquatic habitats along the borders of the ancient Tethys Sea. This extended far beyond the limits of the present-day Mediterranean Sea. The habitats of the anthracobunids, moeritheres, barytheres, and *Numidotherium* are very similar—shallow, muddy water environments along fluctuating shorelines. This is consistent with the warm, moist world of the Eocene. Both the Asian and African fossil sites contain numerous marine invertebrates and vertebrates, confirming the proximity of the ocean to the inland proboscidean habitats.

Among these early, primitive proboscideans, we already see a specialization of dental characters from a full complement of teeth, to lost canines and premolars, enlarged incisors, and molars with increased lophs. Considerable increase in body size is also in evidence (one barythere was already the size of a modern elephant). What evolutionary pressures could have driven these changes in the Eocene proboscideans? Although the early-to-middle Eocene represented a peak warming period, the world grew cooler and drier, especially at higher latitudes, between the middle and late Eocene. The lush, tropical kind of vegetation began its retreat in the face of increased dryness and seasonality (remember that such descriptions are all relative; the world was much warmer and wetter than more recent epochs). On a regional scale, even the lower latitudes could have experienced some aridity, creating drier types of vegetation and newer niches to exploit. Larger herbivorous mammals evolved with more prominently ridged (or lophed) teeth to deal with coarser plant forage. Larger body size is partly a response to the nutritional needs for processing greater quantities of lower quality vegetation. The elephantlike size of *Barytherium grave* cannot be explained by a need for immunity from predators; there were no large carnivores during the Eocene. Rather, it can be explained by the changing vegetation, which made it necessary for a herbivore to consume the vegetation at higher rates. Although *Barytherium* fossils are associated with aquatic habitats and its anatomy certainly suggests life in swampy ground, it is also reasonable to think that this creature obtained substantial quantities of its forage from drier woodlands on more firm ground.

Interestingly, all of these Eocene proboscidean genera are now believed to be somewhat removed from the direct ancestry of present-day elephants. Even *Moeritherium*, long considered an ancestor, was possibly too specialized in certain skull and dental characters to be the ancestral stock of all latter-day proboscideans.

1.4   *The Oligocene—Evolutionary quiescence*

The global climate grew even cooler and more seasonal at the transition to the Oligocene (35 My ago). Tropical vegetation and the polar deciduous forests continued to shrink, with the latter eventually disappearing. Antarctica became ice-capped, but ice was yet to appear at the northern pole. Yet, the world was still somewhat wetter than at present, with lesser differences between the tropics and the poles. After the late Eocene extinctions, the Oligocene seems to have been a period of evolutionary stability; thus, this epoch does not attract the attention of many paleontologists.

Primitive Eocene proboscideans such as the moeritheres and barytheres seem to have lived to the end of the Oligocene. At the same time, there appeared in the early Oligocene at the Fayum site at least two types of palaeomastodontids that are closer to the elephants than are the moeritheres or latter-day deinotheres. The palaeomastodontids may actually have originated during the late Eocene and given rise to two major proboscidean branches, the mammutids and the gomphotheres, the latter being the ancestors of the true elephants. One type of palaeomastodontid, *Palaeomastodon beadnelli*, had oval-shaped (in cross section) tusks in both upper and lower jaws. The absence of canines and anterior premolars produced a marked diastema (gap) between the tusks and the cheek teeth. The molars were bilophodont, with cusps arranged transversely in pairs. Standing about 2 m high—the size of a subadult elephant—*Palaeomastodon* is believed to have been a dweller of forest and open woodland.

Another type—*Phiomia serridens*—stood a little taller than *Palaeomastodon* and had more specialized dentition. Molars were trilophodont, with three transverse pairs of conical cusps. Its horizontally projecting lower tusks were shorter and flattened, perhaps aiding the animal in feeding. *Phiomia* is believed to have been a creature of moister lowlands. Both the palaeomastodonts had short trunks, a bit longer than those of tapirs.

Except at the beginning, the quiet, equable Oligocene did not witness any great evolutionary upheavals. Many of the abundant mammals of the Oligocene belong to orders that still exist, although the families they represent are now extinct. The near absence of any proboscidean radiation (at least this is what the evidence suggests) could simply be a reflection of this evolutionary quiescence among mammals. But, 10 million years was too long a vacation for biological evolution, and the stage was already set by the end of the Oligocene for the next explosive radiation of mammals.

1.5   The Miocene—Evolutionary diversification

At the dawn of the Miocene, which spanned 24–5 My, a warming trend set in again, this time accompanied by an even drier climate. Shifts in the continental plates closed the Tethys Sea (creating the Mediterranean), while a passage was opened between Antarctica and South America. These changes, combined with other tectonic events, such as the uplifts of mountains (including the Himalayas, the Andes, and the Cordilleras), brought about changes in oceanic and atmospheric circulation to set up new global climatic patterns. The climatic contrasts of heat and cold increased between higher and lower latitudes. The warming in the middle latitudes seems to have caused some expansion of tropical and subtropical forests here, but the arid trend also encouraged thorn scrub and grasslands. Importantly, the new land bridges formed by lower sea levels and continental tectonics paved the way for vast migrations across continents by the new radiation of mammals.

The Miocene witnessed the greatest proliferation of the proboscidean tree, giving rise to the mammutids and the gomphotheres, the latter leading to the progenitor of the true elephants before the close of the epoch. Before a closer look at the evolutionary adaptations and radiations of these two groups, another bizarre proboscidean must be introduced—*Deinotherium* (the "terrible beast"), whose fossils first appear in middle Miocene strata. The deinotheres differentiated earlier, possibly during the late Eocene, and enjoyed phenomenal evolutionary success with little change over a period spanning the Oligocene, Miocene, Pliocene, and early Pleistocene. Deinothere fossils were first discovered in Europe, where they were wrongly classified with rhinos and tapirs. Later, their remains were found in North and East Africa and in Asia (as far east as India), but none have been recovered in the Americas. One genus, *Deinotherium*, alone lived through 20 My, a testimony to its great adaptability to a changing world. Over this time, it remained remarkably stable in form, save for an increase in body size (*Deinotherium giganteum* reached 4 m in height, much larger than any modern elephant).

The main peculiarity of *Deinotherium* was the absence of tusks in the upper jaw, but it possessed a pair of inward-curving tusks from a down-recurving lower jaw, not seen in any other proboscidean group. (The story goes that the Rev. Dr. William Buckland, Dean of Westminster, hypothesized that the deinothere was an aquatic creature that used its downward-pointing tusks to anchor itself to the riverbank while sleeping.) The tusks were possibly used for digging up plant roots and vegetation. At the same time, their role as merely a sexual display cannot be discounted (see chapter 3).

The deinotheres had a mixture of general and specialized proboscidean characters. The first molar was trilophodont, while the other two molars were bilophodont. Cheek teeth were replaced in a vertical fashion as in primitive proboscideans, rather than horizontally as in advanced forms. To prolong the life of the teeth, the enamel on deinothere teeth was much thicker (5–8 mm) than in the elephantids (1–5 mm). The shearing teeth were ideal for processing soft vegetation. The elevated position of the external nostrils suggests the presence of a trunk, perhaps only a bit shorter than that of the elephants. One of the earlier forms *Prodeinotherium* originated during the early Miocene in eastern Africa and possibly radiated into Asia (*Deinotherium indicum* is one species), Europe (*D. giganteum*), and other African localities (*D. bozasi*).

How did the deinotheres live through a changing world over millions of years with not much adaptive change, but only an increase in size? One possibility is that the deinotheres adapted to increasing aridity and poorer quality forage by increasing body size to process higher quantities of food. Jeheskel

Shoshani feels that the mixture of general and specialized characters in the deinotheres helped in adapting to changing environments across continents through time.

The early Miocene also saw the emergence of mammutids (family Mammutidae). The mammutids possibly differentiated during the Oligocene, but the earliest known fossils of a mammutid, the species *Eozygodon morotenesis*, are associated with the early Miocene of Uganda. The mammutids radiated from Africa into Eurasia (where *Zygolophodon turicensis* from the middle Miocene is a type species) and North America (*Mammut americanum* or the American mastodon from the late Miocene onward is one of the best known of extinct proboscideans). The mammutids were also a very successful proboscidean group, surviving to the end of the Pleistocene.

A mammutid was as different from a mammoth or an elephant as "a dog is from a cat" (to quote Shoshani 1992a, p. 24). Although it had a shortened lower jaw compared to many of the early gomphotheres, a mammutid had a long jaw compared to the mammoth. While some earlier mammutids had a short pair of tusks in the lower jaw, this was completely lost in later forms. The upper jaw had a pair of well-developed tusks. The molars were low crowned with little bonding material, but with thick enamel. Pairs of domed cusps lined the length of the teeth (hence the term *mastodont*, meaning nipple-tooth in Greek). Among mammutids, there are the beginnings of horizontal replacement of the cheek teeth. Only two teeth were in wear at any given time. Mammutids such as the American mastodon were clearly adapted to a browsing mode of feeding.

The gomphotheres are a group of Miocene proboscideans considered to represent the second major radiation of the order. There has been much confusion over the use of the term *gomphothere*. Indeed, Jeheskel Shoshani feels that the gomphotheres have been a "wastebasket" of the proboscideans into which taxa of uncertain position or affinities have been dumped at various times. This is ironic given the importance of the gomphotheres as the stem group of the true elephants. It is beyond the scope of this volume to go into gomphothere taxonomy; I use the term gomphothere in the broader sense to include an assortment of Miocene proboscideans with the exception of the mammutids, stegodontids, and the true elephants. Given the taxonomic and phylogenetic uncertainties, I only briefly trace the radiations of some of the better-known gomphotheres.

As with most of the ancestral proboscidean groups, the gomphotheres originated in Africa, where fossils (of the genus *Gomphotherium*) have been traced to early Miocene deposits in Egypt and Kenya. Depending on how one defines evolutionary success of a taxon, the gomphotheres were the most successful originally, migrating to all continents save Australia and Antarctica (no other group went to these either), diversifying into a large number of forms and living from the early Miocene to the Pleistocene. Unlike the mammutids, the gomphotheres were "long-jawed" proboscideans.

The genus *Gomphotherium* is the most morphologically conservative of this group, with few diagnostic characters to distinguish it from the more advanced gomphotheres. It had tusks in both the upper and lower jaws plus a well-developed, though short, trunk. The molars were typically trilophodont (three transverse ridges), low crowned (brachyodont), with thick enamel. A sequence of progressively larger teeth indicates both horizontal and vertical replacement. *Gomphotherium* was as large as a modern Asian elephant.

From its eastern African origins, *Gomphotherium* migrated into Eurasia, where fossils are known from Arabia, Pakistan, France, Portugal, and even Japan and into North America through the Bering land bridge during the Miocene. Several species are described for the Eurasian sites, but their relationships are still unclear. One early Miocene proboscidean that caught everyone's imagination is *Platybelodon*, which differed from *Gomphotherium* in having reduced upper tusks (which were vestigial in females) but possessing a pair of enormously long and flattened lower tusks juxtaposed to form a shovel. The specialized nature of this character seems to point definitely to a creature that lived in marshy habitats and used its shovel to dig up soft vegetation and roots. Clive Spinage, however, argues that this large gomphothere could not have obtained sufficient nutrition from low-quality aquatic plants (which have large air spaces for buoyancy). Rather, the shovel could have been used to crop land plants just as hippos do with their broad, horny lips. Perhaps, the "shovel-tuskers" adapted to an increasingly arid Miocene by switching from marshy plants to drier ground herbs. A later form, *Gnathabelodon*, lost its lower tusks, and its protruding bony jaw was presumably covered with tough skin. The related genus *Amebelodon*, also widespread across Eurasia and North America, had narrower, more elongated shovels with differences in dentine structure. *Amebelodon* is well known from North American sites, where they may have occupied similar moist habitat niches.

By the middle Miocene, the globe had reached its peak warming since the beginning of the Oligocene.

A cooling trend accompanied by further desiccation set in during the late Miocene, about 10 My ago. Mountain uplift, especially in the tectonically active Himalayan-Tibetan plateau region, during the early-to-middle Miocene had exposed more rock to chemical weathering. In the process, carbon dioxide was removed from the atmosphere and transported to the oceanic sink. This "reverse greenhouse" effect resulted in greater loss of heat from the atmosphere. The increasing aridity promoted the spread of grasslands in the two American continents. Drier vegetation types also spread in the other continents, although true grasslands were not as yet expansive.

The reduced atmospheric carbon dioxide also brought about another ecological change that could have had important consequences for the evolution of herbivores, including the elephants. This was a shift toward grasses with the C_4 pathway of carbon fixation during photosynthesis (see chapter 5). Plants with the more common C_3 photosynthetic pathway are very inefficient at fixing carbon when CO_2 levels fall below a certain threshold (this is partly temperature dependent, but may be in the range of 160–180 ppm). Under such conditions, the C_4 plants (primarily tropical kinds of grasses and sedges) successfully

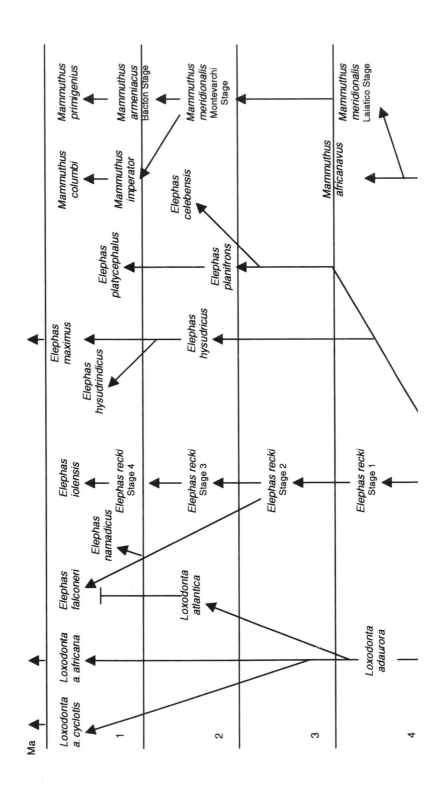

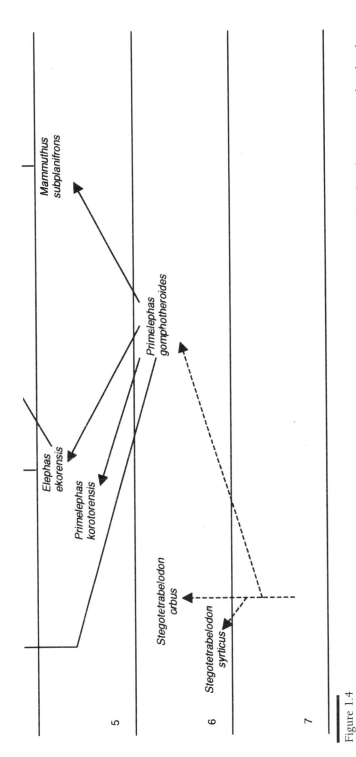

Figure 1.4
Phylogenetic relationships within the Elephantidae. (Updated from Maglio 1973, figure 40, p. 105, and Todd and Roth 1996. Reproduced with permission granted by the American Philosophical Society.)

out-compete their C_3 counterparts. The work of Thure Cerling, Jay Quade, and others on fossil soils and herbivore tooth enamel using carbon isotopic analysis showed that C_4 grasslands underwent a major global expansion during the late Miocene, anywhere between 8 and 6 My ago (see chapter 5 for details of the stable carbon isotopic method and its use in dietary inferences). The evidence for expansion of the C_4 grassland (used here in the broader sense to include sedges) comes from sites as far apart as North America, South America, East Africa, and South Asia.

Grasses had been around for a long time, probably evolving during the early Paleocene. Many herbivorous mammals undoubtedly included grasses as a part of their diets. The grasses initially played a relatively minor ecological role. Their increased success during the late Miocene, however, introduced a new dimension to the equation between herbivores and vegetation. Unlike most other plants, the grasses grow from basal tissues that are not destroyed by herbivory. Moderate levels of herbivory actually stimulate their productivity. Animals adapted to feed on grass ensured themselves a constant supply of a plant that spread across large landscapes. This is precisely what a variety of the later Miocene mammals did; equids, bovids, rodents, and proboscideans are some of the groups that evolved newer structures to take advantage of this resource.

Grasses, especially the perennial siliceous grasses of the C_4 type, have the disadvantage (to herbivores) of being highly abrasive to teeth. The adaptive response of grazing mammals, therefore, is to develop teeth with high crowns (hypsodonty), complex surface patterns, and stronger reinforcement of cement. This is most striking in the evolution of horses, for instance. The proboscideans, too, show dental adaptations to the late Miocene vegetational shift.

The late Miocene saw the third major radiation of the Proboscidea—the emergence of the true elephants (family Elephantidae) (fig. 1.4), which diversified through the Plio-Pleistocene. An "advanced" gomphothere was most likely the ancestor of the elephants. But, before riding the elephant wave, we must briefly attend a sideshow in the great proboscidean drama.

The stegodontids, derived from an advanced gomphothere, were once believed to be ancestors of elephants, but are now considered a sister group of the elephantids. They evolved in Asia around the same time that the true elephants arose in Africa. Actually, one genus with less-specialized characters, Stegolophodon, may have arisen in earlier Miocene times in Southeast Asia (Indochina) and stagnated in molar development, before a late Miocene radiation to other parts of Asia. Stegodontid fossils are known from China, Japan, Southeast Asian islands, and the Indian subcontinent, as well as Europe and Africa. The genus Stegodon diversified more rapidly during the Pliocene.

A particularly impressive form was Stegodon ganesa (named after the Asian deity with an elephantine form; see chapter 2), which stood 3.5 m at the shoulder and sported a formidable pair of tusks. Emerging from the upper jaw, these thick tusks almost touched the ground, curving sideways and upward at the ends. Only vestigial tusks remained in the shortened lower jaw. Molar replacement in the stegodons was horizontal, with only two teeth being in wear at a given time in each jaw half. The molars had up to 14 lophs (transverse ridges), with each loph composed of a row of thickly enameled cusps. The low-crowned teeth, however, suggest that stegodons were adapted to a browsing diet of forest leaves and bamboo shoots.

We must, therefore, seek for the ancestral elephant among the subfamily Stegotetrabelodontinae (fig. 1.4). The two recorded genera, *Stegotetrabelodon* and *Stegodibelodon*, are known from fragmentary remains in Africa. The prefix *stego* is confusing as it implies that these were stegodontids, as earlier believed, but they are now considered true elephantids, or at least intermediate between the gomphotheres and the elephantids, based on their dental characters. They had low-crowned teeth like the gomphotheres, but with a few plates characteristic of the elephantids. The ridged surface, with cusps in the more primitive forms, had now evolved into plates, each plate consisting of a flattened loop or lamella with enamel on the outside and dentine filling inside. The space between the enamel loops was U or V shaped as in the elephants. While *Stegotetrabelodon* had short incisors in the lower jaw, these are absent in the more progressive *Stegodibelodon*, which also had a shorter mandible.

One of these early African elephantids is believed to have given rise to *Primelephas* just prior to the end of the Miocene (5 My ago). Vincent Maglio considered *Primelephas* to be the progenitor of the genera *Loxodonta, Mammuthus,* and *Elephas,* while M. Beden thought that *Loxodonta* could be derived directly from the stegotetrabelodonts. The former view seems the more favored today. A more recent discovery of an unnamed species of *Loxodonta* from late Miocene deposits in Uganda and from Kenya seems to imply that *Primelephas,* although an elephantid and related to *Elephas* and *Mammuthus,* may not be a direct ancestor. The molars of *Primelephas gomphotheroides* show some structural advances over those of the stegotetrabelodonts. Although still low crowned, the molar ridges are more like those of later elephants. A pair of small incisors was still retained in the short symphysis of the lower jaw.

Thus, 6 My ago, or close to that time, there were many proboscidean players, belonging to an amazing 22 of the 38 or so recognized genera, marching across all continents except Australia and Antarctica. They included the primitive deinotheres, the mammutids, the gomphotheres, the stegodontids, and the true elephants. There is no precise figure for the number of species that were found at a given point in time, but this was undoubtedly large.

How could such a variety of large bodied proboscideans coexist? One explanation obviously is that the various genera and species were geographically spread over the different continents. Even where more than one species of proboscidean were found together in the same locality, there could have been ecological separation in use of habitats and plant types consumed. The climatic changes occurring during the late Miocene were also giving rise to newer vegetational compositions, structures, and mosaics, providing the stimulus to evolutionary adaptations among the mammals. Thus, gradation in use of semi-aquatic or soft vegetation, browse from moist forests or drier woodlands, and grass from savannas or true grasslands may have contributed to a certain degree of niche separation and coexistence among proboscideans. By the close of the Miocene, about 5 My ago, the emergence of the true elephants ensured that this amazing run of proboscidean diversity, although in decline, was not going to end in a hurry.

1.6   The Pliocene—Radiation of the elephants

The relatively cool, dry climate of the Pliocene, inherited from late Miocene times, created conditions under which the types of vegetation with which we are now familiar began to appear. Tundra vegetation appeared over permafrost inside the Arctic Circle, followed by a belt of coniferous evergreen forest ("taiga"). Deserts, practically unknown earlier, appeared at lower latitudes. The grasslands that now spread over large continental areas were more arid and treeless compared to the earlier wooded savannas. Tropical forests were squeezed into smaller areas around the equator. Such conditions were not conducive to maintaining a diversity of either plants or animals. Mammalian herbivores had to cope with new challenges in dealing with poorer quality forage. A number of those that could not adapt to a changed world became extinct, especially in North America, which was not connected as yet to an equatorial rain forest zone. Those that did adapt further increased in body size, a trait that equipped them better to deal with unfavorable seasons and to subsist on a diet of coarse plants.

The "third radiation" of the proboscideans, that of the true elephants, now proceeded in earnest. The evolution of the elephantids during the Plio-Pleistocene was correlated with fairly rapid changes in skull architecture and mastication apparatus (fig. 1.5), apparently to deal with the changing vegetation conditions. This involved a transition from the combined grinding and shearing teeth function, characteristic of gomphotheres, to a mostly shearing function, as in the elephantids. Concurrently, there was an increase in the number of plates (lamellae) with U-shaped valleys in between. Horizontal replacement of the molars was well developed. The most striking feature of dental evolution was the rapid increase in crown height (hypsodonty) with thinning of the enamel. Clearly, these changes enabled the elephantids to chew coarse vegetation, including abrasive grasses, fibrous bark, and other plants likely to wear down the molars quickly over a longer life span.

Primelephas gomphotheroides, or a very closely related form, gave rise to three lineages in sub-Saharan Africa. The evidence of the fossil record suggests that *Loxodonta* was the first to differentiate, close to the Miocene-Pliocene boundary, followed by *Mammuthus* (mammoth) and *Elephas* during the early Pliocene. The molecular and morphological data, however, are equivocal on this point.

The earliest known mammoth, *Mammuthus subplanifrons*, is described from early Pliocene fossils in eastern and southern Africa. A more progressive spe-

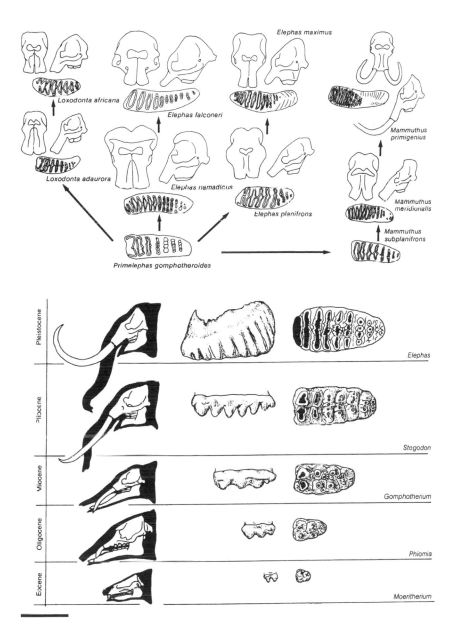

Figure 1.5

A sequence of proboscideans (*bottom panel*) showing general morphological trends; apart from changes in overall skull characters, the increase in number of lophs or cusp rows on each tooth and increase in the crown height are also shown. The upper panel shows in greater detail the changes in molar pattern and skull proportion for each of the three elephant genera, *Loxodonta*, *Elephas*, and *Mammuthus*, during the Plio-Pleistocene. (From Savage and Long 1986. Reproduced with the permission of Michael R. Long, Illustrator.)

cies, *Mammuthus africanavus*, occurred in late Pliocene times in the Chad basin and other northern African sites. These African mammoths clearly lived in a tropical environment, a far cry from the icy wastes of the tundra their descendants finally occupied. South of the Sahara, there is no evidence for mammoths after the late Pliocene. In the meantime, an early mammoth form had migrated into Europe, where *Mammuthus meridionalis* is well known at a number of sites, from England and France to Italy and Russia. Vincent Maglio believed that *M. meridionalis* derived from *M. africanavus*, which migrated across the Gibraltar in western Europe. Mammoth specialist Adrian Lister, however, thinks it more plausible that there was a migration of descendants of *M. subplanifrons* through the eastern land bridge (Middle East to Turkey) into Europe. Standing 4 m in height, *M. meridionalis* would have towered over the modern elephants. The creature inhabited mixed deciduous woodland with browse-trees such as oak, ash, beech, hemlock, wing nut, and hickory. This forest-dwelling mammoth still had low-crowned teeth (for an elephant) with 12–14 thick-enameled lamellae on the last molar. At this time during the late Pliocene, Europe seems to have enjoyed a relatively warm, mild climate.

Meanwhile, *Loxodonta* was well differentiated in Africa. The earliest recognizable species, found in Kenya in deposits 4 My old, is *Loxodonta adaurora*, which lived through most of the Pliocene. Its dental advancement over *Primelephas* was comparable to that seen in the earliest mammoths. Over its evolutionary age of about 2 My, however, it seems to have changed little in its dental characters. By the late Pliocene, *Loxodonta adaurora* was becoming scarce in areas of former abundance in East Africa, even though the local ecology had not changed much. Most likely, this was due to its displacement by a member of the third lineage of elephants, the genus *Elephas*.

Elephas ekorensis, the first recognizable species of this genus, appears along with the earliest mammoth remains in East African deposits. With narrower plates and thinner enamel, it had slightly more progressive dental characters than the earliest loxodonts. During the Pliocene itself, *E. ekorensis* gave rise to two lineages, an Afro-Eurasian lineage that eventually reached a dead end and an Asian lineage that gave rise to the modern Asian elephant. There is little doubt that *E. recki*, the dominant *Elephas* fossil in East Africa at that time, was a descendant of *E. ekorensis*. The Asian derivative of *E. ekorensis* was *E. planifrons*, found in late Pliocene and Pleistocene deposits of the Middle East, Indian subcontinent, and northern China. This species, or another that closely resembled it, may even have reached Java, where it further evolved into distinctive forms.

The earliest, or one of the most important, major cooling event in the Northern Hemisphere actually occurred about 2.5 My ago. Evidence for this event comes from sites around the globe. Loess deposition began in Central China, temperatures dropped in the Andes and the Netherlands, and seasonal climate was established in the Mediterranean. This was the period when the Sahara became a permanent desert, the forests became savannas in eastern Africa, and even western Africa turned somewhat arid. Alan Turner examined mammalian faunas in Africa and Europe and found this climatic phenomenon reflected in distinct evolutionary changes. *Elephas recki* progressed over time through five recognizable evolutionary stages toward higher tooth crowns, more plates, and thinner and more folded enamel. The major shift in hypsodonty occurred between 2.3 and 2.0 My ago. At the same time, the genus *Loxodonta* disappeared locally in the East African fossil record. It is possible that *Loxodonta*, predominantly a browser, was affected to a greater degree by the loss of moist woodlands. *Mammuthus* also made its first appearance in Europe around this climatic event 2.5 My ago.

The radiation of the elephantids was yet to reach its peak diversity; this was retained for the momentous Pleistocene. Apart from witnessing the rise of the three major elephantid lineages, the Pliocene was also the stage for other interesting proboscidean events. The amazing *Deinotherium* survived through the Pliocene. The stegodons continued to push into the corners of Asia, differentiating into newer species in the Indian subcontinent, China, Japan, Indochina, and Southeast Asia. At least three species (*Stegodon bombifrons, S. ganesa*, and *S. insignis*) are recognized from the Indian subcontinent, with the last probably endemic. The *S. ganesa* here was most likely an invader from South east Asia. The distribution of *S. zdanskyi* in both northern China and Japan suggests that a land connection existed between the Japanese islands and mainland Asia during the Pliocene. Several stegodon species are known from the East Asian region. *Stegodon elephantoides* from Myanmar (Burma) is considered a classic stegodon, but has been poorly studied. It is safe to assume that, prior to the arrival of *Elephas*, a vast territory from South Asia into Southeast and East Asia was a stegodon kingdom. Interestingly, among the stegodons, there is probably the only instance of a proboscidean migration into Africa. *Stegodon kaisensis* is derived from one of the early Asian stegodonts that migrated back during the Pliocene to the cradle continent of the proboscideans.

The very early Pliocene, about 4.5 My ago (the late Hemphillian in North American stratigraphy), was a period of the highest mammalian extinctions in North America in the preceding 10 My. These were associated with a trend toward a cooler, drier climate in the continent's temperate belt. A mammutid (*Pliomastodon*), a gomphothere (*Gomphotherium*), and an amebelodontid (*Amebelodon*) did not survive this episode. The mammutids and the gomphotheres, however, left behind successors.

Autochthonous speciation in the continent ensured that one mammutid and at least three gomphothere genera continued to reign the Pliocene New World. The American mastodon (*Mammut americanum*) first appeared about 4 My ago in the region of the present Washington State. Its eventual distribution over North America encompassed a large tract up to the East Coast, although a considerable degree of ecological separation from the mammoth is evident from their fossil distributions during Pleistocene times. The mastodon continued to be predominantly a browser in woodland habitat. About 3 My ago, the establishment of the Panamanian land bridge triggered the great American interchange of plants and animals across the northern and southern continents.

This passage, however, was a "filter barrier," regulating the exchange through its varying ecological conditions.

Strangely, *Mammut americanum* did not migrate into South America and neither did the gomphothere *Rhynchotherium*, which evolved autochthonously from gomphothere stock during late Miocene times. Other North American gomphotheres, however, took advantage of this passage to move into the southern continent for the first time in proboscidean history. *Cuvieronius*, a gomphothere that may have evolved from *Rhynchotherium* in southern North America, may have been one of the first to reach South America. This creature favored mesic coastal savanna and scrub habitats; it may have thus used the warm dry periods when tropical scrub covered the Panamanian corridor to disperse into South America.

Three other gomphotheres (*Stegomastodon*, *Haplomastodon*, and *Notiomastodon*) are also known from South America. Some of these gomphotheres may have been products of Pleistocene evolution after isolation on this southern continent (a recent discovery of an unidentified "gomphothere" from upper Miocene strata of Amazonian Peru raises other intriguing possibilities, including migrations from South to North America).

By the late Pliocene, the mastodonts, now flourishing in North America, had died out in Europe and Asia.

1.7   *The Pleistocene—The final burst and then collapse*

About 2 My ago, the world entered an even cooler period of alternating glacial and interglacial phases. The Pleistocene, which lasted until 10,000 years ago, is sometimes called the Ice Age, but the intense periods of cold were punctuated by warm episodes called *interglacials*, during which the climate was similar to that of the present. The warm periods were relatively short, lasting only a few thousand or tens of thousands years every 100,000 years or so. At peak glaciation, the polar ice sheets expanded; during the last full glaciation (20,000–16,000 years ago), ice covered Canada, crept into the northern United States, and overran Scandinavia and the British Isles. Average global temperatures at higher latitudes were 5°C lower than present-day values. There have been 20 or more cold-warm oscillations since the beginning of the Pleistocene.

The frigid world of the Ice Age, with contrasting climate between the poles and the equator, had some of the most inhospitable habitats still seen today. Cold desert or tundra at higher latitudes and hot deserts in the tropical belt are symptomatic of the most arid habitats the globe has seen. Tropical forests disappeared altogether in places or were squeezed into pockets—the so-called Pleistocene refugia. At peak glaciation, the global sea level was much lower, providing land bridges across island archipelagos such as the Sunda shelf (connecting mainland Southeast Asia to Java, Sumatra, Borneo, and other islands). New opportunities were created for the migration of mammals and their subsequent evolution.

The start of the Pleistocene has been variously dated at 1.7 to 2 My ago or even earlier, depending on the evidence for the first glacial event in different parts of the world. The Pleistocene witnessed a great geographical expansion of the elephantids and a high rate of speciation and phyletic evolution. Rapid climatic change, habitat isolation accompanying the glacial events, and increased competition among species may have contributed to this rapid evolution. At the end, the curtains also came down swiftly on a bewildering array of proboscideans, from dwarf elephants not unlike the moeritheres in size to the towering mammoths.

A primitive stage of *Loxodonta atlantica* appeared by early Pleistocene in southern Ethiopia. The genus *Loxodonta* never left the African continent. As with *L. adaurora*, *L. atlantica* became scarce in eastern Africa with the rise of *Elephas recki*. By the middle Pleistocene, however, *L. atlantica* became the dominant elephant in northern and southern Africa. In the later Pleistocene, *L. atlantica* disappeared concurrent with the rise of *E. iolensis*, presumably a derivative of *E. recki*. It was only after the extinction of *Elephas* in Africa that *Loxodonta* reemerged as the dominant elephant in the two forms known today.

Elephas evolved more rapidly. Although it reached a dead end in Africa, with the last recorded species being *E. iolensis*, the genus continued its march across Eurasia. A derivative of one of the middle stages of *E. recki*, possibly *E. recki atavus*, probably migrated through the Middle East into Eurasia, where it appeared as *E. namadicus* during the later Pleistocene and the closely related *E. antiquus* in Europe. This lineage is also commonly known as *Palaeoloxodon*. Fossils of *E. namadicus* are widespread, from Germany, through India (Narmada and Godavari River valleys), and to Java, southern China, Mongolia, and Japan. *Elephas namadicus* showed further specialization in skull and dental characters. Its molars were narrower, higher crowned, and more progressive in number and spacing of plates.

It was, however, the earlier migration of *Elephas* into Asia that finally led to the modern *Elephas maximus*. The late Pliocene migration of a derivative of *E. ekorensis* resulted in new phyletic lines. The first species to appear in Asia was *E. planifrons*, well known from the Siwalik Hills in the Indian subcontinent. This species is also found in deposits over a wide area, from Bethlehem in the west to the island of Java in the east. Depending on its evolutionary stage, the molars of *E. planifrons* are variable. The species that was the direct ancestor of the modern Asian elephant is, however, *E. hysudricus*, also from the Siwalik beds. Some paleontologists considered *E. hysudricus* to be descended from *E. planifrons*, but their contemporaneous occurrence in the Siwaliks suggests that they had a common ancestor. According to Vincent Maglio, it seems probable that both *E. planifrons* and *E. hysudricus* had a common ancestry from the *E. ekorensis–recki* complex, with *E. planifrons* being more conservative, while *E. hysudricus* evolved rapidly, as did *E. recki*. The discovery of *E. platycephalus* from India poses a problem. This later Pleistocene elephant, with a flattened primitive skull and small tusks, was probably an offshoot of *E. planifrons*.

Elephas hysudricus spans a relatively short period during the early Pleistocene in the Siwalik and upper Irrawady (Myanmar) deposits. The most striking feature of this elephant was the greatly expanded parietal and occipital regions of the skull. Being even taller than the modern Asian elephant, *E. hysudricus* thus had two very prominent domes or "bumps" on the top of the head, a feature that is retained, although less prominently, in *E. maximus*. *Elephas hysudricus* spread further east and evolved into *E. hysudrindicus*, known from Java. The last species converged toward the earlier *E. recki* type of skull, in some ways reversing the overall evolutionary trend. *Elephas maximus* is believed to be derived from *E. hysudricus*, after the mid-Pleistocene, by progressing further in dental characters. The number of plates more than tripled in *E. maximus* compared to the earliest form of this genus. The enamel became thinner and attained its maximum folding, while crown height quadrupled (over *Primelephas*).

Pleistocene evolutionary changes in the *Mammuthus* lineage were equally as, if not more, remarkable as those in *Elephas*. *Mammuthus meridionalis*, which had evolved from earlier mammoth forms during the late Pliocene, continued to thrive through the earlier Pleistocene in Europe and Asia. By about 1 My ago, the global cooling had further intensified, causing the woodland habitat of the ancestral mammoth to retreat and grassy landscape to take its place. *Mammuthus meridionalis* responded to this deterioration in climate and vegetation in Europe. Mammoth fossils dating to 750,000 years ago and later show progressively higher tooth crowns, thinner enamel ridges, and more enamel bands or plates per tooth.

The steppe mammoth, *M. trogontherii*, was clearly recognizable by this time in grass-dominated habitats across Europe. Newer interpretation from the work of Adrian Lister and Andrei Sher suggests that *M. trogontherii* did not evolve in situ in Europe as previously believed, but migrated from Siberia, where it had arisen earlier, perhaps as early as 1.2 My ago. A 1990 discovery of *M. trogontherii* at West Runton in England suggests that about 600,000 years ago this species still inhabited some woodlands, but elsewhere in Europe, its association with open habitat is clear.

The evolution of the mammoth culminated in the familiar woolly mammoth, *M. primigenius*, which first appeared in Europe about 200,000 years ago, but was again seen in Siberia perhaps 800,000 years ago. The early onset and persistent severity of glacial conditions in northeastern Siberia may have triggered this evolutionary trend.

Although smaller than the steppe mammoth, the woolly mammoth represented the most advanced adaptations among the proboscideans in skull and dental characters, no doubt driven by the most inhospitable habitat in which a proboscidean had ever survived. *Mammuthus primigenius* not only possessed molars with the highest crowns among the elephantids, as did *M. trogontherii*, but also had molars with even thinner enamel and up to 26 enamel ridges. To accommodate the higher-crowned teeth, the skull morphology changed through a deepening of the upper and lower jaws. The top of the skull also became more prominent (single dome, unlike the double-dome *Elephas*), thus providing greater area for attachment of the tendons and muscles needed to support its enormous tusks. To cope with the frigid cold of the last Ice Age, *M. primigenius* had a coat of thick fur, as entire frozen carcasses in the tundra have shown.

About 1.8 My ago, *M. meridionalis* or the advanced early Siberian *M. trogontherii*–like mammoth migrated across the Bering Strait during a period of low sea level into North America. Here, it underwent autochthonous speciation to give the Columbian mammoth, *M. columbi*. The Columbian mammoth was one of the largest of the mammoths, standing about 4 m high, but it lacked the dense fur of the woolly mammoth as it lived in a more pleasant southern habitat. However, it possessed the imposing, spirally curved tusks characteristic of the mammoths. The range of this mammoth extended south to Mexico, the farthest that *Mammuthus* was to reach after its migration out of Africa.

Some paleontologists describe two other mammoth species for North America, the imperial mammoth, *M. imperator*, with characters between *M. meridionalis* and *M. columbi*, and *M. jeffersonii*, which seems more advanced than *M. columbi*. These two are of uncertain validity; they may be considered subspecies of *M. columbi*.

The woolly mammoth, *M. primigenius*, which ranged widely across northern Europe and Siberia, also eventually migrated across Beringia about 100,000 years ago into North America. This represented the second and last mammoth migration into the New World. As in Eurasia, the woolly mammoth occupied the same northern range of latitudes in North America, maintaining reasonable separation overall from the Columbian mammoth, which had already established itself further south, although some overlap did occur.

1.7.1   Dwarf elephants and mammoths

No account of proboscidean evolution would be complete or accurate without mention of the remarkable reversal in body size that occurred during the Pleistocene. Several species of elephants (including mammoths) isolated on islands during the fluctuating sea levels of the Pleistocene underwent rapid dwarfing. This phenomenon was not necessarily confined to the Pleistocene, but may have occurred much earlier in the Southeast Asian islands, although the evidence is fragmentary. There are some clear examples from these islands for Pliocene dwarf proboscideans. The best-studied examples of dwarf proboscideans, however, come from islands off the Californian coast and those in the Mediterranean during Pleistocene times (fig 1.6).

Many of the Southeast Asian islands (Java, Sumatra, Borneo) have been repeatedly connected to or isolated from the mainland, depending on past sea levels. Other islands, such as the Philippines, Sulawesi (Celebes), Flores, Sumba, and Timor, have apparently remained isolated, but the surrounding sea was not a barrier to proboscideans swimming to these islands. The remains of a dwarf proboscidean from Sulawesi dating to the late Pliocene were described by Dirk Hooijer as *Archidiskodon celebensis*. This species was later recog-

Figure 1.6
A model of the dwarf elephant *Elephas falconeri* found during the Pleistocene in certain islands of the Mediterranean. (Photo courtesy of A. M. Lister.)

nized as belonging to *Elephas* and hence was named *E. celebensis*. Vincent Maglio considered this to be derived from a dwarfing of *E. planifrons*, but others think it also was likely to have descended directly from the more primitive *Stegotetrabelodon*. The advanced characters of *E. celebensis*, such as the short, high skull or high-crowned molars, are consistent with either an *E. planifrons* origin or a parallel evolutionary trend from a more primitive ancestor. Interestingly, a dwarf *Stegodon* is also known from the mainland Javan fauna of Kedung Brubus during the middle Pleistocene, while another *Stegodon* of large size or mainland proportions is known from the island of Flores. Dwarfing of proboscideans in Southeast Asia thus demands explanations that go beyond habitat insularity and probably are related to factors such as time of isolation, habitable area, vegetation, predation, and so on.

A more straightforward "island effect" explanation is clear for other instances of dwarfing. Several islands in the Mediterranean have shown such dwarf proboscideans. The best known among these is *Elephas falconeri* from the islands of Malta and Sicily, dating to at least 500,000 years ago when the two islands were joined. Believed to be derived from *E. namadicus* (or *E. antiquus* as the European branch of *E. namadicus* is sometimes named), *E. falconeri* stood only 1 m tall as an adult and is the smallest known elephant. In comparison to body size, the molars of *E. falconeri* were proportionately larger than in *E. antiquus*. A second arrival of *E. antiquus* here during the later Pleistocene gave rise to a somewhat larger dwarf named *E. mnaidriensis*. A dwarf mammoth is known from the island of Sardinia, while some dwarfs from Cyprus were descendants of *E. antiquus*. Other dwarfs of uncertain affinities have been discovered in Crete, Cyclades, and Dodecanese.

The Channel Islands off the coast of California have the best example of dwarf proboscideans in the New World. During the late Pleistocene, the Columbian mammoth *M. columbi* seems to have colonized these islands by swimming across the 30-km oceanic separation from the mainland rather than using a land bridge. The resulting dwarf mammoths, *M. exilis*, found on these islands, particularly on Santa Rosa, typically stood 1.2–1.8 m (4–6 feet) tall as adults. Allometric scaling suggests body weights between 200 kg and 2 tons compared to 5–10 tons for the Columbian mammoth. These survived until the very late Pleistocene, about 12,000 years ago.

An amazing discovery was reported from the remote Wrangel Islands of the Siberian Arctic in 1993 by S. L. Vartanyan, V. E. Garutt, and A. V. Sher. The woolly mammoth had not become extinct by the end of the Pleistocene, 10,000 years ago, as earlier believed, but survived as a reduced form until as recently as 4,000 years ago. Normal-size woolly mammoths also lived here 12,000 years ago when Wrangel was still connected to Siberia. Rising sea levels at the end of the Pleistocene cut off Wrangel from the mainland. By about 7,000 years ago, the mammoth had reduced in size to about 1.8 m (6 feet). Over a 5,000-year period, or about 100 mammoth life spans, the height of the species was reduced by over 40% and there was an even greater reduction in body mass, an extremely rapid evolutionary transition, if not as extreme as that of the Mediterranean and the Southeast Asian species.

Several explanations are possible for this dwarfing of elephantids on islands. Often, an island has not been colonized by a large predator or is too small to hold a viable predator population. Once it is free from predation pressure, large body size is not of much advantage to a herbivore. An island habitat has limited food resources and also increases competition. A smaller body size and a need for fewer resources would thus be favored. Interestingly, the island rule is reversed for small mammals such as rodents, for which gigantism is favored under insular conditions.

1.7.2   *Evolutionary rates in the elephants*

The rates of evolution can be measured in many different ways. Among the elephants (including mammoths), the rate of change of teeth characters has been quantified in detail by Vincent Maglio. Over the first 2 My after their emergence in Africa, all three genera—*Loxodonta*, *Mammuthus*, and *Elephas*—did not differ much in their rates of molar evolution. While *Loxodonta* continued to be conservative in molar development through the late Pliocene and the Pleistocene, *Mammuthus* and *Elephas* then surged ahead, with the woolly mammoth representing the most advanced stage.

A major dental change that characterized the evolution of the elephants was reduction in the grinding component of mastication in favor of the shearing component. A simplified "shearing index," suggested by Vincent Maglio and based on lamellar frequency and molar width, gives one indication of the relative adaptation of dental characters among various species (table 1.2).

Changes in individual molar characters, such as the number of lamellar plates, enamel thickness, and crown height, among the three genera reflect not only the differences in evolutionary rates, but also the nature of adaptive responses to changing ecological conditions encountered (fig. 1.7). It is clear that, in all these characters, the rates of change were much greater in *Mammuthus* and *Elephas* than in *Loxodonta*, especially from about 3 My ago.

The noted evolutionary biologist J. B. S. Haldane suggested the use of a unit, the darwin, to depict the rate of evolutionary change. A rate of evolution

Table 1.2
Shearing ability of an elephant's third molar calculated from the mean lamellar frequency (LF^3 = upper third molar; LF_3 = lower third molar) and lower molar width (W_3) as $(2LF^3 \times 2LF_3 \times W_3)/1000$.

Species	LF^3	LF_3	W_3	Shearing Index
Stegotetrabelodon syrticus	3.0	3.1	119.2	4.43*
Stegotetrabelodon orbus	2.8	2.9	97.9	3.18
Primelephas gomphotheroides	3.1	3.3	94.5	3.87
Loxodonta adaurora	3.7	3.4	90.2	4.54
Loxodonta atlantica	4.2	4.6	89.1	6.89
Loxodonta africana	4.1	4.2	75.4	5.19
Elephas ekorensis	4.4	4.0	91.4	6.34
Elephas recki	5.1	5.0	90.6	9.24
Elephas iolensis	4.0	5.3	104.7	8.88
Elephas antiquus	5.6	5.7	75.1	9.59
Elephas planifrons	4.2	4.2	94.0	6.63
Elephas celebensis	7.9	6.2	42.5	8.33
Elephas hysudricus	5.1	5.4	91.7	10.10
Elephas maximus	6.6	7.2	77.0	14.90
Mammuthus subplanifrons	3.5	3.3	94.4	4.36
Mammuthus africanavus	4.1	3.8	91.9	5.37
Mammuthus meridionalis	4.6	4.6	97.2	8.76
Mammuthus armeniacus	6.3	6.5	87.6	14.35
Mammuthus primigenius	8.5	9.0	87.6	26.81

Source: From Maglio (1973). Reproduced with the permission of the American Philosophical Society.
*Corrected from Maglio.

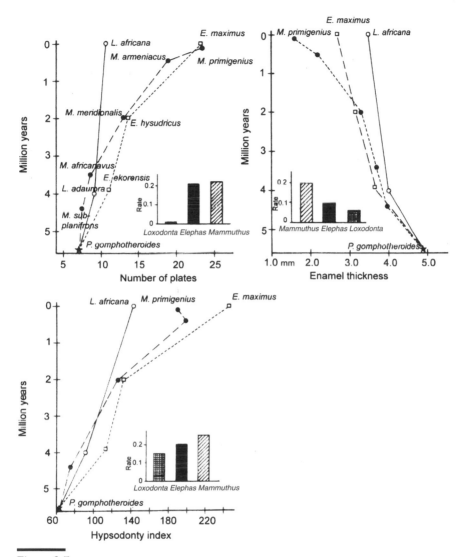

Figure 1.7
Evolutionary changes in plate number, enamel thickness, and hypsodonty index for
the molar M^3 of three lineages of elephants: *Loxodonta* (open circles), *Elephas* (open
squares), and *Mammuthus* (solid circles). The absolute rate of change, measured in
darwins, is also given for each lineage for each of these characters. (From Maglio
1973. Reproduced with the permission of the American Philosophical Society.)

of 1 darwin indicates doubling or halving of a character in 1 My. The rates of change in molar characters averaged around 0.2 darwin in *Mammuthus*, a little less in *Elephas*, and under 0.1 darwin in *Loxodonta*. Considering that all three genera arose in Africa, it is interesting that the rates of evolutionary change are also positively related very broadly to the distance of their eventual dispersal.

Variations in rates of change of particular characters within a lineage have been linked to local selective pressures in some cases. The rapid change in *Mammuthus* during the middle Pleistocene, for instance, is believed to have been driven in part by the appearance in Europe of *Elephas antiquus*, a potential competitor. Northern Europe also experienced a major glaciation at this time. With *E. antiquus* occupying the southern forests, *Mammuthus* was pushed further north and thus may have adapted more rapidly to the frigid conditions. Adrian Lister now believes that the entry of *E. antiquus* might have hastened the extinction of *M. meridionalis* in its woodland refugia. The rapid evolutionary change in the African line of *Elephas*, culminating in *E. iolensis*, during the later Pleistocene also coincided with the expansion of a competitor, *Loxodonta atlantica*, in the same regions. The dwarfing of elephants in several Mediterranean islands proceeded at the remarkable rate of about 10 darwins.

After the origin of the elephant family about 6 My ago, the extinction rates were initially low. The number of species began to increase gradually, concurrent with an increase in average species duration. About 3 My ago, the duration of a species averaged a high of 1.8 My. From the middle Pleistocene, 1 My ago, the elephant family witnessed a rapid phase of evolution with a spectacular increase in the number of species. As the pattern seen toward the end of the Pleistocene was one of "active diversification," Vincent Maglio and others have argued that the equally phenomenal extinctions at the end of the Pleistocene strongly suggest a cause such as human intervention.

1.7.3   *The rapid extinctions of the late Pleistocene*

The burst of elephant evolution during the Pleistocene, driven in part by the fluctuating glacial-interglacial climate, was to culminate in rapid extinction of the proboscideans under the possible influence of the same factor. Close to the end of the Pleistocene, 10,000 years ago, the mammoths of Eurasia and North America, the mastodons of North America, and the gomphotheres of South America made a sudden exit. Although the extinction of the mammoths and of the mastodons are the events best known to the public, several other proboscideans also disappeared at indeterminate periods during the Pleistocene. *Deinotherium* made a quiet exit in Africa during the middle Pleistocene. Likewise, *Stegodon* became extinct in Southeast Asia, and several species of *Elephas* became extinct in Eurasia and Africa during the Pleistocene.

The extinctions near the end of the Pleistocene have evoked the greatest interest and have been studied in some detail as these were rapid, well represented in the fossil record, and contemporaneous with prehistoric humans.

Not only the proboscideans, but also a host of the larger mammals (weighing more than 40 kg) became extinct during late Pleistocene times, beginning about 40,000 years ago. North America lost about 40 species or 70% of the larger mammals, South America lost 75%, while Australia was devastated by a 90% loss. Unlike the previous "major extinction" during Pliocene times, the late Pleistocene event was notable for the selective loss of the larger mammals. Of all mammals heavier than 5 kg, about 50% of genera were lost worldwide in the latter event.

Geographical variations can be discerned in the timing of these extinctions. In North and South America, the majority of extinctions, including those of the mammoths and the mastodonts, are clustered around 11,000 years ago, while in Europe and over most of Siberia, this seems to have occurred about a thousand years earlier. The southernmost populations of the woolly mammoth in Eurasia, such as those in China, died out earlier, around 20,000 years ago. A gradual shrinkage of the range of mammoths northward is thus indicated in Eurasia, but more recent evidence suggests a complex picture, including fragmentation of the range into many small populations. The Australian extinctions of mammals began as early as 30,000 years ago. Explanations for the late Pleistocene extinctions must thus account not only for the loss of a host of species other than the proboscideans, but also for this geographical variation in timing.

Climate change and associated environmental changes probably explain the earlier major extinctions of mammals in the geological record, and it is true that the late Pleistocene was a period of significant climatic fluctuation. The association of prehistoric human artifacts with fossil proboscideans at some sites, however, raises the possibility that hunting could have been a major factor in these extinctions.

The proponents of climate change as the cause of the late Pleistocene extinctions usually relate these to proximate mechanisms, such as vegetational change and associated shifts in diet, disruption of reproductive cycles, or even a "coevolutionary disequilibrium" resulting from break-up of previous associations of species. The late Pleistocene was indeed a period of changing and unstable climate. Beginning from about 16,000 years ago, the earth warmed, and the ice sheets retreated over a large area of the Northern Hemisphere. Around 11,000 years ago, there was a sudden reversal to cold conditions for a short period (the so-called Younger Dryas) before the warming trend continued into the early Holocene. Some of these changes seem to have occurred with unprecedented rapidity. For instance, there are suggestions that the temperature may have soared by 6°C within 10–20 years around 13,000 years ago. Such an increase would have been even greater than climate model projections for the twenty-first century as a result of human-induced greenhouse gas increases. In spite of such climatic instability, a possible direct impact of the weather on large mammals has not generally found favor among paleontologists. It is believed that even woolly mammoths, with their thick fur coats, could survive under warmer conditions by retreating to their cooler northern refugia. The Columbian mammoth ranged as far south as Mexico and thus could not have been dependent on only cold conditions.

David Webb, one of the chief proponents of the climate change hypothesis, has described six major extinction pulses in North American mammals over the past 10 My. The late Pleistocene episode, the last of these six events, is only the second most severe in its loss of mammalian genera (the most severe being the Pliocene event of about 4.5 My ago). Climate change effects are harsher at higher latitudes. Webb argues that one test of the climate hypothesis is to look for patterns in extinction across a latitudinal gradient. The latitudinal pattern of extinction-survival in North America is in conformity with this expectation. Webb proposed two fundamentally different mechanisms for climate-related extinctions, one resulting from environmental stress and the other from biological interactions of new species assemblages following migrations. Several paleontologists have explored these and other climate-related themes.

The simplest proximate causation linked to climate change is a change in the vegetation patterns. However, it is not an easy task to reconstruct precisely the vegetational changes over large landscapes, even for a relatively recent period. One problem is that our present-day definitions of vegetation into grassland, woodland, savanna, tundra, and so on do not fit the vegetational patterns of the Pleistocene. The evidence suggests that each of these vegetational communities, or their analogs, was more diverse during the Pleistocene. An example is the extensive dry northern grassland, termed the "mammoth steppe," which does not have a modern equivalent. Further, a more complex mosaic of grassland and woodland communities also existed at that time in northern latitudes. This can perhaps be traced to a longer and more varied growth season. All this changed with the warming trend after the last peak glaciation. Seasonality seems to have become more pronounced with a reduction in growing season. The warmer, moister climate encouraged the spread of forest into the vast expanse of steppe-like vegetation that had supported the mammoths. The greater seasonality actually increased snow cover. This, along with melting water from ice sheets, seems to have created the poor tundra vegetation of the far north. Neither the nutrient-poor, slow-growing tundra plants nor the coniferous forests to the south could support mammoths used to a diet of more nutritious grasses and herbs.

Picking up the threads of vegetational change, Dale Guthrie has woven a more complex theory of extinctions that links herbivore feeding strategies with changes in plant nutrients and chemical defenses. His basic arguments are as follows. Herbivorous mammals are adapted to different diets in terms of plant type (browse versus graze), nutrient content (structural carbohydrates, protein content, etc.), and the nature of plant antiherbivore defenses (tannins, alkaloids, etc.) based on gut anatomy (ruminant versus nonruminant) and body size (see chapter 5). A shortening of the growing season and increased latitudinal zonation of vegetation types and decreased plant diversity would have changed the herbivore-dietary equations. Not only could the herbivores have found it difficult to obtain the correct mix of nutrients, they also could have been unable to cope with new combinations of plant chemical defenses encountered in the altered habitats. These changes were more likely to affect larger, nonruminant mammals such as the proboscideans. The fossil record shows that virtually all the larger monogastric (nonruminant) grazers and browsers became extinct by the end of the Pleistocene.

A more direct effect of the shorter growing season and increased seasonality could have been a disruption in a mammal's ability to synchronize its reproductive cycle with the seasonal availability of resources. This argument, championed by Richard Kiltie, links the possible changes in gestation times resulting from changes in seasonality to a lowered long-term reproductive output and eventual extinction of populations. Here again, larger mammals such as proboscideans with gestation periods longer than 1 year were less likely to be able to adapt to a changing climate.

The idea that humans may have caused the extinction of certain mammals through hunting first gained credence during the mid-nineteenth century. Jacques Boucher de Perthes, a French civil servant, uncovered the bones of several Pleistocene mammals, including the woolly mammoth, along with human artifacts in the Somme River Valley (see Martin and Klein 1984, pp. 3 and 25). It took a while, however, for the leading naturalists of his time to recognize the significance of his discoveries. In recent times, Paul Martin has been the foremost proponent of the hunting hypothesis. His arguments are based on the association of human artifacts, including hunting tools, with proboscidean remains at several sites in North America as well as a computer-based model simulating the hunting of megafauna concurrent with population expansion of the hunters.

Although the exact timing of arrival of humans in the North American continent is controversial, it is believed that small bands of Paleolithic people from Asia crossed into Alaska through the land bridge existing during late glacial times (about 12,000 years ago) in Beringia. These Paleoindians or "Clovis hunters" (the term is derived from Clovis, New Mexico) used characteristic fluted stone spearpoints hafted into long shafts (fig. 1.8). These characteristic Clovis points are associated with mammoth remains at fossil sites across North America, especially in the arid Southwest, only from about 11,500 to 11,000 years ago. They are then abruptly replaced by different stone points of the Folsom culture associated with smaller animal remains.

The most dramatic example of overkill or "blitzkrieg" begins with a hypothetical band of 100 Paleoindians located at Edmonton, Alberta, Canada, around 11,500 years ago. The computer model of James Mosimann and Paul Martin (actually based on an earlier model of the Russian scientist M. I. Budyko) then simulates the population of hunters increasing exponentially, hunting the megafauna wastefully, and advancing along a broad "front" southeastward to the Gulf of Mexico.

Many scenarios of human population growth, hunting patterns, prey densities, and preferences can be simulated. The basic simulation incorporates a

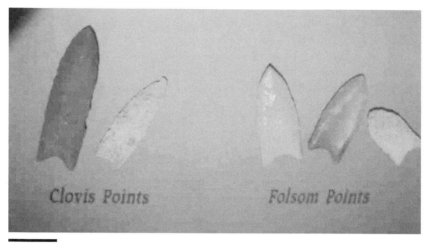

Clovis Points   Folsom Points

Figure 1.8
Clovis stone points associated with the remains of large animals such as mammoths,
and Folsom points associated with the remains of smaller animals such as bison.
Fixed to a long wooden shaft, a Clovis projectile point with a razor-sharp edge was
a formidable weapon capable of inflicting grievous injuries on large animals such as
mammoths. (Photographed at the Milwaukee Public Museum.)

doubling time of 20 years (the actual long-term doubling time is 30 years or
2.4% growth per annum) of the hunters, who take an average of 13 animal
units (1 unit equals 450 kg biomass) per person per year, wasting half the
meat. If mammoth and mastodon were preferred prey, hunters increasing at a
much lower rate could still wipe out a hypothetical population of 3.3 million
proboscideans in about 500 years.

The Mosimann-Martin model demonstrated that it was entirely plausible
for these hunters to wipe out 100 million large animals over 3 million square
miles (about 7.5 million km^2) as the hunters increased to a population of
300,000 within 300 years. During this short period, many species of mammals
were hunted to extinction—the blitzkrieg allows no time for these animals to
adapt to such an effective predator. Only such rapid extirpation times are consistent with the radiocarbon dates of mammoth kill sites across the continent.
The argument of blitzkrieg is that the killing spanned such a short time that
little evidence has been preserved in fossil sites.

There have been several criticisms of both the climate change and the
human overkill hypotheses as causes of late Pleistocene extinction of megafauna. A major objection to the climate change theory is that the mammoths
and mastodons survived through a number of other Ice Age cycles during the
Pleistocene, including one transition that may have been more severe than the

recent event. Why did these and other larger mammals die out only at the end of the last glaciation? Arguments that the last climatic warming was the most severe or that the response of the vegetation this time was the most unfavorable to the herbivores are not yet backed by hard evidence. If climatic and vegetational change had forced proboscideans to alter their diets drastically, it should be possible to determine this directly from preserved food remains and indirectly from stable carbon isotopes in fossil bone or tooth over a time sequence. The last method can distinguish between a diet of C_3 plants (browse) and a diet of C_4 plants (warm season or tropical grasses), although the C_4 plant type would have been scarce in the cooler northern latitudes (see chapter 5).

As yet, few details are available from analyses of plant remains in mammoths or mastodons over a time period. One isotopic study by P. I. Koch of late Pleistocene mammoth and mastodon from the Great Lakes region indicates a near 100% C_3 diet. Thure Cerling and associates found that *Mammuthus* in the more southerly latitudes of Florida, Texas, and Arizona had a predominantly C_4 plant diet, while *Mammut* from the same locations consumed C_3 plants preferentially. Both had a mainly C_3 diet in the more northerly Idaho. Clearly, more work needs to be done before dietary changes, if any, and their significance in the extinction process become clearer.

Objections to the overkill hypothesis are even stronger. A computer-based model does not prove that hunters across three continents behaved in a manner that wiped out their teeming megafauna within a few hundred or a couple of thousand years. While it is not disputed that late Pleistocene people hunted mammoths, perhaps even commonly in places, there are few sites where there is incontrovertible evidence of hunting. Of the dozen or more sites in the United States where Clovis spearpoints have been found along with mammoth (or mastodon) remains, only at one or two sites (such as Naco, Arizona) is there clear evidence that mammoths were actually hunted. The evidence for hunting at other sites is more circumstantial or absent. In many instances, the association of spearpoints and proboscidean bones may merely indicate the scavenging or butchering of dead or dying animals.

The evidence for regular mammoth hunting in Eurasia is even weaker. The large Paleolithic dwelling sites constructed from ivory, bone, and skulls of mammoths, as well as remains of other creatures, uncovered in Central and Eastern Europe are more likely to have been collected from naturally dead animals and not the result of overkill. Indeed, some of these sites may have been occupied over several centuries. There are clear indications of mammoth hunting in the Jersey Islands in the English Channel and of the hunting of the straight-tusked elephant, *Elephas antiquus*, at the Lehringen site in Germany, but these date to the middle Pleistocene. Siberia, a key mammoth region, was only very sparsely populated prior to the Holocene.

In short, prehistoric people did hunt proboscideans, but they also scavenged carcasses for meat or butchered bones for marrow and collected bones, tusks, and hide for their dwellings. The crucial question is whether they killed proboscideans as well as a variety of other mammals at a rate that triggered the mass extinction of the late Pleistocene. Studies of continental hunting societies indicate that they did not usually hunt their prey to extinction. The subsistence base of hunters during the Pleistocene and Holocene was much broader than the largest herbivores; in fact, medium-size animals seemed to be preferred.

To be fair to the Mosimann-Martin model, further simulations by Stephen Whittington and Bennett Dyke that incorporated lower human densities and prey offtake, while discarding the concept of a "front," still indicate that overkill is a possibility. They believe that M. I. Budyko's original model without the rapidly advancing front actually makes a better argument for the human overkill hypothesis.

A theory of humans as the cause of the Pleistocene mammalian extinctions but not through hunting may seem to be very radical. This is precisely what Ross MacPhee and Preston Marx have proposed—a "hyperdisease" hypothesis in which migrating human populations spread lethal pathogens during their first contact with the animal species encountered. This is similar in its features to Paul Martin's blitzkrieg theory with a crucial difference in the causality. Entire populations of mammalian species succumbed rapidly to new pathogens for which they had no immunity. The much longer coexistence of humans and animals in Africa, the cradle of human evolution, and parts of Eurasia also meant that the faunas here were resistant. Although an attractive hypothesis, this is yet to be backed by evidence. A major problem is to demonstrate that a few pathogen species could infect a host of mammalian species and spread over continental scales to cause population extinctions. Using genetic (DNA) sequences from known pathogens that show characteristics of hyperdisease, a search is on among fossil specimens to identify ancient pathogens.

Perhaps the strongest argument in favor of a human role in the Pleistocene extinctions is the increasing evidence for the disappearance of megafauna at different locations and at various times, coinciding with the first arrival of humans. Thus, the bird *Genyornis newtoni*, which was double the size of a modern emu, became extinct in Australia around 50,000 years ago (when climate change cannot be invoked) or only a few thousand years after the first arrival of humans on the continent. Ground sloths became extinct across North America during the late Pleistocene but survived in Cuba until 6,000 years ago, around the time of human arrival. More recently, the island of Madagascar experienced a major episode of extinction after humans reached there about 2,000 years ago. We can find other such examples of vertebrate extinction around the globe.

Other interesting approaches using life history theory have been taken to examine proboscidean fossil assemblages for evidence of climate change or hunting as the cause of extinction. Fundamental differences in life history traits of populations that have died out due to environmental stress as opposed to hunting can be expected. An elephant population declining from climatic and associated vegetational change could be expected to show decreased growth in body size, increased age of sexual maturity, and decreased fecundity. This would translate into an age structure, preserved in the fossil record, with a relative predominance of older individuals.

Analogies can be drawn with modern elephant populations, as in parts of East Africa, that have shown such traits (see chapter 7). Some evidence for the climate/vegetation hypothesis is seen not only in the reduced body size of the mammoths of Wrangel, which may be explained purely as the effect of insularity, but also to a lesser extent in the mainland populations of the late Pleistocene.

By contrast, a population that has been heavily hunted would show the opposite life history characteristics. Daniel Fisher has been examining in detail, using innovative techniques such as tusk growth patterns, the life history traits of fossil American mastodon assemblages. The preliminary data do not indicate mastodon populations suffering from severe environmental stress, but rather those of normal productive populations. Larger fossil samples across various sites have to be examined before any conclusions can be drawn.

There have also been attempts to incorporate both climate change and hunting in a synthetic theory of late Pleistocene extinctions. This recognizes that climate change played an important role, but that hunting by people may have been the last straw in the extinction of the larger mammals, such as mammoths and mastodons. Gary Haynes has argued, for instance, that proboscideans subject to environmental stress could have congregated around water sources, much like African elephants do in times of drought, where they would have been easy prey for hunters. He proposed that "humans opportunistically spread their worldwide range in northern regions only after they had found a resource (mammoths) that was becoming more and more vulnerable because of environmental stress." According to him, "A sweeping conclusion that would indisputably pin the blame for proboscidean extinction on Clovis hunters would be a literary triumph but a scientific impossibility. . . . Clovis hunters perhaps made an already bad situation worse for megamammals: While climatic changes were driving proboscideans to die off, the added stress of Clovis hunting drove them to *die out*" (pp. 316–317).

A crucial question is, Why were the megafauna the most vulnerable during the late Pleistocene extinctions? Whether it was because of climate change or hunting or any other related factors, the relatively low population sizes and slow demographic response of the larger mammals would have rendered them more vulnerable to extinction. Picking up the threads of extinction of the larger herbivores, Norman Owen-Smith proposed that a host of carnivores, smaller herbivores, and other vertebrates that had coexisted with the megafauna now hurtled down the path to extinction. The megaherbivores were "keystone" species that modified the vegetation substantially, facilitating the survival of smaller mammals. Extinction of these keystone species triggered the decline of a host of smaller species. The curtains had fallen decisively for the extraordinarily diverse mammalian fauna of the Pleistocene, and humans were at least in part responsible for this collapse.

1.8   *The Holocene—Calm after the storm*

The ice sheets had retreated and the sea levels had attained their present limits about 10,000 years ago. A thousand years later, the world had warmed to perhaps a slightly higher degree than it is at present. The Asian summer monsoon intensified, while global precipitation reached a new peak in recent times. Forests expanded in the tropical belt. This was the "Holocene Optimum," a period of warmth and high rainfall.

Loxodonta and *Elephas* were left as the sole elephant inheritors of the African and the Asian continents, respectively. A few woolly mammoths may have still roamed the Siberian wastes, while some were certainly stranded on Wrangel Island, destined to reduce in size with succeeding generations. Relict dwarf elephants also possibly remained on some Mediterranean islands. It was of no consequence. Their fates were already sealed.

During the Pleistocene, *Loxodonta* were literally in hiding in the moist forests of Central Africa, as their cousins from the genus *Elephas* roamed over the drier regions, which were far more extensive in the continent. The warming and wetter trend, which set in after the last glaciation about 18,000 years ago, contributed to the expansion of woodlands in Africa, a process that continued into the early Holocene, when peak warmth and precipitation was reached. Although evolutionary rates had been slow in *Loxodonta*, the very traits that were more suited for a life of browsing in forests may have favored their dispersal out of the moist forests into the expanding woodlands.

It is not known how and why *Elephas* disappeared from Africa. In any case, at some point in time, the late Pleistocene climatic and habitat conditions conferred on an earlier form of modern *Loxodonta* a selective advantage over *Elephas* (a late stage of *recki* or *iolensis*), thereby enabling it to become the sole proboscidean inhabitant of the African continent.

Loxodonta spread throughout the continent, with the exception of the central Saharan region, by the dawn of human history. When the earliest Egyptian dynasties were established 5,000 years ago, the African elephant was found in the lower Nile region, as well as throughout coastal North Africa bordering the Mediterranean. This original range of over 40 million km^2 has since shrunk to about 5.8 million km^2. Two subspecies of the African elephant were recognized until recently (the smaller forest elephant, *Loxodonta africana cyclotis*, and the larger bush or savanna elephant, *Loxodonta africana africana*), but a case has now been made for treating them as distinct species (see section 1.9.4).

There is no precise date for the origin of *Elephas maximus* in Asia as the fossil record for this species is virtually nonexistent. All that is known is that the modern Asian elephant was derived during the later Pleistocene from *E. hysudricus* found in the Siwaliks of the Indian subcontinent. Since the last glaciation, the southern and eastern Asian region, covering the historical range of *Elephas maximus*, also came under the influence of a warmer, moister climate when forests expanded. Unlike its African cousin, the Asian elephant had an evolutionary history of adapting to a coarse, grazing diet characteristic of more arid habitats. How the species coped with the reversed trend in habitat is not clear.

By the mid-Holocene, about 5,000 years ago, another period of aridity set in over South Asia and possibly a wider region. Desert appeared in the northwest of the subcontinent, while the great Indus River valley civilization, which may have been the first to tame the Asian elephant, declined by 4,000 years ago. The stable isotope investigations of southern Indian peat deposits by my research group clearly show that arid conditions were established here around the same time.

About 4,000 years ago, the Asian elephant ranged from Mesopotamia in the west through a narrow belt along the Iranian coast into the Indian subcontinent and further east into Southeast Asia and China at least as far north as the Yangtze-Kiang. This earlier range of over 9 million km^2 has shrunk to less than 500,000 km^2 at present. Three subspecies of the Asian elephant have been commonly described: *Elephas maximus maximus* from Sri Lanka, *E. m. indicus* from the Asian mainland, and *E. m. sumatranus* from the island of Sumatra. The basis for this differentiation, however, is less clear than it is for *Loxodonta*.

Today, the Asian elephant is thought of as a creature of the forest and the African elephant as one of the savanna. This is misleading for several reasons. If the actual distribution of Asian elephants is considered, then it is true that most of their range is forested habitat. However, this may simply be due to the occupation of the drier habitats by humans and not a reflection of their favored habitat. Similarly, large populations of African elephant are still found in woodlands and moist forests. Evolutionary history and dental characters suggest that *Elephas maximus* is more adapted to a grazing diet than are *Loxodonta*. When the feeding habits of the two genera are compared, there is little to differentiate between them in the degree of browsing versus grazing (see chapter 5). African forest elephants and Asian elephants in moist forests are almost entirely browsers. African savanna elephants and Asian elephants in deciduous woodlands include almost identical proportions of grass in their diets, as seen from carbon isotopic analysis of bone collagen and from direct observations. In spite of differences in evolutionary adaptations, the two species inhabit a variety of habitats, from semiarid savanna to moist forests, where they show similar feeding behavior.

1.9 *Genetics, phylogeny, and population differentiation in the elephants*

The historical tendency of proboscidean taxonomists to be splitters to an extreme degree in naming genera and species also extended to subspecies. Henry Fairfield Osborn listed 18 subspecies for *Loxodonta africana* in his 1942 tome. For *Elephas maximus*, P.E.P. Deraniyagala alone named eight or nine subspecies, including several for Sri Lanka. With the available morphological data, these were whittled down to two subspecies for *Loxodonta africana* (but see section 1.9.4) and three for *Elephas maximus*. The development of new techniques in molecular biology now offers the possibility of offering greater clarity to the issue of speciation or subspeciation in terms of the underlying genetics. With the recent evidence for recognizing two or more distinct species of elephants in Africa, the splitters may still have the last laugh.

Molecular techniques also have the potential of teasing out the complexities of population structure and differentiation across a range of spatial scales, from local herd to regional and continentwide scales. Several laboratories around the world are currently addressing questions relating to the molecular genetics of the elephants. Unlike for many other mammal species, only limited results are presently available for elephants. These should thus be interpreted with caution. Some of the early studies, especially those related to genetic diversity in elephant populations, were based on variation in proteins or enzymes (allozymes) that are the products of genes. These have been quickly overtaken by the more direct examination of DNA, the repository of genetic information. I thereby confine this account only to the DNA studies.

The DNA studies can be broadly categorized into those that profile DNA found in mitochondria, the tiny cell organelles or "powerhouses" inherited only maternally, and those that profile the DNA in the cell nucleus and combine both maternal and paternal inheritance. For technical reasons, the elucidation of much smaller quantities of mitochondrial DNA (mtDNA) in a cell has been easier; incidentally, the mtDNA changes through mutation about 10 times as fast as nuclear DNA in evolutionary time and is thus particularly suitable for studies of phylogeny. Most of the early DNA studies of elephants focused on mtDNA. Only very recently have techniques to profile nuclear DNA in certain variable segments been developed and applied to elephants. It is obviously important to profile the nuclear DNA because this constitutes the bulk of the genetic information of an individual and has both maternal and paternal contributions.

1.9.1   *Molecular phylogeny of the elephantids*

The traditional view of phylogenetic relationships among the elephants (i.e., including mammoths), based on skeletal and dental morphology, is that *Mammuthus* is more closely related to *Elephas* than it is to *Loxodonta*. In their detailed cladistic analysis of the proboscideans and related mammalian orders, Pascal Tassy and Jeheskel Shoshani note "a sister-group relationship" between *Elephas* and *Mammuthus* based on morphology, although they recognize that the biochemical data do not support such a strong relationship. It is easy to see that features such as the domed skull in the mammoth (single dome) and the Asian elephant (twin dome) and molar characters like numerous lamellae and high degree of hypsodonty in these genera would place them side by side in morphological analysis.

Jerold Lowenstein used radioimmunoassay to compare the proteins albumin and collagen of several proboscidean genera. The technique involves reacting antisera with the protein extracts of fossil material as well as living animals. In immunological terms, the proteins from mammoths were nearly identical to those of both Asian and African elephants. Lowenstein thus concluded that *Mammuthus, Elephas,* and *Loxodonta* were equally related among themselves.

The early DNA studies gave conflicting results, with some favoring a closer relationship between *Mammuthus* and *Loxodonta* and others favoring a *Mammuthus-Elephas* relationship. The most recent study on this subject (published in 2000 by Mark Thomas, Adrian Lister, and their associates) reviewed the previous data plus obtained new results from analysis of up to 545 nucleotide base pair sequences from the cytochrome *b* (cyt *b*) gene of mitochondrial DNA in the three elephant genera. While the earlier studies used sequence data from only one or two individuals each from the various genera, this study compared sequences from 5 mammoths, 14 Asian elephants, and 8 African elephants. A variety of statistical analyses turned up very similar results; *Mammuthus* clustered more closely with *Loxodonta* than it did with *Elephas*, although the difference was not strong. This underscored the need to use multiple lines of evidence in both morphological and molecular approaches to reconstructing phylogeny.

1.9.2   *Population structure and differentiation of the living elephants*

The population structure of the African savanna elephant *Loxodonta africana africana* across eastern and southern Africa was first studied by a team led by molecular geneticist Nicholas Georgiadis. The team used a combination of blood, tiny amounts of skin, and tissue scrapings from tusks representing 270 elephants from five countries (Kenya, Tanzania, Zimbabwe, Botswana, and South Africa) for their analysis. A segment of mtDNA of 2,450 nucleotide base pairs spanning the ND 5–6 region was examined. Using several restriction enzymes, which cleave the DNA molecule at specific sites, they looked at variation in base sequences across this region of the mtDNA. They mapped 47 restriction sites; of these, 23 sites showed polymorphism or variation. There were 10 haplotypes at this segment of mtDNA among the elephants examined in this study (table 1.3).

Several unexpected patterns emerged from the mtDNA analyses. The two most common haplotypes (numbers 3 and 4) occurred throughout the range of countries sampled at varying frequencies. This clearly argued for protracted gene flow across the eastern and southern African elephant populations in the past. The other eight haplotypes were more localized, with some of them occurring only in eastern African populations and others in Zimbabwe and Botswana. Interestingly, the only two haplotypes found in the relatively isolated Kruger population of South Africa were the two most common ones. Thus, there was a marked differentiation of populations at the continental

Table 1.3
Frequency of mitochondrial haplotypes at
ten locations in eastern and southern Africa.

Country	Location	Sample Size	Haplotype and Frequency (%)									
			1	2	3	4	5	6	7	8	9	10
Kenya	Amboseli	29	37.8	3.5	55.2	3.5	—	—	—	—	—	—
Kenya	Tsavo	14	57.1	14.3	14.3	14.3	—	—	—	—	—	—
Tanzania	Tarangire	35	—	17.1	77.1	—	—	—	5.7	—	—	—
Zimbabwe	Sengwa	22	—	—	50.0	—	36.4	13.6	—	—	—	—
Zimbabwe	Hwange	24	—	—	12.5	29.2	29.2	—	—	25.0	4.2	—
Zimbabwe	Zambezi	28	—	—	14.3	3.6	3.7	—	—	75.0	—	3.6
Botswana	Chobe	40	—	—	50.0	20.0	—	—	—	30.0	—	—
Botswana	Savute	27	—	—	7.4	—	—	—	—	67.7	22.2	3.7
Botswana	Mashatu	17	—	—	11.8	88.2	—	—	—	—	—	—
South Africa	Kruger	34	—	—	26.5	73.5	—	—	—	—	—	—

Source: From Georgiadis et al. (1994). Reproduced with the permission of Nature Publishing Group, U.K.

scale, but no such differentiation was apparent at the regional scale of eastern or southern Africa.

The elephants sampled also separated into two exceptionally divergent mitochondrial "clades." Haplotypes representing both these divergent clades coexisted at the same location, not in just one location, but at several distant locations. This is indeed a puzzling result as the two major clades are thought to have diverged 4 My ago (in hindsight, probably an overestimate); this idea is based on standard calculations of evolutionary rates using mtDNA sequence divergence.

In other species, there are rarely such widely separated mitochondrial haplotypes coexisting in the manner seen in the African savanna elephant. One explanation for such a pattern is that populations were allopatric or reproductively isolated at some distinct ancestral time and later came into contact. There is no evidence as to whether this occurred in *L. a. africana*. Another explanation, a more parsimonious one, is that these representatives of such differing mitochondrial clades have persisted by chance alone over the indicated evolutionary timescale of 4 My. Given the absence of any barrier to gene flow, these divergent haplotypes now coexist at distant locations. Calculations based on neutral coalescent theory indicated that the observed pattern of coexistence of divergent haplotypes could have occurred by chance alone. Given the long generation time of 20 years in elephants, a genetically effective population size of over 50,000 females, maintained by gene flow, needed for this chance persistence of a subdivided, but not isolated, population over 4 My was entirely plausible.

Another study of African elephant genetics, on a more localized scale, is that of Silvester Nyakaana and Peter Arctander. The savanna elephant population of Uganda had declined precipitously, from about 60,000 in the 1960s to only 1,200–2,000 by the 1990s (chapter 8). Nyakaana and Arctander sampled 72 elephants at three locations to look at the genetic patterns using both mtDNA (a 400-bp [base pair] segment of the control region) and nuclear DNA (microsatellite analysis of four variable loci). They distinguished 11 mtDNA haplotypes, of which 3 were represented by only one individual each. Of the remaining 8 haplotypes represented by multiple individuals, 6 were specific to certain localities, suggesting considerable genetic differentiation. Sequence divergence among the mitochondrial haplotypes varied from 0.25% (representing one substitution) to as much as 6.1% (representing 23 substitutions). The nuclear DNA also showed fairly high variation in the four microsatellite loci examined as well as differentiation among the populations, although to a lesser extent than the mtDNA, suggesting that gene flow was maintained largely by the males.

Genetic studies of Asian elephant populations also have generally kept pace with those of their African counterparts. A team led by geneticist Günther Hartl amplified mtDNA from hair follicles obtained from 53 elephants originating in Sri Lanka, southern and northeastern India, northern and southern Myanmar, northern and eastern Thailand, and Vietnam. A 480-bp sequence of the cyt *b* gene was screened for variation. Based on a 335-bp scored sequence of this gene, they found eight mitochondrial haplotypes. As in the continental African study, they found two common haplotypes, representing 18 and 12 individuals each of the 53 screened, distributed throughout the continent. The other six haplotypes had more restricted distributions. The eight haplotypes also clustered into two major clades, with one difference from the African savanna elephant: The two common haplotypes each went into a different clade.

A genetic study by Prithiviraj Fernando and associates was novel in that it used the dung of 118 elephants, mostly free ranging, in Sri Lanka, Bhutan-India, and Laos-Vietnam to extract DNA. They amplified a 630-nucleotide-bp sequence of mtDNA encompassing the highly variable control region as well as adjoining segments, including a part of the cyt *b* gene. They distinguished 17 mitochondrial haplotypes across these samples; these segregated into two assemblages or clades, one labeled α with 7 haplotypes and another labeled β with 10 haplotypes (fig. 1.9).

Two of these haplotypes, representing the most common haplotype in each of the two assemblages, were also the only haplotypes that were shared by elephant populations both in Sri Lanka and in mainland Asia. As many as 12 haplotypes were found within Sri Lanka, with high differentiation across the northern, central, and southern parts of the island. In comparison, fewer haplotypes were found in the mainland, although the data have to be interpreted cautiously because far fewer elephants were sampled there. The average divergence in the nucleotide sequences between the two haplotype assemblages

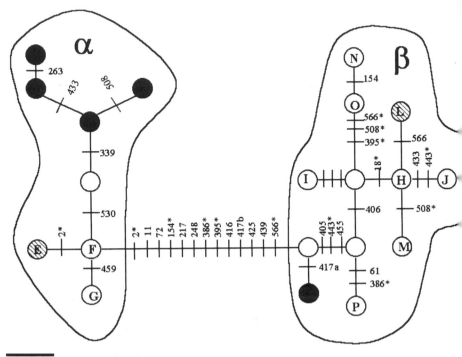

Figure 1.9
Parsimony network of Asian elephant haplotypes (letters) based on mitochondrial
DNA analyses. Circles without a letter denote haplotypes assumed, but not observed, in this study. Shaded circles represent Asian mainland haplotypes; striped circles indicate those shared between the mainland and Sri Lanka; and open circles indicate those limited to Sri Lanka. Dashes between haplotypes represent mutational
steps between haplotypes. Asterisks mark assumed instances of homoplasy. (From
Fernando et al. 2000. Reproduced with the permission of Nature Publishing Group,
U.K.)

was 3.1%, about half the divergence between the Asian and the African elephant.

Using an estimated long-term sequence divergence rate of about 1% per
million years, Fernando and associates suggested that the two clades had diverged about 3 My ago. Although there are several possible explanations for
the observed patterns of mtDNA structure, they favored allopatric subspeciation of the two lineages, in Sri Lanka and the mainland, with subsequent migrations during the Pleistocene glaciations, when sea levels were lower, which
would have resulted in regional mixing and coexistence of haplotypes.

A combination of cyt *b* and control region sequence was also used by
Robert Fleischer and associates in their genetic survey of Asian elephant popu-

lations based on 57 captive animals of known origin. Their samples also separated into two major clades, with a broad north-to-south gradient across the continent. All the Sumatran and Malaysian elephants grouped into only one clade (termed the Indonesian clade), while elephants from other regions further north and west grouped into either clade. They speculated that the Indonesian clade haplotypes could have descended from *Elephas hysudrindicus*, the extinct Pleistocene species with fossils that are known from Java, while the other clade may have originated from the northern *E. hysudricus*, known from fossils in the Siwaliks in the Indian subcontinent. They also stressed that the historical trade in Asian elephants and subsequent escape of captive animals into the wild could have shaped present-day population genetic structure, in addition to natural dispersal facilitated by Pleistocene sea level fluctuations.

The distinct character of the Sumatran and Malaysian elephants is also supported by the more recent work of Prithviraj Fernando and Don Melnick. Their preliminary work on the elephants of Sabah, on the island of Borneo, has also shown a distinct mt haplotype not seen anywhere else in Asia (this finding has an important bearing on whether the elephants of Borneo are native or have descended from captive stocks presented to the Sultan of Sulu in A.D. 1750 and later released; the evidence now points to the former explanation but more data are needed). The elephants of the Indian subcontinent have been poorly represented in all these genetic studies. T.N.C. Vidya and I have been collaborating with Fernando and Melnick to rectify this deficiency. One interesting result that has emerged is that the southern Indian populations are represented by few mt haplotypes. In fact, the largest global population of Asian elephants (estimated at about 8,000 individuals or over 15% of total *Elephas maximus* in the wild), which ranges over the Nilgiri-Eastern Ghats region there, is represented by a single mt haplotype. The southern Indian mt haplotypes are also found in Sri Lankan elephants.

1.9.3   *Genetic diversity in elephant populations*

Genetic variation in a species can be examined at the level of individuals, within populations, and across populations. We are still at a preliminary stage with respect to making judgments about the levels of genetic diversity in elephant populations and their significance for conservation. Nevertheless, some revealing patterns have been emerging from the genetic studies.

Some early work I did with Lalji Singh involved the use of a DNA probe called Bkm 2(8), developed by Singh for human DNA fingerprinting but also used in several animal studies later. When applied to Asian elephants, we found that elephants from northeastern India had higher levels of heterozygosity than elephants from southern India. This is consistent with the pattern that has since emerged from the more detailed studies using other means of investigation. Mitochondrial haplotype diversity seems to be highest among the Sri Lankan elephants, followed by those in northeastern India and northern Myanmar. On the other hand, mitochondrial nucleotide diversity is highest in this last region. The southern Indian elephants have shown one of the lowest diversities overall of all populations.

Several elephant populations are known to have gone through a "bottleneck" (reduced to a small size and then recovered) in historical times. It would be ideal to study the possible loss of genetic variation in such populations. The Ugandan study revealed relatively high genetic variation, presumably because population sizes still remained in the hundreds. In contrast, elephant populations in southern Africa had been hunted to very low numbers during the nineteenth century. While many had become extinct, two places where the populations recovered under protection are Kruger and Addo National Parks. The bottleneck had been more severe in the case of Addo, where the present population of over 300 elephants could be traced to only 11 founding individuals that remained in 1931.

Anna Whitehouse and Eric Harley examined nine genetic (microsatellite) loci among living individuals in these populations, as well as two museum specimens from Addo. They found significantly reduced variation, in terms of fewer alleles and lower heterozygosity, in the Addo elephants compared to those at Kruger. The museum specimens also showed two alleles not seen in the present Addo population.

1.9.4   How many species and subspecies of elephants are there?

The molecular data from both Asian and African elephant populations, although still in early analysis, are already threatening to overturn the traditional systems of classification. At our present level of understanding of the genetics of Asian elephants, there is no support for the subspecies status of the Sri Lankan elephant population (*Elephas m. maximus*) and its differentiation from those in mainland Asia (*E. m. indicus*). These studies and unpublished data clearly indicate that several mitochondrial haplotypes found in Sri Lankan elephants are shared with those in the mainland, particularly southern India. On the other hand, there is some support for the differentiation of the Sumatran elephant (*E. m. sumatranus*) and the Malaysian elephant, although more work needs to be done.

The more revolutionary shift in elephant taxonomy seems to be happening with *Loxodonta*. The wide variation in body size (appendix 2) and morphology of African elephant populations has always brought demands for subspecies or species status for some of these forms. For decades, the legend of the pygmy elephant persisted in Central Africa. David Western investigated this legend in 1986 and found that, in regions where savanna elephants and forest elephants intermingled to a certain extent, the forest subspecies was naturally regarded as a "pygmy" relative to the much larger savanna animals. Based on morphological examination of skulls from savanna and forest elephant populations, Peter Grubb, along with Colin Groves and other associates, made a case in 2000 for giving species status to the savanna elephant (*Loxodonta africana* Blumenbach, 1797) and the forest elephant (*Loxodonta cyclotis* Matschie, 1900). They also recognized that some hybridization could be occurring where the two populations mingled.

In 1997, an article in the journal *Science* had hinted that the African forest elephant (*L. a. cyclotis*) may also be sufficiently differentiated in genetic terms from the savanna elephant (*L. a. africana*) to warrant distinct status as a species. The results of this work by Alfred Roca, Nicholas Georgiadis, and their associates, finally published in the same journal in 2001, also make a strong case for elevating the forest elephant to the status of a distinct species (*Loxodonta cyclotis*). The team sequenced four nuclear genes (1732 nucleotide base pairs) from 195 elephants in 21 populations (locations) across Africa to examine patterns of genetic divergence. Of this sample, 36 forest elephants from 3 locations (Dzanga-Sangha, Lope, and Odzala) and 121 savanna elephants from 15 locations formed two genetically distinct groups on the basis of each of the four genes as well as collectively. Within each of these two categories, it was difficult to differentiate individuals from their DNA sequences. For instance, the savanna elephant populations across the continents were indistinguishable, while the forest elephants of Dzanga-Sangha could not be differentiated from those at Lope. The forest elephants were also much more genetically diverse compared to the savanna elephants. At one site, Garamba, in the forest-savanna transition region of the Congo, the sampled elephants showed a combination of the otherwise distinct forest and savanna elephant genes, indicating a limited history of hybridization among their ancestors. The team concluded that the genetic distance between the forest elephant and the savanna elephant was 58% of the distance between *Loxondonta* and *Flephas*, and that the former had diverged about 2.6 My ago, which was sufficient time for differentiation at the species level.

One deficiency of the above study was the absence of samples from the scattered West African populations (see appendix 1), which include both the savanna-type and the forest-type elephants. When Lori Eggert, Caylor Rasner, and David Woodruff rectified this anomaly (by collecting samples from 10 locations there) and pooled the genetic results from the West African elephants from published results elsewhere in the continent, they came up with a far more complex picture of the phylogeography and taxonomy of *Loxodonta*. Their analyses included a portion of the mtDNA (from the standard *cyt-b* control region) and four microsatellite loci of the nuclear DNA.

Five clades emerged from the continent-wide mtDNA analysis, namely, (1) East, north Central, and South African savanna elephants, (2) West African forest and savanna elephants, (3) East, West, north Central, and South African savanna elephants, (4) Central African forest and savanna elephants, and (5) West African forest and savanna elephants. The microsatellite DNA analysis also showed rather similar clustering of populations from different regions of the continent. Of these divisions or clades, the Central African forest elephants were the most similar to the Asian elephant, perhaps not a surprising result. Eggert and associates suggested that the earliest members of modern *Loxodonta* (*africana*) may have inhabited the Central African forests, about 5 My ago, and then repeatedly dispersed to other parts of the continent in response to episodes of climate change that resulted in contraction and expansion of forest or savanna. Three broad groups—the Central African forest elephants; the savanna elephants of central, eastern, and southern Africa; and the West African forest and savanna elephants—could be recognized at a minimum on the basis of genetics, geography, and ecology.

This study has obviously opened up a virtual Pandora's box of African elephant taxonomy. Thus, it seems premature at this time to differentiate *Loxodonta* into two species. The IUCN/SSC African Elephant Specialist Group decided at their 2002 meeting to retain the traditional classification of two subspecies (*L. a. africana* and *L. a. cyclotis*) until further studies resolve the taxonomic uncertainties. Although rapid progress is being made, there is still some distance to go before the molecular genetic studies of elephant populations provide us with a satisfactory understanding of their phylogeny, differentiation, and diversity. The molecular studies are still based on unevenly distributed samples across the elephant's distributional range; the elephants of the Indian subcontinent are only now being analyzed. The nuclear DNA that constitutes the bulk of the genetic material in an organism has yet to be characterized in sufficient detail among elephant populations. The relationship between fossil and molecular dates for differentiation of populations is unclear; for instance, the population coalescent dates derived from mitochondrial haplotypes are not necessarily the same as the population divergence dates, as sometimes is assumed in genetic studies. More standard molecular genetic comparisons with larger samples of elephants, along with morphological data, would help to resolve these issues.

Elephants, Gods, and People
The Interrelationship
of Culture and Ecology

2

By the end of the Pleistocene or last glaciation, about 10,000 years ago, the end was inevitable for a host of the larger mammal species, including the mammoths and the mastodons. Climate change and associated environmental change and "overkill" by humans are the most likely explanations for this extinction spasm toward the end of the last Ice Age. The Holocene thus dawned on prehistoric man with a highly impoverished megafauna over a substantial land area of the Northern Hemisphere as well as in the southern continents of Australia and South America. Exceptions to this extinction spasm were Africa and southern Asia.

The tropical and subtropical belts were possibly better buffered against the vicissitudes of a rapidly changing global climate. Here, in the African and Asian continents, in the relatively more benign climate, two proboscidean genera survived, their survival aided perhaps by a longer history of evolved coexistence or by the absence of humans with advanced technologies for indulging in overkill of the megafauna. Perhaps the *Homo sapiens* here relied on a variety of mammal species, which would have been more diverse toward the tropics, for their protein and thus were not near-obligate carnivores on proboscideans. In tropical forests or woodlands, the hunting of an elephant involves considerable costs in pursuit and harassment, unlike the containment and mass killing of mammoths, already weakened through environmental stress, at waterholes in the temperate grasslands. The foraging decisions of Paleolithic humans would

have been influenced by cost-benefit considerations that are not clearly understood today.

In any case, at the dawn of recorded history, the surviving proboscideans
Loxodonta africana and *Elephas maximus* had extensive distributions in the African and Asian continents, respectively. *Loxodonta* roamed over most of Africa
except for the Saharan region. *Elephas*, of course, was more restricted in its
distribution to the southern part of Asia, but nevertheless ranged from the
Tigris-Euphrates basin in West Asia eastward through southern Iran and Pakistan, to the Indian subcontinent, into continental Southeast Asia, and northeast
to beyond the Yangtze-Kiang in China. Further, *E. maximus* also occurred on
several islands, including Ceylon (Sri Lanka), Sumatra, Borneo, and possibly
Java.

We have little basis for reconstructing the elephant-human relationship
during the early Holocene (10,000–5,000 years before the present). The fossil
record of *Loxodonta* and *Elephas* is scanty or nonexistent for this period. The
dawn of the Holocene was also the beginning of a major shift in the diets of
humans. The domestication of animals such as sheep, goats, cattle, and pigs
and the cultivation of crops, including cereals and pulses, had their beginnings
around 10,000 years ago in western Asia. The spread of agriculture and animal
husbandry during the early Holocene changed the patterns of food procure-
ment by humans over a broad region covering the three ancient civilizations—
the Nile, the Tigris-Euphrates, and the Indus.

Undoubtedly, hunter-gatherer societies in Africa and Asia would have continued to rely on elephants for meat, hide, bone, and ivory. Unlike the mammoths and the mastodons, there are virtually no known sites of mass deaths
of *Loxodonta* and *Elephas* in the fossil record; hence, it is virtually unthinkable
that early Holocene humans slaughtered either of them in mass kills. The killing of elephants would have been restricted to one or a few individuals at a time
and scavenging of those that died naturally or during drought.

About 4,000 years ago, there arose a new relationship between elephants
and humans, a relationship that was to influence the sociopolitical and cultural
life of peoples and the eventual fate of the elephant itself in a profound manner. Such a relationship between beast and human never existed before nor is
it likely to evolve in future generations. I refer, of course, to the taming of the
elephant in Asia.

The domestication of the dog, the ox, the horse, the pig, and the camel
have, in a distinctive fashion, left an indelible mark on human cultures and
history. True, the cow has been venerated as much as the elephant and contributed far more to nourishing human populations, the horse has fought battles
with more success than the elephant, and the dog has been a faithful companion to humans over more continents than the elephant. Yet, the elephant occu-
pies a higher pedestal in human cultural history by virtue of the sheer contrast
and splendor of the elephant-human relationship.

There are several detailed descriptions of the role of elephants in Asian
cultures, but none of these explored in depth the ecological context of this

interaction. A species that, at the same time, not only has been worshipped as god and slaughtered for meat or ivory, carried us and our heaviest burdens but also has trampled crops and people alike, and acted as a gentle ambassador of peace as earnestly as it has fiercely fought battles through the centuries would be a fascinating subject for exploring the interrelationship of culture and ecology.

According to the "dare theory" of the origin of domestication, the control of a fierce or large animal was a challenge to the physical prowess and intelligence of humans in ancient societies. This would have been especially true of the elephant, the largest of the land mammals. The dare motive could also explain how such animals (whether cattle, horses, or elephants) became associated with ceremonial and religious rituals.

Several other questions, however, come to mind when we consider the elephant-human relationship. Why has the tradition of capturing and taming elephants persisted in Asia for over four millennia, while it died out very early in Africa? How did the elephant occupy a pivotal position in the culture of Asian peoples? What is the real significance of the worship of the elephant (in the form of the elephant-headed god, Ganesha) in Hindu culture? Would this elephant culture continue to persist in Asia, and could such a culture arise in Africa? Drawing on historical evidence, I explore the answers to these questions within an ecological framework.

2.2   *Historical antecedents of the elephant culture in Asia*

The earliest evidence of the taming of the elephant goes back to the spectacular Indus Valley civilization, also known as the Harappan culture, which flourished during the third millennium B.C. over an area much larger than that of either the Egyptian or the Mesopotamian civilizations. This included a city culture maintained from surplus agricultural produce of the surrounding country, in the Punjab, Sind, northern Rajasthan, western Uttar Pradesh, and Kathiawar areas in present-day Pakistan and India. Associated with the Harappan culture are small steatite seals with a pictorial motif, animal or human, and an inscription. The elephant is a common motif in these seals (fig. 2.1), depicted in some with what appears to be a long piece of cloth draped over its back. Tame elephants were obviously present in or known to people of the Harappan culture. We cannot conclude from this that the elephant was first tamed by the Indus people, but merely that this represents the earliest known evidence of captive elephants. The elephant may well have been tamed earlier by peoples who inhabited the Indian subcontinent prior to the rise of the Harappan culture.

If wild elephants were present in the Indus River basin at that time, this must have been the northwestern limit of their distribution. Paleoecological evidence from pollen studies suggests that this region was under denser natural vegetation cover in a moister climate during 3000–2000 B.C., although this has

Figure 2.1
One of numerous depictions of
an elephant on steatite seals
associated with the ancient Indus
Valley civilization in the northwestern Indian subcontinent.

been questioned recently. There is certainly no evidence that the elephant's
range ever extended further west of the Indus River basin, except in the extreme south within a very tenuous belt along the coastline of the Arabian Sea
and the Persian Gulf (even this is only inferred from its historical presence in
the Tigris-Euphrates basin).

Beginning about 2000 B.C., the Indus civilization began to decline, a process that seems to have been completed by 1700 B.C. Scholars are still debating
the causes of this decline. Earlier accounts, especially those of European historians, generally blamed this on invasions by the so-called Aryan people from
the Iranian plateau, who came in through mountain passes in the Hindu Kush
range. This theory has been found to be without basis by present-day historians. First, the migration of the Aryan people took place over an extended
period of time after the decline of the Harappan culture. It is possible that the
people of the Harappan culture had, prior to the Aryan migrations, moved into
the subcontinent (and perhaps it may have been the Dravidian race that the
Aryans encountered in southern India). The paleoecological evidence points to
a period of desiccation of the northwestern part of the Indian subcontinent
that preceded the period of decline of the Harappan culture. I have mentioned
the evidence from my studies that point to a similar decline in precipitation
over southern India prior to about 2000 B.C. (see chapter 1, section 1.8). It
thus seems likely that climate change, resulting in less precipitation, desertification of northwestern India (this vegetation transformation perhaps was hastened by the biomass needs of an advanced and populous culture, not unlike
that of modern times, for over a millennium), and lowered agricultural productivity may have compelled the Indus people to migrate east and south into the

subcontinent. Given the vast geographical spread of the Harappan culture sites, no single cause can perhaps explain its decline in key places.

The impact of this ecological transformation of northwestern India on the wild elephant would also have been significant. The limit of elephant distribution would have shifted further east, perhaps leaving some isolated herds in moister vegetation patches of the Indus basin. The relationship of the Indus people with the elephant is not clear. Although elephants were presumably caught and tamed, the methods of capture and the use to which they were put are not known from unambiguous sources.

The Indo-Europeans or Aryans, a pastoral people from Central Asia, reached the Indian subcontinent around 1500 B.C. It is here that the Aryans must have first come into contact with elephants, wild ones as they pushed into the Indo-Gangetic basin and captive ones held by the pre-Aryan tribes who inhabited the region. The hymns, prayers, poems, rituals, and incantations of the Aryans, a series of compositions known as the *Vedas* (1500–600 B.C.), provide the earliest sources of information on the human-elephant relationship. Following these are the *Ramayana* and the *Mahabharata* (the two great Indian epics), which deal with events that may have originally taken place during 1000–700 B.C., and the *Jataka* stories (the stories of the Buddha's former births), which are believed to have been compiled by the second century B.C. Dhriti K. Lahiri-Choudhury has elaborately described the references to the elephant in these sources. I confine my interpretations to the ecological significance of the elephant-human relationship.

The immigrant Aryans confronted, absorbed, and modified the "elephant technology" with which they came in contact as they moved into the Gangetic plains. The domesticity of the elephant is well established, even during the earliest Vedic times. The ownership of an elephant was a status symbol, and an important person such as a king would ride a richly caparisoned elephant. However, one notable feature of the animal-human relationship during the Vedic times has been pointed out by Lahiri-Choudhury. Horses were still the most important animals of the *Vedas*, the elephant having not yet supplanted the horse as the vehicle of the Aryan god Indra. This reflected the early years of contact between the horse culture of the Indo-Aryans and the elephants of the territory into which they had moved.

2.3   *The rise of elephant armies in Asia*

The Aryans undoubtedly realized the potential of the elephant as a beast of burden and an instrument of war as they pushed east and south into the Gangetic basin. Forests had to be cleared, goods and people transported, and local tribes (some possessed captive elephants) had to be kept at bay. An elephant force would have been a valuable asset under these circumstances.

In the *Ramayana*, there are descriptions of noblemen and people riding elephants, the giving of elephants as gifts, and the use of elephants in battle.

There are several references to *chaturanga bal* (four-arm forces consisting of elephants, chariots, cavalry, and infantry) (fig. 2.2), and Rama (the lord and hero of the *Ramayana*) encounters a large elephant force led by his principal protagonist, Ravana (who, however, rides a horse-drawn chariot). Strangely, there are few descriptions of elephants in actual battle and their role is not defined, which seems to indicate that most of the references are later interpolations.

The method of capturing wild elephants with the help of trained captive elephants (or *koonkies*) was known at this time. The hunting of elephants (at least by royalty) was accepted practice (King Dasharatha, father of Rama, mistakes the sound of a young hermit drinking from a pool as that of an elephant and kills the hermit with an arrow).

Lahiri-Choudhury concludes that the captive elephant was much more abundant and its presence in the common life of people better established in the (Dravidian) land beyond Aryavarta (the land of the Aryans). I would add that, while the use of elephants in battle by the Dravidian people seems almost certain, the same has not been established for the period prior to about 1000

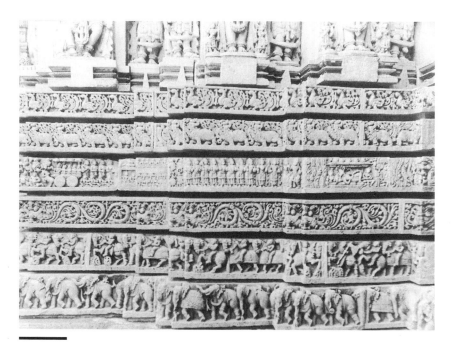

Figure 2.2
The four-arm fighting force of ancient India depicted in this sculpture at Somnathpur (Hoysala period, about eleventh through thirteenth centuries) in Karnataka. From the bottom, the panels show elephantry, cavalry, and infantry/chariotry. Chariotry is believed to have declined in the subcontinent during the Christian era.

B.C. for the Aryans. With the ancient texts, the possibility of interpolations in later versions (the revised form of the *Valmiki Ramayana*, for instance, known to us dates to the fifth century A.D.) must be kept in mind.

The *Mahabharata* has more vivid descriptions of the use of elephants in battle and provides the earliest authentic account of the war elephant. The elephant is such an integral part of the *chaturangini sene* (or four-arm fighting force), which is so basic to the descriptions of the war in the *Mahabharata* that Lahiri-Choudhury believes these could not possibly be indiscriminate later additions. However, in spite of the use of elephants in warfare, the horse-drawn chariot was still the main fighting arm of the two forces, those of the Pandavas and Kauravas, in the *Mahabharata*. Experts in elephant warfare are specifically identified as coming from aboriginal hunting tribes.

Lahiri-Choudhury points to one interesting aspect of the elephant and horse cultures during these times. While the elephant culture had developed considerably in the wetter eastern regions of India, the horse culture continued to dominate the drier west. This was a reflection of not only the relative abundance in the distribution of wild elephants, but also that they had military significance (Bhishma's advice to Yudhishtira was that horses and chariots were to be deployed during the dry season, but infantry supported by elephants was to be favored during the wet season).

The ecological status of northern India during the first millennium B.C. is thus a distinct west-east gradient, the west being dry and often devoid of any forest, the result of climate change and centuries of exploitation by a large human population, and the east a relatively wetter, forested tract with a lower human density. The paleoecological evidence indicates that the weakening of the Indian monsoon that set in during the third millennium B.C. over the subcontinent persisted at least up to the dawn of the Christian era. Without sufficient natural vegetation to support elephants, the Northwest remained practically devoid of wild elephants and had only relatively small herds of captive elephants, while both wild and captive animals increased in abundance in the procession eastward.

From the middle of the first millennium B.C. onward, we are on firmer ground with respect to the chronological record of Indian history. By about 600 B.C., northern India saw the establishment of republics and kingdoms. While the monarchies were concentrated in the Gangetic plains, the republics were established in the peripheral hilly country to the north along the Himalayan foothills and in the northwestern Punjab. It is plausible that the republics, consisting of a single tribe or a confederation of tribes, pre-dated the monarchies. The earliest of the major kingdoms known was that of Magadha, situated in the wetter eastern Gangetic basin in present-day Bihar. The nearby forests provided timber for building and a good supply of elephants for the army.

The rise of Magadha during the sixth century B.C. was contemporaneous with the preachings of two great thinkers, Mahavira and Gautama Buddha, whose teachings form the basis for two major religions, Jainism and Buddhism, respectively. Both Jainism and Buddhism put great emphasis on *ahimsa* or nonviolence toward all creatures. (Incidentally, the metaphor of the six blind men each touching a different part of the elephant and interpreting the object accordingly can be traced to Jaina teaching.) The elephant came to have a special symbolism in the practice of Buddhism. The Buddha himself is considered the reincarnation of a sacred white elephant (fig. 2.3), while images of Ganesha abound in Buddhist countries as far as China and Japan. The Jataka stories, a collection of folklore on the Buddha's former births, were possibly originally compiled by the second century B.C. Several of these are set in eastern India and speak of royal elephants, elephant festivals, elephant trainers, and killing of elephants for ivory; in short, there is an emphasis on elephant culture. This is consistent with the increased emphasis on elephants as opposed to horses in the moister Himalayan foothills and the eastern region of the subcontinent.

According to Greek sources, the Nandas, who inherited the kingdom of Magadha during the fourth century B.C., were reputed to have maintained an army with 3,000 elephants. Even if this figure and those of other components of the army were exaggerations, the elephant is seen to be established firmly as a war machine by this period. The scene then shifts briefly to the Northwest, where a famous battle was fought on the banks of the Jhelum. Alexander of Macedonia marched with his formidable army through West Asia, defeating Darius of Persia, whose army fielded 15 elephants, and reached the Jhelum (Hydaspes) in 326 B.C., where he confronted the impressive elephant army of King Porus. Different sources mention between 80 and 200 elephants in Porus's army; H. H. Scullard mentions 200, but states that only 80 were used in the main battle. Although Alexander's brilliant strategy carried the day and overcame Porus's elephant army, the Macedonians turned back shortly after

Figure 2.3
Queen Maya's dream that a white elephant is descending on her to enter her womb and be born as Gautama Buddha. This depiction is from Bharut, Madhya Pradesh, India (second century B.C.). (From the Indian Museum, Kolkata.)

reaching the Beas (Hyphasis). Apparently, the Greek soldiers had been shaken up by Porus's elephant force and did not wish to face the vast numbers of elephants they heard were beyond the Beas in the east. This was not entirely without substance. Apart from the much larger elephant army of the Nandas, there were certainly similar forces held by other tribes of the subcontinent. Chandragupta Maurya, who usurped the Nanda throne in 321 B.C., reputedly had 9,000 elephants in his army.

The Greek campaign in northwestern India did not have any significant political impact on the east; in any case, the campaign lasted for only two years. Ecologically, too, there was a void between the Northwest, watered by the tributaries of the Indus and the fertile Gangetic basin further east. The decline in precipitation, which had set in by the third millennium B.C., and perhaps tectonic activity changed the hydrology of the rivers considerably in the Indus basin. The dry plains between the Indus and Gangetic basins thus may not have been territory that was much sought after, and few wild elephants, if any, may have survived there. The retreating Macedonians, however, took with them several dozen elephants; these, along with the elephants acquired by Alexander's successors, were to make a lasting impression on and influence the military history of the Mediterranean.

With the rise of Chandragupta Maurya, the culture of capturing and training elephants, their veterinary care, their deployment in the army, and even the protection of wild elephants was firmly established. The Mauryan Empire, which controlled a vast territory over the subcontinent, was a formidable one by any standards. A highly centralized bureaucracy, with a role that was well defined, was needed to administer it, and a vast army, described as an economic liability in peacetime, was needed to secure its borders. Pliny the Elder, the famous Roman writer, cites a figure of 9,000 elephants in the Mauryan army, with a further estimate of at least 5,000 elephants held by other tribes in the subcontinent. We have no reason to disbelieve these figures entirely. The subcontinent held large stocks of wild elephants, and their overexploitation through an elaborately organized system of management was certainly possible. This would also have resulted in local extinctions of elephant populations in the Gangetic basin.

Chandragupta was the protégé of the Brahman Kautilya (also known as Chanakya), the chief architect of the elaborate system of administration recorded in the *Arthasastra* (a manual on statecraft originally devised around 300 B.C., although the present-day version is believed to have interpolations until about A.D. 300). The *Arthasastra* advised that the king should set up sanctuaries in the forests along the periphery of the kingdom for the protection of wild elephants as sources for the Mauryan army, and that any person killing an elephant was to be put to death. Kautilya was quite explicit in asserting the importance of these sanctuaries for supplying the army with elephants. The *Arthasastra* records that, "Some teachers say that land with productive forests is preferable to land with elephant forests, because a productive forest is the source of a variety of materials for many undertakings while the elephant forests supply only elephants. Kautilya disagrees. One can create productive forests on many types of land but not elephant forests. For one depends on elephants for the destruction of an enemy's forces." Obviously, a debate over forest and land use, much like in modern times, had raged during the Mauryan times!

There is also a strong hint of the production forests and elephant forests being ecologically different; the former could have been moister tracts, yielding timber, and the latter drier tracts or secondary growth preferred by elephants. The administration included a superintendent of elephants, who was responsible for the management of elephant forests and captive elephants. As many as 15 different job posts are also prescribed (in comparison, there are just four or five such posts in vogue today).

The *Arthasastra* also gives instructions for the capture of elephants and their classification, training, diet, health care, and deployment in battle. It also mentions the distribution of wild elephants at that time. Eight *gaja vanas* or elephant forests are listed in the *Arthasastra*, while later texts provide more information about these forests and their elephants. Historian Thomas Trautmann provides descriptions of the geographical extent of each of the *gaja vanas*, spread over the subcontinent, with the curious exception of the extreme south (perhaps understandable because the Mauryan Empire or its successors never extended to the southern tip of the peninsula). With the exception of the *Pancanada Vana* in the north, the Indo-Gangetic basin is clearly seen as largely devoid of elephants.

These Sanskrit texts also rank the forests in terms of the quality of their elephants, perhaps an indication of the nutritional status of the elephants and, hence, of the ecological status of the habitat. Interestingly, the elephants of Saurashtra in the west and the Indus to the north, the most arid regions within the range of elephant distribution, are described as being of the lowest quality.

The system of elephant management that had developed by the Mauryan times seems to have changed little over the next 2,000 years or so until the arrival of the British in the subcontinent.

2.4   *The rise of the elephant-headed god*

We now come to the central figure in the evolution of the elephant culture in India, the elephant-headed god, Ganesha (fig. 2.4). One of the most widely adored of Hindu gods in the subcontinent, Ganesha ranks almost on a par with the supreme gods of the Hindu triumvirate. His popularity and worship have not been confined to India, but have historically extended over a wide area to places as far as Afghanistan, Central Asia, Myanmar (Burma), Thailand, Laos, Cambodia, Vietnam, China, Japan, and even the islands of Java, Bali, and Borneo.

The present therianthropomorphic divinity of Ganesha has a relatively late origin, perhaps as late as the fifth century A.D. according to Alice Getty, although

Figure 2.4
The elephant-headed god,
Ganesha, depicted in a
temple (twelfth century A.D.)
at Jalasangi, Karnataka, India
(Photo courtesy of D. K.
Bhaskar.)

other authorities, like M. K. Dhavalikar, believe that some images may date to
the late second or early third century A.D. The earliest literary references to the
modern Ganesha are also relatively recent, say around the fifth century A.D.
There is no mention of Ganesha during the pre-Christian era; for instance,
Ganesha does not appear in either the *Ramayana* or the *Mahabharata*.

The classic Ganesha is actually the culmination of a complex and confusing process extending to pre-Vedic times in the subcontinent. A multiplicity of
independent traditions relating to sacred symbols, spirits, deities, and cults
seem to interact over a 2,000-year period before the almost sudden appearance
of the fully developed classic Ganesha. Historians of religion have devoted
considerable attention to the precise antecedents of this elephant-headed deity.
As Wendy O'Flaherty has written, "Ganesa has everything that is fascinating to
anyone who is interested in religion or India or both: charm, mystery, popular-

ity, sexual problems, moral ambivalence, political importance, the works. One can start from Ganesa and work from there in an unbroken line to almost any aspect of Indian culture" (Courtwright 1985). Thus, historians have delved into the ethnographical, linguistic, archaeological, numismatic, and art historical data—in short, all the conventional sources used by historians.

Conspicuous by its absence is any attempt to place this therianthropomorphic deity in an ecological context. I believe that any attempt to provide a satisfactory and comprehensive theory of a deity linked to a species that has historically been one of the most dominant features of the biological landscape and has played a pivotal role in the political and economic (not to repeat socioreligious) life of the subcontinent has to be seen in the interface of culture and ecology. In this, I would differ from Paul Courtwright, who states that there is no need for a theoretical construct about Ganesha's origins. Indeed, an elephant-headed deity would beg for a satisfactory theory of its origin—unless one would like to believe that a 2,000-year history of intense conflict between animal and humans, the taming of the largest terrestrial mammal and its extensive deployment in political conflict, the imposition of a taboo on consumption of its flesh, the sacred symbolism of the beast albeit in a dualistic negative/positive nature, and the ultimate rise of the classic deity are simply a series of independent, unconnected events.

Before attempting to place the antecedents in an ecological context, I now briefly trace these antecedents of Ganesha as discovered by historians of religion. Then, I also compare this with the cultural context of the African elephant, which took a rather different historical course in its relationship with people.

The representation of the elephant as an independent figure in the seals of the Harappan culture does not seem to have any connotation of sacredness. However, the elephant's inclusion among four animals surrounding a seated figure may indicate an association with a major deity according to A. K. Narain. Although no other visual representations of the elephant seem to have survived from the pre-Aryan cultures, it is generally agreed that the elephant was worshipped by the aboriginal populations of the subcontinent. An elephant-headed deity was possibly a totem of Dravidian tribes and associated with agrarian rites. Their primitive effigies often had animal heads, and it is certain that the elephant would have figured among these animals.

After the Harappan seals, the visual representation of the elephant as a sacred symbol is seen only about two millennia later, during the time of the Mauryan Emperor Ashoka, who placed it in one of his pillars (the *dharmastambhas*). A drawing at Kalsi is labeled *Gajamate*, the supreme elephant. Thus, the sacredness of the elephant is included in Buddhist religious thinking much before orthodox Brahmanical Hinduism. During the Mauryan period, the elephant is also frequently represented in *karshapanas* or punch-marked coins.

The earliest attempts to create a therianthropomorphic elephant deity can be traced to the northwestern region under the patronage of the Greco-Bactrian and the Indo-Greek rulers. An important coin type of the Indo-Greek king

Eukratides, who ruled about 170–150 B.C. over a part of Alexander's territories in Asia, shows the Greek god Zeus on a throne with an elephant head to the right and a mountain to the left. Because the sacred elephant was associated with the mountains and was a symbol for rain and clouds, it is possible that the Greeks identified it with their own Zeus (worshipped as the sky deity, whose presence is marked with lightning, thunder, and rain). In the words of W. W. Tarn, to the Greeks "a mountain god could not well become anything but Zeus."

The earliest representation of an elephant-headed deity, an "incipient Ganesa," comes from a coin of Hermaeus (about 75–55 B.C.), probably the last of the Indo-Greek kings. A. K. Narain was the first to point out that the seated figure in this coin is clearly endowed with the trunk of an elephant. A fascination for the elephant can also be seen among the Greeks of Bactria, whose rulers (like Demetrius and others) used the elephant scalp as a headdress.

During the early centuries of the Christian era, there are few surviving examples of elephant-headed deities prior to the emergence of the classic Ganesha. One of these is a frieze of *ganas* (attendants) on a Buddhist stupa near Mihintale in Sri Lanka. One of the *ganas* clearly has the face of an elephant with trunk and tusk. Interestingly, the elephant-headed figure is seen crouching between two rows of *ganas* bringing him food and drink, one of them holding sheaves of rice or sugarcane, while five others carry jugs of (his favorite) beverage. This is similar in style to an image on one of the Amaravati railings dated as first century A.D. in central India.

There are also several Ganesha-like images in red sandstone from the Mathura region in northern India. In these, the elephant-headed god holds in his left hand a bowl of sweets (which incidentally he is eating with his trunk) and in his right hand a radish or a broken tusk. These figures are dated as late second or early third century A.D. during the reign of the Kushans.

There also is an interesting Mathura frieze of this period that depicts six arches showing worshippers and five elephant-headed figures. Some scholars identify this with the malevolent deities, *vinayakas* who, as discussed below, eventually participate in defining Ganesha.

Finally, our discussion turns to the classic Ganesha sculptures of the Gupta period, which appear around the fifth century A.D. The best known of these are from the Bhumara temple, Udayagiri, and Ramgarh hill in central India. In these, the elephant-headed deity has a potbelly and two or four arms and is holding the axe, the broken tusk (or was this a misrepresentation of a radish?), and a bowl of sweetmeats. This is the "real" Ganesha recognized by historians, an icon that has persisted with all its classic attributes to the present day.

There is no mention of an elephant-headed deity that can be connected to Ganesha in the early Vedic literature associated with the Aryans. The two great epics, the *Mahabharata* and the *Ramayana*, also do not mention this deity. The *Mahabharata*, however, speaks of two classes of *ganas* of Shiva (one of the supreme Hindu gods): a group of benevolent deities and another group of malevolent deities (*vinayakas*), who could be propitiated. Both the *Ramayana* and the *Mahabharata* mention propitiatory rites and ceremonies.

These spirits are encountered again in the *Manava Grhyasutra*, dated at about the second century B.C., which gives the names of four *vinayakas* and prescribes rites for pacifying them. In later texts, such as the *Yajnavalkyasmrti* and the *Baudhayana Grhyaparisesasutra* (both from the second or third century A.D.), the group of four *vinayakas* is merged into a single *Vinayaka*, appointed by Shiva as Ganapati-*vinayakas* or the leader of the *ganas*, who could create difficulties and obstacles if not properly propitiated. Related to *Vinayaka* are names such as *Vighnesa* and *Vighnesvara*, commonly used for Ganesha. These are derived from *vighna* (meaning obstacle), which is used to personify a demigod who is a destroyer. In the *vighna*-related epithets, a dual role, the negative one of malevolence (*vighna-karta*, creator of obstacles) and the positive one of benevolence (*vighna-harta*, remover of obstacles), is indicated.

Some of the later Vedic texts also mention deities related to the elephant, such as *Dantin* (one with tusks), *Hastimukha* (one with the face of an elephant), *Ekadanta* (he of one tusk), and *Vakratunda* (he of the twisted trunk). However, these seem to be theriomorphic cult deities with an independent existence, possibly derived originally from the non-Vedic or Dravidian tradition, which were incorporated as a result of the interactions between the Vedic and non-Vedic cultures. Some scholars like M. K. Dhavalikar connect the above epithets to *Vinayaka* and *Vighna* through their mention in certain texts, an interpretation not accepted by others like A. K. Narain, who considers these references to be of doubtful authenticity. However, this does not deny the eventual identification of a malevolent *Vinayaka* with the benevolent Ganesha in the early centuries of the Christian era. As G. S. Ghurye writes, "Only one step further, and that a very radical transformation, was needed to enthrone Ganesa being the 'Lord of Obstacles,' as the 'Destroyer or Remover of Obstacles.' Such transformations inhere in the very nature of early religio-magical systems of beliefs. One who is the lord of anything can be trusted to control and subdue the thing he is lord of. . . . So *Vinayaka*, the trouble-maker, becomes the much-prayed-to trouble-averter Ganesa" (1962, p. 61). This transformation was probably completed much before the occurrence of Ganesha images of the fourth or fifth century A.D.

The iconography and literary evidences thus broadly point to the emergence of the benevolent Ganesha, the remover of obstacles, by the fifth century A.D. at the latest in central or northern India. From here, the *Puranas* record in greater detail the worship of Ganesha in Brahmanical Hinduism. The *Puranas* refer to a particular group of Sanskrit poetical works dating to around A.D. 300, but elevated to sacral status in Hindu Brahmanism only during the sixth century or later. The detailed narratives of Ganesha's life and character are usually in the later texts (about A.D. 600–1300). Robert Brown points out that some of the confused etymology related to Ganesha can be traced to the Puranic texts.

Ganesha worship spread to the south of the country by the sixth or seventh century. A sculpture of this god at Badami in Bijapur dated at A.D. 578 is considered the earliest representation in the south (a possible exception may be a fragmentary terra-cotta image at Veerapuram in Andhra Pradesh dated prior to A.D. 300). By the end of the seventh century, an independent shrine was consecrated to Ganesha at Tiruchirapalli, further south in Tamilnadu. The seventh century was the period when the Pallavas ruled the south, and their rock-cut works provide some of the most impressive visual accounts of the elephant.

From the Indian subcontinent, Ganesha spread eastward to become a truly pan-Asian god. By the sixth century, he appears in China and soon after in Southeast Asia, a process first traced by Alice Getty and later updated by Robert Brown. Over a large geographical range from Burma, through Thailand, Laos, Cambodia, Vietnam, and Malaysia to Indonesia, the image of Ganesha spread with the migration of Hindu culture. A seventh century Ganesha from Prasat Prei Kuk in Cambodia seems to imply that he was also regarded as a supreme deity. The Southeast Asian iconography, however, tends to resemble the earliest forms of Indian Ganesha, being closer to the imagery of the fifth century or earlier and not the latter-day *Puranic* Ganesha. For instance, the older images of Ganesha that I have examined in Cambodia resemble more a seated elephant than the classic deity. Ganesha is also incorporated into Buddhist worship in Southeast Asia, although he never attains the same importance here as in Buddhist Nepal or Tibet.

The oldest elephant-faced icon in China is surprisingly dated as early as A.D. 531. This "*Vinayaka* form of Ganesha" in the Buddhist grotto-temple of Kung-hsien is labeled the "Spirit King of Elephants." Buddhist monks in China translated Indian texts dealing with Ganesha by the seventh and eighth centuries. The evolution of Ganesha in China and Japan took unique forms, including that of a "dual Ganesha," a fused male and female form, not seen in India. An important characteristic of the Buddhist Ganesha in Tibet, China, and Japan not shared in the Southeast Asian region is his *tantric* character—a malevolent spirit demanding propitiation. This *tantric* nature actually derives from poorly understood antecedents stretching back to the Harappan culture. This important aspect of the evolution of Ganesha demands an explanation: In the Hindu context, the post–sixth-century Ganesha is regarded as a positive force, while in the Buddhist context, he is negative. Thus, a malevolent elephant-headed spirit ultimately rises to supreme, benevolent godhead in the Indian subcontinent, while the positive, sacred elephant of Buddhist Ashoka fails to define the (*tantric*) elephant-headed deity in China.

The evolution of the elephant culture is thus a complex process of interactions spread over time and extending from northwestern India over a large area in East and Southeast Asia. Several independent traditions come together in the Indian subcontinent, and from a process of eclecticism and syncretism, the benevolent, elephant-headed god of learning, the remover of all obstacles, who has persisted for fifteen centuries emerges. The salient features of this evolution can be summarized as follows:

1. The Harappan culture of about 2000 B.C. commonly featured the elephant in seals, and a hint of sacredness is seen in one of the figures.
2. During the second millennium B.C., the Dravidian cultures had tamed the elephant. Elephant-headed spirits were totems.
3. The elephant was used as a war machine during the first half of the first millennium B.C. by Dravidian tribes and then increasingly by the Aryan immigrants. This period saw the emergence of republics and kingdoms in the north. By the second half of the millennium, large numbers of captive elephants were held by emperors, primarily for use in their armies.
4. Several important traditions emerged during the Mauryan period (from about 300 B.C.). Sanctuaries were set up for the protection of wild elephants, presumably to supply the king's army. The elephant was considered sacred by Emperor Ashoka and was incorporated into Buddhist traditions. In the northeast, the Indo-Greeks depicted an elephant-headed deity on coins, and an independent tradition of worship of an elephant god of the mountains seems to have been established.
5. In the early centuries of the Christian era, a taboo on consumption of elephant meat was recorded in northern India. Several representations of an elephant-headed deity were also seen in north-central India before the emergence of the classic, benevolent Ganesha around the fifth century. This is a transformation of an earlier tradition of propitiation of a malevolent *Vinayaka* (or *vinayakas*).
6. The worship of Ganesha spread to East and Southeast Asian countries. In Buddhist China and Japan, Ganesha retained its basic tantric or malevolent character.

2.5   *Ecology, politics, and culture*

The origin of religious ideas can often be traced to the costs/benefits of ecological processes, as anthropologist Marvin Harris has so elegantly done for a variety of cultural food taboos, including those for the pig in the Middle East and the cow in the Indian subcontinent. The imposition of supernatural taboos by a human culture on animal flesh may be the consequence of a deteriorating cost-benefit ratio for the use of a particular species by the community. Several thousand years ago, as human populations increased, production intensified, and natural resources (including forest cover) declined in the semiarid Middle East, the ecological costs of rearing pigs (a moisture-loving creature) gradually became a threat to the entire subsistence system in the region. As ancient cultures and religions responded to this ecological challenge of producing pork, the pig taboo was a recurring theme across a wide zone of pastoral nomadism, from North Africa through the Middle East into Central Asia. Not only the ancient Israelites, but also, before them, the ancient Egyptians and Mesopotamians developed a distinct prejudice against the consumption of pork during the second millennium B.C. The rise of Islam during the seventh century A.D. further reinforced this process of imposing food taboos. The Islamic priesthood incorporated into the *Koran* the divine dicta of the Levitical priests of the Israelites.

The origin of the sacred cow in the Indian subcontinent may have an even more complex cost-benefit ecological consideration. The early Aryan immigrants were pastoral-agriculturalists who seemed commonly to consume beef. Several scholars observe that the Vedic texts up to the first millennium B.C. have ample references to consumption of beef by the Aryans, including by the Brahmans or priests. After an extended period of ambivalence toward beef consumption, a taboo on slaughter of cows and oxen and eating their flesh was firmly established in Hindu India by the middle of the first millennium A.D. This period saw the spread of Aryan settlements over the Indo-Gangetic basin, intensification of production, a virtual disappearance of natural forests, and a population explosion.

Not only did the rearing of cattle for meat become more ecologically difficult, but also the link with agriculture of cattle as draft animals was more firmly established. Agriculture itself was at the mercy of the vagaries of the monsoon. During years of drought, the temptation to slaughter cattle for consumption would have been strong, but cattle were more useful alive than dead. When the rains came, the oxen were needed to plough the fields. Cows were needed for milk, dung, and the production of more oxen and cows. Thus, it may have been adaptive for a farmer to take a longer-term view of the costs/benefits of keeping cattle as opposed to slaughtering them for short-term gain. This inextricable link between cattle and agriculture may have been at the root of the anti–cow-slaughter and anti–beef-consumption sentiments that spread through ancient India.

Explanations for the taboo on elephant flesh and the deification of the species may also be sought in the interactions of culture, the sociopolitical milieu, and ecological processes of ancient India. Among the ruins of the Harappan culture are found the burned bones of several animals whose flesh was presumably consumed at that time. Bones of elephants are also found here, suggesting that the species may have been consumed, even if only rarely, by people of the Harappan culture. Elephants were certainly hunted and their meat consumed by hill tribes in southern India up to at least the fifth or sixth century A.D., as seen from descriptions in the Sangam literature of the Tamils. On the other hand, the taboo on elephant meat in northern India probably arose much earlier and may have been contemporaneous with the general spread of vegetarianism.

When the Aryan immigrants reached the subcontinent, it is certain that elephant flesh was never really a part of their diet. The elephant never existed in the region of Central Asia from where the Aryans migrated, and they would have become familiar with the animal only after reaching the vicinity of the Indus Valley. At the same time, there is no reason to believe that the early Aryans shunned the flesh of elephant once they encountered the species and other cultures that consumed it, especially as the Aryans ate a variety of other animals. The elephant was widespread and abundant and, as the Aryans pushed into the fertile Gangetic plains, would potentially have been a source of meat.

As the Aryan populations and settlements grew, the forests of the Indo-Gangetic tract, and along with it the elephant, gradually retreated. The rise of republics and kingdoms and the growing use of elephants in armies, however, would have created a sustained demand for the supply of elephants from wild populations. Historically, elephants never bred too well in captivity, and thus a steady supply from the wild was needed to maintain or increase the captive stocks. As discussed, the Mauryan Empire maintained a large stock of elephants. The prescription in the *Arthasastra* that sanctuaries should be set up along the periphery of the kingdom for the protection of elephants, and the death penalty imposed on those killing an elephant, implies that a depletion of wild populations had already occurred on a local scale. The demographic traits of elephants are such that their sustainable harvest, even through capture of any sizable proportion of the wild population, is rarely feasible (see chapter 7). Harvest of Asian elephants at a rate exceeding 1.5%–2.0% of the population annually would have resulted in their depletion. The large elephant armies in ancient India certainly suggest higher rates of capture. These Mauryan prescriptions on protection were presumably to ensure a steady supply of elephants for the king's army.

Thus, a taboo on the killing of elephants (presumably for meat) may have been in force since the early Mauryan times. This was further strengthened during the reign of Emperor Ashoka, the grandson of Chandragupta. Ashoka became a Buddhist, and in his famous edicts, he declared that "no living being may be slaughtered for sacrifice" and, by inference, for consumption.

We can thus speculate that, as the elephant was increasingly used by the Aryans as a beast of burden in the colonization of northern India and, more important, deployed in their armies, the elephant at some stage became more useful alive than dead. The Aryan chieftains and kings, perhaps on the advice of the Brahman priests, may have imposed a taboo on the killing of the elephant and consumption of its flesh.

The taboo on elephant meat may have arisen as an independent tradition, but eventually was incorporated into the more general spread of vegetarianism, especially the shunning of beef, in the subcontinent. This was obviously a gradual process that spanned several hundred years. Passages in many of the later Vedic texts show inconsistencies, indicating ambivalence toward consumption of animal flesh. The large-scale animal sacrifices, sponsored by the Aryan chieftains and performed by the Brahman priests, and the feasts at which meat was distributed to the common people were fewer by the middle of the first millennium B.C. The expanding human population and ecological pressures would have made it very difficult for the chieftains and priests to cater to the demands of the people at large for sacrificial meat. Thus, meat eating seems to have largely become a monopoly of the elite—the rulers and the priests. The emergence of Buddhism and Jainism, both with considerable emphasis on not killing any creature, would have posed a challenge to this meat-eating elite of Aryan society. The eventual shunning of meat by the Brahmans and other upper castes and the doctrine of *ahimsa* (nonviolence) may have been a response to this challenge in order to keep the people within the Hindu fold.

Societies outside the Aryan pale, as in southern India, would have continued to consume elephant meat for much longer. It is difficult to say precisely when this practice ceased virtually all over the subcontinent, but this could have been around the seventh or the eighth century A.D., when the worship of Ganesha became established in the south. The Arab traveler and scholar Alberuni recorded during the middle of the eleventh century that the prohibition on killing of animals "applies in particular to Brahmins, because they are guardians of the religion. . . . It is allowed to kill certain animals [by other castes] . . . those which are forbidden are cows, horses, mules, asses, camels, elephants" (Sachau 2002, pp. 559–560). In short, there was universal prohibition on killing of useful animals.

The shunning of elephant meat was roughly contemporaneous with the evolution of the elephant-headed deity. Explanations for the eventual emergence of Ganesha may also be sought in the ecological milieu of ancient India, particularly the conflict between elephants and people for space and resources. Consider the following steps in the evolution of Ganesha. Originally, an elephant related deity was probably the totem of one or more Dravidian tribes and seems to have been associated with primitive, agrarian rites. In earlier times, the elephant deity was propitiated to avoid personal ills. The *vighna*-related epithets make it clear that there was a malevolent side to this deity, who was the creator of obstacles. Later, the deity was transformed into the now-familiar benevolent Ganesha, the remover of obstacles. The symbols associated with Ganesha—the sugarcane, the radish, the bowl of sweet cakes—are predominantly agricultural and related to food. Interestingly, the early Chinese texts, most of which were originally written by Indian monks, refer to Ganesha as *Vinayaka*, an obstacle who must be driven away or removed.

Even prior to the arrival of the Aryans, the small, agricultural societies in the subcontinent would have faced a threat from elephants that ravaged crop fields or even killed people. The elephant was thus to be feared and an elephant spirit or deity to be appeased to avoid personal misfortune. As the Aryans spread into the Indo-Gangetic basin, this conflict with elephants would have intensified. The clearing of forests for settlement and agriculture and the fragmentation of remaining habitats would have increasingly brought the still-abundant wild elephant population into crop fields. The *Gajasastra*, ancient elephant lore (sixth or fifth century B.C.) attributed to the sage Palkapya who lived in eastern India, alludes to the ravages caused by the elephant to agriculture in the kingdom of Anga (in present-day Bihar State). The Aryans would have incorporated some of the tribal deities into Vedic traditions, a recurring theme in the evolution of Hindu worship. Undoubtedly, an elephant deity, still retaining its basic malevolent character, would have been part of these traditions.

At the same time, the capture of elephants for deployment in the armies of the Aryan rulers and the clearing of habitat for settlement would have eliminated wild elephant populations over large tracts of the Indo-Gangetic basin. While people living along the periphery (the cultivation-forest boundary) of such tracts or in the outer plains and hill forests would still have confronted the elephant in their daily lives, those living toward the center of these cultivated tracts would have been safe from its depredations. For the latter, the elite of society, it was no longer necessary to consider the elephant as an evil force. Rather, the very opposite would have been true. The elephant, an indispensable beast of burden and a war machine par excellence, was a very positive force.

Historians of religion have been puzzled by the transformation of a malevolent *Vinayaka* into the benevolent Ganesha. G. S. Ghurye (1962) merely observed that "such transformations inhere in the very nature of religio-magical beliefs" (p. 61) and further that "this last problem [i.e., transformation] defies a perfectly rational and reasonable explanation" (p. 57). It is easy to see that, for the chieftains and kings, the priests and intellectuals, and the farmers cultivating lands free from the threat of depredations (in short, the elite of Aryan society), there was every reason to transform a malevolent deity to a benevolent one. Even though there was a distinct attempt to stress the humble origins of Ganesha, presumably to make the deity more acceptable to the common people, G. S. Ghurye rightly observes that the worship of Ganesha first rose among the elite and was only grudgingly accepted by the commoners, who presumably would still have confronted the wild elephant in their lives.

This differing religiocultural perception of the elephant could potentially have set the stage for social conflict in ancient India. This can be compared with the more contemporary conflicts over the elephant, for instance, between the southern African and eastern African views on elephant management, the internecine conflicts in many African countries between the perceptions of "natives" and "expatriates" over elephant conservation, or even in modern India between villagers and urban-based conservationists (see chapter 9). How then was a potential conflict solved in ancient India?

We can only speculate that the demand for war elephants by the Aryan rulers would have created sufficient economic incentives for the more marginal sections of society, the shifting cultivators and hunter-gatherers who lived among the elephants. As is true even today, these communities would have possessed the skills of capturing, training, and handling elephants. Perhaps a compromise formula was worked out between the two parties. Rather than confront the economically and militarily more powerful Aryan elite, the forest tribes perhaps stopped killing elephants for meat and instead captured them for their rulers' armies. Whatever the interplay of social, economic, political, and religious factors in ancient India, it is a historical fact that, by about 1,200 years ago, the elephant had risen to the status of an important god, and a universal taboo on its killing and consumption was firmly established across the sub-continent. Only certain tribes of the Northeast, who remained outside the influence of mainstream Aryan culture, have continued to this day to consume elephant flesh.

2.6   *From Ganesha to the present*

The mythology of Ganesha blossomed since the seventh century A.D., particularly through the Puranic texts, into myriad tales that made this deity the most popular one across households in India. Ganesha's eventual identification as the son of Shiva, one of the supreme Hindu gods, and of his consort Parvati also aided in the acceptance of this originally demonic figure by Brahmanical sensibilities. Paul Courtwright (1985) interprets Ganesha thus: "Throughout the history of Indian culture the tendency has been to see in the elephant the emblem of the cosmos itself, containing all dichotomies within his more ample form. Ganesha embodies many of these oppositional characteristics" (pp. 30–31).

After the rise of the classic Ganesha, the war elephant continued its march through Indian history until the early nineteenth century, by which time improved weapons based on gunpowder pushed it from the front line to the supply line as noted by Lahiri-Choudhury. The impressive rock-cut sculptures of the Pallava dynasty (A.D. 600–700), the temple sculptures of Orissa (about the eleventh to thirteenth centuries A.D.) and the elaborate bas-reliefs of fighting forces in temples of the Hoysala kingdom (twelfth to early fourteenth centuries A.D.) all testify to the importance of the elephant in the political history of peninsular India.

It is, however, with the arrival of the Afghan and Turkish Islamic rulers in northwestern India, beginning in the early eleventh century, that the best historical accounts of the use of elephants in war are provided. Simon Digby provides a detailed history of the war elephant during the eleventh to fourteenth centuries. The Ghaznavid kingdom centered in Afghanistan seems to have deployed large numbers of elephants. Mahmud of Ghazni, whose invasions left a wide swathe of destruction across northwestern India, is reputed to have inspected 1,300 elephants at the muster of A.D. 1023–1024, while his son Masud inspected 1,670 elephants in A.D. 1031. Given that Afghanistan was devoid of wild elephants, it is clear that the Ghaznavids captured or obtained as tribute their war elephants from rulers in northern India.

The Hindu Rajputs had successfully repelled the invading Turkish forces of Muhammad Ghuri in A.D. 1191 at Tarain, but a year later, the Rajput king Prithviraja Chauhan was defeated by Ghuri after the former apparently changed his mount from an elephant to a horse.

The Turkish Empire thus established in northern India, referred to broadly by historians as the Delhi Sultanate, was to last until A.D. 1398. At the height of their power (about A.D. 1340), the sultans of Delhi possessed about 3,000 elephants, of which 750–1,000 animals were of sufficient size and condition to be used in battle. Most of these elephants were captured from other rulers or obtained as tribute from places as far apart as Bengal, Orissa, the Deccan, and even the Pandyas in the extreme south. There is also a distinct possibility that elephants were imported by the Sultanate from Ceylon and Pegu (Burma).

A complex pattern of trade in elephants seems to have prevailed among these regions during this time. This also implies that the wild elephant populations in northern India had declined considerably. The *pilkhana* (elephant stables) of the Delhi Sultanate, however, declined precipitously to only 120 animals by the time it was defeated by the invading Mongol forces of Amir Timur (Tamerlane) in A.D. 1398. The Malikzada Sultan Mahmud's war elephants were "surging like the ocean and trumpeting like thunder clouds, armoured and with structures placed on their backs," each with several archers. They were no match, however, for Timur's strategy. Lahiri-Choudhury has pointed out that the line of buffaloes and camels used by Timur as a barrier to the advancing elephant force of the Sultanate is possibly the first instance of a biological repellent of elephants!

Although a shadow of its former glory, the Sultanate managed to survive for over a century, first under the Sayyids, nominees of Timur, and later under the Lodis. Ibrahim Lodi, the last of this line, fielded about 100 elephants (one exaggerated report mentions 1,000) at the battle of Panipat (A.D. 1526), where he was killed by Babur, the founder of the Mughal dynasty. The latter used firearms, possibly the first instance of their use in the subcontinent.

The memoirs of the Mughal kings and accounts by their court historians provide the basis for the military history of elephants during the sixteenth and seventeenth centuries. Babur (A.D. 1526–1530) recorded in his memoirs that wild elephants were to be found in the district of Kalpi, in the present-day Gangetic basin devoid of elephants, and that these increased as one proceeded eastward, an accurate observation. His grandson Emperor Akbar (A.D. 1556–1605), the most illustrious of the Mughal rulers, was a connoisseur of elephants. He ascended the throne at the young age of 13 after his Mughal forces overcame the Afghan forces of Adil Shah in a seesaw battle in which the latter deployed several hundred choice elephants.

Akbar undoubtedly built up a large elephant force. Shireen Moosvi estimates there were 5,000 elephants with the Mughals about A.D. 1595, while nobles and landlords held at least 2,800 animals. Her estimate for the captive population in the subcontinent during the sixteenth century is about 17,000 elephants. There are tales of spectacular battles and individual valor in the clashes between the Mughals and the Rajputs, with both sides throwing in their prized elephants. Akbar's chronicler records wild elephants in many parts of central India.

The number of elephants in the Mughal stables had swelled to 12,000 animals, with over 40,000 in the kingdom, during the rule of Akbar's son

Jehangir (A.D. 1605–1627). The higher figure may refer to both captive and wild elephants estimated for the empire. Jehangir's favorite elephant, Gajraj (king of elephants), finds special mention in the chronicles and is depicted in a painting (fig. 2.5).

Jehangir's memoirs recorded an "elephant hunt" in the Panchamahal hills in western India, a region far removed from wild elephant habitat today. The Mughals interestingly refer entirely to capture and not killing of the animal, thereby implying that the Muslim rulers respected the prevailing sentiments of sacredness of the elephant. At the same time, this would have also suited their personal interests in building and maintaining a large elephant army.

An elaborate system of elephant management was in place during Mughal times, and the animal symbolized the pomp of the royalty. The Mughal expeditions to capture elephants also eventually resulted in the complete disappearance of wild populations, possibly already in advanced decline, over a wide

Figure 2.5
The Mughal Emperor Jehangir's royal mount "Gajaratan" or "Gajraj" depicted in a painting. (From the Indian Museum, Kolkata.)

area in central India. During the declining phase of the Mughal dynasty, the use of elephants as a mount for army commanders was rendered totally ineffective by improved musketry and mobile cannon.

The idea of elephant hunting (i.e., killing) as a sport of the upper classes, alien to the local ethos, was introduced by the British during the early nineteenth century. Unlike previous rulers, Maratha or Mughal, Afghan or Rajput, the British did not absorb or practice culturally rooted taboos against hunting certain animals. D. K. Lahiri-Choudhury explains it thus: "The new rulers, unlike the 'natives,' were not encumbered by any superstitious veneration for the animal; for any animal for that matter, except perhaps the horse" (1999, p. xx). In 1807, Thomas Williamson had declared that "no native of Bengal nor any European resident there, would undertake such a piece of rashness as to go out shooting elephants" (quoted in Lahiri-Choudhury 1999, p. xxvi), even though this was prevalent in Africa. By 1826, however, shooting elephants had become an accepted form of sport among the British in Sri Lanka.

Big-game hunting in Africa and Asia was a distinct cultural phenomenon among the colonial rulers. The primary motive behind hunting was presumably the "Hunt," interpreted by historian John MacKenzie as a "contemporary rediscovery of medieval chivalry" linked to ritualized warfare and killing and symbolizing "manliness." Environmental historian Mahesh Rangarajan's interpretation goes a step further. The elephant, like the tiger, was just another large denizen of the jungle whose killing symbolized for the British the conquest of a vast subcontinent by a small group of armed men. Hunting more than ever was an analog of warfare, and until late into the nineteenth century, many British governors gave out rewards for killing elephants. Hunting for sport and animal control resulted in large-scale slaughter of elephants across the Indian subcontinent, Burma, and Sri Lanka (see chapter 8).

The capture of elephants continued during the British period, albeit with different end uses. Elephants were still part of the army, but were not valued as transport for men and goods over hilly or wet terrain. The elephants' moment of glory in modern times came during World War II (1939–1945), when they were an indispensable part of military operations in Burma. The retreating British forces were heavily dependent on these skilled sappers to build bridges and to transport troops and supplies across the densely forested, hilly Burmese terrain, while the advancing Japanese also coveted these elephants for much the same reasons.

The other major use of elephants was for logging the moist forests of Burma and India beginning in the mid-nineteenth century. This was concurrent with the setting up of forest departments in British-ruled provinces. Drawing on traditional systems of elephant husbandry, the British civil servants organized the elephant workforce and introduced westernized veterinary practices. The "timber elephant" became a familiar scene in the economic and cultural landscape of Burma and India.

The Elephant Preservation Act (1872) of the Madras Presidency, which went into force from October 1873, and a similar act in 1879, which extended to other parts of India and eventually Burma to "prevent indiscriminate destruction of elephants," were presumably measures to ensure the continued supply of wild elephants to the military and the logging operations. At present, it is only in Myanmar that the timber elephant retains its original character (fig. 2.6).

Even as a military asset, the elephant made its presence felt as recently as during the Vietnam War, when American planes reportedly bombed the animal directly along the Ho Chi Minh trail to prevent the Viet Cong using it to move supplies through the jungle.

During the nineteenth and twentieth centuries, the Indian elephant continued to retreat not only from capture, but also from conversion of its habitat into use for plantations of tea and coffee, agriculture, railways and roads, mining, dams, and other developmental projects. This process only accelerated after Indian independence in 1947 as the country strove to raise the economic standards of a growing human population.

The Wildlife Protection Act (1972) placed the elephant in the highest category of protection, while the Forest Conservation Act (1980) helped slow the process of deforestation of wildlife habitats. The wild elephants of the country had by then retracted into four regional populations—southern, north-

Figure 2.6
An elephant engaged in logging operations in the Bago Yomas, Myanmar. This is the only country in which elephants are still used extensively for such work.

western, east-central, and northeastern—each with distinct subpopulations within just about 3% of the original geographical range.

As a final point, during the Indian struggle for independence, the nationalist leader, Bal Gangadhar Tilak (1856–1920), transformed Ganesha into a powerful symbol of cultural and religious unity among the people of Maharashtra in their resistance to the British. Tilak achieved this even though there were no wild elephants, and few captive ones, in his native state. The British administrator, Mountstuart Elphinstone, was sufficiently alarmed at the threat to the imperial rule to write, "One talisman that while it animated and united them all, could leave us without a single adherent. This barbarism is the name of religion, a power so obvious that it is astonishing our enemies have not more frequently and systematically employed it against us" (quoted in Courtwright 1985, p. xxvi). It can be argued that the nationalist elephant finally triumphed over the imperial lion in 1947. Ironically, the lion was declared India's national animal until it was displaced by the tiger in 1968, in spite of the eminent naturalist M. Krishnan suggesting in 1952 that the elephant was the truly pan-Indian species and was fit to be the national animal.

Historians have pondered over the wisdom of the Indian rulers' seemingly blind faith in the efficacy of the elephant as a war machine. The argument is that horse-based cavalry repeatedly proved superior to the elephant in battle. The eminent historian A. L. Basham sums up this view in the following words: "The great reliance placed on elephants was, from the practical point of view, unfortunate. . . . The pathetic Indian faith in the elephants' fighting qualities was inherited by the Muslim conquerors, who, after a few generations in India, became almost as reliant on elephants as the Hindus and suffered at the hands of armies without elephants in just the same way" (1967, pp. 129–130).

Simon Digby takes a somewhat different view of Indian military strategy. According to him, the tactical importance of the elephant, even if it did not match that of the horse, was much greater than has been conceded by military historians. For instance, elephants were much more useful in certain terrain, such as hills and moist tracts, where the horse had its own limitations. As supporting evidence for the importance of elephants in war, Digby emphasizes that the Delhi Sultanate, which once possessed several thousand elephants and successfully warded off invaders, finally succumbed to an elephantless army (that of Amir Timur) only when its *pilkhana* had been reduced to a mere 120 elephants.

Whatever the true achievement of the elephant as a war machine, the perceived role of the animal through history obviously determined the religio-cultural traditions of society. It so happened that the elephant was elevated to a supreme position, unmatched by any other animal, in the cultural life of a major civilization. That this exalted position has persisted for two millennia is itself a testimony to the powerful and vibrant role the elephant has played in the subcontinent. Long after the war elephant has faded into history, the elephant-headed god reigns supreme, more popular than ever before, assuming new roles and adapting to changing circumstances. The elephant itself has assumed the role of a flagship in India's efforts in conserving its forests and wildlife through the launch of Project Elephant in 1992.

2.7   *The capture and use of the African elephant*

The capture and taming of elephants is associated, for good reasons, with the Asian continent. Around the time *Elephas* was being first tamed in the Indian subcontinent, it is distinctly possible that a now-extinct population of *Loxodonta* in northern Africa was also being exploited.

The pharaohs of dynastic Egypt hunted, and maybe even captured, elephants in the Nile River valley. Rock drawings of the early third millennium B.C. in Upper Egypt depict elephants, sometimes being hunted, but one cannot conclude that these were also captured and tamed for use. The evidence for capture is thus very circumstantial; the elephant does not figure in ancient Egyptian monuments or its mythology.

Until the early third millennium B.C., the African elephant was widespread in the north, including substantial areas of a moister and greener Sahara. The onset of arid conditions in northern Africa then seems to have resulted in the retreat of the elephants into the region of the Atlas Mountains, comprising present-day Morocco, Algeria, and possibly Tunisia.

The expeditions of Egyptian rulers during the second millennium B.C. again seem to have been mainly to hunt elephants for their ivory. At the same time, ivory was also being obtained from Asia. Thutmose I (1525–1512 B.C.) and his grandson Thutmose III (1504–1450 B.C.) hunted elephants, but interestingly, they hunted the Asian elephant in the Euphrates basin. One of the Syrian elephants seems to have been taken alive to the Egyptian Thebes, where Thutmose III maintained a collection of plants and animals he encountered during his expeditions.

It is only after the fifth century B.C., by which time the use of the elephant as a military weapon had already been well established in Asia, that the elephant in Africa was clearly sought alive for use in war. By this time, the Asian elephant had disappeared from West Asia, probably as a result of its exploitation by the Assyrian rulers. The Mediterranean basin became a cauldron for the struggles of several kingdoms—the Greeks, the Romans, the Syrians, the Carthaginians, and the Ptolemaic Egyptians—along its Eurasian and North African fringe.

In the meantime, an elephant culture seems to have flourished around 400 B.C. in the kingdom of Meroe, around Aswan in the upper Nile, beyond the influence of Ptolemaic Egypt. The elephant is portrayed in several sculptures and reliefs. One relief at Musaw-warat es-Sofra shows a king riding an elephant while an attendant is kneeling and holding the end of the trunk. The excavations here suggest that some of the large enclosures may have been built to hold elephants.

H. H. Scullard provides a detailed account of the use of the elephant in the Mediterranean region during the second half of the first millennium B.C. Salient features of this account are given here. During the latter part of the fifth century B.C. the Greek writer Herodotus, who had visited Egypt but had never actually seen an elephant, gave an account of several wild beasts, including elephants, in the westward parts (of Libya) and further observed that the Ethiopians sent a tribute of "twenty great elephant tusks" every third year to the Persian court. The Greeks, however, seemed to have first learned about the use of elephants in war from the writer Ctesias, who was the court physician to the Persian king Artaxerxes II from 405 until at least 387 B.C. In one of his accounts, he relates how the elder Cyrus of Persia was defeated (in 530 B.C.) by Amoraius, king of the Derbikes, who used elephants from India (the Indians may have actually commanded the elephants). Another curious tale is about the semimythical Semiramis, who built dummy elephants in her battle against an Indian king's elephant army, which eventually prevailed against her (some historians believe this may refer to the historical figure of Sammuramat, an Assyrian queen who ascended the throne during 810–805 B.C. after her husband's death).

Plato makes a brief mention of the elephant ("a very large and voracious animal") on an island in the Mediterranean or the Atlantic; this was undoubtedly the African elephant, which was known from the Atlas region of North Africa. Aristotle (384–322 B.C.) had an intimate knowledge of the elephant, as seen from his descriptions in works such as *De Partibus Animalium* and *Historia Animalium*. He recognized that elephants existed in North Africa and India, but emphasized similarity rather than differences. It is said that Aristotle briefly tutored the young Alexander, son of Philip of Macedonia, and that Alexander later supported Aristotle's pursuit of natural history.

The Greeks probably first encountered war elephants at the battle of Gaugamela in 331 B.C., when Alexander of Macedonia overcame Darius III of Persia, who had the backing of about 15 elephants fielded by his Indian supporters. Alexander captured these and eventually went on to acquire more elephants during his eastward thrust, including 86 from the ruler of Takshashila (Taxila), for a total of 126 elephants by the time he confronted King Porus across the Jhelum (Hydaspes) in 326 B.C. Interestingly, Alexander did not field any of his more than 125 elephants against Porus' 200-strong elephant army. Perhaps he did not have sufficient faith in his elephant force; Scullard believes that he did not have sufficient time to coordinate the various arms of his forces, including the cavalry, into a cohesive unit and thus did not wish to experiment with his elephants. Alexander's victory and the subsequent outcome were discussed above. In the words of eminent historian Romila Thapar (1966), the two-year Greek campaign "made no impression historically or politically on India, and not even a mention of Alexander is to be found in any older Indian sources. It seems that the Greeks departed as fast as they came" (p. 59).

The encounter with Indian elephants at the Jhelum, however, seemed to have made a lasting impression on the Greeks. After Alexander's death at Babylon, shortly after his retreat, his embalmed body was carried on a magnificent vehicle that was richly decorated, including a painting of war elephants led by their Indian mahouts and followed by armed Macedonians. Alexander's death triggered a complex struggle among his successors, a galaxy of generals, soldiers, and governors, for control of his vast empire. The chief players were Perdiccas, his second in command; Ptolemy of Egypt; Lysimachus, one of his bodyguards; Seleucus, who controlled the east and seemed to appreciate the military importance of elephants the most; Eumenes, head of the imperial chancery; Craterus of Cilicia; Antigonus of Phrygia; and Antipater, the governor of Macedon. Strangely, it was his successors who began to use elephants in a distinctly offensive role in the course of several battles, major and minor, they fought. Elephants were frequently deployed in the internecine struggles, as well as in battles with other neighbors, like Pyrrhus of Epirus, who deployed elephants against them, the Romans, and in Sicily.

Seleucus, who had been operating rather independently along the Indian frontier, made peace with Chandragupta Maurya after ceding him some territories in exchange for a large number of elephants, variously estimated to be between 130 and 500, for use in his western campaign. In one decisive battle, Seleucus's superior elephant force defeated and killed Antigonus, who deployed 75 elephants. After the death of Seleucus (he was killed by Ptolemy Ceranus, one of Ptolemy's sons), his son Antiochus effectively used elephants to beat back the invasions of the Gallic tribes. Glorious in victory and hailed by the Macedonians, Antiochus is reputed to have wept, "shame, my men, whose salvation came through these 16 beasts [i.e., elephants]."

In 312 B.C., Ptolemy I had captured some 43 Indian elephants from Demetrius (son of Antigonus) in a battle at Gaza. These were paraded at Alexandria by his son Ptolemy II Philadelphus in a grand show of splendor and wealth. The Ptolemies now began to consolidate their elephant stocks. They were aware of the elephants at Meroe. Philadelphus organized expeditions along the African coast of the Red Sea in the region around Eritrea in search of elephants. A papyrus of about 255 B.C. speaks of an elephant expedition, while an inscription records that a certain Eumedes "caught elephants in great numbers for the king, and he brought them as marvels for the king." The elephants were transported by sea to Alexandria. The Ptolemies thus built up a sizable elephant force incorporating both the African and the Asian species.

During the second half of the third century B.C., the Seleucids and the Ptolemies were involved in a series of wars for the control of Syria. In 219 B.C., Ptolemy IV Philopator's mixed force of 73 elephants faced the superior Seleucid force of 102 Indian elephants fielded by Antiochus III in the battle of Raphia. The African elephants in Ptolemy's left wing were afraid to join battle with the larger Indian elephants of Antiochus, and this wing of Ptolemy retreated. Ptolemy's right wing, however, held its ground, and this helped him overcome Antiochus. The role of the elephants here is unclear, but Scullard speculates that Ptolemy's Indian elephants, facing their equals, may have helped. Antiochus retreated for the present, but consolidated his forces with more Indian elephants and regained southern Syria from Ptolemy V in 200 B.C.

We now need to go further back in time and further west in the Mediterranean region to the Carthaginian Empire, based in North Africa and controlling Spain and several island territories, and trace its struggles against the emerging Roman Empire. The Carthaginians were familiar, since at least the early fifth century B.C., with the existence of African elephants in the region between the Atlas Mountains and the Mediterranean. An early Carthaginian explorer, Hanno, writing before 480 B.C. in Punic language, described elephants in a lagoon overgrown with cane.

Unlike the Seleucids and the Ptolemies, who had to obtain their elephants from afar, the Carthaginians could exploit a population nearer home. It is not clear when and how they began training elephants for use in war. The earliest documented use of elephants in war by the Carthaginians was during a battle against Rome in Sicily in 264 B.C. The Roman legions had already faced Pyrrhus's Indian elephants earlier in Italy and were able to beat back the Carthaginians, capturing most of the surviving African elephants. The Roman commander Regulus took the battle into Africa itself and gained Tunis in 246 B.C., but the defeat of the Carthaginians was due to a tactical error of fielding their approximately 100 elephants in the hills rather than in the plains. Reorganizing their forces under a professional commander, Xanthippus from Sparta, they effectively used their elephants eventually to rout the Romans.

After crushing a rebellion by their mercenary troops with the help of their elephants, the Carthaginians decided to regain control over Spain and to use this as the launching pad against the Romans. This was a struggle of fluctuating fortunes, revolving around the military strategy of the famous Hannibal, although his brothers Hasdrubal and Mago also played important roles.

As a young boy, Hannibal had accompanied his father, Hamilcar Barca, to Spain in 237 B.C. with a force of 100 elephants and thus had personal knowledge of the use of these animals in warfare. Hannibal's audacious campaign against Rome by crossing the Alps in 319 B.C. with an elephant army is one of the most celebrated tales of history. Overcoming the Gauls at the Rhone, he transported his elephants safely across the river on rafts, but only after some of them panicked and slid into the river, drowning their mahouts. Going across the Alps, he faced hostile tribes, but in the words of ancient historian Polybius, "The elephants were of the greatest service to him; the enemy never dared to approach that part of the column where they were placed, being terrified at the strangeness of their appearance" (quoted in Scullard 1974, pp. 158–159). In addition, there was a very difficult descent because of a landslide, but miraculously Hannibal managed to get all his 37 exhausted elephants to the plains of Italy, although losing many of his men.

The Romans tried to seize this opportunity to repulse a vulnerable Hannibal, but Hannibal's strategy repulsed the Romans. Hannibal was eventually to lose all but one of his elephants, seemingly not in battle, but due to exposure to severe cold. Undaunted by the loss of his elephants, men, horses, and even the sight of one eye, Hannibal rode the sole surviving elephant (quite possibly an Indian animal obtained from the Ptolemies) across treacherous terrain to notch up significant victories.

There were several twists and turns to Hannibal's campaign. He received reinforcements of elephants and even reached the gates of Rome, but was forced to retreat. The power of the Carthaginians, however, steadily declined.

In a final showdown in 204 B.C., Hannibal, with 80 elephants, faced the brilliant Roman general Publius Scipio at Zama in North Africa. Scipio's strategy carried the day. Of Hannibal's elephants, 11 were killed, while the rest were presumably captured. The Carthaginians were forced to surrender all their elephants and to agree to discontinue training any in the future.

The Roman passion (or the lack of it) for elephants had quite a different purpose from that of the Seleucids, Ptolemies, and Carthaginians. When Curius captured a number of Indian elephants from Pyrrhus in 275 B.C., he displayed these to the Roman people, who probably saw these animals for the first time. Metellus likewise displayed in the circus the African elephants he took from the Carthaginians in the battle of Panormus.

The Romans did use elephants intermittently in their wars with Greece and opponents further east, as well as in the west against several tribes. Although their elephant forces were typically small, these made useful contributions to several of their victories. Julius Caesar is reputed to have used one large elephant during his second invasion of Britain in 54 B.C. to suppress the troublesome Gauls. He had no faith in the efficacy of elephants; his elephant-less army finally overcame Pompey's forces with the support of Juba of Numidia (in North Africa), who fielded a considerable number of elephants at the battle of Thapsus in 46 B.C. This was the last battle fought by the Romans with elephants for about 300 years.

The use of elephants by the Romans, however, was overwhelmingly as a public spectacle in processions, as a circus animal, and as an object of torment. Pliny the Elder reports that elephants first fought in the circus in the year 99 B.C. Animal fights, much like the battle of the gladiators, had become popular in Rome. Elephants were pitted against men armed with javelins at the infamous Games of 55 B.C., a lavish but bloodthirsty spectacle organized by Pompey. After Caesar's victory over Pompey, a considerable number of the 64 elephants captured were again on display in 46 B.C. in Rome. Although the show included men fighting from the backs of the elephants, this does not seem to have drawn blood to the extent that Pompey's games did a decade earlier.

Imperial Rome had to demonstrate its power and prosperity both to its citizens and to the outside world. The elephant was a very convenient vehicle to realize this objective from several viewpoints. The parading of elephants in victory triumphs demonstrated that Rome had the wealth and skills to transport these large animals over long distances. When elephants were made to perform stunts in the circus arena or were slaughtered with javelins, the Roman spectators did not necessarily make a distinction between these categories of amusement. Since the Roman territories did not have wild elephants, the elephant was identified with their enemies, such as the Carthaginians. In the words of Jo-Ann Shelton, "The torment of elephants in Roman arenas represented a victory over the defeated enemy, and it enabled the spectators to participate in the process of imposing Roman justice on a barbarian world . . . their enormous size and strength made them appear menacing, but their lumbering gait and strange appearance meant that they could be easily ridiculed."

We now turn to an aspect of ancient Mediterranean warfare that has been much discussed—the role of Asian versus African elephants. Ancient writers were unanimous in their observations that Indian elephants were larger than their African counterparts and were more effective in battle. Describing the battle of Raphia between Ptolemy's predominantly African elephant force versus Antiochus's Asian elephants, Polybius wrote that "most of Ptolemy's elephants were afraid to join battle, as is the habit of African elephants; for unable to stand the smell and the trumpeting of the Indian elephants, and terrified, I suppose, also by their great size and strength, they immediately run away from them." Pliny, in his writings of the Roman Empire, states that "African elephants fear Indian, because the Indian is bigger," but he also wrote that "Ethiopia produces elephants that rival those of India," a statement dismissed by scholars because an exaggerated height of 30 feet was ascribed to the former. The depiction of an African elephant with its rider in relief from Meroe also suggests that it was relatively small.

Such observations have led several scholars to conclude that the African elephant captured and used in war during ancient times was the smaller forest elephant (*Loxodonta africana cyclotis*). Now there are some problems with this interpretation. It is, of course, possible that the *cyclotis* elephants extended into North Africa from their present range in West Africa through the Atlantic coastal belt. These would have been the elephants exploited by the Carthaginians. On the other hand, it is highly unlikely that *cyclotis* was present along the Red Sea in the region of East Africa, the source of the Ptolemies' elephants.

Other explanations are possible for the smaller size of the African elephants vis-à-vis the Asian elephants used in war. The African animals could simply have been younger animals. The Ptolemies or even the Carthaginians may not have had the skills to capture and train adult African elephants (this ability is restricted even today in parts of Asia). There may have been insufficient time for the young elephants to become full grown before deploying them in battle. The elephants sourced from India were adults given the longer tradition of capture and training.

These African elephants could have been a smaller variety of the savanna elephant (*Loxodonta africana africana*). Even today, there is wide variation in the adult body sizes of the African savanna elephant across the continent, with some (like those in Kenya's Shimba Hills) being intermediate between the typical savanna elephant and the forest elephant in size (see appendix 2). The recent genetic evidence from African elephant populations (see chapter 1) also suggests another possibility: the elephants of North Africa were a distinct variety or subspecies, now extinct, as suggested in 1971 by W.F.H. Ansell.

The efficacy of the elephant, African or Asian, in the Mediterranean wars can again be questioned, as with its role in the Indian subcontinent. The greater reliance placed by the Seleucids, the Ptolemies, and the Carthaginians, compared to other powers, on the elephant may be a reflection of the relative proximity of elephant populations or ability to source them. Astute commanders, however, realized that elephants were merely weapons of fear, most effective the first time they were used against an enemy unfamiliar with these animals. With increasing familiarity, a combination of proper weapons and tactics could nullify an elephant force. There is no doubt that the elephant was instrumental in influencing the course of several battles, but by the dawn of the Christian era, the elephant had practically died out as a war machine. During the first three centuries of the first millenium A.D., a few battles were fought with the help of elephants, but these cannot be compared in scale to their deployment over the preceding three centuries in the Mediterranean region. By contrast, the elephant war machine rolled on for a long time further east in Asia, even if its relevance can be disputed.

The crucial question, then, is why did the elephant culture die out, or to state more appropriately, why did the elephant culture remain at the totemic level in Africa while it continued to flourish supremely in Asia? By elephant culture, I mean the entire gamut of elephant-human relationships, including its expression in art and in oral traditions, its symbolic function, its practical use by humans in war and in peace, and its deification. I must emphasize here that the representation of the elephant in native African sculpture, masquerade, dance, and song is common and rich across the continent. A 1992 volume edited by Doran Ross amply demonstrates the importance of elephant symbolism to the lives of modern African peoples (indeed, such documentation has not been put together for the Asian continent). It is but natural or even inevitable that native African peoples relate the largest land mammals to their social lives and the environment in conspicuous symbolism and complex metaphor. At the same time, the actual physical relationship with the elephant has been largely that between adversaries. There are many similarities with Asia in this fundamental relationship of humans and elephants. At a certain stage in Asian history, however, the culture of capturing the elephant for putting it to human use intensified, and ultimately the animal's status was raised to that of a major deity.

What could be the reasons for the early collapse of the culture of capturing and taming elephants in Africa? The culture of organized capturing of elephants is distinctly associated with the rise of major republics, kingdoms, or empires in both the continents. In Africa, this was not backed by the advantage of biogeography. It is true that the supply of elephants to the Carthaginian army does suggest that reasonable numbers were present in North Africa. However, neither there nor along the Red Sea, where the Ptolemies sourced their elephants, is there evidence for populations that could be harvested sustainably for any length of time. The Carthaginians and the Ptolemies did not have access to Africa's large sub-Saharan elephant populations; their influence just did not extend that far. Crucially, however, no major republic or kingdom arose in sub-Saharan Africa at that period of history, when elephant cultures were on the ascent. Even the Assyrians did not have a sizable population of Asian elephants to exploit in the Tigris-Euphrates basin. The elephant had only a tenuous existence in West Asia. The Indian rulers, on the other hand, had the advantage of large elephant populations they could regularly exploit for much longer periods of time. The same is true for the later kingdoms further east from Burma to Indochina.

In more recent times, the only concerted effort to tame African elephants was of the smaller forest elephant in the erstwhile Belgian Congo. Two training camps operated during the first half of the twentieth century, with up to 100 elephants at a time, but this declined to a few animals by the last decade. Asian methods, especially Sri Lankan and Burmese, were used in their capture, training, and management. Although elephants were successfully trained, the camps were never sustained because there was no real use for the elephants here. The African elephant is thus as tractable as its Asian cousin. Why, then, did its taming not catch on in the continent even during the colonial times? It is possible that colonial prejudice in other matters equally extended to the elephants of Africa. The African elephant was valued for its extractable re-source—the ivory trade even partially funded the imperial expansion in its early phase in parts of the continent. Protection of the elephant in Africa came at a much later time, prompted by a fear of ivory shortage. So, the African elephant was more valuable dead for its ivory, while the Asian had reasons to be left alive as a source of captive stock.

As a final thought, human societies that had a more primitive relationship with the elephant, perhaps hunting them occasionally for meat and hide, ex-pressing their art through masquerade, or carving tusks and absorbing the symbolic elephant in their social lives, are also the ones that permitted the elephant to survive in their midst. Exceptions to this can, no doubt, be found. Paul Martin makes the pertinent observation that humans who dispersed fur-ther away from the cradle of elephant and human evolution, Africa, are also those who have exploited the proboscideans the most. Finally, it was the ad-vanced hunting tribes of North America who may have speared the mammoth to extinction, the great kingdoms and empires of Asia that wiped out elephants locally through capture, and the foreign traders who coveted Africa's white gold for prosperous societies in Europe, America, and in more recent times, East Asia, slaughtered the animal wholesale. It remains to be seen if the charis-matic flagship roles of the African and the Asian elephant are powerful enough to meet the exponentially growing challenges of conservation in the two conti-nents during the twenty-first century.

Bulls, Musth, and Cows
The Elephantine Mating Game

3

3.1   Introduction

The breeding system of a species has important ecological and evolutionary consequences. Among the mammals, differences between the sexes in body size and the intensity of secondary sexual characters such as coat color or ornamentation (antlers, for instance) in males are significantly correlated with reproductive strategies. Charles Darwin (1871, Vol. II) noted that, among monogamous seals, the sexes were approximately equal in body size, while in polygynous seals, the males were up to six times larger than the females. The males of polygynous species are also more likely to sport elaborate ornamentation, such as large antlers or horns, which in Darwin's words are "singularly ill-fitted for fighting" (p. 251) but are "used chiefly or exclusively for pushing and fencing" (p. 253).

The elephant is a polygynous mammal, as are 95% of all mammals. Polygyny has been defined by William Shields as a situation when "more females than males breed, with the result that variance in reproductive success is greater in males than in females. The greater the difference in variance, the greater the degree of polygyny." The degree of dimorphism between the sexes is a good indicator of the degree of polygyny in a species. The elephant is one of the most sexually dimorphic of mammals. In African elephants, a full-grown male weighs twice as much as a full-grown female, making these among the most sexually dimorphic (and also polygynous) of all mammals.

One demographic consequence of polygyny is that sex ratios, especially of adults, are biased toward females because the males suffer higher death rates. There could be several reasons for this asymmetry in survivorship. Males pay an additional metabolic price in the process of attaining a larger body size, making them more susceptible to nutritional stress and diseases. There are higher costs (either injuries or death) associated with male-male competition or risks of emigrating from the natal family. Elephant populations universally show a preponderance of females over males, with the disparity progressively increasing with age class. Spatial segregation between the sexes on a seasonal basis may also be a feature of polygynous species. Males and females may use different areas because of variation in nutritional demands or as part of their antipredatory strategies. While there is no evidence for exclusive cow (i.e., female-led family) areas, there is evidence for exclusive bull areas among elephants.

Whatever the social system of a species, the sexes have to meet, even if only during a certain time of the year, for breeding. There are two determinants of mating: dominance hierarchies based on the outcomes of male contests and female choice of mates with certain desirable qualities. For a long time, biologists believed that mating success was decided entirely by the competition among males. Even though Charles Darwin had cautiously proposed that females of some species might select their mates, it took over a century for this idea to be tested and confirmed empirically.

Reproduction in elephants has been described, often in rather imaginary terms, since ancient times. From the ancient Sanskrit and Tamil literature of India, to the writings of the Greek philosopher Aristotle, to the zoological literature of the eighteenth and nineteenth centuries, we obtain glimpses of the mating game in the largest of terrestrial mammals. Scientific details of the reproductive biology of elephants, however, emerged from three major lines of investigation that began around the mid-twentieth century. The elephant control programs in eastern Africa at that time and later in southern Africa provided the material for detailed investigations of the anatomy and histology of reproductive organs. Seminal papers in 1953 and 1964 by J. S. Perry of reproductive biology in African elephants provided the framework for later descriptions of reproductive structures and function. Since then, several physiological studies, chiefly of hormonal control of reproduction, of both Asian and African elephants in captivity have revealed a rather complex female estrous cycle. At the same time, behavioral studies of mating from captive and wild situations have added substantially to our knowledge of reproductive strategies of elephants.

In this chapter, I first describe the estrous cycle of a female elephant and how this state is conveyed to the males. I then describe the phenomenon of *musth*, a rutlike condition in bull elephants. A bull in musth undergoes important physiological changes and exhibits a range of specific behaviors designed to increase its mating success. After describing the behavioral and physiological correlates of musth from studies of both Asian and African elephants, I analyze the evolutionary significance of this phenomenon in the framework of game theory as applied to competing males and female choice of mates. Finally, I consider a possible role for tusks as an indicator of genetic fitness of male elephants.

3.2   *Estrus in the female elephant*

3.2.1   *Physiology of the female reproductive cycle*

As in other mammals, the reproductive tract in female elephants is composed of a pair of ovaries (located near the kidneys), the Fallopian tubes, a uterus with two cornua or horns, and a chamber that leads into the urogenital passage that opens externally at the vulva. A striking feature of the reproductive system in elephants is the long (nearly 1 m) urogenital canal, a common passage for both the genital and urinary tracts that opens at a position anterior to the hind legs. The clitoris is also unusually pronounced in cows; this has often been a source of incorrect sexing of animals in the field, of young captives, or even of museum specimens.

Typically, the estrous cycle in a mammal involves a follicular phase with growth of the vesicular ovarian (or so-called Graafian) follicles containing the ovum (egg); ovulation, which is release of the egg into the fallopian tubes; the luteal phase, in which the corpus luteum is formed inside the ruptured follicle; and finally, if the egg is not fertilized, the degeneration of the corpus luteum to start a new follicular phase. Several hormones mediate this process; the principal hormones are the two gonadotropins, follicle-stimulating hormone (FSH) and luteinizing hormone (LH), secreted by the pituitary gland in the brain, and the two female sex hormones, estrogen and progesterone, produced by the ovaries. The levels of FSH and LH are relatively low during most of the follicular phase, but rise abruptly when the rate of estrogen secretion by the growing follicle increases. The rise in LH is quantitatively higher than that of FSH and induces maturation of the follicle, with ovulation occurring soon after the LH surge. Following ovulation, the corpus luteum, a glandular tissue that forms inside the ruptured follicle, now begins to produce estrogen and another steroid hormone, progesterone. Monitoring the levels of these hormones in the bloodstream or their metabolites in the urine of an animal helps to reconstruct the estrous cycle of the species.

The estrous cycle in elephants is still rather poorly understood. Overt signs of estrus in female elephants are lacking. Some early behavioral observations during 1969–1970 of captive cow elephants and attendant bulls in Sri Lanka (Ceylon) indicated an estrous cycle of 18–27 days, with an average of 22 days. Bulls showed distinct sexual interest in the cows at these intervals, and the animals mated more often during this time. Data on vaginal cytology and urinary estrogens from elephants in western zoos also pointed to an approximately 3-week estrous cycle.

Until this time, it was difficult to detect progesterone in elephants because the levels of this hormone were probably very low. The development of sensitive radioimmunoassay techniques, however, changed this situation. In 1975, Edward Plotka and associates reported the first reliable detection of progesterone and estrogen in the blood of captive Asian and African elephants in various reproductive states. No clear relationship between these hormone levels and the reproductive state of the animal could be discerned in these early experiments. A major shift in our knowledge of the estrous cycle in elephants occurred when Michael Schmidt and colleagues, working at the Washington Park Zoo (Portland, Oregon) with Asian elephants, announced at a meeting in 1981 that the duration of the cycle was about 16 weeks; this was based on clearer progesterone profiles in several cows (fig. 3.1).

Puberty can be considered as the onset of the first estrous cycle, as evidenced by the development of a large follicle, while sexual maturity is the age at first ovulation seen from the presence of at least one corpus luteum. By the above criteria, there may be a difference of 2–4 years between puberty and sexual maturity in female elephants. The age at sexual maturity itself varies quite widely in populations of African and Asian elephants. This seems related to local climate, forage resources, nutritional plane, and other ecological factors (chapter 7). In the wild, female elephants typically attain sexual maturity between 11 and 14 years of age, although the mean age of maturity in populations ranges from 9 years to as high as 22 years. Reports of 6-year-old elephants attaining sexual maturity under captive conditions are exceptional. Some define sexual maturity as the age at first conception, but this may not occur during the first ovulation.

The follicular phase in elephants is also referred to as the nonluteal or interluteal phase. The early histological studies of ovaries obtained from elephants shot during control operations in Africa are still the main sources of information of follicular and luteal structures. These descriptions have been provided mainly by J. S. Perry, Roger Short, John Hanks, Irvin Buss, Norman Smith, and Richard Laws. The ovaries of a mature elephant, pregnant or otherwise, contain multiple follicles in different stages of development. The sizes of follicles reach 30 mm in diameter, with pubertal animals having at least one follicle greater than 6 mm. The dominant follicles in mature animals generally vary from 10 to 20 mm.

Changes in steroid and peptide hormone profiles and their relationship to follicular development are still rather unclear. Some of the early measurements of FSH in the blood of African elephants showed no clear patterns or apparent relationship to age. The more detailed work of Janine Brown and associates in captive Asian elephants reported in 1991 provides a much clearer picture of FSH profiles. A cyclic pattern of FSH lasting 12–14 weeks was seen, with low levels (below 10 ng/ml) during the late follicular and early luteal phases, followed by elevated levels (typically 25–40 ng/ml) over a long period (7–8 weeks) during the late luteal and early follicular phases. FSH levels were also inversely related to those of another peptide hormone, inhibin (as expected,

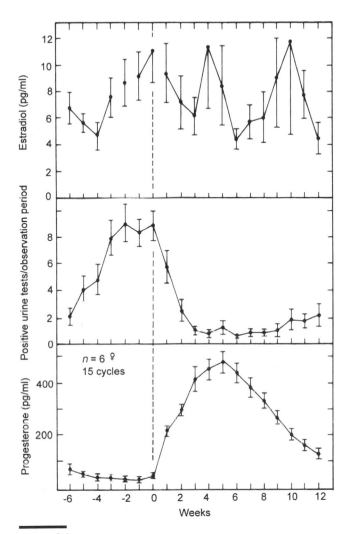

Figure 3.1
Weekly mean (±standard error) progesterone and estradiol concentrations in blood of six Asian elephant cows for 15 estrous cycles. The average frequency of positive urine tests by bulls during the same cycle is also shown. Week 0 is designated as the week preceding one in which progesterone exceeded 100 pg/ml. (From Hess et al. 1983. Reproduced with the permission of the Society for the Study of Reproduction, Inc., U.S.A.)

because inhibin suppresses FSH), with a similar 12–14 week cycle. The inter-luteal or follicular period itself is of a short 4–6-week duration.

After it became apparent from the work of David Hess and the Schmidts that the estrous cycle in Asian elephants is likely to be much longer than earlier suspected, further work on hormone profiles of both species by Edward Plotka and associates confirmed that the cycle was indeed 14–16 weeks. They pro-posed that elevated estrogen levels, although often obscure, reflect possibly five successive waves of follicular growth with a periodicity of about 3 weeks throughout the cycle, and that the clear progestin cycle of 14–16 weeks repre-sents the culmination of one of these waves in ovulation and formation of a functional corpus luteum. They could only occasionally detect multiple peaks of LH within a progestin cycle. Later work, however, clearly indicated more than one LH surge during a cycle, but this did not occur throughout the cycle. LH profiles of African elephants obtained by N. Kapustin and coworkers showed that each ovarian cycle was characterized by two LH surges, separated by 3 weeks, within the follicular phase, and that the second peak was associ-ated with an increase in progestin.

The dynamics of the primary class of female sex hormones, the estrogens, during the estrous cycle are confusing. The concentrations of circulating estra-diol (the predominant estrogen in most mammals) are very low (usually under 15 pg/ml) and seemingly fluctuate without any pattern. Only the study by N. Kapustin's team indicates small but significant estradiol peaks prior to each of the two LH peaks. Estrogen profiles presented by K. Taya and associates for Asian elephants in the Tokyo Zoo have also been interpreted by Keith Hodges to contain multiple peaks within the interluteal phase. It is possible that mea-surements of conjugated estradiol (e.g., to protein) may yield more meaningful results than profiles of the free hormone.

The present evidence, therefore, strongly suggests that the timing of ovula-tion is closely linked to the increase of progestin and to the second of the twin LH surges toward the end of the interluteal phase. Other possibilities cannot be ruled out in view of the multiple LH peaks and possible follicular waves.

There are also conflicting views as to whether the elephant releases one egg (monovular) or several eggs (polyovular) during a cycle. Roger Short fol-lowed an African cow in estrus; the elephant was then shot, and the ovaries were collected. One of the ovaries contained "one fresh haemorrhagic ovulation point, 9 mm diameter," which was taken to be evidence for a single follicular rupture. The low frequency (about 1%) of twinning recorded in both African and Asian elephant populations also seems to argue for monovulation. On the other hand, the large numbers of corpora lutea (CL) present in the ovaries of both pregnant and nonpregnant elephants suggest that the animal is polyovula-tory. After examining the corpora lutea in ovaries of several hundred animals culled in Zambia, John Hanks and Roger Short concluded that the elephant could be either monovular or polyovular. Of course, it is entirely possible that an animal producing only one offspring at a time may be releasing several eggs during a cycle, but only one is fertilized.

If an elephant does not conceive, the luteal phase lasts for about 8–11 weeks, although a shortened phase of only 2–3 weeks has also been noticed. The multiple, large CL in the ovary are a feature the elephant shares with another large mammal, the whale. The CL range in size from 2 to 35 mm in diameter. Both small and large CL bear stigmata of ovulation; thus, size cannot be used to distinguish between primary and accessory lutea. The early biochemical studies that accompanied the histological examinations of fresh ovaries either failed to detect progesterone or recorded extremely low levels of this hormone in the luteal tissue. Roger Short and John Hanks thus advanced the hypothesis that the accumulation of CL from one cycle to another was necessary for production of sufficient quantities of progesterone to sustain pregnancy. So far, there is no evidence for any progressive increase in progesterone concentrations with successive nonfertile cycles. It is not clear why multiple CL should persist structurally, but not functionally, from one cycle to another.

Recent work by Keith Hodges and associates has shown that it is not progesterone, but two other forms of progestin, 5α-pregnane-3,20-dione (5α-DHP) and 3α-hydroxy-5α-pregnan-20-one (5α-P-3α-OH), which are the principal progestins synthesized by CL of African elephants (culled at Kruger, South Africa). In both the elephant species, 5α-DHP is also the predominant progestin in blood, with its concentration 10–20-fold that of progesterone in the African species. The affinity of this 5α-reduced steroid to an endometrial receptor also confirms its biological activity.

Attention therefore now is shifting from progesterone to obtaining profiles of these 5α reduced progestins during the ovarian cycle of elephants. Already, one investigation by Hodges's team led by Michael Heistermann has shown that 5α-DHP profiles in the blood of captive African elephants are more pronounced than those of progesterone during the luteal phase (table 3.1). This could provide a much clearer indication of the time of ovulation. Similarly, 5α-P-3-OH showed a clear cyclic pattern in urine, thereby providing a means to monitor luteal function noninvasively. In Asian elephants, the profiles of the related 17α-hydroxyprogesterone (17α-OHP) in blood and of pregnanetriol in

Table 3.1
Concentration of progestins in the blood of captive
African elephants during the estrous cycle.

Ovarian Phase	Progesterone (ng/ml)	5α-DHP (ng/ml)
Follicular phase	0.14 ± 0.01	1.43 ± 0.11
Midluteal phase	0.71 ± 0.06	13.6 ± 1.09
Luteal/follicular levels	5.1	9.5

Source: Based on Heistermann et al. (1997).
5α-DHP, 5α-pregnane-3, 20-dione.

urine were found by Cheryl Niemuller, also working with Hodges, to be useful in monitoring the ovarian cycle.

Prolactin, a peptide hormone normally elevated during pregnancy, is also known to play a regulatory role in the ovarian cycle of mammals, especially in relation to environmental factors such as photoperiod. One investigation by Ursula Bechert and colleagues on nonpregnant African elephants showed elevated levels of prolactin during the follicular phase and reduced levels during the luteal phase, the inverse of the progestin pattern. This suggested that prolactin could play a role in regulating ovarian function in the elephant.

Based on the information available until about 1998, a model of the ovarian cycle in elephants was proposed by Keith Hodges. In 2000, Janine Brown updated this model to arrive at the following picture of the estrous cycle (fig. 3.2). During the luteal phase, the elevated levels of progestins inhibit follicular development and the release of LH. The subsequent decrease in progestin restores follicular activity. The elevated levels of FSH at the beginning of the nonluteal phase initiate two successive waves of follicular development, each of which culminates in a distinct LH peak. The follicles that develop during the first wave do not result in ovulation, but regress and form CL, which secrete hormones later in the cycle. Over the next 3 weeks, another wave of follicular development results in the formation of one large follicle ("Graafian" follicle) that releases an egg about 24 hours after the second LH surge. The elevated estrogens, which have low concentrations that are difficult to measure, may trigger the LH surges during each follicular wave. The Graafian follicle may also secrete small amounts of progestins in the period leading up to ovulation. After ovulation, the progestin levels rise along with the maturation of CL, followed by a gradual rise in FSH that peaks at the end of the luteal phase.

A key question regarding the elephant's estrous cycle is the significance of the two or more follicular waves during the interluteal phase. A functional explanation may be that the first, nonovulatory, follicular wave may be needed to form accessory CL for producing the small preovulatory progestin rise required for ovulation. An evolutionary explanation could be that this serves as an early signal to a bull of impending ovulation in a particular cow. In regions of low elephant density, it may be advantageous for a bull to be associated with one family group for an extended period and for a cow to maintain a bull's interest over this period to derive reproductive benefits. With a short duration of 2–4 days during an estrous cycle in which a cow elephant can conceive, a missed mating opportunity would mean a delay of 15 weeks before another possibility of conception arises. Perhaps Richard Barnes's model of bull association with an elephant herd (chapter 4) should be revisited.

Should an elephant conceive, the resulting pregnancy proceeds through a gestation of 20–22 months. The persistence of multiple CL through pregnancy has been emphasized by practically all the histological investigations of culled elephants. Some studies did not detect any corpora albicantia in the ovaries of elephants, even during the second half of pregnancy, implying that no regression of CL had occurred. More recently, D. J. de Villiers and coworkers at

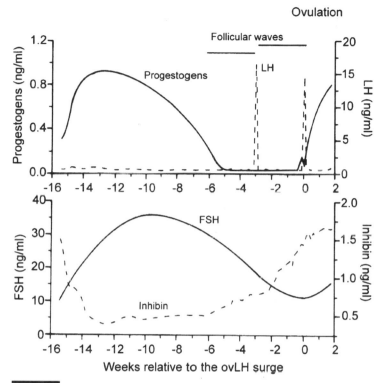

Figure 3.2
Model for the elephant estrous cycle. Smoothed profiles of luteinizing
hormone (LH), progestins, follicular-stimulating hormone (FSH), and
inhibin in blood serum are shown based on various studies of Asian
and African elephants. Time 0 corresponds to the presumed time of
ovulation. (Based on Brown 2000. Reproduced from *Zoo Biology* with the
permission of John Wiley and Sons.)

Kruger found that the volume of CL, but not the number, decreases, indicating
a slow regression through gestation.

Hormonal regulation of pregnancy in elephants is even less understood
than hormonal regulation of the ovarian cycle. The CL appear to be most active
hormonally between 3 and 15 months of gestation. No consistent changes in
the levels of blood progesterone have been recorded, although one study on
the Asian elephant by Cheryl Niemuller recorded up to a twofold rise during
pregnancy. She also demonstrated that changes in the ratio of blood progesterone to 17α-OHP from as early as the second or third week of conception could
be a valuable tool in early diagnosis of pregnancy.

What supports CL function through pregnancy is not clear. No consistent
patterns are seen in gonadotropins, a possible contender for this role. A clear

surge is seen, however, of prolactin, which is known to support luteal function in other mammals. First investigated by A. S. McNeilly and team, the levels of prolactin rise substantially (20- to 100-fold) in the blood of both elephant species, although the timing of its initial increase at 4–6 months into pregnancy is considered too late to support CL activity beyond the normal luteal phase duration (which should occur at 2–3 months). The origin of this prolactin is not known; it is unlikely to be entirely from the pituitary gland. The placenta itself may play a role in progestin production, although the evidence is lacking.

As during the ovarian cycle, the levels of free estrogens remain low with no apparent pattern. Conjugated estrogens, however, increase in both blood and urine during the second half of gestation. There is an interesting suggestion that the ovaries of the developing fetus may be hormonally active. Limited data show an enlargement of the ovaries in the fetus to adult sizes during late gestation, followed by regression before birth. During the week preceding parturition, there is the anticipated decrease in progesterone levels to baseline values.

3.2.2   Signaling and detecting estrus

A female elephant in estrus signals her condition through auditory and chemical signals: An estrous cow may also show one or more distinctive behaviors during this period. Cynthia Moss has described in detail estrous behavior in African elephants at Amboseli in Kenya.

Wariness: A cow is noticeably alert and wary of approaching bulls, quickly moving out of their way and not tolerating attempts to test her estrous condition.

Estrous walk: In response to approaching bulls, an estrous female may walk away briskly from her group with head held high and turned to one side as she watches the bull following her; she makes an arc before returning to her group.

The chase: An estrous cow may increase her pace to a run and may be pursued by one or more bulls. The cow usually describes a wide arc before returning to her group. However, she may stop if a bull succeeds in touching her.

Consortship: An individual cow and a large bull may maintain physical proximity for a short period. The large bull threatens or chases away other bulls that approach the pair, while the cow avoids other bulls by moving toward her partner.

A female elephant in estrus also advertises her condition through chemical signals released through urine or vaginal secretions. The nature of chemical compounds used in communicating estrus and behavioral responses by bulls have been studied in detail by L.E.L. (Bets) Rasmussen and several collaborators, in particular Michael Schmidt at Washington Park Zoo, where captive Asian elephants were studied (also see chapter 4). They carried out extensive tests of responses by bull elephants to urine, organic compounds extracted from urine, and various synthetic compounds. Urine was collected from cows during the preovulatory period, the period of peak interest by the bull, and when they were anestrus. The response of bulls was tested using whole urine and extracts from urine placed in a suitable solution. Behaviors recorded included sniffing, flehmen, blowing, avoidance, and penile erections.

Flehmen behavior in elephants refers to testing a chemical signal using the trunk and the vomeronasal organ. A typical flehmen consists of placing the tip of the trunk on the part or substance of interest (the urogenital orifice of the female, urine on the ground, or temporal gland secretion [TGS], for instance) and bringing a sample of the chemical substance to the pair of vomeronasal organs located on the roof of the mouth (fig. 3.3). The tip of the trunk is curled, inserted into the mouth, and pressed against the twin orifices of the vomeronasal organ, which assays the chemical substances. A flehmen lasts for 3–8 seconds and may be repeated several times.

While a bull elephant may regularly test the urogenital orifice or the urine of a female, the frequency of flehmen responses increases about 10-fold when the cow is in estrus. In one set of experiments, the flehmenlike responses by captive bulls averaged 5.9 responses per 1-hour test with estrous urine, 3.8 per test when estrous urine extracts were resuspended in nonestrous urine, and less than 1.0 response per test when presented with nonestrous urine extracts, nonestrous urine, or other controls, such as organic solvents used in urine extraction.

Naturalist M. Krishnan, several years earlier, described an advertising behavior by a female elephant in which she slapped the tip of her bristly tail against the urogenital region and held it aloft for some moments. This behavior

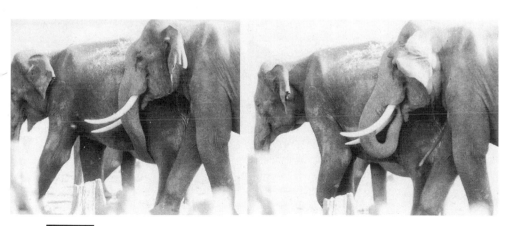

Figure 3.3
Detecting estrous in elephants: (*left*) a bull tests a cow for estrus and (*right*) performs a typical flehmen. (Photo courtesy of R. Rasmussen.)

may be a signal to males or, as other observations indicate, a signal to other females. Maximal tail flicking in captive cows occurs a few weeks prior to ovulation. In the wild, the males seem to bypass such tail-flicking females, but other females check them and perform flehmen.

Bets Rasmussen and coworkers recently identified the chemical compound released in urine by female Asian elephants to signal their estrous state as (Z)-7-dodecen-1-yl acetate, the same volatile compound used by many female insects to attract mates.

Even if courtship in elephants may last for several hours or days, mating itself is a short affair, lasting no more than a couple of minutes. The bull places his trunk lengthways on the cow's back and mounts her by rearing up on his hind legs. Intromission occurs by locking the tip of the S-curved erect penis into the cow's vagina, located in front of her hind legs. Some observers have remarked that the anatomy of the elephants' genitalia demands absolute cooperation by the female if intromission is to be successful. A pair may also mate several times over the period of 1 or more days.

3.3   *Musth in the male elephant*

Compared to other land mammals, a strikingly different feature of the male elephant's reproductive system is that the testes are located within the abdomen. During the fourth century B.C., Aristotle wrote in his *Historia Animalium* that, "The penis of the elephant is like that of the horse, but small considering the animal's bulk. The testes are not visible externally, but are placed inside, near the kidneys." The musculature of the penis gives it an S-shaped flexure when erect, thereby enabling it to hook into the forward-directed vagina of the cow. Another characteristic observed in the male elephant's anatomy is that macroscopically it is not possible to differentiate an epididymis from the ductus deferens, which along with the longer Wolffian duct, conveys the semen from the testes to the urethra. The accessory organs include the seminal vesicles, the prostate gland, and the paired bulbourethral glands.

Puberty in the male can be defined as the first production of viable sperm, while it can be said that sexual maturity has been attained when a dense mass of motile sperm is produced. As with the female elephant, the age of puberty and sexual maturity in a bull may vary across populations, depending on habitat factors. Richard Laws generally found a close correlation between reproductive maturity in males and females of an elephant population, although this could vary by as much as 6–10 years across populations. The onset of puberty in male elephants may occur anywhere between 8 and 15 years of age, while sexual maturity takes 2–3 years longer. I must emphasize here that enormous variation exists, and that observations in zoo animals cannot be taken as indicative of wild populations.

Sexual maturity in a bull elephant eventually has to lead to sociological maturity if it is to reproduce successfully in the longer term. This takes us to an aspect of a bull elephant's biology known in Asian elephants since ancient times, but recognized in African elephants only recently. The adult male elephant goes through a period of intense aggression toward other males and sexual interest in estrous females, a phenomenon termed *musth*. A bull elephant in musth secretes a fluid from its temporal gland and may constantly dribble urine. The term *musth* comes from an Urdu word for intoxication. The phenomenon of musth has been well documented in Asian elephants since ancient times. In the *Rig Veda* (1500–1000 B.C.), the simile of a bull elephant in musth is used to describe the indomitable strength of Indra, the king of the gods. The ancient Indian epic, the *Mahabharata*, speaks of warriors riding into battle on elephants in musth. Perhaps the most apt description of musth is found in Nilakantha's *Matangalila*: "Excitement, swiftness, odor, love passion, complete florescence of the body, wrath, prowess, and fearlessness are declared to be the eight excellences of musth." That single sentence alludes to aggressive behavior, chemical signaling, and the sexual connotations of musth.

The long history of keeping elephants in captivity in Asia undoubtedly provided the opportunity for observing musth and associated behaviors. The scientific literature on African elephants was, however, rather confused on the issue of musth. Both female and male African elephants secrete from their temporal glands, often in response to disturbance or stress in the environment. Observers of African elephants during the 1960s and 1970s thus attributed a chemical signal function to this secretion, which they called musth. They further postulated that temporal gland activity had entirely different functions in the Asian elephant and the African elephant, a sexual role in males of the former and a communication function in both sexes of the latter species.

An article by Joyce Poole and Cynthia Moss in 1981 firmly established that adult bull elephants in Amboseli National Park exhibited the physical and behavioral characteristics of musth similar in all aspects to the male Asian elephant. This was distinct from the temporal gland secretion of immature and adult females and males of African elephants, which should be termed *temporin*, and plays a role in communication among individuals in a social group. The term musth had been wrongly applied to any kind of secretion from the temporal glands in either males or females. Further, female Asian elephants had almost never been observed to have active temporal glands and thus were not considered to come into musth like their African counterparts (see chapter 4).

3.3.1   Behavioral characteristics of musth

The elephant's temporal glands are a pair of modified sweat glands located on each side of the head between the eye and the ear. The onset of musth can be seen from swelling of the temporal glands and the secretion of fluid (the musth fluid), which streams down the cheeks of the animal (fig. 3.4). There are different stages in the manifestation of musth. Toke Gale describes four stages of musth based on his observations of Burmese timber elephants.

Figure 3.4
An Asian bull elephant in musth secreting from the swollen temporal glands (*bottom*). A musth bull is more likely to be associated with a family group (*top*) in which one or more cows may be in estrus. (Photo courtesy of M. Y. Ghorpade.)

Based on this description and other observations in captive and wild elephants, the typical progression of musth is as follows. During the early stage, the temporal glands swell slightly and are clearly visible as small dark patches. When the temporal glands begin to secrete, the fluid is watery and flows down the cheeks as a thin streak 7–10 cm long. Later, the temporal glands swell considerably and discharge more copiously. The pungent-smelling fluid during the "full-musth" phase may be more viscous and stains a wide area of the cheeks, even flowing down to the corners of the mouth. The Burmese term this last stage the "musth drinking stage." At this time, the bull also begins to dribble urine, either as discrete drops or in a regular stream. A particular odor is also associated with the urine discharged when a bull is in musth. When a bull has been urinating for an extended period of time, the proximal part of the penis and the distal end of the sheath show a greenish coloration, termed the *green penis syndrome* by Joyce Poole and Cynthia Moss. These physical manifestations of musth may last from a few days to months, depending on the age and condition of the bull.

It is well known in Asia that captive bull elephants in musth become aggressive and fail to respond to commands from their keepers. Thus, bulls are almost invariably kept restrained for the duration of their musth phase. Observations of musth behavior in Asian elephants have largely remained anecdotal or descriptive. Joyce Poole's accounts of the behavioral ecology of musth in Amboseli's elephants remain the most detailed so far. These include several behaviors, postures, and vocalizations performed almost exclusively by bulls when in musth. I briefly describe some of her observations and supplement them with what is known about musth behavior in Asian elephants.

Musth walk: A musth bull may walk with its head held high, at an angle
such that the chin looks tucked in, and the ears spread and motionless. This, combined with a swinging motion to the head and tusks while walking, would project a formidable image of a musth bull to its opponents.

Tusking: At Amboseli, males in musth were observed going down on their knees to tusk the ground, throwing up lumps of mud or grass. This behavior occurred invariably during fights between bulls in musth. I have observed a variant of this tusking behavior in Asian bulls. A musth male would gently press his tusks against an embankment, and the temporal glands would visibly discharge fluid. A more frenzied act of digging the tusks into the bottom of a pond was once observed in a young bull probably experiencing musth for the first time.

Marking: Although male elephants rub their temporal glands against trees when in musth and out of musth, they were seen at Amboseli to rub their glands much more frequently when in musth. This behavior has also been seen in Asian elephants and may serve to scent mark an individual's identity.

Ear wave: In contrast to other ear signals, when both ears are flapped, a musth bull performs the ear wave by moving only one ear at a time. The inner and upper portion of the ear is thrust forward suddenly, with the outer and lower portion of the ear following. It is speculated that this serves to waft the scent of the musth secretion forward toward other elephants. This behavior has not been reported among Asian elephants. It is possible that only the larger-ear African bulls are able to perform this motion, or that such an act is less frequent and may have been overlooked in Asian bulls.

Musth rumble: Elephants communicate at low sound frequencies (infrasound) that travel over longer distances without attenuation (see chapter 4). African savanna bulls in musth give a distinct set of calls with frequencies as low as 14 Hz (hertz) and sound pressure levels up to 108 decibels (at a distance of 1 m). A musth rumble is usually performed in conjunction with the ear wave. Musth males vocalized more frequently when alone than when they had already joined a family group. Younger males (under 40 years) rumbled only about once every hour, while older males did so about three times more frequently. Female elephants respond to a male's musth rumble with their own characteristic low-frequency sound.

Urination with sheathed penis: Bulls in musth, which dribble urine at a low rate for more than an hour, urinate with the penis retracted within the sheath such that the urine is sprayed onto the insides of the hind legs.

These behaviors basically serve either to repel potential competitors or to attract estrous females. Thus, an aggressive posture with the head held high or scent marking by rubbing the temporal glands on trees may deter other large bulls, while leaving a urine trail (with specific scent compounds) or musth rumbling would attract the attention of receptive cows in the area.

3.3.2   *Age, duration, and timing of musth*

Musth is a postpubertal phenomenon. In an Asian elephant population in southern India, bulls have been observed to come into musth from about age 15 years. In younger bulls (15–25 years), however, the intensity of musth as seen from temporal gland activity is low, and the duration is relatively short, lasting from only a few days to weeks. Older bulls show the characteristic, full-blown musth. Younger bulls may show only the early stage of musth seen in older bulls and not enter into the later, intense phase.

At Amboseli, bulls younger than 24 years were never observed by Joyce Poole to show any signs of musth. The average age of onset of musth was 29 years. However, only about 50% of bulls aged 25–35 years were observed coming into musth, while practically all bulls above 35 years exhibited musth. The duration of musth varied from just 1 day to a maximum of about 4 months. There was also a clear relationship between age and duration of musth that lasted for longer periods in larger, and thus older, bulls, which also achieved higher reproductive success (fig. 3.5).

Musth should not be thought of as a phenomenon that is suddenly switched on in male elephants at a particular age. After attaining sexual maturity, there is a gradual build up in the frequency, duration, and intensity of musth in an individual bull, depending on several factors, of which body condition may be the most important. While an individual male generally comes into musth at the same time each year (over a short timescale), different males in a population show wide variation in the time of the year they come into musth. At Amboseli, the highest occurrences of musth were between the months of January and July, during and just after two rainy seasons, when the numbers of females in estrus also peaked. The larger and more dominant bulls came into musth at the most favorable periods, the rainy seasons when the frequency of estrous cows was also higher. At any given time in the year, however, there was at least one bull in musth.

In South Africa's Kruger National Park, Anthony Hall-Martin recorded a clear wet season peak in the number of bulls (>20 years old) coming into musth during 1982–1986, although some bulls were in musth during other months (fig. 3.6). This seasonality in musth also coincided with the peak in conceptions by the cows in the region, suggesting that musth bulls did most of the breeding. By contrast, in Addo National Park, where rainfall is more evenly spread over the year, there was no evidence for any seasonality of musth in bulls or of conceptions by cows. In southern India, Ajay Desai has also observed that more bulls came into musth during the wet season. My observations indicate that the younger bulls generally exhibit musth during the dry season (January–May), while older, presumably higher-ranking, bulls come into musth during the wet season (June–December). Curiously, Toke Gale's detailed records of the Burmese timber elephants show that most bulls come into musth during the dry months, especially in April–May, just prior to the onset of the monsoon. This does not seem related to any seasonal differences in workload that could potentially influence musth, but could be due to the age profile of the observed bulls.

3.3.3   *Male–male interactions during musth*

The anecdotal observations that male elephants become more aggressive during musth have been quantified at Amboseli by Joyce Poole. She found that the median frequency of agonistic interactions by musth bulls was 7.5/hour compared to 3.5/hour by nonmusth, sexually active bulls. Just as dominance rank in nonmusth bulls is decided by body size, the larger bulls also won most of the agonistic interactions of a pair of musth bulls. Of 75 pairs of such contests observed between musth bulls, the larger bull emerged dominant in 93% of cases. However, in aggressive contests between a musth bull and a nonmusth bull, the winner was determined not by body size, but by musth. Thus, in 49

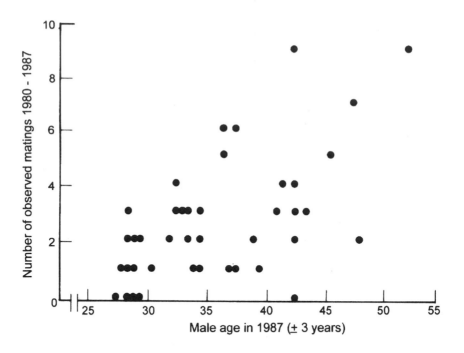

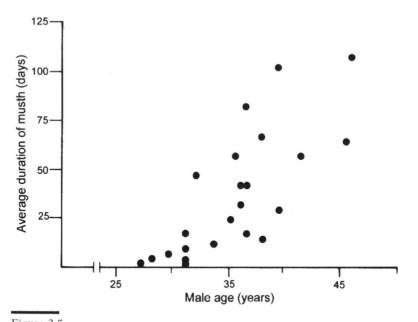

Figure 3.5
The relationship among age, musth, and reproductive success in African bull
elephants at Amboseli: (*top*) age versus cumulative mating success from 1980
through 1987; (*bottom*) age versus average annual duration of musth during 1980–
1981. (From Poole 1989a. Reproduced from *Animal Behaviour* with the permission
of Elsevier Science.)

A) Kruger

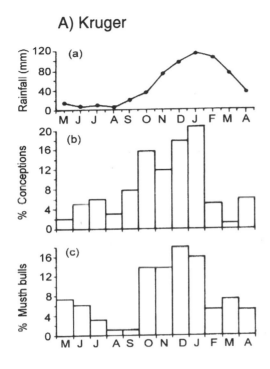

B) Addo

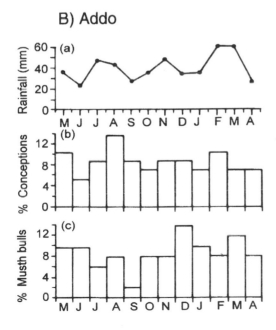

Figure 3.6
The relationship between average monthly rainfall and percentage conceptions by cows and bulls (>20 years old) in musth in two South African elephant populations: (A) Kruger National Park, 1982–1986; (B) Addo National Park, 1976–1986. (From Hall-Martin 1987. Reproduced with permission of the *South African Journal of Science*, National Research Foundation, South Africa.)

such contests observed, when the musth male was smaller in body size, the smaller male emerged victorious in 86% of interactions.

Joyce Poole also observed that, when a large, high-ranking musth bull chased a smaller, lower-ranking musth bull, the latter often stopped showing signs of musth (urine dribbling, temporal gland secretion, and behavioral postures). On the other hand, two high-ranking musth bulls did not cease musth, but tried to avoid each other's company by using different areas if their musth periods overlapped. The musth periods of many large males, of course, were also spaced out during the year to avoid overlap.

The aggressive contests described above are confined to threat displays, chasing, and minor combat using tusks. Escalation of contests into serious fights is rare, even when bulls are in musth. Observations on retreat distances by males of different sizes seem to suggest strongly that male elephants not only believe that musth in an opponent announces aggression, but also enables them to assess the chances that a contest may escalate into a serious one. In 14 years of field observations, Joyce Poole observed only 31 escalated fights between bulls, of which 20 were between pairs of musth bulls; two such contests resulted in the deaths of one contestant. During 1981–1982, I recorded three such elephant deaths in male-male combat in southern India. Since then, I have heard of few such instances, but this could be a reflection of the overall paucity of large males in southern India as a consequence of ivory poaching. Anthony Hall-Martin recorded seven adult bulls killed in fights during 1976–1986 in South Africa's Kruger National Park. Interestingly, all seven victors were bulls in musth, while four of the bulls killed were themselves in musth.

3.3.4   *Physiological and biochemical correlates of musth*

There is extensive anecdotal information from Asia that good nutrition and body condition are necessary for the successful expression of musth in bull elephants. The precise physiological links between body condition and musth are not clear as yet, although some possibilities are mentioned in this discussion.

It is well known that rutting males have increased levels of blood testosterone, which may mediate aggressive behavior. Males may also advertise their rutting condition by releasing scents from various glands. Before we discuss the specific functions of these physiological changes, we should consider the extent and nature of these rutting signals.

During 1969–1970, veterinarian M. R. Jainudeen and associates carried out the first detailed measurements of blood testosterone during the nonmusth and musth phases in captive Sri Lankan bull elephants. They found that bulls showing no signs of musth had testosterone levels of only about 0.2–1.4 ng/ml in blood plasma. During the premusth phase, this rose to 4–14 ng/ml, while bulls in full musth showed dramatically elevated levels of 30–65 ng/ml of plasma testosterone. Within a week of coming out of musth, these values returned to the baseline values of nonmusth bulls.

Similar investigations by Bets Rasmussen and colleagues on Asian bull elephants at the Washington Park Zoo in Portland showed testosterone levels of 20–40 ng/ml during musth. A related hormone, dihydrotestosterone, which normally remained at about 0.2 ng/ml during the nonmusth phase, also shot up to 1.5 ng/ml when a bull was in heavy musth.

Cheryl Niemuller and R. M. Liptrap extended these findings through weekly monitoring of testosterone levels and relating these to a qualitative score of musth intensity in eight captive Asian bull elephants for up to 2 years (table 3.2). While a higher concentration of androstenedione than testosterone was generally seen during the nonmusth phase, the ratio was reversed in favor of testosterone during the musth phase; further, it correlated neatly with the intensity of musth.

The longest duration study of blood testosterone profiles is the weekly sampling over 5 years of six captive Asian bulls in Sri Lanka by G. A. Lincoln and W. D. Ratnasooriya. This clearly showed that short-term fluctuation of testosterone in an individual and high variability between animals may be the natural, erratic pattern in the tropics. Only the oldest bull showed a distinct cyclicity in the blood concentrations of testosterone; thus, the cyclic pattern of musth may develop gradually as the animal ages.

Attempts to measure testosterone in captive adult male African elephants when they showed temporal gland secretion have not as yet yielded useful results because of the confusion over the recognition of true musth by these researchers. Presumably, the male African elephant would show a similar upsurge in androgen levels if musth were properly recognized in zoo animals and sampled. Weekly monitoring of testosterone levels in the blood serum of a captive African forest elephant (*Loxodonta africana cyclotis*), aged 19 years, by K. A. Cooper and associates showed an irregular pattern and lower concentrations overall in contrast to two Asian bulls of similar age; the Asian bulls showed the more characteristic seasonal peaks associated with temporal gland activity.

In wild elephants, it would be an extremely demanding task to collect blood from bulls. Joyce Poole thus hit on an ingenious method of measuring testosterone in the urine of bulls. Soon after a bull urinated, she drove it away and quickly aspirated the urine from the ground with a syringe. The collected urine was filtered and frozen before being sent to a laboratory for analysis. As expected, bulls that were sexually active (but not in musth), in the premusth stage, or in regular musth generally had higher urinary testosterone levels than those not in musth and sexually inactive.

The daunting task of sampling elephants in the wild did not deter Anthony Hall-Martin from mounting a sustained operation during the 1980s of immobilizing elephants for sample collection at Kruger and Addo National Parks in South Africa. By now, there was a clearer recognition of musth versus mere temporin secretion in African elephants. Of the 111 bull elephants 21–40 years of age sampled over several seasons and years for blood and temporal gland secretion, 6 bulls were radio-collared and regularly sampled over a 5-

Table 3.2
Concentrations of androgens in the blood or urine
of male elephants during nonmusth and musth phases.

Captive Asian elephants: serum androgen (North American zoos)

Elephant Group	Age (years)	Severity of Musth	Androgen Levels, Nonmusth (ng/ml)		Androgen Levels, Musth (ng/ml)	
			T	A	T	A
A	16	Mild	3.5	2.4	20.7	6.0
B	17	Mild	2.5	3.4	15.4	5.1
C	18	Mild	6.4	10.0	14.5	16.0
D	17	Medium	6.7	4.2	38.2	8.4
E	22	Strong	7.8	10.3	116.6	37.0
F	35	Strong	2.4	2.6	152.5	35.3

Wild African elephants: urinary androgen (Amboseli, Kenya)

Elephant Group	Musth Category	Testosterone Levels (ng/ml creatinine)
A	Sexually inactive, not in musth	77.7
B	Sexually active, not in musth	146.7
C	Mature, sexually active, not in musth	176.4
D	Premusth	225.7
E	Musth	241.3

Wild African elephants: serum androgen (Kruger, South Africa)

Elephant Group	Musth Category	Testosterone Levels (ng/ml creatinine)
A	Nonmusth (46%)	0.1–2.0
B	Premusth, postmusth (39.5%)	2.0–10.0
C	Musth (13.1%)	20.0–50.0
D	Heavy musth (6.5%)	50.0 ≥ 100.0

Sources: Based on Niemuller and Liptrap (1991); Poole et al. (1984); Rasmussen et al. (1996).
T, testosterone; A, androstenedione.

year period (1985–1989). Bets Rasmussen and David Hess analyzed these samples for androgens and other organic compounds. Two-thirds of female elephants acting as controls had testosterone levels less than 0.1 ng/ml, while the rest showed levels in the range of 0.1–2.0 ng/ml. All bulls had testosterone levels above 1.0 ng/ml. As expected, the levels of testosterone and dihydrotestosterone in blood were distinctly higher in bulls during the musth phase, the former even crossing 100 ng/ml during very heavy musth (table 3.2). Interesting differences in blood androgen levels were observed in relation to the social context of the secreting bulls. These bulls had lower testosterone levels when they were near other adult bulls (about 5 ng/ml) compared to when they were solitary (70 ng/ml) or near family herds (70 ng/ml). These results should be interpreted with caution because of the low sample sizes of the comparisons. In the bulls that were sampled regularly, the characteristic cyclic pattern of androgen concentration was seen, with an elevated level associated with typical musth behaviors such as aggression.

The correlation between blood testosterone levels and temporal gland secretion or other signs of musth is not always clear in some observations of captive bulls. Some of the ambiguity could be due to a failure to distinguish between temporal gland activity and true musth (see sections 3.3 and 4.3.3). Nevertheless, on the basis of these observations it seems reasonable to look beyond the hypothalamic-pituitary-gonadal (i.e., reproductive) axis for a functional explanation of musth. Lisa Wingate and Bill Lasley have suggested that the adrenal glands also may play a role in the expression of musth. Apart from the gonads (testes), the adrenal glands are known to secrete androgens such as testosterone, dihydrotestosterone, and androstenedione. Good nutrition or over-nutrition may stimulate adrenal activity for increasing the production of cortisol (a hormone that regulates blood glucose), while androgens may be secreted at the same time. Musth is thus a secondary effect of adrenal activity. Temporal gland secretions have similarly been analyzed in both Asian and African elephant bulls. Here again, the results of chemical analysis of TGS in Asian bulls in musth are probably more revealing as TGS in African elephant bulls may not necessarily represent the musth phase. In fact, some of the earlier investigations of TGS composition in African elephants were certainly not carried out during the musth phase. In one such early study at Kruger, the sampled elephants were "stimulated into temporal gland secretion by helicopter driving." This TGS was obviously temporin, which does not seem to have any significance in sexual communication.

During the musth phase, androgens are much more concentrated in TGS than they are in blood among Asian elephants. Testosterone levels average about 500 ng/ml in TGS (and may even exceed 2000 ng/ml) or a 5–10-fold concentration compared to serum testosterone. Dihydrotestosterone also shows very high levels, averaging 350–400 ng/ml, a greater than 100-fold concentration compared to serum levels. Various volatile compounds, such as the phenols, are also found in TGS associated with musth. The most exciting of recent findings by Bets Rasmussen, Heidi Riddle, and V. Krishnamurthy on the chemical nature of TGS in Asian elephants, published in the journal *Nature*, is the difference between younger and older musth bulls in the compounds secreted. While sweet-smelling compounds such as esters and 3-hexen-1-ol were found exclusively in the TGS of younger musth bulls (or *moda* musth as stated in ancient Indian elephant lore), foul-smelling compounds (such as the frontalins and nonanones) were found only in older musth bulls. The veracity of observations of musth in ancient Indian writings was thus confirmed through modern science.

3.4   Sexual selection and mate choice

It is reasonable to expect that males and females of a species have evolved behavioral traits related to mate choice that maximize their fitness in reproductive terms. In the case of elephants, consider the following aspects of social organization and physiology. As with other mammalian species, the females spend more energy directly in reproduction compared to males. In a polygynous society with an absence of male parental care, this difference between the sexes in costs of reproduction and rearing of offspring is even more accentuated. Given the long gestation period in elephants, less than a third of females in a population can potentially come into estrus at a given time. Females, however, come into estrus on average only every 15 weeks or so, and estrus lasts for only 3–7 days. It thus makes sense for a male to search actively for as many estrous females as possible rather than try to defend a harem. Once an estrous female is located, a male would normally have to compete with other males before successfully mating.

Male elephants have thus evolved traits that allow them to compete with other males as well as attract the attention of several estrous females. Potentially, a male could evolve honest signals of motivation in competing with rival males or cheat about its real motivational state. Similarly, a male could honestly advertise its true quality to potential mates or cheat about its inherent status. In theory, there could also be some form of mate choice by males. Among elephants, there is certainly much individual recognition given the longevity of the species. The issue of mate choice by males is probably a relatively trivial one among elephants (except to avoid inbreeding) as it would pay for a male elephant to copulate with as many estrous females as possible. This subject, however, is open to further study.

The female elephant, on the other hand, is better off by choosing the fittest male from the pool of males she attracts. A wrong choice of a mate would be expensive for the female as her offspring could be less fit if sired by an inferior male. She should thus be able to discriminate among her suitors, see through dishonest male signals, and recognize honest signals of male quality.

Various traits and behaviors associated with reproduction will thus have to be examined for their adaptive roles in the mating game. Could musth have evolved in male elephants as a means of signaling their fighting ability or announcing their motivation in holding resources (estrous females)? What information do musth males convey to estrous females? How do these relate to the spacing of musth among males in a population? How is female choice of mates influenced by musth and potential sexual ornamentation, such as tusks, in elephants?

3.4.1   *Mate guarding and male reproductive success*

Female elephants in estrus actively solicit guarding from musth males, but only rarely solicit it from nonmusth males at Amboseli. When females were in midestrus they were guarded and mated mainly by the guarding males. Over 90% of the guarding males were in musth, while 38 of 49 matings observed during midestrus were by guarding musth males. Further, nearly 90% of males that guarded females in midestrus were over 35 years old. During early and late phases of estrus, the females were usually not guarded and were frequently chased and sometimes mated by younger, nonmusth males.

Several interesting aspects of elephant reproductive behavior emerge from these observations. By soliciting guarding behavior from large, musth males, the female elephant exercises a certain degree of mate choice. The older the male, the better its success in guarding females in midestrus when conceptions are more likely. Reproductive success per unit time in males thus keeps increasing with age (except perhaps at very old age if a bull survives to its maximum potential longevity) (fig. 3.5). This is in contrast to most other mammals, for which reproductive success seems to peak during middle age and declines subsequently. Unlike other mammals, however, elephants continue to increase in body weight practically throughout their life span, certainly up to 50 or more years of age (see appendix 2). Given the positive correlation between body size and reproductive success, it is not surprising that increased reproductive success with age in male elephants is also seen.

Musth, of course, is crucial to reproductive success in male elephants. Why should this be necessary? If there are two sexually active bulls of similar size and age with different musth status, why should the musth bull have a mating advantage over the nonmusth bull? What has been the adaptive significance of musth in the course of evolution?

3.4.2   *Musth as a signal of intent to males*

There has been much discussion and theory developed around the issue of how rival males should signal their fighting abilities or aggressive intentions. The approach of the more traditional ethologists was that the expression of excitement, aggression, fear, or pain conveys the signaler's motivational state. Some of these views have been challenged by game theory as applied to animal behavior by J. Maynard Smith, G. R. Price, and G. A. Parker. Maynard Smith developed the concept of the evolutionarily stable strategy (ESS), a strategy that, if adopted by most individuals in a population, cannot be invaded by any other mutant strategy. Game theory models have shown that, although signals conveying information about fighting ability (or resource-holding potential as the theorists often put it) can be maintained by natural selection, those that signal motivation (i.e., intentions during conflict situations) would quickly lose their value. Announcing to an opponent what you would do next is like placing all your cards on the table. Cheaters would be able to invade a population of honest signalers.

During conflicts between male elephants, a large male in good condition but not in musth almost always defers to a smaller musth male in poorer condition. It is hard to believe that, in actual combat, the small male would have a decisive advantage even if it is in musth. The musth condition of the small male thus cannot be an honest signal of its fighting ability alone. Why then does the large, nonmusth male give in to the small musth male?

Geoffrey Parker and Daniel Rubenstein developed a model in which they considered two types of asymmetries: (1) asymmetry in fighting ability or resource-holding potential; thus individuals may differ in size, strength, or weaponry, which would translate into probable costs incurred in contests between rivals; (2) asymmetry in resource value or rewards, by which the contested resource (say, estrous female) may be worth more to one opponent than to the other. Parker and Rubenstein considered how animals should behave in a contest when both these asymmetries interact. The mathematical formulation of the model is complex, but the solutions can be expressed in simple terms. When roles A and B refer to the asymmetry between opponents, which sustain costs at rates K_A and K_B, and resource values are V_A and V_B, a unique ESS obeys the following rule: Fight on estimating role A, where $V_A/K_A > V_B/K_B$, retreat in role B. In other words, if you are able to assess your opponent's fighting ability with few mistakes, the rule approximates a commonsense ESS: Retreat if you would be the first to spend more in a contest than the resource is worth to you, otherwise persist.

Joyce Poole applied the Parker-Rubenstein model, for which an interaction exists between fighting ability and resource value, to the observed patterns of musth in the Amboseli elephants. The data from Amboseli showed that, on average, twice as many female elephants come into estrus during the wet season (February–July) compared to the dry season (August–January). Thus, resource value is higher during the wet season. All male elephants have equal chances (assumed to be 75% in this case) of locating an estrous female. However, high-ranking males are able to guard and monopolize all estrous females they find, a medium-ranking male mates with any female not already located by a high-ranking male, while a low-ranking male obtains any female not mated by the others. Musth has certain costs that may reduce future fitness; these are loss of condition and injury or death in escalated contests. Dry season costs from urine dribbling (when water is scarce) are higher (by 50% in this model) compared to wet season costs. Further, fitness costs are higher in low-ranking males as they are more likely to meet higher ranking individuals.

The payoffs (value of winning versus sustaining costs) are considered for three possible strategies by males of different ranks:

1. Come into musth for a full year, but only in alternate years.
2. Come into musth each year during the wet season only.
3. Come into musth each year during the dry season only.

The relative payoffs are summarized for the different strategies and bulls in table 3.3. From this, it is seen that for high-ranking bulls, it is best to come into musth during the wet season each year. The medium-ranking bulls are now able to assume the resource value (estrous females) and costs of high-ranking males during the dry season. Thus, they maximize their payoffs by expressing musth during the dry season. Given the above scenario, the best strategy for low-ranking males seems to be to come into musth during the wet season, overlapping with the high-ranking bulls. When challenged by a high-ranking bull, a low-ranking bull would also do better by retracting the announcement of musth (stop secreting from the temporal gland or urine dribbling, if any). This would also lower their costs of musth and further increase their payoffs.

Some direct evidence for this game theoretic explanation came from sound playback experiments that Poole conducted at Amboseli during 1988–1990 (see chapter 4 for details of sound communication). Two types of infrasonic calls, the musth rumble of males and the estrous call of females, were used in the playbacks. When the musth rumble of a high-ranking bull was played, the other musth bulls in the vicinity approached the speaker with aggressive intent, while nonmusth bulls walked away. Similarly, the estrous call playback attracted the attention of musth bulls, which quickly approached the speaker, whereas the nonmusth bulls listened for some time before moving away from the source of the call.

The observed patterns of musth at Amboseli fit the predictions derived from the application of this model. By and large, the older and bigger males do come into musth during the wet season, the medium-ranking ones come into musth during the dry season, while the younger males come into musth sporadically during the wet season. Even when a large, high-ranking nonmusth male can potentially dominate a smaller musth male, it does not attempt to contest because any risk of injury may reduce its capacity to come into musth

---

Table 3.3
The 2-year payoffs (V/K) for male elephants of high, medium, and low ranks in expressing musth at various times of the year.

Season of Occurrence of Musth	Male Rank and Payoffs		
	High	Medium	Low
Full year in alternate years	0.9	0.2	0.05
Wet season in both years	1.5	0.3	0.08
Dry season in both years	0.6	0.1	0.03

Source: From Poole (1989b). Reprinted from *Animal Behaviour* with the permission of Elsevier Science.
K, costs incurred; V, value of a resource.

during a later (wet) season when its fitness returns would be much greater. Obviously, the spacing of musth in an elephant population would be site specific and depend on a variety of other factors, such as climatic seasonality, density and spacing of other males, forage availability, or even susceptibility to parasitic infections.

Observations by Rob Slotow and associates in South Africa even point to a control of musth in younger bulls by the older, higher-ranking bulls. During 1992–1997, the 10 young orphaned male elephants introduced into Pilanesburg from Kruger (after culls in the 1980s) showed deviant, aggressive behavior such as killing several white rhinos in the park when they came into musth at a relatively young age of 18 years. The introduction of 6 older bulls from Kruger into Pilanesburg rectified much of this behavior by suppressing the onset and duration of musth in the younger bulls.

The recent findings of Bets Rasmussen and associates that the chemical nature of temporal gland secretion is different in younger and suggests a more complex nature of male-male signaling that needs to be unraveled. A combination of sophisticated laboratory chemistry, field testing of the chemical signals of musth, and behavioral observations fitted into the game theoretic framework are perhaps needed to provide a better understanding of the role of musth in male-male competition.

3.4.3   *Musth as advertisement of male quality to females*

Even more important than serving as a deterrent to rival males, musth may influence female choice of mates. As discussed, musth males advertise their condition through a specific infrasonic call that may be heard by females within a radius of 5–10 km. Temporal gland secretion seems to play a similar role in signaling the musth condition to estrous females, although the precise role of the signal is not yet clear (see chapter 4). Urine dribbling by a musth male, however, serves as a strong signal to potential mates in the area. Joyce Poole and Cynthia Moss were the first to point out that female elephants were attracted to musth males that had marked their paths with strong-smelling urine. Females inspected urine-marked trails with interest and were observed to follow such trails.

While high testosterone levels have been recorded in the urine of musth males, there are possibly other compounds as well that serve in communicating musth to females. Elephants may also be able to recognize information about individuals from such chemical signals.

The more fundamental questions are: What precisely are musth males conveying to estrous females? and Why do females evince such interest in mating with a musth male? Theory dictates that females should evolve a preference for mates with high genetic quality so that their offspring may inherit such traits. In this manner, the relative fitness of females discriminating among mates would be enhanced.

A signal used by a male to attract females, in principle, can be either an honest one of its inherent quality or a dishonest signal. According to existing theory, honest signals of genetic quality are costly to produce and maintain. For two individuals of equal quality, one honest and the other a cheat, the cheater is one that incurs less immediate costs for a given signal. In our case, cheating has nothing to do with the inherent quality (high, average, or low) of the signaler, but with incurring lower costs in signaling. If receivers (in this case, females) cannot discriminate between the two individuals, the cheater benefits in the short term. How can honest signals be maintained at all if cheaters can invade a population of honest signalers?

Alan Grafen has developed theory that demonstrates that, in fact, honest signaling of quality is evolutionarily stable, and that a cheater's average fitness would be reduced even when receivers (females) are nondiscriminating. The theory is complex, but can be put in a nutshell. Any variation in genetic quality among the cheater's sons is not expressed in their signals. A cheater's son with higher-than-average genetic quality will not necessarily have a higher probability of being selected by a female. Daughters of nondiscriminating females inherit this trait and end up with lower fitness as they select mates of lower quality on average (remember that some cheaters would have lower-than-average quality and would not be discriminated against). Thus, a costly but honest signal of male genetic quality is evolutionarily stable.

The evidence so far does suggest that musth is an honest indicator of male quality. It is well known among mahouts (elephant handlers) in Asia that captive male elephants do not come into musth if they are not in good body condition. In fact, they have used this knowledge to suppress musth deliberately in (otherwise troublesome) elephants by denying proper feed. Similarly, observations of wild elephants in both Africa and Asia indicate that undernourished or injured bulls do not come into normal musth.

Musth is an expensive proposition in the currency of energy. The reduced amount of time spent in feeding and greater time spent in searching for estrous females also means that a bull has to be in good condition in the first place to sustain the rigors of the musth period. High levels of androgens (e.g., testosterone) also increase metabolic rates and consume more energy. Thus, captive males in musth lose body condition even if they are chained and given normal quantities of forage. The constant dribbling of urine also exacts a physiological cost. A large male in musth may lose 350 liters of urine each day. When water is limiting, as in semiarid habitats or during the dry season, the physiological costs of urine dribbling for signaling can be substantial if the male is to leave uninterrupted trails.

Females choosing males in musth for mating thus seem to be choosing males of high quality. This can be demonstrated even more convincingly when the cost imposed by musth on the functioning of their immune systems is considered—but this is a subject that merits a separate discussion.

3.4.4   *Musth as a handicap: Immune suppression by testosterone*

The innovative biologist Amotz Zahavi proposed in 1975 a novel hypothesis to explain the evolution of exaggerated male secondary sexual characters. At first glance, some of these, such as the peacock's gorgeous train of feathers, do not seem to serve any purpose beyond merely displaying to potential mates. Indeed, these actually seem to draw the attention of predators and directly impair the ability of males possessing these to escape from a predator. Charles Darwin devoted a whole book to this paradox, extensively documenting examples from the animal kingdom. Darwin recognized that "these characters are the result of sexual and not of ordinary [i.e., natural] selection" (1871, Vol. I, p. 258). In other words, such male characters can be attributed solely to female mating preferences.

For several decades, not much thought was given to this problem until, in 1958, mathematician Ronald Fisher reasoned using genetical theory that initially the evolution of a female mating preference should have a reproductive advantage, but later could proceed purely through sexual selection even if any advantage through natural selection has ceased. The process of an increasingly exaggerated male secondary dimorphism is termed *runaway sexual selection*. Biologists have pondered how such male traits could evolve purely through female choice in the absence of any inherent male genetic quality linked to these traits.

Zahavi's explanation was that female preference for what seems to be a handicap in a male has evolved precisely because of the handicap. A male possessing an exaggerated secondary trait has after all survived in spite of this "handicap" and is therefore demonstrating his inherent vigor and quality. Known as the handicap principle, this explanation has been applied to a variety of puzzling biological phenomena, including sexual dimorphisms, patterns of animal coloration, alarm signals, and "dangerous" behaviors. Related theories linking the evolution of sexual secondary traits with parasitism and disease have also been much debated, and I apply these to sexual selection in elephants.

As discussed, musth is an expensive proposition for male elephants in terms of the physiological costs involved. By the end of the musth period, the bull is in poor body condition. To that extent, a bull is "handicapped" by going through musth. There is, however, a much more serious handicap that a bull suffers when it is in musth, an aspect that has been overlooked by elephant biologists. The high levels of the major androgen, testosterone, associated with musth (or the development of secondary sexual characters, for that matter) also seriously impair the functioning of the immune system, exposing the male to debilitating parasitism and disease.

W. J. Freeland was possibly the first to suggest that female choice of mates (in primates) may be influenced by the parasitic burden of males, and that females could even incite male-male competition to identify fitter males. This idea was independently elaborated by William Hamilton and Marlene Zuk to implicate the role of parasites in the evolution of extreme male ornamentation. They suggested that male secondary sexual characters allow females to appraise the male's ability to resist parasites (the word *parasites* is used in the broader sense to include diseases). By preferring males with exaggerated traits, the female ensures "good genes" for her offspring, in terms of parasite resistance, assuming that the trait is heritable. Unlike earlier good gene hypotheses, however, the resistance gene will be changing since the parasites are also evolving; thus, the system remains dynamic and maintains the importance of female choice.

While Hamilton and Zuk recognized their hypothesis to be a variation of the handicap principle, Ivan Folstad and Andrew Karter went a step further in more formally linking the parasite-male handicap idea with the immunocompetence burden. The differences between males and females in hormone profiles need not be elaborated here. These hormonal differences may translate into differences in immune response between the sexes. Typically, the male shows weaker immune response to several antigens than do females. High levels of testosterone, vital to the development of male secondary sexual traits, reduce the immunity of the individual. The physiological interplay of testosterone and the immune system is complex, involving various organs, tissues, and cell types. Testosterone may reduce immunity through shrinkage of the thymus gland and other lymphoid tissue and through humoral and cell-mediated immunity.

Reduced immunity would thus make the individual more susceptible to parasitism. A male elephant in musth, surging with testosterone, is thus advertising a considerable handicap to estrous females. It is also signaling that it can shoulder this immunocompetence burden during the musth period. Thus, musth can again be thought of as an honest signal of male genetic quality.

While there is some empirical evidence from several mammal species for the Folstad-Karter scenarios, hardly any work has been done on this aspect in elephants. However, Milind Watve and I have looked at a related aspect of this issue—that of tusk length and parasite loads in Asian elephants. In the course of this work, we found that the highest recorded level of fecally dispersed parasite loads was from a bull in musth. I discuss this work in greater detail in the next section.

3.4.5   *Tusks, parasites, handicaps, and sexual selection*

The ecological and evolutionary role of tusks in elephants is debatable. Tusks may play a role in obtaining nutrition, such as from debarking of trees. They may be used by males in male-male combat and perhaps even by females (of African elephants) in establishing intrasexual dominance. More important, tusks in male elephants may act as a secondary sexual character that influences female choice of mates.

Among Asian elephants, only males may possess tusks; thus, there is a distinct possibility that tusks may function as a secondary sexual character.

Even when both sexes possess tusks, as in the African elephant or extinct proboscideans such as the mammoth or the mastodon, there is sexual dimorphism for tusk size. Richard Laws's data on tusk weights in Ugandan elephants show that, at 40 years of age, a cow has a combined tusk weight (30 kg) that is only one-fourth that of a bull (120 kg). This dimorphism may further increase to a sixfold difference in tusk weight between the sexes in the oldest age group. Such a difference seems to be the pattern in many extinct proboscideans as well. Alexander Averianov describes the tusks of the male mammoth as "turned medially very strongly and even crossed as their ends" (1996, p. 261). I can think of no other function of such enormous curved tusks in mammoths but their value in attracting the attention of females.

There is considerable variation in tusk length among male elephants. Of course, this could arise due to differences in tusk use and rate of chipping or wear (this may also be region specific), as well as differences in rate of growth. Thus, tusk length by itself is not a reliable indicator of age in male Asian elephants, although the girth of tusks may provide a much better estimate of age. Since tusks keep growing in size throughout the life span of a male, any differences in growth rate may also accentuate differences in size.

Beyond a certain size, the tusks may also become a handicap; heavy, long tusks may slow the mobility of the individuals, while tusks that cross at the tips may actually hamper feeding. I have seen several elephants in southern India with oversized tusks (one of these, a 26-year-old male named Cross Tusks Jr., studied for several years, is illustrated in fig. 3.7) that are distinctly handicaps. The famous elephant Ahmed of Kenya possessed enormous tusks. The tusks are thus potential candidates for Zahavi's handicap principle. Ivory poaching both in Africa and in Asia may have served to lessen the variation in male tusk sizes.

The considerable variation in tusk length observed within an Asian elephant population provided the basis for Watve and I to test the Hamilton-Zuk hypothesis on intensity of male ornamentation and parasite loads. We looked at the elephants of Mudumalai Sanctuary in southern India. We used simple field techniques for aging male elephants and for measuring their tusk lengths. While age of the animal was estimated from its shoulder height, degree of ear folding, and morphology, the tusk lengths were measured from photographs of side profiles. We had to control for differences in tusk length due to age. For this, we constructed a standard growth curve of tusk length with age (obtained from a relationship of tusk girth versus tusk length in 158 museum specimens). The measured tusk length of a wild bull was subtracted from the average tusk length for that given age, and this deviation from the average was used in further analysis.

We looked at parasites dispersed in the dung of elephants (to study other types such as blood parasites would have been very difficult for a protected species). Fresh droppings were collected by following individually identified bulls, and standard techniques were used in identifying parasite eggs and measuring their numbers.

Figure 3.7
An Asian bull elephant (Cross Tusks Jr., pictured at estimated age 23 years) with a long pair of tusks. Oversize tusks could be distinct handicaps to the animal.

Elephants had among the highest parasite loads of any of the mammalian species we investigated. This could be attributed to the low predation pressure on elephants (in other herbivores, such as axis deer, which show much lower parasite loads, the high rate of predation would presumably have weeded out individuals with crippling parasite loads). The parasites of elephants were mostly nematodes. Nematode eggs in dung of different elephants sampled varied from 0 to 20 million per day according to our calculations. There was also a distinct seasonal difference in parasite loads in the population (both female and male), with the dry season loads much higher than the wet season loads (median loads of 25 and 9 eggs/g feces, respectively).

When parasite loads (corrected for seasonal population differences) of 38 bulls (>10 years old) were plotted against their tusk length deviation from the average, a significant negative relationship was seen (fig. 3.8). In other words, bulls with longer tusks had lower average parasite loads. These results are in conformity with the Hamilton-Zuk hypothesis, although there are several other uncertainties.

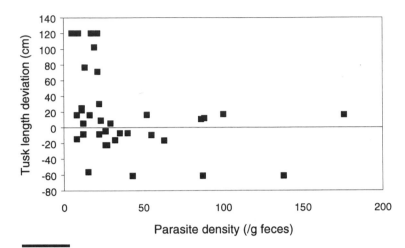

Figure 3.8
The relationship between fecally dispersed parasite egg loads and tusk length deviation from the expected value (best-fit curve) in Asian bull elephants at Mudumalai in southern India. The outlier to the right was a bull in musth condition for at least 3 weeks prior to sampling. (From Watve and Sukumar 1997.)

Such a relationship between tusk length and parasite loads also has important implications for conservation if we assume that these traits are heritable. In recent decades, both the African and the Asian elephants have been subject to high rates of ivory poaching (see chapter 8). Ivory poachers tend to preferentially target elephants with larger tusks. In the process, they may be eliminating genes for resistance to parasites from the population. Poaching has also occurred over historical timescales in both species, and it would be interesting to look at how this may have affected the distribution of parasite abundance in the host (elephant) populations.

Many studies on parasite distributions in animal populations have found that the most common pattern is distinct clustering of parasites, with a large proportion of individuals of a species carrying few or no parasites, and a few individuals carrying large loads. Our studies also found this pattern in herbivores such as axis deer (Axis axis) and sambar deer (Cervus unicolor) with low parasite loads or omnivorous sloth bear (Melursus ursinus) and the carnivorous wild dog or dhole (Cuon alpinus) with high parasite loads. In all these species, the parasite distribution in the population was skewed, with individuals free of parasites or nearly so constituting the modal class. With elephants, however, there were few individuals in the parasite-free class. Could this pattern have come about as a consequence of selective poaching of larger-tusked elephants? Certainly, the Mudumalai Reserve and adjoining areas suffered significantly from poaching over the past two decades.

Our study of tusk length and parasite loads was the first of its kind in elephants; therefore, the results should be interpreted with caution. We were handicapped by the relative paucity (due to poaching) of adult bulls in our study area. Even if a negative relationship between tusk length and parasite loads in male Asian elephants did exist, we have no idea of how female choice of mates is actually influenced by tusk size. Female African elephants do choose older bulls, which on average would have larger tusks, but are they selecting for body size and musth intensity or also tusk size in males? The role of tusks in sexual selection among elephants would be a fascinating topic for research.

Several other questions on sexual selection in elephants come to mind. Tuskless male elephants (called *makhnas*) obviously follow a different strategy in attracting a female. In populations in which both tuskers and *makhnas* are found in roughly equal numbers, as in northeastern India, the *makhnas* seem on average to be larger and more robustly built. Presumably, selection would have favored traits such as larger body size, better musculature of the trunk, and development of the skull in *makhnas* to compensate for lack of tusks. Even among tusked males, those with longer tusks may not necessarily be more robust in physique; in fact, the opposite may be true. The bulls Ahmed of Kenya and Cross Tusks Jr. of Mudumalai, with exceptionally long tusks, were relatively poorly built. No doubt, such subjective comparisons will have to be quantified with more rigor.

The point I am trying to make here is that male elephants may follow alternative stable strategies. Madhav Gadgil has argued that dimorphism among males of many animal groups, from insects to mammals, may arise from selection for alternative strategies on cost-benefit considerations. One form may be superior in combat, but pay the costs of higher expenditure of energy to maintain the needed weaponry, while the other may gain in other ways (such as longevity) by conserving this energy. "This costly arms race comes to an end when those investing in weaponry are just as well off as those which have totally opted out of such investment" (1972, p. 580). With elephants, the situation may be similar, but with the additional role of female choice. Could the tuskless elephants or *makhnas* gain mating advantage through their robust build and intense expression of musth, while other males divert resources into tusk growth by which they gain a reproductive advantage through female choice for tusk size? Even among the tusked males, those with short tusks better suited for actual combat may be able to dominate in male–male competition or expend more energy for musth, while those with oversize tusks may gain from female choice for this handicap.

These theories of sexual selection and the supporting empirical evidence have broader implications for species conservation. Hunters often claim that by shooting only the older males or those sporting the largest ornamentation (whether stags with oversize antlers or elephants with long tusks), they are only removing those individuals past their reproductive prime. In the case of elephants, this is not true. If legal or illegal hunting for several generations removes the most parasite-resistant males, there may be long-term implications for the population. R. M. Anderson has shown theoretically that a high degree of aggregation of parasites is known to stabilize the host–parasite dynamics. Populations with less-aggregated distributions may become more vulnerable to parasitic diseases. Models show that species of parasites that have existed in an endemic state of low virulence for several generations may then become a serious health problem.

Mothers, Children, and Aunts
The Social Life of Elephant Families

4

4.1 Introduction

After a gestation period of nearly 2 years, an elephant calf is born into a typically stable family of closely related individuals. Within this social group, the young elephant will spend long years in physical and behavioral development. The eminent sociobiologist Edward Wilson considers social behavior as a set of devices for tracking changes in the environment, and socialization as the sum of social experiences that alter the development of an individual. He emphasizes the potential of species for rapid evolution of social traits as a means of adapting to changing environments.

From the early years of nutritional dependence on its mother (or perhaps occasionally on an aunt), through social interactions with members of the family and elephant groups within the larger population, an individual elephant experiences a complex social life that reaches into this multitier society during its lifetime. The rich repertoire of behavior exhibited by an adult elephant reflects this long history of social interactions and learning.

While the development of social behavior is a continuous process, the primatologist Frank Poirier defined four stages for the sake of convenience: (1) the neonatal period of complete dependence of infant on the mother; (2) the transition period, in which some adult locomotor and feeding patterns are seen; (3) peer socialization, during which much of the contact is with members of the group other than the mother; and (4) the juvenile-subadult period, during which infantile patterns disappear and adult patterns, including sexual behavior, emerge. This scheme, although developed for primate societies, also broadly holds true for the elephant.

One outcome of this prolonged social exchange among individuals and with their environment is adult-regulated social organization. In fact, the elephant is believed to have one of the most advanced mammalian social organizations. In Edward Wilson's scheme, this would rank among or very close to the highest grades, that of the "generalized learner," among animal social systems. Such animals have a large brain capable of considerable memory and insight learning. Most behaviors are shaped by complex episodes of learning based on the context in which stimuli are received. Socialization is a prolonged and complex process, especially so in a long-lived creature such as the elephant. This is also dependent on recognition of individuals and events through time. The key social feature of such an animal is a perception of history.

The rich fabric of elephant social life has not been unraveled to the extent it has been for other mammals, such as primates and carnivores, or even for social insects. One reason for this is the long generation time in elephants, which allows only snapshots of its social life during the study period of human observers. This chapter provides some of these glimpses of social behavior and development within the family setting in elephant society.

4.2 Behavioral development and social interactions in elephants

The development of behavior among juveniles can be considered in both the nonsocial and the social contexts. The ontogeny of various elements of behavior, such as suckling, locomotion, feeding, drinking, grooming, and solitary play, can be considered essentially nonsocial, while some of these and other behaviors involving contact with other individuals in the group are also components of sociality. Behavioral development is highly species specific, especially among elephants, which differ in several crucial ways from other mammals. For instance, the ontogeny of feeding behavior in young elephants would involve elements relating to use of the trunk and hence is different from that of other herbivores. Outside zoos, there have been surprisingly few studies of behavioral development in elephants. My former colleague Vijayakumaran Nair carried out one of the earliest studies of the ontogeny of behavior among calves in free-ranging groups of tame Asian elephants at Bandipur in southern India. The only observations from a wild situation are those of Cynthia Moss and Phyllis Lee on African elephants at Amboseli in Kenya.

4.2.1 Behavioral development in calves

An elephant calf is considered "precocious" in that it can stand up within minutes or a couple of hours at most after birth (by contrast, an "altricial" offspring is completely helpless at birth). Further, it soon begins walking and following its mother and other elephants in the group. But, this is about the best it can manage in the first few days. The coordination of its limbs is imperfect; it usually stumbles and falls down frequently and needs the support of its mother's trunk and front legs to walk. Its vision is poor, and it finds its mother by smell, touch, and sound. The orientation of suckling is confused. The calf searches for its mother's breasts randomly between her front and her hind legs. During the first week, it has little control over its trunk movements, usually wiggling it about rapidly and even tripping over it.

Much of this changes by the second week of life. The calf's gait is steadier, it can follow or even run short distances with its mother, and trunk maneuverability improves. Vijayakumaran Nair observed Asian elephant calves pick up grass with the trunk tip and objects with the flap of the trunk and the aid of its forelegs by the ninth day, while Cynthia Moss recorded African calves grasping sticks with the tip or the curve of the trunk even earlier. Calves at Amboseli even curiously walked up to a vehicle, inspecting, touching, and even butting it before wandering back to the group. By the end of the first month, the use of the trunk by the calf for manipulating objects improves substantially. It can pick up, hold, and keep in its mouth objects such as grass, leaves, and twigs (fig. 4.1). It cannot, however, suck water into the trunk and drinks directly through the mouth. The calf is essentially still completely dependent on its mother and follows her very closely.

Complete nutritional dependence on the mother continues until the end of the third month. By this time, the trunk maneuverability has improved dramatically. During the fourth month, the calf can pull out grass, herbs, and leaves more easily and, more important, begin consuming them. Around the same time, it begins to use the trunk to suck in water and even transfer some of it into the mouth. It also collects soil and grass with the trunk and throws them on the body. Coordination among lips, trunk, and leg improves, the calf can drop a stick from its lips onto the trunk, step on one end of the stick, and break it. During 3–6 months of age, however, calves continue to suckle at practically the same rate as previously, in addition to some feeding on vegetation, indicating that they need both sources of nutrition for their growth. Nair terms this as an "exploratory period with intense practising" (1989, p. 49).

Independence in feeding quickly picks up between 6 months and a year. By 9 months, the Amboseli calves spent 40% of their time in feeding, with only a small decrease in suckling duration. This is also the period when various actions involving the trunk, feet, and mouth are perfected. The Bandipur calves, for instance, picked up the skill of grasping a bamboo culm, bending it, and standing on it to prevent it from springing back before using its trunk for feeding on the leaves by the seventh month. Later, they even began exhibiting adultlike behavior, such as chasing cattle with spread ears, raised tail, and vocalization. By its first birthday, the elephant calf has developed all the basic skills for independent feeding, drinking, and grooming, although it will con-

Figure 4.1
An African elephant calf trying to grasp a clump of dry grass. A 1-week-old calf can
grasp twigs and grass with the tip or curve of the trunk to a limited extent; by the
age of 1 month, it can deftly manipulate such objects.

tinue to depend on its mother for nutrition and defense against predators for
at least another year.

Using statistical cluster analysis, Nair looked in detail at the ontogeny of
various behavioral elements during the first year in the Bandipur calves. During
the first 3 months, the preparatory steps for feeding formed a significant cluster, while those associated with actual consumption of plants were not yet
significant. During the 6–9-month period, the two significant clusters were of
elements involved in preparation of vegetation and actual consumption of
food. By 1 year, of course, the full sequences of feeding, drinking, and grooming are well developed. The ontogeny of behavior relating to feeding is particularly fascinating in elephants. The ability to clean mud from plants by rubbing
against the legs, belly, or cheeks or by washing in water and the coordinated
use of the forefeet and trunk in uprooting and consuming plants are actions
that require considerable skill and discrimination.

4.2.2   *Maternal investment in offspring*

Elephants show an extended period of maternal care and direct investment of energy through nursing of calves (fig. 4.2). The average suckling duration of 2–4 minutes per hour observed in elephants younger than 1 year is one of the highest rates reported among ungulates. Even though calves have developed the motor skills needed for feeding on plants, they continue to derive signifi-cant amounts of nutrition from their mothers until 3 years or older. The mater-nal contribution beyond 2 years is not needed for survival, but could be crucial for maintaining growth rates, body condition, and ultimate reproductive ability of offspring. Therefore, it can be expected that elephant mothers would regu-late their investment in children in a manner that would maximize their own long-term reproductive success.

In a polygynous species with marked sexual dimorphism, such as in ele-phants, the variance in reproductive success is much greater among males than among females (chapter 3). Mothers should thus preferentially invest in off-spring of the sex that brings them the highest genetic returns. While these ideas had been in the literature for some years, Robert Trivers and D. E. Wil-lard in 1973 presented a theoretical framework for the evolution of parental ability to vary investment in male and female offspring. In a polygynous, sexu-ally dimorphic mammal, it pays to invest preferentially in male offspring when

Figure 4.2
An elephant calf suckling. Among African elephants at Amboseli, Kenya, the mothers bias investment toward male calves.

a mother has ample resources (when she is in good body condition, for instance). The logic here is that a well-provisioned son would grow large, achieve dominance over other competing males in the population, and enjoy a higher than average reproductive success. On the other hand, a weak mother is better off investing in a daughter with an opportunity anyhow to reproduce rather than produce a weak son with a low chance of successful mating. The Trivers-Willard hypothesis, as originally formulated, related largely to parental ability in adjusting the sex ratio of offspring, although it did state that, for species with prolonged maternal investment, this should be extended to the total investment in offspring. Studies on a variety of mammal species have so far been equivocal in support for this hypothesis.

The Amboseli study of Phyllis Lee and Cynthia Moss provides the only detailed observations of elephants on this subject (fig. 4.3). Lee and Moss observed 110 male calves and 125 female calves aged 0–54 months. From about 3 months, male calves attempted to suckle from their mothers more frequently than did female calves. The male calves were also more successful at suckling. When averaged across all ages, male calves suckled once every 37 minutes, while female calves did so every 50 minutes. The duration of each bout of suckling did not vary significantly between the sexes (86 seconds for males and 89 seconds for females). However, when the frequency and the duration of suckling bouts were combined into a single measure of milk intake, it was clear

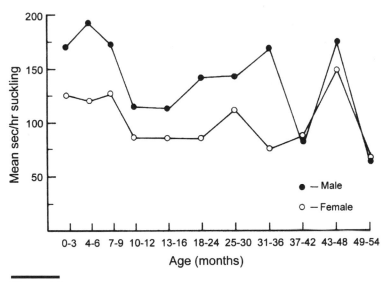

Figure 4.3
The mean estimated milk intake (duration of suckling times number of successful suckling bouts per hour) for male and female elephant calves of various age classes at Amboseli. (From Lee and Moss 1986. Reproduced with the permission of Springer-Verlag GmbH & Co., K.G.)

that male calves spent more time on the nipple than did female calves. This pattern was consistent across all ages from birth to 3 years. While it was the calf that generally initiated suckling, either the calf or the mother terminated suckling. Maternal termination of suckling by male calves became pronounced after 3 years.

Weaning itself was a gradual process. There was no specific age at which suckling suddenly terminated; in a small proportion (15%) of cases, an older sibling continued sporadic suckling along with the younger sibling. The duration of maternal suckling in a calf is obviously important in determining onset of estrus in the mother and interbirth intervals, an important consideration in ultimate reproductive success. The Amboseli data showed that investment in a male calf resulted in interbirth intervals that were longer by 2 months (wet years) to 5 months (dry years) compared to having a female calf previously. There seems to be a certain cost, in direct demographic terms, that goes along with the higher level of investment made in male calves. Obviously, there is a trade-off between investing more in a son in the expectation of increasing his reproductive success and incurring a higher short-term demographic cost through longer interbirth interval.

Lee and Moss (1986) aptly asked whether elephant mothers may "be investing more in males than females *in order* for them to grow faster, or alternatively *because* they grow faster" (p. 360, italics in original) Data from Amboseli indicated that males grew faster than females on average from birth onward, and the dimorphism was clear by 5 years, by which time they had been weaned (in a study of growth rates in Asian elephants born in captivity, I found no difference between male and female calves in growth until 2 years, after which differences surfaced; see appendix 2). Because of their faster growth rates, male calves could be demanding and obtain more milk from their mothers.

The observation that elephant mothers bias postnatal investment toward sons is consistent with the Trivers-Willard hypothesis, although by itself, it is not necessarily substantial evidence for the same. At the population level, mothers may have to invest more in sons than in daughters only because sons grow faster. The crucial question is whether individual mothers in good (higher-than-average) body condition are preferentially investing in sons such that these sons would enjoy greater than average reproductive success (or that mothers in poor condition do the opposite). This has to be integrated over various stages, taking into consideration prenatal mechanisms (adjustments in sex ratios of offspring), postnatal investment (bias in suckling), demographic cost-benefit (changes in inter-birth interval) considerations, and offspring reproductive potential. In a long-lived species, these conditions would vary over the life span, as with age-related body condition, interannual variation in climate and food availability, population densities, and so on. This integration is possible only when a population is studied over the long term, as at Amboseli, although pieces of the jigsaw puzzle may be assessed elsewhere. Among 261 elephants born in captivity in southern India, I found that mothers in the 20–40-year age group produced more sons than daughters, while no bias was noticed for other ages. Middle-aged mothers in their reproductive prime can also be expected to be relatively in good condition, thus lending support to the Trivers-Willard model.

4.2.3   Development of social interactions

Apart from contact with its mother for nutrition or otherwise, an elephant calf has the opportunity to interact with several other family members. The rich repertoire and extended period of such interactions help mold the variety of behavioral traits seen in elephants. These interactions could be through suckling, contact by trunk and body, play, aggression, or even merely proximity ("nearest neighbor").

The caretaking of infants by individuals other than the mother is termed *allomothering* (this does not necessarily imply suckling, for which the specific term *allosuckling* is used). Phyllis Lee observed at Amboseli that calves are overwhelmingly dependent on their mothers for suckling. In spite of many anecdotal accounts of calves being nursed by their "aunts," instances of allosuckling were less than 4% of all observations at Amboseli. Three-fourths of these few instances of allosuckling were from nulliparous females, while most attempts to suckle from lactating females were terminated quickly. Allosuckling thus seems to be a behavior associated with comforting a calf rather than providing nutrition. The captive Asian elephant calves observed by Vijayakumaran Nair at Bandipur, however, seemed to allosuckle more regularly from females that had weaned their own calves.

Young calves are obviously in proximity to their mothers (fig. 4.4). Amboseli elephants aged 0–8 years remained within 5 m (as measured from scan observations) of their mothers for about 80% of the time. This distance between calves and mothers increased gradually with age, especially in the case of male calves. Distance between calves and nonmother neighbors did not, however, change appreciably. Interestingly, young elephants had at least one neighbor, in addition to the mother, when moving in a group, and these neighbors tended to be closer to the immature elephant than the mother. Female elephants, especially juveniles, were more likely to be neighbors of young calves than expected by chance. This pattern could also partly be an outcome of the association of such females with their mothers, to which calves were attached. When the mother was greater than 5 m away, a calf was more likely to have an age-mate, with the exception of juvenile males, as the nearest neighbor.

When a calf is in distress, as when it has strayed several meters away from the mother/group or got stuck in mud or a hole, it lets out a loud bellow or a deep rumble. Both mothers and allomothers in the group respond quickly by rushing to the calf's side to help it. Vijayakumaran Nair recorded that calves would make distress calls when they strayed more than 5 m away from the mother. Phyllis Lee observed that calves of younger females seemed to make distress calls more frequently.

Figure 4.4
An Asian elephant calf well protected by its mother and an "aunt" within the elephant group at Mudumalai, India.

The direct contacts of young elephants with others include friendly inter-actions, such as touching the other's body with the trunk, comforting behavior such as rubbing the body against the other, investigating food by putting the trunk into the other's mouth, or interactions relating to play. The Amboseli calves interacted (suckling excluded) with mothers to a slightly lesser extent (2.3 contacts/hour) than they did with all other individuals combined (2.5 contacts/hour), although with any particular age-sex class this was lower (fig. 4.5). As they aged, the male calves interacted at a lower rate with their moth-ers, but female calves continued their contacts at the same rate.

Interactions of calves can be categorized as those they initiate or receive. Of interactions initiated by calves toward their mothers, the majority were those relating to rubbing or seeking comfort. Those received from the mother were equally likely to be rubbing/comfort or greeting/touching. By contrast, a higher proportion of calf interactions initiated toward and received from others related to greeting. Calves of all ages interacted more frequently than expected by chance with their peers and less than expected with adult females. Interest-

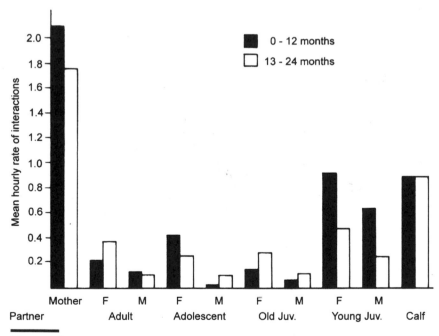

Figure 4.5
The mean hourly rate of interactions of calf with each age-sex class of partners among the young elephants (males and females) observed at Amboseli, Kenya. (From Lee 1987. Reprinted from *Animal Behaviour* with the permission of Elsevier Science.)

ingly, calves of younger mothers were more likely to receive friendly contacts from others than were calves of middle-aged mothers or matriarchs.

Play is a common behavior among immature elephants (fig. 4.6). Young elephants play by pushing with their heads, wrestling with trunks, mounting or rolling on another (including in water), and chasing. In general, the Amboseli elephants tended to play most frequently with age mates. Calves played the most during the first year of life; the bouts of play and time spent in play declined with age (table 4.1). There were gender differences in play behavior. The decline in playing time with age was more pronounced among female calves. By 3 years of age, the males spent about twice as much time in play as the females. Older males also tended to play more with peers of the same sex and also with those less familiar as with peers from other families or social groups. Females were more conservative in that they generally preferred peers more familiar to them, such as within the family or bond group. They were also more likely to direct play toward younger elephants (<2 years old) as compared to males who played with peers of similar age.

All interactions among young elephants and with their elders were not necessarily friendly. Certain behaviors, such as poking with tusks, shoving another away, slapping with the trunk, and chasing or threatening with head and ears shaking were definitely aggressive in intent. The rate of aggressive interactions was very low among young calves, but increased with age, especially in

Figure 4.6
Three African elephant calves indulge in play at Bumi Hills, Zimbabwe.

Table 4.1
Play bouts (as % of all play) among young African elephants of the
same sex with all elephants or with strangers, and play bouts (%)
of juveniles (>2 years old) directed toward calves (<2 years old).

Age (years)	Same-Sex Play with All (%)		Same-Sex Play with Strangers (%)		Play with Calves (<2 years) (%)		Total Play Bouts Recorded	
	M	F	M	F	M	F	M	F
0–1	25.5	29.2	3.3	6.2	—	—	153	162
1–2	31.3	33.4	7.8	6.1	—	—	64	66
2–3	38.6	41.3	6.8	2.2	22.7	45.7	44	46
3–4	45.2	37.2	16.1	3.7	11.3	38.9	62	54
4–5	67.4	41.7	34.9	16.7	9.3	20.9	43	24
5+	83.3	41.7	49.4	25.0	2.1	16.7	48	12

Source: From Lee (1986), reproduced with permission of National Geographic Research and
   Lee (1987), reprinted from *Animal Behaviour* with the permission of Elsevier Science.
M and F refer to male and female calves, respectively, while sample sizes (total play bouts) are
   also given.

the case of females. The calves themselves hardly initiated any aggression. Adult
elephants, especially males associating temporarily with a group, were the most
frequent initiators of aggression toward the young elephants. Significantly,
mothers showed more aggression toward their daughters than toward sons.
The mere fact that daughters were more likely to be present closer to the
mother may explain this observation.

   Early behavioral development among elephants thus reflects the needs of
the sexes for their eventual role within the social organization of adult society.
While mothers may initially invest more in sons because of their greater metabolic needs, the sons become independent from their mothers faster than the
daughters, as seen from their increasing distance and fewer interactions. This
presumably prepares the young males for dispersal from the family at puberty,
several years later. At the same time, young males prefer peers of the same sex
for play and are more willing to interact with strangers. These behaviors again
would allow them to gain experience for interaction as adults with other males,
perhaps in many cases the same age-mates or strangers. Young female elephants,
on the other hand, have a more consistent relationship with their mothers.
This is to be expected in a species with strong kinship. The proximity of young
females to their mothers and the greater likelihood that such females would
also play the role of allomothers by assisting calves may have several benefits.
Daughters may eventually acquire the social status of their mothers and information about resources that may be crucial in both the short and the long term
(when adverse environmental conditions may force elephants to seek resources

outside their normal range). This proximity increases competitive interactions between daughters and their mothers, but any costs incurred could be outweighed by long-term benefits.

4.3   *Communication in elephants*

Communication in animals lies at the heart of the study of behavior. Animal communication mainly involves sight, smell, and sound, although other senses, including touch and electroreception, may also be specific to certain taxa. Communication can be looked at from its production by the organism, its transmission through the environment, its reception and analysis, and its functionality, including its evolutionary significance. There has been much discussion as to how to define communication. Most authors agree that communication involves the provision of information, as conveyed through a signal, by a sender to a receiver, and the use of that information by the receiver in deciding how to respond. A *signal* is distinguished from a *cue* in that the former reflects the intentional transfer of information, while the latter is not associated with any such intent (although determining the intent of an animal is not easy).

The theoretical evolutionary approach recognizes that communication is associated with benefits and costs, in terms of genetic fitness, to the signaler and the receiver. R. Haven Wiley thus recognizes four possible outcomes arising from an act of communication: (1) mutuality, when both the signaler and the receiver experience fitness increases; (2) deceit, when manipulation by the signaler increases its fitness, but decreases that of the receiver; (3) eavesdropping, when the receiver is able to increase fitness to the detriment of the signaler; and (4) spite, when both parties have decreased fitness. While these aspects have been applied to the study of communication in a variety of animal species, our understanding of communication in elephants is, with some exceptions, still largely descriptive.

Elephants actively communicate through a wide repertoire of tactile, visual, chemical, and acoustic signals. Several observers of captive and wild elephants have described the use of the trunk in a variety of contacts: reaching out to each other with extended trunks, entwining trunks, inserting the trunk tip in the other's mouth, placing the trunk over the back, caressing with the trunk, or just touching another with the tip of the trunk. Some of these contacts, such as making trunk contact with the temporal gland or the genitals, are obviously to obtain chemical signals, but many others are purely tactile contacts. Placing the trunk tip in another's mouth, for instance, seems to be part of reassurance behavior under times of stress (fig. 4.7). A calf may put its trunk into an elder's mouth to seek information about food. Leaning against or rubbing another's body is another form of tactile communication.

The African elephant has two fingerlike projections at the tip of its trunk, while the Asian elephant has a single finger. Several observers of the Asian species have noted the sensitivity of the trunk tip in functions such as detecting

Figure 4 .7
Female elephant placing trunk tip in the mouth of another adult cow. In addition to communicating through touch, chemical messages may be exchanged through breath.

ground vibrations, delicately picking up very small objects, and obtaining information on an object's texture, size, and perhaps even temperature. Histological examination of an Asian elephant's trunk tip by L.E.L. (Bets) Rasmussen and Bryce Munger revealed a high density of free nerve endings, convoluted branched small corpuscles, and "vellus vibrissae" or short hairs that barely protrude beyond the skin surface (fig. 4.8). These specialized structures are consonant with the advanced tactile abilities of an elephant, including sensing vibrations, performing delicate manipulations, and conveying chemical signals to other organs in the mouth.

While it is possible to assign a function to certain types or instances of tactile exchanges between two elephants, at other times it is not clear what information is being exchanged through such contact. This is especially true of exchanges between calf and mother. In his study of the Bandipur elephants, Vijayakumaran Nair recorded one young calf (<6 months) touching its mother 24 times an hour and one of its allomothers about half as frequently (fig. 4.9). The mother touched her calf about 9 times an hour, while the allomother did so 3 times an hour. On the other hand, the adults touched each other far less frequently. When Madhav Gadgil examined in detail the mother-calf exchanges

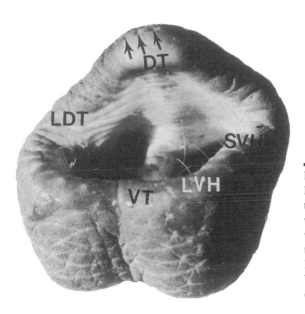

Figure 4.8
Life-size photograph of the trunk tip of an Asian elephant. Small vibrissal hair (SVH) and large vibrissae (LVH) can be seen on the skin surface (DT = dorsal tip, LDT = area lateral to dorsal tip, VT = ventral tip). (Photo courtesy of L.E.L. Rasmussen.)

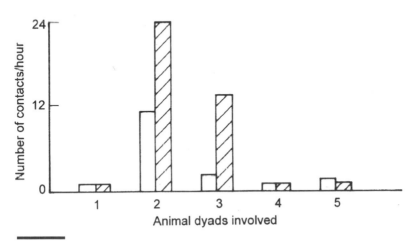

Figure 4.9
Number of contacts made per hour in different captive Asian elephant dyads between (1) two adult females, and between calf (hatched) and (2) mother, (3) I allomother, (4) juvenile, and (5) II allomother at Bandipur in southern India. (From Gadgil and Nair 1984. Reproduced with the permission of the Indian Academy of Sciences, Bangalore.)

recorded for the Bandipur elephants, he found that, in about 80% of instances, no immediate function could be attached to an exchange. He has suggested that these exchanges contribute to monitoring the state of well-being of the calf by its mother and other adults. In a highly social, long-lived animal, it would be advantageous for the mother to have regular information about her off-spring's state so that she could then regulate her investment according to its needs. An active calf would indicate that it is healthy while one with lower activity would be signaling that it needs assistance. The basic idea, of course, is to optimize investment in a manner that maximizes the genetic returns to mother and offspring (or, broadly, the "inclusive fitness" to any individual making such investment). Just as too little investment may not serve this purpose, too much investment in an offspring that has crossed a certain threshold in its health status would not be worthwhile. In principle, a calf may try to misinform the adults to extract extra investment, but Gadgil and colleagues showed through modeling that this is not easy as the calf could also run the risk of receiving lower investment than its actual needs.

4.3.1   Visual communication

Most observers agree that elephants have relatively poor vision. It is believed that elephants see the world in shades of gray under bright light, but may have very limited color vision under dull light. They possibly gain little information about their environment through sight except at very close distances. Nevertheless, several interactions among elephants involve visual signals, some of them very impressive to human observers (especially those directed toward the humans!).

Courtship between the sexes includes the characteristic "musth walk" by the male or the "estrous walk" by the female (see chapter 3). Visual signals are especially apparent in aggressive interactions. Several observers, including Iain Douglas-Hamilton and Joyce Poole for the African elephant and George McKay and M. Krishnan for the Asian species, have provided descriptions of such visual displays. Based on observations of captive African elephants, the ethologist Wolf-dietrich Kühme described body postures related to motivational states, in particular, several variations from the normal in the angle of the head, ears, and trunk.

While many of the descriptions in the literature pertain to displays toward humans or a predator, some of these or their variations are also seen when one elephant (usually a bull) approaches another with aggressive intent. A basic display described by George McKay for the elephant in Sri Lanka (Ceylon) is the approach with "the head raised somewhat and the ears extended forward or rather laterally" (1973, p. 66). A common variation of this is to extend the ears fully and approach the stimulus with the trunk raised. Another display is to extend the ears forward and at the same time "stand tall," sometimes by placing the front feet on a fallen log (fig. 4.10). Both African and Asian bulls indulge in these displays. For a species in which body size is an important determinant of social rank and dominance, such displays designed to exaggerate size are understandable. While these may have the maximum effect in the

Figure 4.10
An impressive visual display by a bull African elephant at Tsavo National Park, Kenya.

larger-eared African elephant, the twin domes on the Asian elephant's skull (or the single dome of the mammoth) may serve the same purpose.

Visual displays may be accompanied by behaviors such as swaying of the body or shaking of the head. Eventually, this may be followed by the classical forms of conflict behavior—displacement activity (kicking the ground with the front foot, throwing mud or leaves over its back, exaggerated feeding rate), redirected aggression (thrashing a bush, breaking a stem), attack (a mock charge or a full-blown attack), and retreat (with the tail held aloft). An elephant may not go through this entire sequence. A submissive animal may quickly flee with its tail held up. Visual displays may be accompanied by auditory signals—a shrill trumpet or a series of short squeaks that indicate conflict. The Asian elephant is also known to produce a loud booming sound by rapping the trunk sharply on the ground, possibly through exhaling rapidly at the same time. Although many of these displays have been described in the context of male-male interactions, several of them may occur, although infrequently and subtly, during competition among females or family groups.

4.3.2   Auditory communication

Elephants use a variety of sounds, described as trumpets, roars, barks, snorts, growls, and rumbles, for communication at close range to long distances. While most of the sounds produced by elephants are true vocalizations (i.e., are generated from the vocal cords within the larynx), there are some that emanate from the trunk that may also convey a signal.

The sound language of elephants, as audible to humans, was described in subjective terms by several observers. The more recent discovery and characterization of "infrasound," along with the possibilities of playback experiments using modern gadgetry, however, has opened new avenues to study acoustic communication among elephants. Problems with studying vocalization are to first identify the individual making the call, coin an appropriate term to describe it, and then interpret the meaning of the call.

A repertoire of "basic sounds," the modification of their properties (such as amplitude and resonance), the resulting sound, and its interpretation for wild Asian elephants was given by George McKay. Several of these had also been described by other observers, including G. P. Sanderson and M. Krishnan. I have taken the liberty of reproducing McKay's repertoire with my own suggestions (table 4.2). For the wild African elephant, Joyce Poole gives a more comprehensive list of calls based on their context, such as group dynamics, distress, and sexual signaling. She observed that, of 26 calls made by adult elephants, 19 are made only by females, 3 by both sexes, and only 4 exclusively by males. Female elephants thus seem to possess a much richer repertoire of acoustic signals compared to males. This may be related to the more

---

Table 4.2
Vocalizations and their possible functions in Asian elephants.

Basic Sound	Modification	Resulting Sound	Context
Growl	1. None	Growl	Short-distance contact
	2. Resonate in trunk	Rumble	Mild arousal
	3. Increase amplitude	Roar	Long-distance contact
	4. Low frequency	"Motorcycle"	Infrasound in different contexts
Squeak	1. None	—	?
	2. Multiple short squeaks	Chirping	Conflict, nervousness
	3. Lengthen, increase amplitude	Trumpet	Extreme arousal
Snort	1. None	Snort	Change in activity
	2. Increase amplitude	Snort	Mild-to-strong arousal
	3. Same as no. 2 plus bounce trunk tip on ground	Boom	Threat display

Source: Modified from McKay (1973).

frequent and more diverse communications in which females have to engage, both within the family and across family groups encompassing the larger clan.

Several elephant observers recognized a call barely audible to humans. G. P. Sanderson, writing about the southern Indian elephants in 1878, briefly noted "an almost inaudible purring sound from the throat" (p. 49) of an elephant he interpreted as expressing pleasure. The Indian naturalist M. Krishnan clearly recognized in a 1972 article that wild Asian elephants communicate at sound frequencies not fully audible to humans. He described these as "throaty, hardly audible," "low-pitched but clearly audible from a distance," and "a throbbing purr." The earliest experiments on the hearing abilities of the elephant were probably those by Rickye and Henry Heffner on a 7-year-old female Asian elephant at the Mitchell Zoo in Independence, Kansas. Using a pair of loudspeakers to broadcast varying sound frequencies this study, published in 1980, determined that the hearing range of an elephant extended from 17 Hz (hertz or cycles per second) to a maximum of 10.5 kHz (kilohertz). By comparison, the auditory range of humans is about 30Hz–20kHz. Thus, elephants can hear low frequency sounds that humans cannot, while humans can hear high frequency sounds that elephants cannot. This was not really surprising because it was known that hearing ability in mammals was related to body size, with smaller mammals better able to hear high frequency sounds. It was the first time this hypothesis was tested on a very large mammal. More precisely, the ability to hear high frequency sound varies inversely with the distance between the ears (interaural distance); smaller mammals with close-set ears are therefore better equipped to hear higher frequencies. In contrast, the elephant had better ability to hear low frequency sound than any other mammal tested.

Judith Berg recorded sounds made by captive African elephants at San Diego Wild Animal Park in California. She described some "low intensity" calls and inferred the existence of sound frequencies between 18 and 28 Hz, although the dominant frequency was above 90 Hz, which is well within the human audible range.

The first complete description of infrasonic calls in elephants came from a 1986 paper by Katharine Payne, William Langbauer Jr., and Elizabeth Thomas. Katharine Payne was observing Asian elephants at the Washington Park Zoo in Portland, Oregon, when she sensed "a palpable throbbing in the air like distant thunder, yet all around [her] was silent" (1989, p. 266). She realized that the elephants could be communicating at low sound frequencies below the threshold of human hearing. Using a tape recorder capable of registering low-frequency sounds, Payne's team found that the elephants were calling at fundamental frequencies ranging from 14 to 24 Hz with a duration of 10–15 seconds and sound pressure levels of 85–90 dB (decibels) at a distance of 5 m. Because low-frequency sound at high pressure can pass through vegetation with little attenuation, this provides a means for communication over distances greater than several hundred meters. A few years later, from playback trials of prerecorded low-frequency calls, they inferred that captive African elephants responded to what seemed to be recognition of biologically meaning-ful signals (fig. 4.11).

The next step was to catalog the repertoire of infrasonic calls, assign a meaning to each, and carry out field trails to document the extent to which infrasounds are used by elephants in various social contexts in the wild. For this, Katharine Payne and her associates collaborated with Joyce Poole and Cynthia Moss at Amboseli (Kenya) and with Rowan Martin and Ferrel Osborn at Sengwa (Zimbabwe) and Etosha (Namibia). Using the considerable expertise of Joyce Poole and Cynthia Moss in the study of elephant social behavior, the team obtained spectrograms of eight distinct "call types" with fundamental frequencies of 14–35 Hz. Only about a third of the rumbles recorded were actually audible to one of the observers in the field. The rest emerged using techniques such as speeding up the tape or through examination of the spec-trograms (table 4.3).

While a catalog of infrasonic calls made by elephants was a basic first step in studying their role in communication, this did not by itself prove that ele-phants in the wild were indeed responding to such calls or show the extent to which these were important in long-distance communication. At Sengwa, sev-eral female elephants were fitted in 1990 with radiotransmitters to track their movements and to relate these to infrasonic calls they made. Although the study had to be abandoned after a year's work (because of an elephant cull at Sengwa), this did indicate that some family groups coordinate their movements through infrasound contact calls. Rowan Martin's unpublished earlier study of elephant movement there had strongly suggested such coordination; at that time, the mechanism was not known.

The team, this time led by William Langbauer, had earlier carried out field trails using playbacks in Etosha National Park, Namibia. Using an array of

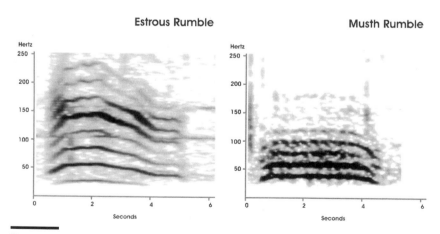

Figure 4.11
Infrasound calls in elephants. Sound spectrogram of estrous call and of musth rumble by African elephants. (Courtesy of Katharine Payne.)

Table 4.3
Characteristics of infrasounds and their biological context recorded at Amboseli.

Call Type	Sound Pressure Levels at 5 m (dB SPL)	Fundamental Frequencies	Description of Social Context
1. Greeting rumble	92	18–25 Hz*	This call is typically used by adult females within the same family or bond group when they meet after separation for several hours.
2. Contact call	101	18 Hz	A relatively soft, unmodulated sound accompanied by steady ear flapping. The contact call and the answer seem to be used when elephants are separated by up to 2 km during feeding.
3. Contact answer	103	18 Hz	In response to the contact call, the answer starts loudly and then becomes softer at the end.
4. "Let's go" rumble	77	15 Hz	As the term suggests, this soft rumble is used by a female to herd the members of the group before moving to a different location.
5. Musth rumble	78	14 Hz	A male in musth gives out a low-frequency pulsated sound (the "motorcycle") several times an hour.
6. Female chorus	98	15–24 Hz*	Several adult females may answer a musth rumble with a low-frequency modulated chorus.
7. Postcopulatory call	102	18–35 Hz*	An estrous female makes a series of loud calls for up to 30 minutes; more common after mating.
8. Mating pandemonium	100	–	This indicates much excitement among members of a mated female's family. They indulge in a frenzy of activity.

Source: After Poole et al. (1988). Reproduced with the permission of Springer-Verlag GmbH & Co. KG.

Note: All sound pressure estimates are based on measurements at a particular distance and extrapolation to 5 m (SD = ±3 in all cases).

*These calls are modulations from the lower frequency to the higher one and back to the lower one.

microphones, recorders, two video cameras, and a loudspeaker mounted on a van, they played back infrasonic calls to elephants that were 1.2 km and 2.0 km from the speaker. The calls were broadcast at only half the sound pressure levels of the strongest calls recorded because of a technical limitation of the loudspeaker. Simultaneously, they made audio and video recordings of the elephants' behavior from a tower overlooking a waterhole. The playback experiments were directed toward both family and bull groups. The infrasonic calls selected for the playbacks included a variety of female social contact and postcopulatory calls.

The results showed that both family and male groups responded, through changes in their behavior, more after the playback than before it at the two distances tested. In statistical terms, the overall response scores were significant for male groups at 1.2 km and 2.0 km, while for family groups they were significant only at 1.2 km. The responses obviously varied with respect to the specific behavior of the elephants and their change in distance from the loudspeaker after the playback. In a typical full response, one or more elephants "would lift their heads within a few seconds of the onset of the playback and raise, spread and stiffen their ears, and then freeze, apparently listening. Simultaneously or shortly after this, one or more animals vocalized. The animals would then 'scan,' slowly swinging their heads from side to side, orient towards and move towards the loudspeaker" (Langbauer et al. 1991, p. 42). One notable difference in the responses by family groups and males was a greater tendency in the former to vocalize and in the latter to move longer distances toward the loudspeaker. This could be related to the need for family groups to maintain regular contact for coordinating their movements and for males to locate an estrous female (which has signaled) quickly to take advantage of a mating opportunity. Because the sound pressure levels of the playbacks were about half (or 6 dB less than) the strongest calls recorded, William Langbauer and the team calculated that the effective range of infrasound could be at least 4 km, or twice the broadcast distance. This translates roughly to a 50-km^2 area over which a strong infrasonic call could be audible.

Although there is still much to learn about auditory communication in elephants, the discovery of infrasound is proving to be a powerful new tool to investigate aspects of elephant social behavior and ecology. Indeed, recent research by Karen McComb in association with Cynthia Moss and her team at Amboseli points to infrasound as the medium for a well-developed network of individual recognition among elephants. Using recordings of female contact calls from several individually identified family groups, they conducted a series of playback experiments to test the ability of adult females to recognize the calls of other females socially related to them to varying degrees. Social familiarity was determined from long-term records of associations among various female-led family groups. Behaviors such as contact calling in response, approaching the loudspeaker, listening with ears extended, bunching together in agitation, and avoidance by moving away from the loudspeaker were used to interpret the subjects' reactions.

The first two positive behaviors were exclusively performed in reaction to playbacks from members of the same family unit or bond group (see section 4.5.2 for definitions of social units). In all but one instance (11 of 12 playbacks), listening only was directed toward members of high-association families. The opposite was true of playbacks from low-association family members beyond the bond group. Playbacks from such members elicited the more negative behaviors, such as bunching and avoidance (in 11 of 12 cases). Interestingly, a female's contact call played back 3 months after her death elicited a positive response from her family members. These experiments confirm the ability of elephants to recognize individuals through discrimination of their vocalizations. McComb and her associates calculated that an adult female elephant at Amboseli would be familiar with the calls of roughly 14 families comprising about 100 adult females in the population, an unusually extensive network of vocal recognition for a mammalian species.

It is well known that the propagation of sound is influenced by environmental factors such as atmospheric conditions (wind, temperature, turbulence, moisture, etc.), topography, ground reflection, and attenuation by vegetation in addition to the physical properties of the sound itself. David Larom and Michael Garstang, along with their associates, have researched the influence of atmospheric conditions over the southern African savannas, using empirical data and computer modeling, on propagation of animal vocalizations. The area of sound propagation changed substantially over a 24-hour period. Strong atmospheric temperature inversions prevail close to the ground before sunset and decay with sunrise. Calm winds may accompany this temperature inversion during the early evening. Under such conditions of clear, cold, and calm nights, about 1–2 hours after sunset, the conditions are optimum for sound propagation. At this time, the spread of a 15-Hz vocalization may be over 10 km and "calling areas" over 200 km^2, as opposed to daytime figures of under 50 km^2 (the calling area is calculated from within the contour of the sound pressure dropping by 67 dB from the source).

One obvious characteristic of low-frequency sound is that it can travel over longer distances with little attenuation by vegetation. From this consideration, I tentatively suggested in 1994 that, in theory, infrasound could be expected to be even more useful for forest-dwelling elephants compared to those in the savannas. Recent recordings of infrasound in African rain forest habitat seem to support this expectation. Several recordings of the forest elephant (*Loxodonta africana cyclotis*) made in Central Africa by Katharine Payne and Stephen Gulick (unpublished 2001) show strong calls at much lower frequencies of 5 Hz (the lowest frequency recorded for *L. a. africana* in the savannas is 14 Hz).

The inverse relationship between body size (or interaural distance) and frequencies of auditory communication in mammals is well known. At the same time, there is a broad positive correlation between body size and home range area in terrestrial mammals. The larger mammals thus need to communicate over longer distances, which is facilitated by infrasound.

The diurnal variation in sound propagation (of not just infrasound, but a range of frequencies) through the atmosphere also suggests that it would be adaptive for animals to link their communications to the more favorable periods. The collared elephants at Sengwa also used loud, infrasonic calls most frequently during the late afternoon when they trekked to a waterhole. I have observed a high frequency of "roaring" by Asian elephants during evening and early night hours.

Sound propagation characteristics would also vary in the short term from one day to another and with the longer seasonal climatic changes. This brings up the possibility of more complex linkages among auditory communication, movement patterns, social organization, and behavior among elephants. The social dynamics of elephants, from maintaining contact while foraging during the day, gathering at a waterhole in the evening or making sudden seasonal movements, could all be related to the windows of communication opportunity.

Malan Lindeque has suggested, for instance, that elephants may make early seasonal movements to areas receiving rains by detecting infrasounds generated by thunderstorms. This could be in addition to or superior to their ability to smell moisture, as suggested by other observers. Clearly, there are many opportunities for research into the complex world of elephant communication.

4.3.3   Chemical communication

Elephants have a highly sophisticated system of chemical communication. A wide variety of chemical compounds are broadcast from modified skin and mucous membrane structures, including glands. These chemicals may be secretions, excretions, or filtrates. To sense these signals, the elephant is endowed with a sensitive olfactory apparatus for gaseous compounds and a vomeronasal organ for detecting liquid compounds. Centuries-old elephant lore from India (Nilakantha's *Matangalila*) recognized the role of chemical signals in the following observations: "And from the smell of their sweat, dung, urine, and must-fluid other elephants instantly are excited." "Upon smelling their own dung and urine, let them always produce a tickling of the palate" (Edgerton 1931, p. 53).

The leading researcher on this subject is Bets Rasmussen, who has collaborated with several veterinarians, physiologists, chemists, and ecologists, notably Irvin Buss, Michael Schmidt, David Hess, Bruce Schulte, Anthony Hall-Martin, and V. Krishnamurthy, over three decades to bring us a detailed picture of the anatomy, histology, physiology, chemistry, and behavior associated with chemical communication in elephants, especially the Asian species. Much of the work on chemical communication relates to signaling between the sexes for mating. Thus, the physiological and behavioral attributes of chemical signaling as they relate to reproduction are dealt with in chapter 3. In this section, I provide the background to the anatomical structures associated with chemical production and detection, the chemistry and function of the compounds, and only a brief account of the associated physiology and behavior.

The compounds that act as signals in elephant communication are produced and released from several parts of the body. Research is just beginning on secretions from the elephant's skin itself. Asian elephants have been observed exuding liquid around the toes on hot days. Recently, it has been established that Asian elephants possess well-developed sweat glands in the interdigital region, presumably for secreting liquids that contain chemical messages. A specialized skin gland, the temporal gland, is of course a very visible producer of chemical secretions. Located on each side of the head in the temporal depression, this modified apocrine sweat gland opens to the cheek surface through a thick-walled duct. The gland itself, lying just below the skin, consists of numerous lobules joined by connective tissue. A network of smaller ducts interconnects the lobules and leads into the main duct, which expels secretions in both male and female elephants. The temporal glands also release gaseous compounds that may act as signals. Messages may also be broadcast through saliva produced by glands in the oral cavity and by the mucous-lined trunk through expelled breath. The urogenital tract is also an important source of chemical signals released in urine or through cervical mucus (in females) and accessory sex glands.

The trunk of the elephant has a more complex structure than earlier believed (fig. 4.12). Its role in chemosensory function is only partially understood. The specialized vibrissae or hair on the dorsal trunk tip, although mainly tactile in function, may also play a chemosensory role (fig. 4.8). The long nostril passages have an olfactory membranous lining that clothes the well-developed ethmoturbinates and nasoturbinates. The epithelial cells associated with these turbinates are the smell receptors. The elephant's nose is believed to be five times as sensitive as that of a bloodhound, a remarkable olfaction capacity. Running through the trunk are the facial nerves and the maxillary branch of the trigeminal nerve. The elephant possesses one of the most developed trigeminal systems, with nerve endings that are important in detecting noxious compounds.

Two other chemosensory organs in the elephant have to be mentioned. The first is the vomeronasal organ (or Jacobson's organ) found in many amphibians, reptiles, and nonprimate mammals. In the elephant, the vomeronasal organ is a paired tubular structure (about 4 cm in diameter) located on the roof of the mouth (fig. 4.13). It is surrounded by connective tissue and cartilage and partially embedded in the vomer bone. This organ seems to be the key detector of chemical signals in less-volatile liquid substances such as urine. Small samples of the substance are transferred via the trunk tip to the roof of the mouth by the so-called flehmen response. From there, the neuroreceptors of the vomeronasal organ transmit the information to higher brain centers for identification. The vomeronasal organ is especially important in processing signals relating to reproduction, such as detection of the estrous chemical signal in female urine by bulls. At the same time, it also seems to play a role, through the

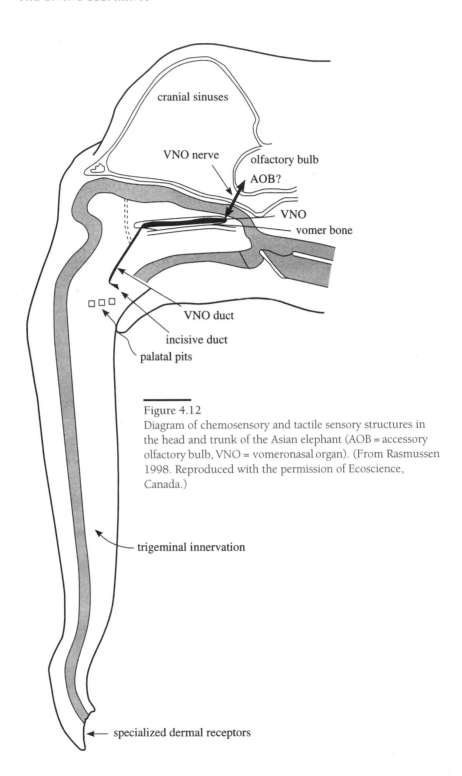

Figure 4.12
Diagram of chemosensory and tactile sensory structures in the head and trunk of the Asian elephant (AOB = accessory olfactory bulb, VNO = vomeronasal organ). (From Rasmussen 1998. Reproduced with the permission of Ecoscience, Canada.)

Figure 4.13
The pair of vomeronasal
organs located on the roof
of an elephant's mouth.
(Photo courtesy of L.E.L.
Rasmussen.)

flehmen response, in other contexts, such as male-to-male and male-to-female
musth signals and female-to-female signals of social significance.

The other possible chemoreceptor system is the palatal pits, which are
small paired structures, numbering from 5 to 21, located at the junction of the
trunk and the hard palate. The palatal pits seem involved in the commonly
observed trunk-to-mouth contacts by individuals within a family. Although
some of this contact may be tactile, it is certain that chemical signals are being
transmitted through breath.

A bewildering array of chemical compounds may be present in the temporal gland secretion (TGS), exhaled breath, or excreted urine. It is not an easy
task to find the specific identity of the compounds that act as biological signals
in a given context. The first task is to identify the precise chemical nature of
the compounds released, then identify likely candidates for bioactivity before
carrying out field trials with elephants to recognize their possible signaling
function. This is precisely what Bets Rasmussen and her associates have been
doing for over three decades—a combination of sophisticated laboratory chemistry, field behavioral trials, and observation in captive and wild situations.
They have so far focused on temporal gland secretions, breath, and urine in
the context of sexual signals. Most of their work pertains to the Asian species
unless stated to the contrary (table 4.4).

Secretion from the temporal glands of male Asian elephants when they
come into musth, a rutlike sexual state, has been described since ancient times
(see chapter 3). Female Asian elephants, too, on occasion secrete from their
temporal glands. I have seen this happen only when a cow is in an advanced

Table 4.4
Conspecific chemical signals of Asian elephants: exudate-elicited behaviors and identified compounds.

Directionality→	Exudate (Putative Pheromone)	Chemosensory response* (Observed Behavior) [Postulated Intent]	Receiver (Olfactory System)
Female→ male	Urine: preovulatory ((Z)-7-dodecenyl acetate)	Flehmens: high frequency (Precopulatory behaviors) [Concentration assessment]	Mature males (Sequentially MO, VNO)
Female→ female	Urine: follicular	Checks and flehmens (Aggression) [Estrous detection]	Mature female, follicular stage (MO and VNO)
	UG mucus: prior LH-1	Checks (Sender: tail flicking maximum) [Detection: impending estrus]	Mature female, follicular stage (MO and VNO)
Male→ female	Urine: musth	Approaches, checks, places (Reciprocal urination, vocalizations, tail erect) [Assessment of musth status]	Mature female, follicular stage (MO and VNO?)
	Secretions: TG† (Whole)	Flehmens	Mature females: (MO and VNO)
	(Cyclohexanone)	Checks, flehmens	Subordinate females: (MO, VNO, palatal pits)
	(C$_5$–C$_9$ Ketones)	Sniffs, repulsion	Subordinate female: (MO)
	(Frontalin)	Attraction / Indifference / Moderate repulsion	Mature female, follicular stage (MO) / Mature female in luteal stage (MO) / Pregnant female (MO)

Source	Secretion	Response	Recipient
Male→ male	Urine: musth	Attraction	Most males (MO)
		Flehmen	Young males (VNO)
	Breath: musth	Deterrent	Teenage males (MO)
		Sniffs	Males
		Retreat [Spacing]	Subordinate, nonmusth males
	Secretion: TG (Whole)	Repulsion	Teenage males
		Attracted, indifferent, repelled	Adult males
		Indifferent	Adult males
	(Frontalin)	Flehmen, check, retreat	Teenage males
Mother→ offspring	Maternal urine	Flehmen	Offspring
			(VNO)

Source: Modified from Rasmussen (1998), courtesy L.E.L. Rasmussen.

LH-1, first serum luteinizing hormone elevation; MO, main olfactory system; TG, temporal gland; UG, urogenital; VNO, vomeronasal organ system.

*Significantly elevated over controls.

†In male Asian elephants only during musth.

stage of pregnancy or just after calving (fig. 4.14). It is therefore not unreasonable to attribute a communication function to this secretion. Given that the
protection of a newborn and allomothering are important within elephant family groups, an adult cow could be communicating this need to other family
members.

Among African elephants, or at least those in savanna and woodland habitats, both males and females secrete rather freely from their temporal glands,
often in response to disturbance, such as being chased. The scientific literature
on the African species was initially rather confused on this subject. Elephant
observers during the 1960s and 1970s loosely termed this as musth in both
the sexes. They further postulated that temporal gland activity or musth had
entirely different functions in the Asian elephant and the African elephant, a
sexual role in males of the former and a more general communication function
in both sexes of the latter species. An article on Amboseli's elephants by Joyce
Poole and Cynthia Moss in 1981 cleared this confusion. They firmly estab-

Figure 4.14
Female elephants secreting
from their temporal glands.
While female African
elephants (*top*) seem to secrete temporin quite freely,
Asian females (*bottom*) do so
only when in advanced stage
of pregnancy or soon after
calving.

lished that African bull elephants also come into musth, with the accompanying physical and behavioral traits with strong sexual overtones, as do their Asian counterparts. Secretion from the temporal glands of African bulls in musth is different from the secretion of immature and adult females and males at other times, which should be termed *temporin*. The temporin possibly plays a role in communication among individuals in a social group, as suggested above.

The early studies of temporin in African elephants by Irvin Buss and his associates focused on analysis of proteins and lipids (chiefly the steroid cholesterol), but later turned to the phenols, cresols, and the sesquiterpenes. Three sesquiterpenes (farnesol and two derivatives) were initially isolated from the temporal gland secretions of mature African elephants culled at Kruger National Park, South Africa. Prior to sample collection, these elephants had been stimulated into secretion by chasing them from a helicopter, thereby inducing stress. Recently, Thomas Goodwin identified two more farnesol-related compounds, one a bumblebee pheromone never seen before in a mammal, and the other known only from a Greek variety of the tobacco plant.

Although not much is known about temporal gland secretions in female Asian elephants, over the years Bets Rasmussen has been assembling chemical profiles of volatiles from temporal glands of individuals in various physiological states. Two sick females dying from foot infection had high levels of isoprenes and ketones in addition to phenols. Some of the pregnant females had high levels of aldehydes. A female that secreted when she ran excitedly had an interesting compound that is a precursor of a farnesol. Secretions from the temporal gland, either visible liquids (temporin) or gaseous volatiles, may thus provide information to other members of the family group about health, physiological status, and stress.

Temporal gland secretions from musth bulls also contain a variety of lipids, proteins, steroids, and other organic volatile compounds, many of which are also seen in exudates of other mammals. The lipids in TGS include cholesterol, while protein concentrations may vary from about 25 mg/ml (in one Asian bull sample analyzed by P. S. Easa) to about twice this figure in African bulls. TGS in musth bulls also shows very high concentrations of testosterone, the male sex hormone, compared to its levels in blood serum during the same phase. None of these compounds, however, has demonstrated bioactivity as chemical signals, although they could in principle serve as long-duration signals given their greater persistence. For this, we should turn toward the volatile compounds, a mixture of several alcohols, ketones, dienes, and aldehydes found in TGS. All these are also seen in musth breath and urine, with the addition of several hydrocarbons in breath and furans in both (table 4.4).

Not all of these volatiles, however, may convey a specific message or evoke a response from other elephants. A signal about the musth status of a bull may be contained in some of these volatiles, either singly or in combination. It is not clear which of these volatiles are responsible for causing other nonmusth males to avoid a musth male, a behavior observed frequently in the wild. A complex natural mixture of 10 compounds, including 8 ketones, an alcohol, and frontalin, elicited a distinct retreat response from subordinate and young female elephants during trials. These compounds of low molecular weight and high volatility (thus short-duration signals) are not seen in exudates of females or nonmusth males.

As a bull goes through various phases of musth, the chemical composition of the signals may also change. The TGS of young Asian bulls in musth have sweet-smelling ("honeylike") compounds, such as esters and 3-hexen-1-ol, that are not detected in the TGS of older bulls. Among the older animals, the chemical 2-butanone seems to signal the premusth period before TGS is visible. Compounds such as the frontalins and 2-nonanone, which are foul smelling, appear in the TGS of older bulls, especially during late musth.

A compound found in trace amounts in musth TGS and urine was fortuitously discovered to act as a male-to-female signal. This ketone of higher molecular weight, cyclohexanone, elicited a high frequency of flehmen responses from subordinate female elephants, although the response from dominant females was less. In fact, the females responded with a greater frequency when presented with an extract of cyclohexanone compared to the original male urine. Another behavior noticed when a group was exposed to this compound was a tendency for adult cows to bunch protectively around the juveniles. Males do not respond to this compound.

The search for a compound that acts as a female-to-male signal of estrous status led to a remarkable discovery by Bets Rasmussen and her associates. Among captive elephants, it was well known that bulls pay increasing attention to cows as the cows approach their estrous periods. While a bull may regularly test the urogenital region or the urine of a cow, the frequency of flehmen responses increases about 10-fold when the cow is in estrus. The chemical released in preovulatory urine by female Asian elephants to signal their estrous state has been identified as (Z)-7-dodecen-1-yl acetate (Z7-12:Ac), a compound of low molecular weight and high volatility.

The location and the biochemical pathway of synthesis are not known, although it is speculated that the acetate is produced in the liver. The playback experiments also show that a full response from Asian male elephants is obtained only when this acetate is presented in the medium of control urine, thereby suggesting that other compounds may be important for the estrous signal (fig. 4.15). Free Z7-12:Ac in urine will gradually combine with water to form the alcohol Z-7-dodecenol. Proteins can bind to the acetate and prolong its pheromonal lifetime. Many other volatile compounds are also released in urine. While some of these elicit a mild response, it is not yet clear whether any of these act singly or as cofactors with Z7-12:Ac in signaling reproductive condition. An odorant binding protein (OBP), similar to a class of compounds known as lipocalins, has been recently isolated from mucus in the elephant's trunk. The OBP is believed to regulate the transfer of acetate from urine to the vomeronasal organ during the flehmen response.

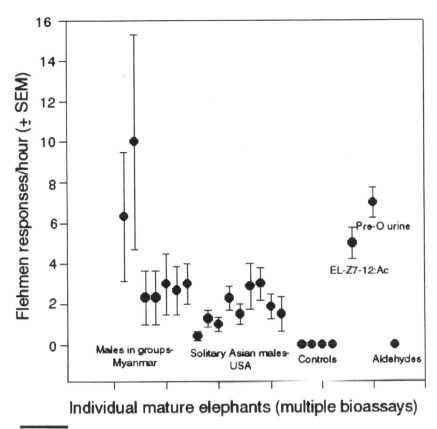

Figure 4.15
Bioassays of the female estrous signal, 1.0 mM (Z)-7-dodecen-1-yl acetate, tested on
Asian bull elephants in Myanmar timber camps and in U.S. zoos. The results are
expressed as mean (±SE) flehmen responses per hour. Note that with the "control"
elephants, a full response was obtained only when the acetate was presented in
(preovulatory) urine. (From Rasmussen 1998. Reproduced with the permission of
Ecoscience, Canada.)

The same compound (Z7-12:Ac;) is used by many female insects, especially the Lepidoptera (moths and butterflies), as pheromones to attract mates,
an amazing example of convergent evolution. Interestingly, African male elephants hardly respond to Z7-12:Ac; female *Loxodonta* must thus be using a
different compound to attract mates.

Several other aspects of chemical communication in elephants are poorly
understood. Female elephants provide information to other females about their
estrous state through urine, but the identity of the compounds is not known.

This signaling could be for social reasons within elephant family groups or for promoting synchrony of estrous periods among females. The role of chemical signals in interindividual recognition among elephants needs to be explored further. In this long-lived species, it can be expected that social interactions would be based on individuals recognizing each other in the long term. There is already some evidence that an elephant calf can recognize its mother from her urine. This chemical memory from early imprinting may be retained for years or decades. In fact, bulls even show reduced flehmen response to the estrous urine of their mother several years after separation from her. This could be one mechanism for avoiding inbreeding irrespective of the precise nature of male dispersal from the natal family. Further research on chemical communication in captive elephants and the corroboration of results when possible in a wild situation would undoubtedly uncover fascinating new details about elephant society.

4.4   Home range of elephants

Every animal describes, in the words of Robin Baker, an invisible "lifetime track" in space. Animals move for feeding, finding mates, avoiding predators or conspecific competitors, avoiding unfavorable environmental conditions, and so on. From the time of its birth, an animal establishes a familiar area or "home range" through its movement. Among elephants, this familiar area is determined in prepubertal individuals by the movement behavior of the matriarch. A bull that disperses from the family will establish its own familiar area. Extension of familiar area of an elephant unit may occur throughout its life, both by its own exploratory movement and through social contact with neighboring groups. Once such a familiar area is established, the movement within this area may be largely a "calculated" movement based on previous experience. Robin Baker argues that the movement strategy of an animal should aim at "increasing the ratio of calculated to non-calculated movement" (1978, p. 45).

The ranging behavior of elephants is obviously strongly influenced by their need for water and forage of a certain type and quality (chapter 5). Much less is known about how movement patterns and home ranges are influenced by social mechanisms such as male dispersal, female philopatry, breeding, and interfamily or intermale competition. We do have a fairly good idea of home range area (varying by two to three orders of magnitude!) and the major ecological determinants of this size. But our understanding of the social determinants of the "familiar area" of elephant groups is still very inadequate. Part of the reason is the sheer logistics of having to organize and sustain the simultaneous monitoring of a large enough sample of elephant groups over a sufficiently large area and a long period of time. Possibly the most comprehensive monitoring of this type carried out by Rowan Martin at Sengwa in Zimbabwe about two decades ago remains largely unpublished and unavailable to a wider audience. Even if this study had the potential to answer many of the unknown facets of social organization in elephants, the subsequent culling of elephants at Sengwa has altered the basic social fabric at Sengwa.

This brings up the questions of how and where to understand the "natural" ranging pattern and social organization of elephants. Obviously, these would vary with habitat type and local ecology, but even within a given range, it is increasingly difficult to find populations with habitats that have not been transformed by humans. This is especially true of Asia, but is also increasingly so in Africa. While it is important to study the overall ecology of a species under relatively natural conditions, this is all the more important for studying movement, home range, and social organization. This would provide the base line information needed for understanding how human influences on elephant habitats and, more directly, on populations would alter the behavior of the elephants.

4.4.1   Home range size

The big-game hunting literature of colonial Asia and Africa has many tales of the propensity of elephants to trek long distances using well-trodden paths, often across steep mountain slopes. Elephant bulls and family herds usually restrict their daily movements, as measured in a straight line, to a few kilometers or at most 10–20 km, but exceptional distances of 90–180 km have been observed in the dry Etosha region of Namibia. Of greater ecological interest is the range size of elephants on a seasonal or annual basis. Some of the earlier scientific studies in both continents used observations of resightings of elephants identified from morphological features or painted with numbers to obtain crude estimates of home range size. In one such early study, Don Rodgers and William Elder immobilized and conspicuously marked 37 male elephants in Zambia's Luangwa Valley. Though home range areas could not be obtained from subsequent resightings, one observation was that the bulls were relatively sedentary during the dry season, staying close to permanent water, and moving over longer distances with the coming of rains.

The early studies of the Sri Lankan elephant, in the northwest of the island by John Eisenberg and Melvyn Lockhart and in the southeast by George McKay, indicated small home ranges, on the order of a few tens of square kilometers. Recognizing the limitations of chance resightings of identified elephants, I estimated minimum home ranges of 105–115 km^2 for two clans and 170–320 km^2 for three bulls in the Biligirirangans of southern India. Assuming that elephant clans utilized the entire area of habitat types in which they were sighted, I suggested that their home ranges could be about 250 km^2. Based on a much larger number of resightings, Ajay Desai later came up with figures of 111–266 km^2 for three clans in the adjoining Nilgiris.

It was only after radiotelemetry was perfected and used to track elephants over periods exceeding an annual movement cycle that an objective picture of ranging behavior and home range size emerged (table 4.5). One of the earliest applications of radiotagging to elephants was at Lake Manyara National Park

Table 4.5
Home range sizes of elephants based on telemetry studies. The range sizes are based on 100% minimum convex polygon (MCP).

Region/Country	Female Home Range (km^2)		Male Home Range (km^2)		Source
	Mean	Range (n)	Mean	Range (n)	
African elephant					
Lake Manyara NP, Tanzania	~40	14–52 (?)	—	—	Douglas-Hamilton (1972)
Tsavo NP, Kenya					
Tsavo West	409	369–448 (2)	>843	—	Leuthold (1977b)
Tsavo East	2,380	1,009–2,975 (5)	1,182	516–1,756 (4)	
Kruger NP, South Africa	436	?	—	—	Hall-Martin (1984)
Zambezi Valley, Zimbabwe	178	37–380 (8)	—	—	Dunham (1986)
Etosha-Kaokoland, Namibia	5,860	2,136–10,738 (7)	—	—	Lindeque and Lindeque (1991)
Laikipia-Samburu, Kenya			—	—	Thouless (1996)
Ranch	121	102–143 (3)	—	—	
Ewaso Ngiro	1,967	1,567–2,294 (3)	—	—	
Lewa	1,414	624–2,180 (3)	—	—	
Migrant	4,348	2,650–5,527 (6)	—	—	
Mathews	1,180	953–1,406 (2)	—	—	

Location					Reference
East Transvaal, South Africa	238	115–465 (11)	238	67–342 (14)	De Villiers and Kok (1997)
Waza NP, Cameroon					Tchamba et al. (1994, 1995)
Resident	785	785 (1)	—	—	
Migrant	2,775	2,484–3,066 (2)	—	—	
Dzanga-Nouabaie, Central African Republic and Congo	880	880 (1)	—	—	Blake et al. (2001)
Amboseli NP, Kenya	—	—	175	140–210 (2)	Douglas-Hamilton (1998)
Asian elephant					
Nilgiris, India	551	531–800 (3)	293	211–235 (2)	Baskaran et al. (1995)
West Bengal, India					
Northwestern	3,708	3,708 (1)	—	—	Chowdhury et al. (unpublished)
Buxa-Jaldapara Reserves	450	232–618 (4)	—	—	Sukumar et al. (unpublished)
Rajaji NP, India	267	~100–400 (4)	—	—	Williams (in review)
	34	34 (1)	200	200 (1)	Joshua and Johnsingh (1995)
Ruhuna NP, Sri Lanka	100	61–121 (3)	—	—	Fernando and Lande (2000)

Only telemetry studies that have followed elephants for longer than about 8 months are reported here; for other studies, see text. n refers to sample size of animals observed. The home range sizes at Lake Manyara do not seem to be 100% MCP, but are obviously small. The sample size of locations for the study in the Zambezi Valley are small (mostly <10) and should be interpreted cautiously. NP, National Park.

in Tanzania during the late 1960s by Iain Douglas-Hamilton. His findings of small home range sizes of only 14–52 km^2 for several family units probably reflect, in part, a confinement within a valley bordered by human settlements, a large lake, and a steep escarpment, although the last-mentioned feature is not a true barrier. At the same time, it must be recognized that Lake Manyara is also a very productive habitat for elephants.

The first detailed telemetry study of elephant home range, involving a large sample of elephants, was by Walter Leuthold and John Sale (1973) in the Tsavo National Park of Kenya. The home ranges of two female-led groups averaged over 400 km^2 in the western region, while in the drier eastern region, the ranges of five female groups followed for over 6 months were much higher (average 2,400 km^2) and more variable. Four male elephants tracked in Tsavo East averaged less than 1,200 km^2, which was smaller than the female ranges. Both the female and male home ranges showed considerable overlap within themselves and across the sexes.

More recently, another detailed telemetry study by Chris Thouless in the Laikipia-Samburu region of Kenya, outside formal protected areas, revealed interesting variation at the population level (fig. 4.16). Several elephants were radio-collared over a wide variety of habitats within this large population range. The home ranges of 20 collared females followed for at least 9 months varied from about 100 km^2 to over 5,500 km^2, with the five subpopulations these represented having similar variation in average range sizes. This is one of the widest variations in elephant home ranges demonstrated within one population. Here again, there was overlap in the ranges of females from different subpopulations, and occasionally these family units were even seen in the same elephant group. Overall, there was a negative relationship at Laikipia-Samburu between home range size and rainfall, although the rainfall varied only twofold (400–750 mm per year) compared to a 50-fold variation in the home range size.

A similar variation in range size was also seen in female elephants in semi-arid northern Botswana tracked during 1992–1994 through satellite and very-

---

Figure 4.16 (*facing page*)
Home range sizes (minimum convex polygons) in female elephants monitored through radio telemetry. (*a*) Representative home ranges for each of six elephant subpopulations in Laikipia-Samburu region of Kenya. The scale is the Universal Transverse Mercator (UTM) grid. (Simplified from Thouless 1996. Reproduced with the permission of Blackwell Science Ltd., U.K.) (*b*) Home ranges of three elephant clans in the Nilgiris in southern India. The region around Ooty is a raised plateau under settlement; hence, only the hatched forest area actually used by one of the clans is shown. The forest divisions shown are Bandipur National Park (BNP), Coimbatore Forest Division (CFD), Mudumalai Wildlife Sanctuary (MWS), Nagarahole National Park (NNP), Nilgiri North Forest Division (NFD), Satyamangalam Forest Division (SFD), and Wyanad Wildlife Sanctuary (WWS). (From Baskaran et al. 1995. Reproduced with the permission of the Bombay Natural History Society, India.)

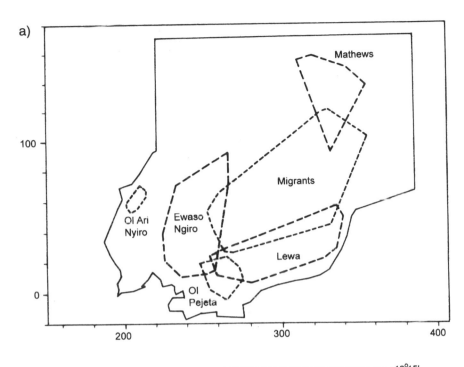

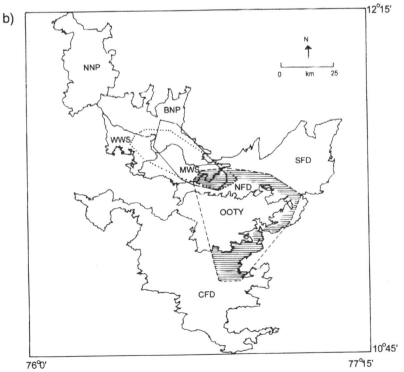

high-frequency (VHF) telemetry by A. Verlinden and I.K.N. Gavor (1998). Two types of movements by the female groups were seen. Some groups were mostly resident close to water sources and had smaller home ranges compared to others that were migratory and moved between specific dry and wet season habitats. Average home range sizes are possibly not very meaningful when the enormous variation, from as low as 50 km^2 to as much as 6,400 km^2, recorded for this population is considered. Sample sizes of locations were very low in this study, but nevertheless the differences are clear given the rainfall variation of only 450–650 mm/year across this range. The Kruger National Park in South Africa has a very similar rainfall variation (375–750 mm/year), but a much smaller variation in elephant home range size was recorded by Anthony Hall-Martin.

Adjacent to Kruger, the female elephants monitored through telemetry by P. A. De Villiers and O. B. Kok in several private nature reserves showed even lower variation. While five females collared at Timbavati Private Nature Reserve had a mean home range of over 400 km^2, similar to the Kruger average, another six females in Klaserie Private Nature Reserve had a smaller mean range of less than 200 km^2. In both regions, the variation in range size was low. The more interesting ranging patterns from this study pertain to the large numbers of male elephants that were monitored. Three categories of males could be discerned on the basis of their movement strategies. Some males used the same home range during the 5 years of study, others shifted their home range every year, while yet others relocated their ranges intermittently during 1 or more years. Such variations in movement patterns of bull elephants had been suspected earlier, but this was the first convincing demonstration.

Two studies of the desert elephant in southwestern Africa deserve special mention. The Namib Desert region extending over the Kaokoland and Damaraland westward into Etosha National Park receives only 20 mm rainfall annually in the driest regions of the east, with an upper figure of 350 mm in parts of the west. A small population of the desert elephant ranges over a region receiving about 50–150 mm rain annually. The first study of this population during 1980–1983 by P. J. Viljoen, through aerial tracking of identified individuals, came up with home range sizes of 1,876 km^2 for females and 2,780 km^2 for two bulls. These are roughly similar to the range sizes in Tsavo East. A second study in northwestern Namibia, this time through satellite telemetry, by M. Lindeque and P. M. Lindeque came up with the largest home ranges ever recorded for elephants. Four females from Kaokoland had an average range size of over 5,000 km^2, while three females from Etosha had a range size of nearly 7,000 km^2. The smallest size recorded was 2,136 km^2 and the largest 10,738 km^2. Even if these older satellite fixes may be prone to some error, the movements of desert elephants undoubtedly cover by far the longest distances of any elephant population.

The earliest attempt to determine home range sizes of Asian elephants through radiotelemetry was in the rain forests of peninsular Malaysia during 1975–1976 by Robert Olivier. Given the difficulties in tracking elephants through rain forest, even from an aircraft, the few observations and the short duration of the study preclude any but a bare minimum estimate. A radiotelemetry study of Asian elephants in the medium rainfall, seasonal deciduous forests of the Nilgiris in southern India during 1991–1993 by N. Baskaran, A. Desai, and associates provided the first detailed account of home ranges in this species (fig. 4.16). With an average home range of 650 km², the three female elephants followed initially over a 2-year period showed relatively low variance. This was about threefold the earlier estimates by Desai of some of the same elephants in this region. The female home ranges also overlapped considerably. A tuskless adult bull had a range of 211 km², while a younger bull that had dispersed from its family ranged over a larger area of 375 km². These were smaller than those of any of the female group range areas.

Two other studies in South Asia provide interesting variations to the above patterns. The first, during 1996–1998 in the eastern dry zone of Sri Lanka by Prithiviraj Fernando, revealed surprisingly small home ranges among family groups. Four female groups followed through telemetry had a mean range size of only 90 km². Another study by Christy Williams and A.J.T. Johnsingh during a similar period and with a similar number of females in the Rajaji National Park along the Himalayan foothills in northern India came up with a figure between the Sri Lankan and the southern Indian figures.

While there is now a fair idea of movement patterns and home range sizes in the low-to-medium rainfall regions of Africa and Asia, there is still a paucity of information from the high-rainfall zones of the two continents. One female African forest elephant (*L. africana cyclotis*) monitored through Global Positioning System (GPS) telemetry by Stephen Blake in the aseasonal rain forests of the Dzanga Sangha region of Central African Republic and Congo ranged over 880 km² within a year. Two female forest elephants monitored through satellite collars by James Powell in Cameroon had an average home range of 266 km². The actual range sizes are likely to be somewhat larger as one of the elephants was tracked for only 8 months. One bull tracked for over a year had a larger range of 528 km². Four female Asian elephants being followed by my research team in the high seasonal rainfall (about 400 cm/year) area of the Buxa-Jaldapara Reserves in West Bengal State in India had an average annual range of about 450 km² during 2001–2002.

The home range estimates of elephants in the larger and relatively more intact habitats provide the background for understanding movement behavior in the more fragmented and human-impacted habitats. The elephant "population" in central India comprises a series of small, isolated populations within a highly fragmented landscape (see appendix 1). A subpopulation of about 50 elephants that had been largely confined to the Dalma Sanctuary and its environs began to make deep forays eastward into southern West Bengal since 1987 (see chapter 8). Hemant Datye and A. M. Bhagwat, who followed the course of some of these identified elephants, estimated a home range of nearly 3,400 km² for one female clan and an average of about 3,850 km² for two bulls. Much of this area, of course, encompassed agricultural land in which conflict was intense. These elephants were still expanding their range when the study concluded in 1992. A bull attached to a small resident herd, however, had a home range of only about 250 km². Another study by Sushant Chowdhury and associates using telemetry in the fragmented landscape of northern West Bengal recorded a range of about 450 km² for one female group during the noncrop season. This expanded considerably during the two crop seasons to give an overall range size of 3,700 km², much of it again agricultural land, over the year. This elephant group ranged to the west of the more compact Buxa-Jaldapara Reserves, where my team recorded a smaller range size.

A similar pattern has been observed by Martin Tchamba and colleagues in the relatively fragmented elephant range of northern Cameroon. A female group that was resident in the Waza National Park had a home range of 785 km², while two other groups that moved between seasonal ranges and came into conflict with agriculture had a mean range size of 2,775 km².

4.4.2   Ecological determinants of range size

What are the ecological correlates of home range sizes in elephants, and what do these patterns tell us about the social dynamics of elephant groups? Before we examine the patterns in range size within or across elephant populations, it is useful to look briefly at the biological determinants of home range among mammals in general and, more specifically, among herbivorous mammals. One approach taken by several biologists, and championed by ecologist Robert H. Peters, is to derive allometric relations between body size and ecological attributes such as home range (this broader theme is explored in more detail in chapter 5). A general form of the relationship can be given by

$$\text{Home Range} = \text{Constant} \times \text{Body Weight}^b$$

The general relationship then becomes the starting point for exploring the more complex variations. It can be intuitively expected that larger animals have larger home ranges. Based on a study of small mammals, Brian McNab suggested in 1963 that home range scales with body weight in a manner similar to that of basal metabolic rate (BMR) and body weight (M. Kleiber had earlier demonstrated BMR to scale as $W^{0.75}$). He thus concluded that home range size in mammals is determined by their rate of metabolism or energetic needs.

Several comparative studies have since provided new insights into ecological influences on home range. Carnivorous mammals have larger home ranges than herbivorous mammals of similar size (this was also recognized by McNab in terms of "hunters" versus "croppers"). The more interesting finding has been that the exponent relating body weight to home range is much greater than the value of 0.75 established for basal metabolic rate (or even average daily metabolic rate, which is similar to BMR and significantly less than 1.0). For herbivorous mammals, R. H. Peters gave the relationship as

$$\text{Home Range} = 0.032 \ W^{1.0}$$

while A. S. Harestad and F. L. Bunnell gave a very similar exponent of 1.02 based on North American species. Incorporating a new measure of time into home range use, R. K. Swihart and associates derived an even higher exponent of 1.56 for McNab's croppers. For female home range sizes (expressed in km^2) among large African herbivores, N. Owen-Smith derived the relationship as

$$\text{Home Range} = 0.0135 \ W^{1.25}$$

An exponent greater than about 0.75 indicates that home range size increases with body size more rapidly than does metabolic rate with body size. One explanation for this is that the mean abundance of resources within the home range decreases with larger area as these include blanks or patches of low productivity. J. Damuth has argued that the home range area of larger animals is shared with more individuals of the same species (i.e., greater range overlap); hence, there is the need to cover even larger areas to obtain the necessary resources. Home range areas may thus have to be transformed to an individual basis before making comparisons across species. Michael Reiss provides a concise review of several of these ideas in a 1988 article.

What do some of these theoretical relationships imply for elephant home ranges? One interesting observation is that the predicted home range of an adult female elephant (say, 3,000 kg in weight) as computed from the range of exponents and associated functions in the literature goes from the smallest recorded area (about 10 km^2 when using the Kleiber/McNab value of 0.75) to the largest area (about 10,000 km^2 when employing the Swihart value of 1.56). As the majority of elephant populations studied have intermediate-size home ranges, a function such as that derived by Owen-Smith using an exponent of about 1.25 seems to be the most appropriate. We still have to seek explanations for the wide variation in elephant home range sizes both across and within populations.

One obvious pattern that emerges when home range sizes across elephant populations are considered is a negative relationship between rainfall and range size (fig. 4.17). As the annual rainfall increases, the home range area of female elephants decreases. Actually, this is not a simple linear relationship, but one that scales linearly as the logarithm of home range versus rainfall. In comparisons of this kind, there are numerous problems. Is total annual rainfall an adequate measure of environmental moisture, or is the seasonal distribution of rainfall more appropriate? How does one derive a figure for rainfall when this itself varies widely across the home range of an elephant group? The elephants themselves may be tracking spatial variation in rainfall over the year. The variability in home range size within a population also has to be considered. Does an average figure adequately represent home range size for a population? We are only just beginning to get information on home range sizes for elephants in the high rainfall regions of the two continents.

In spite of these potentially confounding factors, the rainfall–home range relationship is clear, at least for habitats with very low to medium rainfall. The

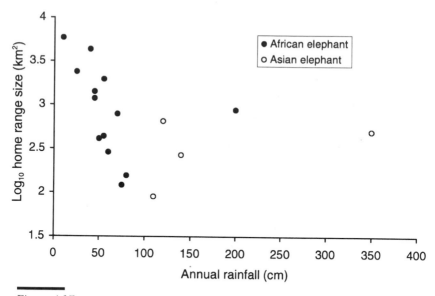

Figure 4.17
The relationship between annual rainfall and home range size in several African and Asian elephant populations (see text). Home range sizes clearly decline with increasing rainfall in the low-to-medium rainfall habitats of African elephants.

simplest explanation for this is that overall productivity decreases and patchiness of nutritional forage (and water) increases with declining rainfall; hence, there is an increase in elephant home ranges. While this may be true for habitats from low-rainfall desert through semiarid savannas and woodlands to deciduous forests with medium rainfall (about 1,000–1,300 mm/year), it is not clear that productivity is indeed higher from an elephant's perspective in the high-rainfall (>2,000 mm/year) areas. In tropical rain forest, for instance, the density and quality of plants palatable to elephants is low even though overall vegetation productivity is high (see chapters 5 and 6). One would then expect a reverse trend in home range size, that is, an increase in tropical moist forest. Unfortunately, our knowledge of elephant movement in tropical rain forests is extremely scant, but we have indications that range size does increase in the moist forests.

Several of the telemetry studies have shown shrinking of home range size during the dry season with expansion during the wet season or during winter. When water or green biomass is scarce, elephants would naturally be confined to small areas where these resources are available. They could also quickly move from one resource patch to another.

Many observers have also noted that female groups are conservative or show fidelity to their home range, at least in the short term of several years. Elephant movement is usually an annual round-trip within this range. This means that an elephant group moving over even long distances comes back to a given locality during a particular season or month (these movements are sometimes precise to the nearest week!).

Elephants seem to track changes in the phenology of vegetation and water availability within their home range and move accordingly. It is not improbable that other tracking mechanisms also operate in elephant movement. I have already mentioned the ability to detect moisture or infrasound from thunderstorms, but it is now well known that animals have navigational abilities based on both terrestrial and celestial cues. We can expect an intelligent, well-traveled animal like the elephant to retain in its memory a detailed "cognitive map" of its home range. Several "experiments" in which elephants, usually problem animals, have been translocated have failed, with the animal returning to its place of capture, sometimes traversing over 200 km through presumably unfamiliar terrain. This certainly suggests a navigational ability that goes beyond a cognitive map of its familiar range.

The evidence so far suggests that, within a population, the home ranges of family groups overlap to varying degrees. However, there may be differences in the time of year when unrelated family groups utilize a particular area of overlap. The observation that several family groups, which associate with each other, also show coordinated movements within a defined home range over the year takes us to the issue of what constitutes such groups. This is still only a partly answered question in elephant social organization, an aspect I deal with below. Depending on the size of such groups, the terms bond/kin groups, clans, and subpopulations have been used from the smaller to the larger groupings. The important question is whether, at the population level, the home ranges of elephants are simply a series of overlapping ranges of individual or a few family groups or whether there exist higher levels of social groupings, each with its unique home range. The association, movement, and spacing of family groups may vary according to population densities, climate, habitat type, and resource distribution.

How can we explain the almost 50-fold variation in home range areas of family groups within a single population observed by Chris Thouless in northern Kenya? At a proximal level, the spatial variation in rainfall can explain some of this variation in home range size. The rainfall, however, varies only twofold across this population, a difference that is common across the range of many other elephant habitats without the accompanying magnitude in variation of home range sizes. One explanation provided by Thouless is that the movements of some of these elephants (or subpopulations) are of recent origin because of disturbances from land-use change and hunting. Elephants having small home ranges within ranches moved to these locations in recent years. Presumably, these ranges could further change in the future.

The short- and the longer-term historical elements in the evolution of elephant home range sizes and spacing of social groups must thus be considered. Even when home range areas of social groups overlap extensively, the temporal partitioning of habitat use suggests avoidance behavior to reduce competition. Home range areas and access to resources within may depend on dominance ranks of matriarchs leading the social groups, an aspect that we are only beginning to understand.

Finally, we must briefly consider how adult male elephant ranges are organized with respect to one another and in relation to female group home ranges. Male home ranges also overlap considerably. The majority of the relatively fewer studies also indicate that adult males have smaller home ranges or smaller core areas than do female groups in the same population. There are, however, some populations, such as Kruger, in which the males clearly have a significantly larger range than do the female groups. The home range of a male also increases substantially when it comes into musth as it searches for estrous females. Bulls may also utilize exclusive habitats (the so-called bull areas) such as steep hill slopes or those considered too marginal or poor in resources for use by female groups. The more intensive use of agricultural areas by bulls also introduces a difference in their movement patterns and home range attributes.

Spatial segregation of the sexes on a seasonal basis has been well documented in several ungulates. One explanation is that, during the nonbreeding season, the males may use certain areas to recuperate their energies in addition to enacting social roles among themselves.

It is important to study male home range over several years or decades beginning with the male's dispersal. Many observers report the sighting of adult bulls not seen earlier over years of watching elephants at particular localities. It is possible that adult bulls may shift their range during their lifetime as opposed to the more conservative behavior of family groups. Of course, all this must remain partly speculative until the "lifetime track" of elephants is studied.

4.5   Social groups and their determinants

4.5.1   Group size dynamics

The size of groups in the larger mammals is a product of social evolution, habitat features, resource availability and dispersion, seasonality, and levels of human disturbance. It is commonly accepted, for instance, that group size is a trade-off between benefits that may accrue from closer social contact and the efficiency of foraging on a limited resource. The term group here does not necessarily imply relatedness among individuals, but merely the close spatial association of members of a population.

With elephants, there are clearly several social benefits to be gained by close association with others (fig. 4.18). Larger elephant groups may also be better able to protect calves and juveniles from predators. On the other hand, the feeding efficiency would decline with increasing group size when nutritive

Figure 4.18
Elephant groups at (*top*) Nagarahole National Park, India, and (*bottom*) Amboseli National Park, Kenya. Group size in both Asian and African elephants is influenced by season, forage availability, density, social needs, and predation pressure.

forage is limited, such as during the dry season. Group size may also be a direct function of random associations of basic societal units, such as mother-offspring. Thus, group size could be positively related to density, which in turn could vary seasonally or across habitat types. Finally, human disturbance in the form of poaching could bring elephants together into larger groups for protection.

Data from across the elephant's range in the two continents show that several of these factors interact in determining group size dynamics of a given population. The various studies are not always directly comparable because of different survey methods used (ground versus aerial counts) and the lack of a clear definition for a group in some cases. Group size data may also be represented by the average size or by the frequency distribution of sizes. Only matriarchal groups are considered here.

The largest elephant group sizes observed are in African savanna populations, such as in East Africa (fig. 4.19). Mean group sizes of over 10 individuals have been commonly recorded in several populations. Very large elephant groups, numbering up to several hundred animals, are also seen here at times. Some of these are not cohesive groups, but represent a loose congregation of several elephant groups, which themselves may be quite large. Richard Laws has suggested that the polymodal frequency distribution of elephant group sizes in savanna habitat could reflect the association of the basic mother-offspring units. Group sizes are more typically in the range of 5–10 individuals in African woodland habitats and in Asian dry forests, such as in southern India. Much smaller mean group sizes of fewer than 5 elephants are characteristic of African rain forests (fig. 4.19).

The simplest explanation possible for the variation in group size across habitat types is food availability and dispersion. Savannas offer an abundance of green biomass in the form of perennial grasses, especially during the wet months, compared to the rain forests, where food plants—a variety of fruits, palms, climbers, and shrubs—are scarce and widely dispersed. The need to avoid competition and increase foraging efficiency in the rain forest habitat would call for smaller group sizes.

Variation between dry season and wet season group sizes within a population also supports the foraging efficiency hypothesis. Walter Leuthold found a consistent positive relationship between rainfall and elephant mean group size during 1965–1973 at Tsavo National Park. Likewise, at Amboseli, David Western and Keith Lindsay observed that elephant herd sizes during 1973–1979 spontaneously increased with the onset of rains and progressively declined through the dry months. A comparison of seasonal group size distributions here during 1985 by Joyce Poole and Cynthia Moss showed that group sizes larger than about 85 elephants were seen only during the wet months.

Other explanations are also possible for variation in elephant group size. Elephants are social animals, and the unit social groups may tend to associate among themselves whenever they meet. Thus, higher elephant density, either in preferred habitat within the range of a population or across the distributional range (savanna versus rain forest), could promote larger group sizes.

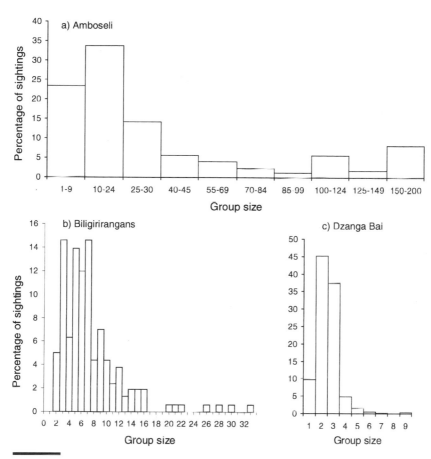

Figure 4.19
Group size frequencies in different elephant populations. (*a*) African savanna elephants in Amboseli, Kenya, during the wet season of 1985. (From Poole and Moss 1989. Reproduced with the permission of the Zoological Society of London.) (*b*) Asian elephants in the deciduous forests of the Biligirirangans in southern India during 1981–1983. (From Sukumar 1985.) (*c*) African forest elephants at Dzanga Bai, Central African Republic, during 1991–1994. (Based on Turkalo and Fay 1995.)

Richard Laws thus found, in North Bunyoro, Uganda, that elephant groups were larger in regions of higher density, but that group sizes did not necessarily vary with season. This is also implicit in Natarajan Ishwaran's observation that Asian elephant group sizes were larger in a Sri Lankan population with a range that had contracted in comparison to another population.

The mean group sizes I recorded during 1981–1983 in the Biligirirangans were clearly larger during the dry season (8.2) and the second wet season (8.8) compared to the first wet season (5.8). My explanation was that elephants tend to congregate at higher densities near water sources within preferred habitat during the dry months, thereby increasing the chances of intergroup contact and association. Their dispersal over a wider area with the onset of the first rains reduced social contact and group sizes. The largest elephant groups were observed during the second wet season, when variability was also the highest. The larger group sizes during the second wet period occurred partly from aggregation of families for movement to lower elevation scrub habitat. Western and Lindsay also observed that the large aggregations of Amboseli elephants occurred immediately following the rains, when food was still scarce, presumably for movement to bushland habitat. Anecdotal accounts of large elephant groups undertaking long-distance migration lend further support to this contention.

Another interesting pattern of group dynamics can be observed in the Nagarahole-Bandipur Reserves of southern India. Elephant groups here begin to frequent the banks of the Kabini Reservoir during the late dry season. The proximate attraction seems to be in part water as well as short grasses that grow along the banks when the reservoir recedes. However, this period is also turned into an opportunity for social interactions among the elephant groups, which can now get quite large. The congregations persist through the premonsoon period, but break up with the arrival of heavy monsoonal rains.

A final point to be considered is that increased group size in elephants is a response to threats from natural predators or humans. The larger group sizes in habitats such as African savannas or Asian forests that harbor the larger predators (the lion and the tiger, respectively) broadly supports this expectation. However, it is difficult to tease out the extent to which antipredatory response influences group size as opposed to other factors, such as food dispersion. The tendency for elephants under hunting pressure to aggregate has also been noticed in East African populations.

Uganda's Queen Elizabeth (Rwenzori) National Park suffered heavily from poaching during the 1970s and 1980s. The mean group size of female herds increased from 5.9 in 1963–1965 to 10.8 by 1976, when Keith Eltringham observed a positive relationship between group size and poaching pressure in different areas of the park. More than a decade later, Eve Abe found that the elephants here had aggregated into two large semipermanent groups. Because poaching had eliminated the older matriarchs, this behavior could have been due to leaderless herds coming together for safety and social needs. In Tanzania's Mikumi National Park, however, a dry season survey in 1992 by K. Γ. Anderson and S. K. Eltringham did not find any evidence for stress-related aggregation of elephants in spite of poaching pressure and lack of older matriarchs.

Thus, elephant groups are not merely random associations of the basic units, but form as a response to specific circumstances and needs. These could be social needs, such as networking among individuals or groups, reinforcing bonds between related members, mating opportunities, or even resource acquisition by kin groups, possibly in addition to seeking safety from predatory or poaching threats. A complex trade-off between these social factors and foraging efficiency in relation to food dispersion could determine elephant group dynamics in a given population.

4.5.2   *Social organization*

The female-centered or matriarchal nature of elephant society was recognized by some astute naturalists of the nineteenth century, in spite of numerous references in the colonial hunting literature to "master bulls" and their likes leading elephant groups. The description of an elephant hunt in 1863 by Victor Brooke and Douglas Hamilton in southern India's Biligirirangans, for instance, alludes to a male-led elephant society. A few years later, however, G. P. Sanderson (1878, p. 46) was to record, from observations in the same region, that an elephant "herd is invariably led by a female, never a male." He considered this a "necessity for the convenience of the mothers of the herd regulating its movement . . . as they must accommodate the length and time of their marches, and the localities in which they rest or feed at different hours, to the requirements of their young ones; consequently the guidance of a tusker would not suit them." Further, he clearly recognized that "each herd of elephants is a family in which the animals are nearly allied to each other." Even earlier, in 1856, the hunter James Chapman had noted in his diary (published in 1971) that the southern African elephants that they are "gregarious and run in herds which separate into families and meet again . . . the males are found separate from the female during most of the year" (quoted in Spinage 1994, pp. 129–130).

A clearer picture of elephant social organization began to emerge from the early scientific studies in East Africa and Sri Lanka. From the population structures of culled elephants in Uganda and Kenya, Richard Laws and his associates recognized that elephants moved in social groups that represent family units comprising closely related individuals. They even constructed kinship diagrams for several cropped herds based on age-sex composition and occurrence of placental scars in adult cows.

Iain Douglas-Hamilton's pioneering study of elephant social organization and behavior at Lake Manyara National Park was the first indication, based on following identified individuals and groups over 4 years, that a stable family unit was the core of elephant society. He defined this family unit as comprising several adult cows and their offspring, including daughters of all ages and sons of prepubertal age. The average size of a family unit was 10 at Manyara. Further, he described a higher level of organization—the kinship group—in which two or more family units had close ties and were often seen together. The formidable matriarch Boadicea's social groups exemplified this situation. While this matriarch led her own family unit (or extended family) of 22 elephants, including 6 breeding cows, she also seemed to be the leader of a larger kinship group that included two other family units, a total of about 40 ele-

phants during the first year. He also observed the process of splitting of Boadicea's family during the third year, when one subgroup of an adult cow, her
young mature daughter, and their three offspring increasingly began to move
independently.

The high degree of stability in the family units or extended families at
Manyara was not seen in other parts of Africa, such as Sengwa and Amboseli,
during subsequent studies. There, the only stable unit seemed much smaller,
consisting of only one adult cow and her immature offspring. The longest-
running study of elephants anywhere, beginning in 1972 at Amboseli by
Cynthia Moss, has given us the most detailed picture of the social relationships
of females and their families. Moss visualizes elephant social organization as
radiating from the family unit "through a multi-tiered network of relationships
encompassing the whole population" (1988, p. 125). Several levels of organization emerge along this axis from the basic unit to the population (fig. 4.20).

Moss illustrates this with the example of the EB family, whose matriarch
is Echo, popularized through a television film. In early 1983, the Amboseli

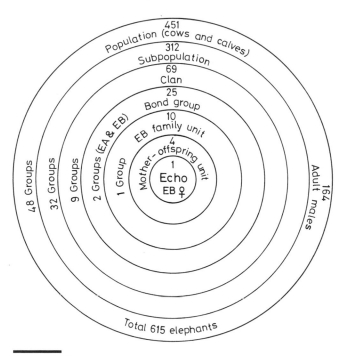

Figure 4.20
Levels of social organization in African elephants at Amboseli,
Kenya, depicted through a multitier network of relationships for
the adult female Echo. (From Moss and Poole 1983. Reproduced
with the permission of Blackwell Publishers Ltd., U.K.)

elephant population stood at 615 elephants—451 elephants in 48 family groups and 164 adult bulls. Echo's mother-offspring unit included three offspring, while her family unit was larger at 10 individuals, including three mother-offspring units. The EB family had been seen in association with each of the other 47 family units in the population, although infrequently with the majority of them. With 19 of these family units, the EB family was seen for more than 15% of the total sightings. Of these, associations with 18 units occurred on 15%–29% of occasions, while with 1 unit, the EA family, this was a significantly higher 53% of sightings. Apart from the spatial closeness of these two families, these elephants also greeted each other with an intensity quite different from greetings with other units. When the two families met after a separation of several hours, their greeting ceremony was accompanied by deep rumbling, trumpeting, screaming, and loud ear flapping. The EA and EB family units thus comprised a bond group, similar to the kin group of Douglas-Hamilton, but without necessarily implying close relatedness between the associating families.

During the dry season at Amboseli, the elephant families were found clustered at several different regions of the park. The families within any single congregation seemed to form a higher level of organization—the clan. This could have been a simple geographical separation of families when dry season home ranges shrank. But the families of a clan have been observed showing aggression toward families of other clans if these intruded into their dry season range. This suggests a biological significance in that matriarchs of higher social rank may defend scarce resources successfully. On the other hand, the families within each clan lived amicably, although they did not necessarily greet each other or form close bonds. Echo was part of a clan that included nine family units. About seven clans utilized Amboseli entirely or partly during the dry season.

The population of elephants at Amboseli could be further resolved into two subpopulations, one of which congregated around the swamps (the "central subpopulation"), while the other was a "peripheral subpopulation." The home ranges of clans overlap considerably. During the wet season, the elephants grouped into larger aggregations and ranged more widely, including over areas outside the park boundaries.

A similar basic social structure has been observed in Asian elephant populations in the dry forests of Sri Lanka and India, although this species has been studied in less detail. The early Sri Lankan studies, by observers like George McKay and Fred Kurt, while recognizing the existence of families of related individuals, used the term *herd* to refer loosely to any elephant group. They further differentiated these into "nursing units" and "juvenile-care units" with a certain degree of spatial separation. Distinct levels of social organization were not explicitly discerned (indeed, they may not exist here).

Charles Santiapillai and associates, also working in southeastern Sri Lanka, used the term *group* to refer to any aggregation of animals, but used *herd* to denote a more cohesive unit of adult cows and offspring. They opined that the larger groups were random associations of the herd units.

My observations in southern India suggested that elephant social groups could be categorized into families, bond groups, and perhaps even clans. The stable family units, however, were small and consisted of only one or two adult cows and their children (fig. 4.21). I therefore suggested that the term *family* is restricted to a single adult cow and offspring unit, while another term, *joint family*, be used to describe larger groups comprising two or more adult cows plus offspring even if these are relatively stable. The existence of bond groups was suspected, but was not based on quantitative data. Over a geographical area of about 1,000 km^2 in the Biligirirangans, I also noted at least five distinct clusters of elephant groups during the dry season. Four of these congregations comprised between 50 and 125 elephants each and corresponded to the clans described at Amboseli. A fifth congregation in a river valley to the southwest of the study area was much larger, with over 200 elephants. This may have been a subpopulation comprised of two or more clans. Baskaran's detailed study of three adult females through telemetry in the Nilgiris also suggested the existence of clans of up to 65 elephants each with overlapping ranges.

Figure 4.21
A family of Asian elephants comprising the matriarch (*extreme left*) and her five offspring of various ages in the Biligirirangans, India.

The few observations in tropical moist forests hinted at a much simpler social organization among elephants in close-canopied forest (fig. 4.22). Confirmation that this is indeed so has come from several years of observations of the African forest elephant (*L. a. cyclotis*) by Andrea Turkalo at a small forest clearing, the Dzanga Bai, in the Central African Republic. Elephants can be seen in this clearing during the late afternoon and night practically every day. An identification file of these elephants has been maintained since 1990 at this site. The overwhelming majority (89%) of family groups that visit the site are units comprising only one adult cow with one, two, or occasionally three offspring. Interestingly, the next most frequent category (10%) has been of solitary females that have passed the reproductive age. Units of two or three adult females with their offspring are seen very rarely. Although there are indications of some form of association or bonding between family groups in a few cases, this is by no means common or evident from behavioral observations at the clearing, unlike the case of savanna elephants. Greeting ceremonies between families have never been observed. There is, however, intense socializing among elephants that gather at the clearing. Much of the social interactions observed here are related to dominance bouts such as at a water hole. Over 2,000 elephants, or a majority of the population in the contiguous Dzanga-Sangha Reserves, visit this clearing; indeed, they may visit several other clearings in the region. Most of the identified groups have been sighted only 1–5 times at the clearing over a 5-year period, indicating a high rate of turnover and perhaps no distinct pattern of movement.

Asian elephants in the rain forests of Peninsular Malaysia again do not seem to have any higher level of organization than the family or bond group. Mohamad Khan's few observations here point to smaller family group sizes than with the populations in the South Asian dry forests, although the groups seem larger than those encountered in the moist forests of Central Africa.

Social relationships of male elephants also can be expected to vary across habitats and populations. The dispersal of a young male from its natal family is related to the age of puberty. This also effectively reduces the chances of inbreeding, although some form of kin recognition through pheromones may also play a role, as does social separation. At Amboseli, the males were observed to become independent of their families at any time between the ages of 10 and 19 years, with an average age of 14 years. In southern India, I also observed most males leading an independent life between ages 10 and 15 years. The dispersal of a young bull may depend both on behavioral development of the bull and on the degree of intolerance shown by its mother or other adult cows in the family group. This is a subject that needs further study.

It is generally agreed that the separation of a male from its family is a gradual process and not an abrupt one. As a male grows older, it spends more and more time in all-male groups or even briefly associates with strange families. By about 14 or 15 years old, the young males at Amboseli spend over 80% of their time away from their families, a stage that can be considered as

Figure 4.22
A typical family of three African forest elephants (*top*) and an adult bull (*bottom*) at Dzanga Bai, Central African Republic. (Photo courtesy of Katharine Payne.)

being independent. Adult females have also been observed showing aggression toward pubertal males, which may hasten their decision to leave the family.

Once a bull disperses from its family, it may range solitarily or in the company of other bulls. Solitariness seems to be the rule in dense forest such as in the Dzanga-Sangha Reserves. Any association between bulls at the clearing lasts for only a few minutes or at most a day. Among Asian elephants in dry forest, the bulls again range mostly solitarily. Data on bull group frequency distributions from Sri Lanka and southern India show that sightings of solitary bulls are by far the most common.

Bulls do associate in groups of two or occasionally more individuals (fig. 4.23). The largest bull group recorded by George McKay in Sri Lanka was seven animals. In southern India, I have observed associations of over two bulls only rarely in several hundred sightings of bull groups, with the largest group being a loosely spaced congregation of eight bulls along the banks of the Kabini Reservoir in the Nagarahole National Park. While there was no evidence for any special bonding between bulls seen in the forest during the day, some bulls associated in pairs for up to a month while raiding agricultural fields at night (see chapter 8).

Figure 4.23
An association of four Asian bull elephants at Nagarahole National Park, India. Such associations are usually quite temporary.

The larger bull groups of over 10 individuals have been recorded exclusively in the African savannas (the largest bull group on record seems to be one of 144 individuals seen by Ian Parker at the Galana Ranch of Kenya). Here, too, the typical association involves only two or three bulls. The nature of the social relationship among associating bulls has naturally attracted the attention of elephant observers. Iain Douglas-Hamilton found the bull groups at Manyara to be very unstable. The longest association of two bulls was merely 14 consecutive days. Bull groups were of ever-changing composition with no evidence of any lasting ties.

The influx of elephants into the Serengeti National Park during the 1960s and, in particular, the destruction of larger trees in the Seronera area by bull groups attracted much attention. These bull associations were studied by H. Hendrichs (cited by Croze 1974a) and later by Harvey Croze. The Seronera bull groups typically had one bull distinctly larger and presumably older than the rest. A close examination of associations among 25 identified bulls showed that, in statistical terms, these were not different from chance associations except in two instances. One such pair spent 51 days moving together, fed "on the same bushes simultaneously, rolled in the same wallows, and even scratched themselves against one another" (Croze 1974a, p. 8). Such observations obviously lend credence to traditional descriptions of friendship bonds between bulls (in northeastern India, such associations, termed locally as *maljuria*, are known from many anecdotal accounts). Eventually, these bulls went their own way.

In Amboseli's more sedentary elephant population, there are stronger hints of associations among bulls. Although the males here do not form stable groups, several pairs have been seen in association; over 30% of the time, each had been observed in the company of a male.

Irrespective of whether the adult bulls range solitarily or in association with other bulls, a complex pattern of changing dominance relationships exists among them. The social relationships depend on frequency of encounter (which in turn is related to habitat, elephant density, and ranging patterns), body size, age, and most important, the sexual state of the bulls. When a bull comes into a state of heightened sexual activity associated with musth, it moves solitarily in search of estrous cows or is seen in the company of female groups (chapter 3). The six oldest bulls at Amboseli were seen solitarily 29% of the time and in association with cow groups 66% of the time on average when in musth. When they were not in musth, the same bulls were seen solitarily 26% of the time and in the company of other bulls 68% of the time. While bulls that are larger or older are generally more dominant, the situation may be reversed when a smaller or younger bull comes into musth. A musth bull shows increased aggression toward other bulls. When bulls are not in musth, they may associate peaceably in bull areas. During such times, the less-aggressive sparring bouts may help decide dominance hierarchies (fig. 4.24). Joyce Poole has suggested that the relationships also may be based on relatedness among bulls. Even when bulls move solitarily, as in tropical moist forests, their visits to

Figure 4.24
Two Asian elephant bulls at Nagarahole National Park, India, lock tusks in a dominance contest. Such contests rarely escalate into a serious fight.

clearings or mineral licks (such as at Dzanga) provide an opportunity to meet and socialize with other bulls.

Finally, we should take a brief look at adult bull associations with cows (this theme is the subject of chapter 3). Male-female associations in elephants are predominantly for the purpose of reproduction. Adult males can successfully mate when they are out of musth, but are far more likely to do so when in musth. At Amboseli, the six oldest bulls that spent two-thirds of their time with cow groups when in musth did so only 7% of the time with cows when out of musth. The available evidence suggests that bulls associate with family groups at random, depending on the presence of an estrous cow. It has been suggested that both cows and bulls may have their preferred partners. This is likely in a long-lived species for which individual recognition plays an important role in social relationships. It would take years of observation of a large number of identified elephants to confirm or reject this speculation.

Before concluding this discussion of male-female relationships by rejecting the "herd bull" concept, we must consider an interesting theoretical possibility. Using a plausible mathematical formulation, Richard Barnes has argued that, in regions of low elephant density, it would be advantageous for an adult bull to be attached to a female group for an extended period of time. Perhaps the last word has not yet been said on this subject.

4.5.3   Genetic evidence for social organization

The observational studies of elephant social relationships have implicitly assumed that association among female groups is directly proportional to relatedness. Thus, in the larger families, the adult cows are related as sisters (or as mother-daughters), those in the kin groups are related as either sisters or cousins, and within a clan as distant cousins, aunts, and so on. Further, it has been generally believed that males establish their own home ranges at some distance away from their natal family or clan after becoming independent. Two recent studies, one in Asia and the other in Africa, using molecular genetic information have come to somewhat different conclusions.

Prithiviraj Fernando and Russell Lande analyzed mitochondrial DNA (mtDNA) sequences in seven female-led groups and several bulls from the Ruhuna National Park and two nearby sites, Uda Walawe National Park (30 km west) and Mirrijjawila (30 km southwest), in southeastern Sri Lanka. After extracting DNA from the dung of these known elephants, they analyzed a 630-nucleotide base pair segment of the D-loop region gene of the mtDNA. Since mitochondrial DNA is maternally inherited, it provides a means to trace maternal lineages (see chapter 1). Thus, individuals with different mitochondrial DNA sequences or "haplotypes" are not related to each other, while those with the same haplotypes may either be related or be unrelated as kin.

All elephants sampled within each of the seven groups had the same mitochondrial haplotype, suggesting that animals constituting a group could very well be related. The social groups, however, showed certain variations in their haplotypes (table 4.6). Two groups at Ruhuna shared the same haplotype (labeled A), while another herd there had a unique haplotype (B). The fourth group sampled at Ruhuna shared a haplotype (E) with another group at Uda Walawe. The second group at Uda Walawe had its unique haplotype (D), and so did the herd at Mirrijjawila (type F). The occurrence of so many different haplotypes in female groups over such short distances is itself rather surprising. The combined results from telemetry (home range and associations) and genetics indicated no higher level of organization than the family group even if these groups are relatively large.

Other surprising results emerged from the haplotype analysis of bull elephants, all of them ranging within the Ruhuna National Park. Although four different haplotypes (A, B, E, and a unique C) were recorded, only 1 of the 11 bulls had a haplotype that differed from those of the female groups that ranged over the same area of the park. Fernando and Lande thus proposed that male dispersal is more limited in terms of distance from the natal area, and that more periodic, long-distance movements of the males during musth could be the mechanism promoting outbreeding.

Table 4.6
The distribution of mitochondrial haplotypes in female-led
elephant groups in southeastern Sri Lanka.

Location	Social Group	Number of Individuals Samples	Mitochondrial Haplotype
Ruhuna NP	Yala I	9	A
Ruhuna NP	Yale II	7	A
Ruhuna NP	Thambarawa	12	B
Ruhuna NP	Katagamuwa	4	E
Uda Walawe NP	Uda Walawe NP I	3	D
Uda Walawe NP	Uda Walawe NP II	4	E
Mirijjawila	Mirijjawila	3	F

Source: From Fernando & Lande (2000). Reproduced with permission of Springer-Verlag
GmbH & Co. KG.
NP, National Park.

Another study of three female groups at Sengwa in Zimbabwe confirmed that these corresponded to clans in the conventional sense. The mtDNA profiles, however, brought another surprise. The members of a clan were not necessarily matrilineally related. Of the two haplotypes found in these clans, two adult females from different families but within the same clan, seemingly associating as a bond group, were of different matrilines. This perhaps was not quite unexpected when Cynthia Moss preferred the term bond group to kin group at Amboseli. The corresponding telemetry data at Sengwa also showed that only some families within a clan coordinated their movements, while others used the space quite independently. A possible explanation is that Sengwa does not represent a natural condition in that large numbers of elephants have been culled in recent times; this may have resulted in significant changes in social organization.

Molecular genetics provides new tools to investigate the social organization of a species. Using both mitochondrial and nuclear DNA profiles, new facets of the mating system, dispersal, relatedness, and social relationships in elephant societies would undoubtedly be unraveled in the coming years.

4.6   *The evolution of elephant society*

The raison d'etre of elephant society has been explained in evolutionary terms as the maximization of the genetic fitness of its members. Cooperation among the larger cows of a family in group defense of young elephants, which are vulnerable to predators such as the tiger in Asia or the lion in Africa, would constitute one such benefit. If group defense is indeed one of the primary functions of elephant families, we could expect larger family groups in regions where predatory threats are greater. The data on family group sizes broadly support this expectation. Larger families are seen in African savannas and in Asian dry forests, where the larger predators are common. In contrast, the small, single-matriarch families are seen in Central African rain forests, which do not have any large predator such as the lion and only low densities of medium-size predators such as leopards.

Group size is also strongly influenced by the availability and dispersion of food resources; the greater the food availability is (as in savannas and dry forests), the larger is the group size. The resources factor in fact could completely obscure any considerations of predatory threat. However, it is interesting to note that elephant family groups are much smaller in Central African rain forests compared to those in Malaysian rain forests, with presumably similar resource availability. The Malaysian forests are home to the tiger, while no predators of comparable size are to be found in African rain forests.

The apparent altruistic behavior of female elephants can be justified by the high degree of relatedness among members of the family; in genetic terms, such behavior enhances the "inclusive fitness" of the donor through "kin selection." After all, by saving a niece or a nephew with whom she shares a significant proportion of her genes, a matriarch also ensures that copies of her genes are passed on to future generations. There is obviously a cost attached to allomothering, especially if this means delayed reproduction through suckling a sibling's calf. Phyllis Lee's observations, however, show that allosuckling is quite rare. In a long-lived species in which individuals recognize not only their immediate kin, but also less-related members within a social group, there is also a high chance of reciprocity in such altruistic behavior. Allomothering thus has to be seen as not only promoting inclusive fitness, but also benefiting from reciprocity.

A stable family also provides the ideal milieu for younger elephants to learn much of their behaviors from the elders. While some of these behaviors, such as knowledge of what plants constitute food, may contribute to longer-term fitness, others (such as the appropriate response to a predatory attack) could be crucial to immediate survival. A calf's brain weighs only 35% of its ultimate weight of about 6 kg during adulthood. This provides considerable scope for learning: What better than an extended stable family setting for a rich learning experience?

We are barely beginning to understand objectively the importance of the leadership role of the matriarch in survival of her family, an aspect that many elephant observers have speculated upon. In a highly social, intelligent, and long-lived animal, the matriarch is virtually an encyclopedia of stored knowledge that her family can draw on. By leading her family or higher social entity to the best foraging and watering grounds on a daily or seasonal basis or rediscovering a water source used in the distant past during a time of drought, the matriarch enhances the fitness of her social group.

While cooperation among adult female elephants has been much emphasized, little attention has been paid to competition among the matriarchs. Competition and conflict, after all, are as much a feature of animal societies as is cooperation, and perhaps they are even more integral to their functioning. Based on her observations in Kenya's Tsavo West National Park during the 1970s, Holly Dublin has drawn attention to several possible arenas of competition among female elephants. All these relate directly or indirectly to the relative reproductive success of female elephants. Antagonistic interactions between female elephants of unrelated social groups have been described by some observers, but their outcome in terms of benefits or costs to the players has never been quantified. A matriarch who successfully defends resources such as food and water, especially at relevant times during the year, could ensure lower mortality and better reproduction within her social group.

Dublin's observations at Tsavo indicated that calves born before the major annual peak in rainfall had a lower mortality than those born after this rainfall peak. Further, she observed that most calves born before the rainfall peak were born to socially dominant mothers, as determined from dyadic interactions, while calves born after the peak were mostly born to subdominant cows. Given the gestation period of about 20–22 months, the inference here is that female elephants that are able to time their ovulation and breeding to coincide with the peak rains, through better access to high-quality forage and mates, would emerge as winners. At the same time, the dominant females would have to suppress the reproductive efforts of other females. At Tsavo, the dominant females seemed to be achieving this goal through increased aggression toward subdominant females. In several mammals, it is well known that intrasexual competition could result in suppression of or delayed ovulation, failed implantation, or even abortion among the subordinate animals. The physiological mechanisms of such action are poorly understood. Dominant females could also monopolize access, through overt and subtle behaviors, to the dominant musth bulls for mating during the most favorable season. How elephant societies achieve the right balance between cooperation and competition is clearly a subject wide open to investigation.

The subject of intelligence in elephants itself has been hardly investigated since the pioneering efforts of Bernard Rensch reported in 1957. The ability of an elephant to understand and respond to a substantial vocabulary of commands from its trainer is legendary. Rensch carried out a series of experiments to actually measure the learning capacity of a 5-year-old female Asian elephant at the Münster Zoo in Germany. The elephant was trained to discriminate among various visual patterns through a system of rewards for the correct response. A surprising result was that the elephant could simultaneously keep in memory the meaning of 20 visual stimulus pairs, having mastered these superbly. The scores in these tests suggested that the elephant could have mastered a bigger vocabulary given more time and training, but the observers felt this would not add any significant information about the animal's learning abilities.

Tool use by an animal is generally considered characteristic of higher intelligence. It is well known that Asian elephants use twigs to scratch their skin and branches as tools to repel flies from parts of the body they cannot reach with their trunks (fig. 4.25). This behavior has also been observed in African elephants, although less frequently. Benjamin and Lynette Hart studied such tool use and its context in captive Asian elephants used for tourist rides in Nepal. They concluded that elephants indeed use branches as switches to dislodge parasitic flies, and this was not merely stereotypic behavior related to confinement. Further, they estimated that fly switching reduced fly count by 43%, a level significant in reducing loss of blood. Elephants also fashioned the branches intelligently to increase their efficiency as tools. The ability of elephants to create images with a paintbrush and colors is also being viewed as a demonstration not only of its manipulative skills, but also its superior discriminatory powers.

Intelligence in the social sphere, especially among the matriarchs, could be an important determinant of biological fitness of their social groups. Perhaps the most exciting new research on this subject is that of Karen McComb, who worked with Cynthia Moss and other associates at Amboseli. Their playback experiments of infrasonic calls revealed an unusually high ability among

Figure 4.25
A captive Asian elephant uses a branch for switching flies off its skin. Such tool use is indicative of higher intelligence in mammals. (Photo courtesy of Ben Hart.)

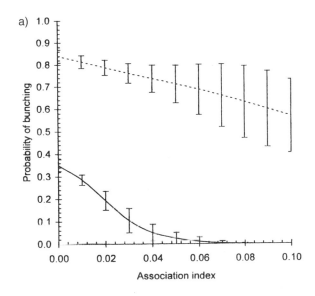

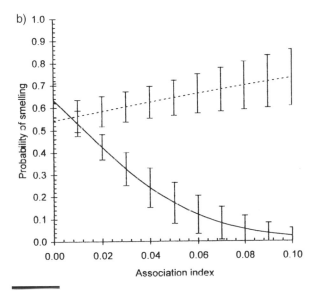

Figure 4.26
The discriminatory ability of Amboseli's elephant matriarchs
to infrasound playback calls of other females. The association index is a measure of previous association observed
between the matriarch and the caller. Two age categories of
matriarchs are depicted: younger matriarchs (<35 years,
dashed line) and older matriarchs (>55 years, solid line).
The graphs describe probabilities of (a) bunching and (b)
smelling. (From McComb et al. 2001, *Science*, **292**, 491–
494, Figure 1. Reprinted with the permission of the American Association for the Advancement of Science.)

female elephants to discriminate between calls of individuals associated with them to varying degrees (see section 4.3.2). The typical response to a playback from a closely associated female was to call in return, while with a less-familiar female, it was negative behavior, such as bunching together or smelling with raised trunk. Families, however, differed in their abilities to discriminate between calls and respond appropriately; the age of the matriarch was a key determinant of this ability. The tendency to bunch in negative fashion declined with increased association with the calling family (the association was represented as an index calculated on the basis of field observations of these families). With older matriarchs (>55 years), there was virtually no bunching when calls of high-association families were played back (fig. 4.26). The discriminatory abilities of younger matriarchs (<35 years) were much poorer. Not only did their families show a much higher probability of bunching in response to playback calls, but they also continued to bunch at relatively high frequencies even in response to calls from high-association families. With respect to the behavior of smelling, the younger matriarchs could not discriminate between calls of low- and high-association families. Several other variables, such as number of females in the family group, the age of females other than the matriarch, the number and age of calves, and the presence of adult bulls that could confound the results of such experiments were not statistically significant. McComb and associates thus concluded that families with older matriarchs have either "larger networks of vocal recognition or greater social confidence" than do families with younger matriarchs.

The most interesting part of this work was the translation of these observations to biological fitness of the family groups. From the demographic records of identified elephants of Amboseli, it was seen that "the age of the matriarch was a significant predictor of the number of calves produced by the family per female reproductive year" (McComb et al. 2001, p. 493). In other words, families with older matriarchs possessing superior discriminatory abilities were also more successful in reproducing. Populations such as that at Amboseli, where long-term records of identified individuals are being kept, provide the best opportunity for understanding the evolution of social life in this long-lived animal.

Bamboos, Bark, and Bananas
The Diet of a Megaherbivore

5

5.1   Introduction

The feeding habits of the largest land mammals have naturally attracted a lot of attention, if only for the sheer quantity and variety of plants they consume and the impact they make on their habitats. Both in Africa and in Asia, there have been numerous studies of the foraging ecology of the elephant. Given the diversity of habitats in which elephants are found across the two continents, we can naturally expect considerable variation in the types and parts of plants they consume. Yet, we must search for commonality amid the myriad patterns of foraging behavior recorded. Can the elephant's feeding strategies throughout its range be explained by a simple set of rules?

An animal's feeding behavior is fundamentally explained by its anatomical and physiological adaptations, products of its evolutionary history. Among mammalian herbivores, structures of the teeth and of the gastrointestinal tract are obviously important determinants of plant types eaten. Their ability to degrade cellulose in the plant cell wall through microbial symbionts for obtaining energy is closely related to the structure of the gastrointestinal tract. Body size exerts a great influence through its physiological consequences, such as metabolic rate. The sexes may have differing nutritional requirements or may use habitats in a different manner; females and young may have greater need to avoid predators, for example. In the case of the elephant, the very large body size imposes special constraints on its feeding ecology. At a more proximal level, the food choices of a herbivore will depend on what is available. The theoretically "ideal" diet for a species may never be achieved, except in very localized regions, by most populations because such an ideal variety and quantity of plants may just not be available.

Allometry has been used as a predictive tool in the comparative ecology of species within functional groups. Using data on body size, for instance, the quantity of forage or even a particular nutrient such as protein required by a herbivorous mammal could be derived from a standard relationship. Allometric functions could also fail completely with certain ecological characteristics. With the elephant, it fails to predict home range (which varies over two orders of magnitude) or, say, the proportion of the diet constituted by grasses. Predictive relationships, of course, could be explored with a species that spans a diverse range of habitats, from rain forest, through deciduous forest and savanna-woodland, to near desert.

Optimal foraging theory, which has been successfully applied to animals such as insectivorous birds or predatory mammals, has only had limited application to large mammalian herbivores. Apart from qualitative accounts, the foraging behavior of elephants has not been examined within such a theoretical framework in spite of numerous studies on their feeding. One reason could be the relative paucity of specific physiological data for elephants. A more important reason could be the sheer logistical problems involved in studying the food choices year-round of a long-ranging species, quantifying the distribution and availability of a variety of herbaceous and browse plants, and simultaneously keeping track of changes in plant phenology and nutritional qualities.

I begin with a description of the plants actually consumed by elephants across their distributional range, the quantities ingested, and the variations across seasons and habitats. The issue of whether the elephant is a browser or a grazer is then tackled through the newer evidence of carbon isotopes. The ecological determinants of diet in elephants in relation to body size, gut anatomy and physiology, and nutritive requirements are finally explored.

5.2   The nature of the elephant's diet

5.2.1   Plants and plant parts in the diet

The ancient Sangam literature (first–fourth centuries A.D.) of the Tamils makes numerous references to the elephant's fondness of bark. There is also an interesting observation that a pregnant elephant would abort its fetus if it fed on the young shoots of bamboo, one of the earliest references to a plant toxin (today, it is known that growing shoots of many plants may be protected from herbivory through the production of cyanogenic compounds).

Most modern-day elephant observers in Africa and in Asia have commented on the diversity of plants in the diets of the two species. A unique organ, the trunk, makes it possible for the elephant to delicately pluck the tiny inflorescence of a touch-me-not (*Mimosa pudica*) herb or bring crashing down the stout branch of a large *Acacia* tree. The elephant's diet includes short and tall grasses, forbs, aquatic plants, leaves and twigs of several shrubs, trees and lianas, fruits, bark, roots, and the pith of baobabs and bananas (fig. 5.1).

There are several figures in the literature on the number of plant species consumed by elephant populations in various habitats. These can be looked at broadly in dry habitats, such as savannas and woodlands, or in moist habitats, such as rain forests. One of the earliest scientific studies of feeding in elephants was in the savanna habitat of Uganda. Examination of stomach contents, reported by Irven Buss in 1961, revealed 25 plant species in the diet of these elephants. Similar examination of culled elephants during 1971–1972 at Wankie (Hwange) in Zimbabwe by B. R. Williamson identified 61 browse species. Direct observations of elephant feeding have turned in even higher species numbers. Peter Guy, on foot, followed elephants at the Sengwa Reserve in Zimbabwe during 1973 to record their feeding habits. His records, which covered all the major seasons in this dry woodland region, included 133 species of plants belonging to 95 genera and 41 families. George McKay, who studied the elephant in Sri Lanka (Ceylon), reported in 1973 that its diet in dry thorn forest and grassland comprised at least 88 species of plants, including trees, shrubs, vines, and herbs. My own observations of a southern Indian population of elephants during 1981–1983 in deciduous and thorn forest showed at least 112 food species, with the bulk of the diet comprised of plants from about 25 species belonging to five botanical groups—grasses, sedges, palms, legumes, and malvaceous shrubs and trees.

There are fewer studies of elephant feeding in moist forests; these have usually relied on indirect evidence of feeding, such as plant components in dung (fig. 5.2). Two studies on the African forest elephant in Ivory Coast's rain forests during the late 1970s brought out the importance of fruits in the diet. G. Merz noted that seeds constituted up to 35% of the dry weight of elephant droppings during the fruiting season, which was December to February. As many as 29 species of fruits were recorded during a single month. D.-Y. Alexandre identified a total of 37 fruits in elephant droppings. A few of these dominated the elephant's diet seasonally, with seeds from only 2 species making up half the weight of droppings. Another study by J. Short of the diet of forest elephants in moist evergreen and semideciduous forests of Ghana recorded 35 species of fruit consumed with traces in 93% of elephant droppings examined. More recently, Lee White and colleagues recorded the fruit of 72 species in the diet of forest elephants in Gabon. Remains of at least 1 fruit species were found in 82% of dung samples. Most fruit species, however, were recorded only over 1 month, indicating that the elephants were consuming whatever was available seasonally. Overall, the elephants of Lope Reserve consumed various parts of at least 230 plant species.

In an indirect survey of food plants in Malaysian rain forests, Robert Olivier listed over 400 species as potential food for Asian elephants. Of these, nearly 350 species were palms. No individual elephant or herd may feed on

Figure 5.1
A representation of the diversity of plants and plant parts in the diet of elephants, with elephants feeding on (clockwise from top) bark, grass, and bamboo. (The photograph at the top is courtesy of D. K. Bhaskar.)

Figure 5.2
Remains of fruit (arrows) in the dung of elephant. Dispersal by elephants may be important for some species of trees, especially in rain forest.

all of these, but the point to emphasize here is the diversity of an elephant's diet.

Certain plant families consistently appear as providing much of the elephant's diet in both the continents. These are Poaceae (or Graminae—the grass family), Cyperaceae (the sedge family), Palmae (the palm family), Fabaceae (or Leguminosae—the legume family), Euphorbiaceae (the spurge family), Combretaceae (the combretum family), Rhamnaceae (the buckthorn family), Anacardiaceae (the cashew family), Moraceae (the mulberry family, which includes the figs), and the botanical order Malvales, comprising Malvaceae (the mallow family), Sterculiaceae (the sterculia family), and Tiliaceae (the basswood family).

The elephant is also a versatile feeder when it comes to handling different plant parts. From the grasses, not only are the leaves consumed, but also the entire clumps are uprooted, and the succulent basal portion is eaten along with the roots (after cleaning them of mud by thrashing against the front feet or even immersing in water). From bamboo clumps, the lateral shoots with leaves are commonly taken, but entire culms are sometimes split and eaten. Small herbaceous plants are consumed whole. Taking foliage from shrubs and trees is the most common way of browsing. The same plants may also provide other sources of nourishment, such as bark and fruits. From acacias, for instance, the leaves, bark, and fruits are often consumed. The short, hooked thorns or long spines on acacia branches do not deter elephants from taking them entirely.

Although fresh foliage is preferred when elephants browse, they still consume dry branches and twigs when the need arises, such as during the dry months. From many other shrubs and trees, such as the malvaceous plants, only the bark is consumed, and any leaf taken in is largely incidental. The growing central rachis is pulled from palms, often killing the plant. Short palms are also dug and pulled out to consume the basal portion of the stem and the root. Smaller fruits are consumed whole, while larger ones such, as the jackfruit, are first crushed under the foot.

The consumption of fruits is obviously seasonal. Elephants may spend long periods of time at a particular tree or a cluster of trees, literally gorging themselves with ripe fruit. They may even get drunk if these happen to be fruits, such as from certain palms, that ferment. The stem of a baobab is gouged out to get at the central succulent pith. Banana stems are likewise split to reach the soft pith. The elephant can also be very selective, spending long periods picking the tiny flowers of favored herbs, such as mimosa. In the variety of plant types and parts consumed, the elephant does not seem to have any equal among terrestrial herbivorous mammals.

5.2.2   Feeding rates and quantity consumed

There is, of course, considerable interest is estimating the quantity of food required or consumed by an elephant daily (table 5.1). There are several ways of empirically determining this figure. The stomach contents of dead elephants can be weighed and the daily consumption calculated from knowledge of the rate of passage of food. Richard Laws and his team made several calculations of food consumption by elephants in Uganda by weighing stomach contents of a large sample of culled elephants at Murchison Falls National Park. Using a passage time of 12 hours, they initially concluded that adult males consumed 4.8% and adult females 5.6% of their body weights as fresh fodder daily. These figures were later revised to 4% of body weight for elephants of all age classes with the exception of lactating females, for which a much higher figure of 6% of body weight was computed. Thus, an adult bull weighing 6,000 kg would consume 240 kg, and a lactating female weighing 2,700 kg would eat 162 kg of fresh plant material each day. If one were to make adjustments for the moisture content of plants, the dry matter of plants would reduce to only 1% of body weight for most elephants and 1.5% for lactating females.

Another approach is to make observations of the elephant's daily routine and feeding behavior and estimate the following figures: time spent in feeding daily, rate of picking vegetation, number of trunksful of forage eaten per unit time, and weight of a trunkful of forage. As the moisture content of plants varies considerably with time of day and seasons, it is best to express all forage weights as dry weights. In practice, this manner of computing the quantity of food eaten is not an easy task. The observer has to follow elephants both during the

Table 5.1
Feeding rates and forage intake in African and Asian elephant populations.

Locality (Country)	Sex	Season	Time of Observation	Feeding Time (%)	Trunkful/minute G	Trunkful/minute B	Trunkful Weight (g)	Daily Intake (kg)	Daily Intake as % Body Weight	Source
Sengwa (Zimbabwe)	F	Wet	D	57	3.7	2.6	75 WM	200 WM		Guy (1975)
	M	Wet	D	57	3.0	4.2	75 WM	225 WM		
	F	Dry	D	41	2.0	1.6	75 WM	128 WM		
	M	Dry	D	41	1.5	1.8	75 WM	140 WM		
Gounda-St. Floris (Central African Republic)	F/M	Wet	T	78	5.2	4.8	—	55 DM		Ruggiero (1992)
	F/M	Dry	T	65	5.0	4.5	—	46 DM		
Amboseli (Kenya)	F	Wet	T	74	5.7	2.2	14/16 DM	45 DM	1.7	Lindsay (1994)
	M	Wet	T	70+	5.4	1.6	20/30 DM	63 DM		
	F	Dry	T	73	3.5	1.9	10/19 DM	52 DM	1.9	
	M	Dry	T	71	4.4	2.6	17/25 DM	68 DM	1.4	
Gal Oya (Sri Lanka)	F/M	Wet/dry	D	75	1.4	1.6	60 DM	60 DM		McKay (1973)
Biligirirangans (India)	F/M	Wet	D	50	0.8–1.7		77 DM	44 DM	1.9	Sukumar (1989a)
	F/M	Dry	D	50	0.8–1.7		58 DM	34 DM	1.5	

The trunkful weights for Amboseli are for grass and browse, respectively.
B, browse; D, daytime; DM, dry matter; F, female; G, grass; M, male; T, 24 hours; WM, wet matter.

day and at night to determine the time spent in feeding over a 24-hour period. There may be active and more passive phases of feeding in which feeding rates differ. The weight of a trunkful of forage may vary between grass and browse and from one season to another. Nevertheless, many observers have made such estimates based on partial or complete information.

A related way of estimating food quantity is to find out the rate of defecation by elephants and weigh a sample of droppings or collect and weigh all droppings over a 24-hour period. A correction has to be made for digestibility of the plants consumed. In F. G. Benedict's classic physiological study of a female Asian elephant named "Jap" published in 1936, the average weight of feces over a 9-day period was 25.8 kg dry weight per day. This 3,672-kg animal had consumed 413 kg of dry hay over this period or 45.9 kg/day. This implied a daily consumption of 1.3% of body weight as dry fodder and an assimilation efficiency of 43.8% for hay. Controlled experiments by Tom Foose on digestibility in two Asian and three African zoo elephants, using timothy hay and alfalfa (lucerne), yielded similar values. Such high digestibility, however, is unlikely under natural conditions. The forages used in these experiments were high-protein, temperate C_3 grasses, while elephants in the wild would be mostly consuming lower-quality tropical C_4 grasses. Some digestibility trials by R. A. Rees and field estimations by Richard Ruggiero on African elephants indicate digestibility of only 18%–23% of dry plant matter. Estimates of food intake by elephants based on weights of feces thus have to contend with different digestibility of forage, depending on plant type, parts, and even season.

If we assume a body weight of about 1,400 kg for "Eleanor," the 10-year-old female African elephant studied by Malcolm Coe, the 25 kg of dry feces (100 kg fresh weight) it evacuated daily translates into 2.4% of body weight consumption, assuming 25% digestibility of forage eaten. Several others have estimated weights of elephant droppings, but these figures cannot be expressed as forage intake in relation to animal body weights.

Observations of time-activity budgets of elephants indicate that they may spend anywhere between about 40% and 75% of their time in feeding. Peter Guy recorded that both sexes at Sengwa spent only about 41% of their time in foraging during the dry months, a figure that rose to 57% during the wet period. His figures, however, were extrapolations from daytime observations. J. R. Wyatt and S. K. Eltringham followed seven elephants continuously over 24-hour periods at Rwenzori National Park in Uganda. They found that these elephants spent three-fourths of their total time in feeding, with three activity peaks—one in the morning, another in the afternoon, and the third around midnight. The detailed observations of Keith Lindsay at Amboseli also suggest that elephants may overall spend 70%–75% of their time in feeding. The studies of George McKay and B.W.B. Vancuylenberg in Sri Lanka reported even higher figures (up to 94% in males), but these refer only to observations made in open areas when elephants were actively feeding and do not reflect either diurnal or 24-hour feeding budgets.

A comparison of feeding rates among different populations suggests that African elephants feed more rapidly (i.e., transfer forage more often to the mouth with the trunk), but that they take in less per trunkful compared to Asian elephants. The lowest rates of 1.5 trunksful per minute recorded at Sengwa and Amboseli are close to the highest rates (1.6–1.7 trunksful/minute) recorded in Sri Lanka or India when observations were made of elephants actively feeding on grass. African elephants feed as rapidly as 5–6 trunksful/minute. On the other hand, the quantity of grass per trunkful is substantially higher in Asian elephants (58–77 g) compared to African elephants (10–25 g). When these are translated into daily intake expressed as a percentage of body weight, the range of values is very similar. Elephants in both continents seem to consume between 1.5% and 2.0% of their body weight as dry forage each day. I have also pointed out that Asian elephants can comfortably achieve this level of intake in just 12 hours at normal rates (0.8 trunkful/minute) of feeding. When feeding on cultivated grasses such as paddy or millets, they can consume this amount in just 6–7 hours of feeding. It is thus possible that, if elephants were to spend over half their time in feeding, they could be consuming higher quantities, as proportions of their body weights, than suggested by most studies.

5.2.3   Choice of plants and seasonal changes in diet

It is often mentioned that elephants are generalist feeders because they consume a wide variety of plants and plant parts. While this is true when we compare the elephant to a specialized grazer or a frugivorous animal, the elephant also exercises considerable choice in the type of plant it eats both on a short-term as well as on a seasonal basis. Feeding behavior in the short-to-medium term of days or a few weeks essentially involves food selection within one or a few vegetation communities, while the seasonal changes in diet may involve complete shifts to different vegetation communities.

The selection of dietary items obviously depends to a large degree on what is available. In the process of consuming an ideal diet from a natural environment, an elephant has to select from a changing mosaic of different plant species, phenological stages, structural types, chemical compositions, relative or absolute abundances, and dispersion patterns. Because a particular plant item is consumed frequently or in large quantity, it does not necessarily mean that this is a "preferred" food plant. A positive or a negative preference for a particular plant species or part has to be scored in relation to its availability vis-à-vis other plant species. Some observers have looked at the selection of browse in a woodland habitat, while others have evaluated preferences among a variety of herbaceous plants, including grasses in grassland habitat. It is not an easy task to determine feeding preference in habitats that offer a mixture of browse, grass, and forbs as there are practical difficulties in quantifying the relative availability of these plant types.

In one of the early studies of elephant feeding, Peter Guy followed elephants at Sengwa in Zimbabwe, recording in detail the plants they ate and quantities consumed. In addition, he estimated tree densities and canopy volumes to measure availability of potential food plants. Using these data, he calculated three indices of plant selectivity by elephants—one based on tree canopy volumes, another based on tree densities, and the third combining the two measures plus also factoring in plant availability below 6 m height (the maximum reach of an elephant).

Guy evaluated the feeding habits of elephants for selection in two major woodland types, *Colophospermum mopane* woodland and *Acacia tortilis–Grewia* riparian community. In the mopane woodland, there was positive selection for only 2 (both *Combretum* species) of 11 species with a greater than 10% frequency (*frequency* is defined as percentage occurrence of a species in a sample of sites). The rest were either eaten in proportion to their availability or negatively selected. Several species with very high frequencies and abundances, such as *Boscia matabelensis* and *Commiphora pyracanthoides*, were not eaten at all. In the riparian community, 6 out of 17 species with high frequency were positively selected, 4 were not selected, and the rest were negatively selected. Here again, several abundant species were not consumed. *Grewia flavescens,* a species positively selected in the riparian community, was negatively selected in the mopane woodland. Overall, he concluded that "the majority of species in the woodlands are eaten in quantities proportional to their occurrence" (p. 59), but that elephants also selected for certain plants and avoided others.

While Peter Guy did not look closely at seasonal changes in the elephant's diet, another study in Kidepo Valley National Park, Uganda, published in the same year by C. R. Field and I. C. Ross, documented distinct seasonal differences in plant species and types consumed. Over a period of 3 years (1969–1971), when their study covered distinct dry and wet months, the most striking observation was a seasonal shift in the proportions of browse and grass in the diet (table 5.2). During the dry months, browsing on trees and shrubs constituted 59% of feeding observations (this went up to 71% when herbs were included as browse). Grazing, on the other hand, increased, on average, from 29% during the dry months to 57% during the wet months.

Studying elephants at Ruaha in Tanzania during the mid-1970s, Richard Barnes observed that grasses comprised 62%–74% of the diet during the wet months, while browse leaves, woody material, and bark constituted 77%–91% of the diet of bulls and 89%–99% of the diet for cows during the dry months.

My study of Asian elephant feeding habits during 1981–1983 in the Biligirirangans (table 5.2) and later during 1988–1989 in the Nilgiris of southern India showed strikingly similar patterns to the Kidepo study. Within a particular habitat type, the choice of browse or grass was influenced by the availability of these plant types. Thus, as much as 90% of feeding in browse-rich habitats during the dry season (January–April) was on browse. In this habitat, grazing on short grasses picked up only during the second wet season (September–December) when the grasses reached half a meter in height. In deciduous

Table 5.2
Proportion of browse and grass during different seasons in
the diet of elephants as determined by direct field observations.

Plant Type	African Elephant (Kidepo, Uganda)		Asian Elephant (Biligirirangans, India)		
	Dry Season	Wet Season	Dry Season	Wet Season 1	Wet Season 2
Browse (%)	58.6 ⎫	20.7 ⎫	69	46	56
	⎬ 71.4	⎬ 42.9			
Herbs (%)	12.8 ⎭	22.2 ⎭			
Grass (%)	28.6	57.1	31	54	44

Sources: Field and Ross (1976) and Sukumar (1985, 1989a).
Elephants in the Nilgiris, India, spent a higher proportion of time grazing during the wet season (see text).

woodlands, about three-fourths of feeding during the first wet season (May–August) was on tall grasses. In grasslands, elephants obviously grazed most of the time they spent there. When data from all habitat types, correcting for seasonal utilization, were pooled, the importance of browse in the dry season diet was very clear. Adult elephants spent, on average, 75% of their time browsing during January–February; this figure dropped below 70% during March–April, the later part of the dry season. During the early wet months of May–June, grazing by adults peaked at about 68%, reducing only slightly over the next 2 months. Feeding preferences during the second wet season of September–December were roughly intermediate between the other two seasons.

In seasonal habitats, the switch between a predominantly grass diet during the wet season and a browse diet during the dry period by elephants thus has been established by several observers. Even at Amboseli, where woodlands have been largely transformed to grassland, Keith Lindsay observed that elephants had a distinct tendency to go for browse during the dry period even though their diets otherwise comprised mostly grass and aquatic plants from swamps. This seasonal dietary shift could occur either within a given habitat, as seen in some of the African studies, or through change from one habitat type to another, as seen in parts of southern India. Either way, elephants exercise considerable selectivity for plant types to optimize their energy-nutrient intake over the year, an aspect I discuss below.

5.3   *Isotopic tracking of the elephant's diet*

The issue of which plant types elephants (or other herbivores) actually consume and how these are important nutritionally to growth processes in the animal can be traced through an elegant analytical method. Plants vary in their isotopic composition of carbon depending on the photosynthetic pathway of fixing carbon dioxide. The ratio of the two stable isotopes of carbon (the common ^{12}C and the rarer ^{13}C) differs widely between the so-called C_4 plants (mainly the tropical grasses and sedges) and C_3 plants (most dicot trees, shrubs, and herbs, as well as bamboos and temperate grasses). The $^{13}C/^{12}C$ ratio, expressed conventionally as $\delta^{13}C$ per mil, has a range of about −30 to −26 per mil in the C_3 plants and −14 to −11 per mil in the C_4 plants.

The carbon isotope ratio in organic tissues of an animal could be expected to reflect the isotopic values of its diet. Typically, these analyses are carried out on a relatively inert protein, such as collagen in animal bone. A correction has to be incorporated for a shift in the isotopic ratio from the dietary source, through discrimination along metabolic pathways, to the final protein product (for collagen, this correction factor of about +5 per mil is known both through experimental work and through empirical studies of diet in pure C_4 and pure C_3 plant feeders). Similarly, the stable nitrogen isotope ($^{15}N/^{14}N$) ratio may reflect environmental conditions (e.g., rainfall and water stress) or even dietary components (e.g., leguminous plants), but much less work has been done with this technique.

5.3.1   Carbon isotopes and browse : grass ratios in the diet

In a southern Indian population of Asian elephants, I looked at the stable carbon isotopic ratios in bone collagen with the assistance of R. Ramesh of the Physical Research Laboratory at Ahmedabad. We had bone samples from 56 elephants that had died of various causes. The elephants ranged in age from newborn individuals to a 60-year-old adult female with sixth molars that had almost completely worn out. The carbon isotope ratios of the most common browse (C_3 plants) and grasses (C_4 plants) consumed by elephants averaged −27.2 per mil and −12.8 per mil, respectively (we corrected this by +4.5 per mil for relating to the values in bone collagen). Several interesting patterns emerged from the bone isotopic analyses.

The carbon isotope ratios varied to a much greater degree in younger elephants compared to older individuals (fig. 5.3). Thus, elephants less than 25 years old had $\delta^{13}C$ values from −10.5 per mil to −22.7 per mil, indicating a diet composed of 85% grasses in the former to their virtual absence in the latter case. Part of the reason for this wide range of values could be that the "isotopic signature" in younger, growing individuals is not stable because bone collagen is still being synthesized and replaced at relatively high rates. As an individual shifts its diet from browse to grass on a seasonal basis, the isotopic values also keep flipping back and forth. On the other hand, older elephants that had stopped growing showed values in the range of −16.0 per mil to −20.3 per mil, suggesting that their isotopic signatures are more stable.

However, there was another aspect of the isotopic difference between younger and older elephants. The average $\delta^{13}C$ value was −15.3 per mil for

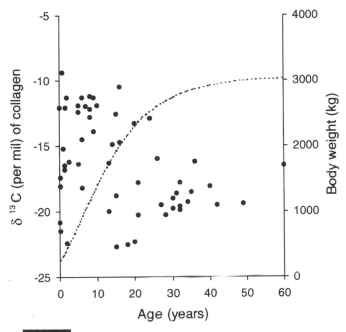

Figure 5.3

Variation in $\delta^{13}C$ (per mil) of bone collagen with age (years) in a southern Indian elephant population. The growth curve for body weight (kg) versus age (years) in female Asian elephants is also shown; this is based on the function (see appendix 2) Weight (at time t) = 3055 $(1 - e^{-0.092(t+6.15)})^3$ kg. (From Sukumar and Ramesh 1992.)

younger elephants compared to −18.6 per mil for older elephants. This suggested that carbon from browse plants contributed about 50% of the total carbon in younger animals, while this figure was just over 70% in older individuals. That younger elephants ate less browse was corroborated by my direct observations of feeding habits of the elephants in this study population. When averaged over the year, the younger elephants spent only 42% of their time feeding on browse (the remaining 58% being spent in feeding on grass), while the older elephants spent 50% of their time browsing. Perhaps it is easier for older elephants to reach out for branches from trees, strip bark, and browse than it is for the younger ones.

    An even more important aspect of dietary nutrition emerged from the study. Even though adult elephants spend only half their time browsing, the browse or C_3 plants contributed over 70% of the organic carbon that went into the synthesis of collagen. Thus, the browse plants provided proportionally higher quantities of protein used in the growth of the animal. This is again consistent with the differential crude protein content of browse (range 3%–26% dry weight) versus C_4 grasses (range 1.5%–10%) for food plants consumed by elephants in this region. Added to this, there may be differences in digestibility of grass versus browse leaves, the former being highly siliceous, fibrous, and unpalatable during the dry season.

The elephants of this southern Indian population have access to a variety of vegetation types, from semievergreen and moist deciduous forest to dry deciduous and dry thorn forest. The home ranges of several adult bulls and family groups studied cover virtually this entire diversity of habitats. Although a certain degree of dietary variation among elephant clans and solitary bulls exists due to constraints imposed by their spacing patterns, individual preferences, and home ranges, the 55%–83% range in protein contribution from C_3 plants to adult elephants brings out the importance of browse in the overall diet.

Similar isotopic studies in several African elephant populations also show the importance of C_3 plants in their diets. A survey of carbon isotopic ratios in elephants from a wide geographical African range by Nikolaas van der Merwe and coworkers showed a simple linear relationship between tree density and $\delta^{13}C$ values (or proportion of C_3 plants in the diet). As expected, the diet of elephants in rain forests, such as in Sierra Leone and Liberia, was 100% C_3 plants. After all, in the near absence of C_4 grasses, elephants would have no choice but to browse on trees and shrubs or feed on C_3 herbs and palms. What is surprising is that even in the drier habitats such as the bushveld savanna of Kruger in South Africa, where C_4 grasses are plentiful, the C_3 plants contributed 97% (range 80%–100%) of protein to bone collagen. C_3 plants also contributed 65%–85% of the diet in elephants inhabiting other dry regions with C_4 grasses, from East Tsavo in Kenya to mopane woodland in Malawi. When isotopic data from various African and Asian elephant populations are related to rainfall (fig. 5.4), it is clear that C_3 plants constitute virtually 100% of the diet in African regions with high rainfall (>1,500 mm/year). In regions with lower rainfall, there is lot of variation, but a broad positive relationship between rainfall and C_3 plants in diet can be seen.

5.3.2   Tracking temporal changes in habitat use and diet

The changes in vegetation in the African semiarid regions, induced by elephant activity or other causes, have implications for how elephants have adapted to their changing landscape. Two regions where ecosystem change has been well documented are Tsavo and Amboseli in Kenya (chapter 6). The Tsavo landscape changed from predominantly woodland to grassland during the 1960s and 1970s. Larry Tieszen and coworkers reasoned that, as woodland changed to grassland, it was possible that elephants changed their diets from browse to grass. This would be reflected in the carbon isotope ratios of bone collagen. It was more likely that the dietary shift would be reflected in the bone collagen of younger elephants, rather than in older elephants whose isotopic values would reflect an earlier period when browse was still available to them in intact

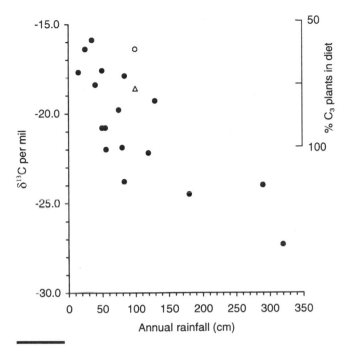

Figure 5.4

The relationship between rainfall and mean carbon isotope ratio, expressed as $\delta^{13}C$ (per mil), in bone collagen across several African (closed circle) and Asian (open circle and triangle) elephant populations. An approximate scale for proportion of C_3 plants in diet is shown on the right Y axis. The data for African populations are based on van der Merwe et al. (1988, 1990), Tieszen et al. (1989), Vogel et al. (1990), and Cerling et al. (1999). The data for Asian elephants pertain to a single population in southern India (open triangle includes all ages and open circle includes only adults older than 25 years) and are based on Sukumar and Ramesh (1992). The rainfall data are based on various sources.

woodlands. When they analyzed a sample of 56 elephants representing all age groups from Tsavo, they surprisingly found no difference in the $^{13}C/^{12}C$ ratios across this age range. Elephants of all ages obtained an average of 75% of their carbon from C_3 plants. It was obvious that, in spite of dramatic change in the habitat from woodland to grassland, the elephants seemed to be conservative in their dietary preferences, perhaps changing their movement patterns to continue to browse to the same extent as previously.

A more recent study in Amboseli found that some elephants did change their diet in response to vegetation change. In the 1950s, the Amboseli basin contained a vegetation mosaic, including dense and open woodlands (with C_3

browse), as well as swamps and grasslands (of C_4 grasses and sedges). By the early 1970s, there was a 90% decline in woodlands in the basin. The slopes of the Kilimanjaro mountain range to the south, however, are still covered with woodlands. Cynthia Moss, one of the authors of this study, has been studying the elephants here since 1972 and had collected the lower mandibles of several identified elephants that died. Elephants that died in the early 1970s, when woodland was still present, showed an average $\delta^{13}C$ value of −18 per mil, as opposed to a value of −13 per mil for those that died in the late 1980s. Clearly, the proportion of C_3 plant contribution to collagen synthesis dropped from 75% to 40% over this period. Among those that died during the late 1980s, younger animals, whose bone growth was more recent, showed higher proportions of C_4 plants in their diets compared to older individuals whose bone growth would have largely occurred prior to the changes in vegetation.

More interesting insights came from microanalysis of elephant teeth. While bones hold a relatively longer-term record of an animal's diet because of slower turnover, the tooth dentin grows by adding layers and thus retains a subannual record of body chemistry. P. L. Koch and coworkers took microsamples of sequential growth laminations from the molar roots of four elephants at Amboseli. Each microsample of dentin represented about 3 months of growth. Three of these elephants showed a regular cyclic $\delta^{13}C$ variation, most likely the result of seasonal shifts in the proportions of browse and grass.

In spite of an overall shift in diets from browse to grass, two elephants at Amboseli defied this trend and continued to feed mainly on browse into the 1980s. Another female elephant, which died in 1987 at an estimated age of 49 years, showed a shift to browse just prior to death. These animals obviously found a way to obtain browse from areas outside the park boundary. More important, even those elephants that lived their entire lives in the Amboseli lake basin, transformed into grassland by the 1980s, still obtained between 35% and 50% of their protein from C_3 plants. The Amboseli elephants thus engaged in relatively local movements to obtain browse, possibly adapting to the changing habitat through feeding at night in the woodlands at the southern edge of the park. A diminishing supply of browse was preferentially exploited by these elephants.

5.4   Ecological determinants of diet in elephants

Body size is a very obvious determinant of foraging strategy and diet in a herbivorous mammal. Norman Owen-Smith argues persuasively that animals weighing over 1,000 kg—the megaherbivores—are distinct in almost all aspects of ecology compared to smaller-size species. In other words, the megaherbivores do not necessarily represent a continuum from trends seen in other large herbivores in several ecological features. Individual species may deviate markedly from the general allometric relationship, suggesting adaptations that free the species from the constraints imposed by body size.

While body size is one important influence, the diet of a herbivorous mammal has coevolved with various other anatomical and physiological features; habitat and vegetation characteristics; competition with other species, especially closely related ones; and even its social organization. Among the two extant rhinos of the genus *Rhinoceros* in Asia, the larger *R. unicornis* (greater one-horned rhino), with its moderately high-crowned molars, is adapted for grazing, while the smaller *R. sondaicus* (Javan rhino), with relatively low-crowned and high-cusped molars, is a browser. The former evolved in moist grasslands of river valleys of South Asia, while the latter was a creature of moist forests in Southeast Asia. Both species have very restricted distributions today, the latter reduced to just two small populations; a third species, *Dicerorhinus sumatrensis* (the Sumatran rhino), which inhabits more hilly forests, is also a browser. In Africa, the larger *Ceratotherium simum* (white rhino), with its broad lips and high-crowned teeth, is essentially a grazer, while in the smaller *Diceros bicornis* (black rhino), the fingerlike upper lip and low-crowned molars are adaptations for browsing. Interestingly, both these species inhabit similar habitat—dry savanna and arid bushland.

The elephants are possibly unique among the larger herbivores in that populations may be almost entirely browsers (as in rain forest) or predominantly grazers (as in savanna). Evolutionary changes in mandible and dental structure of *Elephas* and *Loxodonta* suggest that *E. maximus* is adapted for a grazing diet to a higher degree than is *L. africana*. This difference is not necessarily seen in the actual diets of the two species over their range of habitats, although the carbon isotopic data does hint at such a difference. Dietary compositions are virtually indistinguishable, with a possible exception of higher quantities of bark in the African elephant's diet in woodland habitats. The foraging strategy of a mixed feeder is much more difficult to dissect compared to that of a pure grazer or a pure browser.

5.4.1   *Anatomical and physiological adaptations*

In any discussion of the elephant's feeding strategy, the role of the trunk cannot be ignored. From selectively picking up tiny flowers or fallen fruits from the ground to reaching up 5 m for a stout branch, this unique organ enables the elephant to feed on a wide variety of plants and plant parts. Whatever other functions may be attributed to the trunk, its mere possession and versatility could have been a strong determinant of dietary diversity. In other words, if you have it, you might as well use it.

Over evolutionary time, the jaws and teeth of the proboscideans show adaptations toward an increasingly coarse and abrasive plant diet. The high-crowned molars, the complex pattern of folded enamel plates, the rasplike (occlusal) surface, sequential replacement of molars, and the mechanics of shearing plants between the jaws are all adaptations toward a diet of plants, such as coarse grasses, that cause greater wear on the teeth.

When the anatomy of the digestive system and the process of digestion and nutrient assimilation in herbivorous mammals adapted to a cellulosic plant diet are described, a comparison between ruminants and nonruminants becomes inevitable. Each has its own advantages and disadvantages; the evolutionary determinants of these contrasting strategies were traced by Christine Janis in a classic article published in 1976. I mention the salient differences between ruminant and nonruminant digestion before discussing the implications for elephant foraging.

In contrast to herbivores, which feed mainly on plant reproductive parts such as fruits or seeds, those that subsist on a diet of structural parts such as stems or leaves have to find a way to break down cellulose. The cellulose, a complex carbohydrate of the plant cell wall, has to be degraded not only to obtain energy from the products of its breakdown, but also to release nutrients from the cell. Only microbes such as bacteria produce the enzyme that can degrade cellulose. Among ruminants, the stomach, or rumen, is the site of microbial fermentation of the plant cell wall, while in the nonruminants, this is usually achieved in the cecum or colon.

Although there is little difference in the fermentation process itself, with volatile fatty acids (VFAs) being the products of polysaccharide breakdown, there are interesting consequences for protein and carbohydrate metabolism among the ruminants and nonruminants. In ruminants, not only cellulose, but also simple carbohydrates and proteins are fermented in the forestomach before the ingesta reach the small intestine. As simple sugars are fermented into VFAs, there are limitations to rapid mobilization of energy through absorption of glucose in the small intestine among many ruminants. The fermentation of protein into ammonia and subsequent recycling of nitrogen through urea and microbial protein synthesis, however, ensure that ruminants do not suffer from amino acid imbalances in the diet. Nonruminants, on the other hand, do not have the same advantage of digestion of microbial proteins. The proteins and simple carbohydrates are already absorbed in the small intestine before the ingesta reach the site of fermentation. The significance of hindgut absorption of amino acids from the digestion of microbial proteins is not clear. A nonruminant, therefore, may have to sample a greater variety of plants to meet its protein (amino acid) requirements.

A nonruminant scores over a ruminant in its ability to achieve a higher throughput rate of forage. While a ruminant has physical restrictions, due to the complex structure of the stomach, in the rate of passage of food and, hence, in the quantity of food it can consume, a nonruminant has much less limitation. Thus, a nonruminant can tolerate a diet of lower quality, but has to increase its feeding rate or proportion of time spent in feeding. The above comparisons are for animals of similar body size.

The elephant is a nonruminant having a simple, balloon-shaped stomach, a small intestine, a relatively small cecum, and a noncompartmentalized colon, with most of the ingested food found within the proximal two-thirds of the large bowel (fig. 5.5). The most recent study of the digestive physiology of the

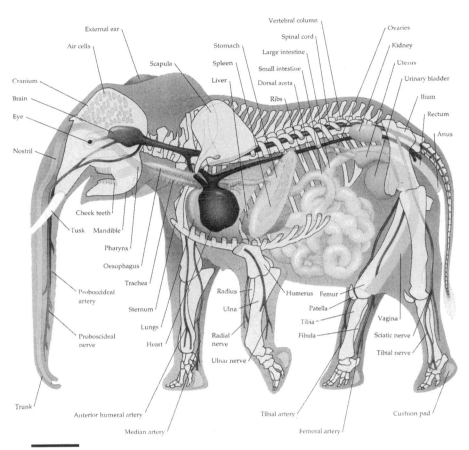

Figure 5.5
A diagram of a female African elephant showing the internal organs. (From Shoshani 1991. Reproduced with the permission of Jeheskel Shoshani.)

elephant (and two other large herbivores) by E. T. Clemens and G.M.O. Maloiy (1982) indicated that the concentrations of the VFAs, chiefly acetate, propionate, and butyrate, in the cecum and colon are comparable to those attained in the rumen of cattle. The efficiency of hindgut fermentation in the elephant is therefore high. The low pH (acidic) and low sodium ion concentration of the small intestine suggest decreased effectiveness of pancreatic and biliary secretions. How this influences intestinal digestion is not clear.

5.4.2 Body size and nutritive requirements

The quantity of food, energy, and specific nutrients, such as protein, required by an elephant may also be crudely derived from the allometric scaling factor of body mass or weight $W^{0.75}$. There are, however, difficulties in extrapolating this relationship all the way up (or down) to a herbivore as large as the elephant. Broadly, the elephant consumes less food and has lower nutrient requirements per unit of body weight compared to small herbivores (fig. 5.6). Its consumption and requirements, however, are higher than predicted by simple allometric scaling. The observed daily food consumption of 1.5%–2.0% (dry matter) of an elephant's body weight is higher than that derived from regressions for herbivores. Norman Owen-Smith uses a value of under 1% of body weight for African elephants; this is based on estimates by Richard Laws and team, who derived this from stomach fill and passage times. Field observations both in Africa and in Asia now clearly show these to be underestimates. Thus, the mass-specific food intake of an elephant is nearly comparable to that of a medium-size ruminant, although it is lower than for a nonruminant such as the zebra. This follows from the higher throughput rate of food possible in a nonruminant.

Owen-Smith rightly points out that, as regards energy and protein requirements, the available data for elephants from gut fermentation rates and crude protein concentrations in the stomach lie above the regression line for herbivores. Experimental studies on energy and protein metabolism in elephants have only been of an exploratory nature. These include the early experiments

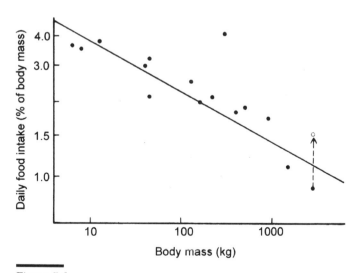

Figure 5.6
The relationship between daily food intake (% of body mass) and body mass (kg) in several African herbivorous mammals. (Based on Owen-Smith 1988. Reproduced with the permission of Cambridge University Press, U.K.) The value for the African elephant has been underestimated (arrow points to probable value); thus, the slope of the regression line would change slightly.

by F. G. Benedict and later independently by C. R. Ananthasubramaniam, Tom Foose, and M. K. Hackenberger.

When daily energy requirements of an animal are to be computed, at least three basic formulations must be kept in mind. Basal metabolic rate (BMR), proposed in 1947 by M. Kleiber, a pioneer in the field of animal energetics, is considered to be an exponential function of body weight described by the equation BMR = $70 \times W^{0.75}$ kcal/day for placental mammals. Active metabolic rate (AMR), including normal activity such as foraging, movement, and resting, is usually taken to be a simple multiple (usually 2) of BMR. In addition, females incur energy costs associated with pregnancy and lactation, the latter being the more important according to O. T. Oftedal. This can again be taken as a simple multiple (e.g., 2.7) of BMR or computed from more complex formulations of milk production and energy yield.

Using allometric equations in the literature, Keith Lindsay worked out energy and protein needs for adult elephants (table 5.3). As pointed out by Ellen Dierenfeld, however, balance trials such as those by C. R. Ananthasubramaniam indicate 50%–100% higher requirements of digestible energy for normal maintenance and activity compared to that derived from a generic Kleiber equation. Ananthasubramaniam found, in his balance trials, that adult Asian elephants need over 100,000 kcal of digestible energy daily; in contrast, a Kleiber function ($140 \times W^{0.75}$ kcal) for placental mammals gives values of only about 50,000 kcal for an adult female (say, 2,500 kg) and 70,000 kcal for an adult male (4,000-kg) elephant.

Protein requirements in elephants may similarly be wrongly estimated if one were to go by allometric functions derived for comparisons across species.

Table 5.3
Daily requirements of adult elephants for metabolizable energy (MJ/day) and digestible protein (kg/day) using allometric functions.

Sex and Status of Animal	Energy (MJ/day)	Protein (kg/day)
Female (weight [W] = 2,739 kg)		
Basal metabolism (BM)	110.9	—
Active metabolism (AM)	221.8	0.63
Peak lactation	308.5	1.29
Male (W = 4,688 kg)		
Basal metabolism (BM)	165.9	—
Active metabolism (AM)	331.9	0.94

Sources: Lindsay (1994) and various literature sources.
The allometric expression used in these derivations are $0.293W^{0.75}$ (for BM); $2 \times$ BM (for AM energy); $0.00166W^{0.75}$ (for AM protein); mean of various functions (for peak lactation energy); and mean AM $\times 0.01703W^{0.52}$ (for peak lactation protein).

A problem is deciding whether such a function applies to an adult individual (and, if so, to a male or a female) or an "average"-size individual of the species. One formula used by K. G. McCullagh (based on D. B. Smuts) computes digestible protein requirement for body maintenance (active metabolism) as $1.76 \times W^{0.75}$ g/day. For an adult elephant weighing 3,600 kg, this implies a daily need of 818 g of digestible protein. Assume that 50% of crude protein in plants is digestible and that an elephant weighing 3,600 kg consumes 72 kg (dry matter) plants daily (at 2% of its body weight). A diet of 2.3% crude protein would be sufficient for meeting the daily requirements, an extremely low figure. The balance studies of Ananthasubramaniam gave a figure of 2,370 g digestible protein daily for maintenance in an adult elephant (37 years old/3,600 kg). This translates into a diet of 6.6% crude protein, a more probable figure based on field empirical observations. For a subadult elephant (10 years old/1,337 kg), Ananthasubramaniam provided a figure of 1,300 g/day, which translates into a plant diet of nearly 10% crude protein.

Putting all these data and formulations together, it can safely be assumed that a diet of 5%–6% crude protein is necessary for adult maintenance, and a higher figure is necessary for younger, growing elephants. Pregnant and lactating cows would also need higher amounts. The crude protein level in plants needed for maintenance, of course, would vary with digestibility, an aspect that is still poorly understood. Digestibility could vary enormously with plant type and part, and this is important to a mixed feeder such as the elephant.

Mineral nutrition in elephants has been a generally neglected subject. The key to understanding certain behaviors, such as feeding on bark or on agricultural crops, may lie in a better assessment of mineral requirements and the role of minerals in elephant dietary preferences. In the absence of specific data for elephants, Ellen Dierenfeld suggested that mineral levels adequate for horses, another hind-gut fermenter, should also be grossly suitable for elephants. She summarized these for adult maintenance as nutrient concentrations in forage (dry matter) of 0.1% for sodium and magnesium, 0.15% for sulfur, 0.2% for phosphorus, 10 mg/kg for copper, 40 mg/kg for manganese and zinc, 50 mg/kg for iron, and 0.1 mg/kg for selenium, iodine, and cobalt. Based on tusk growth rate in male Asian elephants between the ages of 10 and 30 years, I computed that this alone would need 1.7 g calcium daily. Based on human calcium needs, a 10-year-old male elephant (2,000 kg) may need an additional 16 g/day for normal metabolism. Similarly, a pregnant or lactating cow elephant may need about 60 g/day. Based on his balance trials, however, Ananthasubramaniam suggests a much higher calcium requirement for maintenance, computed as 0.5 g per unit metabolic body weight ($kg^{0.75}$). An elephant may be prone to sodium imbalances according to the trials of F. G. Benedict with Jap and Robert Olivier on Malaysian elephants. These trials suggest that 75–100 g sodium may be needed by an adult elephant daily.

With the exception of vitamin E, there has been little work on the elephant's need for vitamins. Ellen Dierenfeld has suggested that the vitamin A concentration of 2,000 IU/kg and the vitamin D concentration of 300 IU/kg of plant forage (dry weight) needed by horses are adequate for elephants. Her work further showed that plasma retinol (vitamin A) values measured in zoo-bred African elephants were nearly twice those in Asian elephants. The low reproductive rate of captive elephants in most Western zoos has encouraged research on vitamin E requirements. The work of Ellen Dierenfeld and others suggests that zoo elephants may be prone to vitamin E deficiency. Levels of plasma α-tocopherol (vitamin E) in captive Asian elephants (mean of 0.54 μg/ml) are nearly double those in African elephants (0.29 μg/ml). These levels suggest deficiencies as wild African elephants had much higher levels of α-tocopherol (0.8 μg/ml). Virtually nothing is known of requirements of the water-soluble vitamins.

While on the subject of nutritive requirements of a herbivore, it is also appropriate to consider the imperatives of avoiding a variety of plant chemicals. After all, every plant contains protein, carbohydrates, lipids, minerals, and vitamins. Why, then, do herbivores avoid feeding on a large number of plant species even if they are physically able to do so? The answer lies in the chemical defenses that plants possess to avoid being eaten. Broadly, these so-called plant secondary compounds have been categorized as quantitative and qualitative defenses.

The quantitative defenses are compounds such as tannins, which reduce digestibility and are dosage dependent. Tannins bind to soluble proteins and render them inert to hydrolysis by protease enzymes. They have a characteristic astringent taste since they tan the proteinaceous mucosa and proteins of receptor cells in the mouth. About 80% of woody dicot plants are believed to produce tannins in varying quantities, in contrast to 15% of herbaceous dicot plants. The qualitative defenses or toxins, such as alkaloids and cyanogenic compounds, are present in smaller concentrations in herbs and weedy plants. They affect the physiological functions of the animal and may even be fatal if ingested in sufficient amounts.

Herbivores can deal with these chemicals to a certain extent. Enzymes produced by microbes in the gut can detoxify many of these compounds, especially in ruminants, in which the stomach medium is alkaline. The same advantage may not be enjoyed by nonruminants, which have an acidic stomach; the elephant's stomach has a very acidic pH of 3.2. Herbivores can also detoxify compounds through other metabolic means, such as the microsomal enzymes in the liver. The observed diets of browsers such as the black rhino and elephants suggest that they may be able to deal with plant defenses no less efficiently than do the ruminants.

5.4.3   *Observed diets, nutrition, and foraging strategies*

The observed diets of elephants in rain forests have not been related to nutrition in any study, with the exception of descriptive remarks by Robert Olivier.

Thus, I confine this discussion to dietary studies of elephants in tropical dry forests and savannas, where more detailed studies have been carried out both in Africa and in Asia.

The proximate factors that influence an elephant's decision to reject or consume a particular plant or part are obviously its sensory properties. Sight, smell, touch, and taste all convey varying information to the animal. Tastes are associated with certain categories of chemical compounds—sweetness with soluble carbohydrates, sourness with organic acids, saltiness with sodium chloride, and bitterness with toxic compounds such as alkaloids. Selection of dietary items based on sensory properties (palatability) may be coupled with a memory for the associated effects of particular foods on the animal. In the ultimate sense, it would be adaptive for a herbivore to select plants with higher nutritive value and avoid those with toxic effects.

The palatability of various grasses during their different stages of growth is obviously important to elephants. In southern Indian deciduous forests, I found that the tall perennial grasses, such as *Themeda* and *Cymbopogon*, are sought after during the early wet months when they flush tender leaves, especially in patches where the dry grasses have burned. As the grasses grow and mature, their leaves turn increasingly fibrous and siliceous. Elephants then avoid consuming the abrasive leaves, but selectively consume the basal succulent stems. They also search for the more tender shorter grasses growing in shaded localities. N. Sivaganesan also stresses that elephants seek soft-textured grasses, including fresh leaves sprouting from livestock-grazed clumps during the dry season. Estimates of fiber contents of grasses are available from the work of Keith Lindsay. In the *Acacia* woodlands of Amboseli, he found that grasses such as *Cynodon plectostachys* virtually double their fiber content as they progress from the wet to the dry season. Tall grasses in certain other habitats, such as grasslands, however, maintained a relatively constant and high fiber content.

Apart from the physical attributes of grasses or other plants, there are correlations between the nutrient/energy content of plants and choice by elephants. The selection of grasses is clearly related to protein content, on a seasonal basis both within habitats and across habitats. In the deciduous forests of southern India, the leaves of tall grasses typically have a crude protein content of 8%–10% (dry weight), a level sufficient for maintenance, during the wet season. The protein levels, however, drop to below 4% during the dry period. During both the late wet season and the dry season, the basal portion of tall grasses, which elephants selectively consume, is also deficient in protein (1.5%–4.0%). The succulent bases may, however, be rich in soluble carbohydrates. In any case, elephants have to seek their protein requirements from other plants when the levels fall below 5% in tall grasses, or specific parts that constitute a staple part of their diet. One way to achieve this during the late wet season is to switch to short grasses, including annuals, which have now grown sufficiently and maintain a high protein level. During the dry season, even the short grasses in woodland habitats may have insufficient protein.

Thus, the strategy of switching from grass to browse seems primarily for obtaining sufficient protein.

Browse plants maintain much higher levels of protein than do grasses throughout the year. My analyses showed that the leaves of woody legumes such as *Acacia* maintain 10%–20% protein, while several other browse plants have 8%–10% protein during the dry months. These are several times the values in the basal portion of tall grasses consumed at this time of the year. In southern India, the overall transition from a grazing to a browsing diet with the progress of the rainy season and into the dry season is achieved more through a shift in habitat type utilized rather than a dietary shift within one habitat.

There has been some discussion as to whether protein or energy is the appropriate currency for evaluating diet choice in a herbivore. The situation becomes more complex when, as pointed out by O. T. Oftedal, the two factors are interrelated; thus, protein malnutrition usually accompanies calorific deficiency. Keith Lindsay made a detailed analysis of diet choice of Amboseli's elephants, mainly in grassland habitats, in relation to energy, protein, and fiber. He found that diet choice by adult females was positively correlated with protein during the wet months and with energy during the dry months. Adult males attached to female groups showed similar patterns, while bachelor bulls showed positive correlations with energy intake throughout the year. Lindsay's direct observations, however, recorded lower levels of browsing than revealed for Amboseli's elephants by carbon isotopic analysis. There were interesting differences between the sexes in feeding patterns. Males browsed to a greater extent during the dry season than did the females. Bachelor males also differed from the female groups in their spatial distribution throughout the year, suggesting that some segregation between the sexes was occurring so that males did not incur the energetic costs of feeding alongside the female groups.

The high mineral content in bark of many woody plants consumed was highlighted by some of the earlier studies of East African elephants. These minerals include calcium, manganese, iron, boron, and copper. I also noted the high calcium content in dicot bark (18–57 mg/g) compared to grasses (1–5 mg/g) in southern Indian habitats. Calcium availability and metabolism are governed by several factors, including fiber and oxalate in forage and vitamin D levels in the animal. What may seem to be excessive intake of calcium in fact may not necessarily be so. One study by G. D. Anderson and B. H. Walker at Sengwa, Zimbabwe, did not find any relationship between the degree of debarking of various woody plants and their mineral content, with the exception of a weak correlation with sodium in the soil. It is well known that elephants seek water sources and soils rich in sodium salts (fig. 5.7). J. S. Weir showed that the distribution of elephants corresponds nicely to the concentration of environmental sodium in parts of East Africa. Another study in the Central African Republic by Richard Ruggiero and Michael Fay found that old termite mounds excavated by elephants for use as "licks" had eight times the sodium levels, in addition to higher concentrations of total salts, compared to surrounding soils.

Figure 5.7
A herd drinking at a pond in Bandipur National Park, India (*top*), and elephants consuming soil salt licks in Mudumalai, India (*bottom left*), and Bumi Hills, Zimbabwe (*bottom right*). Elephants distinctly prefer to drink water and eat soil rich in certain minerals.

Bark may serve other functions in elephant nutrition. During the wet season, when fresh grass low in fiber is a major component of the diet, it may be necessary to supplement this with fibrous material such as bark. This would help maintain an optimum fiber-to-protein ratio of ingesta for a correct throughput rate. Richard Laws suggested that the protein in grass would then be properly digested; elephants could otherwise suffer from colic. As an offshoot of the studies in Uganda by Richard Laws, the blood sera of two female elephants shot at Murchison were analyzed for fatty acids by K. G. McCullagh. He compared these values with an earlier study, by J. H. Moore and S. K. Sikes (noted in McCullagh 1973), of five elephants from a different East African population that had access to plentiful browse, unlike the Murchison elephants. The Murchison elephants were deficient in certain essential fatty acids, such as linoleic acid. The pulp and bark of trees such as the baobab and *Terminalia* are rich in linoleic acid compared to grasses. McCullagh's contention was that the high degree of debarking by savanna elephants could be a search for essential fatty acids. Unfortunately, this line of research has not been followed up.

Browsing herbivores may have thresholds in their tolerance to chemical defenses such as tannins. The barks of many dicots, such as the acacias, which are a favorite among elephants, have tannin contents as high as 10%–20% dry weight. Apart from physiological mechanisms for overcoming plant chemical defenses, other dietary components may aid this process. Fiber in diet may bind a certain proportion of tannins. Geophagy (soil eating) may also serve a similar purpose. The high clay content and electrical conductivity of preferred soils may serve to adsorb several types of plant toxins, especially low molecular weight ones such as alkaloids. At the same time, we must also remember that plant secondary compounds may have a therapeutic function in animals. This is a subject that is still in its infancy. There is anecdotal evidence from captive elephant keepers in Asia suggesting that elephants preferentially feed on certain plants when they are ill.

Even if a complete understanding of the elephant's foraging strategy is still beyond us, we can summarize what is known within the following framework.

1. The early mathematical models of optimal foraging are derived from J. M. Emlen, who postulated in 1966 that an animal should maximize the net energy intake per unit time. While these models are useful for predators, they are insufficient to explain the diets of mammalian herbivores. Even if the "energy-maximizing" and "time-minimizing" principles hold true for a herbivore, there may be constraints set by the need for specific nutrients, such as protein or minerals, plus a need to avoid plant toxins. Alternatives include the "contingency model" approach of Norman Owen-Smith and Peter Novellie applied to the kudu, and the "linear programming model" first formulated by Mark Westoby and later applied by Gary Belovsky to the moose and other

species. Linear programming, which permits simultaneous treatment of energy, other nutrients, and toxins, seems to come closest to predicting actual diets of herbivores. Elephant foraging has not yet been examined within any such theoretical framework.

2. A large generalist herbivore such as the elephant is adapted to feeding on plants that are usually available in abundance, but low in quality. Forage quality varies in space and time as a consequence of habitat (soil, rainfall) and phenological changes. As there are constraints on how fast food material can be processed by the digestive system, a large herbivore has to obtain the best mix of nutrients from a relatively fixed bulk ingested.

3. Being a nonruminant, the elephant may have a requirement for specific amino acids. It thus has to sample a large variety of plants to fulfill this need.

4. Dietary constraints may be set by minerals such as sodium or calcium. If an elephant has to balance its sodium budget, it may have to preferentially consume plants rich in this mineral irrespective of other nutrients.

5. Elephants may have to avoid a large number of plant species because of the chemical defenses they possess.

6. The decision to consume or reject a plant may depend on the animal's previous experience. This involves a complex process of learning by associating the sensory properties of foods with the physiological consequences of their consumption, either immediately or over a longer term.

7. Elephants should thus feed on the staple foods most familiar to them and continuously sample other foods.

8. An elephant must treat a new plant it encounters with caution since it has no way of predicting which toxic compounds may be present. There are several examples of cautious approach by elephants to a novel food that is otherwise very palatable.

9. For a generalist feeder such as the elephant, an important consideration would be the relative choice between browse and grass. Browse is rich in protein and several minerals, but is also high in plant toxins. Further, palatable browse species are unevenly distributed in space. More time is required in search and "preparation" for feeding. These last factors entail certain "costs" to a browsing animal. Though low in nutrients such as protein, grasses are also low in secondary compounds. In tropical dry habitats, grasses are available in plenty, require little preparation for eating, and even have sufficient protein during the wet months. Feeding on mature, abrasive grasses, however, entails the costs of excessive wear on the teeth. The best strategy for the elephant is therefore to track phenological changes in potential foods and consume a mix of browse and grass, depending on the season and their availability in different vegetation types within

its home range. The carbon isotope studies clearly show that browse plants contribute more amino acids to protein synthesis in most elephant populations. In other words, elephants can be entirely browsers or mixed feeders, but not entirely grazers.

10. All elephants in a population may not have the same diet. Differences may arise from specific needs of younger versus older individuals, females versus males, and reproductive status of females. Foraging strategies of different herds or clans in a region may also vary to a certain extent, as seen from carbon isotopic data. These seem related to differences in seasonal patterns of movement and home range arising from intraspecific competition, spacing, and learning mechanisms (if your mother or grandmother followed a particular pattern of movement and ate certain plants, it would be best for you to do likewise).

5.5   *Nutrition and the condition of elephant populations*

In ultimate terms, a particular diet is expressed through body condition, health, and reproductive vigor in the evolutionary fitness of an individual. It has been well documented in African savannas that adverse changes in habitat conditions, such as during a drought, result in loss of body condition among elephants and demographic changes through higher mortality and lower reproduction at the population level. Under normal conditions, systematic differences in diet among herds or clans could also be reflected in their physiological and demographic status. These relationships are not straightforward, and empirical data for elephant populations are scanty.

One of the early studies by Peter Albl on physical condition among elephants culled in the Luangwa Valley, Zambia, found that the kidney-fat index (weight of kidney fat/weight of kidney), a proxy of physiological condition, declined sharply in all age and sex classes by the end of the dry season (table 5.4). He suggested that an index of 10% was the threshold between good and poor condition. Morphological criteria such as buccal, temporal, and scapular depressions were generally related to age. The lumbar depression, however, correlated with the kidney-fat index and could be used for evaluating body condition.

When Richard Laws and Ian Parker examined various ecological traits in the elephants culled at Murchison (Kabalega) Falls National Park in Uganda during the 1960s, they found several differences between the populations to the north and the south of the Nile River. The South Bank population existed at a higher density in habitat that was in a more advanced state of transformation into grassland. The more nutritionally stressed elephants here also had a lower rate of reproduction, as calculated from the intercalving interval. To compare metabolic and nutritional status of the two populations, a series of biochemical investigations was undertaken. The amount of hydroxyproline, an amino acid derived from the breakdown of collagen, excreted in urine was

Table 5.4
Seasonal comparisons of certain indices of physiological
condition in African elephant populations.

Population	Season of Sampling	Hydroxy-proline: Creatinine Ratio	Kidney-Fat Index (%)	Femur Marrow Fat (%)	Source
Luangwa (Zambia)	Wet	—	50		Albl (1971)
	Dry	—	7–15	—	
Wankie (Hwange) (Zimbabwe)	Dry	—	54.4	—	Williamson (1975)
Kabalega North (Uganda)	Wet	52.1	20.0	58.5	Malpas (1978)
	Dry	26.4	26.9	69.7	
Kabalega South (Uganda)	Wet	47.6	14.3	61.8	Malpas (1978)
	Dry	10.7	36.3	72.2	
Rwenzori (Uganda)	Wet	39.7	23.4	62.7	Malpas (1978)
	Dry	34.5	18.2	64.3	

examined by K. G. McCullagh in various age classes from both populations. The results, usually expressed as the ratio of hydroxyproline to creatinine, provide an index of the rate of growth. Surprisingly, the results indicated that the South Bank elephants had a higher growth rate than the North Bank ones. It turned out that the South Bank population had been sampled during the wet season, while the North Bank samples had been collected during the dry period. The seasonal differences in nutrition and growth obscured any inter-population differences that may have existed. When Laws's team examined another proxy of physiological condition, the kidney-fat index, no significant differences were again seen between the two populations.

To rectify this anomaly in sampling, Robert Malpas undertook even more detailed investigations of diet and condition of elephants at the same sites about a decade later. Another surprising result awaited him. The kidney-fat index of elephants, both to the north and the south of the Nile, was higher during the dry season than in the wet season. Forage consumed during the wet season actually had higher protein levels, as seen from stomach content analysis. Blood urea levels also reflected this higher protein intake during the wet season. Why then did the kidney-fat index show this unexpected reversal? One explanation is that in seasonal habitats it is better for elephants to mobilize protein and other energy resources for growth during the wet season and not for fat storage. As the quality of forage declines with the approach of the dry season, it is adaptive to change strategies and to build up fat reserves to tide over a difficult period. Bone marrow fat was also slightly higher during the dry months in Malpas's samples. B. R. Williamson's investigations on elephants culled in 1971 at the Wankie (Hwange) Park in Zimbabwe showed even higher kidney-fat indices during the dry season. He concluded that the Wankie elephants, which incidentally were mainly browsers, were in good condition.

Comparable data on Asian elephants are not available. From visual criteria, such as those described by Peter Albl, I observed that an elephant clan in the Biligirirangans, which mainly browsed in bush habitat during the dry season, seemed in much better condition compared to another that grazed more in deciduous forest (fig. 5.8).

A possible alternative to the kidney-fat content and hydroxyproline excretion is intestinal parasite loads. T.N.C. Vidya and I examined intestinal parasite egg densities in elephant dung, but did not find any clear relationship between body condition and parasite loads. Dry season parasite loads, however, were higher than wet season loads. This line of investigation has to be pursued in more detail.

Figure 5.8
An adult female Asian elephant in poor body condition at the end of the dry season in Mudumalai Wildlife Sanctuary, India. This elephant died less than 2 weeks after this picture was taken.

The links between body "condition" and fitness in demographic terms are not clear from the empirical data. Perhaps too much should not be read into assessments of condition in elephants.

It is known that elephants lose fat stored under the skin during the dry period. There could be redeployment of fat reserves between the seasons. The loss of subcutaneous fat and body weight during the dry, hot season could also aid in efficient thermoregulation. Excessive protein intake is also undesirable during the dry season because nitrogen excretion requires more water, which may be scarce. It can be expected that animals are physiologically adapted to a recurring dry season. Only extreme conditions, such as a severe drought, could threaten their survival and test the resilience of a population. Ideally, a measure of vigor and resilience, incorporating demographic and physiological traits, should capture the condition of a population. For the elephant, however, such a measure still eludes us.

Forests, Fires, and Grasslands
The Impact of Elephants
on Their Habitats

6

6.1   Introduction

It is not surprising that the largest terrestrial animals can make a tremendous impact on their habitats through their feeding activities. Imagine an elephant clan moving through a wooded savanna at an ecological density of 10 animals per square kilometer, each individual having a fresh forage requirement of up to 10% of its body weight each day. With an average individual weight of 1,800 kg, this elephant clan would consume 1,800 kg of vegetation each day from each square kilometer of habitat. Another 1,200 kg of vegetation would be wasted in the process. A 200-strong elephant clan would thus remove 60 tonnes of vegetation each day or 21,900 tonnes each year over a 20 km^2 landscape. Even if such a high elephant density is seasonal and unlikely to be sustained over the year, an average density only a third the seasonal figure would still remove a considerable biomass of woody vegetation over large landscapes.

Now, if most of the forage removed by elephants were to be grass or other herbs, there probably would not be much concern. After all, there seems to be no shortage of grass in the African savannas for elephants and other herbivores. Elephants, however, also feed on shrubs and trees, breaking branches, stripping bark, and uprooting huge trees. When a centuries-old stately baobab is reduced to pulp by elephants trying to get at its succulent pith or a fever tree (a major attraction for tourists, who wish to see lions under its shade or a leopard perched on a branch) is pushed over by a bull elephant for just one trunkful of leaves, there is justified cause for concern. It can be argued that the loss of a local clump of trees, attractive to tourists, is not sufficient cause from an objective biological perspective to label the elephant as a destructive creature. When trees begin to disappear over hundreds of square kilometers and the landscape resembles a battlefield with flattened trees, the stage is set for scientific curiosity over elephant-vegetation dynamics to give way to a political war over elephant management.

The "elephant problem," as it was commonly labeled in Africa, dominated the debate over management of the species in the continent during the 1970s. One school of thought considered such drastic impact on vegetation by the elephants as unnatural. The reasoning was that compression of elephants into protected areas or insular habitats by expanding human settlements resulted in artificially high elephant densities and damage to vegetation. A contrary view was that elephant utilization of woody vegetation was merely natural foraging and that "damage" to trees was part of the natural ecology of semiarid habitats. Much has been written about this issue in the African context and less on the Asian situation. My intentions are to review briefly the nature and extent of vegetation change in elephant habitats, consider the role of elephants and other agents of habitat change, and discuss various theories and models of elephant-vegetation dynamics, especially as to their implications for the management of elephants.

6.2   The nature of vegetation change in elephant habitats

That the heaviest of terrestrial mammals had a propensity to damage trees has been recorded since ancient times. The stripping of bark from trees by elephants is a common metaphor in Tamil poetry from the Sangam period (first to fifth centuries A.D.) of southern India. A twelfth century A.D. inscription from central India records that the elephant-headed god (and hence the elephant itself) revels in the sport of uprooting large numbers of trees. Early European travelers in Africa observed that elephants were prone to strip bark and flatten an entire forest. While some accounts are nonspecific about the kinds of trees and shrubs damaged by elephants, others refer more specifically to plants such as acacias being favorite targets.

Scientific accounts of elephant damage to vegetation emerged during the 1960s. Comparing aerial photographs of Murchison (Kabalega) Falls National Park in Uganda taken in 1932 and again in 1956, Hal Buechner and H. C. Dawkins estimated in a 1961 publication that the tree population in the park had roughly halved during this period. There was, however, considerable spatial variation in the extent of decline of trees. The work at Murchison Falls was carried forward by Richard Laws and his team. Based on aerial photographic transects in areas of significant habitat change, they observed that densities of trees and bushes were low inside the park, but much higher outside. Often, an abrupt change in vegetation density coincided with the park boundary. In the southern part of the park, the pattern of damage showed a progressive radial increase in tree cover and variety away from the foci of elephant concentrations. A 15-km cross section of such a zone showed that 95% of *Terminalia glaucescens*, one of the worst-affected species, were dead in the north, where elephant densities were highest, reducing to only 2% dead in the south, where elephant densities were lowest (table 6.1). *Combretum binderanum* was another tree that suffered considerable damage from bark stripping.

Other studies in East Africa also reported on similar patterns of damage. C. R. Field, who studied elephants in the Queen Elizabeth (Rwenzori) National Park in Uganda, found that trees had declined at an annual rate of 14.6% during 1954–1968. The famous Serengeti National Park in Tanzania also had an elephant problem. In 1967, Hugh Lamprey and his associates reported two studies, one describing damage to *Acacia* and *Commiphora* woodland in the northern Serengeti and the other concerning destruction of the fever tree *Acacia xanthophloea* by bull elephants in the Seronera area to the south. Elephants had been absent in the Serengeti prior to about 1955, when they were first recorded here. Their population increased to about 2,000 individuals over the next decade. Consequently, the larger trees were declining at the rate of 6% per year.

The Seronera bull problem, as it came to be known in the southern tourist area, was investigated in greater detail by Harvey Croze during 1968–1971. He found conspicuous effects on three acacias: the fever tree *Acacia xanthophloea*, the gum arabic *A. senegal*, and the umbrella acacia *A. tortilis*. A bull pushed over three trees on average every 4 days. At specific locations, the elephants were removing the canopy acacias at a rate of 6% per year, although the loss of the larger trees was only 2.5% per year over the entire Seronera region. *Acacia tortilis* was also a prime target for elephants at Lake Manyara National Park during the 1960s, when Iain Douglas-Hamilton recorded a density of 5 elephants/km^2, one of the highest recorded in African habitats.

Table 6.1
Proportion of adult trees of *Terminalia glaucescens* scarred or dead in 1967 because of damage by elephants in the Murchison (Kabalega) Falls area of Uganda.

Sector	Number of Trees	Unscarred (%)	Scarred (%)	Dead (%)
Northeast of Waisoke River	133	0	4.5	95.5
Southwest of Waisoke River	218	5.5	67.9	26.6
Northeast of Sonso River	95	6.3	82.1	11.6
Northwest of Sonso River	112	74.1	24.1	1.8

Source: Based on Laws et al. (1975).

Moving to the even drier bushland of Tsavo National Park, R. M. Watson's analysis in 1967 showed that destruction of trees by elephants was uniformly spread over the 20-km long aerial photographic transects. On average, 27% of trees (over 65-cm crown diameter) were killed, equivalent to a 6% annual rate of death following the drought of 1961. Apart from the decline of the *Commiphora-Acacia* woodlands, the attractive baobab (*Adansonia digitata*) tree, once characteristic of Tsavo, had also almost disappeared. The elephant population of Tsavo suffered substantial drought-related mortality during 1970–1971. Following this population reduction, Walter Leuthold conducted ground surveys of four common trees in the park during 1970 and 1974. He found that three of these (*Commiphora* spp., *Acacia tortilis*, and *Delonix elata*) declined substantially in both mature and recruitment-age classes due to browsing by elephants, while a fourth species (*Melia volkensii*) not utilized by elephants increased slightly. It seemed as if a significant decline in elephant numbers was not sufficient to reduce browsing pressure on palatable trees.

In another dry habitat, the Ruaha National Park in Tanzania, a serious impact on *Acacia albida* and the baobab during the 1960s was first reported by J. M. Savidge. In the larger acacias, damage to bark exposed the tree to attack by borer beetles and eventually it fell. More serious was the heavy localized impact on regeneration, with 94% of stems showing damage by elephants and 55% so severely damaged that permanent deformity or death was certain.

The elephant problem at Ruaha was studied in greater detail by Richard Barnes (fig. 6.1). During a survey in 1976, he found that 40% of *Acacia albida* trees were dead, while 67% of *Commiphora ugogensis* had been killed over the preceding 6 years, a 17% annual rate of mortality almost entirely due to elephant feeding. The baobab was declining at a 3% annual rate, while recruitment had dropped considerably over the preceding 25 years. Barnes surveyed the baobab population again during 1982 and 1989. Baobab tree density declined considerably between 1976 and 1982, but not significantly by 1989. The poaching of most bull elephants during the latter period could have been the reason for the arrest in tree decline. The size structure of the baobab, however, changed over the period 1976–1989, with a shift to larger sizes and the complete disappearance of the smallest stems (fig. 6.2).

The picture was no different in many parts of southern Africa. P. J. Thomson recorded a rapid decline of *Brachystegia boehmii* woodlands since the mid-1960s on highlands that formed the watershed of the Chizarira Game Reserve in Zimbabwe. Over a period of 16 months ending December 1973, nearly 67% of the 500 original mature trees marked were dead, while another 20% were damaged (the dead and damaged included trees recorded originally as damaged). Fire was also implicated in these deaths, but seemed secondary to elephants. In the Sengwa Wildlife Research Area, Peter Guy observed a much higher rate of tree pushing by bull elephants than that recorded in the Serengeti. The bulls he followed each pushed over 9 trees per day during the dry season or 4.5 trees per day over the year as tree pushing was negligible during the wet season. Considering, however, that only one bull per social group

Figure 6.1

A landscape in Zimbabwe (*top*) where the elephant's impact on the woody vegetation can be clearly seen in the sharp contrast along the boundary of Mana Pools National Park, with fewer trees inside the park. (Photo courtesy of Richard Hoare.) A living baobab tree (*bottom left*) with the base of its stem hollowed by elephant feeding at Sengwa, Zimbabwe (photo by author), and another baobab (*bottom right*) reduced to pulp by elephants at Ruaha, Tanzania (photo courtesy of Richard Barnes).

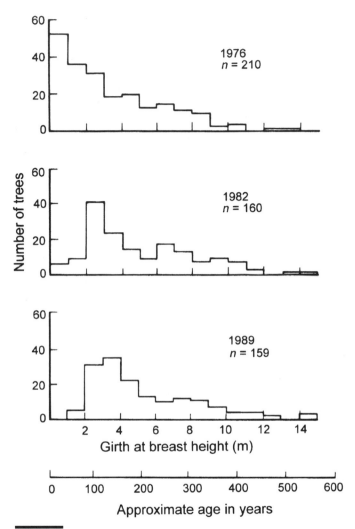

Figure 6.2
Changes in the size distributions of baobab trees recorded in each
of three surveys at Ruaha, Tanzania. (From Barnes et al. 1994.
Reproduced with the permission of Blackwell Science Ltd., U.K.)

would push over trees, Guy calculated that, on average, a male in the Sengwa
population might fell 1.6 trees per day. Female elephants pushed over far fewer
trees. Still, the estimated 56,000 trees felled each year by the elephant population over a 390-km² area of the reserve was significant considering that tree
recruitment rates were likely to be lower (these were not measured).

The Luangwa Valley of Zambia, then home to one of the largest concentrations of elephants in the continent, had a problem with its mopane (*Colopho-*

spermum mopane) woodlands. A Food and Agricultural Organization (FAO) team working there during 1966 estimated that elephants were felling trees at the annual rate of 138 trees/km^2 or 4% of the standing crop (Hanks 1979). A decade and a half later, Dale Lewis, working in South Luangwa, calculated that production of mopane stems was severely restricted by elephant browsing. Elephants also had an impact on succulent thicket rich in endemic plants, as in the Cape Province of South Africa, although this was secondary to feeding by goats. Kruger National Park, home to most of South Africa's elephants, also had a problem of damage to woody vegetation, although this was surprisingly not well documented in the literature as with other regions in Africa.

The impact of elephants on woody vegetation is not confined to semiarid Africa. Robert and Martina Höft documented the impact of elephants on a coastal rain forest that had previously been logged in Kenya's Shimba hills. They listed nearly a hundred species utilized by elephants. The saplings of several potential canopy and subcanopy trees were browsed by elephants; these constituted 19% and 48% of all browsed species, respectively. Elephants could thus have a major impact on the succession and structure of this moist forest.

Transformation of Asian elephant habitats as a result of browsing has not been as dramatic. In a 1971 paper, Dieter Mueller-Dombois described the distortion to young tree crowns caused by elephant utilization in the dry forests of Sri Lanka's (Ceylon's) Ruhuna National Park. As much as 79% of the thorny evergreen tree *Feronia limonia* showed crown distortion, while other woody plants suffering high levels of damage included *Streblus asper* (72%), *Manilkara hexandra* (59%), *Elaeodendron glaucum* (55%), *Salavadora persica* (55%), *Cordia gharaf* (53%), and *Randia dumetorum* (53%). Of 62 species recorded, 17 others were affected to the extent of 25%–50% of stems scored in the survey. Elephants preferentially utilized secondary growth forest to the near-climax seasonal forest. In spite of a large proportion of woody species being damaged to significant degrees by elephants, Mueller-Dombois did not express any concern about a transition from forest to grassland at the existing elephant densities. One reason was that hardly any tree was pushed over or had its bark damaged adversely; the very low numbers of tusked elephants here contributed to this pattern.

Working in Gal Oya, another part of the Sri Lankan elephant's dry zone range, Natarajan Ishwaran also recorded a large number of woody plants browsed on by elephants. However, most (78%) of the damage consisted of breaking or twisting of branches and stems, with only 8% of observed damage being partial or complete pushing over of trees. Crown distortion also was uncommon and restricted to a few species, such as *Bauhinia racemosa*. Thus, there have been no real concerns of a decline in woody vegetation because of elephants in the Sri Lankan dry habitat.

Similar patterns of woody plant utilization by elephants are also seen in the dry thorn forests of southern India. However, it is mainly in the deciduous forests that significant declines of certain tree species can be directly attributed to elephants. During the early 1980s, I observed in the Biligirirangan hills that malvaceous trees and shrubs such as *Grewia tiliaefolia, Kydia calycina, Eriolaena quinquelocularis,* and *Helicteres isora* suffered a high degree of damage from bark stripping and branch or stem breaking by elephants. Even though 80% of *Kydia* and *Grewia* stems had some degree of damage, less than 15% of stems (>10-cm girth) were dead. In drier habitats, two tree acacias, *Acacia suma* and *Acacia leucophloea,* were favorite browse for elephants. There was no evidence for decline of these species. Damage to *Acacia suma* was very high during 1981 and 1982, but this declined in later years (fig. 6.3). The *Acacia suma* woodlands are still intact, although a little thinned, two decades after my initial observations. One change in the structure of the woodland is a shift from smaller size to larger stems as these have grown over the years (fig. 6.4).

Tree population declines, however, have been recorded in permanent vegetation plots I established, beginning in 1988, in the Mudumalai Sanctuary in southern India (table 6.2). In one large plot of 50 hectares, an understory tree, *Kydia calycina,* the most abundant species in 1988, declined steeply: from an

Figure 6.3
A young Asian bull elephant in an *Acacia suma* woodland in the Biligirirangans, India. This woodland suffered heavy damage due to elephants breaking stems and stripping bark during 1981–1982, but thereafter much less damage occurred.

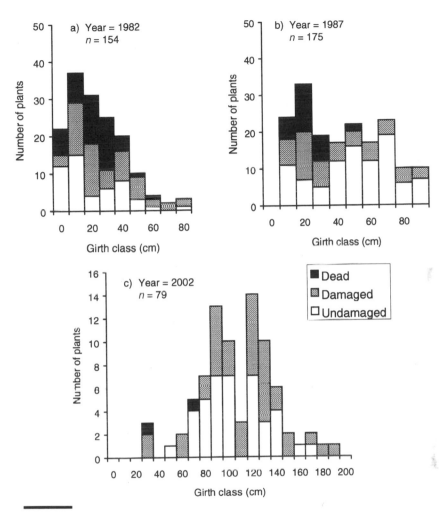

Figure 6.4

Changes in size distribution and damage intensity of *Acacia suma* trees in each of three surveys at Karapallam in the Biligirirangans in southern India. (From Sukumar 1989a and unpublished data of R. Sukumar and H. S. Suresh 2002.)

initial population of 5,175, by 90% to only 525 stems in 1994, and thereafter more gradually to 147 by the year 2000. Damage by elephants has been the main cause of decline. Three other woody plants from the order Malvales have also declined over this period. *Helicteres isora*, a shrub, and *Grewia tiliaefolia*, a canopy tree, have declined from a combination of fire and elephant utilization, while *Eriolaena quinquelocularis*, an understory tree, has lost ground mainly due to the elephant. The demography of these woody species is poorly understood.

Table 6.2
Changes in population sizes (stems > 1 cm diameter at breast height [1.3 m])
of four woody plants (order Malvales) consumed by elephants
in a 50-ha permanent plot at Mudumalai in southern India.

Year	Kydia calycina (Understory Tree)	Eriolaena quinquelocularis (Understory Tree)	Grewia tiliaefolia (Canopy Tree)	Helicteres isora (Shrub)
1988	5,175	250	540	2,569
1989	3,931	234	518	2,228
1990	3,047	228	506	1,918
1991	1,792	221	483	1,299
1992	1,096	186	459	808
1993	762	162	448	725
1994	525	124	434	549
1995	409	67	420	460
1996	247	54	396	307
1997	190	41	390	285
1998	156	37	387	271
1999	147	32	381	289
2000	174	26	374	562

No clear pattern of utilization by elephants can be discerned as yet. Long-term monitoring of these populations could provide better insights into the interaction of elephants, fire, and other influences on their dynamics.

6.3   Hypothesized causes of vegetation change

Many observers realized that it was necessary to look beyond the elephant to explain the decline of particular trees or vegetation change at a landscape level. Vegetation change, even over short timescales of a decade or two, could be influenced by climate, soils, fire, insect pests, herbivorous mammals, or humans. The elephant was only one agent, albeit the most important, in a complex interplay of natural forces and human interventions. Several hypotheses emerged to explain the observed changes in the vegetation.

6.3.1   The compression (overabundance) hypothesis

The decline in woody vegetation is traced directly to an overabundance of elephants, especially in protected areas. The overpopulation of elephants is caused by a compression of their range due to expanding human settlements, combined perhaps with a release from traditional hunting in habitats that are now protected as wildlife reserves. This hypothesis has been stated in various forms by Buechner and Dawkins in their study at Murchison Falls; Lamprey and colleagues, based on their Serengeti study; and Laws, who synthesized a variety of examples in a key 1970 publication. Laws even speculated that elephants may have been responsible for the creation of deserts in Africa.

Implicit in the hypothesis is the assumption that elephants and woody vegetation can be at equilibrium, or nearly so, when the former do not exceed the "carrying capacity" of the habitat under natural conditions. The problem of elephant overabundance may be the result of one of several factors. Given its positive rate of population growth, an elephant population would quickly exceed the carrying capacity unless regulated through expansion of its range or dispersal to other habitats. The boundaries of elephant population ranges, however, were becoming fixed or even contracting in the face of human expansion. The end result was the same in both instances—too many elephants, due either to a positive population growth rate or their being squeezed into smaller and smaller habitat areas even if population sizes were not increasing. A combination of these two factors was also possible. The creation of protected areas added to this problem by reducing or eliminating mortality from hunting. In times past, the mortalities from hunting would have helped to maintain the growth rate at zero.

Evidence for loss of habitat, compression of populations, and hence, increase in elephant densities, coincident to loss of woody vegetation, had been presented for several East African habitats. Graeme Caughley, however, argued in a 1976 article that no significant loss of habitat or compression of elephants could be demonstrated for the Luangwa Valley in Zambia, a region that faced a similar situation, with its declining woodlands seemingly under pressure from elephants. He further stated that compression may not be a "logical necessity" to explain this problem, but that "the crux lies in whether elephants would have changed habitats in much the same way if compression had not occurred" (p. 275). The Luangwa experience suggested otherwise. A decade later, Dale Lewis suggested that some compression had indeed taken place along the eastern boundary of the South Luangwa National Park due to human disturbance, such as hunting, resulting in redistribution of elephants. While this functional "compression" may have imposed a localized pressure on woodlands, this does not seem to be a general explanation for the earlier woodland loss in the Luangwa.

6.3.2   *The fire hypothesis*

Several ecologists studying landscape change recognized that fire may act synergistically with elephants and other herbivores in the decline of woodlands (fig. 6.5). As elephants felled large trees, the increased light stimulated the growth of grasses, which now provided more fuel for dry season fires. The more fierce and frequent fires affected both large trees and young saplings. Thus, Buechner and Dawkins recorded that the stripping of bark of even large trees by elephants at Murchison exposed the inner tissues to fire damage and

Figure 6.5
A fire-burned patch of forest in Bandipur National Park, India. In the short term, fire reduces the availability of forage for elephants and other herbivores, although the flush of grass after the rains arrive attracts these grazing mammals.

death. P. J. Thomson observed, in the Chizarira Reserve, that the burning of grass and woody vegetation in the lower stratum removed this food resource for elephants, which then turned to mature trees for palatable food in the *Brachystegia* woodlands. The presence of thick rootstocks with numerous fire scars in these woodlands also indicated that regeneration had been suppressed by fires in the past.

The synergistic effect of fire and elephants in the decline of woodlands was also stressed by Peter Guy for the Sengwa region in Zimbabwe. A game fence surrounds a wildlife research area that has a much higher concentration of elephants than the communal lands outside. Fire and elephants have an impact on woodlands in the research area, while fire is the main agent of impact on the woodlands outside. While the biomass of shrubs was the same in both these strata, the biomass of trees was clearly lower in the research area (8.5 t/ha) compared to outside (26.2 t/ha). Both these were lower than a theoretically computed biomass of 40.3 t/ha for undamaged woodland.

None of the above studies, however, factored in the regeneration and re-cruitment potential of woody species in the absence of fire. In other words, an important question is whether a woodland affected by elephants can maintain a stable biomass through its natural regeneration capacity if fire is absent. The

Serengeti, where several studies have been carried out since the late 1960s, provides some answers.

In the Seronera region of the Serengeti, Harvey Croze made detailed estimates of elephant damage to and regeneration potential of the tree acacias, particularly *Acacia tortilis* during 1968–1971. He argued that the regeneration potential of this species was adequate to replace large trees killed by elephants, but that the saplings had to be protected from fire. There was a possibility of cycles in the recruitment and dynamics of acacias, but Croze was categorical that the large acacias would not disappear because of elephants, but perhaps as a result of fire. Others, such as Mike Norton-Griffiths, were even more emphatic in pinning the blame on fire for the decline of woodlands. Using large-scale time series maps of fires in the Serengeti during 1963–1972 and superimposing these, along with spatial data on elephant numbers and climatic parameters, on maps of woodland changes, Norton-Griffiths showed statistically that fire was the most important variable in explaining the change in tree cover. Robin Pellew added another dimension to the problem of declining acacia woodlands. Browsing by giraffes on recruitment-size acacia trees was not only checking their growth into mature trees, but also was making them highly susceptible to mortality from fire.

The *Acacia tortilis* woodlands in the Serengeti were reassessed in 1982 by R. W. Ruess and F. L. Halter. By this time, the elephant population of the Serengeti had declined substantially due to hunting. In spite of this, there was a greater than 70% reduction in the abundance of *A. tortilis* trees over 5 m compared to the 1971 situation. This was attributed to two factors: the browsing pressure from giraffes, which arrested the trees to below 3 or 4 m in height, and the occurrence of fire, although less frequent now, which killed the small trees. The longer-term assessment thus provided broad support to the indictment of fire by Croze and Norton-Griffiths and to Pellew's observations of the interaction between giraffe and fire in causing the eventual decline of mature acacias.

Fire could also manipulate the vegetation and elephant distribution in a manner that has a bearing on damage to woodland. By removing grass cover and woody undergrowth, fire could influence the movement of elephants and their feeding on trees. At Kasungu National Park in Malawi, Richard Bell and Hugo Jachmann observed, in experimental fire plots established in *Brachystegia* woodland, that elephants browsed on trees to a significantly lower extent in early-burn plots (21.7% of trees) compared to unburned plots (29.2%). Further, from aerial surveys during 1978–1982 of the park, they also observed that elephants were preferentially distributed during 4 of these 5 years in unburned areas. From these patterns of elephant distribution and feeding in burned versus unburned areas, they concluded that pressure on woodlands would be lower in burned areas, and that fire could be used to achieve management goals. Obviously, the pressure of elephants on trees in unburned areas would correspondingly increase.

In Zambia's Luangwa Valley, Dale Lewis made similar observations of lower browsing pressure on burned mopane woodland. Lewis observed that this was achieved in spite of elephants preferring to feed on mopane branches scorched by fire compared to unburned trees.

Measurements of feeding patterns on burned and unburned areas of mopane woodland in Kruger National Park, South Africa, by Andrew Kennedy, however, found the opposite to be true. The elephants here distinctly preferred the fibrous stems of unburned trees over the charred shoots of mopane. Thus, the African observers differed in their views as to the precise role played by fire in vegetation change.

6.3.3   The climate change hypothesis

One of the more interesting explanations for the decline of a woodland was provided by David Western and C. van Praet in 1973. The fever tree *Acacia xanthophloea* at Amboseli in Kenya was declining through the 1950s and the 1960s. This species was heavily utilized by elephants; in fact, over 83% of trees examined during the study showed signs of debarking, although very few trees had been pushed over.

A casual observer would have blamed the elephant for the decline of fever trees, but Western and van Praet took a more holistic approach to the problem. Analysis of soil samples revealed that tree stands in advanced stage of collapse were found in highly saline soils, while healthy stands grew in non- or mildly saline soils (fig. 6.6). Further investigations showed that groundwater levels had risen 3–4 m between 1961 and 1964. It seemed obvious that the rising water table had introduced a high level of soluble salts to the rooting layer of fever trees, creating a physiological drought. For once, the elephant was clearly not to blame for decline of a tree. Long-term climatic cycles, not well understood, were driving the vegetation dynamics of the Amboseli basin.

The Amboseli phenomenon of changing water tables was possibly a special case that did not apply to most other regions where trees had declined. Amboseli continued to witness an overall decline in tree canopy through the 1980s in the face of an expanding elephant population. David Western later conceded that elephants, indeed, were also responsible for this continuing vegetation change.

6.3.4   The dispersal-foraging maladaptation hypothesis

The regional elephant populations of Africa have fluctuated considerably since the seventeenth century as a result of an upsurge or abatement in ivory poaching (chapter 8). By the end of the nineteenth century, the elephant populations of West Africa, southern Africa (south of the Zambezi River), and East Africa had been largely wiped out. These regions suffered greatly because of their relative accessibility to trade routes out of the continent.

Hugo Jachmann and Richard Bell proposed that the Central African elephants, which were not affected to the same extent, dispersed into southern and eastern Africa as the populations there depleted. The moist forest-dwelling

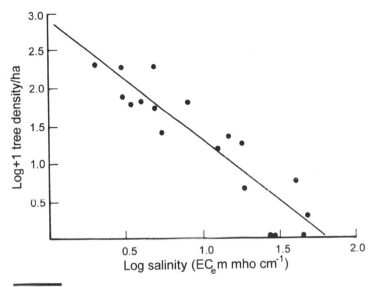

Figure 6.6
The relationship between density of *Acacia xanthophloea* trees and soil salinity in Amboseli, Kenya. A sharp inflection point at about 7–8 EC_e divides sparse from dense stands when plotted on a normal scale. (From Western and van Praet 1973. Reprinted by permission from *Nature*, **241**, 104–106. Copyright 1973 Macmillan Publishers Ltd.)

migrants were adapted to feeding on trees. The feeding behavior of their descendants is thus maladaptive in the more arid regions of eastern and southern Africa, where grass should have been the preferred forage. There is no evidence as yet to support the view that the Central African forest-dwelling elephants dispersed to the drier parts of Africa in recent centuries. Studies on genetic relatedness among the regional populations could shed light on this issue.

6.3.5   The ecosystem nutrient status hypothesis

It is by now well recognized that the abundance of mammalian herbivores over a landscape or regional scale is linked to the nutrient status of the soil. Samuel McNaughton (1988) showed, for instance, that animals in the Serengeti concentrate in areas of higher availability in forage of minerals such as magnesium, sodium, and phosphorus. Daniel Botkin and colleagues emphasized the role of soil nutrient status and cycling in the abundance and dynamics of vegetation and large herbivore populations. The retention of nutrients in the soil is linked to rainfall in a region, as shown in an early East African study by R. M. Scott. Under very low rainfall (<500 mm/year), nutrient saturation is maintained at nearly 100% in all soil types. With increasing rainfall, the saturation drops steeply to 15% at a threshold of about 750 mm/year, after which it increases again through the subhumid regions to a smaller peak of 55% at 1,200 mm/ year, only to drop again beyond this level. Botkin and colleagues thus view the dynamics of vegetation and large herbivores like elephants in semiarid habitats as a complex interaction in which nutrient cycling plays a pivotal role. The removal of large herbivores (e.g., through culling of elephants, for instance) could also remove nutrients and lower the productivity of the vegetation.

6.3.6   The herbivore interaction hypothesis

While the role of fire and of other herbivores such as the giraffe in the wood-land-savanna transition have been described by several observers, Herbert Prins and his associates emphasized the role of many other herbivores, including impala and buffalo, in this process. The seedlings of trees such as *Acacia* estab-lish only infrequently; these rare windows of opportunity arise when popula-tions of browsers such as impala are reduced through disease epidemics. Com-petition for grass from superior grazing ungulates such as buffalo may force elephants to overexploit woody vegetation. A complex interaction of the com-petition-facilitation process within the browser-grazer community, with fire playing the role of a "superherbivore," determines the transitions between woodland and grassland in semiarid Africa.

6.3.7   The natural cycles hypothesis

The hypothesis that probably aroused the greatest curiosity was the "stable limit cycle" between forests and elephants proposed in 1976 by Graeme Caughley. Whereas several of the earlier descriptions assumed that elephants and wood-lands could exist in equilibrium under natural conditions, Caughley began with a radically different view. He argued that there was no natural equilibrium between elephants and woodlands in parts of semiarid Africa. Rather, he visu-alized a cyclical relationship in which elephants increase and thin out the for-ests, only to decline later when the forests become sparse, thus allowing the forest to regenerate. This in turn allows the elephants to increase, and the cycle repeats. This constitutes a stable limit cycle in which the trends in tree and elephant densities resemble sine waves with a time lag (fig. 6.7).

To make estimates of the period of the cycle, Caughley went by evidence provided by the trees themselves in the Luangwa Valley. Patterns of forking of stems in mopane trees, indicative of breaking by elephants, showed low fre-quencies at intermediate sizes compared to small or large sizes, which are suggestive of cycles in elephant usage. There was no basis for fixing ages to mopane trees. On the other hand, size measurements of baobab trees and their transformation to ages showed a peak in abundance (and hence recruitment) at sizes corresponding to 140-year-old trees. Since baobabs seem to regenerate most abundantly in grasslands, this indicated a low forest cover and a low elephant density prior to this time. If the peak in baobab regeneration corre-sponded to the trough in tree density, which occurred about a quarter period

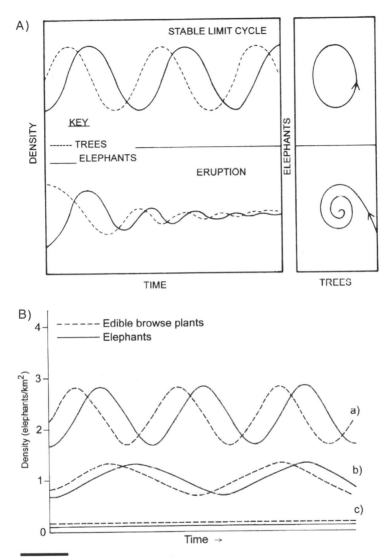

Figure 6.7

Caughley's stable limit cycle (A) between elephants and trees (from Caughley 1976; reproduced with the permission of Blackwell Science Ltd., U.K.) extended (B) to a gradient of climatic/vegetational types. (From Sukumar 1989a.)

or 50 years before the trough in elephant density, then a period of nearly 200 years between successive peaks or troughs in tree or elephant density was indicated.

Caughley recognized that human interference through hunting, fire, and agriculture in the natural system could arrest the cycle and impose an artificial equilibrium. He further reasoned that the period and amplitude of a stable limit cycle could change along a climatic gradient, contracting to a stable equilibrium eventually, but he did not elaborate further.

The Caughley hypothesis requires proximate mechanisms that could drive the cycles between elephants and trees (or, more broadly, woody vegetation). Many have questioned whether any such mechanisms exist in real populations. For a stable limit cycle to operate, there should be a coupling between elephant demography and woody plant biomass. Once woody plants begin to decline in abundance, could the elephant population also follow this trend after only a lag of a few decades? After all, if browse declines in the diet, elephants could switch over easily to grass. They also seem to thrive well on a diet of grass.

Actually, more than one study in East Africa has shown that elephants do not necessarily do too well on a diet in which tall coarse grasses predominate. Richard Laws's extensive studies in Uganda did show that fecundity rates fell considerably in elephant populations living at high densities, in habitats transformed from woodland to grassland, and when presumably their diets had changed from predominantly higher-quality browse to lower-quality grass. The slowing in reproduction was the consequence of both delayed age in first calving by females and longer intercalving intervals. The Murchison South population was clearly a declining one as a result of this demographic shift.

Sylvia Sikes also presented evidence that African elephants could suffer from cardiovascular diseases due to stress caused by loss of tree cover. She even argued that a diet of low-quality grass could make elephants more prone to clogging of arteries, much as a high-fat diet could do in humans.

The main question was whether these conditions were sufficient to produce the regular elephant-tree cycles that Caughley envisaged. This could be modeled much like predator-prey dynamics, but although Caughley provided the basic mathematical formulation in his 1976 article, this was attempted only two decades later. The empirical evidence for the Caughley model is weak. The pattern of age-size distribution of baobab trees (or other trees, for that matter), showing cycles in the form of peaks and troughs, could result in ways other than long-term variations in recruitment. Richard Barnes showed through modeling that such a pattern could arise from a growing elephant population feeding preferentially on young baobabs. My observations of *Acacia leucophloea* and *Acacia suma* show that bimodality in size distributions can arise without any significant change in elephant numbers. Nevertheless, I believe that the Caughley model represented a conceptual jump in attempts to understand the complex relationship between elephants and their habitats.

I qualitatively extended the Caughley model to span the spectrum of habitat types from the semiarid savanna woodlands to aseasonal tropical rain forests where elephants are found (fig. 6.7, table 6.3). Elephant demography can be properly understood only in the light of the evolutionary history of a population. This would have been important in shaping life history traits such as age at first reproduction or longevity. Similarly, the structure of a forest would depend on how the individual species have evolved in relation to climate, soil, competition, herbivory, and so on. The link between elephant population dynamics and forest dynamics would depend on what the latter has to offer in terms of forage. Rain forests have a high biomass of plants, but few of these are palatable or available to elephants. Savanna woodlands have a low biomass, but a high proportion of this is food for elephants. Thus, Caughley's limit

Table 6.3
Characteristics of elephant-vegetation dynamics in different habitats.

	Semiarid Savanna Woodland	Equatorial Rain Forest
Rainfall		
Total quantity/year	Low (<70 cm)	High (>180 cm)
Coefficient of variation	High (>50%)	Low (<20%)
Vegetation		
Density of large trees	Low	High
Total biomass of vegetation	Low	High
Proportional availability of woody plants as food	High	Low
Proportion of total trees that can be pushed over by elephants	High	Low
Quantity of edible woody plants	High	Low
Seasonality in forage resources	High	Low*
Carrying capacity K		
Mean K (elephant/km^2)	High (>1)	Low (<0.1)
Variation in K	High	Low
Demography		
Age at first conception in female elephants	8–12	>18
Mean age in years	Low (10–14)	High (>20)
Variance	High	Low
Mortality rates	High range	Low range
Maximum population growth rates per year	Up to about 5%	<1%
Elephant-woodland dynamics	Highly fluctuating	Relatively stable

Source: Modified from Sukumar 1989a.
*An exception may be fruit availability.

cycles model can be examined in the light of selection pressures on elephants and trees across this climatic gradient.

Selection pressures would obviously have varied considerably across the gradient from semiarid to tropical moist habitats. Rainfall in the semiarid habitat is not only very seasonal annually, but also highly variable from one year to another (in statistical terms, the coefficient of variation in rainfall is inversely related to the quantity of rainfall). High-quality food may be superabundant seasonally or during certain years, while it would be scarce in other periods. Elephants can also feed on a large proportion of plants—herbs, shrubs, and trees—in the structurally simple savanna-woodland. If the availability or quality of one type (say, grasses) declines at any time, they can switch over to another plant type or part (say, bark). On the contrary, rainfall is much less variable in aseasonal rain forests. Food, on the other hand, is more dispersed, much of it being of low quality. The rain forest is structurally complex and rich in species, but most plants are virtually useless as forage. Elephants have to search widely for nutritionally poor palms, lianas, selected fruits, or grasses and weeds growing in tree-fall gaps. The remaining plants have deadly chemicals—the so-called plant secondary compounds—that deter feeding. What little is available, however, is more predictable on a seasonal or interannual basis.

Let us consider what life history traits elephants should evolve in these different habitats. I elaborate on this subject in chapter 7, but it would be useful to state briefly the main arguments here. In the highly fluctuating semiarid habitat, it would be advantageous for the elephant to have traits necessary for a rapid rate of increase when favorable conditions return after a population decline. An early age at first reproduction (in females) and a shorter intercalving interval are two traits of fecundity that would be adaptive in response to favorable conditions. Individuals should be able to delay reproduction (late age at maturity or longer calving intervals) when conditions are unfavorable. Thus, one could expect to see greater flexibility in reproductive traits in elephants of semiarid regions. The opposite can be expected in elephants that have evolved in more stable rain forests.

Observed demographic traits are not entirely genetic in origin, but also have strong environmental components. Nutrition would obviously have a major influence on reproductive traits. The relative abundance of high-quality forage in the semiarid savanna woodlands could thus enable elephants to be highly productive. Elephants in the rain forest have to spend energy in searching far and wide for suitable food. During one season, few species or trees might be in fruit. Food is also of lower overall quality. Such populations cannot be as productive as their counterparts in the savanna woodlands. Indeed, given their more stable environment, they do not need to be as productive for their survival and persistence.

The savanna woodlands have a higher carrying capacity for elephants. Densities anywhere up to three elephants/km^2, or even five elephants/km^2 in localized areas, can be attained here as opposed to not more than one elephant/ 5 km^2 in the aseasonal rain forests. Elephants in the former habitat can increase at a rapid rate of up to 4% per annum or even higher to large populations. Rain forest elephants can possibly grow at a more modest rate of less than 1% per annum.

What would be the fate of trees across the vegetation spectrum in response to elephant foraging? In savanna woodlands, a rapidly increasing elephant population would result in a noticeable decline of canopy trees, most of which are palatable to elephants. Charles Fowler has produced compelling evidence that large mammal populations are most productive when they are close to the carrying capacity of the habitat and not at half the carrying capacity, as called for by the logistic function of population growth. If this were to be true for elephants, the steepest growth in a population would be seen when the decline in woody vegetation has begun and elephant density is near its peak. Density-dependent brakes operate slowly in such a situation. Elephants, by virtue of their life history traits, are resilient to sudden population changes. Their ability to switch from browse to grass is also an insurance against immediate nutritional stress. Trees would continue to decline at a rapid rate. Recovery would be possible only when elephants decline to sufficiently low numbers or, alternatively, move to another area. Elephants and trees would fluctuate in their population numbers or biomass with a high amplitude and a low period.

One would hardly notice any damage to trees in the rain forest. The bark or leaves of most trees are unpalatable to elephants. Larger trees are immune to being pushed over by elephants. Considerable biomass is locked up as wood in these trees and thus is unavailable for elephants. Life history traits that result in a more stable demography in elephants and the lack of any elephant-related declines in woody vegetation would result in a near-stable equilibrium between elephants and vegetation. I am aware that rain forests are not necessarily the highly stable entities depicted in popular writing or even the earlier scientific literature; hurricanes, fires, and droughts can ravage these forests, albeit rarely. Under natural conditions, however, the rain forests of Africa and Asia inhabited by elephants are relatively stable over timescales of decades or centuries compared to savannas.

In regions of medium rainfall, the deciduous forests could be intermediate between the semiarid savannas and the rain forests in the nature of elephant-vegetation dynamics. Elephant life history traits would have medium plasticity. Structurally, the deciduous forests could witness considerable fluxes in the understory trees, but much less in the canopy trees. Elephant-vegetation cycles could have a lower amplitude and longer period here than in the savanna woodlands.

What is the evidence that elephant life histories and vegetation dynamics actually vary in the fashion described above? The earliest ages at first reproduction in female elephants, in the range of 10–13 years, are known only from the semiarid habitats such as Etosha, Hwange, Kruger, Gonarezhou, Mkomazi, and Tsavo (all African sites) and eastern Sri Lanka, while elephants in moist forest habitats such as Budongo (Uganda), Congo, southern India, and Myanmar (Burma) begin reproducing much later (chapter 7). Intercalving intervals also seem to be slightly lower in such semiarid habitats, although the difference with moist habitats seems less pronounced. Variability in fecundity traits is also high in semiarid regions, as seen from the example of the Kabalega Falls elephant population in Uganda. These patterns broadly support my contention of life history variation across habitats. We need to know more, however, of the rain forest elephant both in Africa and in Asia.

Vegetation change across habitats also seems to follow the expectations outlined above. Tsavo is one example of a semiarid ecosystem in which the vegetation has fluctuated between grassland and woodland during the past century. There is historical evidence that the Tsavo region had few elephants (possibly in part due to hunting for ivory) and a largely grassland habitat (settled by pastoralists) toward the end of the nineteenth century. The region has since seen the establishment of woodland, an increase in the elephant population, decline in woodland, and a crash in elephant numbers during the great drought of 1970–1971 and later by poaching, followed by a resurgence in woodland. In the Luangwa Valley, too, a decline in fecundity was recorded by Dale Lewis during 1980–1981, about a decade after the high fecundity observed there by John Hanks. Lewis's explanation that a skewed sex ratio was responsible for this decline in fecundity is not tenable (a ratio of 1 adult male to 2.5 adult females is hardly skewed in elephant populations; see chapter 7). It is more likely that some poorly understood feature of habitat change caused this decline.

In southern Indian deciduous forests, interestingly, the impact of elephants on the vegetation is felt most acutely in understory trees and shrubs. In vegetation plots my research team has set up at Mudumalai, the greatest impact has been on the understory tree *Kydia calycina* and a shrub, *Helicteres isora*. *Zizyphus xylopyrus* is another small tree pushed over by elephant. Some of the canopy trees, such as *Tectona grandis* and *Grewia tiliaefolia* suffer damage to bark by elephants, but death due to elephants is rare in adult trees, especially in the former species. Other common canopy trees, such as *Lagerstroemia microcarpa, Terminalia crenulata*, and *Anogeissus latifolia*, are hardly affected by elephants. The deciduous forest thus witnesses considerable flux in the understory, but is more stable in its canopy layer. I know of no large rain forest where elephants have caused (perceptible) instability in woody vegetation, although elephants could potentially inflict selective damage and change species composition if introduced into a forest where elephants have never existed.

The key question is whether limit cycles as visualized by Caughley can be generated in an elephant-tree system by incorporating realistic parameters of elephant and tree densities or biomass. This has been recently modeled by Kevin Duffy and associates. Using a range of realistic parameters, they showed that a fixed equilibrium between elephants and trees was the eventual outcome, and that an elephant-tree limit cycle was highly unlikely.

Even if the Caughley model itself is only of historical interest, the relationship between elephants and woody plants can still be visualized as going from near stability to a highly unstable dynamics in relation to environmental variability across a rainfall gradient. Human-transformed habitats could further add to this complexity. How would vegetation respond to a rapid compression of elephants to high densities from loss of habitat?

6.4   *Modeling the elephant-vegetation dynamics*

Field measurements of damage to woody plant species, plant biomass and population changes, fire extent and its influence on mortality, elephant or other herbivore population changes, and other such variables can provide clues to the plausible causes of vegetation change. These are not usually sufficient in themselves to provide a complete understanding of the demography of plant populations. Simulation modeling based on the field empirical data can greatly strengthen our understanding of the elephant-vegetation dynamics. Apart from the test of the limit cycle model, several other modeling approaches using field measurements have been published. I trace the salient features of these models and their verdicts on the role of various agents on vegetation change in semi-arid African habitats.

6.4.1   *Differential tree mortality patterns and dynamics in the Ruaha National Park, Tanzania*

The available data on tree population changes in the Ruaha National Park, Tanzania, during 1965–1977 were used by Richard Barnes to model future trends in relation to elephant usage and possible elephant population management through culling. Four species of trees that differed from each other in their mortality patterns were considered. Tree populations were assumed to follow the logistic growth curve. Regeneration was taken as zero at an elephant density of 3 animals/km^2 (based on observations of regeneration by A. Bjornstad in 1971 referred to in Barnes 1983b), while this was 100% of the potential when elephant density was zero. The mortality patterns of the four tree species were as follows:

1. Tree species I (e.g., *Commiphora ugogensis*) experiences density-independent mortality, that is, each elephant killed a fixed proportion of trees over a period of time. In this case, an elephant density of 1/km^2 caused a loss of 5% of trees per annum.
2. Tree species II (e.g., *Acacia albida*) experiences density-dependent mortality, that is, the mortality rate decreases with lower tree density.
3. Tree species III (e.g., *Colophospermum mopane*) experiences inverse density-dependent mortality, that is, the mortality rate accelerates with decreasing tree density.
4. Tree species IV (e.g., *Adansonia digitata*) experiences fixed-number mortality, that is, each elephant killed a fixed number of trees over a period of time irrespective of tree density.

Beginning from hypothetically identical population sizes in 1946, the four tree species populations obviously behaved very differently under the influence of the same elephant population. As expected, species IV crashed to extinction the fastest. On the other hand, species II persisted beyond 1990 because of a declining rate of utilization with decreasing tree density and population. Species III and I became extinct by about 1985 and 1990, respectively.

Barnes then introduced various options of culling the elephant population. A single cull of 50% of the elephants at different elephant densities of $1-2.5/km^2$ merely delayed the time of extinction of all tree species, with the possible exception of species II, which seemed to persist longer as culls were progressively delayed. Even when 100% of the elephants (at a density of $2/km^2$) were culled, this failed to arrest the extinction of tree species IV, although the other three recovered. Culling the elephants whenever their densities exceeded $0.5/km^2$, however, stabilized tree species populations. The benefit-cost ratio of culling (number of trees saved per elephant shot) varied from one tree species to another. Overall, very large numbers of elephants had to be culled at the higher densities to save the trees. Barnes came to the general conclusion that culling must begin early to be effective in terms of the benefit-cost ratio, but that managers usually realized they had a problem only after elephant densities had become too high.

It is a different matter that, in the case of Ruaha and many other African parks, the spate of ivory poaching during the 1980s drastically reduced the elephant populations. A survey of the Msembe study area in Ruaha during 1989 showed little change in baobab numbers or size distribution from the previous assessment of 1982. Since most of the past baobab mortality was caused by bull elephants, their selective elimination by poachers had spared the surviving trees. Barnes thus recommended that selective culling of bull elephants was sufficient to protect baobabs.

6.4.2   The dynamics of mopane woodlands in Botswana

The impact of elephants, fire, and other agents on the woody vegetation in semiarid northern Botswana was studied by Raphael Ben-Shahar during 1991–1993. The various plant species were affected quite differently by elephants and fire. Thus, *Acacia* spp. and *Colophospermum mopane* were utilized heavily by elephants, while others, such as *Burkea africana, Brachystegia boehmii,* and *Dicrostachys cinerea* were affected more by fire.

Ben-Shahar constructed a model of the dynamics of mopane because this was the dominant feature (30% of stems) of the vegetation and constituted an important part of the elephant's diet. The model incorporated field data on biomass of mopane trees and shrubs as well as elephant density at various study sites. Growth rates of mopane and rates of biomass production were related to rainfall isohyets for the region. The model predicted that mopane trees and shrubs could approach maximum biomass in 6 years under high rainfall and no elephant browsing, while they could attain this limit in about

10 years or a bit longer under low rainfall when growth rates averaged only 50% of the highest rates. Browsing by elephants obviously inhibited biomass production. Interestingly, the model showed that, even under the impact of 15 elephants/km^2, an unusually high density, the mopane woodlands could increase their biomass over the short term (5 years) and later stabilize when rainfall conditions were optimum (fig. 6.8). At this high elephant density, a decline in mopane biomass occurred only when dry conditions depressed growth rates to below 70% of the maximum rates. When the maximum plant growth rates in different rainfall zones were achieved, the region could sustain 3–9 elephants per square kilometer. Ben-Shahar came to the overall conclusion that "there was no substantial evidence to imply that elephants will reduce the biomass of mopane woodlands below a sustainable level if their numbers are allowed to increase considerably beyond the current estimate. Elephant culling as a means to prevent woodland loss is unlikely to meet the objective" (1996, p. 514).

Chris Styles and J. D. Skinner, who studied the utilization of mopane trees in Botswana's Northern Tuli Game Reserve, came to a similar conclusion. In spite of heavy browsing by elephants during summer and by other herbivores such as eland, causing plants to remain shrubs, there was no indication that mopane was in decline.

6.4.3   *Acacia woodlands, oscillations, and multiple stable states in the Serengeti-Mara*

The Serengeti-Mara region (Tanzania-Kenya) has undergone considerable changes in vegetation, fauna, and human populations over the past century. In the early 1880s, a severe drought killed large numbers of livestock kept by the Maasai. Soon, rinderpest entered the African continent from Asia and swept through the Serengeti-Mara region. Populations of both domestic ungulates and wildlife species, including giraffe, buffalo, and wildebeest quickly succumbed to this exotic viral disease. The Maasai herdsmen were further impoverished. Ivory hunters arrived on this scene by the late nineteenth century, and aided by some of the destitute Maasai, almost wiped out the elephants there.

The natural vegetation of the Serengeti-Mara region was, at this time, grassland and lightly wooded savanna. Beginning around the turn of the twentieth century, the woody vegetation grew profusely over this region. *Croton* thickets and various species of *Acacia* became the conspicuous features of the landscape by the middle of the century. Proliferation of tsetse flies, which caused the parasitic blood disease trypanosomiasis in cattle and sleeping sickness in humans, also kept the Maasai away.

By this time, the elephant population had recovered. Increasing human settlements around the periphery also forced elephants into the Serengeti-Mara area, which had by now been declared parks by the colonial administrators. In the early 1960s, unusually high rainfall produced lush growth of grasses, which fueled hot fires. Expansive meadows now began appearing amid the wood-

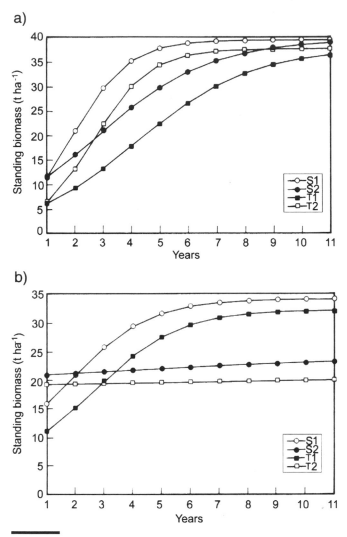

Figure 6.8
Biomass production of *Colophospermum mopane* woodlands comprised of trees (T) or shrubs (S) under (*a*) dry conditions when growth rate $r = 0.5$ (T1, S1) and optimal rainfall conditions when $r = 1$ (T2, S2) and there is no elephant browsing; (*b*) impact of 15 elephants/km^2 at optimal rainfall conditions when $r = 1$ (T1, S1) and dry conditions when $r = 0.7$ (T2, S2). (From Ben-Shahar 1996. Reproduced with the permission of Cambridge University Press, U.K.)

lands, attracting grazing animals. The stage had been set for a dramatic decline in woodlands. Fire frequencies and extent increased, with two or even three fires in some years. The fires not only cleared the bush or suppressed regeneration, but also, at their peak, killed the larger trees. The increasing elephant population and their use of woody vegetation through breaking of branches or stripping bark made the trees more vulnerable to fire. Elephants also directly caused the death of trees.

The various studies on decline of woodlands in the Serengeti also spurred efforts to model the dynamics of the vegetation in relation to fire and mammalian herbivores. Mike Norton-Griffiths took a landscape approach to modeling the changes in the Serengeti. He began by studying patterns of changes in woodland density. He based the study on aerial photographs at different scales and coverage of the park between 1958 and 1972, annual extent of fire during 1963–1972, densities of 13 species of mammals, including elephants, on a seasonal basis between August 1969 and July 1972, and data on climate across the park. There were considerable spatial differences in the loss of woodlands; the higher rainfall regions of the north ("dry subhumid woodlands") lost 26% of their cover density during 1962–1972 compared to only 7% loss in the central semiarid acacia woodlands. A statistical multiple regression analysis using square grids of 100 km^2 and six variables relating to climate, fire, and elephant abundance showed that, in the semiarid central region, the two elephant indices (wet and dry season densities), followed by fire, best explained woodland change. For the subhumid north, where woodland decline was steeper, fire was the most important factor explaining this change.

Norton-Griffiths then simulated, over a 30-year period, the response of the size structure of tree populations to various mortality and growth-retarding influences, such as fire and browsing by elephant and giraffe. No provision was made for seedling establishment because of lack of data. Although a "pessimistic" scenario, this was possibly not important over the short timescale of the simulation. The model suggested that the woodlands were capable of stabilizing, under the conditions prevailing in 1972, provided that they were protected from fire even if elephants increased utilization of the woody vegetation, but not if giraffe increased browsing. Over the longer term, the dynamics of the Serengeti would also be influenced by the production of grasses and their offtake by herbivores such as buffalo and wildebeest. Norton-Griffiths thus felt it feasible that the Serengeti could oscillate between more-woodland and more-grassland phases, mediated by fire and grazers. The addition of browsers or animals such as elephants that can alternate between grazing and browsing introduces levels of complexity not easily tractable.

Robin Pellew constructed a more detailed model that specifically simulated the *Acacia tortilis* woodlands of the Seronera region of the Serengeti. The variables in the model were much the same as previously—fire, elephant, and giraffe—but with seedling input being proportional to the number of mature trees. Projecting ahead from the year 1978, the model showed that the mature tree population would decline when burning frequency exceeded once in about 5–6 years. While reducing elephant numbers would have a short-term benefit in arresting tree decline, a more significant longer-term benefit accrued through reducing browsing pressure from giraffe. The prevalent low elephant densities and high giraffe densities in the Serengeti resulted in a system that oscillated between mature canopy and regeneration-grassland phases. Pellew concluded that, rather than culling elephants, the reduction of giraffe numbers and protection from fire were more likely to help in achieving management goals in the Serengeti.

A very different conclusion, however, was reached by yet another modeling exercise. During 1960–1980, the Serengeti-Mara habitat changed dramatically back to grassland. Wildebeest increased fivefold during this period and removed much of the grass. The lower intensity of fires, however, did not result in recovery of the woodlands. Holly Dublin, along with A.R.E. Sinclair and J. McGlade, modeled the woodland-fire-elephant-wildebeest interactions in the Serengeti-Mara. Their model tracked the fate of trees in relation to burning rate, browsing by elephants and resident antelopes, and trampling of seedlings by wildebeest. Burning rate was assumed to be related to fuel loads and density of humans in the region. Fire only affected trees less than 3 m high, as in previous models. Elephant browsing on trees was proportional to elephant density, not only affecting trees above 1 m in height during the 1960s, but also affecting seedlings during the 1980s, when larger plants had disappeared. Small, browsing antelopes such as impala, dikdik, and Grant's gazelle affected trees less than 1 m only. Similarly, wildebeest damage to trees through trampling was confined to plants less than 1 m.

The model was based on several constants and variables derived from field research by various workers. It was run by varying individual factors such as fire, elephants, wildebeest, or browsing antelopes while holding other factors constant. The synergistic effects of combinations of these factors were also explored. Aerial photographs of the Serengeti-Mara region since 1950 provided the data on actual status of woodland and grassland in the past and rates of change.

Several interesting results emerged from the simulations (fig. 6.9). The observed rates of woodland decline during the 1960s could clearly not be attributed to even the maximum possible rates of browsing by elephants and antelopes. On the other hand, minimal burning rates recorded in this region over the same period could explain the decline in woodlands. This was largely consistent with the hypothesis of Norton-Griffiths that fire was the primary cause of woodland decline in the Serengeti-Mara. The simulations showed, however, that the combined effect of fire and elephant browsing best explained the observed rate of habitat change in the 1960s.

During the 1980s, the wildebeest population had proliferated to such high levels that most of the grass was being consumed. Fire frequencies and intensities had thus declined. This should have promoted the regeneration of woodlands, as predicted by the model when only fire and wildebeest were considered. There was no sign of such a reversion of woodland in the northern Mara

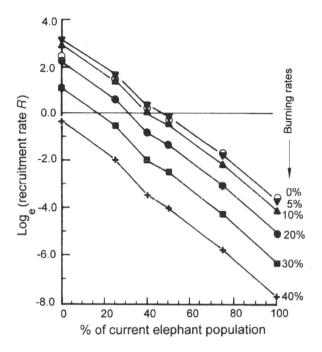

Figure 6.9
Recruitment rates
R of *Acacia* woodland
in the Serengeti-Mara
in relation to varying
elephant population
sizes and burning
rates. The impacts of
wildebeest are held at
0 and those of
browsers at their
1980s rate. Positive
values of R indicate
woodland recovery
and negative values
woodland loss. (From
Dublin et al. 1990.
Reproduced with the
permission of the
British Ecological
Society.)

region. Holly Dublin's observations of elephant feeding revealed an aspect that had been largely overlooked earlier; when the larger trees had disappeared, elephants began pulling out seedlings and eating them. This behavior was obvious only to a careful observer; to a casual observer, it seemed that elephants were just eating grass or other herbs. When elephant feeding on seedlings was plugged into the model along with fire and wildebeest variables, it was clear that the grassland could not revert to woodland. This was consistent with the observations in the Mara during the 1980s.

In the northern Serengeti, bordering the Mara there were signs of woodland recovery. Anthony Sinclair used photographs of identifiable areas of the Serengeti taken between 1926 and 1933 and compared these with his own "photopoints" monitored since 1980. He also used available aerial photographs for looking at changes in woodlands, particularly those of *Acacia clavigera*. Since the 1970s, there was clear evidence of woodland regeneration, a process that continued through the 1980s. The explanation for this contrast with the Mara was simple. There had been a marked change in numbers and distribution of elephants. Poaching had removed up to 80% of elephants in the Serengeti, while the rest had probably moved into the Mara, which now had a high elephant density year round. Released from elephant browsing, the woodlands recovered in the northern Serengeti. They could not do so in the Mara. Caughley's hypothesis assumed that seedlings were immune to browsing by elephants, a condition not met in the Mara.

A major outcome of this work was the "multiple stable states" hypothesis. The savanna woodlands of Africa could oscillate between two equilibria or stable states, one a woodland with few elephants and the other a grassland with many elephants. The elephants by themselves were unable to change a woodland to grassland—an external perturbation such as fire was needed for this to occur. Once a grassland was formed, however, elephants on their own could hold it in this state. The concept of different stable states in ecosystems had been proposed earlier on theoretical grounds by several people, including C. S. Holling (1973) and Robert May (1977). The Serengeti-Mara example was one of the first direct tests of the hypothesis.

There were interesting implications for the management of elephants. If the goal of management was to bring back the woodlands in the Mara, this would be possible only if burning rates were held at less than 10% per year and the elephant population was reduced to less than 40% of the current (1990) levels, both very unlikely in the present context. Thus, the Mara seemed to be locked into its present grassland state.

The future of vegetation in the Serengeti-Mara obviously depends on the outcome of several individual and interacting factors. At some future time, could the Mara elephants move back into the northern Serengeti, perhaps after discovering its recovered woodlands, a rich source of browse? If wildebeest populations continue to remain at high densities in the Mara, could they keep the grass sufficiently low such that the burning rate is negligible? Could there then be a resurgence of woodlands in the Mara?

The important point that emerges from the recent history of the Serengeti-Mara ecosystem, documented by Holly Dublin, is that the concept of "climax" vegetation or community that pervades ecological thinking has no place in such a system. Even if no significant human interference is indicated, it is conceivable that the system could naturally oscillate between different states.

Whatever the actual characteristics of elephant-vegetation dynamics in the various kinds of habitats in which elephants are found today, the credit should go to Graeme Caughley for a radical departure in thinking on this subject. The stable limit cycles with smooth trajectories he envisaged may never occur in an elephant-tree system. Chance fluctuations in elephant births and deaths (demographic stochasticity) and environmental factors such as climate (environmental stochasticity) could cause both elephant populations and woodlands to oscillate rather erratically. Indeed, the development of stochastic models of elephant vegetation dynamics, as has been done with elephant demography (chapter 7), would be a significant step forward in understanding semiarid ecosystems.

6.5   The role of elephants in the ecosystem

A large herbivore such as the elephant obviously makes a tremendous impact on the habitat through its feeding and other activities. This has several consequences for the plant and animal communities in the ecosystem. The transformation of woodland into savanna favors the populations of grazing ungulates. Browsing by elephants on trees keeps the trees in a stunted, shrubby stage that facilitates feeding by smaller browsing mammals. The creation of gaps in forests likewise promotes the growth of herbaceous plants that provide forage for many other herbivores. The paths that elephants make through dense undergrowth also help smaller mammals. The holes that elephants dig in dry riverbeds for subsoil water are also used by other animals. Elephants eat soil or rock (geophagy) to satisfy their appetite for salt. This may result in considerable erosion of land and even the formation of caves along the steep-sided walls of river valleys or cliffs. Some of the larger caves discovered, such as at Mount Elgon in Kenya, have been formed through rock-crunching by elephants over many thousands of years. In semiarid East Africa, the Maasai have long recognized that an abundant elephant population that reduces the density of bushland also keeps down the population of tsetse flies that cause sleeping sickness in humans.

The role of elephants in dispersing fruits and their seeds is well documented, especially in rain forest habitats (see chapter 5). The key question, then, is to what extent is such dispersal important to the regeneration of these plants. One obvious advantage is the mere transport of seeds away from the vicinity of the parent tree, where they may suffer higher destruction from pathogens and seed predators. The passage of a seed through the gut of an animal is also known in several cases to improve the chances of germination by softening or scarification of the seed coat.

Seeds of leguminous plants such as acacias are known to germinate more successfully after being voided by a large herbivore. In semiarid African and Asian habitats, the seeds of such legumes are very common in the dung of elephants. Joseph Dudley found that the seeds of *Acacia erioloba* alone made up 12% of the dung weight, with some piles having over 5,000 seeds of this plant during the dry season in Zimbabwe's Hwange National Park. James Powell recorded 91 plant species germinating from the dung of forest elephants in Cameroon, these representing 14% of the species recorded in this region. Experiments by Diana Lieberman and associates on seeds of 11 species in Ghana's moist forests showed that, in three of these, the rate of germination was clearly higher in ingested seeds than in fresh seeds. In two species, there was no difference in germination rates, while in the rest the experiments were incomplete. While smaller fruits and their seeds may be dispersed by a variety of animals, a tree with large fruits and seeds may be exclusively dispersed by the megaherbivores.

Would such tree species fail to regenerate and decline over time if elephants disappear from an area? Daniel Janzen and Paul Martin proposed that the demography of many Neotropical plants that had evolved for dispersal by megafauna (e.g., gomphotheres) would have altered after the late Pleistocene extinctions (chapter 1). Several traits of extant plants, such as large fleshy fruits, large seeds protected by hard coats, or seemingly passive dispersal are "anachronisms" in today's world. Henry Howe has questioned this hypothesis as being vague; in particular, it is not clear how so many species with "megafaunal syndromes" have persisted for over 10,000 years.

A careful inventory by William Hawthorne and Marc Parren of West African rain forest plants in Upper Guinea, where elephants have declined greatly, found little evidence for a collapse of plant populations, including those most likely to be dependent on elephants for dispersal. One exception was the forest date (*Balanites wilsoniana*), a dry forest tree with seeds that germinate much better and seedlings that grow faster after passage through an elephant's gut. This tree may suffer a decline over a centennial timescale if elephants disappear from a region.

To evaluate the role of elephants in seed dispersal and plant demography, one has to consider several factors, including seed survival from ingestion to voiding, dispersal distance, germination success, and the eventual growth and establishment of the seedlings up to at least the sapling stage. Only then can the role of elephants in seed dispersal be objectively described.

Birth, Death, and Chance
The Dynamics
of Elephant Populations

7

7.1   Introduction

The dynamics of elephant populations hold great theoretical and practical interest. The elephant shares many demographic traits with humans—age of sexual maturity, long gestation, single offspring, low death date, and high longevity. It is not only the statistical details of elephant demography, but also the evolution of life history traits and population regulation in this large mammal that are of considerable interest. From a practical viewpoint, an adequate understanding of demographic processes in elephant populations is essential to making sound conservation judgments. Whether it is comprehending how density influences demography or how populations respond to the pressures of poaching, a fundamental consideration in conservation is the trajectory of animal numbers.

Understanding the dynamics of populations requires not only good empirical data from the field, but also the backing of robust mathematical models. Often, very subjective assessments are made about the dynamics of a population. I have, for instance, commonly heard statements to the effect that, "Every elephant group has a calf and thus the population must be doing very well." This could be correct, or it could be completely wrong. The mere presence of a calf in every group does not by itself say anything about the trends in a population. If the population is suffering a high death rate, it could be declining. "Rule-of-thumb" assessments sometimes can be made about the dynamics of a population based on fragmentary data, but this requires additional knowledge about its demographic attributes. More important, mathematical models allow us to explore the conditions under which a species population is likely to be increasing, stable, or declining. Even if the population itself is increasing, its structure may be getting distorted; for instance, the sex ratio may be skewing in favor of females, as in many parts of southern India, because of selective poaching of male elephants.

Field data on all aspects of demography are not easily available for elephant populations, especially for those living in forests. Even when these have been collected, they are usually snapshots of the population in time. A long-lived species perforce calls for a long-term demographic profile before we can begin to understand its dynamics. Only at Amboseli in Kenya have detailed birth and death records of identified elephants been maintained for longer than one elephant generation. Useful, long-term annual records are also being maintained at Dzanga Bai (Central African Republic), Addo and Kruger (South Africa), eastern Sri Lanka, and the Nilgiris (India). None of these has yet been fully analyzed and presented.

Several methods have been used to estimate demographic variables such as age at first reproduction, interbirth interval, reproductive senescence, and age-specific death rates in the sexes. Postmortem examination of reproductive organs in large samples of culled elephants has provided a wealth of information relating to fecundity in populations such as those in North Bunyoro (Uganda), Luangwa Valley (Zambia), Kruger (South Africa), Hwange (Zimbabwe), and Etosha (Namibia). Field observation methods have been used to derive demographic variables in other places, including Lake Manyara (Tanzania), Amboseli (Kenya), Kasungu (Malawi), Ruhuna-Yala (Sri Lanka [Ceylon]), and Biligirirangans-Nilgiris (India). Some very useful demographic data also come from captive elephants held under seminatural conditions, especially in southern India and Myanmar (Burma). The mathematical models needed to make sense of the empirical data have fortunately become progressively sophisticated. These have given us useful insights into demographic factors that could regulate elephant populations. These have also tackled the issue of minimum viable elephant populations for their persistence. Innovative means, such as the use of tusk size in the trade to derive ages of dead elephants, have been used to understand population dynamics in relation to poaching. Models that link population genetics to demography in elephants, however, are still rudimentary. For instance, we have little understanding of the genetics of tusk inheritance in elephants; the modelers, therefore, have relied on the most basic assumptions for linking demography to changes in the tusk trait of elephant populations.

I first provide a comparative account of observed demographic traits across elephant populations and try to relate these to life history evolution in relation to their specific environments. Beginning with the simplest of population models, I then trace the development of the more sophisticated models and the understanding they provide of the dynamics of African and Asian elephant populations.

7.2   *Demographic variables in elephant populations*

The most fundamental consideration in tracking the dynamics of a population is the estimation of birth rates and death rates. In some instances, the rates of immigration and emigration may also be important. While the overall birth and death rates of a population provide a simple picture of its trends, our understanding of its dynamics is considerably enhanced if we can estimate age-specific fecundity and age-specific mortality. We need to know the age at which a female first gives birth (and not merely becomes sexually mature, although the two are related), the number of young born with each pregnancy, the interval between successive births at different stages in life, the age of last birth, and the death rate at different ages for both males and females. Observations of both captive and wild elephant populations show that the birth of twin calves constitutes less than about 1% of all births (one exception being Etosha, with a 4% rate) and thus can be practically ignored for analyzing their dynamics.

7.2.1   *Age span of reproduction and birth rates*

Puberty is generally taken as the onset of the first estrous cycle in the female and the production of viable sperm in the male. Sexual maturity is the age at first ovulation in the female and the presence of a dense mass of motile sperm in the male. In both sexes, there may be a difference of 2–4 years between puberty and sexual maturity among elephants. Although there is tremendous variation across elephant populations in the age of sexual maturity, the early East African studies showed that females and males within a population generally attain maturity around the same age. This seems broadly true across African and Asian elephant populations, with possibly the cows maturing 1 or 2 years prior to the bulls.

For the purposes of demography, the age of first conception (and subsequent calving) in cows and the successful siring of a calf by a bull are the relevant variables. Cow elephants may conceive within their first few estrous cycles (each lasting 14–16 weeks), but successful mating by a bull may be postponed by as much as 10 years for sociological reasons. The difference between age at sexual maturity and age at first conception is not always explicitly stated in figures provided by some studies; the former can be computed only when a sample of culled elephants is available, while the latter is implicit in results from field observations. As the two figures are related and the difference between them is likely to be generally small for female elephants, I use these terms interchangeably.

The age at sexual maturity and at first conception in female elephants seem related to local climate, forage resources, nutritional plane, and other ecological factors, such as density among wild populations. This varies both across regions and populations as well as within a population over time (table 7.1).

Table 7.1
Reproductive parameters of female elephants in various populations.

Location	Period of Study	Mean Age at I Conception (year)	Mean Calving Interval (year)	Elephant Density (per km²)	Source
African elephant					
Kabalega North (Uganda)	1966	16.3	9.1	1.16	Laws et al. (1975)
	1974	9.6	5.1	1.10	Malpas (1978)
Kabalega South (Uganda)	1967	17.8	5.6	2.70	Laws et al. (1975)
	1974	9.0	3.5	1.22	Malpas (1978)
Rwenzori (Uganda)	1973	12.3	4.5	2.14	Malpas (1978)
Budongo (Uganda)	1966	22.4	7.7	3.12	Laws et al. (1975)
Mkomazi East (Tanzania)	1968	12.2	2.9	0.82	Laws et al. (1975)
Mkomazi Central (Tanzania)	1969	12.2	4.2	0.82	Laws et al. (1975)
Lake Manyara (Tanzania)	1966–1970	11.0	4.7	5.0	Douglas-Hamilton (1972)
Tsavo (Kenya)	1966	11.7	6.8	1.00	Laws et al. (1975)
Amboseli (Kenya)	1970s and 1980s	13.5	4.9	>1.0	Moss (1988), Lee and Moss (1995)
Luangwa (Zambia)	1965–1969	14.0	3.8	2.17	Hanks (1972b)
Gonarezhou (Zimbabwe)	1971–1972	12.5	3.7	1.85	Sherry (1975)
Hwange (Zimbabwe)	1972	11.0	4.0	0.62	Williamson (1976)
Mana Pools (Zimbabwe)	1969–1972	12.5	3.5	0.35	Kerr (1978)
Kruger (South Africa)	1970–1974	12.0	4.5	0.41	Smuts (1975)
Kasungu (Malawi)	1978	11.0	3.6	0.35	Jachmann (1980, 1986)
Etosha (Namibia)	1983–1985	11.2	3.8	0.05	Lindeque (1988)
Asian elephant					
Biligirirangans (India)	1981–1983	15.0	4.7	0.53	Sukumar (1985, 1989a)
Nilgiris (India)	1988–1994	14.0	4.5	~2.0	Sukumar (unpublished)
Ruhuna-Yala and Southeastern (Sri Lanka)	1960–1990	~10.0*	4.0–6.5*	0.25	McKay (1973), Kurt (1974), Katugaha et al. (1999)
Wasgomuwa (Sri Lanka)	1980–1982	~10.0*	4.0*	0.50	Ishwaran (1993)

*The Sri Lankan studies do not explicitly compute the mean age at I conception or mean calving interval; all studies assume that females are generally mature/adult at about 9 years old, while the calving interval has to be deduced from population structure.

Most studies of African savanna elephant populations report a mean age of sexual maturity of 11–14 years, although the range varies from about 9 to 22 years. Individual elephants, of course, may attain maturity earlier (8 years seems the lowest in the wild) or as late as 30 years. The typical population values come from studies at Lake Manyara and Hwange (both 11 years), Tsavo (11.7 years), Kruger (12 years), Mkomazi (12.2 years), Rwenzori (12.3 years), Gonarezhou (12–13 years), and Luangwa Valley (14 years).

One of the lowest mean ages of sexual maturity seems to apply to the elephant population of Etosha in Namibia. Depending on the method of computing this figure, Malan Lindeque reported values of 9.1–13.5 years in 1983 and 10.7–11.9 years for the same population in 1985. The highest mean age of sexual maturity is 22.4 years, registered for the Budongo population by Richard Laws. Also notable is the change in the mean age of maturity for the Murchison (Kabalega) Falls elephants, from 16.3 years and 17.8 years for the northern and southern subpopulations, respectively, during 1966–1967 when Laws examined them, to 9.6 years and 9.0 years by 1974 when Rob Malpas investigated the same subpopulations.

Female Asian elephants also seem to show wide variation across populations in the age of sexual maturity. Although the data are scanty, cows in Sri Lanka seem to have the lowest age at first conception. There are reports of cows mating as early as 7–9 years old; even if these are exceptional, a mean age of maturity of 10–12 years old is likely here. In southern India's Biligirirangans, I estimated the mean age of first calving in female elephants during 1981–1983 to be about 17–18 years; from this, it follows that the age of first conception would have been about 15–16 years. Later observations in the Nilgiris indicated a slightly lower age of first conception and calving. Khyne U Mar's detailed compilation of demographic records of several thousand timber camp elephants, both captive born and wild caught, in Myanmar shows that the cows have their first calf on average between 20 and 25 years, indicating that they first conceived between 18 and 23 years. These elephants are kept in forest areas under seminatural conditions and thus broadly reflect a relatively late age of sexual maturity even if these figures cannot be directly applied to wild populations.

The gestation period in elephants is accepted to be generally between 18 and 23 months, with a mean of about 21 months. There are no objective data to determine differences, if any, between African and Asian elephants or between male and female calves, as claimed in some anecdotal accounts. After successful parturition, a cow elephant would be in lactational anestrus for about 2 years before she begins to cycle again. An interbirth interval of about 4 years is thus about the minimum expected in most cases.

As with the age of maturity, the calving interval can also be expected to vary with environmental conditions. There are also problems in comparing estimates based on number of placental scars in culled samples with percentage of adult cows pregnant or records of successive births to identified cows in a population (fig. 7.1). The data from Asian and African populations mostly

Figure 7.1
A well-identified adult female Asian elephant (note the deep tear in the left ear) with two of her offspring aged less than 1 year and about 5 years. Intercalving interval in a population can be computed from a sample of such examples.

indicate mean intercalving intervals of 4–5 years. In the Biligirirangans, I recorded a mean intercalving interval of 4.7 years during 1981–1983 and a slightly lower value in the Nilgiris during later, longer-term observations.

Some African populations, such as in Luangwa Valley, Etosha, and Kasungu, have recorded even lower intercalving intervals of 3.8–3.9 years, presumably when they have been observed during an expanding phase. One of the longest mean intervals is 7.7 years for the population in the moist Budongo Forest. Intervals of 9.1 years and 5.6 years were reported for the northern and southern subpopulations, respectively, at Murchison (Kabalega) Falls during 1966–1967, which declined to 5.1 years and 3.5 years by 1974. The point to emphasize, therefore, is that calving interval may vary over time for a population or even over the life span of an individual and thus could potentially be a mechanism for regulating population growth.

An interesting aspect of intercalving intervals has been pointed out by Phyllis Lee and Cynthia Moss from their long-term study at Amboseli. When a cow had a male calf, the interbirth interval for the next calf was 2–5 months longer on average than when she had a female calf because of the higher investment needed for nurturing a male calf (chapter 4).

The age of reproductive senescence in female elephants would generally not be an important consideration in demography because the oldest individuals would only constitute a small fraction of the total adult females in a population. An exception to this would be a declining population with a preponderance of older individuals. Female elephants in the 56–60-year age class examined by Richard Laws and colleagues at Murchison (Kabalega) Falls showed them to be reproductively inactive; Laws and colleagues thus proposed that elephants might experience "menopause" similar to humans. Their observations were made for a very stressed population.

Although an overall decline in fecundity can be expected in the older age classes in an elephant population, these individuals may also be reproductively active. Postmortem examination of culled elephants at Kruger and Etosha showed that most cows in the 50- to 60-year age class were reproductively active as they were pregnant or lactating. Captive elephants aged 50–55 years in southern India also gave birth as frequently as did the younger cows, although a decline in fecundity could be seen beyond this age (fig. 7.2). The highest age of calving among these elephants was by a cow (named Tara) when she was 62 years old (she lived to 75 years).

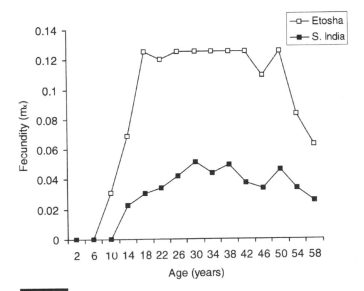

Figure 7.2
Age-specific birth rates in elephants. Fecundity m_x is expressed as the number of female offspring born each year to a female elephant of a particular age. The values shown are for a wild African elephant population culled at Etosha, Namibia, in 1985 (based on Lindeque 1988) and for captive Asian elephants in southern Indian timber camps (based on Sukumar et al. 1997 and newer analysis).

Senescence should be indicated by a depletion of primary follicles or oo-cytes. John Hanks has suggested that reproductive senescence in elephants could result from disorders of the reproductive system as well as a reduction in oocyte number, but the evidence for the latter is weak. In the wild it would be rare for an elephant to survive beyond 60 years; for demographic purposes, it can be assumed that reproduction ceases at this age.

While on the subject of birth rates, we should examine the data for any seasonality to conception and birth in elephant populations. If reproductive activity is influenced by the availability of high-quality forage, seasonality in conceptions and births can be expected in habitats in which rainfall is clearly seasonal, but not in those in which it is distributed over the year. Thus, John Hanks demonstrated a clear seasonality in conceptions during 1965–1968 in the Luangwa Valley, corresponding to the peak in rainfall (fig. 7.3). While peak conception lagged behind peak rainfall by about 1 month, the peak in births would have occurred about 2 months prior to the peak rains. Seasonality in reproduction has also been demonstrated at several other climatically sea-sonal sites in southern Africa, including Etosha, Hwange, and Kruger, but not at Addo, where rains are distributed throughout the year. Among captive ele-phants in southern India and in Myanmar, calves are born throughout the year. Long-term records show an interesting peak in births toward the end of the wet season and much before the arrival of the monsoon in both regions

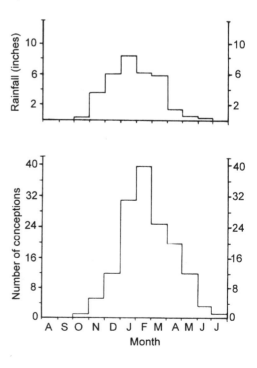

Figure 7.3
Monthly frequency of elephant conceptions and monthly rainfall averaged for 1965–1968 in the Luangwa Valley, Zambia. (From Hanks 1969. Reproduced with the permission of Blackwell Science Ltd., U.K.)

(table 7.2). It is not clear if conceptions are influenced by climate or by seasonal work schedules of these "timber elephants."

Large interannual fluctuations in births may also arise for several reasons. The elephants at Amboseli virtually stopped cycling during the long drought of 1976–1977, presumably when their fat reserves fell below a critical level. Over the next 2 years, practically every adult female in the population conceived, resulting in a baby boom during 1979–1980. An even more pronounced boom occurred over a 6-month period in 1983. Synchronized breeding by females in a population may thus result in large interannual fluctuations in births if more than an average proportion of cows conceive during an exceptionally good year. The long gestation period and lactational anestrus following parturition would ensure that a year of high conception/birth rate would be followed by at least 2 years of low conception/birth rates. Thus, Richard Laws interpreted a polymodal frequency distribution, with peaks and troughs, of the younger age classes in the North Bunyoro elephants as indicating such fluctuations in recruitment. This would be accentuated by low calf survival during a drought year. I also found evidence for cycles in recruitment, with a period of 3 years among 88 elephants, representing several family groups, captured in 1968 by *kheddah* at Kakankote in southern India. Malan Lindeque showed through modeling that, after two episodes of synchronized births, the age structure of the population deviates significantly from the starting age distribution.

Table 7.2
Seasonality in the birth of Asian elephant calves in captivity.

| | Percentage of Total Births | |
Month	Southern India ($n = 261$)	Myanmar ($n = 3,070$)
January	15.3	11.4
February	11.1	10.4
March	5.4	10.9
April	7.3	8.6
May	8.1	6.7
June	6.1	6.0
July	8.4	6.1
August	8.1	5.9
September	4.2	7.6
October	6.1	8.7
November	8.4	7.7
December	11.5	10.2

Sources: Based on Sukumar et al. (1997) and Khyne U Mar (unpublished. Reproduced with permission.)

7.2.2   Causes of death and mortality rates

The causes of death and the mortality rates are notoriously difficult to estimate for most wild mammalian species, including the elephant. Carcasses in the field are usually putrefied, making it difficult to identify the cause of death, especially if a pathogen is involved. Juveniles in the population are usually underrepresented in a collection of remains discovered; thus, estimation of age-specific mortality rates for the younger age classes, vital for understanding population dynamics, usually becomes guesswork. With the elephant, the mixture of natural and human-caused deaths further complicates the study of mortality. The ratio of natural to human-caused deaths among elephants obviously varies with time across populations and the sexes, depending mainly on the pressures of ivory poaching, although deaths related to agricultural conflict may also be regionally significant (chapter 8).

Elephants may die of natural predation; a host of viral, bacterial, parasitic, or noninfectious diseases; malnutrition; thirst; injuries; and accidents (fig. 7.4). It is beyond the scope of this discussion to provide a detailed treatment of causes of elephant diseases or metabolic disorders. However, I highlight the possible

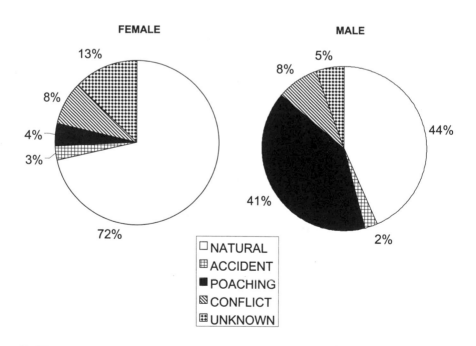

Figure 7.4
Causes of mortality in wild female and male Asian elephants in a large sample of deaths ($n = 1,189$ for females and $1,531$ for males) in southern India during 1976–2000.

importance, as seen from their contribution to overall mortality rates, of some of these causes.

Adult elephants are immune even to the largest natural predators (lions and tigers), but young elephants are certainly vulnerable. Malan Lindeque attributed a significant 32% of all deaths of elephants less than 3 years old during 1971–1987 in Etosha National Park to predation, mainly by lions. Otherwise, the death of calves is mainly due to premature birth, malnutrition if the mother's condition suffers during a drought, infections, and accidents.

Parasitic infections of elephants seem common, but these are poorly understood. James Barnett reported that, during culling operations from 1967 to 1972 in Zimbabwe, the commonly found parasites were "oestrid fly larvae in the stomachs of young elephants, flukes (flatworms) in the small intestine, hookworms in the bile duct and a number of nematodes (roundworms) mainly in the caecum and large intestine" (1991, p. 103). Elephants may normally be able to tolerate the presence of such parasites, but suffer from clinical disease only when they are stressed, such as through malnutrition.

Nematodes and helminths are also common in Asian elephants. Protozoan parasites such as trypanosomes are seen in Asian elephants, but clinical symptoms are restricted to captive animals or certain wild populations, such as in northeast India.

Among the several bacterial diseases known in elephants, only anthrax, which is usually endemic, seems also to reach epidemic proportions. Anthrax epidemics are known both for wild Asian elephant populations in northeastern India and for African elephant populations in countries such as Namibia. The prevalence of anthrax epidemics in Etosha, an extremely arid habitat, runs contrary to the belief that these epidemics only occur in moist regions.

Pneumonialike infections, possibly by bacterial and viral agents, also contribute to a significant number of deaths. The herpes virus is known to infect both African and Asian elephants and in recent years has been identified as the cause of death in several Asian calves in captivity.

A large number of noninfectious diseases have been described for various organs and organ systems among elephants. Those involving cardiovascular, pulmonary, gastrointestinal, urogenital, and reproductive systems are known to result directly in the premature death of elephants, although their prevalence in wild populations is poorly documented.

Sylvia Sikes related several signs of ill health in elephants in East African grassland habitat to arteriosclerosis or progressive thickening and blockage of arteries. This condition was much more common in habitats in which elephants had a diet dominated by nutritionally poor grass than in the riverine habitats in which they also browsed. She differentiated two major types of sclerosis. Medial sclerosis (deposition of lime on the artery wall), as a consequence of abnormal calcium metabolism or excessive vitamin D, was attributed to increased exposure to sunlight as well as an incorrect calcium-phosphorus balance in the diet. Another condition, atheroma (excessive fat deposits on the inner artery wall), also seemed related to a poor diet. The clinical significance of these conditions has been questioned. It is possible that the fermentation products of a predominantly grass diet include a high concentration of saturated fatty acids.

Disorders of the reproductive system may be significant as causes not only of direct mortality in mature female elephants, but also more indirectly through inducing miscarriage, stillbirths, and premature births. Dystocia may be associated with some of the birth disorders. There are hints of increased risk of death among cows during their first pregnancy.

Drought-related mortality, common in African semiarid regions, may be due to both dehydration and starvation from a diet of poor quality. Injuries and accidents also are responsible for a substantial proportion of deaths among elephants. Calves or even adults may fall down steep slopes or into pits, get stuck in rocky clefts or trapped in soft mud, be trampled by a stampeding herd, drown in swiftly flowing water, or be bitten by poisonous snakes. Male elephants, of course, may be fatally injured in sparring bouts or serious fights; more commonly, they break a tusk, which eventually results in infection of the pulp cavity. Cow elephants may likewise be seriously injured by the tusks of an aggressive bull.

Mortality rates in elephants are relatively low, in line with their expected decline with increased body size among mammalian herbivores. I have mentioned the difficulties in estimating age- or sex-specific mortality rates in mammals. Several approaches have been taken to come up with such estimates in elephant populations. The "life table" approach treats a sample of naturally dead elephants (typically aged from their dentition) as a cohort or group of individuals born at the same time and dying at different ages to compute age-specific death rates. An alternative is to age a sample of living elephants or age a one-time cull and look at the shrinkage of successively older age classes to compute death rates.

Several tautologies can arise in the life table approach, as pointed out by Graeme Caughley. An underlying assumption is that the population has a stable age distribution, and that its growth rate r is zero. If r is not zero but its value is known, a correction can be introduced; however, this may make it redundant to estimate age-specific death rates because its purpose could have been to estimate r in the first place!

Nevertheless, a life table, even if imperfect, allows us to understand how the risk of death varies with age for a population. I have constructed survivorship curves from the life table carefully computed by Malan Lindeque from the age structure of culled elephants at Etosha and from demographic records of captive elephants that V. Krishnamurthy and I have maintained in southern India (fig. 7.5).

The survivorship curve for elephants follows the typical "type I" pattern associated with many large mammals—a moderate risk of death during the juvenile stage, a very low death rate from there onward through most of adult life, and an increased risk in old age. The data from Etosha indicated a 25% mortality rate during the first year of life and about 10% during the second

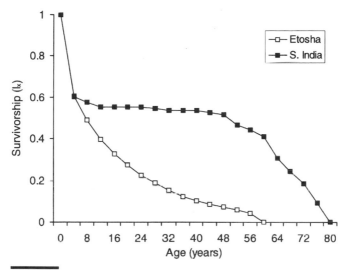

Figure 7.5
Survivorship l_x curves for female elephants, plotted as the
proportion of individuals surviving from birth to a given age. The
survivorship values for African elephants at Etosha are based on a
culled sample in 1985 (from Lindeque 1988), and for captive
Asian elephants in southern Indian timber camps they are based
on actual ages at death (from Sukumar et al. 1997.)

year, with these figures declining to about 4%–5% per year from the third year
to 50 years of age, and thereafter progressively increasing to 10% per year by
60 years of age. Mortality rates seem the most variable during the first year. At
Amboseli, they have gone from a few percent during a good year to as much
as about 75% during a drought year (a 33% mean annual rate has been indicated for 1973–1978, when the population was in general decline). In the
highly productive Lake Manyara, a mortality rate of 10% per year was computed for calves less than 1 year old during 1968–1970. Mortality rates in
subadult and adult females can be expected to vary much less; mean annual
rates of 1%–5% are reported for various African savanna populations.

As with the fecundity variables, we can expect lower variance in death
rates of elephant populations in moist forests compared to those in semiarid
habitats. While we have yet to see natural mortality data for elephants from
tropical forests, my observations over two decades in the deciduous forests of
the Nilgiris indicate that interannual variations in mortality are certainly low
relative to African savanna habitats. During the period 1980–2000, only during one year (1996) was there any appreciable increase in number of female
elephants dying naturally, possibly a response to stress induced by the early
withdrawal of the winter monsoon the previous year. In the adjoining Biligirirangans, I estimated female mortality rates of 5%–15% for calves less than 1

year old and about 3% per year for subadults and adults between 5 and 40 years old. There was also a clear indication that young males died at about twice the rate of young females from birth to age 5 years.

In most elephant populations, we can expect male elephants to die at a higher rate than the females, at least from the age of postpubertal dispersal from the natal family. This follows from the higher risk of injury during fights with other males and also from the higher metabolic costs believed to be imposed by the larger body size in the male of a polygynous mammal. The slightly female-biased sex ratios, progressing with increasing age, in many elephant populations supports this expectation. However, there are populations in which sex ratios do not deviate from equality, suggesting that longer-term mortality rates may not vary naturally between males and females.

Timothy Corfield's detailed analysis of mass elephant deaths in Tsavo during the great drought of 1970–1971, possibly the worst in recent memory for a major elephant population/habitat, brought out an interesting difference in the resilience of male versus female elephants. He not only found a dramatic overall increase in mortality rates (it is now believed that a fourth of Tsavo's 40,000 elephants died) and a prolonged phase of juvenile mortality, but also found a much higher increase in adult female mortality compared to adult male mortality. Clearly, there is much to learn about determinants of mortality across age and sex in elephants.

7.3   *Evolution of life history traits in elephants*

The term *life history* broadly refers to a host of anatomical, physiological, and behavioral characteristics of a species, although it is often restricted to demographic traits, such as age-specific birth and death rates, or developmental traits, such as growth rates and body size. While aspects of reproductive behavior, social organization, or feeding ecology in elephants have been recognized as the outcome of natural selection, there has been little attempt to discuss demographic traits in populations in relation to selective forces. A possible exception is the discussion of changes in birth rates with density, for which the evidence in any case is equivocal. There has been insufficient appreciation of the possible influence of habitat and its characteristics in the evolution of (demographic) life history phenomena in elephant populations. Elephants after all inhabit regions from near-desert conditions to tropical lowland rain forests and montane forests. Adaptations needed to deal with variations in resource abundance (forage type, quality, and dispersion), climate (incidence of drought), or even energetics (physiological costs of moving over steep terrain or long distances across arid landscapes) could surely be expected to be reflected in demographic traits. The problem of interpreting life history traits does not lie only with elephants, but extends to other mammals. In the words of Mark Boyce, "There certainly is a wealth of theory, [but] much of it fails to adequately link demography with environment and it is mostly untested" (1988b, p. 358). I therefore only attempt a rudimentary discussion of this topic as it relates to elephant demography.

The concept of r (intrinsic growth rate) and K (carrying capacity) selection, originally formulated as a theory of density-dependent natural selection, is one framework in which to consider the evolution of life history traits. Unfortunately, the rather indiscriminate application of this theory has led to its virtual abandonment by the theorists, even though the r-K terminology still prevails in the ecological literature.

Basically, this theory suggests that there are trade-offs between the ability to do well under conditions of low density (r selection) and high density (K selection), with the comparisons made in relation to the carrying capacity of the habitat. The prediction is, therefore, that at low population density, those genotypes with high r (reproductive ability) will have a selective advantage, while at high population density, this is reversed in favor of genotypes with high K (say, adult survival). Among mammals, a suggested response to increased crowding is a sequence of (1) increased juvenile mortality, (2) increased age of sexual maturity, (3) decreased birth rates, and (4) increased adult mortality. Even when real populations do show short-term demographic responses to changing density, it is important to differentiate the proximate response of a variable such as age of sexual maturity from the process of natural selection.

The evidence for density-dependent changes in reproduction among elephants is generally weak. The only population for which clear evidence is available to the best of my knowledge is that in Uganda. When J. S. Perry examined a sample of culled elephants there during 1946–1950, he observed that a cow "often begins to breed at an age of 10 years or less" (1953, p. 104) (rather vague and not referring to mean age of conception), and that the intercalving interval (based on more objective criteria) was just under 4 years. By the time Richard Laws and his team examined the high-density population of Murchison Falls during 1966–1967, these fecundity measures had increased considerably, but following a steep reduction in density through culling and poaching had again swung back when Rob Malpas conducted his study during 1974 (see table 7.1).

There have been attempts to derive the relationship between density and fecundity from data across African savanna elephant populations (for instance, by Charles Fowler and Tim Smith, see section 7.2.2). Malan Lindeque's more critical examination of the data showed that the relationship between elephant density and age at first conception is not significant for southern Africa and is weakly significant for eastern African populations only after removal of the anomalous data for Lake Manyara.

It of course might be argued that elephant density per se is not the appropriate variable given a certain variation in habitat productivity even across savanna woodland habitat, but the density as a proportion of the carrying capacity (notoriously difficult to estimate) is the appropriate variable. The strongest argument against density dependence in reproduction comes from Addo, where the elephants have consistently maintained a phenomenal 7% annual population growth rate, obviously spurred by high fecundity, over half a century to attain a very high density (see chapter 9). Obviously, a slowing in growth eventually will have to occur in this fenced-in population, but no one is sure when the tide will turn. Asian elephants in southern Indian habitats, now reaching densities comparable to the highest known values in Africa, also do not as yet show any slow down in fecundity.

We know much less about how mortality rates change with increasing density in elephant populations. There are hints of lower survivorship among young elephants, but no evidence that adults suffer similarly under conditions of high density, except during a drought.

A more interesting framework for life history evolution in elephants is, in my opinion, that of fluctuating versus stable environments. This is quite distinct from density-dependent selection; the predictions of r-K selection theory do not directly apply to selection under fluctuating environments, although they may share certain common features.

Environmental fluctuation can be a powerful force in evolution, but is not easy to unravel. To quote Mark Boyce again, "Environmental variability is a virtual Pandora's box of selective forces which can influence the evolution of life histories, and there is still much that we do not understand about the nature of selection in fluctuating environments" (1988a, p. 16). All environments fluctuate to a certain extent, both seasonally and from one year to another; what is of interest is the relative degree of fluctuation across environments. A well-established climatic pattern is the inverse relationship between annual rainfall and its variability. Thus, a region with low rainfall experiences high variability (or "coefficient of variation" in statistical terms), while one with high rainfall has low variability. The semiarid savanna is thus a highly fluctuating environment not only on a seasonal scale, but also on an interannual scale, while the equatorial rain forest is a relatively stable environment, with rainfall being more evenly distributed over the year and more predictable from one year to another.

Let us consider how elephant life histories should be molded to deal with a highly fluctuating environment, such as in the semiarid savannas. When high-quality resources are available only seasonally, traits promoting rapid (metabolic) growth and high fecundity to take advantage of this distinct seasonal flush would be favored. Larger body size could be one consequence in the more fluctuating habitat, and this could be reflected in other traits correlated with size (see chapter 5 and appendix 2). Likewise, higher fecundity would be expressed in female elephants through an early age of sexual maturity and shorter intercalving interval. This would enable a more rapid population growth when favorable conditions return after a drought and a population decline.

I am not arguing for "group selection," but rather that selection operating on individual elephants in semiarid habitats over the centuries has given us populations with individuals that have reproductive traits that promote rapid growth. Obviously, it may also be true that individuals should delay reproduction (late age at maturity or longer calving intervals) when conditions are unfavorable. Thus, one could expect to see greater flexibility in reproductive traits in elephants of semiarid regions. The opposite can be expected in elephants that have evolved in more stable rain forests. A later age of sexual maturity and longer intercalving intervals, with less plasticity in these fecundity traits, would be sufficient as long as these are close to or above replacement-level rates. Fecundity traits would also be influenced by lower-quality forage in rain forests. Even if they were to exist at much lower densities, elephant populations in rain forests would themselves have fluctuated little and persisted at close to the carrying capacity for longer periods. I would therefore argue that it is more likely for rain forest elephants to have been selected for K-related rather than r-related traits. This could provide a link, however crude, between models of selection under density dependence and selection under environmental variability.

What is the evidence that elephant life histories conform to the above expectations? The earliest ages at first conception in female elephants, in the range of 9–13 years, are known only from arid and semiarid habitats such as the southern and eastern African savannas. These include Etosha, Kruger, Hwange, Gonarezhou, Tsavo, Mkomazi, and Kabalega. With an average annual rainfall from as low as 10 cm to not more than about 75 cm, an exception being Kabalega (more than about 100 cm), these are also the most variable environments across the elephant's range. Mean intercalving intervals are also shorter (in the range of 3.5–4.5 years) in semiarid Africa. The elephant population at Kabalega has also shown considerable plasticity in reproductive traits.

What about the elephants in regions of high rainfall? A late age of first conception and a long intercalving interval is reported for the moist Budongo forest, where annual rainfall averages over 150 cm. It is also interesting that J. S Perry, quoting H. Hedigar, observes that captive African forest elephants in the erstwhile Belgian Congo "do not reach puberty until about 15 years of age" (1953, p. 104). This is a clear hint that African forest elephants inhabiting the high rainfall zone may have a relatively late age of sexual maturity. Asian elephants in the regions of medium-to-high rainfall (100–200 cm) of southern India and Myanmar also show a relatively late age of sexual maturity (13–20 years).

These patterns broadly support my contention of life history variation across habitats. We need to know more, however, of the rain forest elephant both in Africa and in Asia. Most biologists study elephants in dry habitats, in which they are plentiful and far more visible. Study of the rain forest elephant is a much more challenging task. The ongoing studies in Central African rain forests may perhaps provide some of the much-needed answers.

7.4   *Modeling the dynamics of elephant populations*

The dynamics of elephant populations have been modeled by several investigators. The type of model used and the demographic variables introduced into the models have depended on the aspect being investigated—population growth and regulation, productivity, viability of populations, elephant-vegetation dynamics, impacts of poaching on demography, tusk harvest or tusk inheritance, and so on.

The two major classes of models used in population dynamics are deterministic models and stochastic models. A *deterministic* model uses fixed values of demographic variables such as birth rates and death rates to track the fate of a population over time. Thus, an average birth rate and death rate may be applied to a population to determine its growth rate. These values could be varied, if needed, in relation to other variables, such as elephant density. A *stochastic* model, on the other hand, tracks the fate of individuals in the population by taking the birth and death rates to be probabilistic at the individual level. A degree of randomness or chance is introduced, with the result that the fate of a population can only be predicted with a certain probability. When a population is simulated using a computer, the outcomes are different for each run, and typically, an average of several hundred or thousand simulations is taken.

Results from deterministic and stochastic models are also different. It can be shown mathematically that population growth rates derived from a stochastic model are lower than those from a deterministic model. Actually, for a large population the differences are negligible but for smaller populations these are significant. Thus, a deterministic model of population dynamics provides, for practical purposes, an adequate representation of average trends in large populations.

These models are, however, grossly inadequate for application to small populations, for which a stochastic model is more realistic and appropriate. A deterministic model may indicate, for instance, a positive population growth rate for a small population, but a stochastic model may indicate a negative growth rate and high probability of extinction within a given period.

Stochastic models are mathematically complex, and analytical solutions are beyond the reach of most biologists (and many mathematicians). It is, however, much easier to use computer simulations to provide solutions with stochastic models. Concurrent with the spread of personal computers, there has naturally been an explosion in the use of stochastic simulation models in ecology. I first describe the application of deterministic models in elephant population dynamics before considering the more recent use of stochastic models for elephants.

7.4.1   Population changes in elephants of North Bunyoro, Uganda

The elephant population in the North Bunyoro region of Uganda had been affected during 1925–1965 through controlled shooting by license. A minimum of 14,416 elephants had been killed during this 40-year period according to official records. In addition, an unknown number probably succumbed to injury sustained during these operations and to ivory poaching. The population structure of these elephants was thus already distorted considerably by 1965 when the Ugandan National Parks began a further round of cropping to keep a check on the population size. During 1965–1967, another 2,000 elephants were culled in the Murchison Falls National Park. These provided the material for detailed scientific investigations by Richard Laws and his collaborators.

When a population in near equilibrium with its habitat is reduced through hunting, we can expect compensating factors. As a result of increased availability of food and other resources per capita, the remaining individuals in the population could show one or more of the following: faster growth, earlier puberty, increased fecundity, and lower natural mortality. These demographic traits of the culled sample of elephants from Murchison Falls examined by Richard Laws and coworkers, however, showed exactly the opposite tendencies. There was slower growth, an (presumed) increase in age of puberty (to 16.3–17.8 years) in females, decreased fecundity (intercalving interval of 5.6 and 9.1 years in the northern and southern populations, respectively), and increased mortality (by over 50%) of calves compared to the more productive African elephant populations. The sharp reduction in recruitment clearly showed up in the age structure of the culled sample as a deficiency in the younger age classes. From the age structure, it seemed as though the decline in fecundity had commenced about 20 years earlier, that is, around 1946.

In an attempt to explain what may have happened to the Murchison Falls elephant population, Laws and his team used a simple deterministic model based on the fundamental equation of population growth modified for their purpose, $N_t = N_0 e^{-zt}$, where N_t is the abundance of age t, N_0 is the number of newborns, e is the natural exponent, and z is the instantaneous mortality rate.

They took N_0, the number of newborns, to be an arbitrary 1,000 (later adjusted to 1,197), sexual maturity in females to be 12 years, an intercalving interval of 4 years, and an equal ratio of male to female calves at birth. Taking the calculated adult mortality rates, but with a little adjustment of calf mortality rates, they generated the age structure of a "steady state" population, in which the births were balanced by deaths. They believed this represented the age structure of the 1946 elephant population, before the decline in recruitment and increase in calf mortality started (fig. 7.6).

The model was then run to describe the 1966 situation. Sexual maturity in females was changed to 18 years and the intercalving interval to 7 years. By 1966, the number of newborns had declined (from 1,197 newborns in 1946) to 457 individuals. Based on observed age structures from the culled sample, the model further indicated that calf (0–4 years old) mortality rates had increased anywhere between 50% and 100% of the pre-1946 rates. There was no indication that postweaning (after 4 years old) mortality rates had changed. The model was then taken forward to the year 1971, which predicted further decrease in the number of recruits (407 newborns) and the abundance of elephants up to 4 years of age.

Summing the population sizes from various age classes, beginning with an adjusted value of 1,197 newborns, the model indicated a total population size in 1966 of 21,195 individuals compared to the 9,400 elephants indicated by

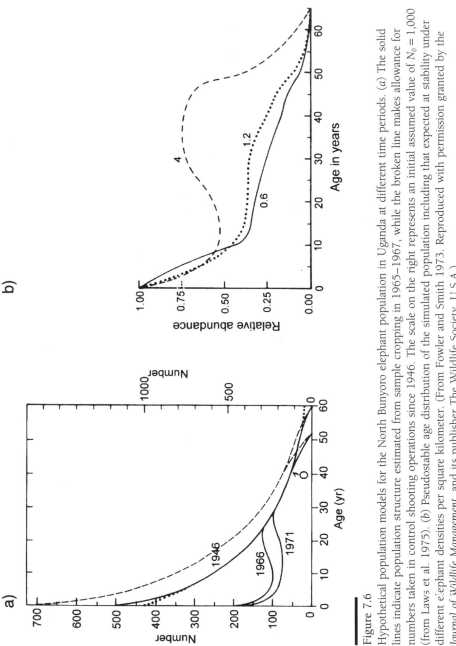

Figure 7.6

Hypothetical population models for the North Bunyoro elephant population in Uganda at different time periods. (*a*) The solid lines indicate population structure estimated from sample cropping in 1965–1967, while the broken line makes allowance for numbers taken in control shooting operations since 1946. The scale on the right represents an initial assumed value of $N_0 = 1,000$ (from Laws et al. 1975). (*b*) Pseudostable age distribution of the simulated population including that expected at stability under different elephant densities per square kilometer. (From Fowler and Smith 1973. Reproduced with permission granted by the *Journal of Wildlife Management*, and its publisher The Wildlife Society, U.S.A.)

actual census figures. The relative abundances of various age classes for 1966 were thus proportionately scaled down by a factor of 0.44. The model-derived population for 1946 was now calculated to be about 16,000 elephants. To this, the 6,000 elephants killed during 1946–1966 in controlled shooting and sport hunting had to be added, giving a total of 22,000 elephants for the 1946 North Bunyoro population. The overall population trends at North Bunyoro were 22,000 elephants in 1946, declining to 9,400 by 1966 and further projected to 7,900 by the year 1971.

A model such as this has limitations because of several assumptions made in respect to functional relationships and a stationary and stable aged population in 1946. Drawing inferences about demography from cross-sectional sampling of age structures is always a tricky business. Nevertheless, the model was useful in at least describing qualitatively the demographic trends in the North Bunyoro elephant population over a period of a quarter century. In this case, the standing age structure during the 1965–1967 cull clearly showed that recruitment had declined substantially, and it strengthened the conclusions drawn independently on reproductive rates from postmortem examinations of the elephants. There still remained the question of why the demography of this population had slowed rather than sped up after a population reduction.

Laws and his colleagues hypothesized that density-dependent compensatory mechanisms served to slow the demography of this population. In spite of a substantial decline in elephant numbers since 1946, there was also a decrease in habitat area. From 6,300 km^2 in 1946, the elephant range contracted by almost half to 3,200 km^2 by 1966. The elephant density thus decreased only marginally from a mean of 3.50 elephants/km^2 in 1946 to 2.94 elephants/km^2 by 1966.

At the same time, there was an increase in the mean weight of an elephant over this time, from 1,894 kg in 1946 to 2,234 kg in 1966 (with reduced recruitment, there was a preponderance of older, heavier animals). A biomass calculation showed that the unit weights of elephants changed from 6,633 kg/km^2 in 1946 to only 6,561 kg/km^2 by 1966, or a 1% reduction. During this time, there was significant decline in habitat quality (conversion of woodland to grassland), strongly suggesting that density-dependent regulatory factors were responsible for the reduced birth rate and increased calf mortality rate.

7.4.2   Age-structured models of population dynamics

The numerous studies of elephant demography in relation to habitat changes in eastern and southern Africa during the 1960s gave indications that population regulatory factors may operate under high densities. The model used by Richard Laws and colleagues to track changes in the North Bunyoro elephants was relatively crude and had several assumptions. For instance, calculations of mortality rates assumed a stable aged population, which may not have been true. None of the studies actually calculated the instantaneous rate of growth r of a population using appropriate demographic models. John Hanks, in collaboration with J. McIntosh, attempted to calculate the actual r and maximum possible growth rate r_m using the well-known Euler equation.

They calculated the instantaneous growth rate r under different values of age-specific fecundity and mortality. The mean age of first conception in females was varied from 12 years to 22 years, while reproductive cessation was varied between 45 and 55 years in 5-year steps. Intercalving interval was changed in 1-year steps from 3 years to 9 years. In most field studies, the estimation of mortality rates poses the greatest problem because many carcasses are not discovered; further, there is underrepresentation of younger animals among the carcasses found. Hanks and McIntosh took three rates of mortality (low, medium, and high) across the age classes. Thus, juvenile (0–4 years) mortality was 5%, 10%, and 20% annually under low, medium, and high rates, respectively, while these were 1%, 1.5%, and 4% for ages 5–45 years. Rates were higher above 45 years of age.

The growth rate r calculated from various combinations of the above birth and death rates gave insights into which factors might regulate populations. Under ideal conditions, an elephant population experiencing low mortality and high reproductive rates (short intercalving interval and long reproductive life span) could grow at an intrinsic rate r of 0.047. This actually translates into an annual population growth of 4.8%. Considering that it is unlikely for a population to experience such ideal conditions for long, Hanks and McIntosh concluded that, in practice, the r_m of an elephant population is more likely to be about 0.040 and the annual growth rate to be just under 4%. This result also corrected earlier estimates of "cropping rates" of 6% as the sustained yield quotas for elephant populations in Africa based on crude estimates of birth rates alone. The overall results were even more interesting from another perspective. The model clearly showed that, while intercalving interval influenced growth rates the most among various reproductive parameters, the mortality rates operating on a population were more important than reproductive rates in regulating the population. The population growth rate was especially sensitive to changes in juvenile mortality rate.

Such a sensitivity analysis is also important from a management perspective. If an elephant population is to be controlled, a mere reduction of the birth rate is usually not sufficient; it is more important to increase its death rate.

In the same year that Hanks and McIntosh published their results for simulated population growth in African elephants, a more sophisticated age-structured model using the "Leslie matrix" was used by Charles Fowler and Tim Smith to characterize the demographic conditions under which an elephant population attains equilibrium with its habitat. The Leslie matrix is an elegant method of projecting into the future an age-structured population under the influence of age-specific birth and survival rates. In the basic application of the Leslie model, the values for each element (age-specific fecundity and age-specific survivorship) of the matrix are constant with time. This is obviously unrealistic for real populations because both fecundity and mortality can be expected to vary with changes in habitat and population density. More-crowded populations could experience lower fecundity and higher mortality.

Fowler and Smith thus used a variable matrix in which fecundity and survivorship values were related to population density. Using demographic data from earlier studies in East Africa by Helmut Buechner, Irven Buss, George Petrides, Richard Laws, and their associates, they derived mathematical expressions for the relationships between elephant population density and fecundity (age at first calving, intercalving interval) and between density and survivorship (of elephants younger than 2 years old). These relationships were plugged into the basic Leslie model such that the age-specific fecundity and survivorship values of the matrix were determined by the density of the population. Survivorship values above 2 years old were assumed to be constant.

The Fowler-Smith model indicated that an elephant population would reach stability at a density of about 0.6 individuals per square kilometer. At this density, the age of sexual maturity in females is 12 years (the first calf being born 2 years later), and the intercalving interval is 4.6 years. Mortality rates during the first and second years are 5% and 3%, respectively.

When this model was applied to the estimated population structure and density data of Laws and Parker for the Murchison Falls elephants during 1945, it was seen that the population size changed very little. Fowler and Smith then increased the elephant density linearly from 0.8–1.2 individuals per square kilometer in 1945 to 4 per square kilometer in 1965. The resulting age distribution was not unlike that seen in the field during this year (fig. 7.6). Although the assumption of a linear increase in elephant density during 1945–1965 was almost certainly an error according to Laws and his associates, they accepted the contention of Fowler and Smith that such a variable matrix model incorporating density dependence was a useful predictive tool for management decisions. For this to happen, however, the relationships between density and fecundity or mortality will have to be based on much better empirical data.

7.4.3 Age-structured model of sex ratio changes in Asian elephants

Even though some demographic data for Asian elephant populations were available from Sri Lanka, these had never been formally used in an appropriate model to study population dynamics. Based on my study of a southern Indian elephant population during 1981–1983, I used the Leslie matrix to model aspects of its dynamics. The models used for the African elephant populations described the dynamics of only the female segment of the population. In the conventional approach to modeling population dynamics, the male segment is often discarded as only females contribute directly to reproduction. However, in some Asian elephant populations, the male was being selectively killed for its tusks. Thus, I was interested in seeing how the differential mortality rates in females and males, the latter being selectively impacted by ivory poaching, would translate into changes in sex ratio and population growth.

The demographic data came from the elephant population of the Biligiriran-gans in southern India. The mean age of sexual maturity in female elephants was about 15 years, with the first calf being born at 17.5 years. Intercalving interval was 4.7 years. Mortality rates for both sexes were estimated from field data on carcasses discovered and from life table analysis for female elephants. For incor-poration into the model, three rates of mortality—low, medium, and high—were used (table 7.3). The low mortality rates were the minimum rates that could be expected to operate in the population based on carcasses found in the field. The medium rates were those suspected to operate in the population over the long term, while the high rates could have been achieved during adverse periods such as a drought or a spurt in poaching. The mortality rates in any one category were higher for males than for females. Nine simulations were run using combi-nations of the three mortality rates each for the sexes (fig. 7.7).

The simulations began with an adult (>15 years old) sex ratio of 1 male to 5.4 females and made population projections over 50 years, by which time the stable age distribution was nearly reached. In all instances, the adult sex ratio skewed further in the short term (5 years). With low male mortality rates, the sex ratio narrowed after 5 years to stabilize between $1:2$ and $1:3$. With medium male mortality, the ratio stabilized at levels very close to the initial ratio. Thus, with medium male and medium female mortality schedules, the adult sex ratio eventually stabilized at $1:5.7$. When male mortality was high, the sex ratios reached $1:13$ or $1:27$ under medium female and low female mortality, respectively. These simulations suggested that the medium male mortality schedules probably had been operating in this and other southern Indian populations over a long term. Sampling of age structures from the Nil-giris, a western extension of the Biligirirangans population, during 1981–1983

Table 7.3
Annual mortality rates for female and male Asian elephants used in population modeling.

Age Class (years)	For Deterministic Model Annual Death Rate (%)		For Stochastic Model Annual Probability of Death (%)	
	Female	Male	Female	Male
0–1	5–15	8–20	10–15	15
1–5	4–12	6–16	4–8	8
5–15	2–4	6–15	2–3	6–16
15–50	2–10	6–15	1.5–3.2	6–16
50–60	10–15	10–15	1.5–3.2	6–16

Source: Based on Sukumar (1985, 1989a, 1992, 1995b).
The mortality rates used in the deterministic modeling span the range from low to high (see text), while those for the stochastic modeling represent rates used to obtain potential intrin-sic population growth rates r varying from 0 to 0.02.

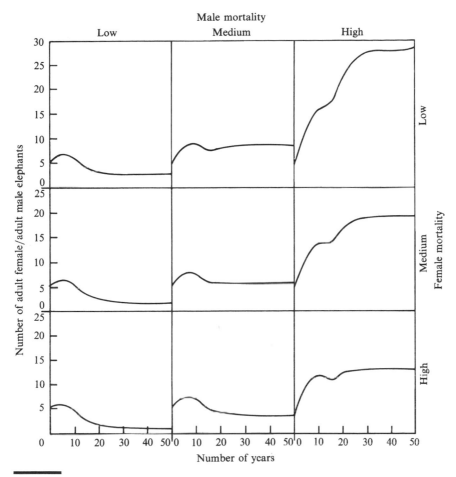

Figure 7.7
Simulated trends over 50 years (base year 1982) in the adult sex ratio of an Asian elephant population in southern India under different mortality schedules. (From Sukumar 1985, 1989a.)

also indicated a 1 : 5 adult sex ratio, while a survey in Periyar during 1969 by G. U. Kurup gave an adult sex ratio of 1 : 6.

The increase in ivory poaching during the 1980s, however, strongly indicated that sex ratios would further skew. The model projected a decline in the proportion of adult males in the population, from the initial 6.5% to about 4% by the fifth year, corresponding to a further widening of the sex ratio to about 1 : 8. Field work during 1987 in the larger Nilgiris-Biligirirangans population showed that the proportion of adult males indeed had reduced to the level predicted by the model. If male mortality continued to be high, the sex ratios would widen to between 1 : 10 and 1 : 20 over the next decade, a level that was reached by 1997.

The model also explored population growth rates and age structure changes under the various scenarios. As with other elephant population models, this also showed that the most sensitive parameter of population growth is female mortality. Unlike some of the earlier estimates of maximum growth rate in African elephant populations, my simulations showed that Asian elephant populations would increase at lower rates of not more than about 2% per annum. Further, I showed that age distributions or ratios are not good predictors of population trends, a point that had also been argued from a theoretical viewpoint by Graeme Caughley. Thus, a population that was clearly declining under a high male–high female mortality schedule had a higher percentage of calves (7.5%) at stable age distribution than another population (5.7% calves) that was increasing under low male–low female mortality.

Consider two populations: A increases largely because of increase in birth rate, and B increases because of a decrease in death rate. In population A, the age distribution would shift toward the younger age classes, while in population B, there will be no change in age distribution if mortality is proportional for all age classes. The interpretation of growth rates in populations based merely on their standing age distributions can be very misleading unless other information is available. In the case of the Murchison Falls elephant population in Uganda, studied by Laws and associates, the sharp depletion of age classes below 20 years did suggest a declining birth rate, but did not necessarily reveal the value of r, the population's intrinsic growth rate.

My model had two possible limitations: it did not incorporate density-dependent relationships, unlike the Fowler-Smith model, and it did not provide for change in fecundity as a consequence of a skewing adult sex ratio. The issue of density dependence is obviously important in population regulation of large mammals. Later work by Charles Fowler strongly suggested that large herbivorous mammals are most productive when they are close to their carrying capacity (and not at half the carrying capacity, as implied in the standard logistic growth equation). Density-dependent brakes begin to operate only when such populations are very close to or have exceeded the carrying capacity. In my study population, I had no evidence that the elephants were near the carrying capacity and thus saw no need to invoke density dependence for the short-term projections.

On the issue of the link between sex ratio and fecundity, there was no empirical basis for deducing the relationship. However, I did carry out further simulations by increasing the calving interval and found that, with a low female mortality, the population growth became zero only at a calving interval of 7.7 years. In retrospect, this factor was again not important for applying the model to my study population. More recent studies by our team in southern India indicate that no measurable effect on fecundity is likely until the adult sex ratio has skewed to about 1 male to 20–25 females. In only one of the simulations did the sex ratio exceed 1 : 25 marginally. Thus, the results are broadly robust in describing the dynamics of the Nilgiris-Biligirirangans elephant populations.

7.5   *Stochastic models of elephant population dynamics*

To reiterate, a stochastic model of population dynamics that incorporates individual life histories is more appropriate for long-lived species with overlapping generations than are deterministic models. It is particularly appropriate for small population dynamics or, in the case of larger populations, those in highly variable environments.

Lilian Wu and Daniel Botkin presented in 1980 the first stochastic model designed specifically for studying the dynamics of African elephants. Their mathematical model provided the analytical framework for female life histories. Using a matrix approach, the model provided methods for calculating the relationship between change in population size and age-specific fecundity and mortality, the average number of female offspring produced by a female in her lifetime, the probability of extinction of a population, and if the population did not become extinct, composition of the population after a certain period of time.

Wu and Botkin then considered the age distribution of female elephants obtained from a 1972 cull in Wankie (Hwange) National Park, Zimbabwe. The age distribution of this sample was irregular, suggesting that it could be due to one or more of the following factors: (1) chance errors in sampling individuals from a stable aged structure; (2) some unknown past event had disrupted the population, which was now moving toward a stable age distribution; or (3) variations in rainfall could have caused this nonstationary population age structure. Using data on birth and death probabilities from the East African study by Richard Laws, they showed from their formulation that the irregular age distribution of the Wankie sample could not possibly represent a stable aged population. They concluded that variations in rainfall were the most likely cause of time-varying birth and death processes and of irregular age profiles.

Since its publication in 1980, the Wu-Botkin stochastic model has never actually been applied to any elephant population except for a test of the Wankie age structure. The complex mathematical formulation of the analytical solutions would have inhibited biologists from even attempting to use the model. The spread of personal computers made simulations of stochastic dynamics more attractive to use. I now discuss the use of simulations in determining probability of extinction and population viability in Asian and in African elephants.

7.5.1   *Modeling viable populations:*
An application to Asian elephants

I used the simulation model Vortex, developed by Robert Lacy (1993), to model Asian elephant population viability. Because a majority of Asian elephant populations are small and found in fragmented habitats, my primary goal was to determine the probability of extinction of small populations and what constitutes a viable population. Apart from looking at chance variations in birth and death processes (demographic stochasticity), I also looked at how varying sex ratios influenced population viability. The sex ratio factor was important in the context of the selective hunting of male Asian elephants for tusks.

The presentation in chapter 9 of conservation gives definitions of population viability analysis (PVA) and minimum viable population (MVP). Briefly, PVA is a process that evaluates data and models to arrive at a probability that a population will survive over a given period of time. The MVP has a predefined probability (say, 95% or 99%) of surviving for a given period of time (100 or 1,000 years, for instance).

The simulation program Vortex has capabilities for modeling demographic, environmental, and genetic stochasticity, catastrophes, and trends in carrying capacity. Monte Carlo simulations are used to determine the outcome of population events. I modeled Asian elephant populations of up to 150 individuals over a period of 100 years. Demographic stochasticity was modeled by assigning age-specific probabilities of birth and death based on field data. The demographic parameters used in the simulations were largely based on my study of the southern Indian populations. The reproductive life span of female elephants was taken to be 15–60 years. Birth probability was 0.20–0.22 per mature female per year, while 80% of males above 15 years old were assumed to be in the breeding pool. Mortality rates (given in table 7.3) were varied to yield a desired population growth rate and sex ratio under a deterministic analysis.

Environmental stochasticity is modeled as variation in the year-to-year probability of birth or death. This is achieved by sampling a statistical distribution, with the standard deviation (SD) of the mean probability of birth or death specifying the interannual fluctuations. To capture this, I set the SD to 20% and 40% of the mean probability of death to represent low and moderate environmental variation, respectively. Correspondingly, the SD on fecundity was set at 25% and 50% of the mean probability of births. I also allowed for two types of catastrophes. A serious drought could occur with a 2% probability (once every 50 years on average), reduce birth by 40%, and kill 20% of individuals in the population. A disease epidemic could occur every 200 years and kill 25% of individuals. The carrying capacity K of the population was set at 150 (SD = 20%).

In small populations, there could be additional demographic problems arising from inbreeding depression. This was incorporated using a "heterosis model," in which homozygotes with lethal genes have higher juvenile mortality compared to heterozygotes.

The age structure of the initial population was set to reflect a stable age distribution under constant fecundity and mortality. The female fecundity and mortality probabilities were adjusted to yield annual population growth rates of zero ($r = 0$), 0.5% ($r = 0.005$), and 2% ($r = 0.02$) under a deterministic scheme. For the scenario with a 2% growth rate, the male mortalities were varied to give adult male-to-female ratios of 1 : 4, 1 : 8, and 1 : 16 at stable age distribution. Under any one scenario, the population was simulated 500 or 1,000 times for 100 years.

The simulations showed that, under a potential growth rate of 2%, a population of 25–30 elephants would have a 99% probability of surviving for 100 years (fig. 7.8). When growth rates were potentially lower at 0.5% or stable, a population size of 65–80 individuals was needed to ensure its survival with the same probability. These sizes are arrived at when the adult sex ratios begin at 1 male to 4 female elephants. With a skewing of the ratios to 1 : 8 or 1 : 16, which is more commonly observed at present in most southern Indian populations, the probabilities of extinction increase considerably even at 2% potential growth rate. With a 1 : 16 ratio, for instance, a starting population of 150 elephants (at $K = 150$) has only a 92% probability of surviving for 100 years. It is only when K is increased to about 250 that this population would have a 99% survival probability.

The fact that a population of a certain size has a high probability of surviving over a period of a century does not necessarily imply its continued viability. When fecundity and mortality schedules indicate a low growth rate, such a population would almost certainly show an average negative growth rate under stochastic modeling. In brief, a population may be expected to survive for 100 years, but it would almost certainly be reduced in size at the end of this period. This would have a bearing on its future viability. Extending the time frame of the simulations, Peter Armbruster and colleagues found a 200-year lag during which extinction probabilities were low, but then increased significantly.

Simulations incorporating inbreeding depression and those omitting this factor showed negligible differences in survival probabilities for population sizes above 30 individuals. Interestingly, the survival probabilities for populations with low and moderate levels of environmental variation were hardly distinguishable, suggesting that long-lived species such as the elephant are relatively well buffered against moderate environmental fluctuations seen in Asian habitats. In semiarid regions of Africa, the degree of environmental variation could be much higher and hence be a more important consideration in determining population viability.

In brief, populations of 100–300 individuals, depending on demography, sex ratio, and ecological pressures, are indicated for their viability in the relatively short term of one or two centuries.

7.5.2   *Modeling long-term viability in African elephants*

The longer-term viability of African elephant populations in semiarid regions was modeled by Peter Armbruster and Russell Lande. Their stochastic model of individual births and deaths used twelve 5-year age classes and discrete 5-year time steps. The main feature of their model is the range of environmental fluctuations incorporated in the form of 10-year (mild), 50-year (moderate),

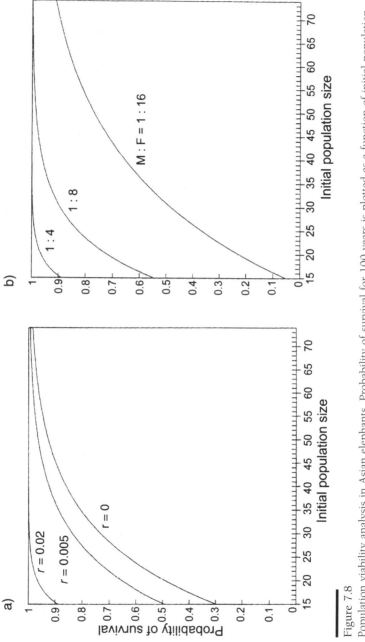

Figure 7.8

Population viability analysis in Asian elephants. Probability of survival for 100 years is plotted as a function of initial population size for populations subject to demographic stochasticity, moderate environmental stochasticity, and small chances of catastrophes: (a) populations with varying potential intrinsic growth rates r and adult male : female ratio of 1 : 4; (b) populations with varying adult male-to-female ratios and potential intrinsic growth rate r = 0.02. (From Sukumar 1992, 1995b.)

and 250-year (severe) droughts. The demographic data for their model came from the East African studies, particularly those in Tsavo National Park, Kenya, by Richard Laws and later by Timothy Corfield.

Births were modeled by relating age at first reproduction and intercalving interval to density in accordance with the functions derived for the Fowler-Smith model. In addition to the normal background rates of mortality, these were also varied under the three different drought regimes, which in turn were based on John Phillipson's (1975) analysis of rainfall patterns in Tsavo. While Phillipson described a mild 10-year drought superimposed on a more severe 50-year drought, Armbruster and Lande added a very severe 250-year drought based on the probability of three consecutive drought years. Carrying capacity constraints were placed by varying habitat or reserve area available to elephants from about 50 to 2,500 km^2.

A baseline simulation was run for 625 years of an initial population of 11 males and 11 females in an area of 10,000 km^2 (roughly the size of Tsavo East National Park). Using normal mortality rates without environmental variance, the population grew to an equilibrium density of 1.2 individuals/km^2 following the classical logistic growth curve. At the lower population densities, the growth rate averaged about 3% per year. The population was again simulated by incorporating mortalities during droughts, but now starting with the equilibrium population size of over 12,000 individuals. When this is simulated over 5,000 years, the volatile dynamics seen from sharp decreases and increases suggest that drought-driven deaths could have a considerable impact on populations (fig. 7.9).

Subsequent simulations were also initiated with a density of 1.2 elephants/km^2 and the population at stable age distribution. Populations in one of the six habitat areas (50 km^2, 125 km^2, 250 km^2, 500 km^2, 1,250 km^2, 2,500 km^2) were simulated over 1,000 years. The simulations show that an area of 1,250 km^2 with an initial population of 1,500 elephants is needed to ensure a 99% probability of persistence for 1,000 years (see chapter 9).

Armbruster and Lande also explored how various options of culling would affect the survival of populations. They found that the probabilities of survival did not decrease appreciably until culling reached about 50% of the carrying capacity. This was especially true for habitat areas above 1,250 km^2.

The Armbruster-Lande model is useful in looking not only at future survival of elephant populations, but also at how they may have behaved in the past under natural cycles of drought in semiarid African regions. A crucial assumption in their model is that practically no young elephant would survive a very severe drought. Their demographic data also came entirely from the Tsavo population. Data from a broader spectrum of habitats in the African savannas would enable the model parameters to be adjusted for more generalized results to emerge on population viability. In particular, the extraordinarily detailed demographic information from Amboseli would provide interesting comparisons with the Tsavo situation. While the model results may be applicable to the extremely fluctuating semiarid zones of the elephant's range, it would

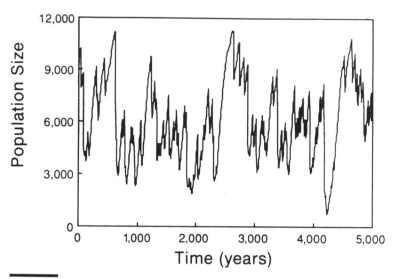

Figure 7.9
Simulation of total population size over 5,000 years in an African elephant population subject to 10-year, 50-year, and 250-year droughts of varying severity. (From Armbruster and Lande 1993. Reproduced with the permission of the Society for Conservation Biology, U.S.A.)

still be necessary to modify it for the more benign habitats, such as moist forests in Africa and in Asia.

7.6   Modeling the dynamics of exploited populations

Elephants in both continents have been exploited through historical times for several purposes. The capture of Asian elephants in large numbers over the past four millennia for taming has not necessarily been a random process, but often was selective in targeting males bearing tusks. The tusked males have also been selectively targeted for their ivory. The exploitation of African elephants is ancient and has been largely for ivory. While both sexes have been hunted for ivory, there has also been selection for large-tusked individuals, which are usually the older males and old females. Thus, human exploitation of elephant populations could be expected to have influenced their dynamics even more significantly perhaps than natural environmental factors. Added to the direct impact on elephant numbers and population structures is the complication introduced by the compression of elephant populations with the spread of human populations.

When the debate on the role of elephant "overabundance" in damage to woody vegetation in African savanna-woodlands was raging, Clive Spinage wrote that, "We need look no further for an explanation as to why elephant numbers may have fluctuated, than the exploitation of elephants for ivory" (1973, p. 281). He was referring to the extensive historical evidence for ivory exploitation that resulted in dramatic declines of elephants, especially since the early seventeenth century (chapter 8).

The exploitation of elephant populations has several demographic and genetic consequences. Many African elephant populations have remained depressed at a young age structure because of disproportionate removal of older individuals. Not only do age structures distort, but also sex ratios skew as males suffer higher rates of exploitation. Demographic changes also include changes in birth rates of the population. Thus, I found that a sex ratio extremely biased in favor of female elephants at Periyar in southern India had clearly depressed the birth rate. Similarly, Richard Barnes and E. B. Kapela recorded a decline in recruitment among the elephants at Ruaha in Tanzania that had been impacted by ivory poaching. The population genetic consequences include a reduction in the frequencies of genes for tusks, thus favoring the increase of tusklessness in the population. Among Asian elephants, the selective hunting of males is usually the most significant determinant of demography and population genetics.

The modeling of human-impacted elephant populations is thus even more important and relevant than modeling "natural" population dynamics. It is not an easy task, however, to obtain reliable field information on exploitation. Modelers therefore have relied on a variety of indirect evidence, such as the sizes and volumes of tusks in the trade, carcass ratios in the field, and standing age structure to simulate the dynamics of individual populations or those at a regional or subcontinental scale. I consider some of these models and what they have revealed about the nature of exploitation or its consequences for the dynamics and conservation of elephant populations.

7.6.1   *Modeling hunting patterns from tusks in the ivory trade*

The enormous volume of the international trade in African elephant tusks during the 1970s and 1980s generated the basic information on mortality patterns to explore population dynamics through simulations. Tom Pilgram and David Western used data on sizes of tusks that originated in Kenya and Tanzania to generate age structures for male and female elephants killed (appendix 2). They then used a deterministic Leslie matrix model to simulate and interpret the mortality patterns seen from the ivory trade. Reproduction was taken to be density dependent following Richard Laws and the Fowler-Smith model. Changes in birth rate with density, however, were varied in a stepwise fashion rather than as a continually varying function. Age at sexual maturity was set at 10 years and intercalving interval at 3 years at the lowest population density. These were increased by 0.5 year each year the population exceeded a set target. Mortality rates were based on studies by Richard Laws, Timothy Corfield, and Iain Douglas-Hamilton. The lower juvenile mortality rates of about

10% during the first year and 2% subsequently until 5 years described by Douglas-Hamilton were used, while above 5 years, the more detailed data of Laws were incorporated.

Two hunting patterns were simulated with the freedom to choose the actual hunting rates. The first hunting pattern assumed was that of a random cropping across all ages and both sexes, much like that used in population control. The second pattern attempted to mimic selective hunting by relating effort to size of tusks. To achieve this, the base hunting intensity was multiplied by the average tusk weight for a given age and sex class being hunted. Older, and thus larger-tusked, elephants suffered proportionately higher mortality from hunting, while males suffered more than females. The hunting intensity factor was varied to achieve set targets of ivory harvest. For these two hunting scenarios and varying intensities, the simulations produced outputs of age structures of elephants alive, dying naturally, and killed. These were compared to the observed patterns for interpreting the prevailing hunting patterns.

The simulations showed that the observed mortality patterns were indicative of selective hunting of a relatively young population. The age structure during year 15 of such a selectively hunted young population showed a characteristic peak in the young-to-middle-age classes. This matched most closely with the age structure of the elephant population at Kasungu National Park, Malawi, studied by Hugo Jachmann. Here, a combination of high fecundity and selective poaching maintained the population at a relatively young stage.

Other simulations based on ivory trade data showed that random cropping or selective hunting of a mature population was unlikely. Pilgram and Western further explored the population consequences of hunting scenarios. Under one scenario, the amount of ivory harvested was fixed at a level equal to 150% of the yield from natural mortality of a mature population. With selective hunting, the population became younger, and mean tusk weight declined. Thus, the intensity of hunting increased to maintain the ivory harvest at a constant level, taking the population to the verge of collapse by the fifteenth year. Another scenario maintained a constant total number of deaths at 150% of natural mortality. Ivory harvest declined with time, but the population stabilized, with deaths being replaced by increased recruitment.

As with other models, the Pilgram-Western model makes various assumptions. In particular, their assumption that selective hunting has a linear relationship to tusk size is unlikely to be true. Their data on age and sex structures of hunted populations derived from tusk sizes in the trade are pooled for several populations in the continent. There may be differences in hunting patterns between various populations that would be obscured from pooled data from the ivory trade. Nevertheless, the Pilgram-Western model represented an important first step in understanding the patterns underlying the exploitation of African elephants for ivory. It also helped resolve one of the most contentious debates on the African ivory trade (chapter 8).

Ian Parker had claimed that most of the ivory came from natural deaths, commercial hunting was generally not a threat to African elephant populations, and competition from expanding human populations was the greatest threat to elephants. Opposing all these views, Iain Douglas-Hamilton contended that most of the ivory in the trade came from elephants killed illegally, and populations were being overexploited in all but the most inaccessible areas. Further, the increase in human populations and loss of habitat could not explain the increased rate of hunting of elephants. The results of the Pilgram-Western model clearly favored Douglas-Hamilton's explanations.

A different approach was used by M. P. Wells to model human-impacted African elephant populations. Instead of using data on tusks in the trade, Wells used the ratio of dead elephants found in the field to live elephants counted during surveys. The "carcass ratio" was used to infer trends in population growth and degree of selective hunting for tusks. This exercise showed that trends in carcass ratios over a period of 15 years showed distinct patterns related to the type of mortality experienced by an elephant population. If data on carcass ratios had been collected in the field during aerial censuses of elephant populations, it may have been possible to infer mortality patterns from the results of such models.

At the gross, continentwide scale, the data on ivory exports during 1950–1987 from Africa were used in another modeling effort by Graeme Caughley, Holly Dublin, and Ian Parker. They used the logistic function with a carrying capacity set by the estimated population size in 1950. Production of "live ivory" was substituted for elephant numbers in the function, with 1 tonne of ivory representing 100 elephants. Ivory offtake effort was related to standing crop of ivory such that the effort increased with declining standing ivory. Assuming an intrinsic rate of increase of $r = 0.06$ on an annual basis, the model produced trajectories of annual production of ivory and deduced elephant population size over the period 1950–2000. This model suggested an overall decline of elephant populations since 1950, with a 3.3% decline throughout Africa during 1990, when the production effort was about 10-fold that of 1950. The reported increases in elephant populations within national parks in East and Central Africa during this period obviously meant an even steeper decline outside the protected areas. The modeled trajectory predicted the near extinction of elephants by 2020. The significant decline in ivory offtake since 1990, however, changed the actual scenario such that the continentwide population probably stabilized during the decade of the 1990s.

One of the more ambitious modeling efforts in scale has possibly been that of E. J. Milner-Gulland and J. R. Beddington, who used continentwide data compiled by Ian Parker on the ivory trade since 1814. In an earlier effort, Milner-Gulland had teamed up with Ruth Mace (1991) to investigate the patterns of hunting for ivory in Africa during 1979–1987 using the Leslie matrix. This exercise showed that the harvest of 12%–13% of elephants annually with a preference for elephants with larger tusks could produce the tusk sizes and quantities of ivory seen in the international trade. Now, instead of a complex Leslie matrix, their model was a "robust simplification" incorporating the range of recruitment and mortality rates observed at several sites across Africa, a factor to describe the density-dependent response, and data on tusk weights in the trade. More important, they used information on elephant distribution areas in various vegetation types determined by Iain Douglas-Hamilton, fixed maximum carrying capacities for each type, and modeled the interaction of hunting for ivory and carrying capacity under different scenarios. Sensitivity analyses showed their model to be robust to the range of parameter values used. Their modeling suggested that reductions in carrying capacity (as a result of agricultural expansion) were the major cause of elephant population declines in the nineteenth century and the early part of the twentieth century, but that hunting for ivory has been the predominant cause of elephant decline since 1950 (fig. 7.10).

The use of changes in the sex ratio over time is another means of determining the levels of poaching for ivory, especially in Asian elephant populations, in which only males possess tusks. This could be especially useful in the case of populations for which reliable official records of poaching are unavailable. Using the basic Leslie matrix, I constructed a model to iteratively simulate changes in the sex ratio of an elephant population under pressure of ivory poaching and applied it to data from the Periyar Reserve with the help of my colleagues. The model made the following assumptions based on studies of

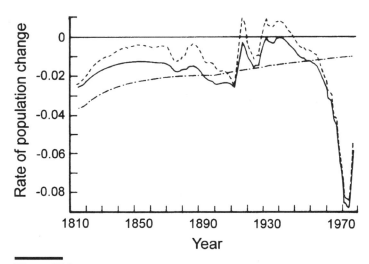

Figure 7.10
A comparison of the mean rate of population change when hunting alone (broken line), when carrying capacity alone (dotted-dashed line), and when both factors (solid line) are assumed responsible for population decline in African elephants. Until about 1970, both factors seemed to play a role, but after this time, hunting was the major factor in population decline. (From Milner-Gulland and Beddington 1993. Reproduced with the permission of the Royal Society of London.)

elephants at Periyar and elsewhere in Asia. The male-to-female ratio of various age classes, especially the adults, in Sri Lankan elephants was taken to be the natural situation that would prevail under the near absence of poaching. This "near-natural" age-sex distribution was therefore simulated using reasonable assumptions of birth rate (intercalving interval of about 4.5 years) and age-specific mortality for the sexes such that the population would be growing at $r = 0.02$ (see section 7.4.3).

Observations at Periyar during the 1950s and 1960s by naturalists such as M. Krishnan had indicated an abundance of large-tusked bulls. G. U. Kurup's survey in 1969 had indicated an adult male-to-female ratio of about 1 : 6, which changed to 1 : 122 by 1987–1989, when Mohana Chandran kept detailed records of elephant sightings. Our surveys during 1994 showed this ratio to be 1 : 101. The basic idea, therefore, was to simulate increased rates of male mortality across the various age classes for a starting population of about 1,000 elephants (from census estimates) with an adult sex ratio of 1 : 6 over a 20-year period (beginning in 1974) such that the resulting population structure (age-sex ratios) would match the observed structure in 1994. The difference between the increased mortality rates and the expected natural rates (of the Sri Lankan situation) would represent the rates of poaching for ivory.

Four scenarios of poaching were simulated: (1) the rate of mortality under poaching was constant over two decades (thus, most of the harvest was during the initial years); (2) the rate was low initially, but then increased as the absolute numbers of tusked bulls declined; (3) there was a background rate of mortality from poaching, but spurts occurred during years 5, 10, and 15; and (4) the spurts occurred during years 3, 6, 9, 12, 15, and 18 of the simulation. We also added a function to lower the birth rate progressively as adult male-to-female ratio skewed beyond 1 : 25 based on field observations.

All scenarios simulated the observed population structure quite well and came up with similar results of poaching intensity and ivory harvest. Over the 20-year period, an estimated 336–388 tuskers had been poached and 3,256–3,334 kg of ivory harvested, with a large proportion of this coming from the 10- to 20-year-old age class (fig. 7.11). Interestingly, the population growth rates indicated even under the extremely skewed sex ratios were only marginally negative. This is actually to be expected because declining birth rates do not result in major changes in population growth compared to increase in death rates (of females). Our more recent observations at Periyar show an increased birth rate, perhaps the result of subadult bulls coming into the adult age category. It would be interesting to monitor changes in the tusker-to-*makhna* ratio in this population in the coming years.

7.6.2   *Modeling long-term trends in tusk inheritance*

The exploitation of elephants would have had several population genetic consequences. Among African elephant populations, the selective hunting of both females and males has made qualitative and quantitative impacts on tusk inher-

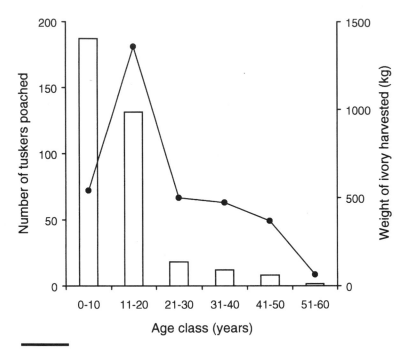

Figure 7.11
Numbers of elephants killed (*bars*) and quantities of ivory harvested (*solid circles*) by poachers in various age classes over a 20-year period (1974–1994) in the Periyar Reserve, India. These represent the averages of four scenarios of poaching simulated by the model. (From Sukumar et al. 1998.)

itance. In qualitative terms, there is evidence for an overall reduction in tusk size. While the mean tusk size in the trade may have decreased because of a demographic shift to younger populations, there has also probably been a corresponding decrease in tusk size for a given age. At the same time, there has also been a noticeable increase in the proportion of tuskless elephants in heavily impacted regions such as Uganda and the Luangwa Valley in Zambia. Some of this change is obviously the outcome in the short term of the selective elimination of tusked elephants. When the poaching pressure decreases, there is again an increase in the proportions of tusked elephants, although not to the original levels, as has been observed in the Luangwa Valley.

The hunting of Asian elephants for tusks, of course, is confined to males. Interestingly, the capture of elephants also may have been biased toward tusked males. The premium on tusked elephants for use in war or ceremonial occasions through history would have resulted in higher rates of "mortality" among tusked males from wild populations. The *Arthasastra*, an ancient Indian manual on statecraft, prescribed the selective capture of 20-year-old tuskers from the wild (see chapter 2). The significant frequencies of tuskless males (fig.

7.12) in several Asian elephant populations hint at a selective advantage for the tuskless trait in the face of human exploitation.

The population genetics of the tusk trait is therefore of obvious interest to elephant biologists and modelers. To model changes in gene frequencies realistically, knowledge of the pattern of inheritance of the trait is needed. At present, there is no clear idea of tusk inheritance in elephants. It is likely that more than one gene locus is involved in the expression of tusks. Tuskless elephants may have rudimentary tusks or incisor teeth (called *tushes* among Asian elephants). These are much smaller than regular tusks. Size frequency distribution of incisors shows a distinct bimodal pattern, with some "tuskless" adult individuals possessing tusks weighing less than 1 kg, while others have full-blown tusks weighing several kilograms. A simple model of tusk inheritance would be a two-locus model in which one locus determines the presence or absence of rudimentary incisors, while the second locus determines if these develop into full-blown tusks. The considerable variation in the size of regular tusks among individuals in a population also suggests polygenic inheritance. Among Asian elephants, an additional complication is the total absence of regular tusks in females.

Attempts to model tusk frequency changes in elephant populations have used the simplest assumption possible. Andrew Dobson and associates, who

Figure 7.12
A tuskless male elephant at Minneriya, Sri Lanka. Such tuskless males are locally known as *aliyas* in Sri Lanka and as *makhnas* in India. They constitute over 95% of males in Sri Lanka, while in India, their proportion is variable across regions. (Photo courtesy of S. Wijeyamohan.)

modeled this in African elephants, assumed a single locus, two-allele (T and t) determinant of the tusk trait. Homozygous dominant TT and heterozygous Tt individuals possess tusks, while homozygous recessive tt individuals are tusk-less. Ralph Tiedemann and Fred Kurt, who modeled Asian elephants, made a similar assumption with the additional condition that tusks are not expressed in females. This requires a role for females as carriers of genes for tusk expression in their sons. Limited records I have examined on tusk expression in sons sired by tuskless males in zoos suggest that females, indeed, play a role in tusk inheritance. A single locus model of tusk expression in elephants is certainly a caricature of reality. Nevertheless, it is a useful starting point in understanding the dynamics of tusk frequencies in elephant populations.

Dobson and his associates combined an age-structured, density-dependent demographic model with a single locus, two-allele population genetic model for tusk inheritance. The ability of males to obtain matings was a function of the proportion of tusked or tuskless males in the population. It was assumed that tuskless bulls would fail to win fights against tusked bulls and thus fail to obtain matings when the proportion of tusked bulls is high. The frequency of matings by tuskless bulls would then increase with a decrease in the frequency of tusked bulls in the population. The initial conditions of the population were set by allowing the simulation to run until age classes and gene frequencies reached stable frequencies and numbers. The population was then simulated with a 5% harvest across all age classes of tusked individuals only. Population numbers decline over the first 50 years to a low level, at which point they stabilize over the next 200 years. As the relative frequency of tusked and tusk-less individuals changes in favor of tusklessness, the mating success of tuskless bulls increases. A predominantly tuskless population then increases to the carrying capacity of the habitat.

The Tiedemann-Kurt model for Asian elephants has been described in much greater detail in their 1995 publication. Their model combines stochastic population dynamics with population genetics at the individual level. The demographic data on birth and death probabilities are based on Kurt's field observations in Sri Lanka during the late 1960s and 1970s and my work in southern India during the 1980s. Males were assumed to begin reproducing at 20 years of age and females at 8 years, giving birth 2 years later. Such an early age in female reproduction is likely to be true only of Sri Lankan elephants, but not other Asian populations. A constraint of an upper limit of six females mated annually by one adult male was set. The minimum intercalving interval was taken as 4 years, with a certain probability that a female would actually conceive in a given year 4 years after a previous conception; this translated into an average intercalving interval of 4.43 years, typical of observed populations.

The initial conditions of age and sex distribution, as well as allelic frequencies, were set by running the simulation for 100 years until equilibrium was established. For the initial simulation, the annual probability of death was set at 5.5% for females and 7% for all males. The above birth and female death rates also produced a stable population size under deterministic dynamics.

These rates were derived from averaging across all age classes for each sex; real populations have different age-class-specific death rates. Further simulations began with a stable age distribution and a population in Hardy-Weinberg equilibrium for allelic frequencies. Thus, the frequencies of genotypes and phenotypes (*makhnas* and tuskers among males) were also stable under random mating between the sexes. The model, however, provides for sexual selection through a mating advantage for tuskers over *makhnas* to a specified degree.

The model was used to explore aspects of population growth in elephants, but the more interesting application was to track changes in gene frequencies for the tusk allele and relative proportions of tuskers and *makhnas* in the population under different selective regimes over a 2,000-year period (fourth century B.C. to early sixteenth century A.D.). Based on some historical data of elephants in Sri Lanka, collated by Fred Kurt and associates in a separate article, the model was applied to the island population. It was assumed that, at the beginning of this historical period, the tuskers constituted about 95% of the male segment, decreasing to less than 15% by the present time. Simple calculations using the Hardy-Weinberg law for allelic frequencies showed that, if tusks were to be determined by a dominant allele T, the initial frequency of this allele would have been 78% (say, 80%). If the allele for tusk expression is recessive (t), on the other hand, its frequency would have to be 97% (say, 95%) initially.

Simulations were run with both scenarios of the tusk allele as dominant and recessive in the absence of sexual selection, but with tuskers suffering a higher annual mortality (10%) compared to *makhnas* (7.5%). None of these simulated populations matched the condition of a decline in tusker proportion from 95% to about 10%–15% of the population over a 2,000-year period. Only when the tusk allele was taken to be dominant and a 50% sexual selection advantage was given for tuskers over *makhnas* in matings was this condition met (fig. 7.13). If the sexual selection advantage for tuskers was lower, at 10%–30%, the result was the extinction of the tusk allele.

The selection against tuskers through capture and hunting, however, has fluctuated historically. Even within the island of Sri Lanka, there are considerable differences in the relative numbers of tuskers and *makhnas*. While southeastern Sri Lanka has a 10%–15% tusker proportion, the Mahaweli basin has practically none. Using different initial population sizes and slightly differing historical mortality rates for tuskers in the two regions, the model was run to simulate the extinction of the tusk allele in the Mahaweli basin by about A.D. 1500. Based on these modeling results, the authors suggested a dominant inheritance of the tusk allele and a moderate degree (about 1.5 times) of sexual selection in favor of tuskers among Asian elephants.

Both the models of tusk dynamics in elephants make crucial assumptions, with little empirical basis, on sexual selection advantage for males. The model of Dobson and associates assumes that tuskless bulls fail to obtain any matings when they are present in low frequencies in relation to tuskless bulls. The mating success of a tuskless bull approaches parity with that of a tusker only when the

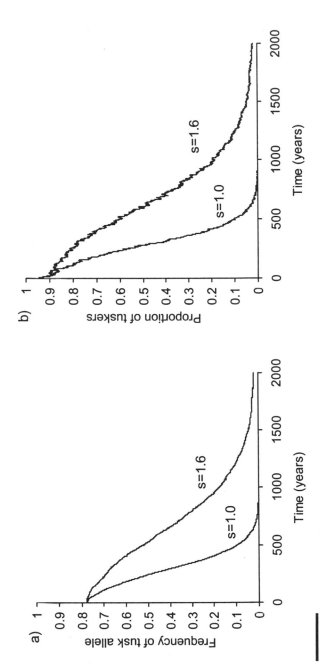

Figure 7.13

Simulated frequency of the (*a*) tusk allele over the long-term in reproductive adults and (*b*) the proportion of tuskers among reproductive male elephants under the conditions that the tusk allele is dominant, tusked males have a 60% reproductive advantage over tuskless males and tusked males suffer higher mortality than do tuskless males (these were simulated by R. Sukumar and G. Pradhan [unpublished results 2003] by modifying the model described in Tiedemann and Kurt 1995; see text for details).

frequency of the latter falls to very low levels. This seems very unlikely. Among Asian elephants, the tuskless bulls are not necessarily inferior to tuskers in fighting ability. The Tiedemann-Kurt model does not explore other possibilities for the low frequency of tusked males in Sri Lanka, including the immigration of tusked males from imported captive elephants that may have become feral.

Gauri Pradhan and I have been modeling the possibilities of captive tuskers contributing the genes for tusks into a largely or entirely tuskless population. There is extensive historical evidence that rulers in Sri Lanka imported elephants, including tusked males, from several regions, including India and Burma, from as early as the sixth century A.D. (see chapter 2), this strongly suggests that tuskers were already scarce locally. Could some of these tusked males have escaped or been released into the wild and infused the tusk gene into the population? We thus explored three possibilities:

1. Tusked males had reduced in the population gradually in accordance with the Tiedemann-Kurt assumption.
2. The island was populated by an entirely tuskless elephant population, the result of genetic drift operating during the Pleistocene in a small founder population, but captive tuskers had successfully mixed with the population.
3. The depletion of tuskers occurred rapidly through selective capture until the sixth century, but the present frequency of the tusk gene has been maintained through the mixing of captive tuskers.

We modified the Tiedemann-Kurt model to incorporate more realistic features such as age-specific mortality for both sexes, age-dependent reproductive success in bull elephants, and frequency-dependent sexual selection of tuskers over *makhnas*. Our results showed that, while the gradual reduction in the tusk gene over the centuries was possible (see fig. 7.13) as in the earlier model, the frequency of the tusk gene (and proportion of tuskers) presently observed in the Sri Lankan elephant population could also have been the result of captive tuskers reverting to the wild in an entirely *makhna* population or mixing with a predominantly *makhna* population after elephant imports commenced during the sixth century A.D.

We are hopeful that the ongoing genetic studies of Asian elephant populations (see chapter 1) will provide more clarity on this issue.

Coconuts, Corn, and Carvings
The Conflict between Elephants and People

8

8.1 Introduction

The relationship between elephants and humans, which was earlier examined largely in the historical sociocultural context, can now be extended into the more contemporary ecological domain. Over the past 100,000 years or more, both elephants and humans have been important forces of transformation of the natural landscape, the elephant through its direct impact on the vegetation and early humans through the use of fire (which actually goes back nearly half a million years). For most of this period, the basic human-elephant relationship was that of predator and prey, with humans also falling victim to the elephant on occasion. The advent of agriculture, about 10,000 years ago, in the Old World introduced a new dimension to the interaction between elephants and people. Cultivated crops attracted the elephant's attention as sources of food, and elephant-human conflicts intensified over this resource and over space as permanent settlement and agriculture gradually spread through the elephant's habitat. At the same time, increased human use of the natural landscape for a variety of products such as wood, fruits, fodder for livestock, and so on had significant impact on the vegetation and consequently on the elephant populations. In addition, there was direct human impact on elephants—hunting for ivory and other products, such as hide and meat.

This two-way interaction—crop depredation and manslaughter by elephants and habitat transformation and elephant hunting by people—has to be placed within an analytical framework drawing on subjects as diverse as foraging theory, landscape ecology, vegetational ecology, social behavior, population dynamics, and population genetics. In spite of extensive research on elephants, their interactions with people have received attention only in recent years. There are several questions that need to be answered satisfactorily if we are to come up with lasting solutions to elephant-human conflicts. The most basic questions are, Why do elephants raid cultivated crops? Is crop raiding merely a response to lack of natural food resources, or is it because of the lure of certain properties of the crops themselves? How do landscape attributes such as shape and degree of fragmentation influence the intensity of crop raiding? How serious is the impact of elephants on the livelihoods and lives of people? As elephants are not carnivores, why are they aggressive toward people? What are the implications of human exploitation of the natural habitat for elephants? In the final analysis, what are the effects of this interaction, including conflict-related deaths and hunting, on elephant populations?

An ecological analysis of elephant-human interaction is important if we are to devise strategies for minimizing conflict and promoting the coexistence of elephants and people across the two continents. In this chapter, I provide the ecological framework for describing elephant-human conflicts or other interactions, drawing on the few studies carried out so far in Asia and in Africa. The literature, of course, is more extensive, but in this chapter, I only draw on those aspects relevant to the ecological analysis of elephant-human interactions.

8.2   Crop depredation by elephants

Depredation of cultivated crops by elephants is widespread in both Africa and Asia. It occurs to varying extent practically throughout the distributional range of the animals, in different climatic regimes and habitat types, on a variety of crops under different land uses and human densities, and under conditions of low to high elephant densities.

Elephants, or other wildlife for that matter, have undoubtedly damaged crops ever since the advent of agriculture. I have referred to ancient Indian elephant lore (the *Gajasastra*), which speaks of serious conflict between elephants and agricultural communities as early as the fifth or sixth century B.C. (chapter 2). In more recent times, there are extensive, although scattered, records of crop depredation and the consequent policy of elephant control by European colonial rulers in Africa and Asia during the nineteenth and twentieth centuries. In British East Africa, the available records suggest that tens of thousands of elephants were shot in control measures. Elephant hunts were also common in other European colonies. Even in British India and Ceylon (Sri Lanka), where elephant capture was the preferred mode of control, thousands of elephants were killed by colonial hunters. These historical records of crop depredation and elephant control unfortunately have yet to be brought together systematically in the literature. Such records would serve as useful background for understanding the nature of elephant-human conflict and the historical progression of the demise of elephant populations on localized scales.

The issue of crop depredation by elephants received little attention in the early research investigations of African elephants. Either there was a passing mention of the problem or the assessments of damage to agricultural crops were confined to internal reports of the wildlife management agencies. Even James Allaway's doctoral study of elephant-human conflict in newly opened agricultural areas along the Tana River in Kenya during the late 1970s was, in his own words, "more descriptive than analytical." The early reports from Asia also were mostly on the economic dimensions of conflict. J. Mishra provided one of the first published reports of loss to maize and paddy crops due to elephant depredation in Bihar, India. Robert Olivier's doctoral dissertation of 1978 provided a brief account of elephant damage to oil palm and rubber in peninsular Malaysia. The first detailed account of the economics of crop loss and methods to keep elephants out of commercial oil palm and rubber plantations in Malaysia came from James Blair, G. G. Boon, and Nache Noor in 1979.

When I began my doctoral research in the 1980s in the Biligirirangans of southern India, I realized that these earlier accounts of crop raiding by elephants did not provide an ecological analysis of the issue. Therefore, I attempted to provide the basic ecological framework for understanding crop raiding and other elephant-human interactions in my dissertation of 1985. Since then, several studies in Asia and in Africa have taken this process forward; the most notable of these is Richard Hoare's study of elephant-human conflict in Zimbabwe.

8.2.1   The nature of crop depredation

Agricultural crops consumed and damaged by elephants are most commonly the analogs of plants eaten by elephants in the natural habitat (fig. 8.1). Cultivated grasses, particularly the cereals and millets, are the most common targets of elephant depredation. In the moist tropics of Asia, the staple cereal, paddy (*Oryza sativa*), is a favorite target of elephants. In drier regions of both Asia and Africa, elephants consume a variety of cereals, chiefly maize or corn (*Zea mays*), sorghum (*Sorghum vulgare*), and wheat (*Triticum vulgare*) and various millets such as finger millet (*Eleusine coracana*), little millet (*Panicum miliare*), and bulrush millet (*Pennisetum typhoides*). Sugarcane (*Saccharum officinarum*) is another cultivated grass that attracts elephants.

All cultivated legumes (such as beans) are potential food for elephants. A large number of legume species that are specific to different regions can be listed. Elephants often target cultivated palms such as coconut (*Cocos nucifera*), usually grown in homestead gardens, and the commercially planted oil palm (*Elaeis guineensis*). In southern India, elephants are known even to feed on ripe berries of coffee (*Coffea arabica*). A variety of vegetables (potato, tomato, carrot, spinach, pumpkin) and fruits (mango, banana, orange, melon, jackfruit) are consumed. A list of all cultivated plants consumed by elephants would run

Figure 8.1
Damage by Asian elephants to paddy crop (*top left*), coconut trees (*top right*), and a
house (*bottom*).

into several dozen species. Most of these cultivated plants belong to botanical families such as Gramineae (grasses), Palmae (palms), and Leguminosae (legumes), which also constitute substantial proportions of the elephant's diet in the wild.

Elephants are selective with respect to the plant parts they consume. When paddy or millets are in a young, vegetative stage, a clump of plants is uprooted and consumed entirely. More typically, these are preferred when they begin flowering and set grain. At this stage, a clump is uprooted, the terminal portion is chewed off and consumed, while the basal portion with the roots is discarded. By weighing several samples of whole plants and discarded basal parts, I estimated that only 62% by weight of finger millet plant is consumed. With sorghum and maize, the stalks bearing the spikes or cob, constituting about one-fourth of the plant by weight, are selectively broken and consumed, although elephants may also feed on the stem and leaves in the absence of flowering. Young coconut or oil palm may be uprooted and trashed until broken pieces of stem and leaves are suitable for consumption. From older trees, the leaves or the central rachis may be selectively removed; the last action kills the tree. Large coconut trees are even uprooted before feeding. Contrary to popular belief, elephants do not necessarily feed on fruits of banana plants, but rather crush the stem and extract the fibrous pith. Fruits such as mango and orange are usually selectively plucked, although in the process, branches may be broken and the tree damaged.

A substantial part of the damage caused to standing crops in the fields may simply be due to trampling by elephants. In my southern Indian study, I found that only about 60% of the damage in finger millet fields where elephants had been actively feeding was due to actual uprooting and consumption of plants. The remaining 40% of the damage was due to trampling. In addition, elephants may also damage fields merely through trampling without any feeding. When a particular crop or a variety of crops is grown in small plots, the raiding elephants may exercise a distinct choice of one or more plots for feeding. I found, for instance, that bull elephants did not feed in finger millet plots in which the plants were in the vegetative stage. Rather, they walked through these plots, trampling some crop in the process, before reaching a plot with millet plants in the more attractive flowering stage. At any particular time when millet fields were in different phenological stages, the bulls distinctly biased selection toward fields with robust plant growth and crop that had flowered or set grain.

When elephant family groups raid crops, much of the damage may be due to trampling of fields as they pass through but do not use for feeding. I found, however, that damage in finger millet fields utilized by them for feeding was not very different from that caused by bulls. Large elephant groups can obviously trample a considerable area of crop fields. In the Indian state of West Bengal, herds of 50 or more elephants trample paddy fields as they walk long distances between forest patches.

Raiding by elephants is not confined to standing crops in fields. They also attempt to feed on harvested plants stacked in the field for drying (prior to threshing) or even raid grain stores by knocking over mud or thatched house walls. There are amusing anecdotes of elephants raiding locally brewed liquor stores in villages or even the imported, connoisseur's varieties kept in army camps near the jungle.

8.2.2   *Seasonality of raiding*

There seem to be several considerations for seasonal patterns of crop raiding by elephants. These include the extent of availability of crops, the presence of elephants in habitats near cultivated areas, and possibly the attractiveness of crops in relation to wild forage during a particular season. In the relatively aseasonal tropics, such as in peninsular Malaysia, there may be no consistent seasonal pattern of raiding perennial crops such as oil palm. Raiding may peak at a given location when a particular group of elephants moves into the area, but no pattern may be discerned over the larger region. In regions with a clear seasonality in rainfall patterns as well as in cultivation of annual crops, there is much stronger evidence for seasonality in crop raiding by elephants.

In the Biligirirangans, I found two peaks in raiding frequency—a first minor one corresponding to the cultivation of maize by some farmers during the first wet season, and a major peak following the cultivation of finger millet by most farmers during the second wet season (fig. 8.2). There was a time lag of about 1–2 months between peaks in rainfall and in raiding as elephants awaited the maturing crops that they preferred. This pattern is largely true of most other elephant regions in southern India as well as other parts, such as northern West Bengal, where farmers cultivate two cereal crops in a year. At Sengwa in Zimbabwe also, a peak in raiding is seen during the transition from the wet to the dry season.

Martin Tchamba's study in northern Cameroon clearly brought out the influence of movement pattern of elephants, as opposed to merely rainfall patterns or crop availability, in determining raiding frequency. In the southern part of the study area, there was a clear late wet season peak in raiding frequency that was also quite high (fig. 8.3). In the north, raiding by elephants occurred only during the dry months, but the frequency was much lower than in the south. Raiding in the intermediate zone was more irregular. This raiding pattern was clearly related to the seasonal migration of elephants between Waza and Kalamaloue National Parks in the south and in the north, respectively.

We can also examine the influence of rainfall on crop raiding in terms of their variation from one year to another. During 1982, the crop yields in the Biligirirangans were poor because of a drought in southern India related to El Niño. I observed that elephants raided crops only about half as frequently that year compared to the previous year, when rainfall was normal. Richard Hoare's

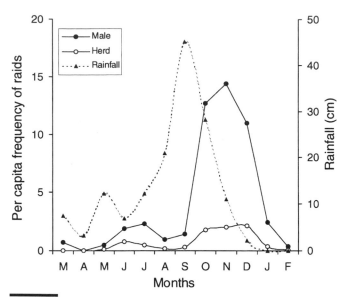

Figure 8.2

Monthly per capita frequency of crop raiding by elephants in relation to monthly rainfall in the Biligirirangans in southern India during 1981–1982. (Based on Sukumar 1985, 1989a.)

study during 1993–1995 in Zimbabwe's Sebungwe region found only a weak relationship between annual rainfall and raiding frequency in a given year. Raiding was highest during the year with intermediate rainfall and lowest during a drought year.

Thus, a complex interplay of factors seems to decide raiding frequencies. While the seasonal availability and productivity of crops is a major determinant, the movement pattern of elephants and the relative difference in productivity or quality of crops versus wild forage may also influence raiding frequency.

8.2.3   Energetics of crop raiding

Elephants raid cultivated crops almost exclusively at night, thereby implying that they have knowledge of the location of crop fields and that raiding is usually deliberate. The movement pattern of raiding elephants during the crop season would thus reflect their foraging needs in the natural habitat during the day, alternating with visits to crop fields at night. While the energetics of such a foraging pattern have not been empirically studied or analyzed even theoretically, I made detailed calculations of quantities of millet plants consumed by solitary bulls, bull groups, and family groups in several villages during 110 nights

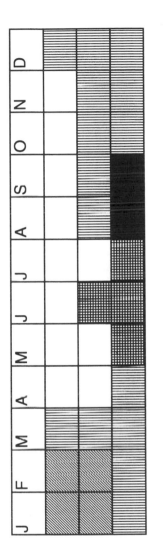

Frequency of raids

| 0 | 1-10 | 11-25 | 26-100 | 101-350 |

Figure 8.3
Average monthly frequency of crop raiding during 1992–1993 in the Waza–Logone region of Cameroon. The frequencies are shown for three zones (northern, central, and southern) in this region. (Based on Tchamba 1996.)

of raiding in 1981–1982. In some instances of raiding by solitary bulls, I was even able to compute the rate of feeding. When finger millet plants were in a vegetative stage, a bull consumed 1.5 kg (dry weight) of plants per hour. This increased substantially to 6.4 kg per hour as the plants grew and flowered. In one instance, a bull managed an intake of over 12 kg per hour when the finger millet had set grain. At this rate, an adult bull can meet its daily requirement of forage in just 5–6 hours of feeding.

The average quantities of finger millet plants consumed by an adult bull during a night of raiding were 44 kg and 30 kg in two sets of villages differentiated on the basis of crop productivity. The maximum quantity consumed was 70–75 kg per night, recorded several times in both finger millet and sorghum fields. For family herds, the average quantities consumed in these sets of villages were 24 kg and 11 kg of millet plant per elephant per night, with an upper limit of 52 kg.

Using data of elephant population density, population structure, and the frequency of raids in the study villages, I made two ecologically relevant estimates of the relative importance of crop raiding in the elephant's diet. The "average" bull in the study area raided crops on 49 nights in the year, while the average family group did so about 8.4 nights. In quantitative terms, the cultivated crops constituted 9.3% of the diet of adult bulls and 1.7% of the diet of family groups during the year.

There were obviously sharp seasonal differences in raiding, with a peak during October–December, when the staple crop, finger millet, was cultivated (fig. 8.2). During these months, the crops constituted 22%–30% of the diet of adult bulls and 4%–5% for family groups.

Averages also obscure other patterns of skewness in the data. Certain adult bulls carried out most of the raids, and presumably so did particular family groups, although this was difficult for me to determine. Two adult bulls (of about 20 bulls in the area) were particularly notorious raiders, one of them entering cultivation about 120 nights of the year. At least one in two of the larger bulls seemed to be regular raiders, while some of the others may have raided more sporadically. Christy Williams and A.J.T. Johnsingh also report from a recent study at Rajaji National Park in northern India that two of four adult bulls monitored through radiotelemetry were crop raiders. Of three radio-collared female elephants from different clans in the Nilgiris in southern India monitored by M. Balasubramanian and associates, only one indulged regularly in crop raiding over the 4-year period of the study. However, all four family groups being tracked through telemetry by my research team in the Buxa-Jaldapara Reserves (section 4.4.1) have indulged in raiding crops.

These patterns indicate that cultivated crops may be significant in the diet of some elephants in a population. In qualitative terms, crops may be even more important than the figures suggested by quantitative intake because of the superior nutritional attributes of crop plants compared to wild plants.

8.2.4   *Group dynamics of raiding elephants*

When elephants move into agricultural areas at night, their group dynamics may be different from that seen during the day in the natural habitat. Adult Asian elephant bulls are predominantly solitary during their daytime movements in the wild. I noticed, however, a distinct tendency among bulls to associate with each other while raiding crop fields at night. While 93% of sightings of bulls in the wild were of solitary bulls, only 58% of bull raids were by solitary ones. A very significant 26% of raids were by two-bull groups, 13% by three bull groups, and the rest by a four-bull group. In most cases, these were not chance associations arising from individual bulls converging independently on a particularly attractive crop field at night. Rather, the associations were formed prior to the bulls entering cultivation from the forest. The group size among raiding bulls, however, was significantly higher only during the second wet season (October–December), when the majority of farmers grew crops in their land. Since raiding involves taking a certain risk (with angry farmers), it is mutually advantageous for bulls to cooperate, rather than compete, when crops are available in plenty.

Bull associations during raiding have been reported from other regions in Asia and also in Africa. Widodo Ramono, in a personal communication, informs me that all-male groups are known to raid plantation crops in Sumatra. Raiding bull groups are known from Sri Lanka. In a study of elephant-human conflict along the western periphery of Malawi's Liwonde National Park, Roy Bhima found bulls raiding in groups of up to six animals. In the Sengwa region of Zimbabwe, where most of the crop raiding is by bull elephants, Ferrel Osborn once observed an all-male raiding group of 17 individuals aged from about 6 years to large adults.

The size of bull groups is a function of the elephant density, proportion and numbers of bulls in the population, predation pressure, and local social relationships. The larger bull groups are generally observed in regions with high population density and numbers of bulls. Other factors, such as human disturbance through hunting, may also serve to increase group size in elephants. On the other hand, selective hunting of male elephants for ivory, such as in southern India, also serves to reduce the numbers of bulls and decrease bull group sizes. Since my study of crop raiding in southern India during the early 1980s, a systematic reduction of the male population through ivory poaching reduced the incidence of bull groups raiding crops. This was reflected not only in my study area, but also elsewhere, such as in the Hosur Division, where Ramesh Kumar observed only solitary bulls raiding crops during 1989–1991.

When family groups raided crops, I did not observe any tendency for them to form larger groups compared to their grouping in the forest. Roy Bhima similarly observed that the group size of raiding herds matched the group sizes of herds in their natural habitat at Liwonde during the wet season.

A possible explanation is that family groups may not gain any extra advantage in facing threats from farmers by coalescing into even larger groups. Rather, this may actually reduce the efficiency of feeding in crop fields. Large family groups do enter cultivated fields; group sizes of 50–80 elephants, including families and adult bulls, are reported from West Bengal State in India. The point I am trying to make, however, is that the group sizes of raiding family groups may not necessarily be different from what one observes in the natural habitat. One exception I found was that mother-calf units rarely seemed to venture for raiding. This is understandable as the mother may not risk exposing a lone calf to danger. At the same time, I must stress that more information is needed from a range of elephant habitats on the group dynamics of raiders.

8.2.5   Raiding frequencies by male versus female groups

When elephants raid crops, they may do so solitarily, as in the case of adult or subadult bulls, or in such social groupings as bull groups, family herds, or families with one or more adult bulls attached. By comparing the relative frequency of crop raids by these categories to the elephant population structure, we can understand possible differences between the sexes in raiding behavior. A striking feature that emerges from most studies is the much higher propensity for male elephants to raid crops. I have mentioned that, on average, an adult bull entered cultivation six times (49 nights) more frequently as a female-led family group (8 nights) during my 1981–1982 study in southern India. In a different part of the elephant's range in southern India, Ramesh Kumar computed a similar difference between the sexes in raiding. Comparable figures are not available from elsewhere, but can be approximated from data on relative raiding frequencies. Of 1,672 instances of raids in northwestern Sri Lanka, Mangala de Silva found 75% to be due to solitary bulls, 7.6% by pairs (which undoubtedly would have been mostly bull pairs), and the rest by larger groups. Thus, adult males were responsible for 80%–85% of all raids, while these probably constituted only about 15%–20% of the population. This again implies a several-fold difference between bulls and family groups in raiding propensity.

The few studies in Africa also point to a similar pattern. At Liwonde in Malawi, about 85% of raids recorded by Roy Bhima were by individual bulls or bull groups. As aerial surveys showed a slight excess of female herds compared to bull groups, it is again clear that bulls ventured out of the park into cultivation far more often. Two studies in Zimbabwe came to similar conclusions. Richard Hoare's documentation of crop raiding in the northern Sebungwe region revealed that 79% of raids were perpetrated by solitary bulls or bull groups, and 9% were by mixed groups in which at least one large male was present. Ferrel Osborn observed that virtually all crop raiding at Sengwa was by bull elephants. The Zimbabwean elephants had a natural population structure, and thus the male bias in raiding is very striking in these two studies.

The majority of studies thus clearly establish that, on average, an adult male elephant is more likely to raid crop fields than would a female-led herd, a behavioral difference that should have a biological basis. Nevertheless, the number of raids by family groups may also be significant and perhaps more than that of bulls on an absolute or even a per capita basis in some regions. These warrant a closer examination.

Some observers loosely report that family groups raid more often than do bulls without relating the raiding frequencies to population data. In some cases, the raiding "herds" may have included one or more adult bulls or even have been an all-male group. One region where family groups seem to raid crops as frequently as the bulls do is Central India, which has been investigated by Hemant Datye. Incidentally, Datye's statement that family herds raid more often than the bulls is not backed by data relating this to the population structure. The small population of elephants of Dalma Sanctuary in southern Bihar (now Jharkhand State) has since 1987 been making deep forays eastward into the state of West Bengal. Utilizing small patches of regenerating forest, these elephants cause heavy damage to paddy fields. Another region where family herds have caused considerably more damage to crops than have bulls on a per capita basis is in the southern Indian state of Andhra Pradesh. After elephants had become extinct at least two centuries earlier, several herds of elephants, including some bulls, immigrated into this state from a much larger population further south beginning in 1983.

Comparable documentation from Africa is scant. A possible example is the Waga-Logone region of northern Cameroon, where Martin Tchamba records that the number of crop-raiding elephants in the rainy season increased from about 50 in 1991 to 330 in 1997. This seems related to shifts in seasonal movement patterns of certain elephant herds. It is interesting to note that the elephants in northern Cameroon have mostly been immigrant from neighboring Chad. Since about 1947, the population here has built up to several hundred elephants with successive waves of immigration.

The overall pattern that emerges is that, in the relatively intact and extensive habitats that harbor large elephant numbers, the males exhibit a much greater propensity to raid cultivated fields compared to female-led herds. Raiding by female-led herds increases with greater fragmentation of habitat. The few recorded instances when family groups had equal or even higher propensity than the bulls to raid were those for which habitats were highly fragmented, populations were relatively small, and environmental factors forced the herds to disperse over long distances, perhaps in search of newer habitats. I discuss the possible significance of this pattern in another section.

As opposed to the per capita frequency of raids by bulls and family herds, the relative absolute frequency of raids by the social groups in a region would depend on their differential propensity to raid and their representation in the population. To take an extreme example, if all adult bulls are eliminated from a population, then 100% of raids (whether few or many) would be by family groups. In the larger elephant populations with a normal age and sex structure, over 80% of all crop raids in the region seem to be due to bulls (the examples being Sri Lanka, Zimbabwe, and Malawi). In such populations, almost free from ivory poaching, the adult bulls are likely to constitute about 15% of the population. As the sex ratios become more female biased through selective hunting of males, the relative proportion of raids by bulls decreases. In my study area, the adult bulls constituted 7% of the elephant population during 1981–1982, but were responsible for 70% of nearly 800 nights of raiding in 12 villages. Bulls were responsible for 54% of about 1,450 raiding incidents recorded by Ramesh Kumar during 1989–1991 in Hosur Division. Although he does not give population figures, it can be assumed that the poaching wave in southern India during the 1980s, which also affected the Hosur Division, would have impacted the adult male segment.

The relative extent of raiding by the various social groups can also be expressed in terms of actual damage inflicted. This would depend on the group size difference (thus, raiding by a family herd could result in greater damage by trampling and consumption compared to that by a solitary bull) and the tenacity of raiding (a solitary bull that spends 10 hours raiding could inflict more damage than a family herd that raids for an hour). Damage itself could be expressed as area of the field that is affected, reduction in crop yield, or economic value of the loss. In my study, the bulls were responsible for about 60% of the total loss in yield to millet and cereal crop. In economic terms, this was slightly higher because coconut trees, which have higher economic value, were almost exclusively damaged by bulls. In contrast, about 65% of the damage was attributed to family herds in a sample of 194 raids in the Nilgiris in southern India, recorded by M. Balasubramanian and colleagues during 1992. Although they do not present population data for this range, it is clear that the reduction in adult males to less than 3% of the population (based on my records) was responsible for this pattern. Interestingly, they concede that, on a per capita basis, the adult bulls raided more often than did the family herds. In absolute terms, the amount of crop damage caused by elephants was reduced significantly in many parts of southern India because of the poaching of tusked males. As this trend continues, the family groups would cause a progressively higher proportion of the reduced damage.

8.2.6   Causes of crop depredation by elephants

Crop raiding is a phenomenon influenced by several attributes of the habitat or landscape, climate, foraging strategies, and behavioral ecology of the elephants. These factors are not mutually exclusive, but are interrelated in a complex fashion that is poorly understood. For the purpose of this discussion, I broadly categorize these factors as proximate causes or ultimate (evolutionary) causes, although I must emphasize here that this division is not always clear.

8.2.6.1   Habitat features and the proximate causes of raiding

There is obviously a certain historical element to crop raiding by elephants in a given region. Let us imagine a large expanse of natural habitat with human settlements and cultivation only along the periphery in the distant past. Some of the elephant herds or bulls would have home ranges that would bring them into contact with the periphery, while others would range entirely over the interior. The former could indulge in some crop raiding, while the latter would be oblivious to the presence of an alternative source of food plants. The incursion of settlements and cultivation into this hitherto natural habitat would bring more elephants into contact with crop fields. If a part of the home range of such a nonraiding elephant herd is now transformed into cultivation, this herd would initially continue to treat this as part of its range and feed on the crops. In the course of time, the confrontation between these elephants and people would result in one of the following outcomes: the elephants shift their range partially or entirely to avoid conflict; the elephants are eliminated; people abandon the area to avoid conflict; or elephants and people coexist at a tolerable level of conflict. The outcome would depend on human cultural factors, the behavioral decisions of the elephants, the availability of alternative habitat for the elephants, the presence of other elephant groups in the region, and even the demography of the elephant herd or population.

The loss of habitat or former home range can thus be a proximate cause of crop raiding in the short term. Examples of this are available throughout the elephant's range in the two continents, especially where deforestation or conversion of natural habitat is rapid. The rapid replacement of large expanses of tropical rain forest with oil palm plantations in Sumatra or Sabah (fig. 8.4)

Figure 8.4
Rain forest cleared for a new oil palm plantation in the Aceh Province of Sumatra, Indonesia. The rapid loss of forest has fragmented the elephant's habitat on this island.

and the establishment of the Handapanagala sugarcane plantation within former elephant range in southern Sri Lanka are some recent examples from Asia.
The response from the elephants has been swift and dramatic—a sharp escalation in raiding and manslaughter. The elephants may also be attracted by
weedy plants such as grasses that invade the open areas. However, the principle of continued utilization (now crop raiding) of their former natural habitat
by elephants, which show a certain fidelity to their home range, is clear.

Raiding in some instances seems related to diurnal or seasonal movements
of elephants, in particular the family groups. Elephants need water, if not daily,
at least every 2 or 3 days. When crop fields intervene between the natural
habitat and the water source, the resulting damage is inevitable. James Allaway
observed that damage to crops in new agricultural areas along the Tana River
in Kenya was essentially due to elephants passing through to drink at the river.
In my southern Indian study, there were several instances of elephant herds
trampling and feeding on crops and then heading toward a pond or reservoir
in agricultural areas at night. It is difficult to ascertain whether the primary
motive in such cases was a quest for water or for attractive crop plants. Elephants can possibly smell moisture-laden air from large bodies of water and
move toward them. Some crop raiding is thus incidental.

Where elephants show distinct seasonal movements to optimize the use of
different habitats (see chapters 4 and 5), a relationship with crop raiding also
emerges. Over most of the elephant's range in southern India, the habitat is a
mosaic of diverse vegetation types arising from a sharp topographic and climatic
gradient. Many elephant herds or clans here show distinct seasonal preferences
for particular habitat types. Some of these raid available crops in settlements
located within or along the periphery of such habitats. In other words, the basic
pattern of seasonal movement of the concerned elephants is natural under the
circumstances and is geared toward optimizing their feeding in the wild. At the
same time, the elephants opportunistically indulge in raiding crops. This is not
to say that elephant herds do not deliberately raid crops. The movement strategy
of some herds could certainly be primarily geared toward raiding.

This brings me to another interesting pattern in raiding that can perhaps
be explained by proximate considerations. As a landscape becomes more fragmented and its ratio of the perimeter of the forest-cultivation boundary to
forest area increases, the frequency of raiding by elephants also increases. The
total number of raids over a year by bull and family groups in 10 enclaves of
cultivation in the Biligirirangans during my study was positively related to the
size of the enclave and also its perimeter (fig. 8.5). In a later study, Cheryl
Nath and I looked at the frequency of crop raids in all villages in the Kodagu
District, also in southern India, during 1992–1996. When these were plotted
on a map, we found the frequencies to be clearly higher in places where the
forest was more fragmented or patchy (fig. 8.6).

Some of the crop raiding in the more fragmented landscapes can perhaps
be explained by chance encounters alone. When elephants move through such
fragmented habitats, there is a higher probability of them encountering culti-

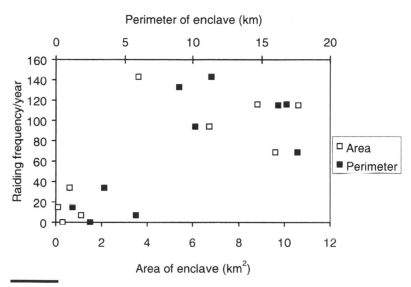

Figure 8.5

The total number of crop raids during March 1981–February 1982 in 10 enclaves in the Biligirirangans in southern India in relation to area of enclave and perimeter of the forest-cultivation boundary.

vated land. It is then natural that the elephants indulge in some opportunistic raiding. At the same time, the forest fragments also provide convenient daytime shelters to indulgent crop raiders that venture out into the surrounding agricultural lands at night.

The status of the natural vegetation in areas bordering cultivation or, indeed, the entire landscape mosaic may also have a bearing on raiding. It is often speculated that "degradation" of the natural habitat is responsible for crop raiding by elephants. The term *degraded* has to be used carefully. What seems degraded from a human viewpoint may not necessarily be so from the elephant's perspective. Secondary vegetation with weedy food plants may actually be more attractive for elephants than the corresponding primary habitat. Degradation in our context should thus be used to denote a reduction in food resources for elephants. Even then, it is not clear that habitat degradation in the immediate vicinity of a cultivated tract would increase the frequency of crop raids. The opposite may also be true. In the course of their movement into the more favorable foraging habitats, elephant herds may make increased contact with cultivation in the vicinity. In his study at Hosur, Ramesh Kumar found that villages situated near superior habitats experienced more raids than those near degraded habitats.

Scaling is thus important when the relationship between the status of the natural vegetation and the frequency of crop raiding is examined. On a localized scale, the observed patterns may be unclear or counterintuitive. Over the

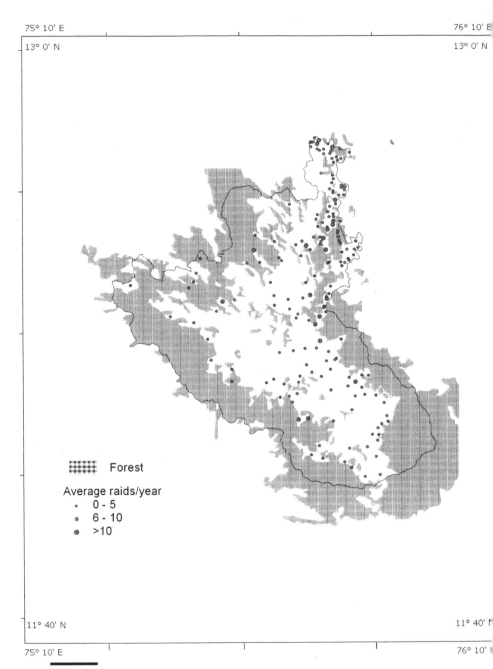

Figure 8.6
Forest cover and the average annual frequency (1994–1996) of crop raiding by
elephants in various settlements in the Kodagu district, Karnataka, India. Note the
much higher frequency of raiding in the more fragmented northeastern part of the
district. (Based on C. Nath and R. Sukumar, unpublished report 1998.)

large spatial scale of the home range of a clan or population, a degraded habitat may increase pressure on elephants to seek a part of their forage requirements from cultivation. This, however, is not a proximate factor, but should be considered as ultimate causation within the framework of foraging theory.

The only detailed study so far of the relationship between habitat features and crop raiding by elephants at the scale of a large landscape has been that of Richard Hoare during 1993–1995 in the northern Sebungwe region of Zimbabwe. This region of about 15,000 km^2 is a mosaic of protected areas for wildlife (national parks and safari areas) and communal lands with varying extent of human settlement. Using data on raiding frequencies and elephant densities from aerial counts in various administrative units or "wards," Hoare also factored in other variables, such as annual rainfall, the frontage of protected areas, human densities, settlement area, and ward area to analyze statistically the possible determinants of crop raiding. Surprisingly, he found that none of these factors could adequately explain the intensity of conflict (table 8.1). There was only a weak association of raiding intensity with elephant density and protected area frontage. Rather, the incidents of crop raiding were irregular and unpredictable, showing considerable variation from one year to another. One reason for this pattern is that most of the raids were by bull elephants; the ensuing elephant-human conflict was thus dependent on the "behavioral ecology of individual bull elephants." More studies of this type at the scale of landscapes are needed before the relationship, if any, between habitat attributes and crop raiding can be better understood.

8.2.6.2 *Foraging strategy and the ultimate causes of raiding*

An adequate understanding of crop-raiding behavior is possible only if we consider this within the framework of foraging theory as it applies to the ele-

---

Table 8.1
Percentage variation for association between variables and problem elephant incidents in 21 wards in Sebungwe, Zimbabwe, during 1993–1995.

| | R^2 (%) | | | |
Variable	1993	1994	1995	Mean
Elephant density	20.8	13.0	4.6	12.8
Protected area frontage	12.8	3.4	0.5	5.6
Human density	1.6	0.1	5.1	2.3
Annual rainfall	0.07	1.8	7.1	3.0
Settlement coverage*	0.01	0.2	0.5	0.2

Source: From Hoare (1999). Reproduced with the permission of the British Ecological Society. The data were transformed as log (incidents +1) and expressed as the coefficient of determination r^2.
*Settlement coverage only for 15 wards with resident elephants.

phant. In ultimate or evolutionary terms, a particular foraging strategy, including crop raiding, is beneficial only if it confers a higher fitness on the individual. It pays to raid cultivated crops if the crops provide better nutrition than feeding on wild plants. Since the advent of agriculture, humans have selected plants for their higher productivity, low toxicity, sensory qualities, and superior nutritive properties. It is therefore not surprising that elephants have also taken advantage of this human-influenced selection in their foraging decisions.

In simple quantitative terms, an elephant can generally feed on cultivated grasses at a higher rate than it can on wild grasses. The reasons for this are obvious. A cultivated field provides a concentrated source of food plants, which are much more dispersed in the natural habitat. At a feeding rate of 12 kg (dry weight) per hour in a millet field, an adult bull elephant can meet its daily requirement of forage in about 6 hours. It is doubtful whether this rate can be achieved in the wild except in the most productive moist grasslands. When elephants enter an oil palm plantation, they can quickly move from one plant to another rather than spend time searching for widely dispersed palms as in the wild.

Qualitatively, the cultivated grasses may be more palatable and nutritious than the wild grasses, especially the perennial species (table 8.2). The tall grasses, such as *Themeda*, *Imperata*, and *Cymbopogon* are soft textured and maintain adequate levels of protein for herbivores during the early stages of growth with the onset of rains. With further growth and maturity, they become fibrous and siliceous. I found that the protein level in the basal portion consumed by elephants during the late wet season fell to much below the minimum 5% level needed by elephant for maintenance (chapter 5). At this time, which was also the peak raiding season, the maturing finger millet and paddy crops had much

Table 8.2
Comparison of nutritive content of cultivated crops
and their analogs among wild forage.

Nutrient	Wild Grasses	Cultivated Grasses
Southern India Protein (%)	2.0–3.8 (Basal half of grass)	5.3–10.4 (Top half of finger millet and paddy)
Calcium (mg/g)	0.8–2.3 (Basal half of grass)	2.4–10.8 (Top half of finger millet and paddy)
Sodium (mg/g)	0.12–0.28 (All grasses)	0.24–0.94 (Top portion of mature paddy and finger millet)
Zimbabwe Protein (%)	9.8 (Mean)	14.8 (Mean)

Sources: Based on Sukumar (1985, 1989a) and Osborn (1998).
All comparisons for second wet season (southern India) or late wet season (Zimbabwe) and for plant parts consumed during this period.

higher protein levels of 5%–10%. Maize cobs, which are selectively plucked by elephants, had protein levels even higher than in fresh growth of tall grasses (all below 10%). Short grasses are more palatable and nutritious than the tall grasses, but even during the late wet season, they do not provide the bulk forage required by elephants.

Similarly, the levels of two minerals, calcium and sodium, were also substantially higher in the millets and paddy. I recorded calcium levels several-fold higher in finger millet plants compared to the bases of wild grasses. Sodium contents in flowering finger millet and paddy were again much higher than in all other wild plants, both grasses and browse, analyzed.

The only other comparison of the nutritive qualities of cultivated crops and wild forage plants comes from Ferrel Osborn's study in Zimbabwe. He found protein levels in crops to be significantly higher than in wild grasses and browse during the late wet season, when most of the raiding occurs, but not during the early wet season. Further, the palatability of crops was also higher, as deduced from its lower fiber and lignin contents compared to wild grasses.

Both in southern India and in Zimbabwe, the rise in crop-raiding intensity seems to occur during the transition from the late wet season to the early dry season. This is also the period when elephants gradually switch from a predominantly grass diet to one with more browse as the protein level in the wild grasses declines. It has been suggested that a mixed feeder such as the elephant has to shift from one plant type to another, such as from grass to browse or vice versa, gradually in order to maintain the correct microbial composition for ensuring proper digestion. If this were the case, then elephants could be obtaining the correct mix of grass (from cultivated sources) and browse (from the natural habitat) during this transitional period. Clearly, more investigations in a variety of situations are needed before the influence of the differential nutritive values of wild and cultivated plants in crop raiding can be clearly evaluated.

Habitat degradation over the home range of an elephant group would further widen the gap between foraging efficiency in the wild and in cultivated land. This may further encourage crop raiding. Elephants living in the relatively resource-poor evergreen forests may find paddy or sugarcane fields even more attractive than those inhabiting deciduous forests or moist grasslands. One prediction that can be tested is that elephants in rain forests would raid crops more frequently on a per capita basis compared to elephants in savannas, woodlands, or moist grasslands, provided that other factors (degree of habitat fragmentation, elephant density in relation to the "carrying capacity," and so on) are kept constant.

Finally, we need to ask the question as to whether elephants really need to raid crops even when they have sufficient wild forage to meet their normal nutritional needs. There are several examples of small elephant populations, inhabiting expansive habitats providing a surfeit of resources, coming into conflict with agriculture. The explanation may lie in the physiological mechanisms that influence foraging choices.

Animals use their senses, particularly taste and smell, to decide whether to accept or reject a potential food item. Each species has presumably evolved the sensory mechanisms appropriate to its particular needs. Sweet, salty, or bitter tastes, for instance, each convey specific information to sensory receptors in the brain about the nutritive attributes of an item. This would have been evolutionarily adaptive; the sweet taste in humans is believed to have evolved for feeding on fruits that are rich not only in sugars, but also in other nutrients. It is well known that the synapses or junctions of the nervous system need regular external stimuli for reinforcement. A positive stimulus is associated with "feeling good." This explains why regular doses of such stimuli could also soon end up in addiction. A child brought up on an excessive diet of sweets would continue this habit into adulthood even if there were no real nutritive advantage (indeed, a "sweet tooth" has several adverse effects on health). Thus, not only children, but also adults may prefer cakes to plain bread when offered a choice at a party (unless they are diabetic, of course!). A crop plant that is richer in nutrients than wild forage conveys superstimuli to receptors in a herbivore's brain. Once an elephant tastes cultivated crops, it may develop an addiction for the same, irrespective of whether it actually needs those extra nutrients. A sugarcane field is an irresistible attraction, even if the overload of sugar may not do the elephant much good.

8.2.6.3   *The behavioral ecology of the sexes and raiding*

There are several features of crop raiding for which we must seek explanations in the behavioral ecology of male and female elephants. One feature is the strikingly higher propensity of bulls to raid crops (fig. 8.7), while another is the heterogeneity among bulls and family herds in their inclination to raid crops even when they have access to cultivated fields.

It is well known that males and females of a species may differ in behavior because of contrasting factors that influence their reproductive success. Robert Trivers has pointed out that, in polygynous mammals, the male is more likely to indulge in risk-taking behavior that promotes reproductive success. The elephant is a polygynous animal, with the sexes showing marked dimorphism in body size. Crop raiding involves taking considerable risks as farmers may injure or kill raiding elephants. The actual risk to a raiding elephant varies according to local cultural perceptions and laws. From records of elephants killed directly during crop raiding and the ratio of raids by bulls and family herds in southern India, I found that the risks to the sexes were virtually identical. As the average adult bull raids crops much more frequently than does a female-led herd, it follows that the male is more willing to take risks to obtain nutritious forage.

How could raiding crops make a difference to the male elephant's reproductive success? Obviously, any foraging strategy that maximizes the intake of energy and nutrients could contribute to better growth, survival, and physical condition. Male elephants can translate better nutrition into larger body size during the postpubertal stage, when they may show a secondary growth spurt,

Figure 8.7
A large bull Asian elephant in Mudumalai, India. In relatively intact habitats, the adult male elephants seem far more likely to raid crops compared to family groups.

or later in adult life as they continue to gain weight (appendix 2). A larger body size would confer an edge to a male during competition with other males. Good body condition is also important for the successful expression of musth in a bull elephant. During musth, a bull is dominant over nonmusth bulls, including older ones, and this greatly increases its chances of mating with an estrous cow (see chapter 3).

In 1988, I published an article along with Madhav Gadgil suggesting that the increased tendency among male elephants to raid crops was the consequence of a "high-risk, high-gain" strategy, molded by natural selection, to enhance reproductive success. We clearly recognized that a crop raiding strategy would not automatically be translated into better reproductive success. Raiding entails considerable risks, and the levels of risks have varied with human technological and sociocultural changes. The risks to an elephant from a trigger-happy farmer are obviously vastly different from the risks associated with one who worships an elephant's footprint in his field. Over the elephant's distributional range in the two continents, the reaction of local communities to elephant depredation varies from vicious retaliation to resigned tolerance. Raiding itself is a behavior acquired over the past few thousand years, clearly insufficient for the natural evolutionary process to select a particular trait. Crop raiding could eventually be a losing proposition to its perpetrators. A raiding bull could be injured, and thus lower its chances of coming into musth, or even be killed in the process. Nevertheless, it is not unreasonable to assume that a notorious bull is only manifesting natural risk-taking behavior that has evolved over the ages.

Female elephants, along with their families, also raid crops, but we must seek alternative explanations for their behavior. A basic explanation for raiding can obviously be found in foraging theory. After all, females also have their extra nutritional needs, such as during pregnancy and lactation. When families raid crops, the matriarchs have to consider not only the risks to themselves, but also the risks to their closely related kin. In the balance, it may not be worthwhile for female elephants to take the same levels of risks as bulls. Could the needs and behavior of subadult males that have not yet separated from the family drive some of the raiding by family groups?

The most visible and spectacular instances of raiding by family herds seem to be associated with long-distance dispersal by these animals. The dispersal of several elephant herds from the southern Indian states of Tamilnadu and Karnataka into Andhra Pradesh, where elephants have been absent for over two centuries, can be attributed to a combination of habitat and climatic factors. Habitat denudation in their original home range could have contributed to the dispersal. It was, however, no coincidence that the first wave of dispersal took place in 1983, after southern India had experienced one of the most severe droughts of the century related to a persistent El Niño, which disrupted climatic patterns globally. Subsequent dispersal by smaller groups did occur, but another major unsuccessful attempt occurred in early 1996 following the failure of winter rains the previous year. Some of the herds that originally dispersed have now moved over a distance of 200–300 km from their original home.

Another example of long-distance movement by elephant herds is from southern Bihar into southern West Bengal in India during the late wet season extending through the winter. In this case, the 50 or so elephants have not completely shifted their home range, but rather have altered their seasonal movements to utilize a new and substantially larger range (chapter 4). There has been severe conflict with agriculture in this process, which has been studied by Hemant Datye and later by Sushant Chowdhury and his colleagues. The first decisive foray from Bihar deep into West Bengal took place in 1987, which was interestingly another drought year in the subcontinent. Ironically, the decision of the elephants to expand their wet season and winter range seems to have been aided by the success of a forestry project in West Bengal, under which large patches of denuded forest have regenerated in recent years. These have provided convenient cover during the day for elephants, which then raid the surrounding crop fields at night.

Crop raiding by family groups therefore seems to be influenced in many instances by their need to seek an alternative habitat when their original home range is unable to sustain their resource needs because of human influence or an adverse climatic event. Such herds may already be utilizing marginal habitats and coming into conflict with agriculture. For long-ranging animals such as elephants, their dispersal into new habitats could have been evolutionarily adaptive in pre-human-dominated landscapes. Elephants are today only manifesting such inherent behavior. The need to avoid competition with more socially dominant family groups in the area, an aspect that is poorly understood, could also influence the decision to disperse under times of stress. It must also be kept in mind that, during such long-distance dispersal by family herds, they may be accompanied or followed by adult bull elephants.

This takes us to the issue of behavioral heterogeneity among elephants in their tendency to raid crops. Why do certain elephants, either adult bulls or family herds, become notorious raiders, while others rarely, if ever, raid crops, even when they have easy access to agricultural fields? In a highly social, intelligent animal, considerable heterogeneity in a variety of behaviors, including crop raiding and response to humans, can be expected. Crop raiding entails taking certain risks. Individuals have to make decisions as regards the levels of risk they are prepared to take in relation to possible benefits they could derive from a course of action. In a higher, more intelligent mammal, the brain has the capacity for longer-term memory, discrimination between different patterns of stimuli, and a nonstereotypic response that draws on its complex episodes of learning. Sociobiologist Edward Wilson terms such a mammal a "generalized learner" possessing a "perception of history." Presumably, elephants that have made contact with agricultural fields would have attempted at some stage to feed on crops. The decision then to persist with or opt out of raiding would depend on how individual elephants or the matriarchs of herds, each with their distinct behavioral personalities, evaluate the risks of confronting humans.

As with foraging choices in the wild, learning within the family setting obviously plays an important role in crop-raiding behavior. Young male and female elephants could thus learn to raid crops from the adult cows in the family. Such behavior could then persist in succeeding generations through cultural transmission. The opposite would also be true. Among elephant clans, this could give rise to raiding and nonraiding (or relatively so) clans. Pubertal males dispersing from raiding herds could turn out to be notorious raiders themselves, while those from nonraiding herds may not raid unless they learn this through association with raiding males. Among family herds, there is a possibility that their competitive interactions with herds of other clans, for use of natural habitat, could influence raiding behavior. The home ranges and foraging strategies of clans could be influenced by the outcome of such interactions.

Only through following the movement, foraging choices, and dispersal patterns of elephant clans and bulls over the long term can the complex interplay of factors that influence their interactions with humans and agriculture be unraveled.

8.3   Manslaughter by elephants

Each year elephants kill several hundred people. The available records from Asia and Africa indicate that the largest number of such manslaughter incidents occur, by far, in India, followed possibly by Sri Lanka. In India, during 1980–2000, about 150–200 people on average lost their lives due to attack by elephants each year—a total of 3,000–4,000 people over these two decades (table 8.3). Information from Sri Lanka suggests that over 50 people are killed annually. Similar figures are suggested for Kenya during the past decade. The much better documentation and larger number of incidents in South Asia can be examined to understand the circumstances of manslaughter by elephants.

Human killing by the larger mammals, such as elephants, lions, and tigers, incites far greater passion among people than do deaths from, say, venomous snake or rabid dog bites. Incidentally, the number of people who die each year of snake or dog bites in India is at least 100-fold compared to elephant-caused deaths. The psychology underlying public outcry against elephants or tigers may be the human perception of greater vulnerability to larger animals than to smaller creatures. Conservation laws that prescribe severe penalties for killing the (endangered) megavertebrates may also contribute to public reaction (you can at least quietly kill a poisonous snake, irrespective of its legal status, without inviting any attention).

Manslaughter by elephants can be considered for two kinds of situations: one under "normal" circumstances in the jungle or in settlements within a large, natural elephant habitat and the other under "abnormal" circumstances, such as when a large herd or clan of mostly crop-raiding elephants disperse to

Table 8.3
Number of people killed during 1991–2000
by wild elephants in four regions of India.

Regions within India	1991–1992	1992–1993	1993–1994	1994–1995	1995–1996	1996–1997	1997–1998	1998–1999	1999–2000	2000–2001
Northeast	98	134	102	82	85	96	95	83	87	43*
Northwest	—	—	9	6	3	—	—	—	—	3
Central	61	57	60	56	73	42	35	24*	36*	59
South	54	34	37	39	71	67	42	47	64	51
Total	213	225	208	183	232	205	172	154	187	155

Sources: Data courtesy Project Elephant Directorate, New Delhi; West Bengal Forest Department, Kolkata; and Karnataka Forest Department, Bangalore.
For each year, the compilation runs from April to March (e.g., April 1991–March 1992).
*Data deficient. In the south, it is also likely that data are incomplete for Kerala and Tamilnadu.

a new habitat. While this distinction may not always be obvious, it is nevertheless useful to illustrate these two types as the management implications may be quite different.

My documentation of over 150 cases of human deaths due to elephants in a southern Indian range comprising Asia's largest elephant population revealed the basic patterns underlying such incidents. While 55% of the incidents occurred in the forest, a significant 45% took place within human settlement and agricultural land. Over three of four people killed were adult men (77.3%), the rest being adult women (17.4%) and children (5.3%). This is not surprising because men venture more often into the forest and almost exclusively guard cultivated fields at night. The pattern is similar elsewhere in South Asia. Hemant Datye reported that, of the people killed in India's Bihar State, 63% were men, and 37% were women. In northwestern Sri Lanka, Mangala de Silva observed that 82% of victims were men, and only 18% were women.

Human deaths in the forest are usually chance encounters between elephants and people walking along a road or path, often created by the regular passage of elephants in the first place. These people may have been walking alone or in small groups from one settlement to another, visiting a small shrine on a hilltop, grazing livestock, collecting firewood and other forest products, or even sleeping under the shade of a tree. Not infrequently, the victim is under the influence of alcohol or is handicapped, thus showing delayed or no reaction to the presence of a wild elephant. There have been the occasional incidents involving photographers approaching elephants and even a curious foreigner possibly unaware of the danger from a wild elephant. While most incidents took place during daytime, it is noteworthy that several of these occurred at dusk very close to human settlement as bull elephants were waiting for the cover of darkness to enter cultivation.

Incidents within the forest were due to both solitary bulls and members of a family group. Identity of the elephant often died with the victim. In contrast, practically all killings within cultivated land could be attributed to subadult or adult bulls. The victims were mostly men guarding crop fields at night from simple structures at ground level, although on occasion these were women or children when a raiding bull broke down a hut. A flashlight shined at a bull or the sound of a dog barking often evoked an aggressive reaction. Another common pattern seen is that a few notorious bulls may be responsible for multiple killings. A recent example of this involved a tuskless bull that reputedly killed over a dozen people during crop raids in the Nilgiris before it was captured in 1998. Another bull in southern Bihar (now Jharkhand) has killed over 40 people over the past few years and still evades being eliminated, although it has been proscribed a rogue. Both in the forest and within fields, elephants killed people by lashing out with the trunk, grasping and flinging, trampling, or goring with the tusks. Instances of elephants dismembering their victims are rare.

In most regions, a male bias in the elephants responsible for manslaughter is obvious. In southern India, I found that 82% of incidents could be attributed unambiguously to male elephants, 10% to female elephants, and the rest to a member of a herd. Mangala de Silva also observed that, in most cases of manslaughter in Sri Lanka, the culprit was a male elephant.

Variations to the above pattern can be seen in places where aberrant behavior in the movement of family herds occurs. When elephants dispersed into the southern Indian state of Andhra beginning in 1983, the local people were oblivious to the dangers of closely approaching wild elephants. The spate of human deaths during the initial years could be mainly attributed to human ignorance. Many people were reportedly killed when they approached elephants within cultivated fields to offer worship. An aggressive adult female elephant was responsible for several deaths. Once the elephants settled down in their new range and awareness increased among the people, the incidents of manslaughter decreased. Similar patterns were seen during the range extension by elephants from southern Bihar. As these elephants, numbering about 50, began making deep forays into southern West Bengal, there was a sharp increase in the incidents of human deaths there (fig. 8.8). Hemant Datye also recorded that a herd of elephants in the Porahat Forest Division of Bihar went on a rampage during August 1989, killing 24 people in the process. Another small herd of elephants that emigrated into the forests of Sarguja in Madhya Pradesh around this time caused similar terror until the animals were removed.

As elephants are not carnivorous, a fundamental question is, Why are they aggressive toward people? As with other aspects of behavior, this question can be approached from different perspectives. An ethologist would interpret aggression in animals as "instinctive" or genetically determined and expressed through their physiological, neural, and musculoskeletal systems. Among mammals, the higher levels of the sex hormone testosterone in males may predispose them to greater aggression compared to females. In elephants, it is well known that testosterone levels rise dramatically when male elephants come into musth and show heightened aggression (see chapter 3). At least among captive elephants, we know that a bull is far more likely to kill people when it is in musth.

Experimental psychologists, on the other hand, stress the role of the environment and learning in the development of aggressive behavior. From this perspective, aggression among elephants can be expected as the outcome of their interactions with humans. Frustration of a goal-oriented behavior such as raiding may provoke aggression. Several observers in Africa and Asia note that elephant populations that have not been harassed by ivory poachers are relatively peaceful toward humans, while affected populations show aggressive or terrified behavior.

Two aspects to learned behavior can be considered. At the first level, an individual elephant could develop aggressive traits as a direct response to harassment by humans. Referring to the formidable threat displays of a matriarch he observed for several years, Iain Douglas-Hamilton mused, "I often wondered what terrible experience Boadicea must have suffered at the hands of man for her to hate and fear us so much" (Douglas-Hamilton and Douglas-Hamilton

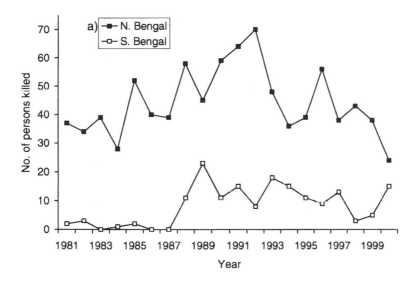

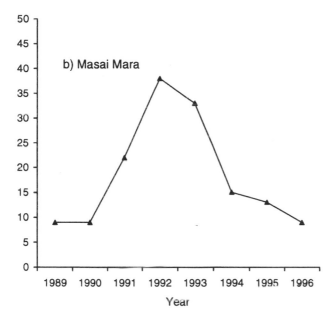

Figure 8.8
(a) Number of people killed by elephants annually in two regions of the Indian state of West Bengal. This state has one of the highest intensities of elephant-human conflict in Asia. (Data courtesy of West Bengal Forest Department and S. P. Choudhury 2001). (b) Number of people killed by elephants annually in the Masai-Mara, Kenya. (From Njumbi et al. 1996. Reproduced with permission of the journal *Pachyderm* published by the IUCN/SSC African Elephant Specialist Group.)

1972, p. 68). The other aspect is that of transmission of behavior from one generation to the next. The elephants in South Africa's fenced Addo National Park are still mainly nocturnal and extremely aggressive toward people, several decades after a sanctuary was set up (in 1931) to protect this once-hunted population. Obviously, cultural transmission of aggressive behavior from elders to children has maintained this trait within this population even though the present-day elephants have never been harassed. It is conceivable that this aggressive trait would disappear in due course at Addo.

While this may be true of elephant response toward people in the elephants' natural habitat, the same may not hold for elephants in contact with agriculture and settlements. David Western believes that after the levels of ivory poaching declined in Kenya toward the end of the 1980s, there was an increase in manslaughter, especially in or near settlements, as elephants seem to have lost fear of people (fig. 8.8).

Over evolutionary time, aggressive behavior among elephants would have arisen as a defense against predators. While adult animals are immune to predators, this would not be true of juveniles. Pleistocene proboscideans were potential prey for carnivores, such as the saber-toothed tiger, the scimitar-toothed cat, and the saber-toothed cat. Young elephants today certainly fall prey to lions in Africa and to tigers in Asia. Group defense and aggressive threat displays by adult elephants are thus aimed at protecting their young from predators. Humans also have been predators of proboscideans since the Pleistocene (see chapter 1). This predatory role of humans has continued into contemporary times through hunting of elephants for ivory in Africa and both hunting and capture of elephants in Asia. In the eyes of an elephant, therefore, humans have always been potential predators. Thus, its aggression toward humans can be thought of as an extension of natural antipredatory strategy.

The interaction between people and elephants, however, has varied through time and changing cultures in the two continents. The elephant's response toward people could therefore reflect this complex interplay of factors through history.

8.4   Habitat manipulation by people

Humans have considerably transformed the natural landscape of the earth. It is estimated that over half of the earth's habitable land surface has already been significantly altered by human activity in some form. The consequences of such manipulation for the overall biodiversity have undoubtedly been profound. The consequences of such manipulation of the habitat for elephant populations in the two continents must be examined. This is not a subject that has been rigorously researched, and only general observations are available.

The most pervasive and detrimental impact has been the loss of habitat and its fragmentation, a process that continues even today in many parts of the elephant's range. The range of the Asian elephant typifies this situation, as does that of the elephant in West Africa (appendix 1). The result has been escalated conflict with agriculture, retaliation from people, and the creation of nonviable elephant populations. The loss and fragmentation of natural habitat is usually accompanied by a corresponding increase in settlements, agriculture, and density of humans. Mutual antagonism between the humans and elephants results in a reduction and eventual elimination of the latter.

Ian Parker and A. D. Graham proposed an inverse relationship between elephant and human densities. Their model indicated that, at the national or subcontinental scale, the density of elephants declines linearly with the natural logarithm of human density.

A more rigorous analysis of higher resolution data from Zimbabwe's Sebungwe region by Richard Hoare and Johan du Toit added a new dimension to this broadly expected trend. There was no clear relationship between human density and elephant density until a threshold human density of about 15 persons/km^2, after which there was a sharp drop in elephant density (fig. 8.9). They suggested that this could arise from elephants moving away from a disturbed region once the threshold of tolerance had been reached and not necessarily from elephants dying out locally.

While this pattern may hold for African savanna habitats, the nature of the relationship between human and elephant numbers may be different in moist forest habitat. Although this has not been examined in a similar manner, Richard Barnes and colleagues found that elephants in remote but intact rain

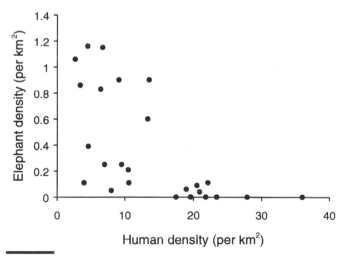

Figure 8.9
The relative abundance of elephants and humans in 25 communal land wards of the Sebungwe region, Zimbabwe. The elephant density is the crude density for the wards. (Based on Hoare and du Toit 1999. Reproduced with the permission of the Society for Conservation Biology, U.S.A.)

forests of Gabon avoid roads and villages, presumably because they associate these with humans who kill a few animals each year near settlements.

As humans expand into natural habitats and fragment them, the verdict is clear—elephants eventually decline. When humans transform the habitat in other ways, such as through extraction of timber and other products, replace natural vegetation with monoculture plantations, use fire to manipulate the vegetation, practice shifting cultivation, graze their livestock, or change local hydrology without actually reducing the area of habitat, the implications for elephants are quite mixed. People may make the habitat less attractive or more attractive for elephants. The implications of such habitat manipulation for the management of elephants will be region specific and will depend on broader conservation goals (chapter 9). Some of these forms of habitat manipulation and consequences for elephants are now examined.

Several observers have commented that elephants in tropical moist forests show a marked preference for secondary growth habitats over primary forest habitat. Logging for hardwoods as structural material or softwood for pulp and fiber is pervasive in tropical forests. Disturbance and light gaps promote the growth of bamboo, grass, and other weedy plants low in secondary plant compounds, thus making them attractive to elephants. Thus, Robert Olivier found that elephant densities in rain forests of peninsular Malaysia were about twice as high in secondary forest than in primary forest. He attributed this to the higher abundance of food plants in the former than the latter (214 versus 157 trunksful per 400 m^2).

The detailed investigation of elephant utilization and impacts in logged versus unlogged rain forests in Kibale, Uganda, by Thomas Struhsaker and associates further reinforces this view. Elephants used heavily logged forest more than lightly logged or unlogged forest. This was not due to any increased abundance of saplings or pole-size stems in the logged forests (the opposite was true), but due to the increased growth of herbaceous and semiwoody plants, which formed a tangle and attracted elephants. Once the elephants began to use the logged forests more intensively, the damage to young woody stems also suppressed their recruitment into trees, thus maintaining gaps and favoring herbaceous growth.

People also extract a large variety of nontimber products from forests and savannas across the elephants' range in the two continents. These include fuel wood; material for house construction and thatching; livestock feed; many kinds of fruits, flowers, roots, bark, and leaves for direct consumption or as ingredients in medicine, food, and nonfood products; lichens; and mosses. While some of this is subsistence-level extraction, these may also cater to a wider commercial market. Extraction can adversely affect elephants if the levels exceed the natural productivity of food plants, resulting in a decline in the available forage biomass and changes in composition of plant communities.

Although there have been several investigations on the nature and volume of extractions in tropical forests, there are practically no published studies that have clearly demonstrated how extraction regimes have affected forage availability for elephants. Often, several factors, such as fire, rainfall fluctuations, browsing by livestock, and even elephant utilization, interact with extraction, making it difficult to separate the various influences. Ramesh Kumar's study of elephant habitat in Hosur in southern India indicated that extraction of forest products by people had the greatest influence in tree population declines, when considered along with fire and damage by elephants.

C. S. Silori and B. K. Mishra documented intense "biotic pressure" through woodcutting, including plants consumed by elephants, in the dry forests of Sigur, adjoining Mudumalai Sanctuary, but did not present any data on changes in biomass or tree populations.

The conversion of natural vegetation to monoculture plantations usually lowers forage availability for elephants. In Asian habitats, these are commonly teak (*Tectona grandis*), sal (*Shorea robusta*), wattles (*Acacia* spp.), pines (*Pinus* spp.), eucalypts (*Eucalyptus* spp.), silver oak (*Grevillea robusta*), and several other species of hardwood, pulpwood, fodder, and fuel wood. In the southern Indian elephant range of the Nilgiris and Biligirirangans, I estimated that about 10% of the natural forest areas under the administrative control of the state forest departments have been converted into monoculture plantations. This does not account for the more historical conversion of forests into plantations of tea and coffee. Several of these plantation habitats, such as wattle, eucalypts, silver oak, and pines, are virtually useless for elephants. Others, such as teak, are utilized to a certain extent (bark of teak is consumed to a limited extent), but the availability of other forage plants, particularly favored species of the Malvales, was much lower in these plantations than in adjacent natural forest.

The use of fire in elephant habitats again has mixed consequences. Fires are set by loggers to cover up illegal extraction, by livestock graziers to promote a new flush of grass, by local villagers and forest produce collectors for better visibility, by poachers to cover their tracks, or even by administrators as part of management objectives. The immediate effect of fire is a drastic reduction of forage, both grasses and foliage of woody stems. This may force elephants to move to other areas to seek green biomass. The new flush of palatable grass, high in protein, attracts them back for intense grazing during the wet season. Fires may also act synergistically with elephants and other browsers to convert woodland into grassland, which may be incompatible with management goals (chapter 6). Even if fires do not create grasslands, they may cause substantial changes in species composition of dry or moist forest by promoting the growth of fire-resistant species.

Grazing of livestock (mainly cattle, buffalo, and goat) within elephant habitat is common in South Asia and East Africa. This may potentially affect elephant populations through competition for forage, changes in vegetation composition, disturbance to herds, and transmission of diseases. Much depends on the local densities of livestock populations. The evidence for competition between livestock and elephants is generally weak for savannas and deciduous forests with tall perennial grasses. The productivity of such grasses is usually far in excess of consumption by elephants and even other herbivores in the community. For instance, I found that elephants managed an offtake of only 3%–4% of primary production of tall grasses in several habitat types examined in the Biligirirangans irrespective of the levels of consumption (2%–42%) by livestock during a drought year.

Competition, however, may occur for short grasses that grow to sufficient height by the late wet season for use by elephants. Excessive livestock densities may remove much of the short grass production, forcing elephants to scarify the soil by scraping with their feet to remove grass stubble.

Livestock grazing in the Nilgiris is also associated with removal of dung for sale outside as manure, a process that results in loss of soil nutrients. In northern India's Rajaji National Park, the lopping of trees by Gujjars, a pastoral community, to provide fodder to their buffaloes has considerably degraded the habitat. The movement of livestock there also poses a direct disturbance to elephants, especially at water holes.

Livestock may also transmit parasites and diseases to elephants. However, Milind Watve found that elephants using areas grazed by livestock did not have higher intestinal parasite loads compared to those using livestock-free areas in the Nilgiris. Anthrax and foot-and-mouth disease are two diseases that could be passed from livestock to elephants. The evidence for transmission of anthrax is only anecdotal, while foot-and-mouth disease occurs only sporadically in elephants.

Shifting cultivation is practiced extensively in Asian seasonal moist forests, including those in central and northeastern India, Myanmar (Burma), Thailand, and Indochina (fig. 8.10). During the early stages of shifting cultivation, the mosaic of primary forest and secondary vegetation in various stages, from grassland to regenerating and medium-stature forests, increases the carrying capacity for elephants. Elephants are attracted to such areas of secondary vegetation. On the basis of the presence of dung, Christy Williams and A.J.T. Johnsingh found higher relative elephant densities in land that had been fallow for 1–10 years compared to pure grassland, plantations, or primary forest in Meghalaya in northeastern India, in line with my qualitative expectations. At the same time, it should be kept in mind that there are increasing human population pressures in many regions that have significantly reduced the period of rotation of sites of cultivation, resulting in depletion of topsoil and its nutrient status and keeping the larger landscape in a degraded state.

Manipulation of the natural landscape is thus a double-edged sword. On one hand, it may create more-favorable habitats for herbivores, including elephants. It also allows pernicious weeds to penetrate and spread, thereby increasing the risk of fire, suppressing native plants and their regeneration, and even decreasing forage for large herbivores. *Lantana camara, Chromolaena odorata*, and *Mikania cordata* are examples of such weedy plants that have spread extensively through disturbed forests in India and other Asian regions. The implications of habitat manipulation for the management of elephant populations have to be evaluated in each instance in relation to broader conservation goals (chapter 9).

Figure 8.10
A former site of shifting cultivation in the Biligirirangans in southern India.
Although this form of cultivation is not much practiced in these parts, it is very
common in central and northeastern India and other parts of Asia. Abandoned sites
of shifting cultivation attract elephants.

8.5   Capture and hunting of elephants

In both the continents, elephants have been captured and hunted through the
centuries. The relative importance of these factors in the decline of Asian and
African elephants has varied regionally through time. Overall, it is clear that
hunting has been the predominant threat to the elephant populations of Africa,
although capturing in North Africa during ancient times may also have contributed to local extinction. In Asia, on the other hand, the regular capture of
elephants undoubtedly has been the major factor in the decline of the species.
The role of hunting as a cause of local extirpation of Asian elephants, however,
has probably been underestimated, especially in continental Southeast Asia.
While the hunting of elephants has been predominantly for their tusks, the
significance of hunting for other products, such as meat and hide, has also
probably not been fully appreciated.

8.5.1   History of the ivory trade with special reference to Africa

Ivory has been treasured since ancient times for its unique qualities. People of
the Gravettian culture of Europe used mammoth ivory during the late Pleisto-

cene to make bracelets, while those of the Magdalenian culture fashioned it into figurines. In more historical times, native peoples have used elephant ivory to express art in the form of simple carvings or jewels. It is difficult to estimate how much of this ivory came from animals that died naturally as opposed to those deliberately killed for tusks (it is known that Thutmose III of Egypt "hunted one hundred and twenty elephants for their tusks" in about 1464 B.C. in Syria, and personally engaged the largest elephant to "cut off his trunk while he was alive" [St. Aubyn 1987, p. 36]). Ivory also always has been considered a luxury and a symbol of wealth. The decorated ivory coffers of Tutankhamen's Egypt or the great ivory throne made by King Solomon are probably good examples not only of this luxury demand, but also of the ancient trade in this substance.

Over the centuries, the trade in ivory has taken various twists and turns as the exploited elephant populations declined, as the demand for ivory changed with the economic prosperity of consuming societies or nations, and with the waxing and waning of the conservation ethos. Although detailed documentation of the ivory art is available, a comprehensive account of the historical trade in ivory is yet to be written.

Tusks are known from early dynastic Egypt. The Egyptian pharaohs of the fifteenth and sixteenth centuries B.C. hunted elephants, presumably Asian, along the Euphrates River. Egypt also sourced its ivory from lands bordering the Upper Nile. There is a record of Egypt importing 700 tusks from Somalia in 700 B.C. The use of tusks and ivory articles in ancient Greece and Rome has also been well described in several tomes on art. The rise of the Roman Empire and its demand for ivory seems to have exhausted supplies from northern Africa. Thus, Pliny wrote in A.D. 77 that, "An ample supply of tusks is now rarely obtained except from India, all the rest of the world having succumbed to luxury." This also was probably a temporary phenomenon; it is doubtful that Asian elephant populations with only the male sporting tusks could have supplied large volumes of ivory for any length of time.

In the Indian subcontinent, ivory articles are known from the Harappan culture of the third millennium B.C. According to historian E. H. Warmington, India itself imported ivory from Ethiopia from the sixth century B.C. onward. It is unclear how much of this ivory was in transit further East or sent back to the West as raw or worked ivory. At the same time, ivory from Indian elephants was certainly exported to the West. There is a reference to the best-quality ivory originating in the region of Orissa. The earliest known ivory carvings in China are from the Shang-Yin period of 1783–1123 B.C. From the second century B.C., however, China seemed to meet most of its requirements for ivory from other regions in Asia, undoubtedly some of this being of African origin. Thus, both ancient India and China made extensive use of ivory, initially from their own sources and later through imports from Africa.

During the early centuries of the Christian era, there seems to have been a relative lull in the use of ivory in the West compared to earlier periods, a reflection of the decline of the Mediterranean powers and their source elephant populations. The Islamic expansion during the seventh and eighth centuries A.D. encouraged Arab traders to send ivory into Europe. Ivory seems to have been used mainly for religious purposes at this time. The Portuguese began to explore the West African coast during the latter part of the fifteenth century. One of the commodities obtained from the natives to take home was ivory. By the sixteenth century, the English also began purchasing ivory in sizable quantities from Guinea. Clive Spinage estimates that, during A.D. 1500–1700, about 100–120 tonnes of ivory may have left Africa on average every year. It must also be noted that, during the latter part of this period, India alone imported 272 tonnes per year, no doubt for trading further to the West and the East.

It was during the seventeenth century that ivory exploitation intensified over a large area of Africa. This was the period of colonial expansion by the European powers. The exploration of Africa and southern Asia was accompanied by a thirst for resources to fuel the emerging industrial nations. Ivory was a much-sought-after commodity for knife handles, combs, toys, piano keys, billiard balls, furniture, or works of art. Native hunting tribes initially provided the ivory demand of the Europeans, to be supplanted later by white hunters and by organized slaughter. Big-game hunting by the colonialists provided trophy-size ivory, adding to the romance of the quest for white gold, a cultural phenomenon interpreted as a contemporary version of ritualized killing (see chapter 2). Hunting was not confined only to shooting large animals for tusks. It extended to more intensive slaughter of elephants, ostensibly to control crop depredation. Thus, the Hunt also served to appease the native people by controlling animals dangerous to their lives and livelihoods. The ivory trade was also inextricably linked to the infamous slave trade in Africa.

The trade in ivory can be reconstructed from the perspective of the primary exporting nations, from the records in entrepôts, or from those of the importing or consumer nations. This is not an easy task given the poor quality or absence of records and the complex entanglement of imports and re-exports. From an ecological perspective, the most important statistics are those pertaining to the number, sex, and age of elephants killed for the trade. Clive Spinage has provided an overview of the trade for the period until 1950, which I summarize here. Beyond this period, a more detailed account based on other sources is needed.

The West African trade in ivory, patronized initially by the Portuguese, flourished until the middle of the seventeenth century, but totally collapsed by the mid-nineteenth century. In the meantime, the British and the Dutch also obtained some of their ivory from this region. The large elephant populations reported from the region of Ghana, Liberia, and the Ivory Coast also would have declined by this period. Regions further south along the coast or hinterland, such as Gambia, Luanda, and the Congo, continued to supply the trade during the nineteenth century. Toward the turn of the century, the volumes of ivory emanating from the Belgian Congo were especially large at 352 tonnes per year (during 1888–1909), representing about half of Africa's total exports at this time. Some of this ivory came from large animals, as indicated by the mean tusk weight of 30 kg during the year 1899; compared to this, the German Cameroons exported much smaller tusks from "young elephants." Spinage estimates that, between 1889 and 1950, about 550,000 elephants were killed in the Belgian Congo to supply these ivory volumes.

The East African trade was also dominated by the Portuguese from the sixteenth century until the nineteenth century, when it was taken over by the Arabs. Several ports along the coast, such as Mombasa, Kilwa, Sofala, Beira, and Delagoa Bay channeled supplies to Europe. Some, like Kilwa, which supplied the Portuguese, dried up by the early sixteenth century; Selago Bay, patronized by the English, ceased trade by 1680, implying reductions in hinterland elephant populations. One hundred years later, the trade at Kilwa had revived with links to Yaoland. By the middle of the eighteenth century, Mozambique had emerged as the leading center of the ivory trade, with an annual turnover of 150–180 tonnes, about 65%–70% coming from the Yao. The export figures for 1759–1761 suggest a total of anywhere from 11,500 to twice this number of elephants killed over these 3 years. The trade continued to flourish with the Yao, Marawi, and Lenje tribes hunting elephants around the lower and middle reaches of the Luangwa River. The pricing policies of the Portuguese, however, saw a gradual shift in the trade out of Mozambique to Kilwa and Zanzibar during the later part of the eighteenth century. A correction in 1793 by the Portuguese contributed to a brief revival, with a peak of 189 tonnes exported that year, only to fall back to nearly half that by 1801 and to 58 tonnes by 1817.

By the early nineteenth century, the East African ivory trade shifted further north along the coast to ports such as Mombasa and Zanzibar. Some of this ivory was destined to ports in the Indian west coast en route to Great Britain or China (fig. 8.11). The Wakamba and the Maasai were two tribes supplying the ivory from their lands in eastern Africa. The ivory trade from East Africa seemed to have peaked during 1830–1856. In 1849, Zanzibar exported 297 tonnes, half of this to India. The average tusk weights recorded at Bombay (now Mumbai) suggest that these represented about 19,000 elephants. In 1856, the total exports from East Africa were estimated at 385 tonnes. A notable feature of this ivory was the average tusk weights, with tusks weighing 45 kg (100 pounds) being "common" and those 80 kg (175 pounds) were "not so rare." Obviously, hunting had taken its toll, perhaps the final one, of the magnificent bull elephants of Africa. In recent times, the average weight of 68 kg for each tusk sported by the legendary bull Ahmed in Kenya's Marasbit National Park was the exception rather than the rule.

A sharp rise in the price of ivory during 1856–1857 saw Arab traders rushing into the region. Soon, a very large number of firearms entered East Africa, further stimulating the hunt for ivory. Zanzibar exported 222 tonnes in 1889 and continued this with an annual average of 180 tonnes until the end of the century. The 40,990 tusks exported during 1893–1894 weighed 351 tonnes. Thus, at least 10,000 elephants were contributing to the trade from the region each year, presumably most of them having been hunted. Apart

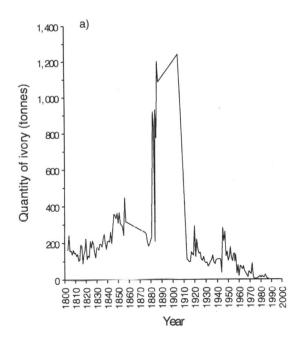

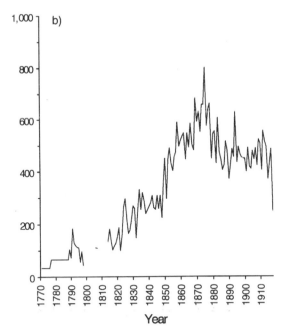

Figure 8.11

Graph of annual import of African ivory by (a) India during 1803–1986 (data for 1887–1912 are incomplete, but imports of over 1,000 tonnes were recorded during the years 1896, 1887, and 1904–1905) (based on Martin and Vigne 1989) and (b) Great Britain during 1771–1918 (based on Spinage 1994; reproduced with the permission of A & C Black Publishers, London).

from Zanzibar, several less-important centers traded in ivory. Taroba in Tanganyika was one such center trading in tusks supplied by the Wanyamwezi tribe. On localized scales, the supplies were exhausted as elephant herds diminished over eastern Africa.

The exploitation of northern Africa, particularly the Sudan and northwest Uganda, was also in progress from the middle of the nineteenth century. This ivory was channeled largely through Khartoum. From 1853 to 1879, an annual average of 148 tonnes was exported from Khartoum to a single purchaser, such volumes falling to 42 tonnes by 1888 and 20 tonnes by 1905. Amid this gloom, there is a hint of conservation efforts by King Kabarega, the young ruler of Bunyoro (in Uganda), who in 1872 imposed a prohibition, with the death penalty for violators, on the free trade of ivory that the explorer Samuel Baker was trying to promote. Five years later, however, two Arabs managed to penetrate this market, but the trade seems to have been relatively restricted.

In 1900, two travelers, Grogan and Sharpe, wrote that, "In the greater part of Africa the elephant is now a thing of the past; and the rate at which they have disappeared is appalling. Ten years ago elephants swarmed in places like British Central Africa, where now you will not find one" (quoted in Spinage 1994, p. 253). Although not entirely true, this was a fair statement of the elephant's status over much of Africa, particularly the savannas, at the entrance to the twentieth century. One exception seems to have been Uganda according to the estimate of 15,000 elephants made by these travelers for the Toro region alone. A trade in firearms by the Ethiopians and their use by the ivory traders began to wipe out the elephant herds during the first decade of the twentieth century.

The elephant populations of southern Africa had also been in decline since the seventeenth century. Common in 1652 around the Table Mountain when the early Dutch settlers landed at the Cape, elephants disappeared south of the Oliphants River by 1775. In the eastern regions of Cape Colony and Kaffararia, they continued to thrive until about 1820–1830; their decline may have been due to ivory being exported to Austria. During 1850–1875, an estimated annual average of 50 tonnes was being exported by South Africa, declining to only 4 tonnes by 1889. Further north in the region of Botswana, the elephant also was being hunted out. The famous explorer David Livingstone records that 900 elephants were killed near Lake Ngami in 1 year following his discovery of the lake in 1849. By 1903, the elephant had virtually disappeared south of the Cunene and Zambezi Rivers.

Recognizing the threat to African elephant populations from the slaughter for ivory, some of the colonial powers did introduce laws to regulate the trade. South Africa tried to regulate the trade from as early as 1822. German East Africa introduced regulations in 1896, making it illegal to possess tusks weighing less than 6.4 kg. The following year, Uganda and the East African Protectorate banned the killing of cow elephants and the possession of tusks less than 4.6 kg (increased to 13.6 kg in 1905 and again decreased to 5 kg in 1933). These measures, combined with the collapse of the slave trade, a fall in ivory prices and in demand for ivory during World Wars I and II, and possibly the greater effort needed to locate elephants, helped the populations to recover over most of eastern, central, and southern Africa during the first half of the twentieth century. The elephants of West Africa, however, were doomed to live as small populations in fragmented landscapes.

Estimates of the numbers of African elephants that contributed to the ivory trade during the eighteenth and nineteenth centuries are confounded by incomplete or duplicate records, fluctuating mean tusk weights, and distinct regional differences. Nevertheless, some crude estimates have been made. The 200 tonnes of ivory that left Africa each year during the eighteenth century may represent about 10,000 elephants (or 1 million over the century) if an average tusk weight of 10 kg is assumed. It is known that average tusk weights for exports from Mozambique varied from 16.4 kg in 1679 to 6.9 kg in 1852. If the lower figure is more representative for the century, then more elephants would have been involved in the eighteenth century trade.

One estimate for the period 1830–1930 is a similar minimum of 1 million elephants killed in Central, East, and West Africa. Spinage argues that the numbers could have been up to five times this figure considering that 60,000–70,000 elephants per year were estimated for the trade during 1880–1894 and over 40,000 a year for the period 1895–1900. The true figure may lie between 1 and 5 million elephants because it cannot be assumed that the intensive exploitation that occurred toward the end of the nineteenth century also prevailed in earlier decades.

On the face of it, these numbers look large, but do not by themselves prove that African populations everywhere suffered catastrophic declines due to hunting. Reductions in habitat area and/or carrying capacity from agricultural expansions or degradation of vegetation, patterns of hunting, and the intrinsic capacity of the elephant populations to withstand these harvests in demographic terms also need to be considered. This calls for detailed and realistic population models (see chapter 7). There is no doubt that, on localized scales, many elephant populations were hunted to extinction in the quest for ivory during the eighteenth and nineteenth centuries.

The models, however, do not pin the entire blame on hunting. One such demographic model by E. J. Milner-Gulland and J. R. Beddington placed equal blame on reduction in carrying capacity as a major cause of elephant decline during the nineteenth century, although the story is different for the twentieth century.

8.5.2   The ivory trade since 1950

The recovery of elephant populations across Africa during the first half of the twentieth century only set the stage for the revival of the ivory trade. The export of raw ivory from Africa climbed steadily from 204 tonnes in 1950 to a peak of 1,164 tonnes in 1980 (fig. 8.12). The ivory trade was back with a vengeance. This time, the indiscriminate slaughter of African elephants (fig.

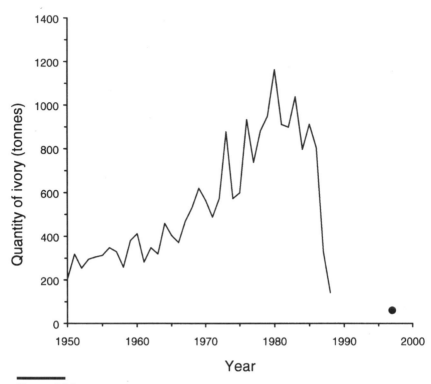

Figure 8.12
Ivory exports from Africa during 1950–2000. (From Barbier et al. 1990. Reproduced with permission granted by Earthscan, Kogan Page, U.K.) In 1997, a one-
time export of 60 tonnes was permitted by CITES.

8.13) set off tremors across the global conservation community that eventually
saw a complete ban on international trade in ivory being imposed in 1989.

The trade in ivory since 1950 and its impact on African elephant populations have been analyzed in detail, sometimes with diametrically opposite conclusions and recommendations. Two individual studies in 1979, one by Ian
Parker and another by Iain Douglas-Hamilton, presented very different perspectives of the trade and its role in the decline of the African elephant. The
gathering momentum toward an international ban on the ivory trade provided
the impetus for an Ivory Trade Review Group; its proceedings, with input from
several authors and viewpoints, were compiled in 1989. The following year,
Edward Barbier and colleagues, part of the earlier review, published their own
economic analysis of the ivory trade; I referred extensively to their analysis for
this summary.

By the late 1970s came the realization that the ivory trade could again be
decimating Africa's elephant populations. By 1975, the annual export of ivory

Figure 8.13
An African elephant poached for its ivory in the Tsavo National Park, Kenya. Both male and female elephants are slaughtered for tusks in Africa. (Photo courtesy of Paula Kahumbu.)

had climbed to about 600 tonnes, and this jumped to 934 tonnes the next year. In 1977, Iain Douglas-Hamilton, who had been carrying out continent-wide surveys of the status of elephants, was the first to raise the alarm over the enormous numbers that may have been involved in the trade. Two years later, he made an estimate of between "50,000 to well over 100,000" elephants a year contributing to this volume of ivory. Given the continental estimate of 1.34 million elephants in 1979, it was clear that such offtake, especially the higher numbers, would send elephant populations on a downhill course.

Ian Parker and Esmond Martin disputed this view based mainly on two points. As opposed to a mean tusk weight of 4.8 kg used in Douglas-Hamilton's analysis, Parker and Martin claimed a much larger weight of 9.7 kg based on customs records in Hong Kong and Japan. This obviously halved the estimate of elephants contributing a particular volume of ivory. Further, they assumed that at least 20% of the ivory came from elephants that died of natural causes. Putting all these together, Parker and Martin estimated that fewer than 40,000 elephants were killed for the ivory trade each year, and this harvest was sustainable provided that the species' range did not shrink further due to human expansion.

Subsequent events and more objective data coming out of the African range states and the trade supported the more alarmist view. Computer-based modeling implicated the ivory trade in elephant population decline. One such model by Tom Pilgram and David Western used data from tusk sizes in the trade to age elephants and concluded that these represented selective hunting of a relatively young population (see chapter 7). Douglas-Hamilton came back strongly in a 1987 article summarizing key elephant population trends across the continent, highlighting the influx of arms and consequent breakdown in law and order and presenting new data from the trade that suggested higher offtake of elephants. A key observation was that mean tusk weights for imports by Hong Kong during 1979–1983 collected by the IUCN's Wildlife Trade Monitoring Unit was only 5.4–5.8 kg, while the Japanese imports also showed a decline in mean weights, from 16.3 kg in 1979 to 9.7 kg in 1982. He summarized his arguments against the Parker and Martin assumptions as "being based upon an illusion of accuracy of ivory trade records, an ignorance of elephant trends then current, and optimistic assumptions about elephant numbers" (p. 22). The ivory trade data provided only minimal estimates of elephant mortality due to ivory poaching. Proclaiming that "elephants are not beetles" (a phrase borrowed from David Western), Joyce Poole and Jorgen Thomsen also presented data on declining tusk weights during 1979–1988, skewed sex ratios in poached populations, and arguments based on disruption of the social fabric of elephant society by poaching to bolster the case against the trade.

Incorporated into a computerized database, the continuing surveys of the IUCN/SSC African Elephant Specialist Group during the 1980s clearly pointed to rapidly declining elephant populations over large parts of their range. From the 1979 estimate of 1.34 million or an improved 1981 estimate of 1.19 million, the African elephant declined to an estimated 0.62 million by 1989.

While precise figures could be questioned, there was no disputing the marked decline in populations. Eastern and Central Africa were the hardest hit by the ivory poaching wave. During 1981–1989, the elephant population of Kenya declined from 65,000 to 16,000 individuals, while in neighboring Tanzania, this dropped from 204,000 to 61,000. Uganda's elephants had already been nearly wiped out during the internecine strife of the 1970s. Other countries, such as Sudan and Somalia, also suffered catastrophic declines, the former more significant in numbers. The East African elephant declined by 75% over this decade. In Central Africa, the decline seemed even more catastrophic in countries such as Zaire (from 376,000 in 1981 to 112,000 in 1989), while the Central African Republic also was hit. The apparent population increases in Gabon and Congo were due to better census techniques being applied in the rain forests rather than any real increase. The scattered West African elephant populations, while insignificant in relation to those of other regions, also suffered from poaching. Southern Africa also experienced rampant poaching during the same time in Zambia (160,000 to 32,000) and Mozambique (55,000 to 17,000).

Countries such as Botswana, Namibia, South Africa, and Zimbabwe represented the only silver lining in the otherwise gloomy African scenario. These countries continued to maintain stable elephant populations or even registered real increases during the decade of the 1980s, a point that was to be a major defense used by these southern African countries to oppose the subsequent international efforts to completely choke the trade in ivory in a desperate attempt to halt the poaching wave.

8.5.3   The ivory consumer nations

The trade in ivory is ultimately driven by economics—there is a market demand from individuals, societies, or nations willing to pay a certain price for the products and a willingness on the part of hunters and traders to cater to this demand. With the possible exception of India over short periods of time, the ivory that originated in the major elephant range countries in recent centuries has almost entirely gone to countries that do not have elephants. Even the large volumes of African ivory that entered India in the past were destined for other consumers.

It is not an easy task to extricate the precise details of the international flow of ivory. The raw ivory imported by a country may not necessarily have catered to a local market, but could have been in transit to other destinations. Part of the ivory could also have been worked by artisans of the importing nation before being sold locally or further exported to overseas markets. India, for instance, was one of the major importers of African ivory from the early nineteenth century until the time of its independence in 1947 (fig. 8.11). Some of this was reexported to Britain and China, while a certain proportion was retained to supply local ivory carvers. A part of Britain's imports eventually reached countries such as the United States. Hong Kong's considerable imports of raw ivory in recent decades, both from Africa and through sources such as Belgium, have been almost entirely exported in finished forms.

Several interesting patterns in the use of ivory by consumer nations can be discerned. The use of ivory by native peoples to fashion simple carvings or jewels now gave way to the expression of more sophisticated art in the form of intricate carvings of very high value or to cheaper articles of mass consumption (fig. 8.14). The major ivory consumers during the nineteenth century were clearly the European countries. The Industrial Revolution had created new levels of economic prosperity for the people, and this was reflected in increased consumption of goods, one of which was ivory.

The imports of ivory by Great Britain, which averaged less than 100 tonnes annually during the late eighteenth century, began to rise steeply during the nineteenth century (fig. 8.11). They imported 250 tonnes by 1825, 400 tonnes by 1850, and peaked at 800 tonnes in 1875. Most, if not all, of the ivory was imported through India prior to 1836, when Great Britain began importing directly from East Africa. While the imports by Great Britain were the highest among the consumer nations, these reflect the general pattern of ivory consumption by Europe, including nations such as Portugal, Belgium, Holland, France, and Germany. Much ivory also found its way to the United States, either through Europe or directly. The use of this ivory was for mundane purposes. Clive Spinage lists the uses during 1889–1993 as knife handles

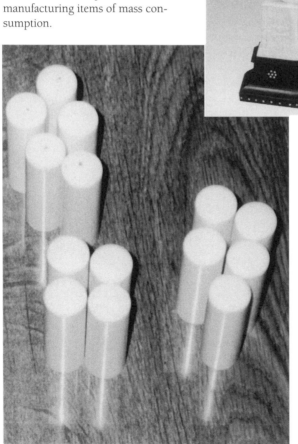

Figure 8.14
An exquisitely carved Ganesha
(*right*; photo courtesy of Karnataka
Police Department) and *hankos* or
Japanese signature seals (*below*;
photo courtesy of Vivek Menon).
The use of ivory through history has
shifted from the expression of art to
manufacturing items of mass consumption.

(34%), piano keys (32%), combs (18%), billiard balls (10%), and miscellaneous items such as prayer book covers. Although the imports of ivory by Great Britain declined since 1875, the quantities reaching Europe as a whole remained high. In 1911, Europe still imported 600–800 tonnes, with 265 tonnes going to Britain.

For centuries, Asia had a sophisticated ivory-carving industry. India and China were the two principal ivory importing and manufacturing nations. I briefly trace the Indian story because of the availability of better records, summarized by Esmond Martin and Lucy Vigne. High-quality ivory carving flourished in Orissa during the thirteenth and fourteenth centuries, possibly from locally available tusks. The Persian style of carving flourished during the Mughal rule in India in the sixteenth to eighteenth centuries. The British colonization of India created a European demand for ivory articles that could be met only through mass manufacturing using machines rather than finely sculpting them by hand. In the words of art historian G. N. Pant, ivory carving declined from an art to a craft by the late nineteenth century as a result. By this period, most of the ivory used by Indian carvers was of African origin.

Although the trade in ivory between Africa and India is ancient, the graph of India's imports begins to climb from the early nineteenth century parallel to the rising demand in Europe. From an annual average of 150 tonnes during the first two decades, the imports rose to over 300 tonnes by 1850. Of this quantity, about 54% was reexported to Britain, 6% went to China, and only 37% was retained in the country for local manufacturing. The imports declined after 1856, but later rose again, peaking at an incredible 1,200 tonnes in 1886. There is some uncertainty about the actual annual imports since 1887, but a rather erratic overall decline is indicated since about 1905 (this may partly reflect lack of data).

Yet, from 1870 until World War I, British India was the largest trader in ivory and one of the three leading ivory manufacturing countries. The annual imports for 1875–1881 were about 250 tonnes, roughly the same as during 1945–1947, just prior to Indian Independence. Thereafter, the strict macroeconomic policies of the government, aimed at conserving foreign currency through imposition of stiff customs duties on luxury goods, resulted in a steady decline of ivory imports.

During 1960–1971, an average of 37 tonnes was imported each year, while in 1979 this was only 5 tonnes, clearly insufficient to meet the requirements of carvers. At this time, there were about 7,200 ivory craftsmen in the country, mainly in the state of Kerala (3,000), Mysore (600), Delhi (2,000), and Jaipur (800). Even though over 50% of the carvers were based in southern India, they consumed much less of the ivory. The southern carvers worked mainly by hand, producing goods of much higher quality and value compared to the north, where machines were used in production. Most of the finished ivory was exported to Europe and the United States. Legal ivory from Indian elephants had always supplied only an insignificant proportion of the demand by carvers, but this may have gained in importance once the African imports became a trickle. In 1978, about 3 tonnes of Indian ivory were sold by the state forest departments to local carvers. In late 1986, the government imposed a complete ban on all trade in Indian ivory.

The period after World War II saw a significant shift in the centers of ivory trade, this time to East Asia. Some of the European countries did continue either to trade in or to consume significant quantities of ivory. Belgium, for instance, was a major entrepôt of ivory during 1950–1978, but consumed little internally. The United Kingdom also traded in ivory again, but consumed little. France had a domestic carving industry that peaked in the early 1970s, with annual imports of 75–85 tonnes. Germany consumed 25–30 annually until the early 1970s, and after 1974 it increased annual imports to about 70 tonnes. The United States imported under 10 tonnes of ivory per annum until 1977, when this rose to 35 tonnes.

However, clearly the postwar centers shifted to Hong Kong and Japan. Hong Kong assumed importance as an entrepôt of trade in raw ivory, while Japan emerged as the dominant end user of ivory products. After 1950, a majority of all ivory flows went into these countries; during the period 1979–1988, this figure was 75% of all ivory traded. From about 100 tonnes per annum during the early 1950s, Hong Kong's imports of ivory steadily rose to about 250 tonnes by the early 1970s. It then shot up to over 500 tonnes (peaks of 597 tonnes in 1973 and 721 tonnes in 1976), and it sustained these levels for a decade before they declined sharply after 1983.

A major part of the raw ivory imported by Hong Kong is used by its own carving industry, with the rest being stockpiled or reexported. During 1979–1988, over 30% of gross raw ivory imports were directly reexported to other Asian countries, principally Japan (60% of exports), but also China, Taiwan, India, and Thailand. About 95% of the processed ivory during the same period was exported to the United States (35% of exports), Europe (29%), Japan (27%), Singapore, and even African countries such as South Africa. Substantial quantities of raw ivory have also been stockpiled in Hong Kong; the estimate of Edward Barbier and colleagues is 3,127 tonnes "retained" during 1978–1988 and 670 tonnes "stockpiled" in early 1990. Overall, Hong Kong has clearly been only an entrepôt of the trade and manufacturer of ivory articles in crude form for the overseas market. Very little ivory has actually been consumed locally.

The above picture is in contrast to Japan, which has an ivory import graph that also began to rise from 1950 onward, paralleling its postwar economic resurgence. Beginning with imports of less than 50 tonnes of raw ivory in 1950, it continued to take an average of 50–100 tonnes per year until the early 1960s, when the graph began to rise steeply to 300–400 tonnes during the 1970s. The imports reached a peak of 475 tonnes in 1983 before declining sharply. To this must be added a certain quantity of worked ivory imports. The local market has largely consumed the ivory entering Japan. About 64% of the ivory is used to make *hankos* or personal signature seals (fig. 8.14).

Indeed, it has been estimated that about 25% of the global consumption of raw ivory has been in the form of signature seals by Japan in recent decades.

8.5.4   *The post-1989 scenario*

An international campaign to ban the ivory trade gathered momentum in the wake of the rising tide of poaching in Africa. In October 1989, the Convention on International Trade in Endangered Species of Wild Fauna and Flora (CITES) voted for a complete ban on all trade in African ivory; the ban went into effect the following year (trade in Asian ivory had been banned since 1976). Following the total ban, the price of ivory crashed in the ensuing uncertainty over the future of the trade. The drop in price was as much as 90% in local African markets and about 50% in the international markets. Just prior to the ban, there were signs that the absolute numbers of elephants being killed across Africa may have begun to drop, although these would have still represented equal or higher proportions of the remaining numbers. However, there was a substantial decline in poaching for ivory after the ban, especially in countries that had lost very large numbers of elephants during the preban years. For instance, Kenya, with an estimated loss of more than 2,000 elephants through illegal killing during 1988–1989, registered only 111 such deaths during 1990–1991. Likewise, the illegal killing in Zambia's Luangwa Valley dropped from over 2,000 elephants to about 650 elephants during the corresponding period.

The influence of the ivory trade ban itself on the reduction in poaching across Africa is a disputed issue. One study by Holly Dublin, Tom Milliken, and Richard Barnes in 1995 suggested that, on the basis of available data from several countries, the trade ban might have contributed only partly to the observed decline in poaching. During the period preceding and accompanying the ban, a sharp enhancement in law enforcement budgets of many countries could have significantly influenced the trends in poaching. Once the enforcement budgets declined, there was again an increase in poaching at several places in spite of the trade ban.

Many observers, especially those strongly in favor of the trade ban, have questioned these conclusions. They point out that ivory poaching declined dramatically following the ban, and that any increase since 1992 has been only marginal or sporadic. Overall, the situation across Africa during the 1990s has been far better than during the previous decade.

The prices of raw ivory have recovered to a certain extent from the initial shock of the trade ban, but are still below the preban levels. A recent survey by Esmond Martin and Daniel Stiles of local ivory markets in Africa found wide variation in the prices and the legality of the trade. The cheapest raw ivory was found in Zimbabwe (U.S.$8–$17 per kilogram), where legal supplies were easily available, followed by Mozambique and the Central African Republic (U.S.$15–$25 per kilogram), where much of the trade was of illegal ivory.

The most expensive ivory was clearly the illegal ivory in nonrange states such as Egypt and Djibouti (range U.S.$68–$137 per kilogram). The overall demand for ivory items was reduced in all countries surveyed with the exception of Nigeria, where it had increased compared to the preban demand.

Ivory was moving across countries in defiance of the ban, while it was also being smuggled out of the continent to East Asia, particularly China. Purchases by diplomats, European tourists, and military and U.N. personnel also suggested that ivory items were being taken out in personal or diplomatic baggage. There was also evidence that the commercial trade in "bush meat" that has ravaged wildlife populations in West and Central Africa also had an impact on elephant populations.

Attempts at CITES Conference of the Parties (COP) during 1992 and 1994 to partially open the international ivory trade failed. The ban was, however, partly relaxed in 1997 to permit one-time sale of 60 tonnes by Botswana, Zimbabwe, and Namibia to Japan under international supervision. No ivory sales were allowed at the subsequent COP in 2000, but again at the COP in 2002 the sale of 60 tonnes by Botswana, Namibia, and South Africa was authorized. CITES and its role in regulating the ivory trade are discussed in chapter 9.

8.5.5   Capture and hunting of Asian elephants

I have described the historical depletion of elephant populations in Asia, chiefly in the Indian subcontinent, through their capture and taming for use in armies (chapter 2). This account looks more closely at the record of captures during the nineteenth and twentieth centuries. While this record is by no means complete, it gives a fair picture of the magnitude of captures and their impact on Asian elephant populations.

The methods of capturing elephants in the Indian subcontinent have varied between the two main elephant-bearing regions—the northeast and the south. In the northeast, elephants were captured through *kheddahs,* by driving entire herds into stockades; also used was the selective capture of subadult elephants through *mela shikar,* noosing with the help of trained captive elephants. In the south, elephants were captured in the erstwhile Madras Presidency through trapping in pits. These were usually solitary animals or mother-offspring pairs. In the princely state of Mysore, however, elephants were captured by the *kheddah* method, which was introduced there by G. P. Sanderson (fig. 8.15). The consequence was that the rate of capture was far higher in the northeast during the nineteenth century, when at least 4,000 elephants were captured within a decade, and again between 1937 and 1980, with over 10,000 elephants captured or killed. In the south, the systematic *kheddahs* of Mysore captured just under 2,000 elephants over the period of a century. The pit captures in other southern regions took even fewer elephants.

For both the north and south, the records of elephants shot to control crop depredation have not been systematically brought together. One record

Figure 8.15
Elephants captured at the Mysore *kheddah* of 1968 being roped with the help of trained captive elephants or *koonkies*. (Photo courtesy of T.N.A. Perumal.)

from the Wyanad in the south suggests that a single person shot about 300 elephants, mostly cows and calves, during the mid-nineteenth century when the government offered rewards for the elimination of elephants. In 1873, the Elephant Preservation Act of the Madras Presidency brought a halt to the regular killing of elephants on government land, although they could still be eliminated on private lands. This act was extended in 1879 to the whole of India and eventually to Burma (Myanmar), seemingly to ensure regular supplies to the government of this important resource. Over the next hundred years, the subcontinent did provide a rich harvest of elephants from the wild for taming. The figures I have compiled indicate that anywhere between 30,000 and 50,000 elephants were captured or killed in the subcontinent over this period, with most of the offtake being from northeastern India.

The Sri Lankan picture has been recently updated by Jayantha Jayewardene. This indicates that the elimination of elephants, through sport hunting and control measures, during the nineteenth century caused even greater depletion than did the capture of elephants. One observer records the wanton killing of 100 elephants in just three days by four Europeans during the year 1837. The destruction of about 3,500 elephants in the Northern Province during 1845–1848 and of 2,000 elephants during 1851–1855 is often cited in the literature. British Government Records actually show that 5,194 elephants were destroyed during 1845–1859. These records also indicate that 3,253 elephants were exported during 1853–1894. On the basis of such records, Jayewardene estimates that 17,000 elephants may have been exported, destroyed, or died in captivity during the nineteenth century. A government ordinance of 1891 seems to have lessened the "wanton destruction" of elephants in later periods.

Myanmar has systematically captured elephants in significant numbers for use in logging operations. Records available for the twentieth century suggest that the captures declined from an average annual offtake of 417 elephants during 1910–1930 to only 100 animals during 1970–1990, for a total of over 17,000 elephants over this period. In 1994, Myanmar imposed a moratorium on captures in view of its greatly reduced wild stocks. The large numbers of captive elephants in Thailand, second only to Myanmar at present, also suggest regular captures from the wild. At the turn of the twentieth century, an estimated 100,000 captive elephants is plausible and 50,000 certainly believable for the country. Although systematic captures halted in the early 1970s, a certain number are still taken illegally.

One Asian country that continues to capture elephants in significant numbers is Indonesia, which does not otherwise have a recent tradition of keeping elephants in captivity. Since 1986, several hundred elephants have been captured on the island of Sumatra, ostensibly to reduce crop depredation. The precise number of elephants captured here is not clear, but a few years ago, at least 520 elephants were reportedly held in several camps across the island. Presumably, more elephants were actually captured, but many died during the operations. These elephants have suffered high postcapture mortality because of a combination of lack of appropriate traditional expertise in training and health care, as well as inadequate resources. By the end of 2000, only 326 elephants seemed to remain in the camps, some having moved to other locations and others having died.

While sporadic poaching of elephants for tusks or other products such as meat undoubtedly existed for a long time in India, the systematic targeting of bulls for ivory began only in the 1970s (fig. 8.13). The written accounts, backed by photographic records of naturalists like M. Krishnan, who observed elephants in several reserves across the country during the 1950s and 1960s, certainly testify to the presence of large numbers of adult tusked bulls in areas where few remained by the 1980s. Systematic poaching for ivory seems to have begun in the southern Indian reserve of Periyar and its vicinity in Kerala State by the mid-1970s, and it wiped out most of the tusked adult male elephants within a decade. Mohana Chandran, a ranger working in this reserve, reported that, during 1987–1989, the adult male-to-female ratio was 1 : 122, while the subadult ratio was about 1 : 6, suggesting that poaching had taken a severe toll of tusked males across virtually all age classes. Observations in this reserve during the mid-1990s by my research team confirmed a very similar elephant population structure. Through computer simulations, I estimated that poachers had killed 336–388 elephants over a 20-year period in this reserve (chapter 7).

By the late 1970s the poaching scourge had spread to other major elephant populations further north in the Anamalais, the Nilgiris, the Biligirirangans, and the Eastern Ghats in the southern Indian states of Tamilnadu and Karnataka. During the 1980s, several independent groups of poachers operated over this southern range, holding some of the largest elephant populations in Asia. The high proportion (>90%) of tusked males in this region also meant that southern India had the largest number of tuskers of any region in the continent. In the Biligirirangans and the Nilgiris, the ratio of adult males to females was about 1:5 during 1981–1982, but it widened to nearly 1:9 by 1987. In the Nilgiris, where I subsequently continued to observe elephants, the adult sex ratio skewed further to about 1:25 by the year 2000.

For the period 1977–1986, I estimated that 100–150 male elephants were killed each year by people. While some of these deaths were possibly of crop raiders and others were failed attempts at poaching, the poachers got away with at least 100 pairs of tusks, yielding 1.8 tonnes of ivory annually. This was a conservative estimate of poaching in southern India. The destination for much of this ivory was the state of Kerala, which was home to a thriving carving industry, although some of this also went to dealers in Mysore and Bangalore cities or smuggled out to the Middle East. From mid-1987 onward, there was a noticeable reduction in poaching in the south.

An upswing in the poaching graph began again in 1991; this time, the phenomenon spread over a wider area in the country, including central and northeast India and finally the northern population. The database that Vivek Menon, Ashok Kumar, and I have been maintaining shows that, between 1994 and 2000, about 80–100 elephants have been recorded as killed by poachers each year in the country. Considering the deficiencies in detecting or recording cases of poaching, this number could easily be over 200 elephants annually. The following broad patterns could be seen in poaching of elephants during the last quarter of a century.

Ivory poaching on a serious scale began in the mid-1970s in the Periyar region of Kerala and soon spread to other elephant populations in southern India. At this time, poaching in other regions of the country seemed to be sporadic. From 1988 onward, there was a relative lull in poaching in the south for a few years, but when it resurfaced in the early 1990s, it became a countrywide phenomenon, peaking in 1997 and affecting central India, the northeast, and finally the northern population of Rajaji-Corbett by the end of the decade. This suggests that the sourcing of illegal Indian ivory has shifted with time, as could be expected from populations depleted of tusked males to others still maintaining sizable numbers of tuskers. Within a population or region, the poaching of tusked males has also shifted from older males to younger males. Several recent poaching incidents in southern India have been of males as young as 3–5 years old (fig. 8.16). This has resulted in skewed ratios not only in the adult segment, but also in the subadult and juvenile segments of the

Figure 8.16
A 4-year-old juvenile Asian male elephant poached for its ivory in Mudumalai in southern India. With the reduction in the numbers and proportions of larger bulls in the population, the poachers in this region have shifted to younger elephants that yield less than 1 kg per pair of tusks.

elephant population. Even in populations or regions for which poaching declined in absolute terms, it may have actually increased in terms of claiming progressively larger proportions of the surviving male segment. Some of the poaching, including that of female elephants, during the 1990s in the northeast was for meat, which apparently was processed and supplied to militant groups. There are also stray reports of elephants being killed for their tail hair (considered a lucky charm) and for parts such as temporal glands for use in medicinal preparations. Today, there is possibly no elephant population in India that has not been affected by poaching.

Unlike India, hard data on poaching of elephants are scarce for other Asian countries. One would expect Sri Lanka to face only a relatively minor problem of ivory poaching as over 95% of its male elephants are tuskless. However, there are many reports of female elephants being killed for their tushes; these reports are corroborated by the availability of carvings from tushes in the local markets. Only sporadic incidents of poaching are reported from Peninsular Malaysia, Sabah, and Sumatra. Reports of raw ivory being available in Sumatra's Lampung Province suggest that poaching may be more common than believed. It is clear, however, that elephant populations across continental Southeast Asia from Myanmar to Vietnam have declined from killing, mostly by traditional hunting tribes, not only for ivory, but also for meat and other products. Poaching has been widespread across Myanmar, especially in the north, in the Rakhine Yoma to the west, and in the southern Tenasserim along the border with Thailand. A newspaper report in 1974 gave figures of 200 elephants killed in the Rakhine Yoma during 1968–1974. Official figures also record 55 elephants killed in the country during 1982–1991.

In neighboring Thailand, at least 91 elephants, representing about 10% of the population, were poached during 1975–1979 in the protected areas. Available figures also suggest 110 deaths of male elephants from poaching during 1987–1997. A report of 42 elephants killed in Laos during 1992 is the only information on poaching for the country. Traditional hunters are active in Cambodia, especially in the Cardamom Mountains to the southwest, which possibly have the largest remaining elephant population there. Hunting of elephants has been widespread in Vietnam during the postwar period, concurrent with the clearing of forests on a large scale for agriculture. Its wild elephant population, numbering less than 100 individuals today in scattered groups, suggests a decline of at least 90% since 1980. Unlike the poaching in India, which has been mostly selective in targeting male elephants, the poaching in Southeast Asia has been relatively nonselective, resulting in declining populations.

Science, Politics, and Pragmatism
Conserving the Elephant Populations

9

Introduction

The continued survival of elephants, or of hundreds of thousands of species unknown to science for that matter, is inextricably linked to a host of environmental, biological, ecological, social, economic, and political factors. As during the late Pleistocene, global climate change, this time human induced, is an environmental factor that could potentially make major impacts on landscapes and species. We can barely speculate upon how elephants and their habitats would respond to climate change in the coming decades.

The biological factors impinging on elephant survival include disease epidemics that could wipe out entire populations, especially smaller ones. The ecological considerations include the demographic viability of small populations in the face of stochasticity, habitat viability in relation to its loss and fragmentation, and changing habitat quality. The resolution of elephant-human conflict is an economic and a social issue with ethical dimensions in developing countries. At the same time, the changing economic contours of nations have witnessed fluxes in the demand for luxury consumption of ivory, with serious consequences for elephant populations. Finally, political structures and conflicts, internecine or international, can influence the course of conservation. Obviously, these factors do not operate independent of each other, but are intertwined.

Futurology is always risky business. However, I think it is fairly safe to say that the twenty-first century will be a defining moment in the earth's history of life. We stand armed with the most sophisticated technologies that can strike at and manipulate the very basis of life—the genetic code. These technologies equip us to play God and drive the future course of the evolution of life. Before that becomes a reality, we are also poised to obliterate a significant proportion of the estimated 10 million or more species of living organisms at a rate that would make the mass extinction of dinosaurs and other creatures at the end of the Cretaceous a minor blip in the geological record.

How would elephants fare under these circumstances? If one were to ask me whether elephant populations in Asia and in Africa could be conserved over their entire present ranges, my answer would be an emphatic "No." The inexorable march of humans across the earth's natural landscapes and current levels of consumption of its resources show no signs of abating as yet. Even if human populations stabilize by the middle of this century, as some demographic projections show, and even if our demands on natural resources plateau by then, large chunks of present-day natural landscapes would have disappeared and along with them many creatures, including several elephant populations. True, the unexpected could always happen. Disease epidemics could curtail human populations on regional scales. Increased urbanization could reduce direct pressures on natural lands. Changes in consumption patterns or alternative energy sources and improved energy efficiency could increase the "carrying capacity" of the planet for humans with minimal impact on natural landscapes. I do not foresee how any of these can halt the loss of natural habitat over the next several decades.

On the other hand, if one were to ask me whether elephants could be saved, my cautiously optimistic answer would be, "Yes." Asian and African elephants have far better survival prospects compared to, say, the tiger, many rhino species now tottering on the brink, or thousands of unnamed insect and plant species destined to perish in the tropics. Elephants are pretty adaptable creatures spread over diverse landscapes in tropical and subtropical Asia and Africa. We can expect them to be resilient overall as a species to some of the knocks they would undoubtedly receive in the coming decades. At this point, science and pragmatism will have to join hands to plan for the conservation of elephants with a long-term perspective. Fortunately, the total population size of African elephants runs into several hundred thousands and of Asian elephants into several tens of thousands, although in fragmented landscapes. I am not trying to project these, especially regarding the Asian elephant, as absolutely safe numbers, but merely as adequate foundations for building conservation edifices. We cannot save every single elephant population surviving today, but we can save several of these populations. Indeed, trying to cling to every single elephant, when conservation resources are limited, may be counterproductive and jeopardize the prospects of the more viable populations.

Charismatic animals such as elephants can act as powerful flagships for achieving broader goals, such as conservation of biological diversity. Some have argued, based on observations in localized areas of semiarid Africa, that elephants are actually inimical to biodiversity. For instance, declines in endemic succulent plants and birds have been seen in vegetation impacted heavily by elephants. Such a narrow focus overlooks the expansive stride of elephants across the two continents, from near deserts through savanna-woodland, and to seasonal forests and rain forests and from lowland forests to mountain habitats approaching the snow line. Many of these are among the most biologically diverse areas on earth. By conserving elephants across these landscapes, the persistence of very significant proportions of the earth's biodiversity would also be ensured. With the Asian elephant, there is the added dimension of the cultural traditions it represents. The landscape approach, termed variously as managed elephant reserves or similarly, is the approach advocated by the IUCN/SSC Asian Elephant Specialist Group in its action plan and incorporated into national conservation plans for the species, such as India's Project Elephant. This action plan also identified several such landscapes across Asia for conservation efforts (appendix 1). The conservation issues and challenges in these landscape units are very different. Many of these elephant populations and their habitats would need intensive management. When resources are limited, it is also necessary to prioritize landscapes or populations for conservation action. I had identified 27 such priority landscapes across Asia based on criteria such as elephant population size, effective population size (see section 9.2.1), habitat area, habitat type, overall biodiversity, regional representation, extent of poaching, levels of elephant-human conflict, local political situation, and so on. To this we must now add measures of genetic variation in elephant populations from the ongoing studies (chapter 1). Priorities may also have to be decided upon on more regional scales. Arun Venkataraman and I have been developing algorithms for prioritizing elephant landscapes and their administrative units.

African elephant landscapes in the eastern, central, and even southern parts of the continent are much more contiguous, although the situation in western Africa is akin to that of fragmented habitats in Asia.

In this concluding chapter, I trace the broad contours of the conservation framework for elephants. Conservation solutions should obviously be region specific in most cases, although certain aspects, such as the trade in ivory, have international ramifications. Science and idealism have to be infused with a strong dose of pragmatism to achieve tangible results that are long lasting. This requires recognition of the complex dimensions to conserving species such as elephants. Socioeconomic forces not within the controlling power of any political system drive land-use changes around elephant landscapes. Our understanding of the dynamics of the international ivory trade and its links to poaching is inadequate. The elephant's ingenuity is more than a match for our technological gadgetry when it has made up its mind to forage in that attractive crop field.

The new science of conservation biology, according to Graeme Caughley, has seemingly progressed along two major lines: the small-population paradigm backed by strong theoretical underpinnings but contributing little to conservation practice and the declining-population paradigm, which is weak in theory but perhaps has more relevance to real-life conservation problems. Obviously, a balanced mix of the two approaches is needed to tackle the conservation issues relating to elephants effectively. The principles listed in the remainder of this chapter are meant to be guidelines for developing strategies for conserving individual elephant populations or the species at regional scales.

9.2   *Minimum viable populations for elephant conservation*

Common sense dictates that the smaller the size of a species population, the more vulnerable it is to extinction. Strictly speaking, though, no species population has a 100% probability of surviving over any period of time. A severe, unanticipated catastrophe can wipe out the largest population of a species. Even if a catastrophe does not strike a small population, chance variations in births and deaths can drive it to extinction.

Mark Shaffer thus emphasized that the continued survival of a population can be expressed only in probabilistic terms within a certain time frame. The "minimum viable population" (MVP) size for a species thus depends on one's definition of the MVP. To the biologist who takes a long-term view of the evolutionary potential of the species, the MVP may be one that has a 99% probability of surviving for 1,000 years. A reserve manager, on the other hand, may be willing to commit resources to conserving a population that has a 90% chance of persisting for 100 or even 50 years. Shaffer further pointed out that there were four major considerations for estimating MVP: (1) demographic stochasticity, chance variations in births and deaths; (2) environmental stochasticity, which arises from interannual fluctuations; (3) genetic stochasticity, the loss of variation from drift (chance); and (4) catastrophes, such as disease epidemics or major climatic events.

Population viability analysis (PVA) is a process that evaluates data and models for a species population to estimate a probability that it would survive for a chosen period of time into the future. A PVA using computer simulations also helps determine the MVP for a species in accordance with an agreed-upon definition. Related to this is the viability of the habitat for the elephant; the two processes can be combined into population and habitat viability analysis (PHVA), an approach championed by the IUCN/SSC Conservation Breeding Specialist Group.

9.2.1   *Viable elephant populations*

The issue of minimum population sizes for maintaining genetic variation to support the natural evolutionary process has been theoretically examined. In 1980, Ian Franklin proposed "rule-of-thumb" estimates of effective population sizes N_e of 50 and 500 for short-term and long-term conservation, respectively. The figure of $N_e = 50$ is the theoretical minimum needed to keep inbreeding at 1% per generation, a level deemed tolerable for domestic animals kept under benign conditions. Such a population, however, would continue to suffer a loss in genetic variation or heterozygosity with succeeding generations. Franklin suggested $N_e = 500$ for gain in genetic variation from mutation to balance loss through drift. These approaches have been criticized as being too vague or general for any application to real populations in the wild.

Interestingly, a review by Mark Boyce indicates that these figures are probably of appropriate magnitude for several vertebrate species, as seen from empirical studies. Several simulation studies of the larger mammals also show that $N_e = 50$–100 is needed for populations to be safe from extinction due to demographic and environmental stochasticity. Further development of theory based on limited empirical data suggests that much higher effective population sizes may be needed for maintaining genetic variation in the long term. While Michael Lynch and Russell Lande estimate that N_e of up to 5,000 may be needed, Ian Franklin and R. Frankham maintain that N_e on the order of 500–1,000 is sufficient for maintaining variation.

A clarification has to be made here about the definition of *effective population size*. In genetic terms, the effective population size is the number of individuals that would be subject to the same amount of genetic drift if it were an ideal, constant population under an equal sex ratio of adults, random mating, and random distribution of offspring among parents in the population. Only adult or reproductive individuals are considered for computing N_e. Thus, N_e has to be distinguished from the total size of a population and is usually only a fraction of it. Among elephants, a skewing of the sex ratio in many populations, primarily because of ivory poaching, is possibly the most important variable that decreases the value of N_e in relation to the number of adults N_s in the population. N_e is computed as $4(N_e \times N_f)/(N_m + N_f)$, where N_m and N_f are the number of breeding males and females, respectively.

What do the theory and the models tell us about minimum viable populations for elephants? Although an arbitrary distinction, the MVP needs to be considered from both the short-term and the long-term perspectives. The simulations I carried out using demographic data from Asian elephants indicated that a population of 65–80 individuals, with a potential (deterministic) growth rate of 0.5% per year and no real constraint on carrying capacity, would have a high (>99%) probability of surviving for 100 years (chapter 7). If adult male-to-female ratios are skewed beyond about 1 : 5, the corresponding population size needed would rise, reaching 120 at a 1 : 16 ratio when the carrying capacity is at least twice this value.

In any case, at these population sizes and sex ratios, the value of N_e would be much below 50. Such populations would continue to lose genetic variation. Therefore, I suggested that maintaining a total population of 100–300 elephants, depending on demography, sex ratio, and basic ecological pressures, should be the goal of managers to ensure the population's survival in the short term in the face of demographic and environmental stochasticity as well as genetic erosion. Populations smaller than these sizes are not necessarily doomed, but would require intensive management to prevent them being drawn into the extinction vortex.

With elephant populations, the main consideration for short-term conservation should be their persistence in the face of demographic and environmental stochasticity. Genetic considerations are secondary for more than one reason. First, the link between genetic variation and short-term fitness of a species population is still rather controversial. Second, the long generation time in elephants also means that any loss of variation will occur over only a few generations within a century. It is only when an elephant population is threatened with strong selection, such as from ivory poaching, that genetics could become an important consideration even in small populations.

Long-term persistence would need much larger population sizes. The Armbruster-Lande model that simulated African elephant populations in semiarid habitats subject to recurring drought cycles indicated a size of about 3,000 individuals to ensure a 99% probability of persisting for 1,000 years (chapter 7). Asian elephant habitats do not seem to be impacted by such severe drought occurrences or climatic variability. Although not explicitly modeled, population sizes smaller than 3,000 would presumably have an equally high chance of persisting over the long term. Therefore, a population of 1,000–3,000 elephants or more, depending on the continent and its climatic zone, may be targeted by managers for long-term conservation. If one were to factor in the more recent theoretical arguments mentioned in the discussion on maintaining genetic variation, about twice the above figures may be appropriate.

There are many African elephant populations larger than these numbers by an order of magnitude or more; an attempt should obviously be made to keep these as large as possible in genetic terms. With Asian elephants, one does not have the luxury of many large populations. There are fewer than 10 populations with over 1,000 elephants each, most of them in India. Even here, the effective population sizes of some are small; one example is Periyar in southern India, with a total population of over 1,000 elephants, but an N_e of only 20–30 due to the extremely skewed sex ratio. It is critical, therefore, that the few remaining large Asian populations be maintained with a long-term perspective.

9.2.2   Viable habitats for elephants

There are three major habitat attributes—size, integrity, and quality—that have to be considered for the conservation of elephant populations. The minimum viable habitat area is related to the minimum viable population and the carrying capacity of the habitat (the density of elephants under so-called equilibrium conditions). An equilibrium density of 0.5 elephant/km^2, typical of many dry habitats in Asia, would indicate minimum habitat areas of 2,000–6,000 km^2 for long-term persistence of a population. If carrying capacity is more likely to be 0.1 elephant/km^2, such as for a tropical rain forest, the minimum area needed increases fivefold over the above figures. The Armbruster-Lande model for African elephants in semiarid habitats arrived at a reserve size of 2,500 km², assuming an equilibrium density of 1.2 elephants/km² and 3,000 elephants as the MVP for long-term persistence (fig. 9.1).

None of these take home range sizes of elephant herds or clans and their overlap into consideration. It is implied that range sizes are incorporated into figures of equilibrium elephant density. Home range sizes of elephant populations vary over two orders of magnitude (chapter 4). Over large landscapes, there could be considerable heterogeneity in elephant usage, densities, and range sizes. All these have to be factored into planning on the ground for viable habitat areas for elephants.

Maintaining the integrity of the overall landscape for an elephant population should perhaps be the most important consideration for long-term conservation. Large, contiguous landscapes would ensure the free movement of groups or individuals on a seasonal basis or when exigencies demand temporary shifts in habitat utilization, as well as permit greater gene flow and dispersal. Even if the size of a population is reduced, a large landscape would facilitate rapid

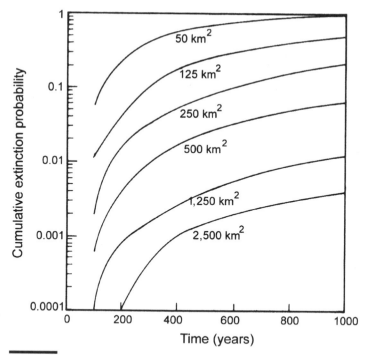

Figure 9.1

The cumulative probability of extinction over 1,000 years in African elephant populations for six habitat areas with a starting density of 1.2 elephants/km². (Based on Armbruster and Lande 1993. Reproduced with the permission of the Society for Conservation Biology, U.S.A.)

recovery when favorable conditions return. Even if observed home range sizes of elephant herds or clans are small now, a long-term perspective requires that larger integral landscapes be maintained.

The well-known "theory of island biogeography," elaborated by Robert MacArthur and Edward Wilson in 1967, is being increasingly applied to insular habitats. Empirical relationships between area and vertebrate species richness in islands submerged since the late Pleistocene suggest considerable species losses in smaller islands. Thus, reductions in the faunal richness of insular reserves have been predicted in the absence of management. John Terborgh has pointed out that, in insular habitats, the species most vulnerable to extinction are those with lower reproductive rates and those at the summit of food chains. Although insular biogeography theory allows for migration and recolonization of habitats in which extinctions have occurred, this would rarely be possible for elephant populations living amid landscapes drastically altered by humans. Fragmentation and insularization are usually irreversible in today's world.

Relatively large, interconnected landscapes are still available for elephants in central Africa and parts of eastern and southern Africa even if sections of these may be devoid of elephants today. Western Africa presents a very different picture with its highly fragmented landscape. Asian elephant landscapes are also highly fragmented, although somewhat less than in western Africa. Several contiguous landscapes of over 10,000 km^2 are still available in countries such as India, Myanmar (Burma) and its border with Thailand, and perhaps Sumatra.

When landscapes are threatened with fragmentation, a system of corridors may be one practical way to ensure connectivity for elephant movement. A *corridor* may be defined in simple terms as a relatively narrow strip of habitat that provides a passage for the target species to move between two larger expanses of habitat (fig. 9.2). The dimensions of a corridor, its location in the broader landscape, and its vegetation attributes are important to its success.

For elephants, a corridor that is 0.1 km wide and 10 km long is obviously a very impractical one. One that is 1 km wide and 10 km long may do the job of ensuring some gene flow, but such a long passage would still entail a high risk of conflict with human settlements and agriculture along the interface.

Field observations in India show that passages 0.5–1 km wide and less than about 5 km long are regularly used by both bulls and family herds. Narrower passages or those with greater length-to-breadth ratios may still be used by some bulls. Narrow corridors situated in the plains are more likely to be traversed than those along steep hill slopes. Because corridors act as funnels for elephants moving between more expansive habitats, there could be a higher incidence of conflict with people along the boundary. The boundaries of a corridor thus may have to be protected (section 9.3). If the objective of a corridor is merely to act as a passage for elephants, it would be better to maintain the vegetation in a state that encourages rapid movement rather than a prolonged stay that could promote conflict.

Figure 9.2
A corridor for facilitating the movement of elephants to the north of this gorge (*top*) was created in 2001 through land acquisition (*bottom*) in the Bandipur National Park, India. This corridor links the western and eastern parts of the largest Asian elephant population's range, the Nilgiri-Eastern Ghats Range in southern India.

Finally, a point has to be made about the location of the potential corridor within the overall landscape. In some instances, a narrow passage may connect an expansive range with a small habitat patch along the periphery of the landscape. Elephants moving through this passage into the small patch may actually come into serious conflict with surrounding cultivation. The pragmatic option here would be to sever the passage and prevent elephants from utilizing the small patch, which might only be an insignificant proportion of the overall home range of the elephant group.

An otherwise large landscape may also be fragmented in functional terms by structures such as roads, railway tracks, dams, and associated canals or pipelines, such as in many parts of India (fig. 9.3). The impediments to animal movement could be partly avoided through appropriate engineering design at the time of construction. Roads across hilly terrain cannot be crossed along stretches lined by steep sides, but can be negotiated where contours are more gentle. Easy passage should be provided at points along identified animal paths.

Elephants may not traverse reservoirs with a very wide waterspread even though they are actually excellent swimmers, but shorter expanses may be crossed regularly, such as in southern India's Periyar reservoir. Canals have had mixed impacts on elephant movement. The Tunakadavu-Sircarapathy canal in the Anamalais has proved to be a death trap for elephants trying to swim across. Some animals have been swept away by the swift-flowing waters into narrow, steep-sided stretches, where they drown or end up at the entry to a tunnel. There has been mixed success in rescuing trapped elephants. Sections of the canal are below ground and do not impede movement. The unpaved, 6-km long Moyar Canal in Mudumalai Sanctuary can be crossed by elephants at several places. The 10-km long Chila-Motichur Canal in Rajaji National Park is paved with concrete; hence, elephants do not venture to swim across. A.J.T. Johnsingh, who has been monitoring the movement of elephants there, observes that only solitary bulls occasionally cross a narrow bridge along the canal, but never the family herds. He believes that herds avoid crossing the bridge because of human disturbances in the surrounding area. In other situations, however, a broader bridge with an earthen surface may be needed to encourage family groups, suspicious of artificial structures, to use it.

Penstock pipes carrying water from a hilltop reservoir downslope to a power-generating plant at several places in the Nilgiris, Anamalais, and Periyar in the Western Ghats obstruct the movement of elephants completely. Possible solutions for such structures would be to bury the pipes underground, at least along certain stretches, or excavate a passage beneath the pipes along elephant paths.

It is difficult to generalize about maintenance of habitat quality for elephants because they range over such diverse habitats. If available, it is best to maintain a mosaic of vegetation types. Studies of foraging ecology indicate that elephants show distinct seasonal preferences for particular habitat types.

Figure 9.3
Open-cut canals (*top*) such as in the Anamalais or (*bottom*) pipelines in many parts
of Western Ghats in southern India hinder the free movement of elephants.

Elephants distinctly prefer secondary forests over primary forests (chapter 8), but this need not be justification for deliberately manipulating primary forests unless there is a very strong need for an artificial increase in carrying capacity to maintain a viable population. Tropical moist forests are unique in their rich biodiversity, which is destroyed through large-scale manipulation. Disturbance also allows alien invasive plants and animals to become established, thereby reducing their biodiversity value. In tropical dry forests, the elephants themselves ensure a high carrying capacity through their mode of feeding on woody plants.

The quality of surface water is also an important attribute of habitat quality, especially when it is likely to be contaminated with parasites/pathogens from other wildlife or livestock, pesticides from nearby agricultural areas, heavy metals and other impurities from mining activities, or untreated sewage from cities and towns. One study by R. K. Singh and S. Chowdhury (1999) on elephant use of riverine habitat in the heavily mined Singhbhum region of central India found significant avoidance of stretches with unregulated mine discharge. They suggest that waste levels in water should be kept below 200 mg/l (total suspended solids, TSS) and 60 NTU (nephelometric turbidity units; turbidity) for it to be fit for consumption by elephants and other wildlife.

Taking all these factors into consideration, the more appropriate approach to making elephant conservation compatible with biodiversity conservation is perhaps the "ecosystem viability analysis" that David Western has advocated.

9.3   *Managing elephant-human conflicts*

Elephants that threaten human lives and agricultural crops have been dealt with historically by society in various ways, from swift retaliation to resigned coexistence. At either end, there is suffering—for elephants or for people. Indeed, the losses suffered due to elephants are only a part of the broader wildlife-human conflict, including depredation by many other animals (table 9.1). In oil palm plantations in Southeast Asia, only about half the damage can be attributed to elephants, while significant losses also occur due to wild pig and porcupine.

Although there are few objective estimates of the economic loss inflicted by elephants, it is certain that the losses run into several tens of millions of dollars each year across the two continents. During the 1970s, it was estimated that the Federal Land Development Agency in Malaysia alone lost oil palm and rubber plantation crops worth U.S.$20 million annually in the export market due to damage by elephants. I made a conservative estimate of U.S.$0.5 million loss to agricultural crops annually in southern India during the early 1980s. The southern state of Karnataka, home to about 20% of India's population of over 25,000 wild elephants, paid an average of U.S.$160,000 per year during 1991–2000 as compensation to farmers for crop loss due to elephants. The losses have been much higher in other parts of the country, such as the north-

Table 9.1

Damage to oil palm trees by various wild mammals in the FELDA plantations of peninsular Malaysia and TIGAMITRA plantations in Aceh, Sumatra.

Species	FELDA, Malaysia*		TIGAMITRA, Sumatra†	
	No. of Trees Damaged	%	No. of Trees Damaged	%
Elephant	1,724,336	58.6	119,068	45.9
Wild pig	902,414	30.7	65,305	25.2
Porcupine	316,045	10.7	30,073	11.6
Rodent			17,201	6.6
Others			27,827	10.7

Sources: Blair et al. (1979) for FELDA plantations and Sukumar (1999, unpublished data) for TIGAMITRA plantations.

*The data for FELDA are up to 1978 with most of the damage occurring during 1976–1978 though plantations were opened up since 1956. Some damage by rodents also occurs but a precise figure is not given in Blair et al. (1979).

†The data for TIGAMITRA are for the period 1995–1998.

east, where conflict has been more severe. The state of West Bengal, which has less than 500 elephants, paid an average annual compensation of U.S.$175,000 during 1996–2000 for crop losses due to wildlife, mostly elephant. In both states, the actual losses would have been higher.

At the same time, many elephants are killed by farmers as a direct consequence of agricultural conflict. Records I have maintained for southern India show that at least 230 elephants died in such conflict during 1976–2000, representing over 8% of all recorded elephant deaths.

Experienced and pragmatic observers of elephants in Asia and in Africa agree that elephant-human conflicts cannot be totally eliminated, except through the elimination of substantial numbers or proportions of elephants. The goal of management should thus be to control and minimize conflict. The available options to manage conflict can be considered under three broad categories: preventing or discouraging elephants from entering settlements and crop fields, elephant population management, and a suite of measures pertaining to social welfare, economic incentives, and land-use planning. A conflict management scheme must obviously be economically viable for it to be sustained in the long term. The Great Wall of China can certainly exclude elephants, but that does not make economic sense. The challenge, therefore, lies in formulating region-specific measures that are both effective in containing conflict and based on sound benefit-cost considerations.

Traditionally, rural societies in Asia and Africa have sought protection from wild animals by organizing themselves into tight-knit communities and cooperating to keep animals away from their settlements and fields. To deal with elephants, farmers have relied on simple means, such as shouting, noise-making with pots and pans, drums, or firecrackers, and hurling rocks or fireballs at them. These are of limited use in keeping elephants at bay. Relatively inexperienced crop raiders may be scared away by such tactics. Veteran raiders, usually adult bulls or even some family groups, are not fooled. When possible, farmers guard their fields from the safety of a treetop platform. Those who try to scare elephants from flimsy structures on the ground are vulnerable to aggressive elephants. A bright spotlight powered by a car battery seems to be effective, but a weak torchlight may only invite a charge from an aggressive bull. Farmers who use dogs to guard their crops may also invite the wrath of raiding elephants.

The northern Bengal region in India experiences very intense conflict, with elephants not only damaging crops, but also demolishing dwellings and killing people. Squads of trained guards and villagers armed with firecrackers and guns, sometimes assisted by trained elephants, have been moderately successful at chasing away marauding elephants in this region. Trenching along the forest-cultivation boundary was attempted around oil palm plantations in peninsular Malaysia during the 1970s, but was soon abandoned because of rapid soil erosion caused by the high rainfall.

Some Indian states, such as Karnataka, have taken to trenching on a significant scale around protected areas (fig. 9.4). The reasoning is that such "barriers" should not only serve to keep elephants away from cultivation, but also prevent livestock from entering the forest. Trenches have been relatively ineffective in higher rainfall areas, such as the western boundary of Nagarahole National Park because of erosion and breaks occurring at places where streams cut across the trench. Trenching has been more effective in areas of low rainfall, such as the northeastern boundary of Bandipur National Park, where the soil is harder and the substrate rockier.

A trench has to be at least 2 m deep, 2 m across at the top, and 1.5 m across at the bottom to keep out an elephant. Even then, a determined elephant could fill up a trench partially by pushing in the soil with its feet and negotiating it. Depending on the nature of the soil, a trench with these minimum specifications costs between U.S.$2,000–$4,000 per kilometer to excavate. Measures to stabilize the wall of a ditch by planting on excavated soil heaped on the outer boundary are inexpensive. Masonry work along the wall is expensive. The considerable additional costs of plugging gullies and streams can result in an unfavorable benefit-cost ratio for a trench. Possible alteration of local drainage by a long trench should also be a consideration. Overall, a trench is most unlikely to be viable in regions with annual rainfall above 100–120 cm, while in those with less rainfall, it could work when a hard substrate keeps maintenance costs low.

A boulder wall held together by wire mesh is an effective barrier against elephants. Its use is limited to areas where boulders are available and transporting costs are low. Dry stone walls in Kenya's Laikipia district have been generally ineffective because elephants push these over with their chests. Barriers

Figure 9.4
Ditches and electric fences are two commonly used barriers to keep elephants away
from agricultural land. At the top is a reasonably effective trench in dry, hard
substrate in Bandipur National Park, India. The bottom shows an official (*left*) of the
Kenya Wildlife Service explaining the features of an electric fence to the author
(*right*).

such as iron spikes embedded in concrete on the ground can be dangerous to elephants.

The high-voltage electrified fence is the most widely used barrier in the two continents (fig. 9.4). The basic principle behind this barrier is to deliver a strong shock that deters an animal, but is neither fatal nor injurious in any manner. This is achieved through the use of a transformer (the energizer), typically powered by a 12-volt car battery, that delivers a current of 5,000–10,000 volts in pulses of very short duration (say, 1/3,000 second) with a gap of about 1 second between successive pulses. A minimum of 7,000 volts is recommended; several observers also point out that a fence in a moist region is more likely to provide sufficient grounding to deliver a strong shock. The battery itself is charged from the mains (110–230 volts alternating current [AC]) or by a solar panel in places where power supply through transmission lines is not available. The fence design itself may vary from a simple singe wire or 2-strand wire attached to existing trees to a sophisticated 12-strand barrier with high-quality accessories such as protected steel posts and insulators.

The effectiveness of an electric fence depends not only on fence design, pulse voltage, and maintenance, but also on the learning capacity and behavioral response of crop-raiding elephants. A fence may be broken by an elephant using its tusks (which are nonconductors) to prise an insulator or even break the wire. Bulls are also known to use the soles of the front feet, again poor conductors, to press down on fence wires. Fence posts may be broken by kicking with the legs or pushing with the tusks, while those protected with live wires may also be dealt with by breaking the wire between posts. Elephants may push trees over a fence, and a determined one may even crash through a live wire without receiving a shock if the timing of the break is between two pulses.

A study of electric fences by C. R. Thouless and J. Sakwa in Kenya's Laikipia district showed no clear relationship between their effectiveness and factors such as sophistication of design and voltage. Some simple fences or those providing a current with only 3,000–4,000 volts were effective over long periods, while some high-specification fences, including a 12-strand one, were repeatedly breached by elephants.

A survey in southern India indicated that sound design, although not necessarily an elaborate one, and good maintenance of electric fences were important for their effectiveness. The ownership of an electric fence was also a key factor in its success because this had a direct bearing on its maintenance. Of 19 fences under private ownership, 16 inspected were functional, while only 3 of 18 fences put up by a government agency were working. The failure of the fences in the latter category was mainly because of breakage of wires by villagers to gain access for themselves and their livestock to the forest and the inability of the forest department to bear the high expenditure for maintenance under the circumstances. The two categories of fence ownership were basically of similar design specification. No elephant has passed through one fence in the Nilgiris for over 5 years because its owner continually incorporated innovative measures, thus keeping one step ahead of elephants. The high-voltage electric fence is thus only a psychological bluff and not a physical barrier. The learning experience of elephants during the initial period of contact with fences may also decide their future response to various fence designs. Innovative measures from farmers are needed against the behavioral response of individual elephants in this "arms race."

What is the overall effectiveness of electric fences? Do these fences have favorable benefit-cost ratios? Malaysia was possibly the first country to use electric fences extensively to protect oil palm and rubber plantations from elephants and other herbivores. A success rate of 80% against elephants has been reported. During early experiments in 1982 by Robert Piesse with a fence in Etosha, Namibia, a total of 259 elephants made 184 contacts without a single break. Caitlin O'Connell-Rodwell and associates recorded no claims against elephant damage in the village of Lianshulu, Namibia, during 1994 after installation of an electric fence, while there had been about 30 claims over the previous 2 years. They attributed this partly to the relative paucity of bull elephants there; the family groups were more hesitant to risk breaking through the fence. The study at Laikipia, Kenya, also concluded that family groups without a bull were much more likely to be deterred, compared to groups with a bull, bull groups, or solitary bulls, by an electric fence (table 9.2).

The cost of an electric fence can vary from about U.S.$500 per kilometer for a 3- or 4-strand fence using local materials up to U.S.$5,000 per kilometer for an elaborately designed 8–12-m strand fence using imported components. With a basic cost of U.S.$200–$1,000 for a good energizer unit, depending on its sophistication, the average costs per kilometer obviously decline with increasing length of a fence. Privately owned fences of simple design in southern India averaged about U.S.$500 per kilometer, while those installed by government agencies cost about twice this amount for a fence with similar specifications, partly because of labor costs.

Table 9.2
Number of elephant social groups crossing electric fence line outward from a ranch before and after erection of fence in Laikipia, Kenya.

Elephant Social Group	Number of Groups		Number of Individuals	
	Before	After	Before	After
Single bull	88	16	88	16
Bull group	114	48	386	168
Cow/calf/bull	97	17	1,154	161
Cow/calf group	146	12	824	51

Source: Simplified from Thouless and Sakwa (1995). Reproduced with the permission of Elsevier Science.

The early Malaysian fences cost U.S.$1,200 per kilometer. Fence costs are reported as U.S.$500–$1,500 per kilometer in Zimbabwe, while costs in Kenya typically are about U.S.$2,500 kilometer or higher because of the need to import several components. A well-designed, experimental, 2-km fence recently put up in Wyanad in southern India cost U.S.$3,700 per kilometer, with partial labor being provided by the villagers. To the above figures 10%–20% can be added as annual costs of maintenance.

There are few published benefit-cost analyses of electric fences. Based on data on fence costs, efficacy, and damage to oil palm plantations in peninsular Malaysia provided by James Blair and associates during the late 1970s, I computed that every dollar invested in fencing would save $74 over a 5-year period. Such a favorable benefit-cost ratio would apply only to commercial crops.

For Hasanur, a seriously affected village in southern India that I studied during 1981–1982, I further computed that the costs of a two-strand fence could be recovered through savings in crop yields within 2 years, and that the annual losses were about three times the annual costs of fence maintenance. The electric fence at Lianshulu, Namibia, costing U.S.$5,900, resulted in an annual saving of crops worth about U.S.$900 during 1994 based on damage during the preceding 2 years.

We need to keep in mind that the favorable economics of an electric fence during initial years could change substantially once determined elephants learn to break through a relatively simple fence. Although electric fencing seems to have been the most successful barrier against elephants, the economics may not justify a high-end fence. Thouless and Sakwa are thus of the opinion that it may be better to build low-cost fences of simpler design and use these as "no-go" areas, rather than impenetrable barriers, combined with management of elephants that persist in breaking the fence. In parts of Africa, this management could include selective shooting of elephants, while in Asia, this has to be confined mostly to capture.

Given the elephant's highly developed sense of smell, there has been interest in identifying possible chemical deterrents. Some experiments in India with the urine of a large predator such as the tiger in scaring elephants have been inconclusive. The use of a deer repellent named HATE-C4 (developed by a German company) in southern Africa against elephants produced equivocal results. A similar repellent used in the high rainfall areas of northeastern India failed completely.

The most promising results so far with chemical repellents seem to be a capsicum-based irritant developed and deployed by Ferrel Osborn in Zimbabwe. Capsicum (or capsaicin), the chemical ingredient derived from dry, ripe fruits of several species of the genus *Capsicum* (peppers and chilies), is a local irritant to sensory nerve endings, but has no lasting effects on mammals. Osborn conducted several experiments with a 10% oleoresin solution of capsicum that was propelled toward raiding elephants from an aerosol canister. The atomized resin floats in a cloud that remains effective for about 20 minutes after traveling a distance of 50–75 m during light wind conditions. The typical response of an elephant exposed to the spray was to freeze, exhale air audibly, test the air with its trunk, shake its head vigorously, and move away rapidly, often after roaring or trumpeting. The experiments were conducted with elephants in the wild at Hwange National Park and with raiding elephants in agricultural areas of the Gokwe Communal Lands. Positive responses were obtained in 19 of 22 tests conducted at Hwange and in 16 of 18 tests at Gokwe. Because of the difficulties in identifying elephants at night, it was unclear whether any of the elephants exposed to the spray returned at a later time to raid crops. While it has been demonstrated that capsicum possesses short-term repellency toward elephants, more experiments are needed to see if animals can be adversely conditioned to avoid crop fields by this method.

Other delivery systems, such as exploding grenades, packed with capsicum powder, may also be useful under field conditions. It has been suggested that the chemical signals of pheromones could be mimicked (see chapter 4) to lure or scare elephants away from crop fields. Preliminary experiments with temporal gland secretion by M. L. Gorman produced ambiguous results. Ongoing research by Bets Rasmussen on chemical repellents seems to hold some promise.

Apart from traditional noise-making, there have been few systematic attempts to use sounds associated with a certain meaning or that convey fear to elephants. A tiger's call played back through a loudspeaker on a large farm in southern India apparently seems to have deterred elephants. The Maasai people of East Africa have a tradition of young men spearing wild animals, including elephants, as part of pubertal initiation rites. Kadzo Kangwana carried out a series of playback experiments with sounds of Maasai-associated cattle bells and mooing. The elephants responded by raising their heads, smelling the air, and retreating from the direction of the sounds. Clearly, they associated these cattle sounds with the Maasai. Such traditional, fear-invoking practices of people could be adopted locally to reduce depredation. Some observations made recently in Kenya suggest that elephants may be repelled by swarms of the African bee (*Apis mellifera scutellata*). Beehives could thus be deployed by farmers around their farms to deter elephants from venturing inside (Vollrath and Douglas-Hamilton, 2002).

The language of infrasound may also hold promise as a deterrent. Caitlin O'Connell-Rodwell played back natural distress calls of elephants recorded at Etosha, Namibia, to family groups and bulls in the same park. In one set of three trials, the family groups tested fled from the site on all occasions, while in other trials, the herds responded aggressively by surrounding the hide from which the calls were broadcast. Bulls were not disturbed by the distress calls. Clearly, much more work needs to be done to see if effective but cheap deterrents based on sound can be evolved.

The impact of elephants on agriculture and people has been kept under check historically through the elimination of the offending elephants, through either capture or killing in Asia and by killing in Africa. Some of this would have been selective targeting of raiding elephants. Much of this form of elephant population management has undoubtedly been haphazard and wasteful.

The large-scale capture of elephants in ancient times or the slaughter of elephants during the colonial period, ostensibly with the goal of control of problem animals, was indiscriminate toward raiders and nonraiders. Conflict control today undoubtedly requires some management of elephant populations through removal of animals, but on a more scientific basis.

Elephant population management can be considered under two kinds of circumstances. The majority of studies relating to elephant-human conflicts in the two continents have shown that, in the relatively intact habitats with large populations, the subadult and adult male elephants show a much higher propensity to raid crops compared to the female-led groups (chapter 7). Also, in economic terms, a major part of the damage to crops may be attributed to these male elephants in populations in which adult sex ratios are close to natural, and not significantly female biased.

Therefore, I have suggested that, when minimal intervention is desired, the first management option to reduce conflict should be to remove identified, notorious bulls selectively. This would not only reduce crop depredation significantly in the short term and appease farmers, but also usually lower the incidence of manslaughter. From an ecological viewpoint, the demography of the population would not be comprised in a polygynous species; field data clearly show that moderately female-biased sex ratios do not lower the birth rate or the population growth rate. Elephant populations that number in the thousands or several hundreds and are not already heavily female biased can absorb the selective removal of some bulls.

In the Indian state of Karnataka, about 60 "rogue" bull elephants were captured during 1985–2000 from regions where "surplus" bulls were available without making any adverse impact on demography. Four of these died during capture or subsequent transportation, while the rest have been trained and held in captivity. During the initial operations, some of the bulls were released into a national park over 100 km away, but at least two of them returned to the original site of capture.

The option of conflict management through selective removal of bulls is much more limited or not available in most other regions of southern India where poaching of male elephants for ivory has resulted in highly female-biased sex ratios (conflict is incidentally much lower in these regions). This form of management through selective removal of bull elephants has undoubtedly been practiced widely in other parts of Asia and in Africa. Interestingly, the *Arthasastra*, an ancient Indian treatise, prescribed the capture of only tusked, postpubertal bull elephants, the most prudent way of managing an elephant population.

Richard Hoare now believes, however, that when an offending bull is removed, a new "problem animal" soon replaces it; thus, this form of management may have to continue indefinitely. Obviously, we do not fully understand the social dynamics of bull elephants in relation to their raiding behavior.

The most common argument against the selective capture of rogue bull elephants is that these are the best breeders, and that the genetic future of the population would be compromised. First, there is no evidence that crop-raiding bulls are indeed the best breeders even if there is that potential; remember, such individuals would be at risk of injury and elimination at the hands of farmers. Second, there are no reasons to believe that rogue bull elephants have any inherent genetic superiority (higher natural longevity or better resistance to disease, for instance) except perhaps by virtue of their dominance over other bulls. If removed from the population, other bulls could easily replace them for breeding. A genetic argument for nonintervention is weak when applied to large elephant populations in serious conflict with people. Where elephant populations are smaller, in tens or a few hundred, interventionist management should be based on population viability analyses that incorporate both demographic and genetic considerations.

A different situation seems to arise in smaller elephant populations ranging over highly fragmented habitats, such as in central India, where family groups indulge in as much, if not more, raiding than the bulls. The larger home range requirements of family groups, compared to bulls, at least in the short term may be one reason for this increased conflict. If such small elephant groups are in serious conflict and nonviable in demographic terms, the only option would be their removal along with the removal of associated bulls from the area. Even if they have a distinct genetic identity, these elephants are unlikely to contribute to the variation of any larger population in view of their isolation.

In Africa, the only way to remove problem animals has been to shoot them; this is unlikely to change in the near future. In Asia, the option of capturing elephants is available in most countries, although the expertise in taming large bulls is restricted to a few regions, such as southern India and parts of Myanmar. In the case of large bulls with a history of aggressive behavior and manslaughter, their elimination through shooting may be the only practical option in other places. Elephants have been captured in recent times by a combination of traditional methods, such as using trained captive elephants (koonkies) to restrain wild elephants after these are sedated or immobilized with a suitable drug.

A decision whether the captured elephants should be retained in captivity would depend on the local expertise available for training them and the demand for captive elephants. The transfer of captured problematic bull elephants to new locations has generally been a failure in Asia. Such bulls have either traced their way back to their original home range area or, if this has been impossible, continued to be in conflict with people in the area where they were released. In one case, a relocated bull in northern Bengal walked over 100 km back to its original range.

Fewer attempts have been made in translocating problematic family groups because of logistical limitations in Asian countries in handling entire herds. The drive has been the most commonly used method with family herds. There are several examples of successfully driving elephant herds, including very large ones, over distances exceeding 50 km in Sri Lanka, Sumatra, and India, but in the absence of postrelocation monitoring, it is unclear whether any of these elephants came into conflict with people.

Translocation of elephants, either bulls or herds, must therefore be accompanied by monitoring through radiotelemetry to decide on the future course of management. It is necessary to continue experimenting with relocation of elephants, especially herds, to learn more about factors that could contribute to its success.

9.4   *Management of overabundant populations*

The most contentious issue relating to the conservation of African elephants during the 1960s and 1970s was the management of locally overabundant populations. A heated debate raged over the issue of whether such populations should be managed through culling of elephants (fig. 9.5). The spate of ivory poaching that swept through Africa during the 1970s and 1980s put an end to this controversy in many countries. However, it is likely that, with the decline of poaching and better protection in many parts of the species' range, the increasing elephant populations could once again rekindle the debate over culling. While there have been no serious demands for reducing Asian elephant populations on grounds of overabundance, we must keep in mind that elephant densities in parts of southern India are among the highest seen anywhere, while those in southeastern Sri Lanka also are relatively high. Although the killing of elephants in these countries can be ruled out, there could be demands for their capture.

Figure 9.5
A team inspects a group of elephants culled in Zimbabwe's Sengwa Wildlife Research Area. (Photo courtesy of Richard Hoare.)

The arguments for culling African elephants have been articulated at length by observers such as U. de V. Pienaar, Irven Buss, and Richard Laws. Many parts of the savanna elephant's range in eastern and southern Africa had become overstocked with elephants. This was the result of loss of habitat, thereby compressing elephants into smaller areas at higher densities, and of harassment of elephants by poachers and people that caused elephants to seek the relative safety of protected areas.

In former times, low levels of subsistence hunting would have held elephant populations under check, but the setting up of protected areas has altered their demography. At such artificially high densities, the elephants were damaging and killing many tree species at rates that exceeded their regenerating capacities, thereby converting woodlands into grasslands. This vegetation change represented an esthetic loss for the landscape apart from having ecological implications for the elephant populations themselves and for the local biodiversity. The changing nature of the vegetation, from woodland to grassland, would be detrimental to elephants through loss of shade and a shift to a less-nutritious diet of grass.

Work by D.M.H. Cumming and associates showed significant declines in the diversity of birds, ants, and certain other taxa in places where elephants had caused a decline in tree canopy. The landscape changes occurring in many parts of the elephant's range were possibly unprecedented and were a threat to the continued existence of these ecosystems.

The most rational way of managing these ecosystems would be to cull elephant populations (and other large herbivores as necessary) to densities below the carrying capacity of the habitat. This would not only benefit the broader community of plants and animals, but also generate revenues for the local rural economy and for park management. It was foolish to argue that we should let nature take its own course because people had created this situation in the first place, and thus intervention was appropriate. Such management through culling of elephants would help maintain a high rate of animal productivity, utilize rather than waste this production, and ensure the persistence of other biological elements in the landscape.

The counterarguments to culling elephants have been equally strong. The evidence for compression of elephant populations was weak in many regions facing a specter of declining woodlands. Factors other than elephants, such as fire or natural climatic factors, were clearly implicated in tree decline in some places. Natural ecosystem processes, including the long-term dynamics of climate, trees, elephants, and other herbivores, were poorly understood. There was historical evidence, for instance, that the Tsavo ecosystem was in a relatively open state with low elephant numbers at the turn of the twentieth century. Clive Spinage argued that elephant populations were now resurgent after being depressed by exploitation for ivory during the late nineteenth century. In short, there was no need for humans to interfere with the natural course of events through any culling of elephants. Comparisons with wildlife management through culling in North America did not prove anything. Anthony Sinclair aptly summed up this view when he stated that culling was based on "the ridiculous conclusion that the only good herbivore population is one vanishingly small" (1981, p. 255)

Ethical arguments further reinforced the anticulling sentiments. Killing a highly intelligent, sensitive, and social animal, and in such large numbers, was morally repugnant. Elephants that were targeted during culls seemed to transmit the trauma of the event to other elephants in the area before being killed. This was initially a very puzzling observation, but the discovery of infrasound communication solved this mystery. The indiscriminate targeting of elephant family groups also meant that several matriarchs, repositories of traditional knowledge crucial for survival, would be killed, resulting in severe disruption of the fabric of elephant society.

Organized culling of elephants in eastern and southern Africa began during the mid-1960s. One of the earliest culls took place in 1966 at Tsavo National Park in Kenya, but was abandoned after about 300 elephants were killed. This made little impact on Tsavo's huge elephant population. Kenya decided to follow a hands-off policy in managing abundant elephant populations, a policy that came under severe criticism after an estimated 6,000 of Tsavo's 20,000 or more elephants died during the drought of 1970–1971. Many more elephants died in the larger ecological unit, and the effects of the drought continued to result in mortality that was higher than average until 1975. Two culls of similar size were organized in Tanzania's Mkomazi Game Reserve (east and central) in 1968 and 1969, but were again discontinued. Uganda was one eastern African country that went ahead with a major cull in the Murchison (Kabalega) Falls National Park (where about 2,000 elephants were taken) and in the vicinity of the Budongo Forest (where 300 elephants were taken) during 1965–1967. It was another matter that political events in Uganda leading to a civil war resulted in overthrowing any rational management plan for elephants, whose population crashed by 90% from indiscriminate killing. Elsewhere in eastern Africa, poaching for ivory also made it redundant to cull elephants.

Southern African countries, with the exception of Zambia, have a longer history of culling as part of their management of elephant populations. Zambia organized a major cull during 1965–1969 in the Luangwa Valley, where about 1,500 elephants were taken. Culling in Zimbabwe has been widespread across the elephant range, including areas where there has been no perceptible damage to vegetation. Records compiled by Rowan Martin show a minimum of 46,775 elephants killed during 1960–1991, with the most (20,000+) being taken from the Matabeleland North, including the Hwange National Park. About 570 elephants were culled in Namibia's Etosha National Park during 1983–1985. South Africa has a persistent history of culling elephants, primarily in Kruger National Park, where most of the country's elephants are found. The objective of culling has been to keep the elephant population at about 7,000 individuals (density to 0.32 elephants/km^2) with accepted fluctuations between 6,000 and 8,500 individuals in the 20,000-km^2 park. To meet these objectives, an organized culling program has been in operation since 1967;

this program removed about 17,200 elephants during 1967–1996, an annual average of 6.7% of Kruger National Park's elephant population estimated through aerial counts. These figures suggest that about 65,000 elephants have been killed in Africa, mostly in Zimbabwe and South Africa, over a period of three decades as part of controlling populations perceived to be overabundant.

The methods of killing elephants and the end use of the carcasses have varied with region and time. The Ugandan culls were carried out by locating elephant groups from an aircraft and then sending in professional teams, which shot entire families on foot within a couple of minutes to prevent any survivors with traumatic memories of the event. The carcasses were used for a variety of scientific investigations on the biology of elephants. The southern African culls have combined research with an end use for most of the elephant products. In Zambia, the elephants were darted with succinylcholine, a drug that kills by paralyzing the respiratory muscles. Carcasses were transported to an abattoir for hygienic processing of the meat for sale. The drug used breaks down on heating, and thus the meat is safe for human consumption. At Kruger also, elephants have been darted, from a helicopter, with massive doses of succinyl-choline, while ground teams quickly move in to shoot the darted animals. The carcasses are processed in an abattoir, with the meat being shared with the park staff or sold to shops in the vicinity and the skin converted into leather goods. In recent decades, Zimbabwe has linked its elephant culling to the much-publicized CAMPFIRE program under which revenues from hunting are shared with local village councils as incentive for protecting wildlife.

What has been learned so far about managing abundant elephant populations? The African observers agree that the more extreme predictions of irreversible population disaster and desertification associated with abundant elephant populations were without basis. Models of elephant-vegetation dynamics have also pointed to the ineffectiveness of culling elephants as a means of preventing the decline of tree populations (chapter 6). By the time a problem is recognized, any cull has to be of unacceptable magnitude for possible stabilization of the situation. Control of fire or even the giraffe could achieve the objective in some situations, such as for *Acacia* woodlands in eastern Africa. Elephant culls have been based on rather arbitrarily defined carrying capacities. The concept of carrying capacity, while of great theoretical interest in ecology, is rather difficult to apply in field management. This is especially true as even the theory has moved away from equilibrium in ecological systems to a better appreciation of the dynamic nature of ecosystems. Steven McLeod is thus in favor of discarding the concept of carrying capacity in describing plant-herbivore interactions in highly variable environments.

We are also slowly realizing that the problem of overabundant elephant populations can be traced to human intervention, not only through compression, but also through habitat management practices, such as creating artificial waterholes. Based on my observations in southern India, I had pointed out that such provisioning of elephant populations with water could result in artificially high animal densities, much above the carrying capacity set by the vegetation. The high densities would occur through a lowering of dry season mortality rates in elephants, resulting in strongly positive population growth rates (section 9.5). A similar mechanism for the growing elephant population in Kruger National Park, South Africa, has been suggested. Added to this is the intriguing suggestion by Antoni Milewski that reproductive rates of elephants may have been boosted by the high iodine content in artificial bore water supplied to animals in conservation areas of southern Africa. A wildlife management practice that is seemingly beneficial may have inadvertently set the stage for a major management dilemma over the longer term.

There have been few objective analyses of the consequences of culling on elephant populations and their habitats. Ian Whyte, Rudi van Aarde, and Stuart Pimm have made a 1998 assessment of culling in Kruger National Park. There were few elephants in the Kruger region during the early decades of the twentieth century. Five years after the park was proclaimed in 1926, there were believed to be only 135 elephants there. The elephant population increased to an estimated 6,600 in 1967, when culling began, and to 8,800 in 1970. Some of the increase was possibly due to immigration from neighboring Mozambique, but after 1972, this factor was negligible. Although the culls prior to 1984 took place all over the park without a clear plan, the park was then divided into four management units for subsequent culls. The annual quota for the park was taken from only one of these subpopulations during a given year. A demographic analysis of Kruger's elephant population showed significant responses to culls. When year to year changes in elephant densities were examined, these were clearly density dependent, as could have been anticipated from theory. This implied that culls immediately following an estimated high elephant density would be premature; the density would have leveled off or even declined without further intervention. The census data also showed that, when elephant densities exceeded 0.37 individuals/km^2, they generally declined without culling. Thus, many of the culls were unnecessary. Another interesting observation was that, immediately following a cull, the elephant numbers declined locally because of disturbance and emigration, but soon thereafter, they increased again as the elephants moved back into the subpopulation. One suggestion from this analysis was that a subpopulation should be culled only when elephant density exceeded 0.37 individuals/km^2 for more than a year.

The ethical dilemma over culling has also prompted new thinking into means of controlling surging elephant populations. If extra iodine in artificial waterholes is stimulating reproduction in elephants, it may be possible to regulate the supply of iodine through selection of watering points.

Birth control aimed at females is one possible means of regulating an elephant population. The technical development of birth control measures requires a better understanding of the elephant's rather complex reproductive cycle (chapter 3) as well as suitable delivery systems. The options include termination of pregnancy, contraception, and sterilization. Each method has its advantages and drawbacks. The likely effect of any particular method on the health of the individual animal and the possible behavioral consequences must be carefully evaluated.

Inducing a pregnant elephant to abort its fetus may have adverse health effects as well as behavioral changes. Contraception is a more acceptable solution, especially if a method with few side effects can be developed. Steroid hormones have the disadvantage of possible health effects and problems in packing sufficient quantity in an implant of a size that can be delivered remotely into elephants. Some experiments at Kruger with implanting capsules of estradiol-17 resulted in continued high concentration of this hormone, prolonged sexual receptivity, harassment by bulls, and separation or expulsion of these female elephants from their breeding groups.

An immunocontraceptive vaccine causes an animal's immune system to produce antibodies that prevent fertilization, with possibly fewer side effects than steroid hormones. R. A. Fayrer-Hosken and a support team have recently carried out trials at Kruger on 41 adult female elephants identified as nonpregnant with a vaccine developed from the pig's zona pellucida (PZP). Of these elephants, 21 were initially vaccinated, while the other 20 controls received a placebo. All elephants were fitted with radiotransmitters for subsequent monitoring. The vaccinated elephants received booster doses after 6 weeks and 6 months. A year later, 19 of the treated elephants were recaptured and scanned by ultrasound for pregnancy; of these, 9 (47%) were pregnant. By contrast, 16 (89%) of the 18 control elephants that were recaptured were pregnant. In a new set of experiments, 10 elephants received the initial vaccination followed by boosters 2 or 4 weeks later. Only 2 (20%) of these 10 elephants were pregnant after 10 months. This immunocontraceptive vaccine was also shown to be reversible, with no deleterious effects on reproductive cycling, as seen from subsequent pregnancy of some of the vaccinated animals.

If the management objectives are to curb elephant population growth, it is insufficient to develop an acceptable contraception method without understanding the actual logistics of the field operations in relation to elephant demography. The demographic characteristics of elephant populations vary from one region to another and with time. It is important to understand a priori which changes in female fertility will be needed to curb or reverse population growth. An elephant population with an adult female mortality rate less than 3% per annum, an age at first calving of 12–15 years, and an intercalving interval of 4–7 years is most likely a growing population. A slow-growing, long-lived species such as the elephant is more sensitive demographically to changes in mortality rates than in fertility rates. By delaying the age at first calving by a few years and by widening the intercalving interval to the desired level, a growing population will not be curbed for at least a decade. It must also be kept in mind that the age pyramid of a population with reducing fertility will shift toward older individuals, thus maintaining equal or higher biomass with corresponding per capita forage requirements.

All this means that an elephant population under some form of fertility regulation will continue to make an impact on its habitat in the short-term. For Kruger, Ian Whyte and associates have estimated that about 75% of 3,000 reproductively active cow elephants would have to be administered contraceptives to ensure zero population growth. The time lag effects in demography also mean that, with a population growing in the short term, a total of about 4,000 female elephants, and not just 2,250 elephants, may have to receive contraceptives by the time the objective of zero growth is actually achieved. An alternative would be to selectively cull 250 of 300 cows at Kruger that are just about to enter the reproductive age class. This would stabilize the population. The word *cull* could be substituted by *sterilize* to achieve the same end. This would need the development of an irreversible contraceptive. The ethics of such an action should be openly discussed before initiating management action. Fertility regulation in elephants, in any case, should be thought of as a management option with a medium-to-long-term perspective.

9.5   *The management of small versus large populations*

With elephants distributed in several populations with varying sizes, diverse habitats, and different densities, it should be obvious that management strategies should also vary across their range. Trying to conserve an elephant population numbering a few tens calls for an approach very different from that for a population comprising several thousand individuals. Whether a small or a large population, the availability of habitat would determine management strategy. Although the sizes of elephant populations and their habitats represent a continuum, it is useful to consider the management of four situations: a small population with either restricted or nonrestricted habitat and a large population with restricted or nonrestricted habitat.

9.5.1   *Small population with restricted habitat*

A small population with restricted habitat represents the most difficult management situation. Let us assume a population of about 10–50 elephants at a density approaching the carrying capacity of the habitat. Examples of such populations can be found in central India, Sumatra, and West Africa. A fundamental consideration in management would be the low viability of this population in demographic terms, even without accounting for environmental fluctuations or catastrophes. This would be accentuated by the low growth rates of populations under density-dependent regulation. Any mortality due to extraneous factors, such as conflict with agriculture or hunting, would be disastrous for population viability. Such a population is, however, also likely to be in serious conflict with humans for several reasons. Its natural ranging propensities would tend to take it beyond the restricted habitat boundaries. The greater ratio of perimeter to area of the habitat would result in increased contact between elephants and agriculture, resulting in some conflict-related deaths.

However, should such a population be managed? The first option would be to relocate the elephants in a much larger area, perhaps where other elephants are found. There are some examples from Sri Lanka and southern India of "pocketed" elephant groups being moved to other areas by driving them across intervening agricultural areas. If the distances involved are considerable, the drive method will not be feasible. With a small group of elephants, a traditional method of capture, such as the *kheddah* (or drive into a stockade), may still work. Immobilizing the animals in the field with drugs and subsequently transporting them to the release site is the preferred method in the more open African habitats, but it is a logistical nightmare in dense rain forest. The experience with capturing and transporting a pocketed elephant from Vietnam's Tan Phu Forestry Enterprise areas generally has been disastrous, with many elephants dying and the head of the first field operations being killed by an aggressive matriarch. With many small Asian elephant populations, the only option may thus be to capture the elephants for taming.

If the decision is to keep the elephants in the wild, a very proactive management plan has to be put in place. A small population with restricted habitat may have to be insulated completely from any contact with people, agriculture, or livestock to avoid mortality from conflict or transmission of diseases. The habitat will have to be maintained for high productivity of suitable forage as well as adequate water sources to reduce dry season mortality. Systematic monitoring of the population's demography and health status will be needed to detect potential problems and make timely intervention. The issue of a narrow genetic base would still remain, but with restricted habitat, the translocation of individuals would be a difficult choice.

9.5.2   Small population with nonrestricted habitat

A small population with a more extensive habitat has better prospects for in situ conservation, but may present a real management challenge. Examples of such elephant populations include the Cat Tien National Park in Vietnam, the Mondulkiri-Dak Lac region of Cambodia-Vietnam, and even some regions of West Africa, such as Niokola Koba National Park in Senegal or forest reserves in Togo.

The demographic viability of these populations is still in doubt, but at least these enjoy the luxury of surviving at much below the carrying capacity of the habitat, with prospects for growth. Such populations are less likely to be in conflict with people, but this is not guaranteed.

Some of the management options suggested for small populations with restricted habitats could still be explored, but several other options should be actively pursued. There may be possibilities of supplementing this population with animals from elsewhere. Where space is not a major limitation, the "immigrant" elephants would have better chances of settling down and thereby increasing the overall demographic and genetic viability of the population. For purely genetic reasons, the introduction of bulls would suffice. This should be carefully monitored to ensure that social conflict among the resident and introduced bulls does not reduce the demographic or even the genetic viability of the population.

The real management challenge, however, lies in nursing the small population to a larger, viable one. There are historical examples of such recovery of elephant populations. A classic example is that of Addo in South Africa. Hunting had reduced the elephant numbers there to an estimated 11 animals in 1931, when a sanctuary was granted. By 1953, when the 117-km^2 park was entirely fenced to keep the elephants inside, the population was under 20 individuals. From here, the population increased at a phenomenal 7% average annual rate to about 325 elephants by the year 2000.

The first goal should be to identify the factor responsible for reducing the population to its present state. In most cases, this would be capture (of Asian elephants) and hunting. Population recovery can be contemplated only when these systematic factors are eliminated (and not just controlled). Intensive management would be needed to aid the recovery process. Dry season mortality of elephants may be reduced through artificial provisioning of water. If the population is nutrient limited, very likely in some habitat types, it may be possible to enrich the habitat with some of these nutrients. Sodium can be provided through artificial salt licks. The suggestion that bore water is enriched with iodine, a nutrient critical for reproduction, is worth investigating. Controlled burns of ground vegetation could stimulate the growth of protein-rich grasses. Obviously, these needs may be locality specific and must be carefully studied before implementation. If the elephants come into conflict with people, it would be necessary to prevent any deaths of either party. If people are killed, there would be demands for removal of elephants or retaliation; the demographic viability of a small population would certainly be compromised if any elephants are eliminated.

The Cat Tien National Park in Vietnam, where I have recently studied the elephants along with Nguyen Xuan Dang and Surendra Varma, is a typical example of this management scenario. Vietnam's wild elephant population is down to as low as 100 or fewer individuals, found scattered in small groups across the country. Cat Tien National Park has remnants of the country's tropical moist forests, with major portions transformed into secondary growth of bamboo and rattan, partly the result of defoliants used by American forces during war. The park itself is divided into two main blocks separated by human settlements; elephants are confined to the southern Nam Cat Tien (383 km^2). Our surveys in Cat Tien indicate there may be as few as 9 elephants and at most 12–15 elephants here, a population with very low viability. The presence of two adult bulls and some breeding cows, as evidenced from a juvenile and a newborn within the herd, offers a ray of hope amid the dismal scenario. Nam Cat Tien is bordered to its west and to its south by forestry enterprises with about 280 km^2 of secondary forest interspersed with cashew plantations. Thus, about 650 km^2 of potential habitat is available for elephants, an area that can easily hold 100 or more elephants. The present small group is largely confined to the southwest of the park, making extensive use of the secondary forests to the south, the cashew trees for their fruit during the dry season, and agricultural fields that are raided beyond.

Saving these elephants by building up the population to a safer level will be a Herculean task; indeed, Cat Tien would be the ultimate test for the survival of the Asian elephant. Our recommendations are to minimize conflict by erecting an electric fence in the southwest, after allowing the elephants the use of part of the enterprise area comprising secondary forest and cashew plantation. The habitat within the park can also be managed in a manner designed to attract elephants. The elephant population itself has to be closely monitored for its demography and health status.

9.5.3   *Large population with restricted habitat*

A large population close to the carrying capacity of the habitat, without scope for expansion of its range, presents several management dilemmas. The elephants could be rapidly transforming their habitat, as in parts of semiarid Africa, or they could be in serious conflict with agriculture. Examples include the Nilgiris-Biligirirangans region in southern India and several populations in southern Africa. Management of such populations should not encourage further growth through habitat manipulation, but rather aim at stabilizing elephant numbers. I am stating this explicitly because there is often a tendency in wildlife management practice to manipulate the habitat excessively without a clear understanding of its long-term consequences for animal populations. For instance, the density of an elephant population, normally determined by vegetation, may be artificially increased through provisioning of water. Within the elephant's range in southern India, water is impounded not only in small ponds, but also by a large number of dams, with a spread of 5–150 km^2. Water is therefore not a limiting factor; it may actually be excessively available in many parks. This may have lowered dry season mortality, resulting in strong population growth and artificially high densities in places. I mentioned the experience of Kruger in South Africa, where provisioning of water could have influenced the strong population growth.

Abundant populations may be at risk of a crash during periods of serious drought. Such populations are also in conflict with people—a headache for park management. Over the long term, it would be impractical and expensive to prop up an abundant population through artificial means. Therefore, the goal of management should be to allow larger elephant populations to regulate themselves at "natural" densities. The point I wish to emphasize here is that field management of large wildlife populations should allow the evolutionary process to operate with minimal interference. A large population has the luxury of being able to absorb normal environmental fluctuations. Some additional dry season mortality may not be a bad thing; in the medium to long term, this would help stabilize an abundant elephant population apart from ensuring the "survival of the fittest."

9.5.4   *Large population with nonrestricted habitat*

A large population existing at a density much below the estimated carrying capacity of the habitat would be in an envious position. By large, I mean a size that would confer long-term demographic viability on a population. This would be in the range of 1,000–3,000 individuals for elephant populations. There are no known Asian elephant populations in this category, but there are several African ones with numbers, ironically, that have been greatly reduced by poaching. Examples would include the larger elephant ranges in eastern and central Africa, as well as in countries such as Zambia. Such elephant populations at relatively low densities can expand if given protection from poaching. Perhaps this should be the main thrust of management without any additional intervention to stimulate population recovery. In semiarid regions, the populations could still become locally overabundant eventually. This may also be an opportunity to regulate population growth through methods such as contraception.

9.6   *Controlling poaching and the illegal trade in ivory*

It has been clearly established that poaching for ivory poses a major threat to the survival of elephants in Africa, and that poaching for a variety of products has likewise contributed to their sharp decline in many parts of Asia, especially the Indochina region. There is universal consensus that poaching of the elephant has to be controlled, but there is much less agreement whether this can be achieved through a complete ban on trade in ivory. The regulation of the international ivory trade has been a contentious issue during the past two decades. We need to consider objectively how poaching of elephants could be controlled both through law enforcement on the ground as well through regulation of trade in their products.

The manner in which elephants are poached varies considerably from one region to another. Uganda's elephants were indiscriminately slaughtered by soldiers during the internecine strife of the 1970s. In southern India, elephants have been poached opportunistically by small groups of villagers armed with crude firearms such as muzzle-loading guns, as well as by larger, better organized gangs armed with more advanced weapons. Elephants in remote areas of Cambodia's Cardamom Mountains are killed by traditional hunters operating singly or in very small groups. Elephants are still hunted across Indochina by local people using old-fashioned weapons such as poisoned arrows. Law enforcement capabilities also vary widely across the range states. Kenya has a professional wildlife service to manage and protect elephants. South Africa's national parks service holds a tight rein on their elephant populations. On the other hand, vast tracts of rain forest in central Africa are outside the pale of any effective law enforcement agency. Likewise, in Asia, countries such as India have an elaborate network of protected areas, laws, and enforcement agencies trained to manage and protect wildlife, while others have little capability or reach. Thus, there can be no universal solution to combating poachers in the field; each country and region will have to develop its own appropriate models for law enforcement.

Law enforcement in wildlife areas of most Asian countries is usually the responsibility of departments of forestry or wildlife, but limited experiments with police or paramilitary forces have been tried. There are hardly any objective analyses available of antipoaching efforts in Asian regions, although success stories of protecting species such as elephants, tigers, or rhinos do exist for individual protected areas over short time periods in countries such as India. Data on wildlife law enforcement in Zambia's Luangwa Valley have been examined in some detail by two studies that are worth describing in brief.

From about 35,000 elephants around 1975 in the Luangwa, the numbers declined through poaching to 15,000 by 1987, and then to 2,400 by 1998 mainly because of movement of elephants out of the area (about 1,000 elephants were poached). Serious law enforcement efforts began only in 1979. Nigel Leader-Williams and E. J. Milner-Gulland argue, on the basis of data for 1979–1985, models, and crime theory, that improved chances of detecting poachers will be a greater deterrent than will an increase in penalty. In Africa, a potential law breaker is likely to value an uncertain distant future much less than the present or immediate future. A stiff fine is unlikely to be paid. Long prison sentences are not necessarily a deterrent when the future is not valued. A very high penalty is likely to turn a part-time local hunter (of small game) into a more serious hunter of species such as elephant or rhino. Programs to provide alternative economic opportunities are more likely to succeed in weaning away local poachers compared to gangs from outside. Local people, however, may be more likely to provide information to authorities about the presence of poachers from outside, resulting in greater detection and less poaching. With organized gangs, the dealer backing them is rarely caught and may continue to fund more poachers even if gang members are caught. The courts may also place a lower priority on wildlife-related crimes than do the enforcement authorities. Under these circumstances, the primary emphasis should be on improving detection of poachers, with secondary emphasis on achieving stiffer penalties. The severity of penalties should be proportional to the crime (thus, the same prison sentence should not be awarded for killing 1 elephant or 10 elephants).

There are two sides to law enforcement: conventional patrols in the field to deter and detect poachers and investigations to identify and arrest poachers and dealers. In 1988, the Luangwa Integrated Resource Development Project (LIRDP) began law enforcement operations. Poaching of elephants decreased substantially. Examining enforcement data for 1988–1995, Hugo Jachmann and M. Billiouw concluded that investigations were much more effective than foot patrols in curbing poaching (fig. 9.6). Each man-day spent in investigation was equal to 23 man-days of field patrol. Even considering the higher expenses incurred in investigations, the overall relative efficiency of investigations over patrols was fourfold. Statistical analyses showed that cash rewards, density of patrol scouts, number of investigation days, emoluments to personnel, and total enforcement budget were positively related to a decline in elephant poaching. Jachmann and Billiouw computed the optimum levels of enforcement in Luangwa as one scout per 24 km^2 and expenditure of $82 per km^2, lower than a more general estimate made earlier of $200/km^2 for African parks. They concluded that variations in elephant poaching during 1988–1995 in Luangwa could be explained merely by resource allocation without having to invoke the international ban on ivory trade.

Some of these observations in Zambia would also apply to Asian countries, such as India, that suffer from poaching of elephants. India has fairly elaborate law enforcement capability, including the institutional framework and manpower spread. Rates of detection of poaching can be said to be moderate to high. Yet, the detection, arrest, and successful conviction of poachers are quite low. Financial resources are limited in some states, but this does not seem to be the main reason for deficiencies in antipoaching efforts. A serious problem

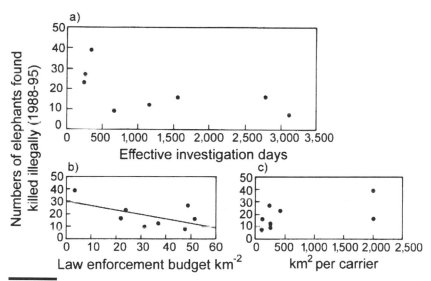

Figure 9.6
The effectiveness of law enforcement in the Luangwa Valley, Zambia, expressed as the relationship among (*a*) number of effective investigation days and elephants found killed; (*b*) total law enforcement budget (U.S. dollars) and elephants found killed (note that the predicted budget for zero elephants found killed is $82/km^2); carrier (i.e., those taking supplies for scouts) density and elephants found killed. (From Jachmann and Billiouw 1997. Reproduced with the permission of the British Ecological Society.)

seems to be inadequacy of investigation and prosecution capabilities. I have long advocated the strengthening of intelligence for identifying dealers of illegal ivory and capabilities for investigation and prosecution of offenders in southern India, in addition to increasing field patrolling efforts.

Control of poaching is much more challenging in countries such as Myanmar, Laos, and Cambodia, where the reach of enforcement agencies is much more limited. In Asia, the need for greater involvement of local communities in protecting wildlife is being increasingly recognized. The Asian models of community involvement in antipoaching efforts will have to be different from African models, which emphasize wildlife harvest and utilization.

9.6.1   Regulation of the trade in ivory

If the consumer demand for raw ivory and ivory products were to be met largely through the supply of legal ivory (i.e., tusks from elephants dying naturally or from the occasional trophy hunting), there would have been no need for elaborate controls on trade. At the peak of the recent wave of poaching during the 1980s, it was estimated that 80% of tusks shipped from Africa were illegal. Similarly, at least two of three Indian elephant tusks used by carvers (who also used imported African elephant tusks) in southern India at this time came from poached elephants. The regulation of trade in ivory, with all its complex dimensions, has thus become central to conservation strategies for elephants. Each country has its own laws and regulations on the local sale and possession of tusks or ivory articles. Most African countries permit local trade in ivory, as do several Asian countries. India is one of the few elephant range states to impose a total ban on all internal trade in ivory, including carvings, although possession is allowed through a permit.

The international trade in ivory and other elephant products is officially regulated by the Convention on International Trade in Endangered Species of Wild Fauna and Flora (CITES), which came into force in 1975. The convention has established lists of species under various "appendices," categorized according to differing perceived threats as voted on by its member states. Thus, species listed under Appendix I, considered the most endangered species, may not be traded internationally for commercial purposes, while limited trade is permitted for those under Appendix II as long as the trade is not detrimental to the survival of the species. The Asian elephant was straightaway placed in Appendix I, thus banning all international trade in its products. It was only in 1977 that the African elephant was placed in Appendix II, which regulated trade in its ivory under a system of quotas and licenses.

It soon became clear that these limited CITES controls on the international trade in African ivory had failed to stem the rising tide of elephant poaching in Africa. In fact, implementation of CITES controls by states such as Hong Kong, a major player in the trade, may actually have triggered a temporary sharp rise in the price of ivory, providing even greater incentive for poaching. The slaughter of elephants across the continent continued, as seen from the large volume of tusks being exported and reports from the field on carcasses and encounters with poachers.

Many countries exporting or importing ivory managed to use loopholes in CITES regulations and enforcement to trade in tusks that were clearly illegal. For instance, Burundi, a country without elephants, was issued ivory export documents that fulfilled CITES requirements. Large volumes of what could only have been illegal ivory went out of this country before the leak was plugged. Traders also took advantage of other loopholes in moving ivory between Japan and Hong Kong.

A global campaign to completely choke the trade in ivory now began to gather momentum. A defining movement in this campaign was perhaps the burning of 12 tonnes of confiscated tusks worth U.S.$3 million by the Kenyan president in July 1989 at a well-publicized event. The campaign culminated in the African elephant being transferred to Appendix I of CITES at the October 1989 Conference of the Parties (COP).

Following this complete ban on the international ivory trade, the price of raw ivory crashed by up to 90% in parts of Africa and about 50% overall in outside markets. The incidence of poaching also decreased sharply, giving African elephant populations a much-needed respite. The price of African ivory did recover partly after the initial shock of the ban, but with a very wide variation across the continent, and in outside markets, it is difficult to draw any general conclusions. There have been sporadic reports during the 1990s of a rise in poaching on localized scales, but the situation can in no way be compared to the previous two decades.

Several southern African countries—Zimbabwe, Botswana, Namibia, and South Africa—that have managed their elephant populations well, with very little impact from poaching, had been campaigning for at least partial lifting of the ban to allow them to trade in ivory and other elephant products. In June 1997, the CITES Conference of Parties (COP) voted at Harare to transfer the elephant populations of these southern African countries back to Appendix II with a one-time sale of 60 tonnes of ivory from Zimbabwe, Botswana, and Namibia to Japan the following year. Sales were not permitted at the COP in 2000, but during the COP at Santiago in 2002, three countries—Botswana, Namibia and South Africa—received the necessary votes to sell 60 tonnes of ivory during 2004 after they and the purchasing countries satisfy the CITES conditions.

There are opposing views on the international ban in trade of African elephant ivory and other products. While an outright ban is strongly favored by many conservationists and governments, others have argued for controlled trade. These views are examined next, as are the possible implications of the African ivory trade for Asian elephant populations.

9.6.1.1   Pro-trade arguments

Those who favor limited trade in ivory point to the wide variation across Africa in the status of elephant populations and incidence of poaching. Elephant populations in southern African countries, particularly Botswana, South Africa, and

Zimbabwe, are healthy ones that are expanding at a high rate and are subjected to very little pressure, if any, from ivory poaching. For example, Zimbabwe's elephant population more than doubled by 1995, from an estimated 33,000 in 1960, in spite of culling. Even if there were to be little or no culling, considerable quantities of tusks would continue to be retrieved from elephants dying of natural causes. These countries badly needed the revenues from ivory sales for boosting the local economy, for supporting community-based conservation projects, and eventually for financing the protection of elephants. An outright ban on international trade in ivory would penalize such African countries that have efficiently managed their elephant populations, a counterproductive strategy.

The underlying philosophy was simple—wildlife in parts of Africa will have to pay for itself if it is to survive. A mere ban in trade is no guarantee that a species would survive. The two species of African rhinos had been placed in Appendix I of CITES since 1976, but had declined extensively due to poaching for horn, with the black rhino nearly hunted to extinction.

Economics is obviously central to the trade in ivory. A key question is how this could be harnessed in a fashion to allow legitimate aspirations of producers and consumers to be met without endangering the elephant itself. The only published work on the economics of the ivory trade is that of Edward Barbier, Joanne Burgess, Timothy Swanson, and David Pearce. This team was part of the preban assessment produced by the Ivory Trade Working Group that recommended a complete ban, although the Barbier et al. team had a differing view. Fully recognizing the earlier limitations of CITES in curbing illegal trade in ivory, Barbier and colleagues are in favor of "a very limited trade in ivory, designed to maintain the incentive to sustained management in the southern African countries and to encourage other countries to follow suit." They otherwise fear that the trade would merely be driven underground. According to them, "The ivory trade is a 'game' in which there are many players, all with individual motives and concerns. Failure to capture those motives and concerns in an international agreement inevitably risks no agreement or its eventual breakdown" (1990, pp. xi–xii)

After discussing the reasons for failure of several preban CITES regulations, such as the Management Quota System, Barbier and colleagues present their own proposals based on economic theory for effective regulation of the ivory trade. A workable system of international regulation would involve the correction of "investment deficiencies" or reasons for the failure of producer nations to invest in the maintenance of elephant numbers, as well as setting up an "enforcement system" that deters possible attempts by individuals or nations to circumvent the system.

The economic reasons for the steep decline in elephant stocks were not difficult to understand. In Africa itself, the future is much less valued than the present ("a high discount rate") given the social and demographic conditions. Thus, any additional wealth is much more valuable today than in the future.

The decision whether to maintain current stocks of elephants or convert them into other forms of assets would be influenced by the dissipation and capture of rents (profits) from elephants. The rents from sale of ivory are widely dispersed across individuals and governments, including local poachers, chieftains, local dealers, international traders, officials, government agencies, and so on. Compared to the value of raw ivory in a consumer nation such as Japan, the sums that accrue locally to individuals or states are usually very low. Thus, a harvester of tusks in central Africa may only capture 10% (under U.S.$10/kg in 1985) of the value of raw ivory (under U.S.$100/kg) in Japan. A major part of the rent is captured by external traders. Even the putative owners of the assets, the elephant range states, may capture only a small fraction of the rent. This created the conditions for uncontrolled exploitation of elephants. Only a country such as Zimbabwe, with a government that organized the collection and sale of ivory, captured about 70% of the rent; this is perhaps a benchmark for other range states to emulate.

The solution to these problems may lie in the channeling of all rents from the sale of ivory through a single controller. A joint marketing arrangement for ivory, along the lines of, say, the oil-producing nations, would be in the economic interest of the range states. This would eliminate the traders or middlemen, who otherwise would capture most of the benefits. The demand for ivory ("demand elasticity") is relatively nonresponsive to price in Japan, the major consumer nation (as with the price of oil here). Such a marketing agreement can only succeed if the consumer nations are willing to monitor and enforce the agreement for the producers. In the case of ivory, it would clearly be in the interest of a consumer nation such as Japan to provide the enforcement mechanism.

One of several kinds of financial and marketing systems could be used to implement such an arrangement. An annual ivory quota for each state based on elephant population and sustainable offtake could be the basis for an "ivory currency" system distributed among them. Consumer nations would be charged with ensuring that counterfeit currency (ivory) is not imported. A substantial difference in price between certified ivory (higher) and uncertified ivory (lower), arising out of consumer nations investing in monitoring, would also provide the incentive for sustainable management of elephant stocks by the producers.

An alternative system could be the establishment of an "ivory exchange" that would take in ivory from producers only in sustainable quantities, and consumers could enter into purchasing arrangements. An "ivory tax" could also be imposed by consumer nations for redistribution to the range states in accordance with their elephant stocks and degree of sustainable management. This would be an incentive for the range states to conserve their elephant populations.

Any ivory trade regulatory mechanism would need methods to detect illegal ivory. While some of these could be built into the documentation associated with the trade, enforcement authorities have also been looking toward means of identifying the source of ivory. For instance, how does one distinguish between Asian and African elephant ivory or identify the geographical origin of a particular shipment of African ivory?

In 1990, the results of two studies, one led by Nikolaas van der Merwe and the other by J. C. Vogel, that used isotope discrimination in elephant ivory and bone appeared in the same issue of the prestigious journal, *Nature* (fig. 9.7). The principle behind the isotopic method is quite simple (see chapter 5). The ratios of stable isotopes of elements such as carbon, nitrogen, strontium, and lead in animal tissue reflect the diet of the animal and provide an imprint of its habitat. Thus, stable carbon isotope ($^{13}C/^{12}C$) ratios reflect the proportion of C_3 (browse) and C_4 (grasses) plants in the diet, nitrogen isotope ($^{15}N/^{14}N$) ratios are related to rainfall and environmental water stress, and strontium isotope ($^{87}Sr/^{86}Sr$) and several lead (Pb) ratios reflect local geology. The first group analyzed collagen for carbon, nitrogen, and strontium isotopes from ivory and bone samples across 10 African countries representing all regions with the exception of central Africa, while the second group also added lead isotopes, but confined their survey to southern Africa. Obviously, no single elemental isotope ratio is able to differentiate between elephant populations, but the discriminatory power increases as more elements are added. From the stable isotopes of carbon and nitrogen, they were able to differentiate several populations across the continent, although considerable overlap also occurs when all the 20 populations sampled are considered simultaneously. The addition of strontium isotopes provided additional ability to distinguish some populations whose carbon and nitrogen isotope values overlapped. The study in southern Africa used multivariate statistical analysis incorporating carbon, nitrogen, strontium, and lead isotopes to achieve more robust discriminatory power, but it remains to be seen if this holds across the continent.

Research is also under way on the possible use of molecular genetic differences among populations for ivory forensics. This would have to involve building up a reference library of DNA profiles from both nuclear and mitochondrial genes of elephant populations (chapter 1). When the source of any consignment of tusks is in question, it may be possible to obtain minute quantities of tissue from scrapings at the basal portion for molecular amplification and matching with the DNA library. Sometimes, it may be impossible, of course, to obtain DNA from tusks or from worked ivory.

Both the isotopic and the genetic methods have their limitations. They depend on sophisticated science and technology that are expensive. The discriminatory power of the methods has not yet been proven; thus, some ambiguity would always remain.

9.6.1.2   *The antitrade arguments*

The opposition to any international trade in ivory comes from conservationists and administrators who are skeptical that any regulatory mechanism would work in practice. The preban trade in African ivory was characterized by a complete breakdown of law and order in some countries; lack of field enforce-

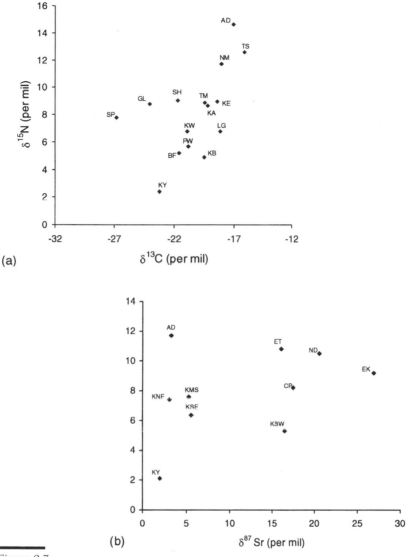

Figure 9.7

Plots of isotope ratios in collagen from elephant bone or ivory in different regions of Africa. Values are expressed in standard notion (per mil). All isotope values are mean values for the population computed from the sources. (*a*) Stable carbon versus stable nitrogen isotope values in collagen for elephants at AD (Addo, South Africa); BF (Burkina Faso); GL (Gola, Sierra Leone); KA (Kasane, Botswana); KB (Kasungu, Malawi); KE (Kruger East, South Africa); KW (Kruger West, South Africa); KY (Knysna, South Africa); LG (Luangwa, Zambia); NM (Namibia); PW (Park W, Niger); SH (Shimba Hills, Kenya); SP (Sapo, Liberia); TM (Tembe, South Africa), and TS (Tsavo, Kenya). (Based on van der Merwe et al. 1990.) (*b*) Strontium versus stable nitrogen isotopes in collagen of elephants at AD (Addo, South Africa); CP (Caprivi, Namibia); EK (East Kaokoveld, Namibia); ET (Etosha, Namibia); KMS (Kruger Mid-South, South Africa); KNE (Kruger NE, South Africa); KSE (Kruger SE, South Africa); KSW (Kruger SW, South Africa); KY (Knysna, South Africa); and ND (North Namib Desert, Namibia). (Based on Vogel et al. 1990.)

ment capabilities; corruption at various levels, including the highest ones of government; inability of CITES to regulate or even to monitor all but a small fraction of the trade volumes; and ineffective controls by the consumer nations to detect illegal ivory.

Iain Douglas-Hamilton's continentwide survey of African elephant populations, poaching, and the illegal ivory trade clearly brought out the chaotic and corruption-ridden situation that prevailed in many countries prior to 1989. There was no reason to believe that the situation would be any better if trade in ivory were to resume, even partially. From an administrator's perspective, Richard Leakey (former head of the Kenya Wildlife Service) argues that any spurt in poaching resulting from opening of the trade would take much-needed resources and attention from infrastructural development. The opponents of trade also point out that the complete ban had caused ivory prices to crash, significantly reduced demand, and rendered the African range states a far safer place for elephants.

Andrew Dobson and Joyce Poole thus questioned the basis of the economic analysis of the ivory trade by Burgess and colleagues, who advocated controlled trade as the best option for elephants. There was no reason to "believe that an illegal, unmonitored trade might cause prices to rise faster than a legal, monitored trade" (1992, p. 151) The high cost of sophisticated isotopic or genetic analysis, even if technically feasible, to back up a controlled trade would actually result in high costs for the legal trade. This would make it possible for dealers offering cheaper illegal ivory to invade the trade.

The laundering of illegal ivory is a danger that many campaigners against the trade emphasize. Even Japanese conservationists like Hideo Obara and Masayuki Sakamoto contend that the country does not as yet have adequate management and enforcement capabilities for a controlled ivory trade. It is impossible to trace certified ivory from its source to the finished form given the several thousand ivory retailers in Japan. Vivek Menon and Ashok Kumar, two leading observers of the illegal wildlife trade in Asia, also fear that even partial opening of legal trade in African ivory would provide the opportunity for Asian ivory, the trade of which has always been banned under CITES, to be laundered. Even if safeguards for legal trade were in place at higher levels of transaction, the message percolating down to lower levels of the trade would be quite diluted, resulting in an upsurge in poaching.

The economics of "sustainable offtake" of elephants through culling has also been questioned. Richard Leakey estimates that, given a maximum sustainable offtake of 3% of the elephant population, the southern African countries at best could expect revenues of only about U.S.$3 million per year. These profits are insignificant in relation to the costs of antipoaching efforts that may be needed if the trade is opened.

Many international conservation organizations have also argued at forums such as CITES that the ivory could easily be purchased by donors and destroyed. They also point to potential revenue loss from tourists, who on ethical grounds may stay away from wildlife parks and countries that practice culling as part of their management. The value of tourism in Kenya, which does not practice culling, has been estimated at U.S.$375 million per year during the 1980s, with the tourism value of its elephant population alone being U.S.$25 million. The culling of elephants for generating revenue through trade in ivory is thus seen as a very shortsighted option.

9.6.2   *The trade in Asian ivory*

The illegal trade in Asian elephant ivory is obscured by its much smaller quantities in the markets compared to African ivory (remember, only male Asian elephants may have tusks, and the overall elephant population in Asia is only one-tenth that of the African species). It is virtually impossible at present to distinguish Asian ivory from African ivory; only a few expert carvers seem to have this ability. Hence, any discussion of the international trade in ivory has almost entirely focused on African ivory and ignored its implications for the Asian elephant and trade in its tusks. Market surveys of the ivory trade in Asian countries do not differentiate between Asian and African ivories on sale, although it is clear that much of the ivory in countries such as Myanmar, Thailand, Laos, Cambodia, and Vietnam comes from local elephants.

The relationship of the illegal trade in Asian ivory to the much larger (potential) trade in African ivory thus has a bearing on the conservation of the Asian elephant. There are several theoretical possibilities of the relationship between the two sources of ivory in the trade. Any rise in the appetite of consumers for ivory would be reflected in increasing flows in laundered Asian ivory, even though the bulk of the supplies could still continue to be of African origin. Thus, the flow of Asian ivory would closely track that of African ivory. There could be a certain preference for Asian ivory, based on its perceived or real superior qualities, hence, there would be a steadier demand for this ivory compared to that for the African product. There could also be a certain minimum demand for ivory, irrespective of source or legality, in consumer nations. Any shortfall in supply of African ivory could result in increased demand for Asian ivory and hence put more pressure on the Asian elephant. The domestic demand for ivory in Asian range states could also drive the trade in relation to the availability and price of imported African ivory.

No clear answers are available as to which of these links may be driving the trade in Asian ivory. One point that emerges is that a price difference has always existed between Asian ivory (in the Indian and East Asian markets) and African ivory (in the international market), the former being more expensive. I noted that, during the period after Indian independence in 1947, the landed cost of imported African ivory became progressively higher due to stiff customs duties, even though a plentiful supply was cheaply available outside the country. The large number of Indian carvers thus began to utilize both legal ivory from Indian elephants (supplied by the government) as well as to obtain tusks from locally poached elephants at rates cheaper than landed African ivory. They also continued to import some legal African ivory, which could then be used as a cover for the illegal Indian ivory being traded. This could at least partly explain the poaching of Indian elephants during the 1970s and 1980s. The Indian government, of course, has banned the internal trade in Indian ivory since 1986 and banned the import of African ivory or its local sale once the 1989 international ban came into effect.

The detailed survey of the Asian ivory markets by Vivek Menon and Ashok Kumar also brought out a little known fact: Ivory from Asian elephants was considered superior in Japan for manufacturing *hankos* and thus commanded a higher price. Japanese carvers were able to distinguish various grades of African and Asian ivory, primarily on considerations of its degree of "softness" or "hardness." Asian hard ivory was considered to possess the best qualities for ink absorption and delivery by the signature seals. Even though there is no scientific basis as yet for differentiating the physical characteristics of modern ivory, any such perception of quality by the trade would be reflected in pricing and eventually in poaching pressures on regional populations.

This suggests that a certain quantity of Asian ivory would continue to be smuggled into Japan. At the same time, the possibility of a rise in demand for illegal Asian ivory if supplies from Africa dry up cannot be ruled out. Clearly, a thorough analysis of the dynamics of the trade in Asian ivory is urgently needed.

9.6.3   What is the future of the ivory trade?

Recent years have seen a sea change in the attitude toward the use of ivory, unprecedented in history. A quarter of a century ago, perhaps no one could have anticipated that the international trade in tusks would grind to a halt, threatening the centuries-old ivory culture. From the simple ornamentals and figures fashioned out of mammoth tusks by the Upper Paleolithic people to the intricate carvings of the Asian masters in more recent times, the expression of art through the medium of ivory has been celebrated through history. Today, the ivory carver has all but disappeared in India, the Chinese carver has to rely on smuggled ivory to continue the profession, and even the Japanese *hanko* manufacturer is uncertain about the future supplies of raw ivory. Almost overnight, the use of ivory in any form is socially frowned on in most Western countries. What then is the future of the ivory culture, even the more genuine one supported by legal raw material? Is a ban on the international ivory trade really necessary? Will the trade be merely driven underground as a consequence, or will it die out eventually?

My views are that the shock treatment to the trade in ivory meted out by the international ban of 1989 was essential in the battle against poaching of African elephants. There is little doubt that the crash in ivory prices and demand soon after the ban and the sharp reduction in poaching have given many African elephant populations a fresh lease on life. Any attempt to reopen the trade within "one elephant inter-birth interval," in the words of Dobson and Poole, could potentially have been disastrous for many populations if it had succeeded. The consequences of the ban for Asian elephant populations are more equivocal.

At the same time, a more pragmatic, longer-term strategy for the trade in ivory has to be worked out. As elephant populations rebound in Africa and elephants die of natural causes, the stocks of ivory in the range states would continue to rise. It is unlikely that most countries would follow the Kenyan example of destroying all ivory stocks, as urged by some conservationists. After the initial shock, the price of raw ivory has recovered to a certain extent in Africa, although it is still depressed compared to the 1989 preban prices. The availability of ivory in the markets of nonrange African states suggests that it still moves across borders in defiance of the ban. Some ivory is still being shipped illegally from Africa to East Asia, as seen from the regular seizures at various places en route. The local ivory markets in Southeast and East Asian countries still continue to do business, some of this undoubtedly of illegal ivory of African and Asian origin. The price of Asian ivory rules firm in the local and international markets, while Asian elephants continue to be under pressure from poachers.

There seems to be no let up in the demand for *hankos* in Japan. While this can be partly met by preban stocks held in the country, the Japanese ivory traders and manufacturers would presumably be actively seeking raw material in the coming years (there are a minimum of 12,000 and maybe up to 50,000 ivory retailers in Japan). Attempts could be made to lower the demand for ivory products through public awareness campaigns; some Japanese conserva tionists are already active in this role.

One problem is the perception, especially since the early 1970s, of raw ivory as a valuable commodity that could be stored as a hedge against inflation. Investors in the prosperous Middle Eastern and East Asian countries have done just that in recent times. The Middle East, especially Dubai, has emerged as a transit and storage point for both African and Asian ivory being smuggled to East Asia. The growing economies of East Asia, in particular that of China, can also be expected to create new markets for ivory in the coming years. The ban has only partly destroyed the economic value of ivory. These are the reasons why synthetic substitutes for ivory have satisfied a few consumers, just as imitation gold has not replaced the demand for real gold.

Concurrently, the demand for partial opening of the ivory trade, especially by the southern African countries, will be voiced at every meeting of CITES. There is a real danger that some African countries might disengage from CITES if continually thwarted from selling their ivory stocks in the international market. One experiment in allowing a controlled transfer of ivory from southern Africa to Japan has already been carried out, with seemingly no adverse impact on elephant populations (although some may dispute this). Another experiment is underway after the vote at the COP in 2002. CITES has embarked, with the technical assistance of the IUCN's Species Survival Commission, on a program of monitoring the illegal killing of elephants (termed MIKE) in the two continents to look at its relationship, if any, to decisions on trade. At the same time, CITES and TRAFFIC-International have also set up a monitoring system for the illegal ivory trade (termed ETIS, or Elephant Trade Information System). These are essentially long-term monitoring mechanisms that cannot necessarily be expected to provide clear answers to decision making by the CITES COP in the short term.

It is highly likely that more experiments in "controlled trade" of ivory will be tried in the near future under CITES sanction. Perhaps a more objective analysis of the links between the ivory trade and poaching of elephants will emerge as this process of trial and error is used in the coming decades. It is important that these experiments are not costly and do not adversely impact elephant populations. There are obviously no easy answers to the dilemma of regulating the ivory trade.

9.7   Management of elephants in captivity

There are fewer than 1,000 African elephants in captivity, most of them in Western zoos. These constitute only a tiny fraction of the total population of *Loxodonta*, estimated at under 500,000; thus, the sustainable management of the captive stocks is not of immediate concern. The IUCN/SSC African Elephant Specialist Group has also indicated that this is not a priority issue for the conservation of the species.

On the other hand, about one-third of all Asian elephants are held captive, mostly in the range states, but also in significant numbers in zoos, circuses, safari parks, and other facilities around the world (fig. 9.8). An estimated 14,500–15,000 *Elephas maximus* are in captivity in the range states, chiefly Myanmar (over 5,000, with about 2,700 held by the Myanma Timber Enterprise and the rest mainly privately owned), Thailand (3,500–4,000), India (about 3,500), Laos (1,100–1,350), Cambodia (over 300), Sumatra (362), Sri Lanka (227), Nepal (171), and Vietnam (165). These elephants are scattered across different facilities—logging camps, nature reserves, village communities, temples, training centers, zoos, tourist resorts, and even individual households. Asian elephants are also kept in zoos and circuses across North America (350–400), Europe (nearly 500), Japan, Australia, and elsewhere. Given the historical trend of the captive stocks of elephants being generally a drain on wild populations, the management of captive elephants in Asia obviously has a bearing on the conservation of the species. The IUCN/SSC Asian Elephant Specialist Group thus recognizes this issue to be of major concern.

There are several issues relating to the management of captive elephants. From a purely demographic viewpoint, it may be important to maintain a self-sustaining captive population, with births balancing deaths overall. Other issues, such as methods of capture, training, and husbandry pertain to the general welfare of this highly social, intelligent animal. Finally, we must consider whether the captive elephant has a future and, if so, what could be its utility to the conservation of the species.

Figure 9.8
Captive elephants kept in social groups in Asian timber camps such as this in
Myanmar (*top*) usually show a better demographic record and need much less
investment than those kept in western zoos (*bottom*).

Captive elephant populations, through history, have never been self-sustaining. The reason for this has mainly been the paucity of breeding, although a high death rate during the process of acquisition, training, and use has also been responsible. The lack of breeding under most captive situations is due to practical difficulties of elephant management, especially of bulls, even under traditional systems. When bulls are in musth (see chapter 3) and are most likely to mate with cows in estrus, they are segregated and restrained because of their heightened aggression and refusal to obey commands. Elephants are kept solitary in many situations, such as when they are under private ownership or kept in a temple. Temples in the southern Indian state of Tamilnadu prefer to keep only female elephants. The famous temple at Guruvayoor in the neighboring state of Kerala is known for its stock of over 50 tusked male elephants. Obviously, breeding cannot occur under such situations. Even when male and female elephants are kept together, such as in logging or forest camps, the reproductive ability of a cow may be compromised by a heavy workload and poor nutrition.

Western zoos have invested in expensive physical barriers of elaborate design to maintain adult bull elephants. Even so, it may be difficult for them actually to breed elephants because of social incompatibility between a bull and the cows. Most zoos prefer not to keep bull elephants because of attendant risks, but send their cows to other facilities for breeding. The zoos also suffer from problems of infertile cows, the reasons for which are not fully known. Even when there is a successful birth, there is a distinct risk of rejection or even killing of the calf by the mother. Such aberrant behavior may be related to the inexperience of the mother, which has been raised solitarily or never observed another elephant giving birth. Much of postnatal behavior of the mother in this highly social animal could be learned behavior in the wild; a captive situation may not provide this enrichment. Zoos in North America also have had a preponderance of male calves over female calves, the opposite of the desired outcome.

While breeding is necessary to maintain self-sustaining populations of elephants in captivity, the survivorship of these elephants has not received sufficient attention. A stable population in demographic terms, after all, is a matter of births balancing deaths. Fewer births are needed to maintain a constant population size in situations in which captive elephants have high survivorship.

I looked at records of several captive elephant populations and found that only those held in seminatural situations, such as forest camps, are usually permitted to feed in the nearby forest at night when wild bulls may mate with cows in estrus. Mating also occurs between captive bulls and cows. Several cow elephants in these camps have lived beyond 60 years, including three cows that lived to 75–79 years, virtually unthinkable in a zoo. The captive elephants held in forest camps by the southern Indian states of Tamilnadu and Karnataka have shown an annual fecundity rate of about 0.1 per adult female during the twentieth century and 0.16 per adult female during the period

1969–1989. Given the relatively high survivorship rates (fig. 7.5), this population could maintain a low growth rate with the lower fecundity rate and a strong positive growth rate with the higher fecundity rate seen in recent decades.

Khyne U Mar has analyzed the records from the Myanmar timber camps (see notes to chapter 7, section 7.2). She reports reproductive rates that are under 0.1 per adult female per year, but given the large captive stock of elephants, a substantial number of calves are born. The survivorship rates are also lower than those in southern India. The timber elephants of Myanmar have been declining at a slow rate under the prevailing birth and death rates. While this decline has been blamed on insufficient breeding, a small change in the survivorship rate through improved health care and husbandry could help achieve the broader objective of a stable population size.

In contrast to the Asian forest camps, elephants in Western zoos are declining at an alarming rate as a result of low birth and high death rates. The North American zoo population of Asian elephants, for instance, is intrinsically declining at about 8% per year. Victoria Taylor and Trevor Poole have compared these situations through a questionnaire survey. They found that only 34% of adult females in the zoos have given birth at least once compared to about 90% or more in Asian forest camps. Further, the low fecundity rate (<0.05 adult female per year), a high rate (25%) of stillbirths, and high juvenile and adult mortality all contribute to the intrinsic decline. Fred Kurt believes that the overweight condition of captive elephants in zoos, by as much as 33%–78% compared to wild elephants, is responsible for much of the reproductive and disease problems. Ultrasonographic examination of zoo elephants by Thomas Hildebrandt and associates revealed that uterine tumors and endometrial and ovarian cysts were responsible for disruption of the estrous cycle. The incidence of such pathologies increased sharply from age 30 years onward, with a corresponding decline in reproduction. Similar examination of male elephants showed much lower incidence of pathologies even in older animals, although semen quality varied widely in ejaculates collected from the same bull and different bulls. Social factors seem to influence the breeding status of these bulls.

Research in Western zoos for nearly two decades on artificial insemination finally succeeded with the birth of an Asian elephant calf in November 1999 at the Dickerson Park Zoo in Springfield, Missouri. Since then, there have also been the births of several African elephant calves conceived through artificial insemination, while six more African cows were pregnant at zoos in North America and Europe (in May 2002). The use of ultrasound technology, which allows the monitoring of the insemination catheter for proper placement of the semen in the female's reproductive tract, has contributed to the successful conceptions.

In the management of captive elephants, equally important issues relating to their training, welfare, and husbandry must be considered. Traditional systems of training and husbandry vary widely across Asian countries and regions.

Some of these systems clearly have undesirable elements that inflict unnecessary cruelty on this highly intelligent animal. Similar issues continue to plague zoos, in which elephants are often confined within small spaces. The Western zoos have also been debating the "protected contact" versus "free contact" system of managing their elephants.

It is beyond the scope of this volume to go into a more detailed discussion of these issues. While there cannot be a uniform system for managing elephants globally, it is imperative that minimum standards for their welfare are developed based on scientific principles. Richard Lair has long advocated the registration of all captive elephants, both in range states and outside, as the first step toward preparing a global plan for their management. Implanting microchips that can be read electronically is one option for marking and registering elephants, although this may be impractical in many parts of Asia. India has begun the process of marking captive elephants with microchips.

What is the relevance to conservation of the captive elephant today? A charismatic animal such as the elephant, which appeals to the sentiments of people, obviously has the potential to act as an ambassador of goodwill and to raise funds for its own conservation as well as for the conservation of other creatures that share its habitat. The birth of an elephant calf in a Western zoo increases visitor numbers and revenue as few other animals do. Zoos have the potential for educating the public not only about elephants, but also about the broader conservation issues. The sacredness associated with the elephant in some Asian countries has undoubtedly contributed to its survival in the wild. I doubt if the elephant would have survived in relatively large numbers in a densely populated country such as India but for its sacred connotations. Thus, elephants kept in temples or participating in cultural or religious festivities can reinforce this sentiment of sacredness among the people. Research on captive elephants has also helped in understanding the biology of the species, especially relating to reproduction and diseases.

However, I think that the captive elephant has a more direct role in the management of wild elephants in Asia. The management of elephant-human conflict can be greatly facilitated through the use of trained captive elephants for chase or capture of marauding wild elephants. Captive elephants can also be used for patrolling protected areas and other forest habitats to deter poaching. The traditional role of elephants in logging has declined in many Asian countries. The ban on logging in Thailand, imposed in 1989 after devastating floods in the country, led to a crisis for captive elephants employed in this industry. The familiar spectacle of the "street elephants" of Bangkok and Chiang Mai, used for begging or to greet visitors to hotels, has been widely reported by the media. In India, the timber elephant also is largely a phenomenon of the past, but the animal has been partly absorbed into other roles, such as tourism in wildlife parks. Only in Myanmar has the timber elephant retained its original character along with the traditional skills of *mahouts* in handling the animals.

There is also the possibility of captive elephants going back to the wild. Such natural experiments have undoubtedly occurred several times in history with a successful outcome. Over large areas in Southeast Asia, there is still sufficient habitat, but a lack of elephants. A major hurdle to reintroducing captive elephants into the wild is the risk that these animals may come into conflict with human settlements. In recent times, one experiment with releasing seven captive elephants (six adult females and one 2-year-old male) into Thailand's Doi Phameung Wildlife Sanctuary produced promising results. More such experiments are needed to evaluate the feasibility of restocking natural habitat with some of Asia's large numbers of captive elephants. When hand-reared elephant calves are to be reintroduced into the wild, under experimentation at Tsavo in Kenya, several precautions have to be taken. They have to be brought up in an environment with minimum contact with humans, especially visitors, and encouraged to learn wild-type behaviors, possibly through contact with wild elephants. The comparative behavior of captive and wild elephants has to be understood before reintroduction programs can be undertaken on a larger scale.

9.8   *Concluding remarks*

The conservation of elephants in Asia and in Africa presents challenges that are central to the broader ecological or social issues in the conservation of landscapes and biodiversity. By saving elephants, we would also conserve a significant proportion of representative landscapes and biodiversity in these two continents. By resolving elephant-human conflicts through the active participation of local communities, we would also be reassuring rural people that they do not have to bear the entire opportunity costs of conservation. The dichotomy in the so-called Northern versus Southern perspectives on conservation or the preservationist versus the utilitarian approaches to conservation is perhaps nowhere as glaring as with elephant conservation. Rigid, dogmatic attitudes at either end of such dichotomies are not necessarily serving the cause of either conservation or of impoverished people. We should recognize that human cultural and value systems are diverse, and that a balanced, pragmatic approach to conservation would be in the best interests of elephants. Only then can we ensure that the living elephants do not follow the path of their Pleistocene relatives.

Appendix 1
Status and Distribution
of Elephants

Asian elephants

The Asian elephant (*Elephas maximus*) is found in the wild in 13 countries across
South and Southeast Asia (table A1.1). More details are available in the action

Table A1.1
Status of Asian elephant populations.

Country	Area of Range Country (km²)	Area of Elephant Range (km²)	Population Estimates Minimum	Maximum
1. India	3,287,590	110,000	26,390	30,770
South		(39,500)	(13,000)	(15,000)
Central		(23,500)	(2,400)	(2,700)
Northwest		(5,500)	(750)	(1,000)
Northeast		(41,000)	(10,200)	(12,000)
Islands		(500)	(40)	(70)
2. Nepal	141,400	>2,500	100	125
3. Bhutan	46,600	1,500	250	500
4. Bangladesh	147,570	1,800	150	250
5. China	9,579,000	2,500	200	250
6. Myanmar	678,000	115,000	4,000	5,000
7. Thailand	513,115	25,500	2,500	3,200
8. Laos	236,800	>20,000	500	1,000
9. Cambodia	181,035	>40,000	250	600
10. Vietnam	340,000	>3,000	70	150
11. Malaysia	329,750	45,000	2,100	3,100
Peninsular	(131,598)	(>20,000)	(1,000)	(1,500)
Sabah	(80,520)	(>25,000)	(1,100)	(1,600)
12. Indonesia	1,919,440	105,000	2,400	3,400
Sumatra	(524,100)	(>100,000)	(2,400)	(3,400)
Kalimantan	(550,200)	(<5,000)	(?)	(?)
13. Sri Lanka	65,610	>15,000	2,500	4,000
Total	17,465,910	486,800	41,410	52,345

The regional figures in parentheses are inclusive of the figures for the country (in the case of
India, Malaysia and Indonesia).

plan of the IUCN/SSC Asian Elephant Specialist Group (Santiapillai and Jackson 1990), which is in the process of being updated. The distribution map (fig. A1.1) is modified from Sukumar and Santiapillai (1995) and can be accessed on the Web at http://iucn.org/themes/ssc/sgs/asesg, as well as at www.asiannature.org.

African elephants

African elephants (the savanna elephant, *Loxodonta africana africana*, and the forest elephant, *Loxodonta africana cyclotis*) are found in 37 countries in the continent, with the savanna elephant distributed over eastern, southern, and western Africa and the forest elephant confined to central and parts of western Africa. The distribution map (fig. A1.2) and the population estimates (table A1.2) are taken from the database of the IUCN/SSC African Elephant Specialist Group, which can be accessed on the Web at http://iucn.org/themes/ssc/sgs/afesg/aed/aed98.html.

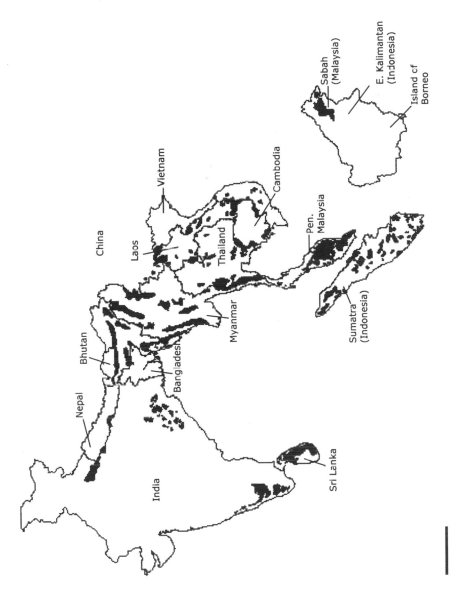

Figure A1.1
Distribution of Asian elephant populations.

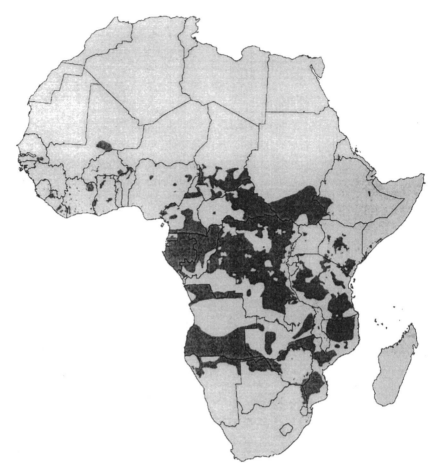

AfESG

African Elephant Database of IUCN/SSC/AfESG
in collaboration with UNEP/GRID

UNEP

Figure A1.2
Distribution of African elephant populations.

Table A1.2
Summary of African elephant estimates on the continent (1998).

Region	Country	Number of Elephants				Total Area (km²)	Range Area (km²)
		Definite	Probable	Possible	Speculative		
Central Africa	Cameroon	1,071	5,285	8,704	675	475,440	229,195
	Central African Republic	2,515	1,600	6,605	8,000	622,980	314,274
	Chad	0	0	1,600	300	1,284,000	219,310
	Congo	0	0	0	0	342,000	255,373
	Democratic Republic of Congo	3,736	20,219	5,618	120	2,345,410	1,476,560
	Equatorial Guinea	0	0	0	80	28,050	14,559
	Gabon	0	0	7,500	54,294	267,760	263,306
	Total	7,322	27,104	27,613	63,469	5,365,550	2,772,397
Eastern Africa	Eritrea	2	0	0	0	121,320	2,967
	Ethiopia	321	0	0	985	1,127,127	59,717
	Kenya	14,364	11,350	4,882	100	582,650	112,988
	Rwanda	39	0	20	10	26,340	1,019
	Somalia	0	0	130	120	637,660	11,783
	Sudan	0	0	0	0	2,505,810	404,908
	Tanzania	67,416	12,196	12,078	0	945,090	458,315
	Uganda	215	565	1,662	280	236,040	11,872
	Total	83,770	22,698	17,216	1,495	6,182,037	1,063,569

Table A1.2
(Continued)

Region	Country	Number of Elephants				Total Area (km²)	Range Area (km²)
		Definite	Probable	Possible	Speculative		
Southern Africa	Angola	0	0	0	170	1,246,700	678,785
	Botswana	76,644	13,414	13,414	0	600,370	81,486
	Malawi	647	1,569	1,649	20	118,480	7,968
	Mozambique	6,898	1,946	4,496	0	801,590	467,062
	Namibia	6,263	1,421	1,421	0	825,418	145,015
	South Africa	11,905	0	0	0	1,219,912	25,847
	Swaziland	39	0	0	0	17,360	188
	Zambia	15,873	6,179	6,694	0	752,610	208,123
	Zimbabwe	63,070	8,034	10,185	0	390,580	109,563
	Total	196,845	17,057	22,623	190	5,973,020	1,724,037
West Africa	Benin	0	0	400	0	112,620	13,036
	Burkina Faso	1,616	606	1,486	0	274,200	18,198
	Ghana	476	218	1,185	443	238,540	30,202
	Guinea	0	0	108	140	245,860	2,277
	Guinea Bissau	0	0	0	35	36,120	331
	Ivory Coast	51	0	495	645	322,460	35,543
	Liberia	0	0	0	1,783	111,370	22,003
	Mali	0	0	950	50	1,240,000	37,024
	Niger	0	0	817	100	1,267,000	2,694
	Nigeria	157	0	860	236	923,770	34,383
	Senegal	9	0	11	10	196,190	8,428
	Sierra Leone	0	0	0	0	71,740	2,914
	Togo	0	0	96	0	56,790	5,430
	Total[1]	2,489	644	6,228	3,442	5,096,660	212,463
	Total Continental Estimates	301,773	56,196	60,780	68,596	22,617,267	5,777,466

Appendix 2
Statural Growth in Elephants

Observers have long recognized differences in the body sizes of elephants from various regions in Africa and in Asia. Apart from the very obvious size difference between the African forest elephant (*Loxodonta africana cyclotis*) and the savanna or bush elephant (*Loxodonta africana africana*), the latter also comes in varying sizes across the continent, the smallest ones approaching the forest elephant in stature. Data compiled by Phyllis Lee and Cynthia Moss (1995) for the African savanna elephant show that the asymptotic heights of females vary from as short as 232 cm at Amboseli, comparable to or even somewhat smaller than the Asian elephant (*Elephas maximus*) in Sri Lanka (Ceylon) and India, to as much as 300 cm at Hwange in Zimbabwe. In Asia, there also is a range of sizes, with the elephants in Sumatra and in Borneo being the smallest, although precise growth data are not available. The oft-repeated statement that the African savanna elephant is larger than the Asian elephant is only true for the males of the two species. Interestingly, the female Asian elephant in Sri Lanka and the mainland is heavier than its African savanna counterpart in most regions, even if the latter is on average taller.

Statural growth in an animal is the product of its genetic makeup as expressed under the influence of resources available in its environment. The environmental influence is possibly more important in determining the dynamics of growth, especially from birth well into adulthood. We know that Asian elephants kept in Western zoos, in which they are provided a high-nutrient diet but little physical activity, grow much faster than do their wild or tame counterparts in the range states. Fred Kurt (1995) observed that the zoo elephants not only grow faster, but also are 33%–78% heavier than captive animals of similar height in Asian timber camps. It is conceivable that levels of nutrition available for wild elephants would also determine their growth rate on both a seasonal or interannual basis and over their life span. Thus, wet season growth can be expected to be greater than dry season growth in highly seasonal habitats. Elephants in tropical rain forest may also be relatively smaller in size because forage is widely dispersed and of poorer quality compared to forage in dry forest and savanna.

Lee and Moss explained the variation in adult body size across savanna elephant populations as reflecting genetic differences and perhaps the past history of hunting, which was selective against larger-size animals. Explanations for adult body size differences among elephant populations can also be sought from considerations of life history evolution (chapter 7). In fluctuating environments, the seasonal regimes of resource availability or interannual variations would favor larger body size, which can endure fasting during the dry season or a drought year. The larger body size of elephants in the climatically fluctuating and highly seasonal semiarid habitats compared to those in the more stable and aseasonal tropical moist forest is in line with this expectation.

Size difference between the sexes is generally considered to be the outcome of selection favoring a larger body in males of polygynous species (chapters 3 and 4). While male and female calves seem to be similar sized at birth in both Asian and African elephants, differences in growth rate between the sexes become obvious by age 2–5 years, although one study at Etosha found a divergence in growth curves between the sexes only after 10 years (Lindeque and van Jaarsveld 1993). At about 10 years, when the elephants may be at the threshold of puberty, the male is distinctly taller and heavier than the female. There are hints of a secondary growth spurt in male African (Laws et al. 1975) and Asian (Sukumar et al. 1988) elephants during the postpubertal years, but this is by no means established as it has not been seen in any other elephant population for which growth has been studied. Female elephants attain their maximum height by age 20–25 years, but continue to gain weight for another 5–10 years. Male elephants reach their asymptotic height by 25–30 years, although growth in body weight may continue well beyond 40 years. The tusks of male elephants keep growing throughout their life span.

Mathematical functions of growth in elephants

There are several mathematical expressions that can represent the growth in body size of an animal. A polynomial function, for instance, can provide a purely empirical fit to growth data, but lacks analytical capability. Two sets of functions, the Gompertz functions and the von Bertalanffy functions, have been extensively used to study growth in vertebrates. The von Bertalanffy functions, in particular, are considered particularly suitable for representing growth in elephants.

The general form of the von Bertalanffy function is

$$S_t = S_\infty (1 - \exp^{-K(t-t_0)})^M$$

where S_t is the size at time t, S_∞ is the asymptotic size (the maximum an animal can attain), K is the coefficient of catabolism (a fitted constant representing the catabolism of body materials per unit weight and time), t is the age of the animal, t_0 is the theoretical age at which the animal would have zero size (this constant is usually an artificial one), and M is the power of the function.

For growth in body length or height, the equation used is

$$L_t = L_\infty (1 - \exp^{-K(t-t_0)})$$

The cubic form of the function best represents growth in body weight:

$$W_t = W_t (1 - \exp^{-K(t-t_0)})^3$$

The von Bertalanffy functions have been applied to aspects of growth in several African savanna elephant populations and in one Asian elephant population. I provide the growth parameters from each of these populations, along with supplemental information on allometric relationships for variables such as height-weight, height-foot dimensions, tusk growth, and so on.

Murchison (Kabalega) Falls, Uganda

Richard Laws and his team (Laws and Parker 1968; Laws et al. 1975) were the first to use the von Bertalanffy functions for describing statural growth of elephants, using data from the culled sample at the Murchison Falls National Park in Uganda.

Growth in shoulder height

Male (birth to 20 years): $h_t = 265 [1 - \exp(-0.114(t + 3.95))]$ cm
Male (21 years and older): $h_t = 307[1 - \exp(-0.166(t - 10.48))]$ cm
Female (all ages): $h_t = 252[1 - \exp(-0.099(t + 6.0))]$ cm

Growth in body weight

Male (1–20 years): $W_t = 3,112[1 - \exp(-0.114(t + 3.95))]^3$ kg
Male (older than 20 years): $W_t = 4,742[1 - \exp(-0.166(t - 10.48))]^3$ kg
Female (older than 2 years): $W_t = 2,744[1 - \exp(-0.099(t + 6.0))]^3$ kg

As the Murchison Falls elephants were believed to be in relatively poor condition at the time of sampling, it was suggested that the "optimal" asymptotic weights were 5,314 kg for male and 2,986 kg for female elephants.

Height-weight relationship

Males (Murchison South): $W = 0.000507\ h^{2.803}$
Males (Murchison North): $W = 0.000306\ h^{2.890}$
Females (Murchison South): $W = 0.001267\ h^{2.631}$
Females (Murchison North): $W = 0.000258\ h^{2.917}$

Luangwa Valley, Zambia

Growth of the Luangwa Valley elephants was analyzed by John Hanks (1972a).

Growth in shoulder height

Males (1–30 years): $h_t = 451[1 - \exp(-0.025(t - 11.84))]$ cm
Females (1–55 years): $h_t = 249[1 - \exp(-0.097(t - 6.36))]$ m

Growth in body weight

Males: $W_t = 5,970[1 - \exp(-0.045(t + 9.77))]^3$ kg
Females (all ages, both pregnant and nonpregnant): $W_t = 2,740[1 - \exp(-0.066(t - 10.48))]^3$ kg

Lower asymptotic weights were obtained when pregnant and nonpregnant females were analyzed separately.

Shoulder height–body weight relationship

Females: The best fit was obtained by a linear regression of log body weight w versus shoulder height h: Log $w = 0.007h + 1.73$

Tusk growth

For length of exposed tusks in females, the following equation is provided: $L_t = 85[1 - \exp(-0.038(t + 1.34))]$ cm. The actual length may be shorter due to tusk wear. For circumference of tusks at the lip line, Hanks provides a plot of the data for males and females, but has not fitted any function to these data.

Amboseli, Kenya

The growth functions at Amboseli, Kenya, are provided by Phyllis Lee and Cynthia Moss (1995).

Growth in shoulder height

Males (younger than 20 years): $h_t = 270[1 - \exp(-0.0967 (t - 4.37))]$ cm
Males (all ages): $h_t = 304[1 - \exp(-0.0713(t - 5.34))]$ cm
Females (younger than 20 years): $h_t = 236[1 - \exp(-0.122 (t - 4.04))]$ cm
Females (all ages): $h_t = 232[1 - \exp(-0.128(t - 3.98))]$ cm

Hind foot length f and shoulder height h relationship

Males: $h = -10.22 + (5.82f)$
Females: $h = 3.04 + (5.47f)$

Etosha, Namibia

Growth in the elephants of semiarid Etosha was analyzed by Lindeque and van Jaarsveld (1993).

Growth in shoulder height

Males: $H_t = 336.89[1 - \exp(-0.07(t + 6.67))]$
Females: $H_t = 262.84[1 - \exp(-0.13(t + 4.05))]$

Tamilnadu and Karnataka, India

Based on growth records of Asian elephants born in captivity or captured from the wild at a relatively young age (younger than 8 years for males and younger than 10 years for females), the following growth functions are provided by Sukumar (1985) and Sukumar et al. (1988).

Growth in shoulder height

The von Bertalanffy function for elephants of all ages does not give a
good fit for very young elephants. For ages 0–2 years, a simple linear regression gives an adequate fit for male and female elephants,
while for older elephants, the von Bertalanffy functions are more appropriate.

Males (0–2 years): $H_t = 92.35 + 27.68t$ cm

Females (0–2 years): $H_t = 92.06 + 27.16t$ cm

Females (3–60 years): $H_t = 256[1 - \exp(-0.133(t + 3.58))]$ cm

Captive males (0–15 years): $H_t = 236[1 - \exp(-0.182(t + 4.82))]$ cm

Captive males (15–60 years): $H_t = 259[1 - \exp(-0.124(t + 2.84))]$ cm

Captive females (0–15 years): $H_t = 215[1 - \exp(-0.133(t + 3.58))]$ cm

Captive females (3–70 years): $H_t = 232[1 - \exp(-0.140(t + 3.85))]$ cm

Captive females (15–70 years): $H_t = 232[1 - \exp(-0.266(t - 6.13))]$ cm

Wild elephants: The above functions were fitted to data for elephants
born in captivity or captured from the wild at a relatively young age
(younger than 8 years for males and younger than 10 years for females). Data from elephants captured after these ages and attaining
maximum heights plus estimates of heights of wild elephants using
field techniques suggest higher asymptotic heights (274 cm for
males and 240 cm for females). Although specific von Bertalanffy
functions could not be generated for wild elephants, these could be
fitted by eye or by substituting the higher H_∞ values in the functions
derived for captive elephants.

Growth in body weight

Captive males (2–60 years): $W_t = 3,255[1 - \exp(-0.149(t + 3.16))]^3$ kg

Captive females (2–70 years): $W_t = 3,055[1 - \exp(-0.092(t + 6.15))]^3$ kg

Wild elephants: From the relationship between weight and height, the asymptotic weight of 3,255 kg of captive male elephants corresponds
to a height of 258 cm. As wild bulls grow, on average, to a height of
274 cm, the predicted asymptotic weight would be about 4,000 kg.
For captive female elephants, the asymptotic weight of 3,055 kg can
also be used for wild females as there was no evidence for reduced
growth in body weight in captivity.

Shoulder height-body weight relationship

A linear regression of cube root of body weight (in kilograms) on shoulder height (in centimeters) gave a better fit than did a semilog plot
of these variables.

Males: $W = [(0.057h) + 0.114]^3$ kg

Females: $W = [(0.060h) - 0.335]^3$ kg

Shoulder height *H*–circumference of front foot CFF relationship

Males and females (all ages): $H = 2.03CFF$

Tusk growth in males

The circumference of tusks at the lip line (CTLL) showed the following
relationship to age *t* in years. For captive males 2–25 years old, this
gave a good fit, and the relationship could also be extrapolated to
wild bulls above this age.

$CTLL_t = 43.3[1 - \exp(-0.064\,t)]$ cm

The growth in tusk weight with age could be plotted from its relation-
ship with CTLL as follows: Tusk weight $= [(0.0715 \times CTLL) - 0.0888]^3$ kg. This results in a sigmoid growth curve.

Notes

This book is written in a style to make it easy for the reader to trace the source of most of the material presented by checking the names of authors mentioned with the reference section. There may be some difficulty in pinpointing a specific reference when a particular author has several articles. These notes are intended to guide the reader more specifically to the sources for various sections in a chapter. While the reference section lists only books, journal articles, doctoral dissertations, and published conference proceedings that are readily accessible, the notes contain additional references to material such as conference abstracts or presentations, unpublished reports, institutional reports, newsletters, master's theses and, in some cases, data kindly made available to me by researchers.

General

The elephant has obviously been the subject of a large number of books catering to different audiences. The selections I list are the more scientific or substantive ones, including personalized accounts of the research of elephant biologists and certain large-format pictorial volumes. The works by Carrington (1958) and Sanderson (1962) are very readable accounts of the natural history of elephants and their relationship to people. Sikes (1971) was possibly the first to provide a technical account of the biology of (African) elephants. Laws, et al. (1975) and Buss (1990) detailed their pioneering research on African elephants in Uganda during the 1960s. The former especially provided much of the basic biological details of elephants for the subsequent African studies. Douglas-Hamilton and Douglas-Hamilton (1975), Hanks (1979), Moss (1988), Poole (1996), and Payne (1998) wrote engaging accounts of their work with African elephants. My early research of Asian elephant ecology was published as a scientific volume (Sukumar 1989a), as well as a popular account (Sukumar 1994a). The pioneering studies by scientists of the Smithsonian Institution on Asian elephants in Sri Lanka (Eisenberg and Lockhart 1972, McKay 1973) were reprinted along with a report by Seidensticker (see Notes 9.3) as a single volume (Eisenberg et al. 1990). Two more recent volumes, one by Daniel (1998) and the other by Lahiri-Choudhury (1999), have likewise brought together very useful pieces of the early literature on Asian elephant natural history, much of it written by hunters.

Eltringham (1982) provided a concise technical overview of the ecology of both African and Asian elephants. Spinage (1994) interwove anecdotal information with the more scientific studies in his descriptive account of the biology of elephants. Among the large-format pictorial books, I would recommend the multiauthor edited volumes of Eltringham (1991) and Shoshani (1992b). Several others on the market focus on the African elephant and are mainly pictorial. A lavishly illustrated recent volume by Gröning and Saller (1998), however, covers considerable ground, from evolution to biology and the cultural history of elephants.

Chapter 1

Sections 1.1–1.8   Work by Osborn (1936, 1942) remains the most comprehensive source of descriptions of fossil proboscideans as a whole, while Maglio's work (1973) is the most detailed account of fossil elephants (family Elephantidae). The edited volume by Shoshani and Tassy (1996a) should be consulted for the most recent information on the evolution of the proboscideans. The reader may also wish to consult earlier reviews on the subject by Aguirre (1969) and Watson (1946). Deraniyagala's work (1955) contains descriptions of elephant material from Asia, especially Sri Lanka. Popular accounts of proboscidean evolution by Shoshani are available in the volumes edited by Eltringham (1991) and by Shoshani (1992b).

The descriptions of geological climate and vegetation change are based largely on the work of Janis (1993). The account of proboscidean evolution through the ages is based on several articles in Shoshani and Tassy (1996a), including the following references from 1996: Agenbroad and Mead, Caloi et al., Dudley, Fisher, Lister (1996a), Roth, Saunders, Shoshani et al., Tassy, Todd and Roth, and Van den Berg et al. Other specialized articles or reviews to which I referred for this chapter are those by Barry et al. (1985), Beden (1983), Cerling et al. (1997), Chakravarti (1957), Court (1993), Hooijer (1972), Gaeth et al. (1999), Gheerbrant et al. (1996), Koch et al. (1989), Lister (1989, 1996a, 1996b), Lister and Sher (2001), Mahboubi et al. (1984), Quade et al. (1992), Sukumar et al. (1993), Tassy and Shoshani (1988), Turner (1995), Vartanyan et al. (1993), and West (1980). Koch's isotopic study of late Pleistocene proboscideans is also available as an abstract in the *Journal of Vertebrate Paleontology*, **11** (Supplement 3), 40A, 1991. Lister and Bahn (1994) provided a good general account of mammoth evolution for the nonspecialist.

The term *mastodont* is sometimes used to encompass both the mammutids and the gomphotheres, but I have used this term in very few places (such as this chapter title) to avoid confusion with the mastodon (refers to only one mammutid—the American mastodon). I have used the term *African elephant(s)* to encompass both living subspecies of *Loxodonta* (*L. africana africana* and *L. africana cyclotis*).

The work of Martin and Klein (1984) still remains the most comprehensive collection of articles on the late Pleistocene extinctions. Individual articles (all 1984) to which I have referred in this volume include those of Gingerich, Graham and Lundelius, Guthrie, Kiltie, Martin, Webb, and Whittington and Dyke. Haynes (1991) carefully examined the fossil record for evidence of Pleistocene hunting. MacPhee and Marx (1997), Miller et al. (1999), Mosimann and Martin (1975), and Owen-Smith (1987) are other articles on this subject.

The dates given for fossils during the late Pleistocene are usually radiocarbon dates, which differ from calendar dates. In most cases, the calendar age is older than the radiocarbon age by 10% 20%. A radiocarbon date of 10,600 years is thus about 12,250 years in calendar age.

Section 1.9   The phylogeny and molecular genetics of the elephants were based on the work of Fernando et al. (2000), Fleischer et al. (2001), Georgiadis et al. (1994), Hartl et al. (1996), Lowenstein and Shoshani (1996), Nyakaana and Arctander (1999), Thomas et al. (2000), and Whitehouse and Harley (2001). The unpublished data for Sumatra, Malaysia and Borneo of P. Fernando and D. Melnick were presented at the Sixteenth Annual Meeting of the Society for Conservation Biology (SCB) held at Canterbury, U.K. in July 2002. The unpublished data from the southern Indian populations were also presented at the same SCB 2002 meeting by T.N.C. Vidya, P. Fernando,

D. Melnick and R. Sukumar. The Bkm 2(8) DNA probe shows extensive restriction fragment length polymorphism in various eukaryotes and is therefore an efficient probe for genetic fingerprinting; the data from Asian elephants are unpublished results of T. Purohit, R. Sukumar and L. Singh (1999).

The case for two species of African elephants has been in the literature since the early twentieth century, when P. Matchie described the forest elephant in the year 1900. For instance, Sanderson (1962) treated the savanna and the forest elephant as distinct species. Based on morphological measurements, a case was presented in the January 2000 issue of *Elephant* (a publication of the Elephant Research Foundation) in two articles by Groves and Grubb (2000), and Grubb et al. (2000). An article by L. Tangley (In search of Africa's forgotten forest elephant. Science 275, 1417-1419, 1997) had hinted at the existence of more than one species of Loxodonta. The genetic evidence for two species of *Loxodonta* was finally presented by Roca et al. (2001), while a more complex taxonomy was suggested by Eggert et al. (2002).

IUCN/SSC refers to the World Conservation Union/Species Survival Commission. The decision of the IUCN/SSC African Elephant Specialist Group to retain the traditional classification of two sub-species of Loxodonta has been reported in page 19 of the January-July 2002 issue of *Species*, the newsletter of the SSC. I have therefore decided to treat the African savanna elephant and the forest elephant as sub-species in this volume.

Chapter 2

The "dare theory" of domestication was applied to the elephant by Baker and Manwell (1983). The major source for this chapter, especially the historical antecedents of Ganesha, was the collection of articles in Brown (1991c). The ones I found especially useful are those by Brown (1991a, 1991b), Dhavalikar, and Narain. Other useful materials on Ganesha are the scholarly books by Getty (1936), Ghurye (1962), and Courtwright (1985) and the popular book by Jagannathan and Krishna (1992). The quotation from O'Flaherty was taken from her foreword to Courtwright (1985).

For ancient Indian history, I used the work of Thapar (1966) and Basham (1967). The term Aryan refers to the "Indo-European speaking people"; it is thus a language or cultural label and should not be confused with race.

The paleoenvironment of South Asia was reviewed by Erdosy (1998). The paleo-ecology of southern India is based on Sukumar et al. (1993). Opinion is divided on the role of climate change in the decline of the Indus Valley Civilization. Enzel et al. (1999) now present evidence suggesting that a period of aridity set in around 4800 years ago in northwestern India, at least 800 years prior to the collapse of this civilization.

Other important sources for this chapter are the works of Digby (1971), Harris (1978), Lahiri-Choudhury (1991a, 1999), Prakash (1961), Achaya (1994), MacKenzie (1987), Rangarajan (2001), and Trautmann (1982). References to the elephant in the Sangam literature have been compiled by E. S. Varadarajaiyer (*The Elephant in the Tamil Land*, Annamalai University, Tamil Nadu, India, 1945). There are now several translations of the *Arthasastra*; the one I used is the most recent of these by L. N. Rangarajan (1992). A good introduction to elephants during Mughal times is the work of Ali (1927). S. Moosvi's estimate on captive elephants during Mughal times was presented at a symposium ("Call of the Elephant") held at the Indian Museum, Kolkata (August 18–19, 2001).

Scullard's (1974) account of the use of elephants in Greek and Roman times was also the main source for the history of captive elephants in Africa. Ansell (1971) suggested that the elephants of North Africa, now extinct, represented a distinct sub-species *Loxodonta africana pharaohensis*. The quotation by J.-A. Shelton was taken from a presentation she made at a workshop ("Elephants: Cultural, Behavioral, and Ecological Perspectives") held at the University of California, Davis (October 26–28, 2000). P. Martin's observations were made in a BBC *Horizon* television program in 1996. Ross's 1992 work is an illustrated collection of articles dealing with the relationship between elephants and people in Africa.

Chapter 3

Several texts on animal behavior deal with the ecological consequences of a polygynous mating system. The definition of polygyny was taken from the work of Shields (1987). Darwin's observations on this subject are found in *Descent of Man and Selection in Relation to Sex* (1871). Descriptions of the anatomy of reproductive systems in elephants are available in the work of Sikes (1971), in the edited volume of Mikota et al. (1994), and in several papers listed below.

Section 3.2   The account of estrus in female elephants is based on the work of Bechert et al. (1999), Brannian et al. (1988), Brown and Lehnhardt (1995), Brown (2000), Brown et al. (1991), Chappel and Schmidt (1979), de Villiers et al. (1989), Eisenberg et al. (1971), Greyling et al. (1997), Hanks (1972b), Hanks and Short (1972), Heister-mann et al. (1997), Hermes et al. (2000), Hess et al. (1983), Hodges (1998), Hodges et al. (1994, 1997), Jainudeen et al. (1971), Kapustin et al. (1996), Krishnan (1972), Laws (1969), Laws et al. (1975), McNeilly et al. (1983), Moss (1983), Niemuller et al. (1993, 1997), Perrin and Rasmussen (1994), Perry (1953, 1964), Plotka et al. (1975, 1988), Ramsay (1981), Rasmussen et al. (1982, 1996b), Short (1966), Smith et al. (1969), Smith and Buss (1975), Taya et al. (1991), and Watson and D'Souza (1975).

Section 3.3   The discussion of musth, its behavioral ecology, and male elephant reproduction are based on the work of Cooper et al. (1990), Gale (1974), Hall-Martin (1987), Hanks (1973), Jainudeen et al. (1972), Lahiri-Choudhury (1992), Laws et al. (1975), Lincoln and Ratnasooriya (1996), Niemuller and Liptrap (1991), Poole (1987, 1996), Poole and Moss (1981), Poole et al. (1984, 1988), Rasmussen et al. (1984, 1996a, 2002), Short et al. (1967), Slotow et al. (2000). Nilakanta's *Matangalila* was translated by F. Edgerton (1931). A. Desai's observations on musth in Asian elephants were presented at a symposium in 1993 and are available as an abstract in Daniel and Datye (1995). L. Wingate and B. Lasley's observations on musth were presented at a symposium (Is musth a reproductive event: An examination of arguments for and against this view, pp. 150-156 in A research update on elephants and rhinos: Proceedings of the international elephant and rhino research symposium, June 2001, Vienna, Austria).

Section 3.4   The discussion of sexual selection and mate choice in elephants is based on the work of Anderson (1991), Averianov (1996), Fisher (1958), Folstad and Karter (1992), Freeland (1976), Gadgil (1972), Grafen (1990a, 1990b), Hamilton and Zuk (1982), Laws (1966), Maynard Smith (1982), Parker and Rubenstein (1981), Poole (1989a, 1989b, 1999), Poole and Moss (1989), Sukumar et al. (1988), Watve and Sukumar (1995, 1997), Zahavi (1975), and Zahavi and Zahavi (1997). A follow-up study by C. D. Nath on tusk size and parasite loads in Asian elephants at Nagarahole in southern India did not find any clear patterns (unpublished master's thesis, Saurashtra University, Rajkot, India, 1999).

The ethological perspective on animal conflict is reflected, for instance, in the work of N. Tinbergen (*The Study of Instinct*, Clarendon Press, Oxford, U.K., 1951) and K. Lorenz (*On Aggression*, Methuen, London, 1966), but also see the work of Hinde in *Animal*

Behaviour (**29**, 535–542, 1981) for an attempt to reconcile the ethological and game theory approaches.

Chapter 4

Many of the references for this chapter on the social life of elephants are the same as for chapter 3. The work of Trivers (1985) is a useful introduction to social evolution in animals. The volumes referred to in the introduction are those of Poirier (1972) and Wilson (1975).

Section 4.2   The Asian studies are based on the work of Gadgil and Nair (1984), Nair (1983, 1989), and Sukumar et al. (1997), while the African studies are from Lee (1986, 1987) and Lee and Moss (1986). The parental investment model was from work by Trivers and Willard (1973).

Section 4.3   I used the work of Bradbury and Vehrencamp (1998) and Halliday and Slater (1983) for a general introduction to the subject of animal communication. There is also a diverse range of material on communication in elephants. I referred to that of Berg (1983), Buss et al. (1976), Douglas-Hamilton and Douglas-Hamilton (1975), Easa (1992), Gadgil et al. (1985), Garstang et al. (1995), Goodwin et al. (1999), Heffner and Heffner (1980), Krishnan (1972), Kühme (1962), Lamps et al. (2001), Langbauer et al. (1989, 1991), Larom et al. (1997a, 1997b), Lindeque and Lindeque (1991), McComb et al. (2000), McKay (1973), Nair (1983), Payne et al. (1986), Poole (1994, 1996), Poole et al. (1988), Rasmussen (1988, 1995, 1998, 2001), Rasmussen and Krishnamurthy (2000), Rasmussen and Munger (1996), Rasmussen and Schulte (1998, 1999), Rasmussen et al. (1982, 1986, 1990, 1993, 1996b, 1997, 2002), Riddle et al. (2000), Sanderson (1878), Schulte and Rasmussen (1999), Sukumar (1994a), Wheeler et al. (1982), and Wiley (1983).

The quote attributed to K. Payne is taken from page 266 of her article (Elephant talk. *National Geographic*, August 1989, pp. 264-277). The recordings of the African forest elephant by Payne and Gullick were from their unpublished data (2001). Nilakantha's Matangalila has been translated by Edgerton (1931).

Section 4.4   The work of Baker (1978) is a massive tome on the subject of animal migration. He defines (pg. 44) "calculated migration" as "migration to a specific destination that is known to the animal at the time of initiation of migration, either through direct perception, previous acquaintance, or social communication", and "non-calculated migration" as "migration to a destination about which, at the time of initiation of the migration, the animal has no information, either memorised, through direct perception, or through social communication".

Published references for home range sizes of elephant populations based on telemetry (both very-high-frequency and satellite based) studies are given in table 4.5. Hall-Martin's telemetry study at Kruger was reported in *The Status and Conservation of Africa's Elephants and Rhinos* (D.M.H. Cumming and P. Jackson, editors, International Union for Conservation of Nature and Natural Resources, Gland, Switzerland, 1984). The other (nontelemetry) studies mentioned are those of Datye and Bhagwat (1995a), Desai (1991), Eisenberg and Lockhart (1972), McKay (1973), Sukumar (1989a, 1989b), Rodgers and Elder (1977), and Viljoen (1989). The telemetry study at Rajaji in India was taken from the work of A. C. Williams (Elephants and their habitats in Rajaji-Corbett National Parks, doctoral dissertation in review, Saurashtra University, Rajkot, India, personal communication). The study of S. Chowdhury and colleagues was taken from an unpublished report (Management of elephant populations in West Bengal for mitigating man elephant conflicts, Wildlife Institute of India, Dehra Dun, 1997). The telemetry study of elephants in the Buxa-Jaldapara Reserves by my research team is ongoing; the results have been presented in a report submitted to the West Bengal Forest Department (Sukumar, R., Venkataraman, A. B., Cheeran, J. V., Majumdar, P. P., Baskaran, N., Dharmarajan, G., Roy, M., Suresh, H. S., Narendran, K. and Mathivanan, A. (2003). Study of elephants in Buxa Tiger Reserve and adjoining areas in northern West Bengal, and preparation of conservation action plan. Centre for Ecological Sciences, Indian Institute of Science, Bangalore).

The discussion on ecological determinants of home range was based on the work of Damuth (1981), Harestad and Bunnell (1979), Kleiber (1947), McNab (1963), Owen-Smith (1988), Peters (1983), and Swihart et al. (1988). Rainfall data are taken from various publications mentioned here as well as from an atlas of rainfall for African sites (Nicholson, S.E., Kim, J. and Hoopingarner, J., Atlas of African rainfall and its interannual variability. Department of Meteorology, The Florida State University, Tallahassee, Fl., 1988).

Sections 4.5–4.6   References for the discussion on social organization include those by Abe (1994), Anderson and Eltringham (1977), Barnes (1982b), Baskaran (1998), Baskaran et al. (1995), Croze (1974a), Douglas-Hamilton (1972), Douglas-Hamilton and Douglas-Hamilton (1975), Dublin (1983), Eltringham (1977), Fernando and Lande (2000), Hart and Hart (1994), Ishwaran (1981), Kurt (1974), Laws et al. (1975), Lee (1987), Leuthold (1976), McComb et al. (2001), McKay (1973), Moss (1988), Moss and Poole (1983), Poole and Moss (1989), Rensch (1957), Sanderson (1878), Santiapillai et al. (1984), Sukumar (1985, 1989a, 1989b, 1994a), Turkalo and Fay (1995), and Western and Lindsay (1984).

The description of Brooke and Hamilton's elephant hunt of 1863 is given in the work of Sanderson (1878). Chapman's observations are mentioned in Spinage's 1994 work. Mohamad Khan has brought out an undated report (about 1992) of his work (*The Malayan Elephant: A Species Plan for Its Conservation*, published by the Department of National Parks, Kuala Lumpur, Malaysia). Heindrichs's observations are given in the work of Croze (1974a). Komar and Melamid (2000) provide a popular account of Thailand's painting elephants.

Chapter 5

A good introduction to the use of allometry in ecology was given by Peters (1983). Owen-Smith (1988) provided a more detailed comparative account of the feeding ecology of the megaherbivores. Benedict's (1936) classic on elephant physiology is still relevant today.

Section 5.2   The general nature of the elephant's feeding behavior and diet was described by Alexandre (1978), Barnes (1982a), Benedict (1936), Buss (1961), Coe (1972), Field and Ross (1976), Foose (1982), Guy (1975, 1976), Laws and Parker (1968), Laws et al. (1975), Lindsay (1994), McKay (1973), Olivier (1978), Ruggiero (1992), Short (1981), Sukumar (1985, 1989a, 1990), Vancuylenberg (1977), White et al. (1993), Williamson (1975), and Wyatt and Eltringham (1974). Merz's study in the Ivory Coast was based on an unpublished master's thesis (University of Heidelberg, Germany) and was quoted in Eltringham (1982), as were Rees's figures on digestibility.

Section 5.3   Two of the early articles on carbon isotopic variation in plants and the application of this method in dietary studies were by Smith and Epstein (*Plant Physiology*, **47**, 380–384, 1971) and DeNiro and Epstein (*Geochimica Cosmochimica Acta*, **42**, 495–506, 1978). The isotopic studies of elephant diet were based on the work of Koch et al. (1995), Sukumar (1985), Sukumar and Ramesh (1992, 1995), Sukumar et al. (1987), Tieszen et al. (1989), and van der Merwe et al. (1988). Data on rainfall are as concerning the discussion of section 4.4.

Section 5.4   The analytical discussion on elephant foraging was based on the work of Ananthasubramaniam (1979), Anderson and Walker (1974), Bax and Sheldrick (1963), Belovsky (1978, 1984), Benedict (1936), Clemens and Maloiy (1982), Dierenfeld (1994), Dougall et al. (1964), Emlen (1966), Foose (1982), Janis (1976), Kleiber (1947), Laws et al. (1975), Lindsay (1994), McCullagh (1969a, 1969b, 1973), Moore and Sikes (1967), Oftedal (1985), Olivier (1978), Owen-Smith (1988), Owen-Smith and Novellie (1982), Ruggiero and Fay (1994), Sivaganesan and Johnsingh (1995), Sukumar (1989a, 1990), Weir (1972, 1973), and Westoby (1974, 1978).

A more comprehensive treatment of plant secondary compounds and their role in herbivory is found in the work of Freeland and Janzen (1974) and Rosenthal and Janzen (1979). M. K. Hackenberger's work is an unpublished master's thesis (1984) from the University of Guelph, Canada.

Section 5.5   The section on physiological condition was based on the work of Albl (1971), Hanks (1981), Malpas (1977), Laws and Parker (1968), McCullagh (1969a), Vidya and Sukumar (2002), and Williamson (1975).

Chapter 6

The literature on the elephant's impact on vegetation is extensive, mostly in the form of scientific articles of individual studies. An early article that reviewed studies from several regions in Africa is that of Laws (1970). The other articles I used for this chapter are listed below.

Section 6.2   The nature of elephant damage to vegetation is described in the work of Barnes (1980, 1983b, 1985), Barnes et al. (1991), Buechner and Dawkins (1961), Croze (1974a, 1974b), Douglas-Hamilton (1972), Field (1971), Guy (1976), Höft and Höft (1995), Ishwaran (1983), Lamprey et al. (1967), Laws et al. (1975), Leuthold (1977a), Lewis (1986), Moolman and Cowling (1994), Mueller-Dombois (1972), Savidge (1968), Sukumar (1985, 1989a), Sukumar et al. (1998a), and Thomson (1975); Watson's study at Tsavo was presented in an unpublished 1968 report. I have also presented some of my unpublished data (1988–2000) from permanent plot observations in Mudumalai Sanctuary.

Section 6.3   In addition to several of the references listed in the preceding section, I also referred to the works by Bell and Jachmann (1984), Botkin et al. (1981), Caughley (1976), Duffy et al. (1999), Fowler (1981), Guy (1989), Jachmann and Bell (1984), Kennedy (2000), Lewis (1987), Myers (1973), Norton-Griffiths (1979), Pellew (1983), Prins and Van der Jeugd (1993), Ruess and Halter (1990), Scott (1962), Van de Koppel and Prins (1998), and Western and van Praet (1973).

Section 6.4   The data and models for this section are based on the work of Barnes (1983a), Ben-Shahar (1993, 1996), Dublin (1991, 1995), Dublin et al. (1990), Norton-Griffiths (1979), Pellew (1983), Sinclair (1995), and Styles and Skinner (2000). An article by Morell (*Science*, **278**, 2058–2060, 1997) also discussed the recent changes in the Serengeti.

Section 6.5   In addition to several articles used in section 5.2 that dealt with seed dispersal by elephants, I referred to the work of Chapman et al. (1992), Dudley (1999, 2000), Hawthorne and Parren (2000), Howe (1985), Janzen and Martin (1982), Powell (1997), Lieberman et al. (1987), and Redmond (1992). Richard Barnes enlightened me about the Maasai's observations on the link between elephants and the tsetse fly.

Chapter 7

For those unfamiliar with the mathematical treatment of population dynamics, any text on ecology or population biology would provide the fundamentals of the subject. Caughley's 1977 work is a good introduction to deterministic models of population dynamics as applied to vertebrates, while Fowler and Smith's 1981 work is a collection of articles from empirical studies of mammalian dynamics.

Section 7.2   References for birth rates in elephant populations are given in table 7.1. Khyne U Mar's compilation for Myanmar timber elephants was presented at a workshop (International Workshop on the Domesticated Asian Elephant, February 5–10, 2001, Bangkok, Food and Agriculture Organization, Thailand). The section on mortality was based on the work of Barnett (1991), Corfield (1973), Dudley et al. (2001), Lindeque (1988), Sikes (1968, 1971), Sukumar et al. (1997), and Watve (1995) in addition to some of the references in table 7.1 and discussions with V. Krishnamurthy and J. V. Cheeran.

Section 7.3   An overview of life history evolution in mammals was provided by Boyce (1988a, 1988b, 1988c). For a discussion of density dependence in relation to life history in mammals, see the work of Fowler (1981). Most of the other references used are as given in table 7.1. Hedigar is quoted in the work of Perry (1953).

Section 7.4   This section was based on the work of Fowler and Smith (1973), Hanks and McIntosh (1973), Laws and Parker (1968), Laws et al. (1975), and Sukumar (1985, 1989a). The reference to the work of G. Petrides is from a conference presentation (Petrides, G. A. and Swank, W. G. Estimating the productivity and energy relations of an African elephant population. Pp. 831-842 in Proceedings of the Ninth International Grasslands Congress, Sao Paulo, Brazil, 1965). The reference to G. U. Kurup was from an article in a newsletter-journal, *Cheetal* (**13**, 5–18, 1971), published by Wildlife Preservation Society, Dehra Dun, India.

The maximum rate of increase in an (African) elephant population was computed by Calef (1988) as 7% per annum, a rate achieved at Addo National Park in South Africa. However, this should not be taken as the norm for all elephant populations as I have argued on considerations of life history variation across habitats. A. Dobson informs me that the medium-term (about 20-year) growth rate of the Amboseli elephant population has been under 2% per annum, very similar to the maximum rate I determined for the Asian elephant in southern India.

Section 7.5   I first presented the results of the stochastic modeling of Asian elephants in the second (1992) edition of my book (see Sukumar 1989a) and later as a full article (Sukumar 1995b). Other references for this section include those of Armbruster et al. (1999), Armbruster and Lande (1993), and Wu and Botkin (1980).

Section 7.6   The tusks of an elephant are premaxillary lateral incisor teeth that are preceded by the deciduous incisors (the tushes). Both the tushes and the tusks develop from one tooth germ. In African elephants, the tushes are replaced at about 1 year by the continually growing permanent tusks in both males and females, while in the Asian elephant, only the males develop permanent tusks.

Tusklessness is much less common in African elephant populations than it is in Asian elephant populations, even when only the males are considered. The overall incidence of tusklessness in African elephants seems to be less than 10% of the population in most regions. It is important to distinguish between the incidence of tusklessness in young animals (a reflection of the underlying genetic patterns) and the observed frequency of tusklessness in older animals (which may be a short-term consequence of poaching for ivory).

Data on tusklessness in African elephants in Uganda were presented by Eve Abe (abstract in *Pachyderm*, **22**, 46–47, 1996), and for Luangwa Valley, they were given by Jachmann et al. (1995). In Uganda, the incidence of tusklessness was very low (less than 2% of elephants shot prior to 1930), but increased to 10% of the overall population by 1988, the direct consequence of the indiscriminate slaughter of tusked elephants during the 1970s. Two-thirds of the elephants over 40 years old were also tuskless, but none younger than 10 years old showed this trait.

A similar trend was seen in the Luangwa Valley, where the frequency of tuskless female elephants in the population went up from about 11% in 1969 (possibly the natural proportion of the population determined by the gene frequencies under Hardy-Weinberg equilibrium) to 38% by 1989 (as a result of the upsurge in ivory poaching), but then declined again to 29% by 1993 (with the growth of younger tusked elephants into the older age classes, given better protection). Most of the female elephants of Addo National Park are tuskless because the founder population, estimated at just 11 individuals in 1931, was a remnant of a heavily hunted population in this region.

Data on tusklessness among males (locally known as *makhnas* in India and *aliya* in Sri Lanka) in Asian elephant populations that I have compiled from various sources (Sukumar 1989a and unpublished data 2002) show that these comprised less than 5% of the male segment of the population in places such as southern India and peninsular Malaysia, about 50% in northeastern India and Myanmar, and over 93% in Sri Lanka. The observed frequencies of *makhnas* in India during recent years are higher among older bulls because of poaching of tuskers; for instance, about two-thirds of adult bulls in northeastern India are now makhnas.

Other references for this section are the works of Barnes and Kapela (1991), Caughley et al. (1990), Dobson et al. (1993), Kurup (as mentioned regarding section 7.4), Kurt et al. (1995), Milner-Gulland and Beddington (1993), Pilgram and Western (1986a, 1986b), Ramakrishnan et al. (1998), Spinage (1973), Sukumar et al. (1998b), Tiedemann and Kurt (1995), and Wells (1989). The reference to P. M. Chandran concerns a presentation made at a symposium on elephants in Kerala, India (February 23–24, 1990, with the proceedings published by the Kerala Forest Department, Thiruvananthapuram).

An excellent overview of the elephant in ancient Ceylon (Sri Lanka) is provided by C.W. Nicholas (The Ceylon elephant in antiquity, (i) The Sinhalese period. The Ceylon Forester 1, 52-28, 1954). While the presence of tusked male elephants on the island between the second century B.C. and third century A.D. is hinted (though not conclusive) from the sculptures of the *hattipakara* or "Elephant Wall" at Anuradhapura, it seems unlikely that wild tuskers existed in any significant numbers after the sixth century A.D. when the rulers of Ceylon imported elephants, presumably Indian tuskers. Writing of this period, Cosmas Indicopleustes, for instance, states that the small tusks (tushes?) of the Ceylon elephant were not used in commerce but that African ivory was being imported into India. Such historical observations and the emerging genetic evidence (Fernando et al. 2000, Fleischer et al. 2001) that the historical trade in elephants have influenced the present-day distribution of elephant genotypes provide justification for seeking alternative explanations for the very low frequency of tuskers in Sri Lanka.

The Tiedemann-Kurt model was modified by us (R. Sukumar and G. Pradhan, unpublished results, 2003) in several respects to make it more consistent with the known biology of the species. Thus, mortality rates were made age-specific in both males and females, while the mean ages at first reproduction in females and in males were higher than in the earlier model; this also gave more realistic population growth trajectories (see section 7.2). The reproductive success of a male elephant was taken to be age-dependent based on Poole (1989a). The sexual selection advantage for a tusker over a makhna was taken to be a constant, irrespective of their relative abundance in the population (as in the Tiedemann-Kurt model) as well as frequency-dependent (with tuskers having the maximum advantage at low frequencies).

Chapter 8

Section 8.2   The Asian studies of crop depredation were based on the work by Balasubramanian et al. (1995), Blair et al. (1979), Datye and Bhagwat (1995a, 1995b), de Silva (1998), Mishra (1971), Olivier (1978), Sukumar (1985, 1989a, 1990, 1994a, 1995a), Sukumar and Gadgil (1988), and A. C. Williams (as mentioned in the discussion of section 4.4). The reference to fragmentation and raiding in Kodagu and fig. 8.6 were based on an unpublished report by C. D. Nath and R. Sukumar (*Elephant-Human Conflict in Kodagu, Southern India*, Asian Elephant Research and Conservation Centre, Bangalore, India, 1998). Ramesh Kumar's data were based on an unpublished report (*Ecology of the Asian Elephant, Final Report*, 1995) of the Bombay Natural History Society, Bombay, India. The study by S. Choudhury and colleagues is available as an unpublished report (as mentioned in discussion of section 4.4), and so is our work in the Buxa-Jaldapara Reserves (Sukumar et al. 2003, discussed in section 4.4). The African studies were based on the work of Allaway (1979, 1981), Barnes (1996), Bhima (1998), Hoare (1999), Osborn (1998), and Tchamba (1996, 1998).

Section 8.3   Statistics concerning manslaughter by elephants are rather difficult to obtain for most of the range states. Data from India were based on my own records for southern India and elsewhere (Sukumar 1985 and unpublished 2001) as well as from the Project Elephant Directorate, New Delhi (courtesy S. S. Bist 2001). For the state of West Bengal, these were also based on records of the state forest department (compiled by S. Pal Choudhury, 2001). Other references for this section are the work of Barua and Bist (1995), Datye and Bhagwat (1995c), de Silva (1998), Douglas-Hamilton and Douglas-Hamilton (1975), and Njumbi et al. (1996). Discussion of David Western's views is based on personal communication (2001).

Section 8.4   There are few objective assessments of how the impact of humans on habitats affects elephants. I referred to the work of Barnes et al. (1991), Hoare and du Toit (1999), Olivier (1978), Parker and Graham (1989), Ramesh Kumar (as discussed in section 8.2), Silori and Mishra (1995), Struhsaker et al. (1996), Sukumar (1985, 1989a), Watve (1994), Williams (as discussed in section 4.4), and Williams and Johnsingh (unpublished report of Wildlife Institute of India, Dehra Dun, 1997).

Section 8.5   There are several volumes that deal with the use of ivory through history; the one that I used is by St. Aubyn (1987). Barbier et al. (1990) provided a detailed account of the economics of the ivory trade. Parker and Amin (1983) and Douglas-Hamilton and Douglas-Hamilton (1992) gave graphic accounts of ivory poaching in Africa, but with very different perspectives and prescriptions.

The general history of the trade in African ivory was based mainly on the work of Spinage (1973, 1994) plus that of Warmington (1974). The trade since 1950 and consumer patterns were based on the work of Barbier et al. (1990), Douglas-Hamilton (1987), Martin (1980), Martin and Stiles (2002), Martin and Vigne (1989), Parker and Martin (1982), and Poole and Thomsen (1989). The trade since 1989 is also reviewed by H. T. Dublin, T. Milliken and R.F.W. Barnes (*Four Years after the CITES Ban: Illegal Killing of Elephants, Ivory Trade and Stockpiles*, A Report of the IUCN/SSC African Elephant Specialist Group, Gland, Switzerland, 1995).

For the final part on capture and hunting of Asian elephants, I drew on my earlier account of this subject (Sukumar 1989a, which also provides a list of references) updated from the work of Jayewardene (1994), Lair (1997), Lahiri-Choudhury (1999), Menon (2002), and presentations made at the Bangkok workshop (see the discussion in section 7.2). Excellent accounts of captive elephants in Asia are also available in work by Sanderson (1878), Williams (1950), Stracey (1963), and Gale (1974). Recent estimates of poaching were based on the database of elephant mortality in India maintained jointly by the Asian Elephant Research and Conservation Centre, Bangalore, and the Wildlife Trust of India, New Delhi.

Chapter 9

I provided an overview of elephant conservation issues in my 1991a work. Priority landscapes for Asian elephant conservation were given in the action plan by Santiapillai and Jackson (1990) and also in an unpublished report prepared for the World Wildlife Fund-US, Washington, D.C. (Sukumar, R. The Asian elephant: Priority populations and projects for conservation. Asian Elephant Conservation Centre, Bangalore, India, 1998). Venkataraman et al. (2002) provide algorithms for prioritizing southern Indian elephant landscapes. A thought-provoking discussion on a possible schism in the field of conservation biology was initiated by Caughley (1994).

Section 9.2   The theory of viable populations and its application to elephants were discussed by Armbruster and Lande (1993), Boyce (1992), Frankham and Franklin (1998), Franklin (1980), Franklin and Frankham (1998), Johnsingh et al. (1990), Lynch and Lande (1998), MacArthur and Wilson (1967), Shaffer (1981), Sukumar (1989a, 1995b), Terborgh (1976), and Western and Gichohi (1993).

Section 9.3   I referred to the work of Blair et al. (1979), Gorman (1986), Hoare (2001), Kangwana (1995), Lahiri-Choudhury (1991b), O'Connell-Rodwell et al. (2000), Osborn and Rasmussen (1995), Sukumar (1989a, 1991b, 1994b), and Thouless and Sakwa (1995). The reference to R. Piesse is an unpublished typescript (1982). The observations on electric fences in southern India were presented in the work by Nath and Sukumar (unpublished report, 1998; see the discussion in section 8.2). J. Seidensticker's prescriptions were given in a report (*Managing Elephant Depredations in Agricultural and Forestry Projects*, The World Bank, Washington, D.C., 1984).

Sections 9.4–9.5   Published references for these sections on population management are the works of Buss (1977), Cumming et al. (1997), Fayrer-Hosken et al. (2000), Laws (1970), Laws et al. (1975), McLeod (1997), Milewski (2000), Pienaar (1969), Poole (1993), Sinclair (1981, 1995), Spinage (1973), Van Aarde et al. (1999), and Whyte et al. (1998). Pienaar's arguments for culling were from an article (Why elephant culling is necessary, *African Wildlife* (**23**, 181–194, 1969). Information on elephant culling is also found in the work of Hanks (1979) and Laws et al. (1975). Martin's compilation of elephants culled in Zimbabwe is found in a report (*Elephant Management in Zimbabwe*, eds. R. B. Martin and A.M.G. Conybeare, 2nd ed., 1992, Department of National Parks and Wildlife Management, Harare, Zimbabwe). There are several reports and secondary references on Zimbabwe's CAMPFIRE; one of these I referred to is by H. Patel (Sustainable utilization and African wildlife policy: The case of Zimbabwe's Communal Areas Management Programme for Indigenous Resources (CAMPFIRE). Indigenous Environmental Policy Center, Cambridge, Mass., 1998).

The reference to the work at Cat Tien is from an unpublished report of the Cat Tien National Park Conservation Project 2002 (Sukumar, R., Varma, S., Dang, N. X. and Thanh, T. V. The status and conservation of Asian elephants in Cat Tien National

Park, Vietnam. Asian Elephant Research and Conservation Centre, Bangalore, India, and World Wide Fund for Nature, Ho Chi Minh City, Vietnam).

Section 9.6   The literature on poaching and the ivory trade and its regulation is extensive, but mostly in the form of articles and reports. The published works to which I referred are those by Barbier et al. (1990), Dobson and Poole (1992), Jachmann and Billiouw (1997), Leader-Williams and Milner-Gulland (1993), Leader-Williams et al. (1990), Leakey (1992), and Milner-Gulland and Leader-Williams (1992). A comprehensive collection of articles (and views) on the trade is available in the proceedings of the Ivory Trade Review Group (S. Cobb, ed., *The Ivory Trade and the Future of the African Elephant*, Ivory Trade Review Group, Oxford, U.K., 1987). Two reports on the post-1989 ban scenario in Africa are those by Dublin et al. 1995 (as discussed concerning section 8.5) and E. Martin and D. Stiles (*The Ivory Markets of Africa*, Save the Elephants, Nairobi, Kenya, 2000). The trade in Asian ivory was covered by V. Menon et al. (*A God in Distress: Threats of Poaching and the Ivory Trade to the Asian Elephant in India*, 1997,) and V. Menon and A. Kumar (*Signed and Sealed: The Fate of the Asian Elephant*, 1998,), both published jointly by the Asian Elephant Conservation Centre, Bangalore, India, and the Wildlife Protection Society of India, New Delhi, as well as the work of S. Nash (ed.) (*Still in Business: The Ivory Trade in Asia, Seven Years after the Ivory Ban*, Traffic International, Cambridge, U.K., 1997), H. Obara (Ivory trade management in Japan, In Proceedings of the African elephant conference, Environmental Investigation Agency, London, 1997), M. Sakamoto (*Analysis of the Amended Management System of Domestic Ivory Trade in Japan*, Japan Wildlife Conservation Society, Tokyo, 1999), and very recently by E. Martin and D. Stiles (*The South and Southeast Asian Ivory Markets*, Save the Elephants, Nairobi, Kenya, 2002), and Menon (2002).

The isotopic variation in elephant ivory was presented in the work of van der Merwe et al. (1990) and Vogel et al. (1990).

TRAFFIC refers to Trade Record Analysis of Flora and Fauna in Commerce.

Section 9.7   The classic on captive Asian elephant management is by G. H. Evans (*Elephants and Their Diseases: A Treatise on Elephants*, Government Press, Rangoon, Burma, 1910). S. S. Bist has recently edited A.J.W. Milroy's *Management of Elephants in Captivity* (original edition published in 1922; reissued by Natraj Publishers, Dehra Dun, India, 2002). The most recent overview of the captive elephant populations in Asia is that of Lair (1997). The health care of captive elephants, especially in Western zoos, was reviewed by Mikota et al. (1994). Other references for this section are the works of de Alwis (1991), Hermes et al. (2000), Hildebrandt et al. (2000a, 2000b), Krishnamurthy and Wemmer (1995a, 1995b), Kurt (1995), Sukumar et al. (1997), and Taylor and Poole (1998). The experiment with releasing captive Asian elephants into the wild in Thailand was reported by T. Angkawanish of the Thai Elephant Conservation Center (typescript 1999), while observations of hand-reared African elephant calves were documented by McKnight (1995).

References

Abe, E. L. (1994). The behavioural ecology of elephant survivors in Queen Elizabeth National Park, Uganda. Ph.D. thesis, University of Cambridge, Cambridge, U.K.

Achaya, K. T. (1994). *Indian food: A historical companion*. Oxford University Press, New Delhi, India.

Agenbroad, L. D., and Mead, J. I. (1996). Distribution and palaeoecology of central and western North American *Mammuthus*. Pp. 280–288 in Shoshani and Tassy (1996a).

Aguirre, E. (1969). Evolutionary history of the elephant. *Science*, **164**, 1366–1376.

Albl, P. (1971). Studies on assessment of physical condition in African elephants. *Biological Conservation*, **3**, 134–140.

Alexandre, D.-Y. (1978). Le rôle disséminateur des éléphants en Forêt de Tai, Côted'Ivoire. *Terre Vie*, **32**, 47–72.

Ali, S. A. (1927). The Moghul Emperors of India as naturalists and sportsmen. *Journal of the Bombay Natural History Society*, **31**, 833–861.

Allaway, J. (1981). The African elephant's drinking problem. *Natural History*, **90**, 30–35.

Allaway, J. D. (1979). Elephants and their interactions with people in the Tana river region of Kenya. Ph.D. thesis, Cornell University, Ithaca, N.Y.

Ananthasubramaniam, C. R. (1979). Studies on the nutritional requirements of the Indian elephant. Ph.D. thesis, Kerala Agricultural University, Mannuthy, Kerala, India.

Anderson, G. D., and Walker, B. H. (1974). Vegetation composition and elephant damage in the Sengwa wildlife research area, Rhodesia. *Journal of the South African Wildlife Management Association*, **4**, 1–14.

Anderson, K. F., and Eltringham, S. K. (1977). Some preliminary observations on possible stress in the elephants of Mikumi National Park, Tanzania. *African Journal of Ecology*, **35**, 278–282.

Anderson, R. M. (1991). Population and infectious diseases: Ecology or epidemiology? *Journal of Animal Ecology*, **60**, 1–50.

Ansell, W.F.H. (1971). Order Proboscidea. In *The mammals of Africa: An identification manual. Part II* (J. Meester and H. W. Setzer, eds.), pp. 1–5. Smithsonian Institution Press, Washington, D.C.

Armbruster, P., Fernando, P., and Lande, R. (1999). Time frames for population viability analysis of species with long generations: An example with Asian elephants. *Animal Conservation*, **2**, 69–73.

Armbruster, P., and Lande, R. (1993). A population viability analysis for African elephant (*Loxodonta africana*): How big should reserves be? *Conservation Biology*, **7**, 602–610.

Averianov, A. O. (1996). Sexual dimorphism in the mammoth skull, teeth, and long bones. Pp. 260–267 in Shoshani and Tassy (1996a).

Baker, C.M.A., and Manwell, C. (1983). Man and elephant: the "dare theory" of domestication and the origin of breeds. *Zeitschrift für Tierzüchtung and Züchtungsbiologie*, **100**, 55–75.

Baker, R. R. (1978). *The evolutionary ecology of animal migration.* Hodder and Stoughton, London.

Balasubramanian, M., Baskaran, N., Swaminathan, S., and Desai, A. A. (1995). Crop raiding by Asian elephant (*Elephas maximus*) in the Nilgiri Biosphere Reserve, South India. Pp. 350–367 in Daniel and Datye (1995).

Barbier, E. B., Burgess, J. C., Swanson, T. M., and Pearce, D. W. (1990). *Elephants, economics and ivory.* Earthscan Publications, London.

Barnes, R.F.W. (1980). The decline of the baobab tree in Ruaha National Park, Tanzania. *African Journal of Ecology*, **18**, 243–252.

Barnes, R.F.W. (1982a). Elephant feeding behaviour in Ruaha National Park, Tanzania. *African Journal of Ecology*, **20**, 123–136.

Barnes, R.F.W. (1982b). Mate-searching behaviour of elephant bulls in a semi-arid environment. *Animal Behaviour*, **30**, 1217–1223.

Barnes, R.F.W. (1983a). Effects of elephant browsing on woodlands in a Tanzanian National Park: Measurements, models and management. *Journal of Applied Ecology*, **20**, 521–540.

Barnes, R.F.W. (1983b). The elephant problem in Ruaha National Park, Tanzania. *Biological Conservation*, **26**, 127–148.

Barnes, R.F.W. (1985). Woodland changes in Ruaha National Park (Tanzania) between 1976 and 1982. *African Journal of Ecology*, **23**, 215–221.

Barnes, R.F.W. (1996). The conflict between humans and elephants in the Central African forests. *Mammal Review*, **26**, 67–80.

Barnes, R.F.W., Barnes, K. L., Alers, M.P.T., and Blom, A. (1991). Man determines the distribution of elephants in the rain forests of northeastern Gabon. *African Journal of Ecology*, **29**, 54–63.

Barnes, R.F.W., Barnes, K. L., and Kapela, E. B. (1994). The long-term impact of elephant browsing on baobab trees at Msembe, Ruaha National Park, Tanzania. *African Journal of Ecology*, **32**, 177–184.

Barnes, R.F.W., and Kapela, E. B. (1991). Changes in the Ruaha elephant population caused by poaching. *African Journal of Ecology*, **29**, 289–294.

Barnett, J. (1991). Disease and mortality. Pp. 102–115 in Eltringham (1991).

Barry, J. C., Johnson, N. M., Raza, S. M., and Jacobs, L. L. (1985). Neogene mammalian faunal change in southern Asia: Correlations with climate, tectonic and eustatic events. *Geology*, **13**, 637–640.

Barua, P., and Bist, S. S. (1995). Changing patterns in the distribution and movement of wild elephants in north Bengal. Pp. 66–84 in Daniel and Datye (1995).

Basham, A. L. (1967). *The wonder that was India.* 3rd ed. Macmillan, London.

Baskaran, N. (1998). Ranging and resource utilization by Asian elephant (*Elephas maximus* Linnaeus) in Nilgiri Biosphere Reserve, South India. Ph.D. thesis, Bharathidasan University, Tiruchirapalli, India.

Baskaran, N., Balasubramanian, M., Swaminathan, S., and Desai, A. A. (1995). Home range of elephants in the Nilgiri Biosphere Reserve, South India. Pp. 296–313 in Daniel and Datye (1995).

Bax, P. N., and Sheldrick, D.L.W. (1963). Some preliminary observations on the food of elephants in the Tsavo Royal National Park (East) of Kenya. *East African Wildlife Journal*, **1**, 40–53.

Bechert, U. S., Swanson, L., Wasser, S. K., Hess, D. L., and Stormshak, F. (1999). Serum prolactin concentrations in the captive female African elephant (*Loxodonta africana*): Potential effects of season and steroid hormone interactions. *General and Comparative Endocrinology,* **114,** 269–278.

Beden, M. (1983). Family Elephantidae. In *Koobi Fora research project. Vol. 2. The fossil ungulates: Proboscidea, Perissodactyla, and Suidae.* (J. M. Harris, ed.), pp. 40–129. Clarendon Press, Oxford, U.K.

Bell, R.H.V., and Jachmann, H. (1984). Influence of fire on the use of *Brachystegia* woodland by elephants. *African Journal of Ecology,* **22,** 157–163.

Belovsky, G. E. (1978). Diet optimization in a generalist herbivore: The moose. *Theoretical Population Biology,* **14,** 105–134.

Belovsky, G. E. (1984). Herbivore optimal foraging: A comparative test of three models. *The American Naturalist,* **124,** 97–115.

Benedict, F. G. (1936) *The physiology of the elephant.* Carnegie Institute, Washington, D.C.

Ben-Shahar, R. (1993). Patterns of elephant damage to vegetation in northern Botswana. *Biological Conservation,* **65,** 249–256.

Ben-Shahar, R. (1996). Do elephants over-utilize mopane woodlands in northern Botswana? *Journal of Tropical Ecology,* **12,** 505–515.

Berg, J. K. (1983). Vocalizations and associated behaviors of the African elephant (*Loxodonta africana*) in captivity. *Zeitschrift für Tierpsychologie,* **63,** 63–78.

Bhima, R. (1998). Elephant status and conflict with humans on the western bank of Liwonde National Park, Malawi. *Pachyderm,* **25,** 74–80.

Blair, J.A.S., Boon, G. G., and Noor, N. M. (1979). Conservation or cultivation: The confrontation between the Asian elephant and land development in peninsular Malaysia. *Land Development Digest,* **2,** 27–59.

Blake, S., Douglas-Hamilton, I., and Karesh, W. B. (2001). GPS telemetry of forest elephants in central Africa: Results of a preliminary study. *African Journal of Ecology,* **39,** 178–186.

Botkin, D. B., Mellilo, J. M., and Wu, L. S.-Y. (1981). How ecosystem processes are linked to large mammal population dynamics. Pp. 373–387 in Fowler and Smith (1981).

Boyce, M. (1988a). Evolution of life histories: Theory and patterns from mammals. Pp. 3–30 in Boyce (1988c).

Boyce, M. (1988b). Where do we go from here? Pp. 351–361 in Boyce (1988c).

Boyce, M. (1988c). *Evolution of life histories of mammals: theory and pattern.* Yale University Press, New Haven, Conn.

Boyce, M. (1992). Population viability analysis. *Annual Review of Ecology and Systematics,* **23,** 481–506.

Bradbury, J. W., and Vehrencamp, S. L. (1998). *Principles of animal communication.* Sinauer Associates, Sunderland, Mass.

Brannian, J. D., Griffin, F., Papkoff, H., and Terranova, P. F. (1988). Short and long phases of progesterone secretion during the oestrous cycle of the African elephant (*Loxodonta africana*). *Journal of Reproduction and Fertility,* **84,** 357–365.

Brown, J. L. (2000). Reproductive endocrine monitoring of elephants: An essential tool for assisting captive management. *Zoo Biology,* **19,** 347–367.

Brown, J. L., Citino, S. B., Bush, M., Lehnhardt, J., and Phillips, L. G. (1991). Cyclic patterns of luteinizing hormone, follicle-stimulating hormone, inhibin, and progesterone secretion in the Asian elephant. *Journal of Zoo and Wildlife Medicine,* **22,** 49–57.

Brown, J. L., and Lehnhardt, J. (1995). Serum and urinary hormones during pregnancy and the peri- and postpartum period in an Asian elephant (*Elephas maximus*). *Zoo Biology*, **14**, 555–564.

Brown, R. L. (1991a). Ganeša in Southeast Asian art: Indian connections and indigenous developments. Pp. 171–233 in Brown (1991c).

Brown, R. L. (1991b). Introduction. Pp. 1–18 in Brown (1991c).

Brown, R. L. (ed.) (1991c). *Ganesh: Studies of an Asian God*. State University of New York Press, Albany.

Buechner, H. K., and Dawkins, H. C. (1961). Vegetation change induced by elephants and fire in Murchison Falls National Park, Uganda. *Ecology*, **42**, 752–766.

Buss, I. O. (1961). Some observations on food habits and behavior of the African elephant. *Journal of Wildlife Management*, **25**, 131–148.

Buss, I. O. (1977). Management of big game with particular reference to elephants. *Malayan Nature Journal*, **31**, 59–71.

Buss, I. O. (1990). *Elephant life: Fifteen years of high population density*. Iowa State University Press, Ames.

Buss, I. O., Estes, J. A., Rasmussen, L. E., and Smuts, G. L. (1976). The role of stress and individual recognition in the function of the African elephant's temporal gland. *Mammalia*, **40**, 437–451.

Calef, G. W. (1988). Maximum rate of increase in the African elephant. *African Journal of Ecology*, **26**, 323–327.

Caloi, L., Kotsakis, T., Palombo, M. R., and Petronio, C. (1996). The Pleistocene dwarf elephants of Mediterranean islands. Pp. 234–239 in Shoshani and Tassy (1996a).

Carrington, R. (1958). *Elephants: A short account of their natural history, evolution and influence on mankind*. Chatto and Windus, London.

Caughley, G. (1976). The elephant problem—An alternative hypothesis. *East African Wildlife Journal*, **14**, 265–283.

Caughley, G. (1977). *Analysis of vertebrate populations*. John Wiley and Sons, London.

Caughley, G. (1994). Directions in conservation biology. *Journal of Animal Ecology*, **63**, 215–244.

Caughley, G., Dublin, H., and Parker, I. (1990). Projected decline of the African elephant. *Biological Conservation*, **54**, 157–164.

Cerling, T. E., Harris, J. M., MacFadden, B. J., Leakey, M. G., Quade, J., Eisenmann, V., and Ehleringer, J. R. (1997). Global change through the Miocene/Pliocene boundary. *Nature*, **389**, 153–158.

Cerling, T. E. Harris, J. M., and Leakey, M. G. (1999). Browsing and grazing in elephants: The isotope record of modern and fossil proboscideans. *Oecologia*, **120**, 364–374.

Chakravarti, D. K. (1957). A geological, palaeontological and phylogenetic study of the Elephantoidea of India, Pakistan and Burma: Part I. Gomphotheriidae. *Journal of the Palaeontological Society of India*, **2**, 83–94.

Chapman, L. J., Chapman, C. A., and Wrangham, R. W. (1992). *Balanites wilsoniana*: Elephant dependent dispersal? *Journal of Tropical Ecology*, **8**, 275–283.

Chappel, S. C., and Schmidt, M. J. (1979). Cyclic release of luteinizing hormone and the effects of luteinizing hormone-releasing hormone injection in Asiatic elephants. *American Journal of Veterinary Research*, **40**, 451–453.

Clemens, E. T., and Maloiy, G.M.O. (1982). The digestive physiology of three East African herbivores: The elephant, rhinoceros and hippopotamus. *Journal of Zoology (London)*, **198**, 141–156.

Coe, M. (1972). Defaecation by African elephants (*Loxodonta africana africana* (Blumenbach)). *East African Wildlife Journal*, **10**, 165–174.

Cooper, K. A., Harder, J. D., Clawson, D. H., Fredrick, D. L., Lodge, G. A., Peachey, H. C., Spellmire, T. J., and Winstel, D. P. (1990). Serum testosterone and musth in captive male African and Asian elephants. *Zoo Biology*, **9**, 297–306.

Corfield, T. F. (1973). Elephant mortality in the Tsavo National Park, Kenya. *East African Wildlife Journal*, **11**, 339–368.

Court, N. (1993). A dental peculiarity in *Numidotherium koholense*: Evidence of feeding behaviour in a primitive proboscidean. *Zeitschrift für Säugetierkunde*, **58**, 194–196.

Courtwright, P. B. (1985). *Ganeśa: Lord of obstacles, lord of beginnings*. Oxford University Press, New York.

Croze, H. (1974a). The Seronera bull problem. 1. The bulls. *East African Wildlife Journal*, **12**, 1–27.

Croze, H. (1974b). The Seronera bull problem. 2. The trees. *East African Wildlife Journal*, **12**, 29–47.

Cumming, D.M.H., Fenton, M.B.B., Rautenbach, R. D., Taylor, R. D., Cumming, G. S., Cumming, M. S., Dunlop, J. M., Ford, G. A., Hovorka, M. D., Johnston, D. S., Kalcounis, M., Mahlangu, Z., and Portfors, C.V.R. (1997). Elephants, woodlands and biodiversity in southern Africa. *South African Journal of Science*, **93**, 231–236.

Damuth, J. (1981). Home range, home range overlap and energy use among animals. *Biological Journal of the Linnaean Society*, **15**, 185–193.

Daniel, J. C. (1998). *The Asian elephant: A natural history*. Natraj Publishers, Dehra Dun, India.

Daniel, J. C., and Datye H. S. (eds.) (1995). *A week with elephants*. Bombay Natural History Society, Bombay, and Oxford University Press, New Delhi, India.

Darwin, C. (1871). *The descent of man, and selection in relation to sex*, 2 vols. J. Murray, London.

Datye, H. S., and Bhagwat, A. M. (1995a). Estimation of crop damage and the economic loss caused by elephants and its implications in the management of elephants. Pp. 375–388 in Daniel and Datye (1995).

Datye, H. S., and Bhagwat, A. M. (1995b). Home range of elephants in fragmented habitats of central India. *Journal of the Bombay Natural History Society*, **92**, 1–10.

Datye, H. S., and Bhagwat, A. M. (1995c). Man-elephant conflict: A case study of human deaths caused by elephants in parts of central India. Pp. 340–349 in Daniel and Datye (1995).

de Alwis, L. (1991). Working elephants. Pp. 116–129 in Eltringham (1991).

de Silva, M. (1998). Status and conservation of the elephant (*Elephas maximus*) and the alleviation of man-elephant conflict in Sri Lanka. *Gajah* (Journal of the Asian Elephant Specialist Group), **19**, 1–68.

de Villiers, D. J., Skinner, J. D., and Hall-Martin, A. J. (1989). Circulating progesterone concentrations and ovarian functional anatomy in the African elephant (*Loxodonta africana*). *Journal of Reproduction and Fertility*, **86**, 195–201.

de Villiers, P. A., and Kok, O. B. (1997). Home range, association and related aspects of elephants in the eastern Transvaal Lowveld. *African Journal of Ecology*, **35**, 224–236.

Deraniyagala, P.E.P. (1955). *Some extinct elephants, their relatives, and the two living species*. National Museum of Ceylon, Colombo.

Desai, A. A. (1991). The home range of elephants and its implications for the management of the Mudumalai Wildlife Sanctuary, Tamil Nadu. *Journal of Bombay Natural History Society*, **88**, 145–156.

Dhavalikar, M. K. (1991). Ganeša: myth and reality. Pp. 49–68 in Brown (1991c).

Dierenfeld, E. S. (1994). Nutrition and feeding. Pp. 69–79 in Mikota et al. (1994).

Digby, S. (1971). *War horse and elephant in the Dehli Sultanate: A study of military supplies*. Orient Monographs, Oxford, U.K.

Dobson, A. P., Mace, G. M., Poole, J., and Brett, R. A. (1993). Conservation biology: The ecology and genetics of endangered species. In *Genes in ecology* (R. J. Berry, T. J. Crawford, and G. M. Hewitt, eds.), pp. 405–430. Blackwell Scientific, Oxford, U.K.

Dobson, A. P., and Poole, J. H. (1992). Ivory: Why the ban must stay! *Conservation Biology*, **6**, 149–151.

Dougall, H. W., Drysdale, V. M., and Glover, P. E. (1964). The chemical composition of Kenya browse and pasture herbage. *East African Wildlife Journal*, **2**, 86–121.

Douglas-Hamilton, I. (1972). On the ecology and behaviour of the African elephant. D.Phil. thesis, University of Oxford, Oxford, U.K.

Douglas-Hamilton, I. (1987). African elephants: Population trends and their causes. *Oryx*, **21**, 11–14.

Douglas-Hamilton, I. (1998). Tracking African elephants with a global positioning system (GPS) radio collar. *Pachyderm*, **25**, 82–91.

Douglas-Hamilton, I., and Douglas-Hamilton, O. (1975). *Among the elephants*. Viking Press, New York.

Douglas-Hamilton, I., and Douglas-Hamilton, O. (1992). *Battle for the elephants*. Doubleday, London.

Dublin, H. T. (1983). Cooperation and reproductive competition among female African elephants. In *Social behavior of female vertebrates* (S. K. Wasser, ed.), pp. 291–313. Academic Press, New York.

Dublin, H. T. (1991). Dynamics of the Serengeti-Mara woodlands: An historical perspective. *Forest and Conservation History*, **35**, 169–178.

Dublin, H. T. (1995). Vegetation dynamics in the Serengeti-Mara ecosystem: The role of elephants, fire and other factors. Pp. 71–90 in Sinclair and Arcese (1995).

Dublin, H. T., Sinclair, A.R.E., and McGlade, J. (1990). Elephants and fire as causes of multiple stable states in the Serengeti-Mara woodlands. *Journal of Animal Ecology*, **59**, 1147–1164.

Dudley, J. P. (1996). Mammoths, gomphotheres, and the great American faunal interchange. Pp. 289–295 in Shoshani and Tassy (1996a).

Dudley, J. P. (1999). Seed dispersal of *Acacia erioloba* by African bush elephants in Hwange National Park, Zimbabwe. *African Journal of Ecology*, **37**, 375–385.

Dudley, J. P. (2000). Seed dispersal by elephants in semiarid woodland habitats of Hwange National Park, Zimbabwe. *Biotropica*, **32**, 556–561.

Dudley, J. P., Craig, G. C., Gibson, D. St. C., Haynes, G., and Klimowicz, J. (2001). Drought mortality of bush elephants in Hwange National Park, Zimbabwe. *African Journal of Ecology*, **39**, 187–194.

Duffy, K. J., Page, B. R., Swart, J. H., and Bajic, V. B. (1999). Realistic parameter assessment for a well known elephant-tree ecosystem model reveals that limit cycles are unlikely. *Ecological Modelling*, **121**, 115–125.

Dunham, K. M. (1986). Movements of elephant cows in the unflooded Middle Zambezi Valley, Zimbabwe. *African Journal of Ecology*, **24**, 287–291.

Easa, P. S. (1992). Musth in Asian elephants. Pp. 85–86 in Shoshani (1992b).

Edgerton, F. (1931). *The elephant-lore of the Hindus: The elephant-sport (Matanga-lila) of Nilakantha*. Reprinted in 1985 by Motilal Banarsidass, New Delhi, India.

Eggert, L. S., Rasner, C. A., and Woodruff, D. S. (2002). The evolution and phylogeography of the African elephant inferred from mitochondrial DNA sequence and nuclear microsatellite markers. *Proceedings of the Royal Society, London, B*, **269**, 1993–2006.

Eisenberg, J. F., and Lockhart, M. (1972). An ecological reconnaissance of Wilpattu National Park, Ceylon. *Smithsonian Contributions to Zoology*, **101**, 1–118.

Eisenberg, J. F., McKay, G. M., and Jainudeen, M. R. (1971). Reproductive behaviour of the Asiatic elephant (*Elephas maximus maximus* L.). *Behaviour*, **38**, 193–225.

Eisenberg, J. F., McKay, G. M., and Seidensticker, J. (1990). *Asian elephants*. National Zoological Park, Smithsonian Institution, Washington, D.C.

Eltringham, S. K. (1977). The numbers and distribution of elephant *Loxodonta africana* in the Rwenzori National Park and Chambura Game Reserve, Uganda *East African Wildlife Journal*, **15**, 19–39.

Eltringham, S. K. (1982). *Elephants*. Blandford Press, Dorset, U.K.

Eltringham, S. K. (ed.) (1991). *The illustrated encyclopaedia of elephants*. Salamander Books, London.

Emlen, J. M. (1966). The role of time and energy in food preference. *The American Naturalist*, **100**, 611–617.

Enzel, Y., Ely, L. L., Mishra, S., Ramesh, R., Amit, R., Lazar, B., Rajaguru, S. N., Baker, V. R., and Sandler, A. (1999). High-resolution holocene environmental changes in the Thar Desert, northwestern India. *Science*, **284**, 125–128.

Erdosy, G. (1998). Deforestation in pre- and protohistoric South Asia. In *Nature and the Orient: The environmental history of South and Southeast Asia* (R. H. Grove, V. Damodaran, and S. Sangwan, eds.), pp. 51–69. Oxford University Press, New Delhi, India.

Fayrer-Hosken, R. A., Grobler, D., Van Altens, J. J., Bertschinger, H. J., and Kirkpatrick, J. F. (2000). Immunocontraception of African elephants. *Nature*, **407**, 149.

Fernando, P., and Lande, R. (2000). Molecular genetic and behavioral analysis of social organization in the Asian elephant (*Elephas maximus*). *Behavioural Ecology and Sociobiology*, **48**, 84–91.

Fernando, P., Pfrender, M. E., Enclada, S. E., and Lande, R. (2000). Mitochondrial DNA variation, phylogeography and population structure of the Asian elephant. *Heredity*, **84**, 362–372.

Field, C. R. (1971). Elephant ecology in the Queen Elizabeth National Park, Uganda. *East African Wildlife Journal*, **9**, 99–123.

Field, C. R., and Ross, I. C. (1976). The savanna ecology of Kidepo Valley National Park. II. Feeding ecology of elephant and giraffe. *East African Wildlife Journal*, **14**, 1–15.

Fisher, D. C. (1996). Extinction of proboscideans in North America. Pp. 296–315 in Shoshani and Tassy (1996a).

Fisher, R. A. (1958). *The genetical theory of natural selection*. 2nd ed. Dover, New York.

Fleischer, C., Perry, E. A., Muralidharan, K., Stevens, E. E., and Wemmer, C. M. (2001). Phylogeography of the Asian elephant (*Elephas maximus*) based on mitochondrial DNA. *Evolution*, **55**, 1882–1892.

Folstad, I., and Karter, A. J. (1992). Parasites, bright males and the immuno-competence handicap. *The American Naturalist*, **139**, 603–622.

Foose, T. J. (1982). Trophic strategies of ruminant versus nonruminant ungulates. Ph.D. thesis, University of Chicago.

Fowler, C. W. (1981). Density dependence as related to life history strategy. *Ecology*, **62**, 602–610.

Fowler, C. W., and Smith, T. (1973). Characterizing stable populations: An application to the African elephant population. *Journal of Wildlife Management*, **37**, 513–523.

Fowler, C. W., and Smith, T. D. (eds.) (1981). *Dynamics of large mammal populations*. John Wiley, New York.

Franklin, I. R. (1980). Evolutionary change in small populations. In *Conservation biology: An evolutionary-ecological perspective* (M. E. Soulé and B. A. Wilcox, eds.), pp. 135–150. Sinauer Associates, Sunderland, Mass.

Franklin, I. R., and Frankham, R. (1998). How large must populations be to retain evolutionary potential? *Animal Conservation*, **1**, 69–70.

Frankham, R., and Franklin, I. R. (1998). Response to Lynch and Lande. *Animal Conservation*, **1**, 73.

Freeland, W. J. (1976). Pathogens and the evolution of primate society. *Biotropica*, **8**, 12–24.

Freeland, W. J., and Janzen, D. H. (1974). Strategies in herbivory by mammals: The role of plant secondary compounds. *The American Naturalist*, **108**, 269–289.

Gadgil, M. (1972). Male dimorphism as a consequence of sexual selection. *The American Naturalist*, **106**, 574–580.

Gadgil, M., and Nair, P. V. (1984). Observations on the social behaviour of free ranging groups of tame Asiatic elephant (*Elephas maximus* Linn). *Proceedings of the Indian Academy of Sciences (Animal Sciences)*, **93**, 225–233.

Gadgil, M., Hegde, M., Joshi, N. V., and Gadgil, S. (1985). On the communication of well-being. *Proceedings of the Indian Academy of Sciences (Animal Sciences)*, **94**, 575–586.

Gaeth, A. P., Short, R. V., and Renfree, M. B. (1999). The developing renal, reproductive, and respiratory systems of the African elephant suggest an aquatic ancestry. *Proceedings of the National Academy of Sciences (USA)*, **96**, 5555–5558.

Gale, U. T. (1974). *Burmese timber elephant*. Trade Corporation, Rangoon, Burma.

Garstang, M., Larom, D., Raspet, R., and Lindeque, M. (1995). Atmospheric controls on elephant communication. *The Journal of Experimental Biology*, **198**, 939–951.

Georgiadis, N., Bischof, L., Templeton, A., Patton, J., Karesh, W., and Western, D. (1994). Structure and history of African elephant populations: I. Eastern and southern Africa. *Journal of Heredity*, **85**, 100–104.

Getty, A. (1936). *Ganeśa: A monograph on the elephant-faced god*. Clarendon Press, Oxford, U.K.

Gheerbrant, E., Sudre, J., and Cappetta, H. (1996). A Palaeocene proboscidean from Morocco. *Nature*, **383**, 68–70.

Ghurye, G. S. (1962). *Gods and men*. Popular Book Depot, Bombay.

Gingerich, P. G. (1984). Pleistocene extinctions in the context of origination-extinction equilibria in Cenozoic mammals. Pp. 211–222 in Martin and Klein (1984).

Goodwin, T. E., Riddle, II. S., Riddle, S. W., Guinn, A. C., McKelvey, S. S., and Rasmussen, L.E.L. (1999). African elephant sesquiterpenes. *Journal of Natural Products*, **62**, 1570–1572.

Gorman, M. L. (1986). The secretion of the temporal gland of the African elephant, *Loxodonta africana* as an elephant repellent. *Journal of Tropical Ecology*, **2**, 187–190.

Grafen, A. (1990a). Biological signals as handicaps. *Journal of Theoretical Biology*, **144**, 517–546.

Grafen, A. (1990b). Sexual selection unhandicapped by the Fisher process. *Journal of Theoretical Biology*, **144**, 473–516.

Graham, R. W., and Lundelius, E. L., Jr. (1984). Coevolutionary disequilibrium and Pleistocene extinctions. Pp. 223–249 in Martin and Klein (1984).

Greyling, M. D., van Aarde, R. J., and Potgieter, H. C. (1997). Ligand specificity of uterine oestrogen and progesterone receptors in the subadult African elephant (*Loxodonta africana*). *Journal of Reproduction and Fertility*, **109**, 199–204.

Groning, K., and Saller, M. (1998). *Elephants: A cultural and natural history*. Könemann, Cologne, Germany.

Guthrie, R. D. (1984). Mosaics, allelochemics, and nutrients: An ecological theory of late Pleistocene megafaunal extinctions. Pp. 259–298 in Martin and Klein (1984).

Guy, P. R. (1975). The daily food intake of the African elephant, *Loxodonta africana* Blumenbach, in Rhodesia. *Arnoldia Rhodesia*, **7**, 1–8.

Guy, P. R. (1976). The feeding behaviour of elephants *Loxodonta africana* in the Sengwa area, Rhodesia. *South African Journal of Wildlife Research*, **6**, 55–63.

Guy, P. R. (1989). The influence of elephants and fire on a *Brachystegia-Julbernardia* woodland in Zimbabwe. *Journal of Tropical Ecology*, **5**, 215–226.

Halliday, T. R., and Slater, P.J.B. (1983). *Animal behaviour. 2. Communication*. Blackwell Scientific Publications, Oxford, U.K.

Hall-Martin, A. J. (1987). The role of musth in the reproductive strategy of the African elephant (*Loxodonta africana*). *South African Journal of Science*, **83**, 616–620.

Hamilton, W. D., and Zuk, M. (1982). Heritable true fitness and bright birds: A role for parasites? *Science*, **218**, 384–387.

Hanks, J. (1969). Seasonal breeding of the African elephant in Zambia. *East African Wildlife Journal*, **7**, 167.

Hanks, J. (1972a). Growth of the African elephant (*Loxodonta africana*). *East African Wildlife Journal*, **10**, 251–272.

Hanks, J. (1972b). Reproduction of the elephant (*Loxodonta africana*) in the Luangwa Valley, Zambia. *Journal of Reproduction and Fertility*, **30**, 13–26.

Hanks, J. (1973). Reproduction in the male African elephant in the Luangwa Valley, Zambia. *Journal of South African Wildlife Management Association*, **3**, 31–39.

Hanks, J. (1979). *A struggle for survival—The elephant problem*. Country Life Books, Feltham, U.K.

Hanks, J. (1981). Characterization of population condition. Pp. 47–73 in Fowler and Smith (1981).

Hanks, J., and McIntosh, J.E.A. (1973). Population dynamics of the African elephant (*Loxodonta africana*). *Journal of Zoology (London)*, **169**, 29–38.

Hanks, J., and Short, R. V. (1972). The formation and function of the corpus luteum in the African elephant, *Loxodonta africana*. *Journal of Reproduction and Fertility*, **29**, 79–89.

Harestad, A. S., and Bunnell, F. L. (1979). Home range and body weight—A reevaluation. *Ecology*, **60**, 389–402.

Harris, M. (1978). *Cannibals and kings: The origins of cultures*. William Collins, Glasgow, U.K.

Hart, B. L., and Hart, L. A. (1994). Fly switching by Asian elephants: Tool use to control parasite. *Animal Behaviour*, **48**, 35–45.

Hartl, G. B., Kurt, F., Tiedemann, R., Gmeiner, C., Nadlinger, K., Mar, K. U., and Rubel, A. (1996). Population genetics and systematics of Asian elephant (*Elephas maximus*): A study based on sequence variation at the Cyt b gene of PCR-amplified mitochondrial DNA from hair bulbs. *Zeitschrift für Saugetierkunde*, **61**, 285–294.

Hawthorne, W. D., and Parren, M.P.E. (2000). How important are forest elephants to the survival of woody plant species in Upper Guinean forests? *Journal of Tropical Ecology*, **16**, 133–150.

Haynes, G. (1991). *Mammoths, mastodonts and elephants: Biology, behavior, and the fossil record.* Cambridge University Press, Cambridge, U.K.

Heffner, R., and Heffner, H. (1980). Hearing in the elephant (*Elephas maximus*). *Science*, **208**, 518–520.

Heistermann, M., Trohorsch, B., and Hodges, J. K. (1997). Assessment of ovarian function in the African elephant (*Loxodonta africana*) by measurement of 5α-reduced progesterone metabolites in serum and urine. *Zoo Biology*, **16**, 273–284.

Hermes, R., Olson, D., Göritz, F., Brown, J. L., Schmitt, D. L., Hagan, D., Peterson, J. S., Fritsch, G., and Hildebrandt, T. B. (2000). Ultrasonography of the estrous cycle in female African elephants (*Loxodonta africana*). *Zoo Biology*, **19**, 369–382.

Hess, D. L. Schmidt, A. M., and Schmidt, M. J. (1983). Reproductive cycle of the Asian elephant (*Elephas maximus*) in captivity. *Biology of Reproduction*, **28**, 767–773.

Hildebrandt, T. B., Göritz, F., Pratt, N. C., Brown, J. L., Montali, R. J., Schmitt, D. L., Fritsch, G., and Hermes, R. (2000a). Ultrasonography of the urogenital tract in elephants (*Loxodonta africana* and *Elephas maximus*): An important tool for assessing female reproductive function. *Zoo Biology*, **19**, 321–332.

Hildebrandt, T. B., Hermes, R., Pratt, N. C., Fritsch, G., Bloyynrt, S., Schmitt, D. L., Ratanakorn, P., Brown, J. L, Rietschel, W., and Göritz, F. (2000b). Ultrasonography of the urogenital tract in elephants (*Loxodonta africana* and *Elephas maximus*): An important tool for assessing male reproductive function. *Zoo Biology*, **19**, 333–345.

Hoare, R. E. (1999). Determinants of human-elephant conflict in a land-use mosaic. *Journal of Applied Ecology*, **36**, 689–700.

Hoare, R E. (2001). Management implications of new research on problem elephants. *Pachyderm*, **30**, 44–48.

Hoare, R. E., and du Toit, J. T. (1999). Coexistence between people and elephants in African savannas. *Conservation Biology*, **13**, 633–639.

Hodges, J. K. (1998). Endocrinology of the ovarian cycle and pregnancy in the Asian (*Elephas maximus*) and African (*Loxodonta africana*) elephant. *Animal Reproduction Science*, **53**, 3–18.

Hodges, J. K., Heistermann, M., Beard, A., and van Aarde, R. J. (1997). Concentrations of progesterone and the 5α-reduced progestins, 5α-pregnane-3, 20-dione and 3α-hydroxy-5α-pregnan-20-one, in luteal tissue and circulating blood and their relationship to luteal function in the African elephant (*Loxodonta africana*). *Biology of Reproduction*, **56**, 640–646.

Hodges, J. K., van Aarde, R. J., Heistermann, M., and Hoppen, H.-O. (1994). Progestin content and biosynthetic potential of the corpus luteum of the African elephant (*Loxodonta africana*). *Journal of Reproduction and Fertility*, **102**, 163–168.

Höft, R., and Höft, M. (1995). The differential effects of elephants on rain forest communities in the Shimba hills, Kenya. *Biological Conservation*, **73**, 67–69.

Holling, C. S. (1973). Resilience and stability of ecological systems. *Annual Review of Ecology and Systematics*, **4**, 1–23.

Hooijer, D. A. (1972). Prehistoric evidence for *Elephas maximus* L. in Borneo. *Nature*, **239**, 228.

Howe, H. F. (1985). Gomphothere fruits: A critique. *The American Naturalist*, **6**, 853–865.

Ishwaran, N. (1981). Comparative study of Asiatic elephant *Elephas maximus* populations in Gal Oya, Sri Lanka. *Biological Conservation*, 21, 303–313.

Ishwaran, N. (1983). Elephant and woody-plant relationships in Gal Oya, Sri Lanka. *Biological Conservation*, 26, 255–270.

Ishwaran, N. (1993). Ecology of the Asian elephant in lowland dry zone habitat of the Mahaweli River Basin, Sri Lanka. *Journal of Tropical Ecology*, 9, 169–182.

Jachmann, H. (1980). Population dynamics of the elephants in Kasungu National Park, Malawi. *Netherlands Journal of Zoology*, 30, 622–634.

Jachmann, H. (1986). Notes on the population dynamics of the Kasungu elephants. *African Journal of Ecology*, 24, 215–226.

Jachmann, H., and Bell, R.H.V. (1984). Why do elephants destroy woodland? *African Elephant and Rhino Group Newsletter*, 3, 9–10.

Jachmann, H., Berry, P.S.M., and Imae, H. (1995). Tusklessness in African elephants: A future trend. *African Journal of Ecology*, 33, 230–235.

Jachmann, H., and Billiouw, M. (1997). Elephant poaching and law enforcement in the Central Luangwa Valley, Zambia. *Journal of Applied Ecology*, 34, 233–244.

Jagannathan, S., and Krishna, N. (1992). *Ganesha the auspicious . . . The beginning*. Vakils, Feffer and Simons, Bombay.

Jainudeen, M. R., Fisenberg, J. F., and Tilakeratne, N. (1971). Oestrous cycle of the Asiatic elephant, *Elephas maximus*, in captivity. *Journal of Reproduction and Fertility*, 27, 321–328.

Jainudeen, M. R., Katongole, C. B., and Short, R. V. (1972). Plasma testosterone levels in relation to musth and sexual activity in the male Asiatic elephant, *Elephas maximus*. *Journal of Reproduction and Fertility*, 29, 99–103.

Janis, C. (1976). The evolutionary strategy of the Equidae and the origins of rumen and cecal digestion. *Evolution*, 30, 757–774.

Janis, C. (1993). Victors by default: the mammalian succession. In *The book of life: An illustrated history of the evolution of life on earth* (S. J. Gould, ed.), pp. 169–217. W. W. Norton, New York.

Janzen, D. H., and Martin, P. S. (1982). Neotropical anachronisms: The fruits the gomphotheres ate. *Science*, 215, 19–27.

Jayewardene, J. (1994). *The elephant in Sri Lanka*. Wildlife Heritage Trust, Colombo, Sri Lanka.

Joshua, J., and Johnsingh, A.J.T. (1995). Ranging patterns of elephants in Rajaji National Park: Implications for reserve design. Pp. 256–260 in Daniel and Datye (1995).

Johnsingh, A.J.T., Prasad, S. N., and Goyal, S. P. (1990). Conservation status of the Chila-Motichur corridor for elephant movement in Rajaji-Corbett National Parks area, India. *Biological Conservation*, 51, 125–138.

Kangwana, K. (1995). Avoidance of Maasai by African elephants (*Loxodonta africana*). Pp. 529–530 in Daniel and Datye (1995).

Kapustin, N., Critser, J. K., Olson, D., and Malven, P. V. (1996). Nonluteal estrous cycles of 3-week duration are initiated by anovulatory luteinizing hormone peaks in African elephants. *Biology of Reproduction*, 55, 1147–1154.

Katugaha, H. I. E., de Silva, M., and Santiapillai, C. (1999). A long-term study on the dynamics of the elephant (*Elephas maximus*) population in Ruhuna National Park, Sri Lanka. *Biological Conservation*, 89, 51–59.

Kennedy, A. D. (2000). Wildfire reduces elephant herbivory on *Colophospermum mopane* (Fabaceae). *African Journal of Ecology*, 38, 175–177.

Kerr, M. A. (1978). Reproduction of elephant in the Mana Pools National Park, Rhodesia. *Arnoldia Rhodesia*, **8**, 1–11.

Kiltie, R. A. (1984). Seasonality, gestation time, and large mammal extinctions. Pp. 299–314 in Martin and Klein (1984).

Kleiber, M. (1947). Body size and metabolic rate. *Physiological Review*, **27**, 511–541.

Koch, P. L., Fisher, D. C., and Dettman, D. L. (1989). Oxygen isotope variation in the tusks of extinct proboscideans: A measure of season of death and seasonality. *Geology*, **17**, 515–519.

Koch, P. L., Heisinger, J., Moss, C., Carlson, R. W., Fogel, M. L., and Behrensmeyer, A. K. (1995). Isotopic tracking of change in diet and habitat use in African elephants. *Science*, **267**, 1340–1343.

Komar, V., and Melamid, A. (2000). *When elephants paint*. HarperCollins, New York.

Krishnamurthy, V., and Wemmer, C. (1995a). Timber elephant management in the Madras Presidency of India (1844–1947). Pp. 456–472 in Daniel and Datye (1995).

Krishnamurthy, V., and Wemmer, C. (1995b). Veterinary care of Asian timber elephants in India: historical accounts and current observations. *Zoo Biology*, **14**, 123–133.

Krishnan, M. (1972). An ecological survey of the larger mammals of peninsular India: The Indian elephant. *Journal of the Bombay Natural History Society*, **69**, 297–315.

Kühme, W. (1962). Ethology of the African elephant (*Loxodonta africana* Blumenbach 1979) in captivity. *International Zoo Yearbook*, **4**, 113–121.

Kurt, F. (1974). Remarks on the social structure and ecology of the Ceylon elephant in the Yala National Park. In *The behaviour of ungulates and its relation to management*, Vol. 2 (V. Geist and F. Walther, eds.), pp. 618–634. International Union for Conservation of Nature and Natural Resources, Morges, Switzerland.

Kurt, F. (1995). The preservation of Asian elephants in human care—A comparison between the different keeping systems in South Asia and Europe. *Animal Research and Development*, **41**, 38–60.

Kurt, F., Hartl, G., and Tiedemann, R. (1995). Tuskless bulls in Asian elephant *Elephas maximus*: History and population genetics of a man-made phenomenon. *Acta Theriologica*, **3** (Supplement), 125–143.

Lacy, R. (1993). Vortex: A computer simulation model for population viability analysis. *Wildlife Research*, **20**, 45–65.

Lahiri-Choudhury, D. K. (1991a). Indian myths and history. Pp. 130–147 in Eltringham (1991).

Lahiri-Choudhury, D. K. (1991b). Keeping wild elephants at bay. Pp. 166–169 in Eltringham (1991).

Lahiri-Choudhury, D. K. (1992). Musth in Indian elephant lore. Pp. 82–84 in Shoshani (1992b).

Lahiri-Choudhury, D. K. (ed.) (1999). *The great Indian elephant book: An anthology of writings on elephants in the Raj*. Oxford University Press, New Delhi, India.

Lair, R. C. (1997). *Gone astray: The care and management of the Asian elephant in domesticity*. Food and Agricultural Organization, Rome and Bangkok.

Lamprey, H. F., Glover, P. E., Turner, M.I.M., and Bell, R.H.V. (1967). Invasion of the Serengeti National Park by elephants. *East African Wildlife Journal*, **5**, 151–166.

Lamps, L. W., Smoller, B. R. Rasmussen, L.E.L., Slade, B. E., Fritsch, G., and Goodwin, T. E. (2001). Characterization of interdigital glands in the Asian elephant (*Elephas maximus*). *Research in Veterinary Science*, **71**, 1–4.

Langbauer, W. R., Jr., Payne, K. B., Charif, R. A., Rapaport, L., and Osborn, F. (1991). African elephants respond to distant playbacks of low-frequency conspecific calls. *Journal of Experimental Biology*, **157**, 35–46.

Langbauer, W. R., Jr., Payne, K. B., Charif, R. A., and Thomas, F. M. (1989). Responses of captive African elephants to playback of low-frequency calls. *Canadian Journal of Zoology*, **67**, 2604–2607.

Larom, D., Garstang, D., Lindeque, M., Raspet, R., Zunckel, M., Hong, Y., Brassel, K., O'Beirne, S., and Sokolic, F. (1997a). Meteorology and elephant infrasound at Etosha National Park, Namibia. *Journal of the Acoustical Society of America*, **101**, 1710–1717.

Larom, D., Garstang, M., Payne, K., Raspet, R., and Lindeque, M. (1997b). The influence of surface atmospheric conditions on the range and area reached by animal vocalizations. *The Journal of Experimental Biology*, **200**, 421–431.

Laws, R. M. (1966). Age criteria for the African elephant *Loxodonta africana*. *East African Wildlife Journal*, **4**, 1–37.

Laws, R. M. (1969). Aspects of reproduction in the African elephant, *Loxodonta africana*. *Journal of Reproduction and Fertility*, **6** (Supplement), 193–217.

Laws, R. M. (1970). Elephants as agents of habitat and landscape change in East Africa. *Oikos*, **21**, 1–15.

Laws, R. M., and Parker, I.S.C. (1968). Recent studies on elephant populations in East Africa. *Symposium of the Zoological Society of London*, **21**, 319–359.

Laws, R. M., Parker, I.S.C., and Johnstone, R.C.B. (1975). *Elephants and their habitats: The ecology of elephants in North Bunyoro, Uganda*. Clarendon Press, Oxford, U.K.

Lazar, J., Greenwood, D. R., Rasmussen, L.E.L., and Prestwich, G. D. (2002). Molecular and functional characterization of an odorant binding protein of the Asian elephant, *Elephas maximus*: Implications for the role of lipocalins in mammalian olfaction. *Biochemistry*, **41**, 11786–11794.

Leader-Williams, N., Albon, S. D., and Berry, P.S.M. (1990). Illegal exploitation of black rhinoceros and elephant populations: Patterns of decline, law enforcement and patrol effort in Luangwa Valley, Zambia. *Journal of Applied Ecology*, **27**, 1055–1087.

Leader-Williams, N., and Milner-Gulland, E. J. (1993). Policies for the enforcement of wildlife laws: The balance between detection and penalties in Luangwa Valley, Zambia. *Conservation Biology*, **7**, 611–617.

Leakey, R. E. (1992). A wildlife director's perspective. Pp. 214–217 in Shoshani (1992b).

Lee, P. C. (1986). Early social development among African elephant calves. *National Geographic Research*, **2**, 388–401.

Lee, P. C. (1987). Allomothering among African elephants. *Animal Behaviour*, **35**, 278–291.

Lee, P. C., and Moss, C. J. (1986). Early maternal investment in male and female Asiatic elephant calves. *Behavioural Ecology and Sociobiology*, **18**, 353–361.

Lee, P. C., and Moss, C. J. (1995). Statural growth in known-age African elephants (*Loxodonta africana*). *Journal of Zoology (London)*, **236**, 29–41.

Leuthold, W. (1976). Group size in elephants of Tsavo National Park and possible factors influencing it. *Journal of Animal Ecology*, **45**, 425–439.

Leuthold, W. (1977a). Changes in tree populations of Tsavo East National Park, Kenya. *East African Wildlife Journal*, **15**, 61–69.

Leuthold, W. (1977b). Spatial organization and strategy of habitat utilization of elephants in Tsavo National Park, Kenya. *Zeitschrift für Säugetierkunde*, **42**, 358–379.

Leuthold, W., and Sale, J. B. (1973). Movements and patterns of habitat utilization of elephants in Tsavo National Park, Kenya. *East African Wildlife Journal*, **11**, 369–384.

Lewis, D. M. (1986). Distribution effects on elephant feeding: Evidence for compression in Luangwa Valley, Zambia. *African Journal of Ecology*, **24**, 227–241.

Lewis, D. M. (1987). Elephant response to early burning in mopane woodland, Zambia. *South African Journal of Wildlife Research*, **17**, 33–40.

Lieberman, D., Lieberman, M., and Martin, C. (1987). Notes on seeds in elephant dung from Bia National Park, Ghana. *Biotropica*, **19**, 365–369.

Lincoln, G. A., and Ratnasooriya, W. D. (1996). Testosterone secretion, musth behavior and social dominance in captive male Asian elephants living near the equator. *Journal of Reproduction and Fertility*, **108**, 107–113.

Lindeque, M. (1988). Population dynamics of elephants in Etosha National Park, S.W.A., Namibia. Ph.D. thesis, University of Stellenbosch, Namibia.

Lindeque, M., and Lindeque, P. M. (1991). Satellite tracking of elephants in northwestern Namibia. *African Journal of Ecology*, **29**, 196–206.

Lindeque, M., and van Jaarsveld, A. S. (1993). Post-natal growth of elephants *Loxodonta africana* in Etosha National Park, Namibia. *Journal of Zoology*, London, **229**, 319–330.

Lindsay, W. K. (1994). Feeding ecology and population demography of African elephants in Amboseli, Kenya. Ph.D. thesis, University of Cambridge, Cambridge, U.K.

Lister, A. M. (1989). Proboscidean evolution. *Trends in Ecology and Evolution*, **4**, 362–363.

Lister, A. M. (1996a). Dwarfing in island elephants and deer: Processes in relation to time of isolation. *Symposium of the Zoological Society of London*, **69**, 277–292.

Lister, A. M. (1996b). Evolution and taxonomy of Eurasian mammoths. Pp. 203–213 in Shoshani and Tassy (1996a).

Lister, A. M., and Bahn, P. (1994). *Mammoths*. Boxtree, London.

Lister, A. M., and Sher, A. V. (2001). The origin and evolution of the woolly mammoth. *Science*, **294**, 1094–1097.

Lowenstein, J. M., and Shoshani, J. (1996). Proboscidean relationships based on immunological data. Pp. 49–54 in Shoshani and Tassy (1996a).

Lynch, M., and Lande, R. (1998). The critical effective size for a genetically secure population. *Animal Conservation*, **1**, 70–72.

MacArthur, R. H., and Wilson, E. O. (1967). *The theory of island biogeography*. Princeton University Press, Princeton, N.J.

MacKenzie, J. M. (1987). Chivalry, social Darwinism and ritualised killing: The hunting ethos in Central Africa up to 1914. In *Conservation in Africa: People, policies and practice* (D. Anderson and R. Grove, eds.), pp. 41–61. Cambridge University Press, Cambridge, U.K.

MacPhee, R.D.E., and Marx, P. A. (1997). The 40,000-year plague: Humans, hyperdisease, and first-contact extinctions. In *Natural change and human impact in Madagascar* (S. M. Goodman and B. D. Patterson, eds.), pp. 169–217. Smithsonian Institution Press, Washington, D.C.

Maglio, V. J. (1973). Origin and evolution of the Elephantidae. *Transactions of the American Philosophical Society of Philadelphia*, n.s., **63**, 1–149.

Mahboubi, M., Ameur, R., Crochet, J. Y., and Jaeger, J. J. (1984). Earliest known proboscidean from early Eocene of north-west Africa. *Nature*, **308**, 543–544.

Malpas, R. C. (1977). Diet and the condition and growth of elephants in Uganda. *Journal of Applied Ecology*, **14**, 489–504.

Malpas, R. C. (1978). The ecology of the African elephant in Rwenzori and Kabalega Falls National Parks. Ph.D. thesis, University of Cambridge, Cambridge, U.K.

Martin, E. B. (1980). The craft, the trade and the elephants. *Oryx*, **15**, 363–366.

Martin, E. B., and Vigne, L. (1989). The decline and fall of India's ivory industry. *Pachyderm*, **12**, 4–21.

Martin, P. S. (1984). Prehistoric overkill: the global model. In *Quaternary extinctions: A prehistoric revolution* (P. S. Martin and R. G. Klein, eds.), pp. 354–403. University of Arizona Press, Tucson.

Martin, P. S., and Klein, R. G. (eds.) (1984). *Quaternary extinctions: A prehistoric revolution*. University of Arizona Press, Tucson.

Matchie, P. (1900). Über geographische Albarten des Afrikanischen elephantens. *Sitzungsberichte Gellschaft natuforschunde Freunde Berlin*, **8**, 189–197.

May, R. M. (1977). Thresholds and breakpoints in ecosystems with a multiplicity of stable states. *Nature*, **269**, 471–477.

Maynard Smith, J. (1982). *Evolution and the theory of games*. Cambridge University Press, Cambridge, U.K.

McComb, K., Moss, C., Durant, S. M., Baker, L., and Sayialel, S. (2001). Matriarchs as repositories of social knowledge in African elephants. *Science*, **292**, 491–494.

McComb, K., Moss, C., Sayialel, S., and Baker, L. (2000). Unusually extensive networks of vocal recognition in African elephant. *Animal Behaviour*, **59**, 1103–1109.

McCullagh, K. G. (1969a). The growth and nutrition of the African elephant. I. Seasonal variations in the rate of growth and the urinary excretion of hydroxyproline. *East African Wildlife Journal*, **7**, 85–90.

McCullagh, K. G. (1969b). The growth and nutrition of the African elephant. II. The chemical nature of the diet. *East African Wildlife Journal*, **7**, 91–97.

McCullagh, K.G. (1973). Are African elephants deficient in essential fatty acids? *Nature London*, **242**, 267–268.

McKay, G. M. (1973). Behavior and ecology of the Asiatic elephant in southeastern Ceylon. *Smithsonian Contributions to Zoology*, **125**, 1–113.

McLeod, S. R. (1997). Is the concept of carrying capacity useful in variable environments? *Oikos*, **79**, 529–542.

McNab, B. K. (1963). Bioenergetics and the determination of home range size. *The American Naturalist*, **97**, 133–140.

McNaughton, S. J. (1988). Mineral nutrition and spatial concentration of African ungulates. *Nature*, **334**, 343–345.

McNeilly, A. S., Martin, R. D., Hodges, J. K., and Smuts, G. L. (1983). Blood concentrations of gonadotrophins, prolactin and gonadal steroids in males and in non-pregnant female African elephants (*Loxodonta africana*). *Journal of Reproduction and Fertility*, **67**, 113–120.

McKnight, B. L. (1995). Behavioural ecology of "hand-reared" African elephants (*Loxodonta africana* (Blumenbach)) in Tsavo National Park, Kenya. *African Journal of Ecology*, **33**, 242–256.

Menon, V. (2002). *Tusker: The story of the Asian elephant*. Penguin, New Delhi, India.

Mikota, S. K., Sargant, E. L., and Ranglak, G. S. (eds.) (1994). *Medical management of the elephant*. Indira Publishing House, West Bloomsfield, Mich.

Milewski, A. (2000). Iodine as a possible controlling nutrient for elephant populations. *Pachyderm*, **28**, 78–90.

Miller, G. H., Magee, J. W., Johnson, B. J., Fogel, M. L., Spooner, N. A., McCulloch, M. T., and Ayliffe, L. K. (1999). Pleistocene extinction of *Genyornis newtoni*: Human impact on Australian megafauna. *Science*, **283**, 205–208.

Milner-Gulland, E. J., and Beddington, J. R. (1993). The exploitation of elephants for the ivory trade: An historical perspective. *Philosophical Transactions of the Royal Society of London*, ser. B, **252**, 29–37.

Milner-Gulland, E. J., and Leader-Williams, N. (1992). A model of incentives for the illegal exploitation of black rhinos and elephants: Poaching pays in Luangwa Valley, Zambia. *Journal of Applied Ecology*, **29**, 388–401.

Milner-Gulland, E. J., and Mace, R. (1991). The impact of the ivory trade on the African elephant *Loxodonta africana* population as assessed by data from the trade. *Biological Conservation*, **55**, 215–229.

Mishra, J. (1971). An assessment of annual damage to crops by elephants in Palamau District, Bihar. *Journal of the Bombay Natural History Society*, **68**, 307–310.

Moolman, H. J., and Cowling, R. M. (1994). The impact of elephant and goat grazing on the endemic flora of south African succulent thicket. *Biological Conservation*, **68**, 53–61.

Moore, J. H., and Sikes, S. K. (1967). The serum and adrenal lipids of the African elephant, *Loxodonta africana*. *Comparative Biochemistry and Physiology*, **20**, 779–792.

Mosimann, J. E., and Martin, P. S. (1975). Simulating overkill by Paleoindians. *American Scientist*, **63**, 304–313.

Moss, C. J. (1983). Oestrous behaviour and female choice in the African elephant. *Behaviour*, **86**, 167–196.

Moss, C. J. (1988). *Elephant memories: Thirteen years in the life of an elephant family*. William Morrow, New York.

Moss, C. J., and Poole, J. H. (1983). Relationships and social structure of African elephants. In *Primate social relationships: An integrated approach* (R. A. Hinde, ed.), pp. 315–325. Blackwell, Oxford, U.K.

Mueller-Dombois, D. (1972). Crown distortion and elephant distribution in the woody vegetations of Ruhuna National Park, Ceylon. *Ecology*, **53**, 208–226.

Myers, N. (1973). Tsavo National Park, Kenya, and its elephants: An interim appraisal. *Biological Conservation*, **5**, 123–132.

Nair, P. V. (1983). Studies on the development of behaviour in the Asiatic elephant. Ph.D. thesis, Indian Institute of Science, Bangalore.

Nair, P. V. (1989). Development of nonsocial behaviour in the Asiatic elephant. *Ethology*, **82**, 46–60.

Narain, A. K. (1991). Ganeša: A protohistory of the idea and the icon. Pp. 19–48 in Brown (1991c).

Niemuller, C., and Liptrap, R. M. (1991). Altered androstenedione to testosterone ratios and LH concentrations during musth in the captive male Asian elephant (*Elephas maximus*). *Journal of Reproduction and Fertility*, **91**, 139–146.

Niemuller, C., Shaw, H. J., and Hodges, J. K. (1993). Non-invasive monitoring of ovarian function in Asian elephants (*Elephas maximus*) by measurement of urinary 5 beta-pregnanetriol. *Journal of Reproduction and Fertility*, **99**, 617–625.

Niemuller, C., Shaw, H. J., and Hodges, J. K. (1997). Pregnancy determination in the Asian elephant (*Elephas maximus*): A change in the plasma progesterone to 17α-hydroxy-progesterone ratio. *Zoo Biology*, **16**, 415–426.

Njumbi, S., Waithaka, J., Gachago, S., Sakwa, J., Mwathe, K., Mungai, P., Mulama, M.,

Mutinda, H., Omondi, P., and Litoroh, M. (1996). Translocation of elephants: the Kenyan experience. *Pachyderm*, **22**, 61–65.

Norton-Griffiths, M. (1979). The influence of grazing, browsing, and fire on the vegetation dynamics of the Serengeti. In *Serengeti—dynamics of an ecosystem* (A.R.E. Sinclair and M. Norton-Griffiths, ed.), pp. 310–352. University of Chicago Press, Chicago.

Nyakaana, S., and Arctander, P. (1999). Population genetic structure of the African elephant in Uganda based on variation at mitochondrial and nuclear loci: Evidence for male-biased gene flow. *Molecular Ecology*, **8**, 1105–1115.

O'Connell-Rodwell, C. E., Rodwell, T., Rice, M., and Hart, L. A. (2000). Living with the modern conservation paradigm: Can agricultural communities co-exist with elephant? A five-year case study in East Caprivi, Namibia. *Biological Conservation*, **93**, 381–391.

Oftedal, O. (1985). Pregnancy and lactation. In *The bioenergetics of wild herbivores* (R. J. Hudson and R. G. White, eds.), pp. 215–238. CRC Press, Boca Raton, Fla.

Olivier, R.C.D. (1978). On the ecology of the Asian elephant. Ph.D. thesis, University of Cambridge, Cambridge, U.K.

Osborn, F. V. (1998). The ecology of crop-raiding elephants in Zimbabwe. Ph.D. thesis, University of Cambridge, Cambridge, U.K.

Osborn, F. V., and Rasmussen, L.E.L. (1995). Evidence for the effectiveness of an oleoresin capsicum aerosol as a repellent against wild elephants in Zimbabwe. *Pachyderm*, **20**, 55–64.

Osborn, H. F. (1936). *Proboscidea: A monograph of the discovery, evolution, migration and extinction of the mastodonts and elephants of the world. Vol. 1: Moeritherioidea, Deinotherioidea, Mastodontoidea.* American Museum Press, New York.

Osborn, H. F. (1942). *Proboscidea: A monograph of the discovery, evolution, migration and extinction of the mastodonts and elephants of the world. Vol. 2: Stegodontoidea, Elephantoidea.* American Museum Press, New York.

Owen-Smith, N. (1987). Pleistocene extinctions: The pivotal role of megaherbivores. *Paleobiology*, **13**, 351–362.

Owen-Smith, N., and Novellie, P. (1982). What should a clever ungulate eat? *The American Naturalist*, **119**, 151–178.

Owen-Smith, R. N. (1988). *Megaherbivores: The influence of very large body size on ecology.* Cambridge University Press, Cambridge, U.K.

Parker, G. A., and Rubenstein, D. I. (1981). Role assessment reserve strategy, and acquisition of information in asymmetric animal contests. *Animal Behaviour*, **29**, 221–240.

Parker, I.S.C., and Amin, M. (1983). *Ivory crisis.* Chatto and Windus, London.

Parker, I.S.C., and Graham, A. D. (1989). Men, elephants and competition. *Symposium of the Zoological Society of London*, **61**, 241–252.

Parker, I.S.C., and Martin, E. B. (1982). How many elephants are killed for the ivory trade? *Oryx*, **16**, 235–239.

Payne, K. (1989). Elephant talk. *National Geographic*, August, 264–277.

Payne, K. (1998). *Silent thunder: In the presence of elephants.* Simon and Schuster, New York.

Payne, K. B., Langbauer, W. R., Jr., and Thomas, E. M. (1986). Infrasonic calls of the Asian elephant (*Elephas maximus*). *Behavioural Ecology and Sociobiology*, **18**, 297–301.

Pellew, R.A.P. (1983). The impacts of elephant, giraffe and fire upon the *Acacia tortilis* woodlands of the Serengeti. *African Journal of Ecology*, **21**, 41–74.

Perrin, T. E., and Rasmussen, L.E.L. (1994). Chemosensory responses of female Asian elephants (*Elephas maximus*) to cyclohexanone. *Journal of Chemical Ecology*, **20**, 2577–2586.

Perry, J. S. (1953). The reproduction of the African elephant, *Loxodonta africana*. *Philosophical Transactions of the Royal Society of London*, ser. B, **237**, 93–149.

Perry, J. S. (1964). The structure and development of the reproductive organs of the female African elephant. *Philosophical Transactions of the Royal Society of London*, ser. B, **248**, 35–51.

Peters, R. H. (1983). *The ecological implications of body size*. Cambridge University Press, Cambridge, U.K.

Phillipson, J. (1975). Rainfall, primary production and "carrying capacity" of Tsavo National Park (East), Kenya. *East African Wildlife Journal*, **13**, 171–201.

Pilgram, T., and Western, D. (1986a). Inferring hunting patterns on African elephants from tusks in the international ivory trade. *Journal of Applied Ecology*, **23**, 503–514.

Pilgram, T., and Western, D. (1986b). Inferring the sex and age of African elephants from tusk measurements. *Biological Conservation*, **36**, 39–52.

Plotka, E. D., Seal, U. S., Schobert, E. E., and Schmoller, G. C. (1975). Serum progesterone and estrogens in elephants. *Endocrinology*, **97**, 485–487.

Plotka, E. D., Seal, U. S., Zarembka, F. R., Simmons, L. G., Teare, A., Phillips, L. G., Hinshaw, K. C., and Wood, D. G. (1988). Ovarian function in the elephant: Luteinizing hormone and progesterone cycles in African and Asian elephants. *Biology of Reproduction*, **38**, 309–314.

Poirier, F. E. (1972). *Primate socialization*. Random House, New York.

Poole, J. (1989a). Mate guarding, reproductive success and female choice in African elephants. *Animal Behaviour*, **37**, 842–849.

Poole, J. (1996). *Coming of age with elephants: A memoir*. Hyperion, New York.

Poole, J. H. (1987). Rutting behavior in African elephants: The phenomenon of musth. *Behaviour*, **102**, 283–316.

Poole, J. H. (1989b). Announcing intent: The aggressive state of musth in African elephants. *Animal Behaviour*, **37**, 140–152.

Poole, J. H. (1993). Kenya's initiatives in elephant fertility regulation and population control techniques. *Pachyderm*, **16**, 62–65.

Poole, J. H. (1994). Sex differences in the behaviour of African elephants. In *The differences between the sexes* (R. V. Short and E. Balaban, eds.), pp. 331–346. Cambridge University Press, Cambridge, U.K.

Poole, J. H. (1999). Signals and assessment in African elephants: Evidence from playback experiments. *Animal Behaviour*, **58**, 185–193.

Poole, J. H., Kasman, L. H., Ramsay, E. C., and Lasley, B. L. (1984). Musth and urinary testosterone concentrations in the African elephant (*Loxodonta africana*). *Journal of Reproduction and Fertility*, **70**, 225–260.

Poole, J. H., and Moss, C. J. (1981). Musth in the African elephant, *Loxodonta africana*. *Nature*, **292**, 830–831.

Poole, J. H., and Moss, C. J. (1989). Elephant mate searching: Group dynamics and vocal and olfactory communication. *Symposium of the Zoological Society of London*, **61**, 111–125.

Poole, J. H., Payne, K., Langbauer, W. R., and Moss, C. J. (1988). The social context of some very low frequency calls of African elephants. *Behavioural Ecology and Sociobiology*, **22**, 385–392.

Poole, J. H., and Thomsen, J. B. (1989). Elephants are not beetles: Implications of the ivory trade for the survival of the African elephant. *Oryx*, **23**, 188–198.

Powell, J. A. (1997). The ecology of forest elephants (*Loxodonta africana cyclotis* Matschie 1900) in Banyang-Mbo and Korup forests, Cameroon, with particular reference to their role as seed dispersal agents. Ph.D. thesis, University of Cambridge, Cambridge, U.K.

Prakash, O. (1961). *Food and drinks in ancient India: From earliest times to c. 1200* A.D. Munshi Ram Manohar Lal, Delhi, India.

Prins, H.H.T., and Van der Jeugd, H. P. (1993). Herbivore population crashes and woodland structure in East Africa. *Journal of Ecology*, **81**, 305–314.

Quade, J., Cerling, T. E., Barry, J. C., Morgan, M. E., Pilbeam, D. R., Chivas, A. R., Lee-Thorp, J. A., and van der Merwe, N. J. (1992). A 16-Ma record of paleodiet using carbon and oxygen isotopes in fossil teeth from Pakistan. *Chemical Geology*, **94**, 183–192.

Ramakrishnan, U., Santosh, J. A., Ramakrishnan, U., and Sukumar, R. (1998). The population and conservation status of Asian elephants in the Periyar Tiger Reserve, southern India. *Current Science*, **74**, 110–113.

Ramsay, E. C. (1981). Monitoring the estrous cycle of the Asian elephant (*Elephas maximus*), using urinary estrogens. *American Journal of Veterinary Research*, **42**, 256–260.

Rangarajan, L. N. (1992). Kautilya: The *Arthashastra* (edited and translated). Penguin Books, New Delhi, India.

Rangarajan, M. (2001). *India's wildlife history: An introduction.* Permanent Black, Delhi, India.

Rasmussen, L. E., Buss, I. O., Hess, D. L., and Schmidt, M. J. (1984). Testosterone and dihydrotestosterone concentrations in elephant serum and temporal gland secretions. *Biology of Reproduction*, **30**, 352–362.

Rasmussen, L. E., Schmidt, M. J., and Daves, G. D., Jr. (1986). Chemical communication among Asian elephants. In *Chemical signals in vertebrates: Evolutionary, ecological and comparative aspects* (D. Duvall, D. Muller-Schwarze, and R. M. Silverstein, eds.), pp. 627–645. Plenum, New York.

Rasmussen, L. E., Schmidt, M. J., Henneous, R., Groves, D., and Daves, G. D., Jr. (1982). Asian bull elephants: Flehmen-like responses to extractable components in female elephant estrous urine. *Science*, **217**, 159–162.

Rasmussen, L.E.L. (1988). Chemosensory responses in two species of elephants to constituents of temporal gland secretion and musth urine. *Journal of Chemical Ecology*, **14**, 1687–1711.

Rasmussen, L.E.L. (1995). Evidence for long-term chemical memory in elephants. *Chemical Senses*, **20**, 762.

Rasmussen, L.E.L. (1998). Chemical communication: An integral part of functional Asian elephant (*Elephas maximus*) society. *Ecoscience*, **5**, 410–426.

Rasmussen, L.E.L. (2001). Source and cyclic release pattern of (Z)-7-dodecenyl acetate, the preovulatory pheromone of female Asian elephant. *Chemical Senses*, **26**, 611–624.

Rasmussen, L.E.L., Haight, J., and Hess, D. L. (1990). Chemical analysis of temporal gland secretions collected from an Asian bull elephant during a four-month musth episode. *Journal of Chemical Ecology*, **16**, 2167–2181.

Rasmussen, L.E.L., Hall-Martin, A. J., and Hess, D. L. (1996a). Chemical profiles of male African elephants, *Loxodonta africana*: Physiological and ecological implications. *Journal of Mammalogy*, **77**, 422–439.

Rasmussen, L.E.L., and Krishnamurthy, V. (2000). How chemical signals integrate Asian elephant society: The known and the unknown. *Zoo Biology*, **19**, 405–423.

Rasmussen, L.E.L., Lee, T. D., Daves, G. D., and Schmidt, M. J. (1993). Female-to-male pheromones of low volatility in the Asian elephant, *Elephas maximus*. *Journal of Chemical Ecology*, **19**, 2115–2128.

Rasmussen, L.E.L., Lee, T. D., Roelofs, W. L., Zhang, A., and Daves, G. D., Jr. (1996b). Insect pheromone in elephants. *Nature*, **379**, 684.

Rasmussen, L.E.L., Lee, T. D., Zhang, A., Roelofs, W. L., and Doyle, G. D., Jr. (1997). Purification, identification, concentration and bioactivity of (Z)-7-dodecen-1-yl acetate: Sex pheromone of the female Asian elephant, *Elephas maximus*. *Chemical Senses*, **22**, 417–437.

Rasmussen, L.E.L., and Munger, B. L. (1996). The sensorineural specializations of the trunk tip (finger) of the Asian elephant, *Elephas maximus*. *The Anatomical Record*, **246**, 127–134.

Rasmussen, L.E.L., Riddle, H. S., and Krishnamurthy, V. (2002). Mellifluous matures to malodorous in musth. *Nature*, **415**, 975–976.

Rasmussen, L.E.L., and Schulte, B. A. (1998). Chemical signals in the reproduction of Asian and African elephants. *Animal Reproduction Science*, **53**, 19–34.

Rasmussen, L.E.L., and Schulte, B. A. (1999). Ecological and biochemical constraints on pheromonal signaling systems in Asian elephants and their evolutionary implications. In *Advances in Chemical Communication in Vertebrates 8* (R. E. Johnston, D. Muller-Schwarze, and P. W. Sorenson, eds.), pp. 49–62. Plenum Press, New York.

Redmond, I. M. (1992). Erosion by elephants. Pp. 128–-130 in Shoshani (1992b).

Reiss, M. (1988). Scaling of home range size: Body size, metabolic needs and ecology. *Trends in Ecology and Evolution*, **3**, 85–86.

Rensch, B. (1957). The intelligence of elephants. *Scientific American*, February, 44–49.

Riddle, H. S., Riddle, S. W., Rasmussen, L.E.L., and Goodwin, T. E. (2000). First disclosure and preliminary investigation of a liquid released from the ears of African elephants. *Zoo Biology*, **19**, 475–480.

Roca, A. L., Georgiadis, N., Pecon-Slattery, J., and O'Brien, S. J. (2001). Genetic evidence for two species of elephant in Africa. *Science*, **293**, 1473–1477.

Rodgers, D. H., and Elder, W. H. (1977). Movement of elephants in Luangwa Valley, Zambia. *Journal of Wildlife Management*, **41**, 56–62.

Rosenthal, G. A., and Janzen, D. H. (eds.) (1979). *Herbivores: Their interactions with secondary plant metabolites*. Academic Press, New York.

Ross, D. (ed.) (1992). *Elephant: The animal and its ivory in African culture*. Fowler Museum of Cultural History, University of California, Los Angeles.

Ruess, R. W., and Halter, F. L. (1990). The impact of large herbivores on the Seronera woodlands, Serengeti National Park, Tanzania. *African Journal of Ecology*, **28**, 259–275.

Ruggiero, R. G. (1992). Seasonal forage utilization by elephants in central Africa. *African Journal of Ecology*, **30**, 137–148.

Ruggiero, R. G., and Fay, J. M. (1994). Utilization of termitarium soils by elephants and its ecological implications. *African Journal of Ecology*, **32**, 222–232.

Sachau, E. C. (2002). *Alberuni's India: An account of the religion, philosophy, literature, geography, chronology, astronomy, customs, laws and astrology of India about* A.D. *1030.* Rupa and Co., New Delhi, India.

Sanderson, G. P. (1878). *Thirteen years among the wild beasts of India.* W. H. Allen, London.

Sanderson, I. T. (1962). *The dynasty of Abu: A history and natural history of the elephants and their relatives, past and present.* Alfred A. Knopf, New York.

Santiapillai, C., Chambers, M. R., and Ishwaran, I. (1984). Aspects of the ecology of the Asian elephant *Elephas maximus* L. in the Ruhuna National Park, Sri Lanka. *Biological Conservation,* **29**, 47–61.

Santiapillai, C., and Jackson, P. (1990). The Asian elephant: An action plan for its conservation. IUCN–The World Conservation Union, Gland, Switzerland.

Saunders, J. J. (1996). North American Mammutidae. Pp. 271–279 in Shoshani and Tassy (1996a).

Savage, R.J.G., and Long, M. R. (1986). *Mammal evolution: An illustrated guide.* British Museum (Natural History), London.

Savidge, J. M. (1968). Elephants in the Ruaha National Park, Tanzania—Management problem. *East African Agricultural and Forestry Journal,* **33** (special issue), 191–196.

Schulte, B. A., and Rasmussen, L.E.L. (1999). Signal-receiver interplay in the communication of male condition by Asian elephants. *Animal Behaviour,* **57**, 1265–1274.

Scott, R. M. (1962). Exchangeable bases of mature, well drained soils in relation to rainfall in East Africa. *Journal of Soil Science,* **13**, 1–9.

Scullard, H. H. (1974). *The elephant in the Greek and Roman world.* Cornell University Press, Ithaca, N.Y.

Shaffer, M. L. (1981). Minimum viable populations for species conservation. *Biosciences,* **31**, 131–134.

Sherry, B. Y. (1975). Reproduction of elephant in Gonarezhou, southeastern Rhodesia. *Arnoldia Rhodesia,* **7**, 1–13.

Shields, W. M. (1987). Dispersal and mating systems: Investigating their causal connections. In *Mammalian dispersal patterns: The effects of social structure on population genetics* (D. B. Chepko-Sade and Z. T. Haplins, eds.), pp. 3–25. University of Chicago Press, Chicago.

Short, J. C. (1981). Diet and feeding behaviour of the forest elephant. *Mammalia,* **45**, 177–185.

Short, R. V. (1966). Oestrous behaviour, ovulation and the formation of the corpus luteum in the African elephant (*Loxodonta africana*). *East African Wildlife Journal,* **4**, 56–68.

Short, R. V., Mann, T., and Hay, M. F. (1967). Male reproductive organs of the African elephant, *Loxodonta africana. Journal of Reproduction and Fertility,* **13**, 515–536.

Shoshani, J. (1991). Anatomy and physiology. Pp. 30–47 in Eltringham (1991).

Shoshani, J. (1992a). Evolution of the Proboscidea. Pp. 18–33 in Shoshani (1992b).

Shoshani, J. (ed.) (1992b). *Elephants: Majestic creatures of the wild.* Rodale Press, Emmaus, Pa.

Shoshani, J., and Tassy, P. (eds.). (1996a). *The Proboscidea: Evolution and palaeoecology of elephants and their relatives.* Oxford University Press, New York.

Shoshani, J., and Tassy, P. (1996b). Summary, conclusions, and a glimpse into the future. Pp. 335–348 in Shoshani and Tassy (1996a).

Shoshani, J., West, R. M., Court, N., Savage, R.J.G., and Harris, J. M. (1996). The earliest proboscideans: General plan, taxonomy, and palaeoecology. Pp. 57–75 in Shoshani and Tassy (1996a).

Sikes, S. K. (1968). Habitat stress and arterial disease in elephants. *Oryx*, **9**, 286–292.

Sikes, S. K. (1971). *The natural history of the African elephant*. Weidenfeld and Nicolson, London.

Silori, C. S., and Mishra, B. K. (1995). Pressure and resource dependency of Masinagudi group of villages on the surrounding elephant habitat. Pp. 270–278 in Daniel and Datye (1995).

Sinclair, A.R.E. (1981). Environmental carrying capacity and the evidence for over abundance. In *Problems in management of locally abundant wild mammals* (P. A. Jewell and S. Holt, eds.), pp. 247–257. Academic Press, New York.

Sinclair, A.R.E. (1995). Equilibria in plant-herbivore interactions. Pp. 91–114 in Sinclair and Arcese (1995).

Sinclair, A.R.E., and Arcese, P. (eds.) (1995). *Serengeti II: Dynamics, management and conservation of an ecosystem*. University of Chicago Press, Chicago.

Singh, R. K., and Chowdhury, S. (1999). Effect of mine discharge on the pattern of riverine habitat use of elephants *Elephas maximus* and other mammals in Siinghbum forests, Bihar, India. *Journal of Environmental Management*, **57**, 177–192.

Sivaganesan, N., and Johnsingh, A.J.T. (1995). Food resources crucial to the wild elephants in Mudumalai Wildlife Sanctuary, South India. Pp. 405–423 in Daniel and Datye (1995).

Slotow, R., van Dyk, G., Poole, J., Page, B., and Klocke, A. (2000). Older bull elephants control young males. *Nature*, **408**, 425–426.

Smith, J. G., Hanks, J., and Short, R. V. (1969). Biochemical observations on the corpora lutea of the African elephant, *Loxodonta africana*. *Journal of Reproduction and Fertility*, **20**, 111–117.

Smith, N. S., and Buss, I. O. (1975). Formation, function and persistence of the corpora lutea of the African elephant (*Loxodonta africana*). *Journal of Mammology*, **56**, 30–43.

Smuts, G. L. (1975). Reproduction and population characteristics of elephants in the Kruger National Park. *Journal of the South African Wildlife Management Association*, **5**, 1–10.

Spinage, C. A. (1973). A review of ivory exploitation and elephant population trends in Africa. *East African Wildlife Journal*, **11**, 281–289.

Spinage, C. A. (1994). *Elephants*. T. and A. D. Poyser, London.

St. Aubyn, F. (ed.) (1987). *Ivory: A history and collector's guide*. Thames and Hudson, London.

Stracey, P. D. (1963). *Elephant gold*. Weidenfeld and Nicholson, London.

Struhsaker, T. T., Lwanga, J. H., and Kasenene, J. M. (1996). Elephants, selective logging and forest regeneration in the Kibale forest, Uganda. *Journal of Tropical Ecology*, **12**, 45–64.

Styles, C. V., and Skinner, J. D. (2000). The influence of large mammalian herbivores on growth form and utilization of mopane trees, *Colophospermum mopane*, in Botswana's Northern Tuli Game Reserve. *African Journal of Ecology*, **38**, 95–101.

Sukumar, R. (1985). Ecology of the Asian elephant (*Elephas maximus*) and its interaction with man in south India. Ph.D. thesis, Indian Institute of Science, Bangalore.

Sukumar, R. (1989a). *The Asian elephant: Ecology and management*. Cambridge University Press, Cambridge, U.K.

Sukumar, R. (1989b). Ecology of the Asian elephant in southern India. I. Movement and habitat utilization patterns. *Journal of Tropical Ecology*, **5**, 1–18.

Sukumar, R. (1990). Ecology of the Asian elephant in southern India. II. Feeding habits and crop raiding patterns. *Journal of Tropical Ecology*, **6**, 33–53.

Sukumar, R. (1991a). Conservation. Pp. 158–179 in Eltringham (1991).

Sukumar, R. (1991b). The management of large mammals in relation to male strategies and conflict with people. *Biological Conservation*, **55**, 93–102.

Sukumar, R. (1992). *The Asian elephant: Ecology and management* (2nd rev. ed.). Cambridge University Press, Cambridge, U.K.

Sukumar, R. (1994a). *Elephant days and nights: Ten years with the Indian elephant*. Oxford University Press, New Delhi, India.

Sukumar, R. (1994b). Wildlife-human conflict in India: An ecological and social perspective. In *Social ecology* (ed. R. Guha), pp. 303–317. Oxford University Press, New Delhi, India.

Sukumar, R. (1995a). Elephant raiders and rogues. *Natural History*, **104**, 52–60.

Sukumar, R. (1995b). Minimum viable populations for elephant conservation. Pp. 279–288 in Daniel and Datye (1995).

Sukumar, R., Bhattacharya, S. K., and Krishnamurthy, R. V. (1987). Carbon isotopic evidence for different feeding patterns in an Asian elephant population. *Current Science*, **56**, 11–14.

Sukumar, R., and Gadgil, M. (1988). Male-female differences in foraging on crops by Asian elephants. *Animal Behaviour*, **36**, 1233–1235.

Sukumar, R., Joshi, N. V., and Krishnamurthy, V. (1988). Growth in the Asian elephant. *Proceedings of the Indian Academy of Sciences (Animal Sciences)*, **97**, 561–571.

Sukumar, R., Krishnamurthy, V., Wemmer, C., and Rodden, M. (1997). Demography of captive Asian elephants (*Elephas maximus*) in southern India. *Zoo Biology*, **16**, 263–272.

Sukumar, R., Ramakrishnan, U., and Santosh, J. A. (1998b). Impact of poaching on an Asian elephant population in Periyar, southern India: A model of demography and tusk harvest. *Animal Conservation*, **1**, 281–291.

Sukumar, R., and Ramesh, R. (1992). Stable carbon isotope ratios in Asian elephant collagen: Implications for dietary studies. *Oecologia*, **91**, 536–539.

Sukumar, R., and Ramesh, R. (1995). Elephant foraging: Is browse or grass more important? Pp. 368–374 in Daniel and Datye (1995).

Sukumar, R., Ramesh, R., Pant, R. K., and Rajagopalan, G. (1993). A $\delta^{13}C$ record of late Quaternary climate change from tropical peats in southern India. *Nature*, **364**, 703–706.

Sukumar, R., and Santiapillai, C. (1996). *Elephas maximus*: Status and distribution. Pp. 327–331 in Shoshani and Tassy (1996a).

Sukumar, R., Suresh, H. S., Dattaraja, H. S., and Joshi, N. V. (1998a) Dynamics of a tropical deciduous forest: Population changes (1988 through 1993) in a 50-hectare plot at Mudumalai, southern India. In *Forest biodiversity research, monitoring and modelling: Conceptual background and old world case studies* (F. Dallmeier and J. A. Chomsky, eds.), pp. 495–506. UNESCO, Paris, and the Parthenon Publishing Group, Pearl River, New York.

Swihart, R. K., Slade, N. A., and Bergstrom, B. J. (1988). Relating body size to the rate of home range use in mammals. *Ecology*, **69**, 393–399.

Tassy, P. (1996). Who is who among the Proboscidea? Pp. 39–48 in Shoshani and Tassy (1996a).

Tassy, P., and Shoshani, J. (1988). The Tethytheria: Elephants and their relatives. In *The phylogeny and classification of the Tetrapods, Vol.2: Mammals* (M. J. Benton, ed.), pp. 283–315. Systematics Association Special Volume No. 35B. Clarendon Press, Oxford, U.K.

Taya, K., Komura, H., Kondoh, M., Ogawa, Y., Nakada, K., Watanabe, G., Sasamota, S., Tanabe, K., Saito, K., Tajima, H., and Narushima, E. (1991). Concentrations of progesterone, testosterone and estradiol-17β in the serum during the estrous cycle of Asian elephants (*Elephas maximus*). *Zoo Biology*, **10**, 299–307.

Taylor, V. J., and Poole, T. B. (1998). Captive breeding and infant mortality in Asian elephants: A comparison between 20 Western zoos and 3 eastern elephant centers. *Zoo Biology*, **17**, 311–332.

Tchamba, M. N. (1996). History and present status of the human/elephant conflict in the Waza-Logone region, Cameroon, West Africa. *Biological Conservation*, **75**, 35–41.

Tchamba, M. N. (1998). Habitudes migratoires des elephants et interactions homme-elephant dans la region de Waza-Logone (Nord-Cameroun). *Pachyderm*, **25**, 53–66.

Tchamba, M. N., Bauer, H., and De Iongh, H. H. (1995). Application of VHF-radio and satellite telemetry technique on elephants in northern Cameroon. *African Journal of Ecology*, **33**, 335–346.

Tchamba, M. N., Bauer, H., Hunia, A., De Iongh, H. H., and Planton, H. (1994). Some observations on the movements and home range of elephants in Waza National Park, Cameroon. *Mammalia*, **58**, 527–533.

Terborgh, J. W. (1976). Island biogeography and conservation: Strategy and limitations. *Science*, **193**, 1029–1030.

Thapar, R. (1966). *A history of India. Vol. 1. From the discovery of India to 1526.* Penguin Books, New Delhi, India.

Thomas, M., Hagelberg, E., Jones, H. B., Yang, Z., and Lister, A. M. (2000). Molecular and morphological evidence on the phylogeny of the Elephantidae. *Proceedings of the Royal Society London B*, **267**, 2493–2500.

Thomson, P. J. (1975). The role of elephants, fire and other agents in the decline of a *Brachystegia boehmii* woodland. *Journal of the South African Wildlife Management Association*, **5**, 11–18.

Thouless, C. R. (1996). Home ranges and social organization of female elephants in northern Kenya. *African Journal of Ecology*, **34**, 284–297.

Thouless, C. R., and Sakwa, J. (1995). Shocking elephants: fences and crop raiders in Laikipia district, Kenya. *Biological Conservation*, **72**, 99–107.

Tiedemann, R., and Kurt, F. (1995). A stochastic simulation model for Asian elephant *Elephas maximus* populations and the inheritance of tusks. *Acta Theriologica*, **3** (Supplement), 111–124.

Tieszen, L. L., Boutton, T. W., Ottichilo, W. K., Nelson, D. E., and Brandt, D. H. (1989). An assessment of long-term food habits of Tsavo elephants based on stable carbon and nitrogen isotope ratios of bone collagen. *African Journal of Ecology*, **27**, 219–226.

Todd, N. E., and Roth, V. L. (1996). Origin and radiation of the Elephantidae. Pp. 193–202 in Shoshani and Tassy (1996a).

Trautmann, T. R. (1982). Elephants and the Mauryas. In *India: History and thought—Essays in honour of A. L. Basham* (S. N. Mukherjee, ed.), pp. 254–281. Subarnare-kha, Calcutta.

Trivers, R. (1985). *Social evolution.* Benjamin/Cumming, Menlo Park, Calif.

Trivers, R. L., and Willard, D. E. (1973). Natural selection of parental ability to vary the sex ratio of offspring. *Science*, **179**, 90–92.

Turkalo, A., and Fay, J. M. (1995). Studying forest elephants by direct observation: Preliminary results from the Dzanga clearing, Central African Republic. *Pachyderm*, **20**, 45–54.

Turner, A. (1995). Plio-Pleistocene correlations between climatic change and evolution in terrestrial mammals: the 2.5 ma event in Africa and Europe. *Acta Zooligica Cracoviensia*, **38**, 45–58.

van Aarde, R., Whyte, I., and Pimm, S. (1999). Culling and the dynamics of the Kruger National Park African elephant population. *Animal Conservation*, **2**, 287–294.

Van de Koppel, J., and Prins, H.T.T. (1998). The importance of herbivore interactions for the dynamics of African savanna woodlands: An hypothesis. *Journal of Tropical Ecology*, **14**, 565–576.

Van den Bergh, G. D., Sondaar, P. Y., de Vos, J., and Aziz, F. (1996). The proboscideans of the south-east Asian islands. Pp. 240–248 in Shoshani and Tassy (1996a).

van der Merwe, N. J., Lee Thorp, J. A., and Bell, R H.V. (1988). Carbon isotopes as indicators of elephant diets and African environments. *African Journal of Ecology*, **26**, 163–172.

van der Merwe, N. J., Lee-Thorp, J. A., Thackeray, J. F., Hall-Martin, A., Kruger, F. J., Coetzee, H., Bell, R.H.V., and Lindeque, M. (1990). Source area determination of elephant ivory by isotopic analysis. *Nature*, **346**, 744–746.

Vancuylenberg, B.W.B. (1977). Feeding behaviour of the Asiatic elephant in southeast Sri Lanka in relation to conservation. *Biological Conservation*, **12**, 33–54.

Vartanyan, S. L., Garutt, V. E., and Sher, A V. (1993). Holocene dwarf mammoths from Wrangel Island in the Siberian Arctic. *Nature*, **362**, 337–340.

Venkataraman, A. B., Venkatesa Kumar, N., Varma, S., and Sukumar, R. (2002). Conservation of a flagship species: Prioritizing Asian elephant (*Elephas maximus*) conservation units in southern India. *Current Science*, **82**, 1022–1032.

Verlinden, A., and Gavor, I.K.N. (1998). Satellite tracking of elephants in northern Botswana. *African Journal of Ecology*, **36**, 105–116.

Vidya, T.N.C., and Sukumar, R. (2002). The effect of some ecological factors on the intestinal parasite loads of the Asian elephant (*Elephas maximus*) in southern India. *Journal of Biosciences*, **27**, 521–528.

Viljoen, P. J. (1989). Spatial distribution and movements of elephants (*Loxodonta africana*) in the northern Namib desert region of the Kaokoveld, South West Africa/Namibia. *Journal of Zoology (London)*, **219**, 1–19.

Vogel, J. C., Eglington, B., and Aurent, J. M. (1990). Isotopic fingerprints in elephant bone and ivory. *Nature*, **346**, 747–749.

Vollrath, F., and Douglass-Hamilton, I. (2002). African bees to control African elephants. *Naturwissenschaften*, **82**, 508–511.

Warmington, E. H. (1974). *The commerce between the Roman Empire and India*. Vikas Publishing House, New Delhi, India.

Watson, D.M.S. (1946). The evolution of the Proboscidae. *Biological Review*, **21**, 15–29.

Watson, P. F., and D'Souza, F. (1975). Detection of oestrous in the African elephant (*Loxodonta africana*). *Theriogenology*, **4**, 203–209.

Watve, M. G. (1994). Ecology of host-parasite interactions in a wild mammalian host community in Mudumalai, southern India. Ph.D. thesis, Indian Institute of Science, Bangalore.

Watve, M. G. (1995). Helminth parasites of elephants: Ecological aspects. Pp. 289–295 in Daniel and Datye (1995).

Watve, M. G., and Sukumar, R. (1995). Parasite abundance and diversity in mammals: Correlates with host ecology. *Proceedings of National Academy of Sciences (USA)*, **92**, 8945–8949.

Watve, M. G., and Sukumar, R. (1997). Asian elephants with longer tusks have lower parasite loads. *Current Science*, **72**, 885–889.

Webb, S. D. (1984). Ten million years of mammal extinctions in North America. Pp. 189–210 in Martin and Klein (1984).

Weir, J. S. (1972). Spatial distribution of elephants in an African national park in relation to environmental sodium. *Oikos*, **23**, 1–13.

Weir, J. S. (1973). Exploitation of water soluble soil sodium by elephants in Murchison Falls National Park. *East African Wildlife Journal*, **11**, 1–7.

Wells, M. P. (1989). The use of carcass data in the study and management of African elephants: A modelling approach. *African Journal of Ecology*, **27**, 95–110.

West, R. M. (1980). Middle Eocene large mammal assemblage with Tethyan affinities, Ganda Kas Region, Pakistan. *Journal of Paleontology*, **54**, 508–533.

Western, D. (1986). The pygmy elephant: A myth and a mystery. *Pachyderm*, **22**, 59–60.

Western, D., and Gichohi, H. (1993). Segregation effects and the impoverishment of savanna parks: The case for ecosystem viability analysis. *African Journal of Ecology*, **31**, 269–281.

Western, D., and Lindsay, W. K. (1984). Seasonal herd dynamics of a savanna elephant population. *African Journal of Ecology*, **22**, 229–244.

Western, D., and van Praet, C. (1973). Cyclical changes in the habitat and climate of an East African ecosystem. *Nature*, **241**, 104–106.

Westoby, M. (1974). Analysis of diet selection by large generalist herbivores. *The American Naturalist*, **108**, 290–304.

Westoby, M. (1978). What are the biological bases of varied diets? *The American Naturalist*, **112**, 627–631.

Wheeler, J. W., Rasmussen, L. E., Ayorinde, F., Buss, I. O., and Smuts, G. L. (1982). Constituents of temporal gland secretion of the African elephant, *Loxodonta africana*. *Journal of Chemical Ecology*, **8**, 821–835.

White, L.J.T., Tutin, C.E.G., and Fernandez, M. (1993). Group composition and diet of forest elephants, *Loxodonta africana cyclotis* Matschie 1900, in the Lopé Reserve, Gabon. *African Journal of Ecology*, **31**, 181–199.

Whitehouse, A. M., and Harley, E. R. (2001). Post-bottleneck genetic diversity of elephant populations in South Africa, revealed using microsatellite analysis. *Molecular Ecology*, **10**, 2139–2149.

Whittington, S. L., and Dyke, B. (1984). Simulating overkill: Experiments with the Mosimann and Martin model. Pp. 451–465 in Martin and Klein (1984).

Whyte, I., van Aarde, R., and Pimm, S. L. (1998). Managing the elephants of Kruger National Park. *Animal Conservation*, **1**, 77–83.

Wiley, R. H. (1983). The evolution of communication: Information and manipulation. In *Animal behaviour. 2. Communication* (T. R. Halliday and P.J.B. Slater, eds.), pp. 156–189. Blackwell Scientific Publications, Oxford, U.K.

Williams, A. C., Johnsingh, A.J.T., and Krausman, P. R. (2001). Elephant-human conflicts in Rajaji National Park, northwestern India. *Wildlife Society Bulletin*, **9**, 1097–1104.

Williams, J. H. (1950). *Elephant Bill*. Rupert Hart-Davis, London.

Williamson, B. R. (1975). The condition and nutrition of elephant in Wankie National Park. *Arnoldia Rhodesia*, **7**, 1–20.

Williamson, B. R. (1976). Reproduction in female African elephant in the Wankie National Park, Rhodesia. *South African Journal of Wildlife Research*, **6**, 89–93.

Wilson, E. O. (1975). *Sociobiology: The new synthesis*. Harvard University Press, Cambridge, Mass.

Wu, L. S.-Y., and Botkin, D. B. (1980). Of elephants and men: A discrete, stochastic model for long-lived species with complex life histories. *The American Naturalist*, **116**, 831–849.

Wyatt, J. R., and Eltringham, S. K. (1974). The daily activity of the elephant in the Rwenzori National Park, Uganda. *East African Wildlife Journal*, **12**, 273–289.

Zahavi, A. (1975). Mate selection—Selection for a handicap. *Journal of Theoretical Biology*, **53**, 205–214.

Zahavi, A., and Zahavi, A. (1997). *The handicap principle: A missing piece of Darwin's puzzle*. Oxford University Press, New York.

Author Index

Subject Index